2nd Edition

Your Introduction to Education

Explorations in Teaching

Sara Davis Powell

Belmont Abbey College

PEARSON

Boston Columbus Indianapolis New York San Francisco Upper Saddle River
Amsterdam Cape Town Dubai London Madrid Milan Munich Paris Montreal Toronto
Delhi Mexico City São Sydney Hong Kong Seoul Singapore Taipei Tokyo

Vice President and Editor in Chief: Jeffery W. Johnston
Executive Editor: Ann Castel Davis
Senior Development Editor: Hope Madden
Editorial Assistant: Penny Burleson
Senior Marketing Manager: Darcy Betts-Prybella
Senior Managing Editor: Pamela D. Bennett
Senior Project Manager: Mary Irvin
Senior Operations Supervisor: Matthew Ottenweller
Senior Art Director: Diane Lorenzo
Cover and Text Designer: Wanda Espanda
Photo Coordinator: Carol Sykes
Permissions Administrator: Becky Savage
Cover Image: Sara Davis Powell and Shutterstock
Media Project Manager: Rebecca Norsic
Full-Service Project Management: Thistle Hill Publishing Services, LLC
Composition: Integra Software Services, Inc.
Printer/Binder: Webcrafters
Cover Printer: Lehigh Phoenix Color Corp.
Text Font: Garamond Book 10/12

Credits and acknowledgments borrowed from other sources and reproduced, with permission, in this textbook appear on page 389.

Every effort has been made to provide accurate and current Internet information in this book. However, the Internet and information posted on it are constantly changing, so it is inevitable that some of the Internet addresses listed in this textbook will change.

Library of Congress Cataloging-in-Publication Data
Powell, Sara Davis.
   Your introduction to education : explorations in teaching / Sara Davis Powell. — 2nd ed.
     p. cm.
   Rev. ed. of: An introduction to education : Upper Saddle River, N.J. : Merrill, c2009.
   Includes bibliographical references and index.
   ISBN-13: 978-0-13-708369-5 (pbk.)
   ISBN-10: 0-13-708369-6 (pbk.)
   1. Teaching—Vocational guidance.   I. Powell, Sara Davis. Introduction to education.
II. Title.
   LB1775.P625 2011
   371.10023—dc22

                                            2010047286

10 9 8 7 6 5 4 3 2 1

www.pearsonhighered.com

ISBN-10:   0-13-708369-6
ISBN-13: 978-0-13-708369-5

Jesse White, to whom the first edition was dedicated, has recently taken his talent and energy to Denver, Colorado. He teaches in an innovative charter school that serves students who live in low-income homes where English is not the primary language. He represents enthusiastic teachers everywhere who make critical differences in the lives of their students. To these teachers, and to Jesse, my son, I dedicate this second edition.

Preface

Your Introduction to Education: Explorations in Teaching

Using an approach that is unique among introduction to education college texts, the second edition of *Your Introduction to Education: Explorations in Teaching* takes you on a journey into authentic classrooms and guides you through issues and dilemmas as they affect real teachers and students in real schools to help you determine whether teaching is for you.

The most distinctive feature of this text is how it weaves the real-life experiences of 10 teachers and 12 students from 4 schools across the country into its content. These people and places are drawn from urban, suburban, and rural settings, allowing us to examine teaching and learning from a variety of perspectives.

The teachers and students are from Summit Station, Ohio; Spanish Fork, Utah; Mt. Pleasant, South Carolina; and Fresno, California. Classroom scenarios, person-to-person features, and nearly every photo in this book—along with hours of video on the accompanying MyEducationLab—are the direct result of time the author spent at each school with every one of the teachers, principals, students, and family members we meet.

This book, built entirely on authentic classroom experience, will empower you, as a future teacher, to *explore* content and classrooms, *reflect* on your learning, and *develop* an image of the teacher you aspire to be.

NEW TO THIS EDITION

- **CHAPTER 12: DEVELOPING PROFESSIONALISM:** This brand-new chapter looks at ways to weave professionalism throughout teacher responsibilities and opportunities, providing examples and advice about becoming a professional teacher.

- **WHERE DO I STAND?** This thought-provoking new inventory begins each chapter by asking you to consider the concepts of the chapter before reading it. As you read through each chapter, you'll have opportunities to reconsider your initial self-evaluation and make connections with what you're learning.

- **POINTS OF REFLECTION** features throughout each chapter ask you to pause and think through what you've read and apply the ideas to your own perceptions of teaching.

- **WHERE DO I STAND *NOW*?** At the end of each chapter, you are asked to reevaluate your personal inventory. Taking into account the reflections you've logged throughout the chapter, consider again where you stand on the chapter's primary topics.

- **DEVELOPING PROFESSIONAL COMPETENCE:** This end-of-chapter case study probes the issues of classroom teaching and helps prepare you for licensure exams by posing a dilemma involving the focus schools, teachers, and students. Following the case study are multiple-choice and essay questions that connect the classroom issues with pertinent standards, thus becoming an excellent study tool for you.

- **DIVERSITY DIALOGUE:** In each chapter we revisit a focus teacher's classroom or school to share an authentic issue related to diversity to help you prepare for the issues you'll face in your own classroom.

- **21ST CENTURY SKILLS:** The knowledge and skills students should possess to succeed in life in the 21st century are emphasized throughout. On page xxii, just after the Special Features Table of Contents, you'll find a complete chapter correlation of all 21st Century Skills coverage.

NEW TOPICAL COVERAGE

- **TEACHER SATISFACTION** New research showing teachers are far more satisfied with their career choice now than in the past three decades: Chapter 1

- **PARTNERSHIP FOR 21ST CENTURY SKILLS** This vibrant organization is influencing teaching and learning in U.S. schools: Chapter 1

- **21ST CENTURY REFORM EFFORTS** Delaware's Vision 2015 is explored as an example of efforts to create the best schools for every student, no exceptions and no excuses: Chapter 1

- **TEACHER EFFECTIVENESS RESEARCH** New research from Teach for America links particular teacher qualities and actions to increased student learning: Chapter 1

- **SCHOOL CHOICE** The possibilities, as well as the pros and cons: Chapter 2

- **CULTURAL PLURALISM** How teacher responsiveness increases the positive potential of diversity to enhance teaching and learning: Chapter 3

- **LANGUAGE MINORITY STUDENTS** Ways of addressing the needs of students for whom English is not the first language: Chapter 3

- **RELIGIOUS DIVERSITY** The issues and how to handle them lawfully and with consideration: Chapters 3 and 10

- **NATIONAL CONTENT STANDARDS** New research and trends lead to strong momentum toward national standards: Chapters 3 and 12

- **CONTROVERSY AND CURRICULUM** New examples addressing controversial issues including intelligent design, Eurocentrism, and sex education: Chapter 4

- **TECHNOLOGY TEACHING TOOLS** The explosion of technology for teaching and learning, including social media: Chapters 4 and 6

- **TRENDS IN INTERNATIONAL MATH AND SCIENCE STUDY** New test results: Chapter 5

- **HIGH-STAKES TESTING** The uses and abuses of state test results: Chapter 5

- **LIFE AND CAREER SKILLS** Methods to incorporate 21st century life and career skills into the classroom: Chapter 6

- **IMMIGRATION AND STUDENTS** The many and growing issues surrounding students who are immigrants, including the controversial DREAM Act: Chapters 3, 7, and 9

- **21ST CENTURY SCHOOLS** Recognizing and using the potential of 21st century innovation: Chapter 6

- **RACIAL AND ETHNIC DIVERSITY** How public schools address the issues: Chapters 3, 7, and 9

- **PHILOSOPHY OF EDUCATION** Interactive methods to help teacher candidates discover and define their philosophies: Chapter 8

- **RECOGNIZING CHILD ABUSE** A frank discussion of this ever-present threat, including an extensive chart of what teachers should look for: Chapters 3 and 9

- **HOMELESSNESS** Ways to recognize and better meet the wide-ranging needs of children in poverty and those who are homeless: Chapter 9

- **CHILDHOOD OBESITY** The recent dramatic increase and imminent threat to student well-being: Chapter 9

- **BULLYING** What teachers can do to heighten awareness and stem harmful relationally aggressive behavior: Chapter 9

- **DROPOUTS** The shocking data now available due to standardization of definitions, and what teachers can do to help students stay in school: Chapter 9

- **RECOGNIZING ETHICAL DILEMMAS** Multiple scenarios bringing to life the day-to-day ethical dilemmas teachers face in their classrooms and schools: Chapter 10

- **RELIGIOUS EXPRESSION** What's lawful for students and teachers, in an easy-to-understand Q&A format: Chapter 10

- **SEXUAL HARASSMENT** Recognizing and addressing sexual harassment: Chapter 10

- **SCHOOL FUNDING** Controversy about how to finance public education, addressed through the continuing funding dilemmas faced by California residents: Chapter 11

- *A BLUEPRINT FOR REFORM* The next reauthorization of the Elementary and Secondary Education Act, as proposed by President Obama: Chapter 12

- **TEACHER EVALUATION AND PERFORMANCE PAY** Controversial proposals to evaluate and pay teachers based on student test results: Chapter 12

- **PROFESSIONAL RELATIONSHIPS** Practical ways to cultivate and maintain professional relationships: Chapter 12

- **PROFESSIONAL RESPONSES TO REFORM** How to view and respond professionally to reform efforts: Chapter 12

Explore

Explore Authentic Classrooms

The focus teachers, students, and schools of this text are discussed throughout. You'll have many specific opportunities to meet and get to know these important people. Look for the *Teaching in Focus* headings to alert you to opportunities to get acquainted.

Teaching in Focus

- The book opens in just a few pages with an introductory *Meeting the Focus Teachers and Students* section, an in-depth exploration of our 10 classrooms. One by one, you will meet each of our focus teachers and their students.

- As each chapter opens, you'll get a glimpse of one of our focus teachers addressing chapter concepts in his or her classroom. The photo on the first page of the chapter is of the teacher in these chapter-opening features to give you an idea of the classroom environment each teacher creates.

Teaching in Focus

Brandi Wade, kindergarten, Summit Primary, Ohio. *In her own words. . . .*

It may not so much be that you choose teaching, but that teaching chooses you. It will be in your heart and on your mind constantly. Although it's never easy for more than 5 minutes at a time, teaching is the most important profession you can pursue. I am truly blessed to be a kindergarten teacher. I get to teach a different lesson, meet a different challenge, and see life from different perspectives every day in my classroom.

Laugh with the children, laugh at yourself, and never hold a grudge. Don't be afraid to say "I'm sorry" to a child when you have done something unprofessional or hurtful. If children do hurtful things, just hug them a little more tightly and make them feel safe. Children learn best when they feel safe and loved no matter what.

I don't teach to be remembered, although it's nice to think that you'll never be completely forgotten. I teach so that I can remember. I remember their personalities and how they grow. I remember the times we struggled with learning and succeeded, as well as those times when we fell short of our goals. I remember the laughter and the tears we shared.

Some people say, "Leave school at school." The best teachers I know often lose sleep thinking about and worrying about their students. It's worth every toss and turn!

- We revisit classrooms of the teachers you come to know as they talk about specific topics that affect their classroom teaching in *Teaching in Focus* features throughout each chapter. Each in-chapter Teaching in Focus is accompanied by a picture of the teacher speaking to us in his or her own words.

- Watch the interviews, room tours, and lessons you read about in these features on the *Teaching in Focus* sections of the MyEducationLab that accompanies this text.

Explore Your Own Positions on Education

Where Do I Stand?

These fascinating new inventories begin each chapter by asking you to think about the concepts before reading. This not only engages you in the chapter to come but also helps you personalize information you are asked to examine and reexamine as each chapter progresses.

Where Do I Stand *Now?*

At the end of the chapter, you are asked to reexamine the initial inventory, think about the chapter you've read, and consider how your ideas about teaching may have evolved.

Explore Issues of Diversity

Diversity Dialogue

Once per chapter we revisit a focus teacher's classroom to share an authentic issue related to diversity. *Diversity Dialogue* gives our focus teachers opportunities to share teaching experiences related to culture, ethnicity, language, socioeconomic status, academic ability, and more as seen in their own classrooms.

Reflect

Reflect on Your Evolving Understanding of Yourself as an Educator

Points of Reflection features ask you to pause and think through what you've read and apply the ideas to your own notions of teaching and learning. You will find Points of Reflection throughout each chapter.

Points of Reflection 9.8

Do you recall being bullied? If so, how did it happen? Did you know students who were relentlessly bullied in school? Did you know students who bullied others? How did you feel toward those who bullied others? How about toward those who were bullied?

Points of Reflection 9.9

Have you experienced theft or violence as a student? Have you seen any of these activities take place in school? What consequences did the perpetrators face? What was your reaction to these crimes?

Reflect on Educational Issues

Through the *In the News* segments, we explore issues in education that have been the topic of a variety of ABC News broadcasts, including *Nightline* and *World News Tonight*.

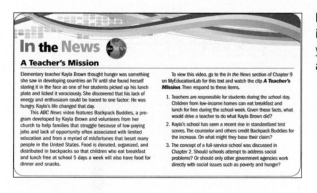

In the News features examine ABC News video clips reporting on specific educational issues, providing opportunities for you to consider issues from all sides.

In the News
A Teacher's Mission

Elementary teacher Kayla Brown thought hunger was something she saw in developing countries on TV until she found herself staring it in the face as one of her students picked up his lunch plate and licked it voraciously. She discovered that his lack of energy and enthusiasm could be traced to one factor: He was hungry. Kayla's life changed that day.

This ABC News video features Backpack Buddies, a program developed by Kayla Brown and volunteers from her church to help families that struggle because of low-paying jobs and lack of opportunity often associated with limited education and from a myriad of misfortunes that beset many people in the United States. Food is donated, organized, and distributed in backpacks so that children who eat breakfast and lunch free at school 5 days a week will also have food for dinner and snacks.

To view this video, go to the *In the News* section of Chapter 9 on MyEducationLab for this text and watch the clip **A Teacher's Mission**. Then respond to these items.

1. Teachers are responsible for students during the school day. Children from low-income homes can eat breakfast and lunch for free during the school week. Given these facts, what would drive a teacher to do what Kayla Brown did?

2. Kayla's school has seen a recent rise in standardized test scores. The counselor and others credit Backpack Buddies for the increase. On what might they base their claim?

3. The concept of a full-service school was discussed in Chapter 2. Should schools attempt to address social problems? Or should only other government agencies work directly with social issues such as poverty and hunger?

- Watch all the ABC videos discussed in these features and answer the questions posed in the text on MyEducationLab.

PEARSON
myeducationlab
The Power of Classroom Practice
www.myeducationlab.com

Develop

Develop Your Opinions on Different Issues in Contemporary Education

Letter to the Editor These features explore issues in education through an actual letter published in a newspaper, asking you to consider the letter, the issue, and your own opinion, and then to compose a letter of your own. The context is set by the chapter content, along with background information about the particular topic or issue involved. Following each letter are questions and prompts to help you form your own opinions. You are then asked to write a letter that supports the writer's views, adds additional information, or refutes the writer's stance. A rubric similar to the one used by the Educational Testing Service (ETS) to assess the writing portions of the Praxis II exams is provided to make clear the quality expectations of this assignment.

Develop Your Sense of Yourself as an Educator

Developing Professional Competence This end-of-chapter feature probes the issues of classroom teaching and helps prepare you for licensure exams by posing a case, again featuring the focus teachers you have come to know. Following the case are multiple-choice and essay questions that connect classroom issues with pertinent standards, providing an excellent study tool.

Answer all *Developing Professional Competence* questions on our MyEducationLab Web site and obtain hints and feedback to better prepare you for your licensure exams.

Supplements for Instructors

Prepare with the Power of Classroom Practice

PEARSON
myeducationlab
The Power of Classroom Practice
www.myeducationlab.com

MyEducationLab's easy-to-assign homework and activities will engage your students and ensure that they come to class more prepared. This saves you the class time that is often spent reviewing the basics and lets you devote that time to higher-level learning experiences. Informed by evidence-based practice, MyEducationLab connects your course content to real classrooms with interactive exercises and activities that enhance students' learning and give them a deeper understanding of teaching. Additionally, all of the activities and exercises in MyEducationLab are conveniently **built around essential learning outcomes** and **mapped to professional teaching standards**.

- Encourage your students to practice applying what they have been learning through **interactive exercises and simulations** including Building Teaching Skills and Dispositions assignments and the Classroom Management Simulations.

- Prepare your students to analyze, reflect, and respond to **real classroom situations** with assignments that provide them with classroom video, case studies, and authentic student and teacher artifacts.

- Address issues and generate class discussion with **ABC News** videos.

- Provide your students with interactive modules, case study units, and podcasts from the acclaimed IRIS Center at Vanderbilt University with the **IRIS Center Resources** on MyEducationLab.

- Assign **Practice Tests** for each chapter of your text, and your students will receive an individualized study plan that identifies their strengths and weaknesses and provides accompanying resources to help them master the concepts covered in your course.

- Explore **Teaching in Focus** footage that takes you inside the classrooms of the 10 focus teachers whose lessons, interviews, and thoughts brighten the pages of the text.

- Assign **Developing Professional Competence** assignments to ensure students comprehend chapter concepts as they prepare for their licensure exams.

- Use the **Lesson Planning Software** to develop high-quality lesson plans. The software also makes it easy to integrate your state's content standards into all of your lesson plans.

- Prepare your students to pass their teacher licensure exam by familiarizing them with **teacher certification test** requirements. This module includes descriptions of what's covered on each exam and opportunities to answer sample test questions.

Online Instructor's Manual with Test Items

An expanded and improved online Instructor's Manual includes numerous recommendations for presenting and extending text content. The manual consists of chapter overviews, focus questions, outlines, suggested teaching strategies, and Web resources that cover the essential concepts addressed in each chapter. You'll also find a complete chapter-by-chapter bank of test items.

Online PowerPoint Lecture Slides

These lecture slides highlight key concepts and summarize key content from each chapter of the text.

The electronic Instructor's Manual and online PowerPoint lecture slides are available on the Instructor Resource Center at www.pearsonhighered.com. To access these resources, go to www.pearsonhighered.com and click on the Instructor Resource Center button. Here you'll be able to log in or complete a onetime registration for a user name and password.

Pearson MyTest

Pearson MyTest is a powerful assessment generation program that helps instructors easily create and print quizzes and exams. Questions and tests are authored online, allowing ultimate flexibility and the ability to create and print assessments efficiently anytime, anywhere! Instructors can access Pearson MyTest and their test bank files by going to www.pearsonmytest.com to log in, register, or request access. Features of Pearson MyTest include the following:

Premium Assessment Content

- Draw from a rich library of assessments that complement your Pearson textbook and your course's learning objectives.
- Edit questions or tests to fit your specific teaching needs.

Instructor-Friendly Resources

- Easily create and store your own questions, including images, diagrams, and charts using simple drag-and-drop and controls that resemble those in Microsoft Word.
- Use additional information provided by Pearson, such as the question's difficulty level or learning objective, to help you quickly build your test.

Time-Saving Enhancements

- Add headers or footers and easily scramble questions and answer choices—all from one simple toolbar.
- Quickly create multiple versions of your test or answer key and, when ready, simply save to MS Word or PDF and print!
- Export your exams for import to Blackboard 6.0, CE (WebCT), or Vista (WebCT)!

Acknowledgments

As a teacher and teacher educator for more than three decades, I found the writing of this text to be a labor of love. I have experienced extraordinary professional development opportunities through this project as I have probed deeply the many and varied issues involved in teaching PreK–12 children and adolescents.

Numerous people have been instrumental in the revision of this text. Here are some to whom I owe special thanks:

- Jeff Johnston, Pearson Vice President and Editorial Director, for his consistent professionalism and faith in me.

- Ann Castel Davis, Executive Editor, through much of the revision, for her skill and insight.

- Meredith Fossel, Acquisitions Editor, through the conceptualization phase of the revision, for her efforts to make this edition possible and her much appreciated encouragement.

- Hope Madden, Senior Development Editor, for her expertise, marvelous sense of humor, creativity, and professional guidance throughout the revision process.

- Darcy Betts-Prybella, Senior Marketing Manager, for her expert sense of what professors and students need and want, in addition to her generous spirit.

- Mary Irvin, Senior Project Manager, for prompt and efficient attention to the details of production.

- Angela Williams Urquhart at Thistle Hill Publishing Services, for overseeing the copyediting, proofreading, and indexing of this edition.

- Carol Sykes, photo editor, for her conscientious help in making the photos an integral part of the pedagogy of the book.

- Principals Laura Hill, Mike Larsen, Carol Bartlett, and Maria Romero, for opening their schools to me.

- Brandi Wade, Renee Ayers, Chris Roberts, Brenda Beyal, Tim Mendenhall, Traci Peters, Deirdre Huger-McGrew, Craig Cleveland, Derek Boucher, and Angelica Reynosa, the text's focus teachers, for opening their classrooms to me and sharing their wisdom with teacher candidates.

- Dylan Todd, Sherlonda Francis, Amanda Wiley, Hector Mancia, Josie Ford, Patrick Sutton, David McBeath, Trista Kutcher, Guillermo Toscano, Mayra Reyes, Khamanny Douangsavanh, and Hugo Martinez, the text's focus students, for teaching me so much.

- Pam Wilson, Melinda Ratchford, Benette Sutton, Judith McDonald, Carroll Helm, Brenda McCraw, and Laura Campbell, my colleagues and dear friends at Belmont Abbey College, for their dedication to the preparation of future teachers that continually inspires me.

- Rus, my husband, for his unwavering support throughout, as well as the many hours of brainstorming and editing.

In addition, I want to thank the professors who contributed time and thought in their feedback: Carol L. Higy, University of North Carolina, Pembroke; Benjamin C. Ngwudike, Jackson State University; Elsa C. Ruiz, University of Texas, San Antonio; BeEtta Stoney, Kansas State University; Mary C. Ware, SUNY Cortland; and Colleen M. Wilson, Jacksonville University.

Brief Contents

Contents

Part II The Work of Teachers

Part IV Growing Toward the Teaching Profession

Special Features

Diversity Dialogue

In the News

Teaching in Focus

Twenty-First Century Knowledge and Skills

The Partnership for 21st Century Skills (P21) is a national organization that advocates for 21st century readiness for every student. The 21st century knowledge and skills proposed by P21 include **outcomes** students should master to succeed in work and life in the 21st century, as well as the **support systems** necessary for this to happen. The outcome knowledge and skills and the support systems are addressed in the text as shown in these correlation tables.

21ST CENTURY STUDENT OUTCOMES	CHAPTER	PAGES
Introduction of the Partnership for 21st Century Skills and 21st Century Knowledge and Skills	1 7	17 202
Core Subjects and 21st Century Themes	3 4 9	69–71 100–106 243–250
Learning and Innovation Skills Creativity and Innovation Critical Thinking and Problem Solving Communication and Collaboration	1 3 3 4 4	20 71–76 85 103–105 111–113
Information, Media, and Technology Skills Information Literacy Media Literacy ICT Literacy	3 4 4 4 6 7	85 101–102 113–114 110–116 154 202
Life and Career Skills Flexibility and adaptability Initiative and self-direction Social and cross-cultural skills Productivity and accountability Leadership and responsibility	1 3 3 6 6 6	6 69–71 78–79 171–173 173 173

21ST CENTURY SUPPORT SYSTEMS	CHAPTER	PAGES
21st Century Standards	1 4 4	20–21 97–98 100
Assessment of 21st Century Skills	5	125–146
21st Century Curriculum and Instruction	4 4	100–106 110–116
21st Century Professional Development	1 12	15–17 329–362
21st Century Learning Environments	6	147–177

Grade Level and Content Correlation

Throughout this text, your attention is drawn to these basic levels: early childhood, elementary, middle school, and high school. Regardless of the school grade configuration, student growth and learning generally move along a continuum that we address within these four broad levels. We approach teaching and learning differently based largely on the developmental level of the students. A first grade teacher in a primary school and a first grade teacher in an elementary school both teach children in the phase of early childhood. Similarly, sixth grade students in an elementary school and sixth grade students in a middle school are all young adolescents in the middle school phase of development. This table indicates where you can find grade-level specific information about a range of content in the text.

CHAPTER	EARLY CHILDHOOD	ELEMENTARY	MIDDLE SCHOOL	HIGH SCHOOL
Chapter 1: Teachers	8: *Teaching in Focus* 9–10: Traditional Paths to Teacher Preparation 11: MEL feature	9–10: Traditional Paths to Teacher Preparation 11: *Diversity Dialogue;* MEL feature	4: *Teaching in Focus;* MEL feature 9–10: Traditional Paths to Teacher Preparation 11: MEL feature 19: *Teaching in Focus*	6: Interest in Subject Matter 9–10: Traditional Paths to Teacher Preparation 11: MEL feature
Chapter 2: Schools	30: *Teaching in Focus;* MEL feature 42–43: Structure and Organization; MEL feature	43–45: Structure and Organization; MEL feature	36: *In the News* 45–46: Structure and Organization; MEL feature	33: *Teaching in Focus* 36: *In the News* 46–47: Structure and Organization; MEL feature 47: *Diversity Dialogue*
Chapter 3: Students	63: MEL feature 65: Developmental Characteristics by Level 74: Language Diversity 76: *Diversity Dialogue*	64: *Teaching in Focus* 65: Developmental Characteristics by Level 73: MEL feature	62: MEL feature 65: Developmental Characteristics by Level 77–78: *Letter to the Editor*	60: *Teaching in Focus;* MEL feature 65: Developmental Characteristics by Level 67: *In the News* 70: MEL feature 73–74: Language Diversity 75: Bilingual Education; MEL feature 86–87: *Getting to Know Trista*
Chapter 4: Curriculum and Instruction	118: MEL feature 119: Instruction	96: *Teaching in Focus;* MEL feature 118: MEL feature 119: Instruction	105: MEL feature 118: MEL feature 119: Instruction 120: MEL feature	104: *Teaching in Focus* 109: *Diversity Dialogue;* MEL feature 118: MEL feature 120: Instruction
Chapter 5: Assessment and Accountability	128: *Teaching in Focus;* MEL feature 113: Assessment of Dylan 144: MEL feature	132: *Teaching in Focus*	138–140: *Letter to the Editor* 143: *Diversity Dialogue;* MEL feature	138: *In the News*
Chapter 6: Creating and Maintaining a Positive and Productive Learning Environment	156–157: Routines; MEL feature 162: Extrinsic Incentives 170: Developing a Classroom Management Plan	150: *Teaching in Focus;* MEL feature 152: MEL feature 157–158: Routines; MEL feature 162: Extrinsic Incentives 170: Developing a Classroom Management Plan	158: Routines; MEL feature 171: Developing a Classroom Management Plan	153: *Teaching in Focus* 158: Routines; MEL feature 161: *Diversity Dialogue* 171: Developing a Classroom Management Plan

(continued)

CHAPTER	EARLY CHILDHOOD	ELEMENTARY	MIDDLE SCHOOL	HIGH SCHOOL
Chapter 7: History of Education in the United States	192: Kindergarten 198: Montessori Method	191: Common Schools	197: Junior High and Middle School	182: *Teaching in Focus*; MEL feature 183: Latin grammar school 188: Academies 192: Secondary schools 204: *Teaching in Focus* 204: MEL feature 205: *Diversity Dialogue* 207: MEL feature
Chapter 8: Philosophical Foundations of Education in the United States		214: *Teaching in Focus*; MEL feature 218: *Teaching in Focus* 228: Brenda's Philosophy Tree		226: *Teaching in Focus*; MEL feature
Chapter 9: The Societal Context of Schooling in the United States.	236: *Teaching in Focus*; MEL feature 237: Child abuse statistics 249: Childhood obesity study	239: *Teaching in Focus* 242: *In the News* 244: Substance abuse statistics	244: Substance abuse statistics 245: Perceptions of harmfulness of substance abuse 246–247: Sexuality-Related Concerns 249–250: Suicide 253: *Diversity Dialogue*; MEL feature	244: Substance abuse statistics 245: Perceptions of harmfulness of substance abuse 246–247: Sexuality-Related Concerns 249–250: Suicide 252: Figure 9.8 Immigration 254: Bullying and Columbine 255: *Letter to the Editor* 258–261: Dropping Out 259: MEL feature
Chapter 10: Ethical and Legal Issues in the United States	271: Recognizing Ethical Dilemmas	271: Recognizing Ethical Dilemmas 288: *Diversity Dialogue*	271: Recognizing Ethical Dilemmas 280–281: Legal cases	268: *Teaching in Focus*; MEL feature 271: Recognizing Ethical Dilemmas 284, 286, 287, 288, 289: Legal cases 289–291: *Letter to the Editor*
Chapter 11: Governing and Financing Public Schools in the United States	314: Characteristics of Principals 315: *Diversity Dialogue*; MEL feature 325: *In the News*	302: *Teaching in Focus*; MEL feature 313: *Teaching in Focus* 314: Characteristics of Principals 316: MEL feature 325: *In the News*	314: Characteristics of Principals 325: *In the News*	314: Characteristics of Principals
Chapter 12: Developing Professionalism	336–337: *Diversity Dialogue* 346: *Teaching in Focus*	342: *Teaching in Focus*; MEL feature	332: *Teaching in Focus*; MEL feature 344: *Teaching in Focus* 358: *Teaching in Focus*	339: MEL feature 342: MEL feature 352: *Teaching in Focus*

Teaching in Focus

Meet the Focus Teachers and Students

"You just had to be there!" we often exclaim when words aren't enough. Learning about teachers, students, and schools is one of those situations when photos or video clips can help convey what a thousand words cannot. Is it as good as being there? No, but it helps.

Throughout this text you will learn about 4 schools, 10 teachers, and 12 students. These people and places are real. You will get to know 10 teachers through interviews, room tours, and lesson clips in MyEducationLab and in *Teaching in Focus* features throughout the book. You will watch 12 students grow through real-life scenarios in both the text and in video segments that include student-teacher conversations and parent interviews. You'll see their smiling faces in the photos throughout chapters.

Explore these classrooms. Reflect on the teaching, the learning, the student diversity you see. Use these teachers, students, and schools to help you develop your own teaching identity. These 10 teachers and 12 students put faces on our discussions of development, diversity, teaching, and learning. Take your time as you read about, watch, and listen to them. Let their stories sink in. Think about the ones who speak to you most deeply. Let them help guide you toward your teaching identity!

FOCUS SCHOOL

Summit Primary School
Summit Station, Ohio
Kindergarten–second grade
Principal: Laura Hill

Summit Primary is a thriving school serving kindergarten through second grade students just outside Columbus, Ohio. Once a rural farm community, Summit Station where the school is located is becoming a suburban area that is increasingly diverse. In the last decade the student population of Summit Primary has changed from basically white and all English speaking to a rich mixture of races and ethnicities speaking at least 17 different languages. It's an exciting time of growth for the community, the school, and the teachers who spend their days with students in the early childhood phase of development.

PEARSON
myeducationlab
The Power of Classroom Practice
www.myeducationlab.com

Get to know the school and its principal, Laura Hill, and follow the teachers and students you are about to meet in the Teaching in Focus section on the MyEducationLab that accompanies this text.

Focus Teachers

Brandi Wade
Kindergarten teacher
Summit Primary School, Ohio
Teaching experience:
Grades 5-6 (2 years),
Preschool and K (14 years)

Brandi says she has found her place in life. From her family to her friends to her teaching career, everything fits for this exuberant kindergarten teacher. One look around her classroom and one brief conversation are enough to know that 5- and 6-year-olds who spend time in Brandi's care are fortunate children.

Brandi believes in active involvement of children. She finds ways to teach the Ohio kindergarten curriculum standards through lots of movement, music, hands-on experiences, and play. Each year she spends whatever time is necessary to help her 15 to 25 kindergarten students per class form positive habits so the necessary routines of the classroom take care of themselves. She knows that classroom management and learning go hand in hand.

"My heart is where the children are" is a phrase Brandi says and lives. She believes that children must feel comfortable and loved in their environment before they can learn and thrive. She laughs and cries with her students, allows herself to be vulnerable to their needs, and provides a warm, developmentally appropriate setting in which children learn and grow.

Brandi and her husband have two sons, a Jack Russell terrier, and two turtles. Brandi enjoys swimming, camping, reading mysteries, and going to movies.

Renee Ayers
Second grade teacher
Summit Primary School, Ohio
Teaching experience:
Reading teacher (2 years)
First grade (3 years)
Second grade (4 years)

Renee exudes enthusiasm for life. From the soccer field to the energy she puts into teaching second grade, Renee's personality shines through. She says summers as a camp counselor influenced her teaching philosophy of infusing active learning and fun into instruction.

Renee is a reflective teacher who spends time in her classroom diagnosing student needs. She says her biggest challenge is to design learning experiences for each child that take into account what the child already knows and is able to do. She believes strongly in individualizing assignments even when her instruction is geared toward the whole class. The children in Renee's class are learning to be reflective too. She saves samples of work from the beginning of the school year and periodically shows the samples to the students so they can compare and recognize their own progress. This is a simple process that's good for children.

At the end of the school year a very shy little boy said, "Mrs. Ayers, can you go to third grade with us?" The children pull at her heartstrings. All the effort is worth it.

Renee and her husband have a baby daughter, the delight of their lives. In addition to her adult women's soccer league, Renee enjoys skiing, snowboarding, mountain biking, and taking evening walks with her family.

Focus Students

Dylan Todd
Kindergarten
Summit Primary School, Ohio

Kindergarten

Dylan with Mom and Dad

Dylan is the only child of Brandon and Lisa Todd. Their pride is obvious as they talk about what a delightful little boy he is. When Dylan smiles, everyone smiles. When he giggles, his pure expression of joy is contagious.

Dylan is in his second year as a kindergarten student. During his first year, Dylan made progress and perhaps could have gone on to first grade. However, in consultation with the school staff, Mom and Dad decided it would benefit Dylan to experience another year of kindergarten, giving him time to mature a bit more socially.

We meet Dylan in the winter of his second year of kindergarten. His teacher, Brandi Wade, says that he has made wonderful progress in learning to read. In terms of the reasoning ability needed for progress in math, Brandi says Dylan is continuously growing and learning.

Sherlonda Francis
Second grade
Summit Primary School, Ohio

Kindergarten

2nd grade

Sherlonda with Mom and Dad

Sherlonda's personality shines. The challenge is to help her develop academically and find success in school so high school graduation will be in her future. Renee Ayers, her teacher, is afraid that if Sherlonda doesn't experience academic success soon, her penchant for socializing may actually get in the way of her success.

Sherlonda is doing fine in second grade. However, in first grade she had some difficulty paying attention and staying on task. Although this isn't unusual for early childhood students, it was chronic enough to concern the Summit Primary staff. Renee talked extensively with Sherlonda's first grade teacher, and they worked together to plan Sherlonda's second grade experience so she would experience success.

Sherlonda's mom is the sponsor of her church dance group, and her dad is very active in Sherlonda's life, saying his daughter loves to learn new things and figure out how things work. Both parents say they have always read to Sherlonda, and now she is reading to them.

FOCUS SCHOOL

Rees Elementary School
Spanish Fork, Utah
Kindergarten–fifth grade
Principal: Mike Larsen

Rees Elementary is a school for kindergarten through fifth grade students in Spanish Fork, Utah, just south of Salt Lake City. Located in a suburban area at the base of the Wasatch Mountains, Rees incorporates an emphasis on the arts supported by an experienced and enthusiastic faculty. While each grade level provides traditional classrooms, Rees also has a dynamic team of three teachers who spend their days in multiage classrooms of third, fourth, and fifth grade students, all learning together.

On the MyEducationLab that accompanies this text, you can hear about Rees Elementary from principal Mike Larsen. You will also hear from each of this school's focus teachers and students.

Focus Teachers

Tim Mendenhall
Third, fourth, and fifth grade teacher
Rees Elementary School, Utah
Teaching experience:
Fifth–eighth grade science (4 years);
Multiage third, fourth, and fifth grade (11 years)

Tim Mendenhall's ready laugh sets the tone for his classroom where third, fourth, and fifth grade students enjoy being actively involved in their own learning. Tim's comfortable manner allows his students to get to know him and one another in his multiage classroom.

Tim's approach to science is to provide interesting objects and books to grab his students' attention. Nothing compares to the excitement generated by the classroom's pet tarantula, Rosie. As Tim teaches his kids how to hold her, Rosie playfully crawls up and down his arm and onto the hand of a willing student (with a little coaxing from Tim!). Take a look at page 102 in Chapter 4!

The reading area in Tim's classroom is surrounded by bookshelves. Inside the area are couches and pillows. Tim says the arrangement is his *kiva,* a Native American meeting space that traditionally was hollowed out with room for seating all around and reserved for important and/or spiritual gatherings. In Tim's reading kiva, his students find a comfortable place to enjoy his collection of varied and interesting books.

Before deciding to teach, Tim was a forestry major. His wife and three sons share his love of the outdoors. Tim finds ways to balance a wonderful family life with his responsibilities as a classroom teacher. Teaching school may not be the most lucrative profession, but it's what Tim loves to do.

Chris Roberts
Third, fourth, and fifth grade teacher
Rees Elementary School, Utah
Teaching experience:
Special education (14 years)
Multiage third, fourth, and fifth grade (13 years)

Chris Roberts's adventurous spirit and active lifestyle permeate both his personal and his professional life. Chris has climbed Mount Kilimanjaro, rafted his way through the rapids of the Grand Canyon, and explored the shores of remote islands.

Chris brings his treasures to the classroom and shares his adventures with his students. Listening to real-life stories of scuba-diving encounters with giant sea rays and six-foot eels makes learning about ocean life and geography pure joy! Imagine spending three straight years in Mr. Roberts's class!

Chris is a fan of all kinds of art. He has posters of some of his favorite paintings on the walls of his classroom along with inspirational poems, essays, and even cartoons. Chris infuses lessons in math, science, social studies, and language arts with a sense of curiosity and elements of critical thinking. One of his goals is for his students to see beyond the classroom walls, beyond Spanish Fork, beyond Utah and the United States, to learn there's a whole world to experience.

Chris's family all share his love of adventure. Chris and his wife raised their children without television. He says there's nothing inherently wrong with television, but it distracts people from doing more worthwhile things like reading and experiencing life rather than just watching other people experience it.

Brenda Beyal
Third, fourth, and fifth grade teacher
Rees Elementary School, Utah
Teaching experience:
Third grade (8 years);
Multiage third, fourth, and fifth grade (13 years)

The teaching profession is very personal to Brenda Beyal, and she approaches it with a sense of calling. The classroom environment she creates is warm and inviting.

Brenda's favorite subject to teach is language arts. She views literature as a child's window on the world, and reading as a way of experiencing both events and points of view. When her class of third, fourth, and fifth graders read a book together, they explore meanings, not just words. They enjoy finding out about the author and rereading the story for deeper meaning. They write in their journals about story themes and act out sequences.

The fact that Brenda is Native American brings extra richness to her classroom. The wisdom of generations of her ancestors influences her. She has meaningful Native American objects and posters in her classroom and feels it's important for her to share parts of her heritage with her students. As they grow and encounter other Native Americans, Brenda wants her students to recall, "I know a Native American. I like the kind of person Ms. Beyal is. I'd like to get to know this person I have just met."

Brenda's family time with her husband, son, and daughter is very meaningful to her. She also enjoys drawing, sculpting, and collecting Native American artifacts.

Focus Students

| *Kindergarten* | *1st grade* | *3rd grade* | *Amanda and Mom* |

Amanda Wiley
Third grade,
Rees Elementary School, Utah

Amanda's mom, president of the Rees Elementary PTA, describes Amanda as "just plain fun." All it takes is five minutes of classroom observation to know the description fits. Amanda loves school now, but reading did not come easily for her, and first grade proved to be very challenging. Toward the end of second grade, things began to click for Amanda. Now in third grade, she is an avid reader.

Amanda is crazy about math. Mom says Amanda doesn't behave like a stereotypical girl. She would rather be involved in rough-and-tumble play than to do what most girls want to do. Amanda is the middle of three sisters and doesn't seem to have time for relationships with other girls.

The summer before going to third grade, when Amanda would be in Tim Mendenhall's homeroom, she talked her family into letting her be the caretaker of Rosie, the class pet. As it turns out, the class pet is not a cuddly guinea pig or a cute little rabbit, but a large hairy tarantula.

Hector Mancia
Fourth grade,
Rees Elementary School, Utah

Kindergarten 2nd grade 4th grade Hector and Mom

Hector's smile would warm the heart of any teacher. As a fourth grader, he is a fluent English speaker, vibrant, curious, and determined to succeed. Hector's family came to Utah from Mexico. One of his biggest challenges is to help his family learn English. Mrs. Mancia understands and speaks some English, but his dad and older brother do not.

Hector enjoys school. He fits right in with other third, fourth, and fifth graders in Chris Roberts's multiage class at Rees Elementary. Hector tells us that he really enjoys reading, sports, recess, and lunch—pretty typical of fourth graders. His mom tells us he enjoys basketball, school, and cleaning his room. This last may seem surprising, but Hector likes to please those around him.

Hector enjoys Mr. Roberts's lessons and says his teacher's travels add a lot to the classroom. Chris Roberts's teaching style draws him in and keeps him excited about school.

Josie Ford
Fifth grade,
Rees Elementary School, Utah

Kindergarten 3rd grade 5th grade Josie and Mom

At age 10, Josie loves school, reads fluently, enjoys math, and is quite proficient on the computer. She thrives in a multiage setting with children in grades 3, 4, and 5. She enjoys spending her days with her classmates, sharing the social aspects of children her own age and younger, as well as the academic challenge of learning fifth grade standards while assisting third and fourth grade students learn their standards. When Josie was a third grader she was assisted by the older children in her multiage classroom. Josie enjoys helping in the same way she was helped.

Josie has a well-rounded life and lots of advantages, evident both in her school performance and her home life. Mom tells us they have an active, outdoor-oriented family. She and her sister and parents often go on adventures in the Utah desert and mountains.

FOCUS SCHOOL

Cario Middle School
Mt. Pleasant, South Carolina
Sixth–eighth grade
Principal: Carol Bartlett

Cario Middle School serves sixth, seventh, and eighth grade students and is located in Mt. Pleasant, South Carolina, a medium-size city just across the Wando River from historic Charleston. Cario provides young adolescents with the foundational components of a true middle school, including teams of teachers who teach specific groups of students, close teacher-student relationships, high expectations, and a support network that boosts both academic and personal growth.

Meet Cairo's principal Carol Bartlett in the Teaching in Focus section on the MyEducationLab that accompanies this text. Here you will also be able to have a look at each focus teacher's classroom and meet each of the students and their parents.

Focus Teachers

Traci Peters
Seventh grade math teacher
Cario Middle School, South Carolina
Teaching experience:
Seventh grade math/science (6 years);
Seventh grade math (2 years)

Traci's classroom is filled with math—the shelves, the walls, the tables—math is everywhere. The seventh graders in her classes know they'll be actively involved in tasks that help them understand concepts. From geoboards to examine perimeter and area, to paper triangles they tear apart to prove the angles add up to 180 degrees, problem solving becomes something they do, rather than something they just read about. One of Traci's primary goals is to show students that learning math can be lots of fun.

Traci offers her students before-school tutoring to help with concepts that may be difficult. The sessions also help students who have been absent to get caught up. The tutoring not only gives an academic boost, but it also gives Traci and her students time to get to know one another better.

Traci believes it's important for teachers to reveal some of their personal selves to students. She freely talks about her son and proudly shows students pictures of him as she encourages students to talk about their families and what they like to do in school and out of school.

Traci is married and has a 2-year-old son. She says she loves the fact that she is his first teacher. Walking on the beach, traveling to see family and friends, and spending everyday time with her husband and son make life a real joy for Traci.

Deirdre Huger-McGrew
Sixth–eighth grade language arts, social studies teacher
Cario Middle School, South Carolina
Teaching experience:
First, fourth, fifth grade (7 years)
Sixth–eighth grade language arts, social studies (4 years)

Deirdre Huger-McGrew has taught a variety of grade levels and subjects. She says each one is interesting and challenging, but none so much as her current assignment on a two-person team charged with implementing a new program at Cario Middle School called CARE: Cario Academic Recovery and Enrichment. The program is designed to assist low-achieving sixth, seventh, and eighth graders in working toward grade-level competency.

Deirdre and her teaching partner, Billy, have been given a unique opportunity to begin a program and design it in ways that are responsive to their students. Principal Carol Bartlett has given them a good deal of professional autonomy. Deirdre says she is thriving in this situation even though her students are among the most challenging at Cario.

Deirdre's ability to talk with students about their interests, hopes, fears, and dreams makes her the ideal teacher for CARE students. She's the "mom" figure for the students.

Deirdre not only has students at Cario to care for, but her own home is brimming over with children. She and her husband have six children, all under 19 years old. Deirdre's attitude is "the more, the merrier." She says she's a teacher 24 hours a day! In her little free time, she enjoys writing and pursuing art activities.

Focus Students

Kindergarten   *3rd grade*   *5th grade*   *David and Mom*

David McBeath
Sixth grade
Cario Middle School, South Carolina

At 6 feet and 195 pounds, David doesn't appear to be 12 years old. However, looking at his childlike face and hearing his soft voice, you realize he is a young adolescent whose emotional and social development are yet to catch up with his physical growth. David wants teachers to be friendly and organized. What he doesn't like are teachers who are boring or who cover material too quickly.

David enjoys music. He plays the bass guitar with a church rock band several times a week. David's mom tells us he hummed before he spoke. Music is his favorite pastime and a way of expressing himself. This kind of interest and talent are particularly important for students with learning disabilities. David has struggled academically since kindergarten.

David's mom makes the most of his auditory skills by encouraging him to listen to books on CD and follow the words as he does so. David will need all the help he can get to succeed in public school for the next six years because of his academic difficulties.

Patrick Sutton
Seventh grade
Cario Middle School, South Carolina

| Kindergarten | 2nd grade | 5th grade | 7th grade |

Patrick is a very self-assured 13-year-old seventh grader who likes school. He enjoys being with friends the most and doing homework the least (no surprise here!). He says he likes teachers who challenge him and dislikes teachers who are mean and yell at kids. Patrick says he would like to join the NFL. But if that's not in his future, he would like to be an architect.

Patrick's mom tells us he is a delight at home. She says he is independent, easy to be around, loves his family, and enjoys attention. The main challenge Patrick has faced is that the family has moved often. Patrick has had to make new friends and start over several times in his eight years of schooling. Mom thinks that has made him stronger and a better student. Her hope for him is that he will retain his love of learning and be true to himself.

Trista Kutcher
Ninth grade
Wando High School, South Carolina

| Preschool | Kindergarten | 3rd grade | 9th grade |

Trista is as friendly as any high school freshman could be. Other Wando students pass her and smile when they say hello. Trista is a cheerleader and an athlete—and she has Down syndrome.

Trista's coach and fellow cheerleaders tell us they anticipated problems because of Trista's disability. They soon discovered that their fears were not justified. Trista has proven to have both the skill and the attitude to be an asset to the squad.

Trista, her parents, ReBecca and Joe, and her two sisters form a loving, supportive family. ReBecca and Joe are both teachers. When at Cario Middle School, ReBecca was there to make sure Trista had every advantage possible in a public school setting. At Wando High School, Joe is her homeroom teacher. Their interest and involvement have played a major role in Trista's success.

FOCUS SCHOOL

Roosevelt High School
Fresno, California;
Ninth–twelfth grade
Principal: Maria Romero

Roosevelt High School in Fresno, California, is a large urban school for ninth through twelfth graders. The student population of Roosevelt is predominantly Hispanic and Asian. Many of the Roosevelt students are children of migrant farm workers, and a significant number have only recently moved to the United States. The dedicated and creative faculty of Roosevelt High provides rich learning opportunities for all students, regardless of race, ethnicity, primary language, or socioeconomic status.

Get to know the school and its principal, Maria Romero, and follow the teachers and students you are about to meet in the Teaching in Focus section on the MyEducationLab that accompanies this text.

Focus Teachers

Craig Cleveland
History, government, economics
Roosevelt High School, California
Teaching experience:
History, government, economics (18 years)

Every day, during lunch as well as in the five-minute passing periods between classes, students gather in Mr. Cleveland's classroom to play a tune on his piano or strum a chord or two on his guitar. Several other students sit on desks and listen or participate. This doesn't happen by accident. It happens because Craig Cleveland welcomes students to express themselves, to be comfortable finding their own voice in his classroom and in his presence.

Craig's philosophical stance concerning teaching and learning involves his belief that students learn best when they are interested and involved through authentic reading, writing, speaking, and listening activities. The lessons he plans in his history, government, and economics classes include reading materials that push students to think and to interact with the text and one another. Students form opinions and write about them. Students speak to both question and persuade, to communicate in order to learn. The first rule of thumb in Craig's planning is "Give the students something worth thinking about."

Craig is an avid observer of human nature and the learning process both at school and in his home. He considers the home a fascinating lab for learning as he and his wife delight in watching their five daughters read, draw, create skits, and solve problems. Craig enjoys playing tennis and writing songs.

Derek Boucher
History, reading
Roosevelt High School, California
Teaching experience:
History (12 years)
Reading intervention (4 years)

Derek Boucher is an intense teacher whose conscientious involvement in the teaching profession sets a standard for all of us. His background in social sciences and his initial years in teaching led him to the realization that until students can read with fluency and comprehension, they will not be the kind of lifelong learners he would hope for them to be.

Although high school may seem much too late to learn to read, the reality is that many 15- to 18-year-olds can read only well enough to barely pass classes, and some not even to that extent. English-language learners often have even more difficulty.

Derek involves the students in all his classes in current events that impact their lives. He helps them put events and ideologies in context. They explore issues such as media influence and bias. He pushes them to think through issues, form opinions, and then find ways to express their opinions. He teaches them to be wise consumers of information.

Derek and his wife enjoy family time with their two sons and daughter. Derek is an avid reader of professional literature. He also contributes to it by writing opinion editorials in the local newspaper, the *Fresno Bee,* and articles in professional journals.

Angelica Reynosa
Modern World History
Roosevelt High School, California
Teaching experience:
World history (3 years)

Angelica Reynosa's tenth grade bilingual modern world history class is filled with enthusiasm. There are 34 students in the class, all of whom have been in the United States for less than two years. Angelica is a young Latina whose fluency in both Spanish and English makes her an ideal teacher at Roosevelt High School.

The students' enthusiasm for the class is enhanced by the fact that Angelica teaches in both Spanish and English. But language is not the only reason students are engaged. Angelica says her goal is to make every day enjoyable, memorable, and meaningful for all her students. She admits that it can be difficult to continually search for interactive, hands-on activities for teaching history, but the effort is worth it.

With a master's degree in school counseling, Angelica sees herself teaching several more years and then becoming a guidance counselor. She has aspirations to pursue a doctoral degree and plans to be part of the education profession for a long time.

Something that is particularly enjoyable for Angelica is the fact that she married a high school history teacher who teaches at a nearby school. Angelica says their conversations are filled with empathy because they each understand the other's dilemmas and can listen attentively and make helpful suggestions when challenges arise.

Focus Students

Kindergarten

3rd grade

6th grade

10th grade

Mayra Reyes
Tenth grade
Roosevelt High School, California

Mayra was born in the United States and is fluent in both Spanish and English. Friends are at the center of her life. Mayra would much rather be at school than at home. She enjoys going out with friends and playing sports. She says she didn't like to read before enrolling in Derek Boucher's class. Now that she has read her first real book, she says she reads better and faster and enjoys it.

On the day that Mayra's mother had agreed to come to school to talk, she didn't show up because of a domestic dispute involving Mom's boyfriend. Mayra's dad has been out of her life for years, and she doesn't understand how he can stay away. She confided that one of her fondest wishes is to be reunited with her father. Her home life often lacks the support that would help her be successful.

Mayra receives support at school through a program for Hispanic students focused on the arts called Folkloria. When asked about her future, she says she would like to be either a teacher or a nurse.

Guillermo Toscano
Eleventh grade
Roosevelt High School, California

Kindergarten   3rd grade   6th grade   10th grade   Guillermo and Mom

Guillermo represents the first generation in his family to go to high school. In conversation, his maturity and thoughtful demeanor are engaging. Guillermo tells us his dad came to the United States to give his family a better life.

Guillermo says he learns best when he experiences the concepts and content to be learned through class activities. He enjoys lots of teacher-student interaction.

Mom says Guillermo is always pleasant and kind. In fact, she affectionately calls him her "gentle bear." She says he enjoys school but is sometimes a little lazy. She lets us know with a giggle that even this trait endears Guillermo to her. He loves sports, both playing them and watching them. Mom hopes Guillermo will go to college and get into a business of his choice. She quickly adds that she hopes he can do all this right there in Fresno so he will be close to her. What a loving environment.

Hugo Martinez
Eleventh grade
Roosevelt High School, California

11th grade   Hugo with Mom and Dad

Hugo is a 17-year-old junior with a very outgoing personality. Are you wondering why there's only one school picture of him? When Hugo, his mom and dad, and three brothers crossed the Mexican border into California 18 months ago, they only brought the clothes they were wearing.

Angelica Reynosa, Hugo's bilingual teacher, interprets the question about what he would like to do in the future. He responds in English, "I have a dream in my life." Then in Spanish he says he wants to graduate from high school, go to college, and be a doctor or a teacher. Hugo's mom and dad, with Angelica interpreting, express their pride in Hugo and say he is responsible, does his chores and homework, and is well rounded. Their hope is that Hugo's teachers be positive and continue to motivate him.

Perhaps the biggest road block for Hugo is his lack of U.S. citizenship. This precludes him from receiving grants and government loans. Without financial assistance, Hugo will likely not go from high school to college.

Khammany Douangsavanh
Twelfth grade
Roosevelt High School, California

| Kindergarten | 2nd grade | 5th grade | Khammany and Mom |

Khammany speaks fluent English at school but only Laotian at home. She participates consistently and demonstrates an appreciation for the value of education. As a learner, Khammany says interest in a subject is the key to motivating her to succeed. Khammany says she likes history in Craig Cleveland's class because there's so much in the past to think about and so much in the future to predict.

Khammany's mom, who speaks no English and relies on Khammany to interpret, is very emotional when she says she wants her daughter to receive a good education to help her succeed. This is especially important since the death of Khammany's dad about a year ago. Mom views her daughter as the hope of their family. She's bright and determined, and her mother is obviously proud of her.

Khammany will be the first in her family to graduate from high school and would be the first to enter college. However, she will likely feel compelled to help support her mom and extended family, making four years of college fairly elusive.

1

Teachers and the Teaching Profession

In *Meet the Focus Teachers and Students* you were introduced to 10 focus teachers with whom you will interact throughout this text. Getting to know our focus teachers helps you explore how accomplished lifelong learners approach the classroom and the profession of teaching. Among the many questions to consider about teachers and teaching, here are some we address:

✦ Who teaches in the United States and why?

✦ How do we prepare to teach?

✦ Is teaching a profession?

✦ What is teacher professionalism?

✦ What are the characteristics of effective teachers?

No African tribe is considered to have warriors more fearsome or more intelligent than the Masai. It is perhaps surprising, then, to discover that the traditional greeting between Masai warriors is *Kasserian ingera,* which means "And how are the children?"

This traditional tribal greeting acknowledges the high value the Masai place on their children's well-being. Even warriors with no children of their own give the traditional answer, "All the children are well," meaning that peace and safety prevail, that the priority of protecting the young, the powerless, is in place, that Masai society has not forgotten its proper function and responsibility, its reason for being. "All the children are well" means that life is good.

If we greeted each other with this same daily question, "And how are the children?" how might it affect our awareness of children's welfare in the United States? If we asked this question of each other a dozen times a day, would it begin to make a difference in the reality of how children are thought of and cared for in the United States?

If everyone among us, teacher and nonteacher, parent and nonparent, comes to feel a shared sense of responsibility for the daily care and protection of all the children in our community, in our town, in our state, in our country, we might truly be able to answer without hesitation, "The children are well. Yes, all the children are well."

Where DO I Stand?

This is the first of 12 self-exploration inventories in this book. Through them you'll explore the world of teachers and teaching. Your responses are based on your opinions and your prior knowledge. As you explore the content of this text, some of your initial responses will likely change. This is how we grow. We consider what we know and what we think. Then we explore and learn more and more, leading to inevitable changes of opinions and broadening of perspectives. Exciting prospect, don't you think?

This first inventory helps you explore your personal reasons for considering teaching as a career. Read each item and decide how meaningful it is to you. If an item resonates very strongly within you, then choose "4: I strongly agree." Reserve a choice of "4" for those items you genuinely care most about. If you agree with a statement, but are not overly enthusiastic about it, then choose "3: I agree." If you really don't care one way or the other about a statement, choose "2: I don't have an opinion." If you simply disagree with a statement, choose "1: I disagree." If you feel adamantly opposed to a statement, choose "0: I strongly disagree." There are no right or wrong answers, just differing experiences and viewpoints. Following the inventory are directions for how to organize your responses and what they may indicate in terms of where you stand.

4	I strongly agree
3	I agree
2	I don't have an opinion
1	I disagree
0	I strongly disagree

_____ 1. Some of my fondest memories involve experiences working with children/teens.

_____ 2. The health insurance and retirement benefits of teaching mean a lot to me.

_____ 3. In K–12 school I enjoyed and excelled in a particular subject.

_____ 4. As a teacher, I look forward to growing professionally.

_____ 5. At least one member of my family is an educator.

_____ 6. I am considering teaching because I believe education has necessary societal value.

_____ 7. Teaching is most worthwhile because of the opportunity to influence students.

_____ 8. Although I may be interested in other professions, the stability of a career in the public school system draws me to teaching.

_____ 9. Both the daily work hours and the yearly schedule of a teacher appeal to me.

_____ 10. Doing the same thing in the same way repeatedly does not appeal to me.

_____ 11. My desire to teach is based on my love of a particular subject.

_____ 12. There was a teacher in my K–12 experiences who had a profound impact on my life.

_____ 13. My family is pleased with my decision to teach.

_____ 14. A teacher's primary task is to help students become productive citizens.

_____ 15. Being with children/adolescents is something I enjoy and look forward to.

_____ 16. I am anxious to read whatever I can about the teaching profession.

_____ 17. A major reason for choosing the teaching profession is the appeal of having holidays and spring break time off.

_____ 18. Being a teacher means always having a job.

_____ 19. Education is necessary for the continued success of our country.

_____ 20. I have very fond memories of my relationship with one or more teachers in K–12 school.

_____ **21.** Having a long summer vacation means a lot to me.

_____ **22.** I have been drawn to a particular subject area for years.

_____ **23.** Professional self-growth motivates me.

_____ **24.** I am interested in teaching because I want to work with children and/or adolescents.

_____ **25.** I plan to teach because someone in my family is encouraging my choice.

_____ **26.** I want to teach because of the promise of job security.

_____ **27.** Being a camp counselor appeals to me.

_____ **28.** I want to teach to positively benefit society.

_____ **29.** Content knowledge is the primary goal of education.

_____ **30.** Someone in my family enjoys teaching and relays positive stories about the profession.

_____ **31.** I would like to be able to personally thank a former teacher for influencing me to be a teacher.

_____ **32.** I like the idea of having days off when my own children will also have time off.

_____ **33.** I have a passion for a content area.

_____ **34.** Even in difficult economic times, the fact that teachers will always be needed appeals to me.

_____ **35.** My family values education and emphasizes the worth of teachers.

_____ **36.** My career goal is to emulate a teacher I have known.

_____ **37.** Without quality public education our society suffers.

_____ **38.** I am still in touch with at least one of my K–12 teachers.

_____ **39.** Being home by about 4 P.M. is important to me.

_____ **40.** Teaching appeals to me most because I love to learn new things.

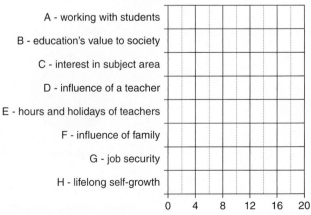

In the tables, record the number, 0 to 4, that you responded for each indicated item. Then find the sum for each table's responses.

ITEM #	MY #	ITEM #	MY #	ITEM #	MY #	ITEM #	MY #	ITEM #	MY #	ITEM #	MY #	ITEM #	MY #	ITEM #	MY #
1		6		3		12		9		5		2		4	
7		14		11		20		17		13		8		10	
15		19		22		31		21		25		18		16	
24		28		29		36		32		30		26		23	
27		37		33		38		39		35		34		40	
Sum A		Sum B		Sum C		Sum D		Sum E		Sum F		Sum G		Sum H	

Now it's time to graph your responses. Mark and then shade your sums on the **Choosing to Teach** *bar graph. The results show how much you value, relatively speaking, eight reasons for becoming a teacher that we discuss in this chapter. Your instructor may ask you to share your graph with others as part of the exploration of teachers and the teaching profession.*

By the end of this book you will have explored many aspects of the teaching profession in very personal ways. As teachers, the better we know ourselves, the closer we come to understanding our students and finding ways to address their needs to help them grow. At the end of this chapter we revisit elements of Where Do I Stand? *by responding to follow-up questions in* Where Do I Stand Now?

Throughout this book you are asked to respond to ideas and questions. **Points of Reflection** *features provide mental exercises that involve you in an extended conversation about teaching.* **Reflection** *requires us to honestly think about what we believe and do, why we believe it and how we do it, and the consequences of our beliefs and actions.*

Are you surprised by your graph? Is this the first time you actually analyzed your reasons for choosing to teach or for at least considering being a teacher?

Choosing to Teach

A - working with students
B - education's value to society
C - interest in subject area
D - influence of a teacher
E - hours and holidays of teachers
F - influence of family
G - job security
H - lifelong self-growth

0   4   8   12   16   20

Teaching in Focus

Traci Peters teaches seventh grade math at Cario Middle School in South Carolina. By all accounts she's an excellent teacher—just ask her principal, her colleagues, and, most importantly, her students. Outside school Traci enjoys a very happy home life with husband Dwayne and young son Robert. The seventh graders in Traci's classes know all about these two very important people in her life, and that's the way Traci wants it. Although math is the subject she has chosen to teach, she is conscious of the fact that her responsibilities go well beyond fractions and equations. She views each student as an individual with relationships and often complex growing-up issues. Traci reveals herself to them, and they, in turn, feel comfortable enough to share with her.

In a prominent place in the classroom Traci has a "Mrs. Peters" bulletin board on which she displays, among other things, family photos (from her childhood to the present), her favorite poems and book titles, her own seventh grade report card, and her 5 x 7 middle school picture. Traci says her students spend lots of time examining the board's contents, laughing and asking questions.

Traci sees herself as a role model of a healthy, positive adult who makes good choices and tries to make a difference in other people's lives. When asked if she would just as freely share with students the not-so-positive aspects of her life, she replies yes. When she's not feeling well, she lets her students know. If her son Robert is sick and she needs to stay home to care for him, she tells her students.

Traci attends her students' basketball games, concerts, spelling bees, Odyssey of the Mind competitions—the typical year-long parade of events. She views this as a tangible way to show her students she is interested in them, their growth, and their lives.

Watch Traci's room tour, as well as her interview, in the Teaching in Focus *section for Chapter 1 in MyEducationLab for this course.*

Who Teaches in the United States and Why?

Teaching is the largest profession in the United States, with almost 4 million teachers in both public and private schools (National Center for Education Statistics [NCES], 2009). Examine Figure 1.1 to see who teaches in the United States.

Figure 1.1 U.S. teachers

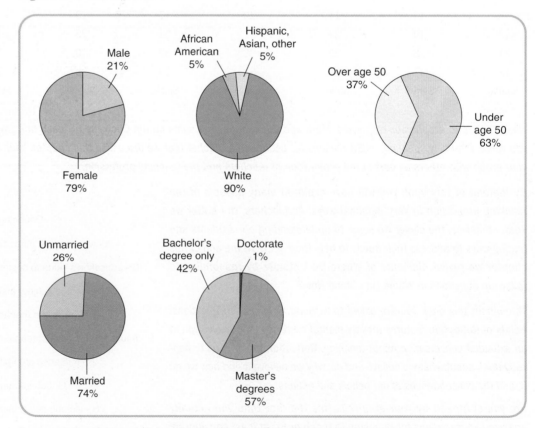

Source: National Education Association. (2003). Status of the American public school teacher 2000–2001. Retrieved May 15, 2005, from www.nea.org/edstats/images/status.pdf.

TEACHERS IN THE UNITED STATES

In Figure 1.1 you'll see that teachers are better educated than ever—more than 50% hold master's degrees. About 75% of U.S. teachers are married, 15% are single, and 11% are widowed, divorced, or separated. About a third of teachers have school-age children themselves (National Education Association [NEA], 2003). However, if you ask, they'll all likely tell you they "have" 20 or more children every year!

Also note that most teachers are white and female. There is considerable need for more diversity and gender balance in the teaching force. Do we want to discourage white women from becoming teachers? Absolutely not. Is there a need for more male teachers and teachers from minority population groups? Absolutely yes.

Most people join the teaching profession purposefully. In a large-scale survey of teachers with fewer than 5 years in the classroom, only about 12% said they "fell into teaching by chance." Some enter directly upon graduation from college, and some become teachers after pursuing one or more other careers. This same survey found that most teachers possess a strong inclination toward their career choice: 86% of the surveyed teachers believe that teaching requires a "sense of calling," and 96% say that teaching is work they love to do. The inference is that entering the teaching profession requires a commitment beyond that required by many other careers and, once in the profession, relatively new teachers overwhelmingly view teaching in positive ways (Public Agenda, 2003). But why did they choose to become teachers?

DECIDING TO TEACH

Helping you first make the decision to teach and then find your teaching identity is at the heart of this book. Exploring why other people choose to teach may help you clarify your own thoughts and desires. In 2001 the National Education Association (NEA) surveyed almost a thousand teachers, asking why they chose the teaching profession. The teachers were given a list of 21 possible reasons and asked to choose their top 3. Our discussion of the reasons for choosing to teach is organized around the eight reasons most often chosen by the teachers in the survey. As you read, think about your own reasons for considering teaching as your career.

> We explore student development in Chapter 3.

DESIRE TO WORK WITH YOUNG PEOPLE.

Because 6 to 7 hours of a teacher's day are spent in direct contact with students, enjoying their company is a must. Getting to know the students we teach allows us to become familiar with their emotional and social needs as well as their cognitive needs. You may hear teachers talk about teaching the **whole child**. This simply means attending to all their developmental stages and needs, along with teaching them grade-level and subject-area content. When we view the whole child, we realize the depth of our responsibilities as classroom teachers.

VALUE OF EDUCATION TO SOCIETY.

Education is widely viewed as the great equalizer. This means that differences in opportunity and privilege diminish as children reach their potential through quality education. In other words, the achievement gap narrows with the increased educational success of the students who historically underachieve. An **achievement gap** is a disparity among students, as some excel while others languish with respect to learning and academic success. Through teaching you will make a difference in the lives of individuals and thereby benefit society as a whole.

Traci Peters values young adolescents as individuals and develops strong positive relationships with them.

INTEREST IN SUBJECT MATTER. According to the National Education Association (2003), high school teachers choose "interest in subject matter" more often than elementary teachers. An intense interest in a subject area is important if you are going to teach that subject all day. Middle school is a happy compromise for people who have both a strong desire to work with students and a passion for a specific subject. Most middle school teachers teach one or possibly two subjects all day to students whose development is challenging and intriguing.

INFLUENCE OF TEACHERS. Can you name the last five vice presidents of the United States? How about the current Miss America? Who represents your home district in the state legislature? Who was your fifth grade teacher? Who taught your favorite class when you were a freshman in high school? The last two questions are the easiest, aren't they? That's because teachers influence us. They are uniquely positioned to shape students' thoughts and interests during the formative years of childhood and adolescence.

LONG SUMMER VACATION. A joke that's been around for a long time goes like this: "What are the three best things about teaching?" Answer: "June, July, August." Here's another. "What's the best time to be a teacher?" Answer: "Friday at 4." Within our ranks we smile at these harmless jokes.

Those who have not taught, or don't understand the pressure of having 15 or 25 or even 100 students dependent on them for at least part of each day, may view the schedule of a teacher as excessively punctuated with days off. However, time away from school is well deserved, even if it is used to catch up on teaching-related tasks. The change of pace is refreshing, allowing opportunities for revitalization.

Aside from summer vacation and days off, other aspects of scheduling make teaching a desirable choice for many. During the school year most teachers do not have students after about 3:30 in the afternoon. To people who work 8 to 5 jobs, 3:30 seems like a luxury. However, most teachers spend additional time either at school or at home planning for the next day and completing necessary administrative tasks. The teaching schedule allows for this kind of flexibility. A teacher's schedule is also ideal for families with school-age children. Having a daily routine similar to that of other family members has definite benefits.

INFLUENCE OF FAMILY. Most of us who consider being teachers grew up in families that valued education and respected teachers. If there are teachers in your family who are energetic and enthusiastic about their careers, they may influence you to follow in their footsteps.

JOB SECURITY. We will always need teachers. Those who are competent are generally assured positions even in difficult economic times. Other benefits related to job security include the availability of group health insurance and a reasonable retirement plan. It's unlikely that a career in teaching is chosen because of salary, although some districts and states are making progress in raising teachers' pay to be competitive with other fields that require a bachelor's degree. Table 1.1 shows average teacher salaries by state.

In almost all states and school districts, teachers are paid for both longevity in the profession and levels of education completed. A beginning teacher with a master's degree will receive a higher salary than a beginning teacher with a bachelor's degree. Two teachers with bachelor's degrees will be paid differently if one has 3 years of teaching experience and the other has 15 years in the classroom. In most cases, the fact that the teacher with 3 years can point to contributing to outstanding verifiable improvement and student achievement whereas the more experienced teacher has little to show with regard to influencing measurable student learning makes no difference in compensation. Is this fair? No. Have we found ways to measure student growth and pay teachers accordingly? Some ideas exist. But for decades school systems have tried to pay teachers based on performance, or

TABLE 1.1 Average teacher salaries, 2006–2007

Rank	State	Salary	Rank	State	Salary
1	California	$63,640	26	Wisconsin	$46,707
2	Connecticut	$61,039	27	North Carolina	$46,137
3	New Jersey	$59,730	28	Colorado	$45,832
4	New York	$59,557	29	Texas	$45,392
5	Rhode Island	$58,420	30	Idaho	$45,094
6	Illinois	$58,275	31	Arizona	$44,700
7	Massachusetts	$58,178	32	Arkansas	$44,493
8	Maryland	$56,927	33	South Carolina	$44,355
9	Michigan	$55,541	34	Tennessee	$43,815
10	Pennsylvania	$54,977	35	Kentucky	$43,787
11	Alaska	$54,678	36	Alabama	$43,389
12	Delaware	$54,537	37	Kansas	$43,318
13	Ohio	$53,536	38	Iowa	$42,922
14	Hawaii	$51,916	39	Louisiana	$42,816
15	Oregon	$51,080	40	New Mexico	$42,780
16	Wyoming	$50,771	41	Oklahoma	$42,379
17	Georgia	$49,836	42	Maine	$42,103
18	Minnesota	$49,719	43	Nebraska	$42,044
19	Nevada	$49,426	44	Montana	$41,146
20	Virginia	$49,130	45	West Virginia	$40,534
21	Washington	$47,880	46	Missouri	$40,384
22	Indiana	$47,832	47	Mississippi	$40,182
23	Vermont	$47,645	48	North Dakota	$38,586
24	Florida	$47,219	49	Utah	$37,775
25	New Hampshire	$46,797	50	South Dakota	$35,378
	U.S. average	**$51,009**			

Source: American Federation of Teachers (2008).

merit, but without the kind of success that perpetuates merit pay to the satisfaction of those affected, the teachers themselves.

When considering salary, investigate the cost of living where you want to live. For example, in 2005, thousands of experienced teachers in the suburbs outside New York City made more than $100,000 a year (Fessenden & Barbanel, 2005). However, an examination of the cost of living in such places as Westchester County, New York, shows that $100,000 there is equivalent to a much lower salary in most of small-town America.

> We look closely at teacher evaluation and possibilities for performance-based pay in Chapter 12.

OPPORTUNITY FOR A LIFETIME OF SELF-GROWTH. This is exactly what teaching offers. Few careers are as exciting or as rewarding on a daily basis, including the satisfaction of positively impacting the future of children. Teachers experience growth, both personally and professionally, in many ways: through relationships, reading, attending conferences, and the wide variety of professional development opportunities available. Teaching is not a stagnant career; rather, it continually presents new experiences, all of which offer opportunities for self-growth.

Sonia Nieto (2009), a respected educator and writer, offers additional, and perhaps more intriguing, reasons for becoming and remaining a teacher in Figure 1.2. Nieto's reasons are somewhat more complex than the eight we just explored and require thoughtful consideration. All of the reasons for choosing to teach are positive of course. Yet only discussing all the benefits and rewards of teaching presents a picture that's out of balance. No career is without challenges; no career is without frustration. Teaching has its share of both, as we discover while considering the many aspects of teaching throughout this book.

Points of Reflection 1.1

We've looked at eight reasons for choosing teaching as a career. Which are your top three reasons for considering the teaching profession and why?

Figure 1.2 Additional reasons for choosing to teach

Desire to engage in intellectual work
Belief in the democratic potential of public education
Anger at the current conditions of education
Sense of mission
Empathy for students
Enjoyment of improvisation
Comfort with uncertainty
Passion for social justice

Source: From S. Nieto (2009). From surviving to thriving. *Educational Leadership, 66*(5), 8–13.

Brandi Wade, one of our focus teachers at Summit Primary School in Ohio, tells us that perhaps we don't choose teaching, but rather teaching *chooses us.* Read about her philosophy in **Teaching in Focus**.

TEACHER SATISFACTION

Regardless of why teachers choose their profession, few will remain if their choice is not satisfying. As in any life's work, there are good days and bad, successes and failures, questions with answers often difficult to find. Talking with real teachers who spend their days with real students yields stories and opinions as varied as the individuals themselves.

For over 25 years MetLife, Inc. has surveyed teachers, encouraging them to express their opinions about many aspects of teaching. Teacher responses concerning their satisfaction with the teaching profession in Figure 1.3 are revealing and encouraging. The graphic depicts a comparison between teacher views in 1984 and teacher views in 2008. In both years teachers said they love to teach at the same rate, 82%. That's where the similarities end. As you can see, in responses to every other statement, teachers were significantly more positive about their profession in 2008 than in 1984, with three quarters of the teachers in 2008 saying they would advise others to enter the profession.

Teaching in Focus

Brandi Wade, kindergarten, Summit Primary, Ohio. *In her own words. . . .*

It may not so much be that you choose teaching, but that teaching chooses you. It will be in your heart and on your mind constantly. Although it's never easy for more than 5 minutes at a time, teaching is the most important profession you can pursue. I am truly blessed to be a kindergarten teacher. I get to teach a different lesson, meet a different challenge, and see life from different perspectives every day in my classroom.

Laugh with the children, laugh at yourself, and never hold a grudge. Don't be afraid to say "I'm sorry" to a child when you have done something unprofessional or hurtful. If children do hurtful things, just hug them a little more tightly and make them feel safe. Children learn best when they feel safe and loved no matter what.

I don't teach to be remembered, although it's nice to think that you'll never be completely forgotten. I teach so that I can remember. I remember their personalities and how they grow. I remember the times we struggled with learning and succeeded, as well as those times when we fell short of our goals. I remember the laughter and the tears we shared.

Some people say, "Leave school at school." The best teachers I know often lose sleep thinking about and worrying about their students. It's worth every toss and turn!

Figure 1.3 25-year perspective on teacher satisfaction

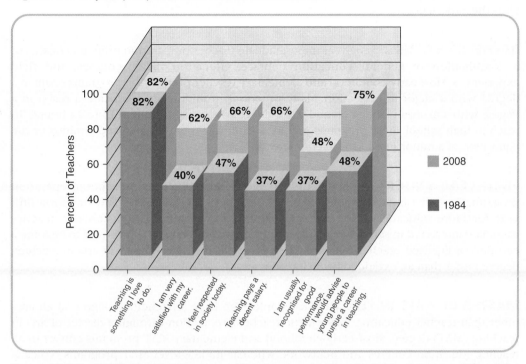

Source: MetLife. (2008). The MetLife survey of the American teacher. Available at: www.metlife.com/assets/cao/contributions/foundation/american-teacher/ MetLife_Teacher_Survey_2009.pdf.

How Do We Prepare to Teach?

You may have heard it said of someone, "He's just a natural-born teacher." There's some truth in this statement. Teaching comes more naturally to some than to others. With varying degrees of natural talent and inclination for teaching, we all have much to do to prepare to effectively make the teaching and learning connection. Our nature-given attributes must be enhanced by the knowledge and skills gained through studying content, learning about theory and methods of teaching, being mentored, reading, observing, practicing, and reflecting.

> We examine the influence of nature on who we are in Chapter 3.

Each state has its own preparation requirements for those who teach in public school classrooms. Most states require a prospective teacher to pass a test before they grant certification or licensure. The most widely used tests are part of the **Praxis Series** published by the Educational Testing Service (ETS). The state issues a teaching certificate or license when a teacher candidate is determined to be sufficiently qualified. Let's examine two broad paths to initial teacher preparation: traditional and alternative.

TRADITIONAL PATHS TO TEACHER PREPARATION

The traditional paths to initial teacher preparation come through a university department of education. National and state organizations carefully scrutinize university programs and evaluate how teacher candidates are prepared. About two thirds of states require university teacher education programs to be accredited (authorized to prepare teachers) through the **National Council for Accreditation of Teacher Education (NCATE)**.

All three of the following initial teacher preparation paths—bachelor's degree, fifth-year program, master's degree—include one or two semesters of **student teaching,** also called **clinical internship**. During this extended fieldwork, teacher candidates teach lessons and, for a designated time frame, take over all classroom duties. A classroom teacher

> Student teaching is discussed in more detail in Chapter 12.

serves as the **cooperating teacher** (host and mentor) while a university instructor supervises the experience.

BACHELOR'S DEGREE. A 4-year undergraduate teacher preparation program consists of a combination of general education courses, education major courses, and field experiences. Most early childhood and elementary teacher preparation programs result in a degree with a major in education. Many programs in middle-level education result in a degree with a major in education and two subject area concentrations (15 to 24 hours). To teach in high school, most programs require a major in a content area and a minor, or the equivalent of a minor, in education coursework.

FIFTH-YEAR PROGRAM. Some universities offer a fifth-year teacher preparation program. Teacher candidates complete a major other than education and stay for a fifth year for more education coursework plus student teaching. For instance, a teacher candidate interested in science may major in biology and then stay a fifth year to become a certified, or licensed, teacher. Some of these programs include a master of arts in teaching degree rather than an extended bachelor's degree.

MASTER OF ARTS IN TEACHING. People who have a bachelor's degree in an area other than teacher education may pursue teacher preparation through a master of arts in teaching (MAT) degree. Most early childhood and elementary MAT programs consist of all teacher education courses and fieldwork, whereas middle-level MAT programs typically require 18 to 24 hours of subject area coursework in addition to education courses. High school MAT programs generally require a degree in a content area or the accumulation of enough content hours to be considered a concentration.

ALTERNATIVE PATHS TO TEACHER PREPARATION

There is a growing movement toward alternative paths to teacher preparation. In the 1980s alternative certification began as a way to address projected shortages of teachers. Since the first efforts, we have seen various models for recruiting, training, and certifying people who already have at least a bachelor's degree and want to become teachers.

Since 1983 the number of teachers entering the classroom through alternative means has rapidly increased. Now all 50 states offer one or more of over a hundred different programs offering alternative certification/licensure, with some estimates stating that as many as a third of new teachers are using alternative routes to the classroom. Adults who decide that teaching is for them after having other careers are likely to enter the profession through alternative paths (Feistritzer, 2009).

Many alternative programs grow out of specific needs and are developed and coordinated through partnerships among state departments of education, school districts, and university teacher education programs. Their structures vary widely, and they tend to be controversial. Some people doubt that teacher preparation is as effective outside the realm of university-based programs.

Perhaps the most widely known alternative path to the classroom is through the nonprofit organization **Teach for America** (TFA). Teach for America's goal is to increase the number of teachers willing to tackle the challenges of classrooms in low-income areas. TFA recruits individuals who are college seniors or recent graduates who agree to teach in high-needs rural or urban schools for at least 2 years in exchange for a salary plus reduction or elimination of college debt. In 2009 there were over 7,000 TFA teachers (Teach for America, 2010).

Diversity is an issue when hiring teachers, regardless of how they are prepared. Read about Mike Larsen's plans to hire a more diverse teaching force at Rees Elementary in *Diversity Dialogue.*

Mike Larsen, principal of Rees Elementary School, Utah

In each chapter you will read about teachers, students, principals, and schools as they struggle with issues involving diversity. All of the scenarios are based on our focus people and places introduced in *Meet the Focus Teachers and Students*. These *Diversity Dialogues* put what we are discussing in context so you can see how teachers, students, and principals address issues in schools and communities.

Mike Larsen of Rees Elementary School south of Salt lake City, Utah, is in his first year as principal of this K–5 school. Rees boasts a rich racial and ethnic diversity. The students are white, black, Hispanic, Native American, and Asian, all the broad racial distinctions recognized by the federal government. Their **ethnicities,** or where their families come from, represent an even greater spectrum of diversity.

Rees is a very good school as determined by multiple measures. The students achieve at levels above the state average, there are few real discipline issues, the facilities are more than adequate, and the teaching staff is both effective and stable. Mr. Larsen is quite pleased to have been appointed principal of such a school. If he simply maintained the status quo Rees would hum along just fine. But one thing bothers him. Although he considers every one of the Rees teachers to be good teachers, Mr. Larsen is concerned that the profile of the teaching staff closely mirrors the national average. Of the 45 teachers, 36 (80%) are female and 42 (92%) are white.

In March of his first year at Rees, Mr. Larsen finds out that three of his teachers are not returning to Rees in August. Two teachers plan to retire and one is marrying a Marine and moving to San Diego. All three are white. Mr. Larsen immediately recognizes an opportunity to introduce more diversity into the Rees teaching staff.

Respond to these items by writing one well-developed paragraph for each.

1. Mr. Larsen is aware that at Rees the tradition is for an entire grade level of teachers to spend time with candidates for teaching positions. The openings will be in second grade, fourth grade, and on one of the third/fourth/fifth grade multiage teams. Mr. Larsen plans to meet with each group of teachers to express his desire to hire teachers who are more diverse. What kinds of things might he say to the groups?

2. Mr. Larsen plans to do some recruiting at local colleges. Why might he find a more diverse pool of teacher candidates in alternative programs?

GETTING TO KNOW SCHOOLS, TEACHERS, AND STUDENTS

Regardless of the route you take to become a teacher, the more experiences you have in schools with teachers and students, the better prepared you will be to have a classroom of your own. The more experiences you have, the more certain your decision will be concerning whether teaching is for you. Experience in classrooms will also lead to more informed decision making about your teaching identity.

Most preparation programs require field experiences throughout. You may begin with observations in one course and then work with individual students and small groups in another, with whole group lessons before and during student teaching/clinical practice. These experiences may hold many surprises for you. Having a 5-year-old nephew you enjoy seeing several times a year is very different from working all day with 20 5-year-olds in a kindergarten classroom. Your memories of senior advanced placement literature that inspired you to want to teach high school English may be a romantic picture of students paying rapt attention as the sonnets of Elizabeth Barrett Browning are discussed. However, this may be a far cry from an actual freshman English class. If you fit the profile of most teachers and are a white woman from suburbia, chances are classrooms in urban America will expand your view of what it's like to be a teacher. You can read about differences in settings and students in this and other books and be somewhat informed. Seeing for yourself brings reality into view.

The Teaching in Focus videos aligned with this text allow you inside four real schools to get to know 10 real teachers and 12 real students. The videos may be accessed through MyEducationLab for this course.

Preparing to teach requires reflection on the many roles involved in the profession.

There are other ways to gain insights into the classroom. Finding opportunities to have conversations with teachers is an excellent way to learn more about the realities of the classroom. Volunteering at schools, places of worship, and community organizations will present opportunities both to get to know kids and to observe adults interacting with them. Being a summer camp counselor, tutoring in an after-school program, and coaching in community recreation leagues all provide valuable experiences.

Is Teaching a Profession?

This text repeatedly refers to teaching as the *teaching profession.* Whether a particular job or career qualifies as a **profession** depends, in large measure, on who is making the determination. We hear references to the plumbing profession, the culinary profession, the cosmetology profession, but there are established guidelines for determining if a career or job is universally considered a profession. These characteristics of a profession will likely not affect common usage of the word, but examining teaching with regard to them helps spotlight aspects of what we do that may need to be strengthened.

CHARACTERISTICS OF A PROFESSION

For decades authors have delineated characteristics of a "full" profession. For equally as long, educators and others have debated whether teaching is indeed a profession. This debate is healthy because as we consider the characteristics of a profession and measure teaching by them, we see what teaching is and is not, what teachers have evolved into, and what teachers may still need to become. A summary of a full profession's characteristics, from both a historical perspective and a modern one, is presented in Figure 1.4. Let's look briefly at these 10 characteristics and think about whether each applies to teaching.

Considering that in the United States children ages 5 through 16 are required to receive a formal education, and that most do this through public schools, a dedicated teaching workforce can collectively deliver this *essential service* (1). Members of this teaching workforce agree that teaching requires *unique knowledge and skills* (2), whether acquired through traditional or alternative paths. On-the-job *training, ongoing study* (2), and development are encouraged, but not necessarily required, although most teachers must renew their teaching

Figure 1.4 Characteristics of a full profession

1. Provides an essential service no other group can provide.
2. Requires unique knowledge and skills acquired through extensive initial and ongoing study/training.
3. Involves intellectual work in the performance of duties.
4. Individual practitioners are committed to service and continual competence.
5. Identified performance standards guide practice.
6. Self-governance in admitting, policing, and excluding members.
7. Allows for a considerable amount of autonomy and decision-making authority.
8. Members accept individual responsibility for actions and decisions.
9. Enjoys prestige, public trust.
10. Granted higher-than-average financial rewards.

Sources: Howsam et al. (1976); Ingersoll (1997); Rowan (1994); Webb, Metha, and Jordan (2007).

certification/license every 5 years or so by completing graduate coursework or participating in other forms of professional development.

Teaching definitely *involves intellectual work* (3). Teachers pass along intellectual concepts and skills, which is the very heart of what teachers do. To enter and remain in a teaching career requires a *commitment to service* (4) and, hopefully, *continual competence* (4) as guided and measured by *performance standards* (5). The word "hopefully" is included because teachers rarely *police their own ranks* (6) to the point of excluding someone who does not live up to accepted teacher standards. If policing occurs, it is generally accomplished by administrators.

When the classroom door closes, teachers have a great deal of *autonomy* (7), sometimes approaching isolation. However, public school teachers must accept any student placed in their classrooms and must teach a set curriculum over which they have little or no control. Even with certain constraints, we are *decision makers* (7), and we must *accept individual responsibility* (8) for the decisions we make.

A great level of *trust* (9) is placed in teachers. After all, for 7 to 10 hours a day families allow teachers to have almost exclusive control over their children. In most communities, teachers enjoy a degree of positional *prestige* (9), but they are rarely *granted higher-than-average financial rewards* (10).

As you can see, not all 10 characteristics of a full profession apply to teaching. We still have few mechanisms for policing our own ranks (6), and the financial rewards of teaching are not higher than average (10). Teachers should continue to work together to perpetuate each of the eight characteristics we exemplify while exploring ways to incorporate the other two. Many associations and organizations are helping teaching to be a profession by allowing teachers through collaborative efforts to set common goals, speak with a collective voice, and build research-based foundations to support what we do and how we do it.

PROFESSIONAL ASSOCIATIONS

National and regional professional associations provide leadership and support for teachers. Some serve the general teacher population; others are specific to a grade span or subject area. Most associations solicit members, hold annual conferences, publish materials, provide information, and advocate for those who teach and those who learn. Participating in professional organizations is a positive step toward growing as a professional.

The **National Education Association (NEA)** and the **American Federation of Teachers (AFT)** are the largest professional education associations in the United States, with a total of more than 5 million members, including teachers, administrators, professors, counselors, and other educators. Both organizations are unions and represent their members in **collective bargaining,** or negotiating with employers and states to gain additional benefits for their members. Large nonunion professional organizations such as ASCD Learn. Teach. Lead., Kappa Delta Pi (KDP), and the Council for Exceptional Children (CEC) serve a wide spectrum of educators. Most national organizations have regional and state affiliate associations. These more local groups provide easily accessible face-to-face opportunities for interaction among members.

An organization that specifically deals with the needs of, and standards for, beginning teachers is the **Interstate New Teacher Assessment and Support Consortium** (INTASC, 1992). The standards endorsed by INTASC address what beginning teachers should know and be able to do. They provide the framework for beginning teacher performance.

Each subject area has a professional organization that provides guidelines for what to teach, sponsors annual conferences, publishes relevant books and journals, represents subject areas in educational and political arenas, and both encourages and disseminates research on teaching and learning. Table 1.2 lists some of the professional associations available to teachers to assist with their professionalism. Visiting their Web sites will give you valuable insight into just how important these, and other professional organizations, are and can be.

We explore professional organizations in Chapter 4.

TABLE 1.2 Professional Organizations

Teacher Unions

AFT	American Federation of Teachers	www.aft.org
NEA	National Education Association	www.nea.org

Subject-Area Organizations

AAHPERD	American Alliance for Health, Physical Education, Recreation and Dance	www.aahperd.org
ACTFL	American Council on the Teaching of Foreign Languages	www.actfl.org
IRA	International Reading Association	www.reading.org
MTNA	Music Teachers National Association	www.mtna.org
NAEA	National Art Education Association	www.naea-reston.org
NATIE	National Association for Trade and Industrial Education	www.skillsusa.org/NATIE/
NBEA	National Business Education Association	www.nbea.org
NCSS	National Council for the Social Studies	www.ncss.org
NCTE	National Council of Teachers of English	www.ncte.org
NCTM	National Council of Teachers of Mathematics	www.nctm.org
NSTA	National Science Teachers Association	www.nsta.org/
RIF	Reading Is Fundamental	www.rif.org

Level-Specific Organizations

ACEI	Association for Childhood Education International	www.acei.org
NAEYC	National Association for the Education of Young Children	www.naeyc.org
NMSA	National Middle School Association	www.nmsa.org

Need-Specific Organizations

INTASC	Interstate New Teacher Assessment and Support Consortium	www.intasc.org
CEC	Council for Exceptional Children	www.cec.sped.org
NAGC	National Association for Gifted Children	www.nagc.org
SCA	Speech Communication Association	www.isca-speech.org
TESOL	Teachers of English to Speakers of Other Languages	www.tesol.org

General Associations

ASCD	ASCD Learn. Teach. Lead.	www.ascd.org
KDP	Kappa Delta Pi	www.kdp.org
PDK	Phi Delta Kappa	www.pdkintl.org

What Is Teacher Professionalism?

Professionalism is a way of being. It involves attitudes and actions that convey respect, uphold high standards, and demonstrate commitment to those served. Fulfilling responsibilities and making the most of growth opportunities are core aspects of teacher professionalism. Patricia Phelps, former academic editor of the *Kappa Delta Pi Record* (a publication of KDP), presents a philosophical framework within which characteristics of teacher professionalism may be placed. Phelps (2003) states that teachers achieve greater levels of professionalism when they are willing to do what it takes, to do what must be done. In other words, professionalism involves hard work. This hard work requires commitment in three broad areas.

COMMITMENT TO MAKE STUDENTS OUR FIRST PRIORITY

Student welfare and learning must be paramount. Ask yourself, as a Masai might, "And how are the children? Are they all well?" Putting students first requires that we become advocates for their welfare.

ADVOCATING FOR STUDENTS. To be an **advocate for students** is to support and defend them, always putting their needs first. How do we become advocates for our students? Here are some components of advocacy to consider.

- Understand that advocacy takes multiple forms with individuals, groups, or causes, in both large endeavors and small actions.
- In all conversations, with educators and noneducators alike, keep the focus on what's best for students.
- Take an informed stance on issues that affect children. Actively promote that stance to have widespread impact.
- Support families in every way possible.

Advocacy guides our efforts and decisions directly toward our goal—improving students' learning, which, ultimately, improves students' lives.

MAKING WISE DECISIONS. As teachers we continually make decisions. Some of the decisions are made on autopilot, especially those that have to do with routines in the classroom. The quality of other decisions often rests on common sense and maturity, characteristics that are enhanced by preparation and experience. It's important to remember that our decisions have consequences and require thoughtful consideration to make sure we are advocating for our students and maintaining a classroom climate that is conducive to learning.

DETERMINING CLASSROOM CLIMATE. Our classrooms can be respectful environments that promote learning, or not. The sobering words of Haim Ginott (1993), a respected teacher and psychologist, should occupy a prominent position in both your classroom and your consciousness.

Points of Reflection 1.2

Does the commitment to put students first sound like something you are willing to do? Explain the reason(s) for your answer.

Advocating for students is important at all grade levels. Renee, a second grade teacher, and her twin sister, Tara, a high school physics teacher, both advocate for their students in developmentally appropriate ways.

I've come to a frightening conclusion. I am the decisive element in the classroom. It's my personal approach that creates the climate. It's my daily mood that makes the weather. As a teacher, I possess a tremendous power to make a child's life miserable or joyous. I can be a tool of torture or an instrument of inspiration. I can humiliate or humor, hurt or heal. In all situations, it is my response that decides whether a crisis will be escalated or de-escalated, a child humanized or de-humanized.

COMMITMENT TO QUALITY

Quality should characterize our knowledge of content and our relationships and interactions with students, colleagues, administrators and families. Phelps (2003) tells us that "modeling quality is the most significant way to motivate others to put forth the same effort" (p. 10). Modeling quality requires that we have positive and productive values leading to teaching that facilitates learning.

FACILITATING LEARNING. Making the teaching and learning connection is the primary role of a teacher. Learning is why students are in school, and teaching is how we guide and facilitate learning. Our effectiveness as teachers should be measured by how much and how thoroughly students learn.

We can categorize the responsibilities involved in facilitating learning in a number of valid ways. Perhaps none is more important than evaluating each of our actions in terms of its contribution to academic rigor and developmental appropriateness. **Academic rigor** refers both to teaching meaningful content and to having high expectations for student learning. **Developmental appropriateness** means that our teaching addresses students' physical, cognitive, social, emotional, and character development. Academic rigor without developmental appropriateness will result in frustration for teachers and foster discouragement and defeatism in students. Developmental appropriateness without academic rigor will accomplish little in terms of student learning. Neither concept is mutually exclusive. In fact, they shouldn't be exclusive at all but rather should interact in supportive ways and balance one another as they guide our decision making.

Points of Reflection 1.3

Are these dispositions part of your personal beliefs? What other dispositions do you think contribute to being a teacher who promotes academic rigor and development appropriateness?

DEVELOPING DISPOSITIONS. **Dispositions** are composed of our attitudes, values, and beliefs. They powerfully influence our teaching approaches and actions. Dispositions that are favorable to effective teaching include, among many others:

- I believe all students can learn.
- I value student diversity.
- I respect individual students and their families.
- I am enthusiastic about the subjects I teach.
- I value other teachers as colleagues and partners in teaching and learning.
- I believe families are important in making the teaching and learning connection.

COMMITMENT TO CONTINUAL GROWTH

Teacher effectiveness is enhanced when a lifelong learning orientation is in place. A commitment to continual growth provides a powerful model for students.

BECOMING A REFLECTIVE PRACTITIONER. We grow when we reflect on our teaching practices. As discussed earlier in this chapter, reflection with regard to teaching is thinking about what we do, how we do it, and the consequences of our actions or inactions, all with the goal of being better teachers. To be **reflective practitioners** means that we deliberately think about our practice, that is, what we do as teachers. We do this with the purpose of analysis and improvement. Sounds pretty automatic and unavoidable, doesn't it? But it's not. A teacher can repeatedly go through the motions of planning, teaching, and assessing throughout a career yet seldom engage in reflection that results in improved practice.

John Dewey (1933), one of the great American educators, described reflection using words such as *active, persistent,* and *careful.* So how do we become reflective practitioners who actively, persistently, and carefully think about how we teach? Here are some concepts to consider:

- Reflective practice requires conscious effort.
- Self-knowledge is vital and can be aided by thoughtfully completing the *Points of Reflection* throughout this text.

- Reading about and researching aspects of teaching will ground our practice and provide subject matter on which to reflect.
- Talking with other educators will both inform and strengthen what we do and how we do it.
- Being deliberate—doing what we do for a reason—will result in better decisions based on reflection.

21ST-CENTURY KNOWLEDGE AND SKILLS. Teachers committed to continual growth are determined to increase their knowledge and skills to keep up with current research and thought concerning teaching practices. During the first decade of the 21st century some major forces both inside of, and external to, the education community recognized and espoused the need for knowledge and skills that reflect the realities of the 21st-century world. Perhaps the most influential source of information about teacher and learner characteristics for the new century is the **Partnership for 21st Century Skills (P21)**.

In 2009 there were 14 states officially and voluntarily aligned with the Partnership for 21st Century Skills: Arizona, Illinois, Iowa, Kansas, Louisiana, Maine, Massachusetts, Nevada, New Jersey, North Carolina, Ohio, South Dakota, Wisconsin, and West Virginia. On the P21 Web site we find the organization's self-description. "The Partnership for 21st Century Skills has emerged as the leading advocacy organization focused on infusing 21st century skills into education. Bringing together the business community, education leaders, and policy-makers, we have defined a powerful vision for 21st century education to ensure every child's success as citizens and workers in the 21st century" (Partnership for 21st Century Skills, 2009).

The Partnership for 21st Century Skills outlines characteristics of teachers that help them teach students in ways that lead to success, including

- Critical thinker
- Problem solver
- Innovator
- Effective communicator
- Effective collaborator
- Self-directed learner
- Information and media literate
- Globally aware
- Civically engaged
- Health conscious
- Financially and economically literate

These are characteristics for teachers to spend their careers developing and improving. A commitment to continual growth requires it.

Points of Reflection 1.4

Do you have a desire to continually grow professionally and personally? If so, how do you know? If you are hesitant to answer this question, what areas of your own motivation do you think you need to consider?

DELAWARE VISION 2015

Teacher professionalism is required for any large-scale education initiative to succeed. Vision 2015 is Delaware's plan to transform its public education system, focusing on student achievement, fairness, and accountability. To accomplish this transformation, teachers who exemplify Phelps's three areas of professional commitment—putting students first, quality, continual growth—are absolutely necessary.

Delaware's stated goal is to create the best schools for every student, no exceptions and no excuses. In other words, Vision 2015 calls for professional educators to respect the uniqueness of each student and provide the schools necessary for all students to succeed. Delaware proposes to make the changes necessary closest to the students—in the schools and in the classrooms—and sets high expectations for every child and every educator. The initiative revolves around six major areas of reform: setting high sights, investing in early childhood education, developing and supporting great teachers, empowering principals to be great school leaders, encouraging innovation and requiring accountability, and establishing a simple and fair funding system (Delaware Department of Education, 2006).

This chapter's *Letter to the Editor* covers a lot of ground, with topics related to Delaware's Vision 2015. The writer suggests that the lofty goals of Vision 2015 will not be accomplished without eliminating ineffective teachers.

Letter to the Editor

This letter appeared in the Wilmington, Delaware, newspaper, the *Wilmington News Journal*.

NOVEMBER 12, 2009 SAME TEACHERS, ADMINISTRATORS WILL NOT GET REFORM JOB DONE

I applaud Marvin "Skip" Schoenhals and his team at Vision 2015 for trying to turn around our public school system here in Delaware and for giving us a report on the current status of education in Delaware.

Unfortunately, his report of some progress contained no quantitative assessments. The only numbers were those related to possible additional federal funding—throwing more money at the problem. Again, unfortunately, the Vision 2015 team is trying to produce a winning team with the same old players (teachers and administrators). Some of these players may well respond favorably to their new coaches.

However, many will probably not, and, at best, will do so grudgingly as new strategies and plays are being developed and attempted to be implemented—these teachers simply carry too much old baggage. In turn-around situations, even the best of coaches will need substantially new players. Players with more talent should be recruited; old players should be given five years to demonstrate new talent or find themselves alternate occupations—they won't make the cut.

Existing players should be given five years to obtain degrees in the subject matter they are teaching—subject matter degrees, not degrees in education or pseudo-subject matter degrees such as physics for non-scientists. All new teachers should be required to have such substantive degrees.

James R. Thomen

Montchanin

Now it's your turn. Write a letter to the editor from the perspective of a future teacher expressing your views concerning the letter writer's concerns. You may comment on any, or all, of the writer's expressed opinions.

The following information and questions may help you frame your thinking but should not limit nor determine what you write.

1. The writer expresses apparent disgust at what he calls "throwing more money at the problem." As a future teacher, how would you answer this common criticism?

2. Does the sports metaphor work in this case? Are there problems with the analogy you want to point out?

3. Is characterizing experienced teachers as "carrying too much baggage" a generalization that's fair? Do you think it likely applies to some teachers?

4. What do you think about the 5-year time frame to demonstrate new talent?

5. Should all teachers, regardless of the grade level they teach, be required to have subject-area degrees as opposed to maybe a degree in elementary education or early childhood education? What about middle and high school teachers?

6. How does what you know about what's considered a full profession relate to the writer's view of getting rid of teachers who are judged to be ineffective?

Write your letter in understandable terminology, remembering that readers of newspaper letters to the editor are citizens who may have limited knowledge of school practices and policies.

Figure 1.5 is a scoring guide that may be used to assess your letter to the editor. It is the same guide that the Educational Testing Service uses to assess the writing portion of the Praxis II *Principles of Learning and Teaching* exam many states require for either initial teacher licensure/certification or at the completion of the first year of teaching. You will refer to Figure 1.5 in subsequent chapters as you write additional letters to the editor.

Figure 1.5 General scoring guide for *Letter to the Editor* features

A response that receives a score of 3:

- Demonstrates a thorough understanding of the aspects of the case that are relevant to the question
- Responds appropriately to all parts of the question
- If an explanation is required, provides a strong explanation that is well supported by relevant evidence
- Demonstrates a strong knowledge of pedagogical concepts, theories, facts, procedures, or methodologies relevant to the question

A response that receives a score of 2:

- Demonstrates a basic understanding of the aspects of the case that are relevant to the question
- Responds appropriately to one portion of the question
- If an explanation is required, provides a weak explanation that is supported by relevant evidence
- Demonstrates some knowledge of pedagogical concepts, theories, facts, procedures, or methodologies relevant to the question

A response that receives a score of 1:

- Demonstrates misunderstanding of the aspects of the case that are relevant to the question
- Fails to respond appropriately to the question
- Is not supported by relevant evidence
- Demonstrates little knowledge of pedagogical concepts, theories, facts, procedures, or methodologies relevant to the question

No credit is given for blank or off-topic responses.

Deirdre Huger-McGrew expresses her views about continual professional growth in the ***Teaching in Focus***.

This text will continue to refer to a career in teaching as the *teaching profession* and to teachers as *professionals*. Commitment to students, quality, and growth—everything a professional teacher does can be placed within this framework. Remember these three commitments as we examine what it means to be an effective teacher.

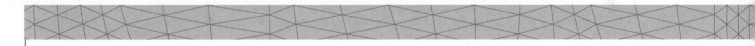

Teaching in Focus

Deirdre Huger-McGrew, language arts/social studies, Cario Middle School, South Carolina. *In her own words. . . .*

Throughout my 12 years as a teacher, I've taken many courses beyond my initial teacher training. I have been involved in teaching-related projects, most by choice and others as directed by my principal to achieve school and district goals. I have taken my professional development personally because I feel it is a part of my responsibility to nurture my growth as a teacher. It is my identity. It is who I am as a teacher. Seeking to enhance my skills makes a difference in my classroom. I take delight in embracing changing views and trying strategies that have the potential to improve my teaching.

What makes athletes, doctors, or lawyers the best in their fields? I believe it is their desire and ability to seek ways to improve what they do as professionals. This gives them an edge. Teachers should want the same. I want to continually accomplish growth-enhancing professional goals.

What Are the Characteristics of Effective Teachers?

"From the moment students enter a school, the most important factor in their success is not the color of the skin or the income of their parents, it's the person standing at the front of the classroom." This powerful statement was made in a speech to the Hispanic Chamber of Commerce in 2009 by President Barack Obama. Sobering, isn't it? The president of the United States is stating what recent research corroborates. Teachers make the most difference when it comes to student learning. Our effectiveness, or lack of it, matters.

The search for a neatly packaged description of an effective teacher dates back for centuries, even millennia. The best we can come up with are lists of characteristics based on observation and available data, along with narrative anecdotal descriptions. There's a lot to be learned from considering a number of perspectives.

Standards for teachers are expectations for what they should know and be able to do. All teacher education standards address teacher effectiveness. School-level organizations such as the National Middle School Association (NMSA) and the Association for Childhood Education International (ACEI) prescribe standards for new teachers. The 10 standards of the Interstate New Teacher Assessment and Support Consortium (INTASC) describe what effective teachers should know and be able to do regardless of the level they teach (Figure 1.6).

The **No Child Left Behind Act of 2001 (NCLB),** the 2001 to 2010 reauthorization of the Elementary and Secondary Education Act, was the most sweeping school legislation in decades. One of the major aspects of NCLB was the requirement that teachers be **highly qualified,** meaning that they have a standard of content knowledge and specialized

Figure 1.6 INTASC standards

1. The teacher understands the central concepts, tools of inquiry, and structures of the discipline(s) he or she teaches and can create learning experiences that make these aspects of subject matter meaningful for students.
2. The teacher understands how children learn and develop and can provide learning opportunities that support their intellectual, social, and personal development.
3. The teacher understands how students differ in their approaches to learning and creates instructional opportunities that are adapted to diverse learners.
4. The teacher understands and uses a variety of instructional strategies to encourage students' development of critical thinking, problem solving, and performance skills.
5. The teacher uses an understanding of individual and group motivation and behavior to create a learning environment that encourages positive social interaction, active engagement in learning, and self-motivation.
6. The teacher uses knowledge of effective verbal, nonverbal, and media communication techniques to foster active inquiry, collaboration, and supportive interaction in the classroom.
7. The teacher plans instruction based upon knowledge of subject matter, students, the community, and curriculum goals.
8. The teacher understands and uses formal and informal assessment strategies to evaluate and ensure the continuous intellectual and social development of the learner.
9. The teacher is a reflective practitioner who continually evaluates the effects of his/her choices and actions on others (students, parents, and other professionals in the learning community) and who actively seeks out opportunities to grow professionally.
10. The teacher fosters relationships with school colleagues, parents, and agencies in the larger community to support students' learning and well-being.

Source: The Interstate New Teacher Assessment and Support Consortium (INTASC) standards were developed by the Council of Chief State School Officers and member states. Copies may be downloaded from the Council's Web site at www.ccsso.org. Council of Chief State School Officers. (1992). *Model standards for beginning teacher licensing, assessment, and development: A resource for state dialogue.* Washington, DC: Author.

preparation for their chosen level. The federal government set guidelines for the quality of teachers in public schools, but each state determines its own policy for what teachers must do to be considered highly qualified. Experienced teachers have options in terms of how to meet the highly qualified stipulations.

WHAT PARENTS SAY ABOUT TEACHER EFFECTIVENESS

In the 41st annual *Phi Delta Kappan/Gallup Poll of the Public's Attitudes Toward the Public Schools*, parents were asked to rank nine teacher traits. From most important to least, the parents polled chose the following:

1. Dedication to, and enthusiasm for, the teaching profession
2. Caring about students
3. Intelligence
4. Ability to communicate, to understand, to relate
5. High moral character
6. Friendliness, good personality, sense of humor
7. Ability to discipline, to be firm and fair
8. Patience
9. Ability to inspire, motivate students (Bushaw & McNee, 2009)

A surprising and welcome statistic to come from the 2009 poll is that 7 of 10 parents report that they would like their children to become public school teachers. This whopping 70% is the highest percentage to respond favorably concerning their own children becoming teachers in over 30 years.

WHAT TEACH FOR AMERICA HAS DISCOVERED ABOUT EFFECTIVE TEACHERS

While attempting to determine why some teachers are significantly more effective than others in facilitating student learning, Teach for America has systematically observed and analyzed the results achieved by TFA teachers. They found some intriguing characteristics linked to teachers who facilitate student learning beyond what might be predicted for the mostly poor, mostly minority, student population taught by TFA teachers. Effective teachers tend to . . .

1. set high, long-term goals for their students
2. perpetually look for ways to improve their effectiveness
3. constantly reevaluate what they are doing
4. recruit students and their families into the teaching and learning process
5. maintain focus, making sure everything they do contributes to student learning
6. plan exhaustively and purposefully
7. refuse to surrender to poverty, bureaucracy, and budgetary shortfalls
8. establish efficient classroom routines
9. possess a relentless mind-set of perseverance
10. reflect on their performance and adapt accordingly
11. show signs of contentment with their lives
12. have a history of personal goal achievement
13. know the content they teach (Ripley, 2010)

Although not necessarily a trait appropriate for this list, Teach for America tells us that a predictor of a TFA teacher's classroom success is grade point average (GPA) in the last 2 years

Effective teachers purposefully and collaboratively plan for instruction.

We discuss student assessment in Chapter 5 and evaluating teachers based on student performance in Chapter 12.

Points of Reflection 1.5

Think about the teachers you have had. What made some effective and others relatively ineffective?

of college, rather than overall GPA. In other words, a GPA that starts out mediocre and then improves appears to be associated with greater teacher effectiveness than a 4.0 all 4 years. Another interesting point is that the more college extracurricular accomplishments, the better the teacher. These are areas you can work on *right now* that will help shape the teacher you will become. Encouraging, isn't it?

WHAT STUDENTS SAY ABOUT TEACHER EFFECTIVENESS

Emphasis has shifted recently from the teacher to the pupil as the focal point for defining teacher effectiveness. Very simply stated, the "ultimate proof of teacher effectiveness is student results" (Stronge, 2002, p. 65). But what results? What seems like a simple statement has complicated nuances because accurately assessing student learning is itself complex. Do we judge the effectiveness of a teacher solely by the standardized test scores of students? That would be easy if standardized test scores told the whole story.

In a survey of about 400 urban, low-income middle and high school students conducted by Corbett and Wilson (2002), all of them identified their teachers as the main factor in determining how much they learned. They listed a variety of characteristics of the diverse teachers most effective in helping them learn, all of which fit into the following six categories. Effective teachers . . .

1. push students to learn
2. maintain order
3. are willing to help
4. explain until everyone understands
5. vary classroom activities
6. try to understand students (pp. 19–20)

EFFECTIVE TEACHERS MAKE A DIFFERENCE

"Substantial research evidence suggests that well-prepared, capable teachers have the largest impact on student learning" (Darling-Hammond, 2003, p. 7). This is not to say that other factors we discuss throughout this book do not significantly influence student learning. However, Linda Darling-Hammond, a noted expert on teacher quality, and others contend that an effective teacher can overcome many of the circumstances in students' lives and positively impact student learning. When the outside influences on student learning result in an achievement gap, Kati Haycock (2003), director of the Education Trust, tells us, "If we insist on quality teachers for every student, we can dramatically improve the achievement of poor and minority students and substantially narrow the achievement gap" (p. 11). Reiterating the need for effective teachers, James Stronge (2002), another respected educator, writes, "Teachers have a powerful, long-lasting influence on their students. They directly affect how students learn, what they learn, how much they learn, and the ways they interact with one another, and the world around them" (p. vii).

Teachers can be effective using very different approaches. You can probably name two teachers in your own experience who were effective but who had different traits. Stronge (2002) tells us "teaching effectiveness draws on a multitude of skills and attributes in different combinations and in different contexts to produce the results that define effectiveness" (p. 64).

An important factor to understand when it comes to the characteristics of effective teachers and teaching is that much of what makes teachers effective comes through experience in the classroom. This is not to say that new teachers can't be effective. Of course they can! But think about this. Teaching is a profession that expects a brand-new teacher to do the same job as an experienced veteran (Johnson & Kardos, 2005). Don't count on someone saying, "Hey, it's okay if only half your kids learn about half of what you attempt to teach. After all, you're new." David Berliner (2000), a noted leader in teacher education, estimates that it takes about 5 years to "get smart about teaching" (p. 360). Some of the characteristics of effectiveness take time to develop: It takes time to be able to make decisions with automaticity and to draw on experience to supplement formal training.

Throughout this text you are urged to ask repeatedly, as the Masai do, "And how are the children? Are they all well?" However, when you are a novice teacher, your primary question may often be "How am I doing?" In *Educating Esme: Diary of a Teacher's First Year,* Esme Codell (1999) reveals that her mentor told her that with experience the question "How am I doing?" increasingly becomes "How are the children doing?"

Effective teachers, regardless of whom or what they teach, share many common characteristics. Teacher professionalism is a thread that binds them all. But although there are many similarities, the day-to-day responsibilities may vary in many ways. Teachers of students with special needs; teachers who specialize in art, music, or physical education; teachers who teach all or most subjects to one group of students; and teachers who teach the same content area each day to several groups of students—all have specific preparation requirements and position responsibilities.

CONCLUDING THOUGHTS

Learning to be a teacher . . . teaching so others learn . . . learning to be a better teacher—this life-affirming cycle can be yours. Think of the cycle as a wheel that gathers momentum and takes you on a profound journey. You have begun to grow toward the profession. As a teacher you'll grow within the profession. Read what becoming a teacher meant to one young man, Jamie Sawatsky, a seventh grade history teacher in Chantilly, Virginia.

> I noticed the change in myself the first time I walked into my classroom. I was no longer Jamie. That was the name of the young man who had delivered pizzas or worked at the office. My newfound teaching life had metamorphosed me into "Mr. Sawatsky." My previous work experiences had taught me a variety of skills, but accepting the title of teacher has cast me into a world where I am charged with the awesome responsibility of sculpting young minds and preparing students for positive participation in their community. When asked why they entered the profession, many teachers respond, "I wanted a chance to make a positive change in the world." In my case, perhaps selfishly, I wanted to be in a profession that would make a positive change in me. With my first year of teaching about to conclude, I can say that I am happy to be a teacher and happy to be "Mr. Sawatsky." (Tell, 2001, p. 18)

After reading the *Chapter in Review,* interact with Traci Peters in this chapter's *Developing Professional Competence.*

Chapter in Review

Who teaches in the United States and why?

- Teaching is the largest profession in the United States.
- Most teachers are white women, leading to a need for more men and people of color in teaching.
- Almost 90% of teachers believe teaching requires a "true sense of calling."

- The most common reasons for choosing to teach include the desire to work with young people, the value of education to society, interest in a subject, the influence of a teacher or of family, the teaching schedule, job security, and the opportunity for a lifetime of self-growth.
- Teacher satisfaction with the profession has grown over the last 25 years.

How do we prepare to teach?

- States issue a certificate or license to teach in public schools based on their own criteria.
- The traditional path to becoming a teacher is through a university-based teacher preparation program.
- Alternative paths to teacher preparation provide timely, but somewhat controversial, routes to teacher certification.
- There are many ways to get to know teachers, students, and schools, including field experiences through teacher preparation programs, volunteer opportunities, watching movies about teachers, and participating online through this and other texts.

Is teaching a profession?

- A profession is an occupation that includes extensive training before entering, a code of ethics, and service as the primary product.
- Teaching meets most of the criteria generally agreed upon for a full profession.
- Numerous professional organizations support teachers and teaching.

- Teachers can and should make contributions to the knowledge base of the teaching profession.

What is teacher professionalism?

- Teacher professionalism involves a commitment to make students the first priority.
- Teacher professionalism involves a commitment to quality in both our work and our relationships.
- Teacher professionalism involves a commitment to continual growth.

What are the characteristics of effective teachers?

- Effective teachers may have very different styles of teaching.
- The most important factor in determining teacher effectiveness is the extent of student learning.
- There are established standards for teacher effectiveness through organizations like the Interstate New Teacher Assessment and Support Consortium and the National Board of Professional Teaching Standards.
- Both individuals and organizations have opinions about what makes a teacher effective. There is much to learn from the differing viewpoints.

Developing Professional Competence

Visit the Developing Professional Competence section on Chapter 1 of the MyEducationLab for this text to answer the following questions and begin your preparation for licensure exams.

You met Traci Peters in *Meet the Focus Teachers and Students* and again in the beginning of this chapter in the *Teaching in Focus* section. She is the math teacher on her four-person interdisciplinary team at Cario Middle School. In March one of her teammates, Melanie Richardson, announced that her husband was being sent to Iraq and that without his help with their five children, she was going to have to move to another state where her parents live. Melanie teaches English-language arts and has been on Traci's team, the Dolphins, for 3 years. This is a big blow to Traci and her two other teammates. Melanie will leave Cario in mid-April. The Dolphin team teachers are very easy to work with and have enjoyed a collegial relationship with Melanie.

Carol Bartlett, principal of Cario, understands the importance of finding the right person to fill the position, but she is told that a teacher from another school will be placed in Melanie's classroom for the remainder of the school year. Ms. Bartlett knows the teacher the district personnel office plans to place on the Dolphin team. Linda Merchant's reputation is that of a veteran teacher who does not collaborate, sits behind her desk during class, and consistently finds ways to undermine administrators. Ms. Bartlett suspects her position was purposefully eliminated at the other school and the district just needs to find a place for her. Ms. Bartlett is certain the Dolphin teachers will not be pleased with the district's choice.

1. Which of the following attributes of a full profession does this scenario directly violate?
   a. A full profession enjoys prestige and public trust.
   b. A full profession admits, polices, and excludes members.
   c. A full profession provides an essential service no other group can provide.
   d. A full profession involves intellectual work in the performance of duties.

2. Which of the following statements applies least to this situation?
   a. The three teachers on the Dolphin team will likely have to put out extra effort to keep their students from being affected by what they anticipate will be substandard teacher performance.
   b. The three teachers are likely most concerned about INTASC Standard 10: "The teacher fosters relationships with school colleagues, parents, and agencies in the larger community to support students' learning and well-being."
   c. The three teachers will continue to instill academic rigor while making their classrooms developmentally appropriate.
   d. Ms. Merchant has a master's degree in education, so the rumors about her are very likely exaggerated.

3. As they have always done, the Dolphin teachers take individual responsibility for the success of their team of students. Which of the following would not be evidence of this?
   a. They use opportunities to say positive things about their students in the community.
   b. They don't get involved in decisions that affect their students because they believe that designated experts know best.
   c. They invite families to come to school to discuss areas of concern for their children.

d. They consistently talk about and act on what they believe to be best for their students.

Now it's time for you to respond to two short essay items involving the scenario. In your responses, be sure to address all the dilemmas and questions posed in each item. Each response should be between one half and one double-spaced page.

4. Traci and her teammates understand that Ms. Merchant will be a temporary member of their team, or at least that's their hope. They have been assured by the school district that they will be able to interview candidates for the English-language arts position and that a new teacher can be in place by August. This helps them get through the remainder of the school year. As they look to the future, what are three qualities you would recommend they look for as they, along with Ms. Bartlett, choose a new teacher for their team?

5. U.S. Secretary of Education Arne Duncan (2009) believes that teacher evaluation is broken. The seventh grade team at Cario is about to experience some of the consequences of a system that not only fails to discriminate between effective and ineffective teachers but also allows ineffective teachers to remain in the classroom. How would meaningful formative assessment help fix the system? What would you recommend be done with the results of annual summative evaluation?

Where DO I Stand NOW?

In the beginning of this chapter you completed an inventory that helped you explore your reasons for choosing teaching as your career. Now that you have read the chapter, completed exercises related to the content, engaged in class discussions, and so on, answer the following questions in your course notebook.

1. If you rated **desire to work with young people** as one of your top reasons for choosing to teach, is it still among your top reasons? If so, why? If not, why not? If **desire to work with young people** was not among your top reasons, has it become more important to you after giving your reasons more consideration? If so, why? If not, why not?

2. If you rated **value of education to society** as one of your top reasons for choosing to teach, is it still among your top reasons? If so, why? If not, why not? If **value of education to**

society was not among your top reasons, has it become more important to you after giving your reasons more consideration? If so, why? If not, why not?

3. If you rated **interest in subject matter** as one of your top reasons for choosing to teach, is it still among your top reasons? If so, why? If not, why not? If **interest in subject matter** was not among your top reasons, has it become more important to you after giving your reasons more consideration? If so, why? If not, why not?

4. If you rated **influence of teachers** as one of your top reasons for choosing to teach, is it still among your top reasons? If so, why? If not, why not? If **influence of teachers** was not among your top reasons, has it become more important to you after giving your reasons more consideration? If so, why? If not, why not?

5. If you rated the **schedule/vacations of teachers** as one of your top reasons for choosing to teach, is it still among your top reasons? If so, why? If not, why not? If the **schedule/ vacations of teachers** was not among your top reasons, has it become more important to you after giving your reasons more consideration? If so, why? If not, why not?

6. If you rated **influence of family** as one of your top reasons for choosing to teach, is it still among your top reasons? If so, why? If not, why not? If **influence of family** was not among

your top reasons, has it become more important to you after giving your reasons more consideration? If so, why? If not, why not?

7. If you rated **job security** as one of your top reasons for choosing to teach, is it still among your top reasons? If so, why? If not, why not? If **job security** was not among your top reasons, has it become more important to you after giving your reasons more consideration? If so, why? If not, why not?

8. If you rated **opportunity for a lifetime of self-growth** as one of your top reasons for choosing to teach, is it still among your top reasons? If so, why? If not, why not? If **opportunity for a lifetime of self-growth** was not among your top reasons, has it become more important to you after giving your reasons more consideration? If so, why? If not, why not?

MyEducationLab

The MyEducationLab for this course can help you solidify your comprehension of Chapter 1 concepts.

- Explore the classrooms of the teachers and students you've met in this chapter in the Teaching in Focus section.

- Prepare for licensure exams as you deepen your understanding of chapter concepts in the Developing Professional Competence section.

- Gauge and further develop your understanding of chapter concepts by taking the quizzes and examining the enrichment materials on the Chapter 1 Study Plan.

- Visit Topic 1, The Teaching Profession, to watch ABC videos, explore Assignments and Activities, and practice essential teaching skills with the Building Teaching Skills and Dispositions unit.

2

Schools

In this chapter we explore schools in the United States by addressing these focus questions:

✦ What are the purposes of public schools in the United States?

✦ What is the culture of a school?

✦ How do school venues differ?

✦ What is school like at different levels?

✦ What are the three principal settings of U.S. schools?

✦ What is an effective school?

Schools are centers of our communities, foundations of our citizenry, targets of political and ethical debate, mirrors and shapers of our society, and keepers of the hopes and dreams of parents and children. Without exception the greeting "And how are the children?" should be on the lips and in the hearts of every adult in every U.S. school.

Before we discuss schools in the United States, explore your own preferences regarding your future career in this chapter's *Where Do I Stand?*

Where DO I Stand?

Responding to these items provides generalizations of where your interests lie in terms of who you want to teach, in what kind of school, and the setting you may prefer. After reading an item, indicate your level of agreement by choosing a number and placing it in the blank before the statement. Following the inventory are directions for how to organize your responses and what they may indicate in terms of where you stand.

4   I strongly agree
3   I agree
2   I don't have an opinion
1   I disagree
0   I strongly disagree

_____ **1.** Teaching routines to young children appeals to me.

_____ **2.** I enjoy living out in the country, away from cities.

_____ **3.** I believe that public schools best serve our country's students.

_____ **4.** Teaching children to comprehend topics through reading is an exciting process to me.

_____ **5.** Having a shopping mall nearby is important to me.

_____ **6.** Teaching middle school appeals to me.

_____ **7.** I would be most comfortable teaching in a private school.

_____ **8.** I am drawn to kids who have fewer advantages than others.

_____ **9.** I want to teach students whose parents have specifically chosen their school.

_____ **10.** Teaching basic math concepts in understandable ways would be fun.

_____ **11.** Social and civic opportunities in the suburbs attract me.

_____ **12.** I want to spend my days with students who are quickly becoming young adults.

_____ **13.** I want to teach one or two specific subjects.

_____ **14.** I have a positive view of public schools.

_____ **15.** Children in grades 3 to 5 are the ones with whom I would most like to work.

_____ **16.** Being somewhat isolated geographically is all right with me.

_____ **17.** Teaching different levels, or branches, of one subject, appeals to me.

_____ **18.** I look forward to the challenges presented by inner-city students.

_____ **19.** Neighborhoods with single-family homes and schools close by compose what I envision as my teaching situation.

_____ **20.** Private schools provide valuable options to students.

_____ **21.** Being part of a team of teachers who share a specific group of students sounds inviting.

_____ **22.** Teaching in a rural setting appeals to me.

_____ **23.** I want to teach in a school that all children have the opportunity to attend.

_____ **24.** I enjoy being with 5-year-olds.

_____ **25.** I want to spend my days with students with whom I can hold an adult-like conversation.

_____ **26.** I function best when I have ready access to stores and services.

_____ **27.** Teaching in a school that aligns with a particular religious faith will be best for me.

_____ **28.** Children who are ready to explore multiple topics and comprehend much of what they read would be a population I would like to relate to.

_____ **29.** Small communities appeal to me.

_____ **30.** The ups and downs of preteens will provide a challenge I am anxious to tackle.

_____ **31.** Students who live in low-income circumstances draw me to the teaching profession.

_____ **32.** The challenges of being a teenager in today's world interest me as a future teacher.

_____ **33.** Teaching children to read is an exciting prospect.

_____ **34.** I want to teach kids who traditionally have had a harder time benefiting from school.

_____ **35.** Within the public schools students have ample opportunity to thrive.

_____ **36.** I would enjoy teaching two subjects and having a homeroom group in grades 4 and 5.

Find the sums as indicated.

ITEM	MY #	ITEM	MY #	ITEM	MY #	ITEM	MY #	ITEM	MY #	ITEM	MY #	ITEM	MY #	ITEM	MY #	ITEM	MY #
1		4		6		12		2		5		8		3		7	
10		15		13		17		16		11		18		14		9	
24		28		21		25		22		19		31		23		20	
33		36		30		32		29		26		34		35		27	
Sum A		Sum B		Sum C		Sum D		Sum E		Sum F		Sum G		Sum H		Sum I	

Now shade this grid with Sums A, B, C, and D to get an idea of how you feel about teaching at a specific grade level.

A = early childhood   C = middle

B = elementary   D = high

16				
15				
14				
13				
12				
11				
10				
9				
8				
7				
6				
5				
4				
3				
2				
1				
	A	B	C	D

Now shade this grid with Sums E, F, and G to get an idea of how you feel about teaching in particular settings.

E = rural

F = suburban

G = urban

16			
15			
14			
13			
12			
11			
10			
9			
8			
7			
6			
5			
4			
3			
2			
1			
	E	F	G

Now shade this grid with Sums H and I to get an idea of your preference for public school or private school.

H = private school

I = public school

16		
15		
14		
13		
12		
11		
10		
9		
8		
7		
6		
5		
4		
3		
2		
1		
	H	I

Does the inventory reflect part of your perceived teaching identity? If not, how do you see yourself differently from these results?

Teaching in Focus

Brandi Wade teaches kindergarten at Summit Primary School in Summit Station, Ohio. She has witnessed many changes at her school as families have moved into the once rural area just outside Columbus. Housing developments have sprung up all around the school, and change has been ongoing for several years. The small town of Summit Station is now surrounded by a thriving suburban-like area, and there are no signs that growth is slowing down. The Licking Heights School District continues to build bigger schools to accommodate the influx of families.

Summit Primary is the only K–2 school in the district. This is a purposeful configuration. Principal Laura Hill says she likes the format because she has every kindergarten, every first grade, and every second grade teacher in the district right in her building. This lends a great deal of consistency to how children are taught and what and when they learn as Summit Primary retains its specialty of early childhood education. The grade-level teachers work together as teams to provide instruction that is developmentally appropriate for young children.

Along with the growth has come diversity. Once a school of predominantly white children with a relatively small African American population, all English speaking, Summit Primary now serves children with a variety of heritages who speak one of 17 different languages. This diversity of languages presents a major challenge for the Summit teachers. In Brandi's two kindergarten classes, five native languages are represented along with twin boys from Somalia. A special teacher works with these learners who speak limited or no English to help them acquire the English they need to make learning kindergarten skills an easier and more natural process. Brandi's dedication to all children in her kindergarten classes, regardless of their background, is evident in her interactions and conversations about "her kids."

Watch an interview with Brandi in the Teaching in Focus section for Chapter 2 in MyEducationLab for this course.

What Are the Purposes of Public Schools in the United States?

Mandatory attendance makes some form of schooling a common factor in our society. As such, we have all experienced schools. But as with all human endeavors, our perspectives differ. Perspective, however, isn't the only reason we view schools differently; the schools themselves are different. We begin our discussion of the similarities and differences among schools by considering distinctions between education and schooling. We then consider the purposes of **public schools** in the United States, those funded *by* the public, and accountable *to* the public, through local, state, and federal governments.

DISTINCTIONS BETWEEN EDUCATION AND SCHOOLING

Remember in geometry class when the teacher told you that a straight line on the chalkboard wasn't a line but rather a line segment? You may have rolled your eyes and mumbled, "What difference does it make?" Well, for the content of the geometry class (and the inevitable test), it certainly mattered. But did your English teacher ever ask you to draw a *line segment* under a prepositional phrase in a sentence? Probably not. Outside the context of geometry class, most of us find it unnecessary to make a distinction between a line and a line segment.

So it is with the words *education* and *schooling*. As teachers, we need to understand the differences. Once we do, we may use the words interchangeably in some contexts, always aware that distinctions do exist.

EDUCATION. Although it may not seem obvious, there is a distinct difference between education and schooling. Education is the lifelong process of learning. Every day of our lives, in every possible setting, we learn. When we see, hear, feel, or sense, we are learning. This is education—our lifelong formal and informal process of learning.

SCHOOLING. Schooling is one specific, formalized element of education. Schools are institutions specifically designed to educate in formal ways. They involve organization and structure, both of which should be determined primarily by the needs of those who learn, as well as those who teach.

A discussion of American schools is often called a discussion of American education. That's fine. It's understood that we are talking about what goes on in school settings. The hope is that education occurring in school is productive and accurate in nature, but regardless, learning of some kind is taking place just like it does continually in every walk of life. As teachers we are called educators. As long as we recognize and acknowledge that the whole world educates children, we may continue to interchange the words *education* and *schooling,* and *educator* and *teacher.*

COMPLEMENTARY PURPOSES OF PUBLIC SCHOOLS

There's no need to settle on, or settle for, narrowly defined purposes for public schooling. Although there are many, we will consider eight. These purposes may be best understood and put into perspective using the concept of balance. Each pair of purposes discussed is more complementary than oppositional. They balance each other.

TRANSMITTING SOCIETY AND RECONSTRUCTING SOCIETY.
Both of these purposes deal with societal knowledge and values. On the more conservative side, *transmitting society* involves public schools both reflecting and supporting our American society. This is a process called socialization. **Socialization** occurs through a variety of influences including home, family, place of worship, print and electronic media, peers, and, of course, school. Students are influenced through the subjects we offer and the content of those subjects, as well as through our instruction, both actions and words. Transmitting society means promoting the concepts that preserve our democratic way of life and discouraging concepts that oppose it. Transmitting society is unifying, emphasizing what we have in common rather than our differences.

Teachers walk a fine line when it comes to achieving the purpose of transmitting society while continuing to respect the students and their families who bring a differing societal view with them to the classroom. What many of us take for granted may be new and unusual to a growing number of our students. A democratic way of life involves acceptance of differences; in American schools, acceptance should escalate to the embracing of differences. This in itself is transmitting a society that preserves democracy.

The complement of transmitting society is *reconstructing society,* challenging knowledge and values with an eye toward improvement. The concept of social reconstruction involves teaching students to recognize what needs to change, identifying the means of change, and encouraging students to work proactively for a common goal. Rather than only passing down knowledge and values to preserve society's status quo, students are urged to examine aspects of our society, keep what is worthwhile, and seek to change or discard what isn't.

As you can see, transmitting society and reconstructing society do not have to be opposing purposes. When they are balanced, it is possible to pass on the best of society while questioning and changing aspects of society for the better.

PARTICIPATION IN SOCIETY AND ACADEMIC LEARNING.
Preparing students to *participate in society* involves socialization plus the teaching of survival skills that will help them get along with others; obtain and keep employment; be politically, morally, and socially proactive; and be productive members of a community with a sense of responsibility. Public schools, along with other institutions and groups, certainly help prepare students for participation in society.

At the same time as we prepare students to participate in society we facilitate *academic learning.* Every subject area includes a body of knowledge that is, by and large, "society free," or independent from what's going on at the time within society. For instance, mathematical formulas, classic literature, history, and geography all have academic aspects that change little with time. Plato maintained that this kind of academic knowledge is the foundation for seeking truth that is not dependent on, or influenced by, current society, and that seeking of truth is a necessary purpose of education. He encouraged students to look at possibilities through the lens of formal academic learning and to question the world around them.

In *A Place Called School*, Goodlad (1984) looked at many documents that have addressed the question "What is the purpose of schooling?" He concluded there are four broad goals:

1. Academic: Imparting knowledge and intellectual skills
2. Vocational: Preparing for the world of work
3. Social and civic: Participating in a democratic society
4. Personal: Developing self-expression and talent

Goal 1 obviously fits into the academic learning purpose, whereas the other three prepare students to participate in society.

INDIVIDUAL NEEDS AND COLLECTIVE NEEDS. These two purposes most certainly go hand in hand. A citizenry of formally educated individuals serves the collective good. American public schools provide opportunities for children to reach their learning potential. Some schools make this opportunity more feasible, more readily attainable, than others. Throughout this book we explore differences in schools that either bring out the best in individual children or that, in either overt or sometimes subtle ways, stand in the way of individual student learning potential.

Meeting the *individual needs* of students is sometimes referred to as the development of *human capital*. These words seem mechanistic and cold until we consider them separately. The word *human* describes us. The word *capital* in this sense is a noun meaning the knowledge and skills derived from education, training, and experience. The development of human capital is directly related to the well-being of individuals. It takes groups of people—the collective—to preserve our democratic way of life.

To serve *collective needs*, then, is to view the purpose of American schools as ensuring strong, free communities by teaching knowledge and values, such as honesty, hard work, civility, respect, compassion, and patriotism. The goals for the collective include economic prosperity, maintenance of our national security, and the development of a sense of both humanity and democratic ideals.

In American public schools we teach individual students who, together, form the collective of our country. The stronger the collective, the more opportunities there are for the individual. These two purposes of public education are complementary and interdependent.

SUSTAINING FOR TODAY AND PREPARING FOR TOMORROW. Schools *sustain for today* by providing a set of experiences for students. Yes, many of them will be successful in school. Some will go on to college and most will have productive careers. But some will not. Not because American public schools want it to be so, but because the reality is that not all students will make the step from school to adulthood to be citizens who contribute in positive ways. Some will drop out of school and lack the knowledge, skills, and/or credibility to fulfill their potential in adult life. Some will experience debilitating life circumstances or even death before they complete high school. What we need to remember in terms of schools serving to sustain for today is that children, regardless of what their futures hold, deserve a warm, caring, nurturing environment where they have opportunities to learn and grow. Ideally, home and family provide this environment. Whether that's the case or not, American public schools should provide this environment day after day, year after year as we ask one another, "And how are the children?"

Elliot Eisner (2004), one of our most influential educators, wrote, "Preparation for tomorrow is best served by meaningful education today" (p. 10). American public education that sustains for today, *prepares for tomorrow*. It's a building process, a self-perpetuating cycle.

Preserving our democratic way of life is accomplished through the fulfillment of these eight purposes and other related goals. Craig Cleveland writes about the learning that occurs both inside and outside of school, the education that you, as teacher candidates, are experiencing. He tells us that both education and schooling, as defined earlier, lead to

Points of Reflection 2.1

With which three of the eight complementary purposes of public schools do you identify most? Explain your choices.

Teaching in Focus

Craig Cleveland, history teacher, Roosevelt High School, California. *In his own words. . . .*

Much of what you need to know about effective teaching and learning is found within yourself already. The environment and circumstances in which you learned powerful and life-changing lessons may have been in school or elsewhere in life. The relevant and meaningful lessons your students learn will need to be both inside and outside the school if education is going to have the power to transform them into thoughtful mature people.

Essential to creating a learning environment in the classroom is a researched and clearly articulated philosophy about how learning happens. When such a philosophy is in place, teachers are able to make sound and reliable instructional decisions and refinements.

Continuing my education in a graduate program, reading professional literature, regularly reflecting on my teaching with an eye toward improvement, and having ongoing conversations with friends and colleagues help make more concrete my beliefs about how learning happens. A ninth grade student of mine made the insightful statement, "Learning is natural." I believe learning is natural when the learner has interest and a voice as a participant within the learning environment of school.

learning for our students. He advises us to continue to develop as professionals in his *Teaching in Focus* feature.

Now let's look inside schools in the United States to examine both their commonalities and some of their differences, beginning with what may seem like an intangible but actually can be sensed in every aspect of schooling: the culture of a school.

What Is the Culture of a School?

School culture is the context of learning experiences; it's the prevailing atmosphere of the school. As places where people work together and learn together, schools function according to their cultures. Noted educator Roland Barth (2001) tells us, "A school's culture dictates, in no uncertain terms, 'the way we do things around here.' Ultimately, a school's culture has far more influence on life and learning in the schoolhouse than the state department of education, the superintendent, the school board, or even the principal can ever have" (p. 7).

A school's culture can be a positive force for learning or a negative influence that interferes with learning. It is important to recognize elements of a school's culture, both the forces that created it and those that perpetuate it. If the culture is positive, acknowledging the influential forces and then reinforcing them keeps the culture vibrant and growing. If the culture is negative or apathetic, altering it begins with looking closely at the influential forces and finding ways to begin the change process.

From a new teacher's standpoint, a positive school culture may be evident when experienced teachers consistently ask how things are going and offer to help with lessons, materials, managing student behavior, paperwork, and so on. Hearing teachers talking and laughing together, sharing what works in their classrooms, and speaking of students with caring and concerned attitudes demonstrates positive culture. On the other hand, when a school seems to have a territorial atmosphere with cliques of teachers criticizing other teachers and the principal, when offers of assistance are few, when students are spoken of primarily in critical terms, a new teacher will likely sense a negative culture. Because most of the adults in a school are teachers, their influence on school culture is immense.

TEACHERS AND SCHOOL CULTURE

Teachers' instructional skills and professionalism either improve a school's culture or keep it stagnant or negative. The level of respect teachers engender among their colleagues and in the community either builds a positive culture or serves to drag it down. This level of respect has much to do with the relationships that exist among a school's adults, which, in turn, influence the ways teachers relate to students. Because all teachers, experienced and new, have considerable influence on school culture, they must be instrumental in maintaining a positive culture or helping to change a negative culture into a more positive one.

CHANGING SCHOOL CULTURE

A school's culture can change. Can it change quickly or easily? Definitely not when improvement is the goal. Positive culture shifts require strong leadership, ownership of the problems and potential solutions by the adults in the school, and a steady, conscious influx of both attitudes and actions that produce the desired results. In contrast, changes in a school culture from positive to negative may only require apathy and neglect.

All components of American education discussed in this text influence a school's culture. For instance, what is taught in a school can be dynamic and challenging, or mediocre and boring. Not only *what* is taught, but *how* it is taught, influences culture. The level of respect teachers and students have for one another influences school culture as does the level of teacher expectations for student success. Remember that the context of schools is complex; schools are living systems. Because students, teachers, parents, communities, policies, and politics all potentially influence school culture, many variances exist among schools, even those with the same basic structure.

How Do School Venues Differ?

U.S. schools vary greatly, from the traditional neighborhood public school to the ultimate private school: the home. This section looks at **school venues,** the variety of ways American students are educated in the more than 130,000 schools in the United States (National Center for Education Statistics [NCES], 2010).

PUBLIC SCHOOL VENUES

School governance is addressed in Chapter 11.

The vast majority of educational settings in the United States are public schools, with most of the funding to support them coming from some form of taxation. Public schools are accountable to the community through elected or governmental officials who have policy and oversight responsibilities.

Public schools come in all shapes and sizes. They are not only open to every student regardless of socioeconomic status, disability, race, or religion, but in fact they must provide a school setting for every child—that's part of being public.

TRADITIONAL PUBLIC SCHOOLS. The traditional, or **neighborhood, school** is still the predominant form of public schooling in the United States. **Traditional public schools** have no admission criteria, other than perhaps residency in a particular attendance zone. Their educational programs are designed to meet the needs of almost all students, with the possible exception of some with severe physical or mental disabilities. Most of the more than 55 million students in grades K to 12 in the United States attend traditional public schools (Snyder, Dillow, & Hoffman, 2009).

A traditional public school that provides a comprehensive program of education and includes student and community services, such as after-school and family-education programs, may be considered a **full-service school**. Many of the components of a full-service school are made possible through community partnerships with businesses, health-care providers, foundations, and government agencies. These services help students and their families cope with a variety of dilemmas. The goals of a full-service school may include the following:

- Meeting students' needs, both academic and nonacademic, through extended-day programs, counseling groups, homework assistance, and the like
- Increasing family stability through parent education
- Creating a safe haven for the community
- Providing role models for all family members
- Responding to physical and psychological needs
- Providing easy access to government services
- Involving community members from all walks of life in public education

Three particular venues of public schools draw specific groups of students. Each has a structure that uniquely matches the needs and interests of its student population.

MAGNET SCHOOLS. A school with a specific emphasis or theme may be known as a **magnet school**. The curriculum and/or instructional program of a magnet school is tailored with unique opportunities that attract certain students. A magnet school's focus may be math or science (or both), performing arts, technology, or high academic expectations and student qualifications. For example, a magnet school with an emphasis on preparation for a career in the trade arts, sometimes called a vocational magnet, would attract students interested in careers in construction, mechanics, cosmetology, culinary arts, and so on.

Magnet schools are more expensive to operate than traditional neighborhood schools. Their special programs may require funds for career-related equipment, performance studios, staff with specific expertise, smaller teacher-to-student ratios, and transportation beyond immediate neighborhoods More and more magnet schools are opening and drawing specific groups of students out of the traditional neighborhood schools as parents and students seek more specialized environments. Magnet schools account for about 2% of public schools, with approximately 3% of students enrolled in public schools attending them.

CHARTER SCHOOLS. A **charter school** is a public school that is freed in specific ways from the typical regulations required of other public schools. For instance, teachers and administrators in charter schools usually have more control over how they spend their funds and the kinds of classes they offer than their counterparts in traditional public schools. Charter schools are open to all students within a school district and must attract students to stay in operation. They must get the word out to the public, convince parents that they can better meet the learning needs of their children, and then follow through with their plans and promises to keep students coming back year after year.

Charter schools are created by people who see a need or an opportunity to fix a problem, such as declining student achievement, or to enhance a particular area, such as student ability in the arts. They may be started from scratch or converted from preexisting schools. Themes may revolve around a subject area, particular teaching techniques, a social problem, specific grade levels, or anything else the creators imagine, propose, and get approved by a state board of education. Once approved and in operation, charter schools are usually governed through **site-based management,** meaning that the school is in the hands of those closest to it, generally teachers, administrators, and parents. There are more charter schools than magnet schools in the United States, but only about 1.2% of students in the United States are enrolled in them.

ALTERNATIVE SCHOOLS. Magnet and charter schools are both alternative forms of school organization. However, in public education, the term *alternative school* takes on a unique meaning. If a school is called an **alternative school,** more than likely it is a school designed for students who are not successful in a traditional school setting. Because school districts can't exclude students and attendance is compulsory until age 16, alternative settings have emerged that may be categorized in two ways: remedial and last chance.

In The News abc NEWS

One Last Chance

Ted Koppel and ABC news correspondent Michelle Martin introduce us to a unique charter school. The Seed Public Charter School is the only public urban boarding school in the United States. Located in Washington, D.C., Seed provides housing, meals, a safe and clean environment, and an education for seventh through twelfth grade students chosen by lottery. Believing that millions of students are being shortchanged, the founders of Seed created an educational structure that allows students previously thought to be destined to drop out of school because of their environment an opportunity for success.

Watch the video to learn more about Seed and the students and teachers who learn together there by visiting the *In the News* section of Chapter 2 on your

MyEducationLab for this course. Respond to these questions and prompts.

1. Why do the founders of Seed claim that the students they serve need an "entirely new environment" to succeed in school?
2. The math teacher says it takes courage for the students to move forward academically. What are two things the Seed students must overcome to be successful in school?
3. What are the purposes of "gates" at Seed? Is the success rate related to them higher or lower than you would have anticipated? Why?
4. What caused Jonathan to say, "You may think because you know my neighborhood that you can judge me for who I may become"?

Students who need more focused attention to be successful than what the traditional school can provide are in need of remediation: academic, social, emotional, or some combination of the three. Once remediation is completed, a student may return to a more traditional setting. Often students who are characterized as being **at risk**—those in serious danger of not completing school and who may be heading toward nonproductive or counterproductive

TABLE 2.1 Public School Venues

Venue	Definition	Admission Criteria	Advantages	Disadvantages
Traditional	Neighborhood school	None	Close to home; sense of ownership	May not have programs of interest or that meet specific student needs
Full-service traditional schools	School that offers student and community services that go beyond academics	None	Draws families in; provides services such as health promotion and community education	None
Magnet	School with specific emphasis or theme	Interest; talent; academic achievement	Specialized curriculum or instruction	May exclude some students; requires more funding
Charter	School freed from some regulatory control of district or state	None; generally first come, first admitted	Site-based decision making; specialized curriculum or instruction	May lack sufficient oversight; danger of "ends justify means" mentality
Alternative	Usually a school for students who are not successful in other public school settings	Behavioral or academic problems	Can provide specialized assistance for students who need it most	May neglect some aspects of school while targeting specific needs; may stereotype or stigmatize students

lifestyles—are strongly urged to attend remedial alternative schools. Students who are not successful in a remedial setting may attend public alternative schools that are considered last-chance schools. In most cases the students have gotten into significant trouble in a traditional or remedial school, have been suspended multiple times, have consistently been disruptive in the classroom, or generally have not benefited from other, less intrusive programs. A school that qualifies as both a charter school because of its vision and unique structure and an alternative school because it was developed to meet the needs of students at risk of not succeeding in traditional public schools is the Seed Public Charter School in Washington, D.C., featured in this chapter's *In the News*.

The wide variety of public schools provides opportunities and choice. Table 2.1 summarizes the commonly available public school options. This chapter's *Letter to the Editor* deals with the possibility of public schools in Tulsa, Oklahoma, reverting to all neighborhood schools, an interesting proposition.

Points of Reflection 2.2

Did you attend public schools? Were they traditional neighborhood schools, magnet schools, charter schools, or alternative schools? If you attended a variety of public school venues, what differences among them did you experience?

Letter to the Editor

This letter appeared in the Tulsa, Oklahoma, newspaper, *The Tulsa World*. It was written by a citizen responding to recent local budget deliberations and the possibility of returning to a system of neighborhood schools.

DECEMBER 17, 2009

FOR NEIGHBORHOOD SCHOOLS

With the continuous hand-wringing that has been publicized almost daily with budget cuts and potential budget cuts to Tulsa Public Schools, it appears the proposal to make some of the schools community centers has gone underground. Not one mention of the first remedy many school districts nationwide, including Seattle, implemented prior to this school year: returning each child to a neighborhood school. I have not seen the costs TPS spends in transporting children outside neighborhood schools but it must be large. Not only would this cut costs, but it would give the impetus to returning school pride and a sense of ownership to local neighborhoods/ communities, students and parents. Most children could then walk or ride their bikes to and from schools providing exercise each day. This would allow Tulsans to volunteer in local schools surrounded by neighborhood children and their parents. Where extra emphasis or resources are needed it would be much easier to implement before and after school programs with travel and time distances reduced. It is time to pool resources and combine programs such as health initiatives, library, career counseling, and academic programs. Quit whining about potential budget cuts that are based on economic realities and get to work. Tulsans deserve the quality public school options that existed prior to 1980 when neighborhood schools were the norm!

Roger Hilst

Tulsa

Now it's your turn. Write a letter to the editor from the perspective of a future teacher expressing your views on this issue and any broader issues you feel it invokes. You may comment on any, or all, of the writer's expressed opinions. The following questions may help you frame your thinking but should not limit nor determine what you write.

1. Do you agree that changing most or all of the Tulsa schools to neighborhood schools is a good idea? If so, why? If not, why not?

2. The issue of the budget led to this letter, but what else about neighborhood schools appeals to many people and would justify changing schools to this format?

3. What does the writer mean by community centers, and would elaborating this point be helpful?

4. Would consolidating services and placing them in schools be helpful? Why or why not?

5. Although it's not directly addressed in this letter, changing school formats will likely mean doing away with magnet and/or charter schools. Do you agree or disagree with this? Why?

6. What recommendations do you have for Tulsa officials as they consider reverting to neighborhood schools they once had? Are there studies they might do or research that could help them decide if this would be the best move for Tulsa?

7. Do you agree or disagree with the letter writer about the relative importance of the issue? Is there a larger issue here that needs to be addressed?

Write your letter in understandable terminology, remembering that readers of newspaper Letters to the Editor are citizens who may have limited knowledge of school practices and policies. Remember to refer to the letter assessment rubric in Chapter 1.

PRIVATE SCHOOL VENUES

The two elements that make schools public—public funding and public accountability—are both absent in **private schools**. About 10% of students in the United States attend private schools (NCES, 2010). Families choose private education for a variety of reasons. Some choose private schools for potential benefits such as smaller class size, specific instruction to meet the needs of students with learning disabilities, or travel and extracurricular opportunities. Still others may choose private education because of family history. Perhaps generations of family members have attended a particular private school.

Some families choose private schools because of negative perceptions about local public schools. They may consider public schools inferior or inadequate. Still others want their children to have religious instruction or believe that their children's specific mental or physical needs require a private setting. Then there are other families who perceive that a private school may be more prestigious than the public schools available.

In most instances, public and private schools exist side by side in a community with little rancor. Yet there may be differences in underlying philosophy that cause friction. Unlike their public school counterparts, private schools are not obligated to educate all students but are able to choose and dismiss students. Thus their classrooms typically have fewer behavior problems, a smaller teacher-to-student ratio, and stronger parental support. Some private school teachers see this as a trade-off because most of them are paid less than teachers in public schools.

PAROCHIAL SCHOOLS. Most private schools are affiliated with a particular religious sect (denomination) and are often called **parochial schools**. Most religion-affiliated schools are aligned with the Catholic faith.

Private schools that are not aligned with a religious group exist in many forms and cater to a wide spectrum of student and family needs and wants. They may resemble charter schools with themes and areas of emphasis, but they are free from all government regulation because they are privately funded.

SINGLE-GENDER SCHOOLS. Some private schools are **single gender,** enrolling either all boys or all girls. Because **Title IX of the Education Amendments Act of 1972** prohibits government money from being used for programs that discriminate on the basis of gender, most single-gender schools are private.

HOMESCHOOLING. Students who receive most of their academic instruction in their homes are considered to be **homeschooled**. Although it's hard to pinpoint an exact number, we know there are over 1 million homeschooled students in the United States (NCES, 2004). This figure represents less than 3% of the total U.S. student population. The reasons for parents choosing homeschooling vary but are similar to parental reasons for choosing private over public school venues.

Homeschooling has become a social movement, with parents as political activists, organizers of national networks, and developers of curriculum and instructional materials. As you can imagine, the quality of the education received in the home varies widely. However, on standardized academic achievement tests homeschoolers tend to score 15 to 30 percentile points higher than students in public schools (Ray, 2006). How students fare socially has not been measured, only openly speculated about. A concern is that children who are homeschooled may miss out on the civic perspective and experiences gained only through going to school with students who are not like themselves in religious beliefs, racial or cultural background, socioeconomic status, or academic aptitude.

Homeschooling has always been part of the human experience. Some notable homeschooled students include Florence Nightingale, Thomas Edison, Margaret Mead, Charles Dickens, Benjamin Franklin, Orville and Wilbur Wright, Woodrow Wilson, and former U.S. Supreme Court justice Sandra Day O'Connor.

FOR-PROFIT SCHOOLS. Nonreligious private schools are often **for-profit schools**. These schools are managed by some entity that receives a percentage of the money generated. Even some public schools may be for-profit. While for years public schools have contracted with private companies to provide aspects of schooling such as transportation, custodial work, and food services, when companies contract with states or districts to take over all aspects of schooling and make money by doing so, then it's capitalism in the schoolhouse. These for-profit schools are given the federal, state, and local money per pupil that a public school receives and are referred to as **Education Maintenance Organizations, or EMOs** (the educational equivalent of health care's HMOs). Public schools run by private companies are controversial.

The largest EMO is managed by EdisonLearning, Inc., with the schools called Edison Schools. In 2008–2009, Edison Schools served over 350,000 students in 24 states and the United Kingdom (EdisonLearning, Inc., 2010). Although they make claims of increased student learning, EdisonLearning, Inc. data calculations are often questioned by those who oppose privatization. Another controversial claim made by opponents of privatization is that when profit is the bottom line, services to the students with special needs may be neglected. More research is needed to determine the efficacy of for-profit companies managing public schools.

As you consider the variety of schools in Table 2.2, keep in mind that what some may view as advantages may be considered disadvantages by others, and vice versa.

Both public and private schools create choices for families. Let's explore how school choice is manifested in U.S. schools.

Points of Reflection 2.3

Did you attend private schools? If so, were they religiously affiliated? If you attended more than one venue of private school, what differences did you experience? Did you attend a combination of public and private schools? If so, what differences did you experience between public and private schools?

SCHOOL CHOICE

School choice—letting parents and students decide which schools meet their needs—has a very democratic feel, doesn't it? Increasing parental involvement, providing learning environments more suited to individual students, attempting broader integration, accommodating particular interests and talents, and affording more desirable settings to at-risk or underprivileged students are just a few of the reasons for choice among schools.

TABLE 2.2 Private and for-profit school venues

Venue	Definition	Admission Criteria	Advantages	Disadvantages
Religious	School with a religious affiliation	Agreement to either uphold or not interfere with the principles of the affiliation	Allows parents and religious groups to include their traditions and beliefs	Not accountable to any government agency
Nonreligious	School without a religious affiliation	Interest; can afford tuition; students may be rejected for any reason	Specialized curriculum or instruction	Not accountable to any government agency
Single gender	School for boys only or girls only	Must be gender of school; generally first come, first admitted	May better meet specific learning styles of either boys or girls	Not accountable to any government agency; may not mirror reality of the coed world
Homeschooling	Students are taught at home or in a home environment	Family member	Provides very specific one-on-one instruction in a manner desired by parents	Not accountable to any government agency; may isolate student from other cultures and viewpoints; may neglect some aspects of what is commonly agreed upon as necessary curriculum
For-profit	Schools run by individuals or corporations that make and keep monetary gain	Any criteria set by school managers	Can be very specialized	If private, not accountable to any government agency

Figure 2.1 School choice options supported by government funding

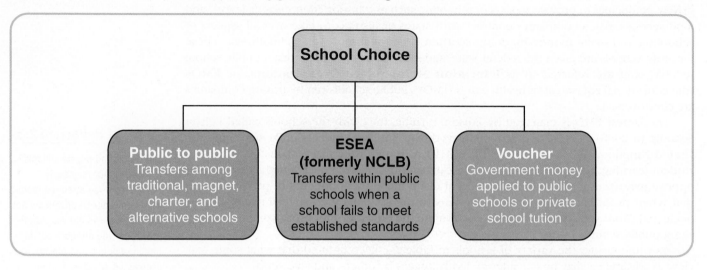

Let's consider school choice in the context of competition. Marketplace theory says that competition leads to improvement. But does this apply to schools competing for student enrollment when more students mean more money? If all schools were high performing and differed only in theme or focus, then competition would simply mean appealing to student interests or learning preferences. But when schools gain enrollment while others lose because of real or perceived failure to meet the needs of students, the failing school is left in an even more untenable situation. If we close them down, we may be eliminating the possibility of improving the predominant public school setting, the neighborhood school. However, no child should be in a school that is not making progress toward improved levels of learning. Answering the question, "And how are the children?" becomes even more complex and important.

For any choice plan, there are two key ingredients for success: information and transportation. Without provisions for both, a choice plan only gives choices to families who seek out information and have the capability to provide transportation out of their neighborhoods. Figure 2.1 illustrates three ways that public school choice may be manifested.

PUBLIC-TO-PUBLIC SCHOOL CHOICE. Allowing for choice among public schools occurs in a variety of ways. The option of attending magnet, charter, and alternative schools versus a traditional neighborhood school within a district is by far the most common manifestation of school choice. Taking this option a step further, **open enrollment** allows students to choose from among all the schools in a school district with a few exceptions, such as magnet schools with specific student qualifications and alternative schools with student enrollment controlled by the district. Open enrollment may extend across district lines as well.

ELEMENTARY AND SECONDARY EDUCATION ACT. In 1965 President Lyndon B. Johnson proposed, and Congress passed, the **Elementary and Secondary Education Act** (ESEA) as a part of the "War on Poverty." The ESEA emphasizes equal access to education and establishes high standards and accountability (U.S. Department of Education, 2010). From 2001 to 2010, the ESEA was reauthorized as the No Child Left Behind Act (NCLB). One provision of the act is that parents and students have school choice under certain conditions. The act includes guidelines for grading schools based on their progress toward reaching designated goals dealing with, among other factors, student achievement on standardized tests and attendance. Schools are evaluated and given report cards called **Adequate Yearly Progress,** or simply AYP reports. After 2 years of failing AYP, students at schools with a high percentage of students in poverty may transfer to schools with passing AYP reports. The school district has the responsibility to provide at least two designated recipient schools that passed AYP for each student and to make transportation available for students.

TABLE 2.3 Advocates' and critics' views of school choice	
Advocates	**Critics**
Competition raises the standards, and consequently the performance, of all schools.	Competition destroys cooperation among teachers, schools, communities.
Competition gives parents decision-making power to choose for their children.	Only parents who are vocal advocates for their children will take advantage of options.
Competition forces low-performing schools to go out of business.	Students remaining in low-performing schools suffer.
Choice better accommodates diversity.	Choice leads to the possibility of further segregation.
Choice provides equal opportunities.	Choice exacerbates inequities.

Are parents and students likely to take advantage of the choices provided by ESEA? Maybe, maybe not. More will if they are informed of the options in a timely fashion, if they are comfortable that long bus rides won't be necessary, and if the students are not socially committed to staying with their neighborhood friends who opt not to move. These are powerful "ifs." Here's another to consider: *If* their parents do not explore options, students will likely remain in schools designated as failing.

VOUCHERS. Perhaps the most controversial of current efforts to provide school choice is the **voucher,** a government-issued form that represents part of the state's financial contribution for the education of a student. Parents choose a school and present the voucher, and the government allocates funding accordingly to the school.

Some vouchers are only for students living in poverty, allowing them to choose a school that perhaps better meets their needs. Other vouchers are awarded to any student within a designated area to use within a school district, or even across district lines. Some vouchers may be used only in public schools, whereas others may be applied to private school tuition or even to schools with a religious affiliation. The viability of voucher plans often sparks debates in state legislatures.

Consider this. Private schools are free to admit or refuse any student. They can decide not to take vouchers from students who don't fit in for any reason, including gender, race, past or potential achievement, or disability. Likewise, they can recruit and admit the most motivated, highest achieving students. Public money in the form of vouchers thus has the potential to become a tool of discrimination.

The use of vouchers to attend schools with a religious affiliation is perhaps the most controversial aspect of the program. Many people consider it a violation of the separation of church and state, and this obstacle may lead to the demise of vouchers as school choice alternatives.

ADVOCATES AND CRITICS OF SCHOOL CHOICE. School choice, regardless of the format, has its advocates and its critics. If we simply pose the question, "Should parents have the right to choose a school that best meets the needs of their children?" most Americans would say yes. Table 2.3 lists several opposing views of school choice.

Points of Reflection 2.4

Does a particular school venue appeal to you? If so, what elements of the particular type of school make it a possible career choice?

What Is School Like at Different Levels?

U.S. schools are organized and structured in four basic levels: early childhood, elementary, middle, and high school.

Summit Primary School,
Summit Station, Ohio

STRUCTURE AND ORGANIZATION OF EARLY CHILDHOOD EDUCATION

Early childhood education is commonly divided into three basic age spans: preschool, kindergarten, and primary grades. Educators tend to agree that early childhood settings should be characterized by warmth, sensitivity, and nurture. Learning through play, with healthy doses of experimentation and discovery, describes a commonly held and balanced early childhood philosophy. Let's briefly explore some of the structural and organizational components of early childhood educational settings.

PRESCHOOL. Experiences of 3- and 4-year-olds in the United States vary enormously. Some children stay home with a parent; some are provided simple child care. Others have a more structured **preschool** environment housed within a primary or elementary school. In this setting, often designated as a prekindergarten for 4-year-olds, care is enhanced by exposure to basic educational concepts. Preschool education may follow many different models.

The **Montessori** approach to early childhood education, with mixed-age grouping and self-pacing, is growing in popularity and has the reputation of being high quality when faithfully implemented (Morrison, 2008). Teachers in a Montessori setting are primarily guides, with children acting independently to choose learning activities. The **High/Scope** approach, widely used in preschool through early elementary settings, is built on consistency and few transitions during the day as children construct meaning for themselves in problem-solving situations within learning centers. The **Reggio Emilia** approach to early childhood education for ages 3 months to 6 years is based on relationships among children, families, and teachers. Close long-term relationships are built because the teachers in each classroom stay with the same children for up to 3 years (Kostelnik, Soderman, & Whiren, 2004). **Head Start** is the largest provider of government-funded preschool education, employing 1 of every 5 preschool teachers in the United States (Barnett, 2003).

KINDERGARTEN. Once considered an optional bridge between preschool, or no school at all, and the beginning of formal education in first grade, **kindergarten** (meaning "children's garden") has become part of almost every 5- to 6-year-old child's educational experience, some for half a day and others for the entire day. However, kindergarten is mandatory for 5-year-olds in only 12 states, with 42 states requiring that kindergarten be offered in every school district (Morrison, 2008).

Some children enter kindergarten with many readiness skills; others do not.

What occurs in both whole-day and half-day kindergarten classrooms across the country varies. In some kindergarten classrooms children are involved in literacy-building activities; in others there's little evidence of any emphasis on literacy. Some kindergartens are housed in K–5 or K–6 elementary schools, while others are in primary school settings that may include prekindergarten or kindergarten through grade 2 or 3. Figure 2.2 displays a possible schedule for half-day kindergarten, with teachers following a similar schedule twice a day. The step from kindergarten to first grade is a giant one, so it is crucial that the term *readiness* has become a major part of the vocabulary of early childhood education.

Figure 2.2 Sample half-day kindergarten schedule

9:25–9:40	Arrival, morning exercises
9:40–10:40	Learning centers
10:40–10:50	Cleanup
10:50–11:10	Outdoor or gym play/snack
11:10–11:30	Whole group instruction
11:30–11:45	Small group time, cooperative activity
11:45–12:00	Art projects
12:00–12:15	Closing exercises/dismissal

Repeat with another group of children 1:20–4:05

PRIMARY GRADES. Teachers in primary classrooms, grades 1 through 3, are faced with the challenge of meeting the needs of children with widely varying levels both of readiness for learning and of acquired knowledge and skills. Imagine a first grade classroom with 5 children who have received very little home encouragement for learning and did not attend kindergarten, 10 children who attended three different kindergartens that varied widely in their approaches, and 4 students who are reading independently. The challenge is to engage them all in learning based on where they are, with a view of unlimited potential. Figure 2.3 shows a general schedule for a primary classroom.

Our early childhood focus school, Summit Primary, does not have a preschool program. Children must be 5 years old to enter one of Summit's three levels of kindergarten. The *Boost* class is for children who need more basic guidance and instruction. The *Average* class is for most of the children. The *Enrichment* class is for children who have already mastered some of the typical kindergarten skills, such as recognizing and writing the alphabet, reading one-syllable and often-used sight words, recalling a story orally in correct sequence, counting to 100, and making and explaining simple graphs. Some children go directly from one level of kindergarten to first grade, and others have the opportunity to stay in kindergarten for another year to build a stronger foundation for first grade. In addition to kindergarten, Summit Primary offers first and second grade.

STRUCTURE AND ORGANIZATION OF ELEMENTARY EDUCATION

Elementary classrooms may be **self-contained**, meaning that one teacher has responsibility for one group of children most of the school day. In some schools, teachers may share responsibility for a group of children, each specializing in one or two subject areas. A sample schedule for a third grade self-contained classroom is provided in Figure 2.4. A sample

To learn more about the structure and organization of Summit Primary School, where Brandi Wade and Renee Ayers teach, take a school tour and watch an interview with principal Laura Hill in the Teaching in Focus section for Chapter 2 in MyEducationLab for this course.

Points of Reflection 2.5

Now that you know more about early childhood education, can you envision spending your days with the youngest students in American schools? What aspects appeal to you? What aspects do not appeal to you?

Figure 2.3 Sample primary grade schedule

8:50–9:10	Arrival, daily business, opening activities
9:10–9:30	Whole group instruction in literacy
9:30–10:30	Small groups rotate through reading and writing centers
10:30–10:45	Recess
10:45–11:45	Math instruction
11:45–12:15	Lunch
12:15–12:30	Read aloud
12:30–1:15	Science (physical education on Tuesday and Thursday)
1:15–1:30	Silent reading
1:30–2:15	Social studies (art on Monday; music on Wednesday)
2:15–2:45	Center Time
2:45–3:10	Whole group review of day, clean-up, dismissal

Rees Elementary School,
Spanish Fork, Utah

To learn more about the structure and organization of Rees Elementary, where Brenda Beyal, Chris Roberts, and Tim Mendenhall teach, take a school tour and watch an interview with principal Mike Larsen in the Teaching in Focus section for Chapter 2 in MyEducationLab for this course.

Points of Reflection 2.6

Does teaching all subjects to the same group of elementary children sound like something you would enjoy? Elementary schools provide opportunities for professionals who are guidance counselors, media specialists, and teachers of students with special needs. Do these fields interest you?

schedule for a fourth grade classroom with a team of three teachers, each teaching a core subject area, is provided in Figure 2.5. A team of three teachers would accommodate three classes of fourth graders.

Our three focus teachers at Rees Elementary School, Utah, have **multiage,** or multigrade, **classrooms,** where children in three grade levels learn together. Chris Roberts, Brenda Beyal, and Tim Mendenhall each have homeroom classes made up of third, fourth, and fifth graders. They teach all four **core subjects**—language arts, math, science, and social studies—to their own classes, but each specializes in a fine arts area. Chris teaches movement and dance, Brenda teaches visual arts, and Tim teaches theater to all three classes. Let's consider Brenda's class as an example of a multiage classroom. In the beginning of the school year, she has third graders who are new to her class, fourth graders who have already been in her class 1 year, and fifth graders who have already been in her class 2 years. At the end of the school year, the fifth graders move on to middle school after having been in Brenda's class for 3 years, and a new group of children who have finished second grade will be assigned to their first year with Brenda. One third of her class will be new each school year.

Another possible elementary school teacher-student configuration with benefits similar to those of multiage grouping is **looping,** which occurs when a teacher stays with a particular group of students for more than 1 year. As the students go, for instance, from first to second grade, the teacher moves with them. Among the many positive reasons to loop are the following (Roberts, Kellough, & Moore, 2006):

- A consistent relationship develops between teacher and students and lasts for 2 or 3 years.

- Student learning styles, strengths, weaknesses, interests, behavior patterns, potential, family circumstances, and the like, are well known to the teacher.

- The last few weeks of the school year are often used more productively, with summer reading and project assignments more meaningful.

- The beginning of the school year requires fewer getting-acquainted and routine-practicing experiences.

Figure 2.4 Sample third grade schedule (self-contained)

8:50–9:15	Whole class morning meeting
9:15–9:35	Small group reading
9:35–9:55	Whole class instruction in writing/spelling
9:55–10:20	Reading and writing activities
10:20–10:40	Recess and snack
10:40–11:15	Whole group math instruction/activities
11:15–12:00	Alternating physical education (M), art (T), physical education (W), music (Th), physical education (F)
12:00–12:35	Lunch, recess
12:35–1:15	Alternating social studies and science
1:15–1:45	Alternating computer and library time
1:45–2:00	Read aloud
2:00–2:30	Free choice centers
2:30–2:50	Reading and writing activities
2:50–3:10	Whole group class meeting
3:15	Dismissal

Figure 2.5 Sample fourth grade schedule (three-teacher team)

8:50–9:05	Whole class meetings in homerooms
9:05–10:10	Block time:
	Group 1: Math
	Group 2: English language arts
	Group 3: Science/social studies
10:10–10:30	DEAR (Drop Everything And Read) in homeroom
10:30–10:50	Journal writing in homerooms
10:50–11:10	Recess and snack
11:10–12:15	Block time:
	Group 1: English language arts
	Group 2: Science/social studies
	Group 3: Math
12:15–12:35	Lunch
12:35–1:00	Computer or library time
1:00–2:05	Block time:
	Group 1: Science/social studies
	Group 2: Math
	Group 3: English language arts
2:05–2:40	Physical education
2:40–3:00	Alternating art and music
3:00–3:10	Whole class meetings in homerooms
3:15	Dismissal

STRUCTURE AND ORGANIZATION OF MIDDLE SCHOOL EDUCATION

Some schools that serve sixth, seventh, and eighth graders are **departmentalized,** with teachers teaching their own subjects and meeting occasionally with other teachers who teach the same subject. With departmentalization, a teacher who, for instance, has Jamal in math does not collaborate with Jamal's social studies or science teacher. The math teacher may not even know who Jamal has for social studies or science.

According to the **National Middle School Association** (2010), the preferred organizational structure for middle level education is the student-teacher team, known as an **interdisciplinary team**. A team generally includes four core subject area teachers and the 80 to 100 or so students they share. If Jamal is on a team, all his teachers know exactly who teaches him each core subject. The team of teachers meets at least three times a week to plan together and discuss student progress and concerns. This kind of teaming is developmentally appropriate for **young adolescents**.

In some **middle schools,** students attend six or seven classes a day, each 50 to 60 minutes long. These classes include the core subjects, as well as other subjects that are considered **exploratory** or **related arts**. These may include art, music, physical education, industrial arts, languages, drama, and computer education, among others. Figure 2.6 shows both a traditional six-period student schedule and a schedule allowing for longer class periods, commonly called a **block schedule**.

Teaming is successfully implemented at Cario Middle School, where focus teachers Traci Peters and Deirdre Huger McGrew teach. At Cario, each core class is taught for 70 minutes. The students also have one class period for a variety of special classes that are rotated every 9 weeks. They have

Cario Middle School, Mt. Pleasant, South Carolina

To learn more about the structure and organization of Cario Middle School, where Traci Peters and Deirdre McGrew teach, take a school tour and watch an interview with principal Carol Bartlett in the Teaching in Focus section for Chapter 2 in MyEducationLab.

Points of Reflection 2.7

Does teaching young adolescents on an interdisciplinary team in a middle level setting appeal to you? Would you prefer teaching a core subject area or perhaps a special area such as a foreign language, art, or choral music? Does working as a guidance counselor, media specialist, or teacher of students with special needs interest you?

Figure 2.6 Middle school student schedules

Traditional schedule (5 minutes to change classes)

8:00–8:10	Homeroom
8:15–9:10	Math
9:15–10:10	English language arts
10:15–11:10	Band/art/foreign language/drama (9 weeks each)
11:15–11:45	Lunch
11:50–12:45	Science
12:50–1:45	Computer education/physical education (one semester each)
1:50–2:45	Social studies
2:50–3:00	Homeroom
3:00	Dismissal

Block Schedule

8:00–8:15	Homework
8:20–10:00	English language arts block
10:05–10:55	Related arts rotation
11:00–11:30	Lunch
11:35–1:15	Math block
1:20–2:10	Science and social studies (rotating days)
2:15–3:05	Related arts rotation
3:05	Dismissal

a 30-minute lunch period and 5 minutes to go from class to class. Cario teachers provide a rich array of clubs and after-school activities from which students may choose.

STRUCTURE AND ORGANIZATION OF HIGH SCHOOL EDUCATION

High school may be a very recent experience for you, or it may have occurred decades ago. Virtually everyone agrees that high school represents a unique time of life. The 4 years of 9th, 10th, 11th, and 12th grade provide vivid memories that many of us choose to relive every 10 years or so as we make our way back to reunions to reminisce, to see what and how our classmates are doing, or perhaps to show off or embellish our own accomplishments. Then there are those of us who would rather forget that time of our lives. Regardless of our feelings or memories from both an academic and a social perspective, high school experiences have a significant and long-lasting impact on most of us.

High school teachers typically specialize in one major subject and teach different areas or levels of that subject. All teachers of a subject form a department and meet periodically to discuss issues such as course materials, innovations and dilemmas in the subject field, and professional development opportunities. Departmentalization is the primary organizational structure of high schools.

Some high schools adhere to a traditional schedule of six or seven classes a day, each about an hour long. Students attend these classes for two semesters to earn a credit in each. However, alternative schedules are gaining popularity. Some schools are choosing to use blocks of 90 to 100 minutes per class that allow for more complete cycles of learning, such as completion of labs, reading and reflecting on literature, and proving as well as applying math theories.

Block schedules take one of two forms. Each has benefits. One form is composed of four classes per day of 90 to 100 minutes, every day, thus

Roosevelt High School, Fresno, California

allowing four courses to be completed in a semester. One of the major benefits of this type of schedule is that students have only four subjects to study at a time, rather than six or seven. With four courses per semester, students have the opportunity to earn 32 credits in 4 years of high school. The other basic form of block scheduling is the alternating-day model. With this schedule, students also receive credit for eight courses a year, but each course meets for 90 to 100 minutes every other day for two semesters.

As an urban high school, Roosevelt is actually two high schools in one. Most of the students (about 2,100) attend the comprehensive program, and about 500 students attend the arts magnet school, Roosevelt School of the Arts. The student population of Roosevelt High School, primarily Hispanic and Asian, is not typical of most high schools in the United States but is more common in California, Texas, and Florida. Most of you did not attend high schools that mirror Roosevelt. Most of you will not teach in high schools like Roosevelt, but some of you will. The majority of Roosevelt's students are from low-income homes. The majority of you are not. So why is Roosevelt our focus high school? There are several reasons. First, you need to see that effective teachers engage students in interesting and relevant lessons in all schools, regardless of the student profile or school setting. Second, because the high school so fresh in many of your memories is most likely a rural or suburban high school with families in middle- to upper-income brackets, you need to be exposed to a high school that's outside most of your zones of awareness and comfort. And, perhaps most important, adolescents are adolescents. Similarities outweigh elements of diversity.

In this chapter's ***Diversity Dialogue***, we read about Advanced Placement (AP) classes and the dilemma surrounding the lack of minority students in them. This issue exists in many high schools across the country.

To learn more about the structure and organization of Roosevelt High School, where Craig Cleveland, Derek Boucher, and Angelica Reynosa teach, take a school tour with assistant principal John Lael and watch an interview with principal Maria Romero in the Teaching in Focus *section for Chapter 2 in MyEducationLab.*

Points of Reflection 2.8

Does teaching in a high school appeal to you? Is there a teacher who had a profound influence on the direction of your life that you would want to use as a model for your own teaching?

DIVERSITY DIALOGUE

Derek Boucher, social science and reading teacher, Roosevelt High School, California

Roosevelt is a dual-purpose school campus, with both a comprehensive high school and an arts magnet program housed on the same campus. Looking at the student populations side by side reveals an out-of-balance picture with regard to race. Roosevelt's general population is predominantly of Hispanic ethnicity, with a growing population of students from countries such as Laos and Cambodia. The arts magnet is a healthy mix of a number of races; about half of the students are white.

When inequities are evident, or suspected, programs in schools may become controversial. The difference between the two high school populations is not unusual, but the discrepancies are much more pronounced in the AP classes, which are the most academically challenging in any school and designed for students who have mastered foundational content. At the end of an AP course students take a rigorous exam, with passing scores resulting in college credit. AP classes are often more expensive to run than others because they are typically smaller, with teachers required to attend special institutes to qualify to teach the courses. Some research studies show that students who take AP classes, regardless of how they do on the exam, fare better in college.

Derek Boucher acknowledges that opportunities to be part of AP classes are available to all Roosevelt students because they cross the regular/magnet barrier. He also knows that walking into an AP class reveals a visible gap regarding which students actually enroll in these advanced courses. They are mostly, and some are exclusively, white. Derek is aware that this is a controversial and complex issue with no easy remedies.

Respond to these dilemmas by writing one well-developed paragraph for each.

1. Because doing well in AP classes requires students to have foundational knowledge and skills, how might Derek and his colleagues go about beginning the process of increasing diversity in AP classes at Roosevelt?
2. When students are chosen for AP classes, would adding several minority students who come close to qualifying have a positive effect on them? If you believe this to be true, explain your reasoning. If, on the other hand, you think this would not be good for the students who do not actually qualify, explain your reasoning.

We return to discussions of school levels as we address various aspects of the teaching profession. Each time the information will build on previous topics so you will have a view of the big picture of what teaching is like in each level. Regardless of the level you decide to teach, your school will be in one of three settings.

What Are the Three Principal Settings of U.S. Schools?

When it comes to schooling, geography has a major impact. Sometimes a mile or two is significant with regard to educational experiences. The commonly accepted categories of rural, suburban, and urban schools that exist in all 50 states probably conjure up images in your mind, generalized impressions of what each embodies. This section refines those images.

An in-focus view will reveal some generalities about the context of schooling in each of three areas: rural, suburban, and urban. The day-to-day realities of children both in and out of school within these three settings may be vastly different in terms of home, socioeconomic circumstances, and school opportunities. These differences may reflect the expectations held by parents, community, and educators of what children can do and be. Most teachers can do little to alter the out-of-school realities faced by schools and schoolchildren. However, what teachers can alter are the ways they view students and their potential. It's a matter of values—both teachers' and students'.

RURAL SCHOOLS

About a third of schools across the United States are in **rural** communities. In Montana, over 70% of the state's schools are rural. Twenty percent of Alaska's schools employ three or fewer teachers each (Carter, 2003).

Most rural schools are smaller than urban and suburban schools. However, some draw students from an area that may encompass hundreds of square miles and have large student populations. A single primary school, elementary school, middle school, and high school, each with more than 800 students, may serve such a large geographic area.

Geographic isolation often means that students may have few of the opportunities and experiences found in more populated areas, such as museums and performing arts. Even basic services that people in suburban and urban areas take for granted, such as hospitals and large libraries, may not be readily available.

A high school of 100 to 200 students that is over an hour away from a medium-size town may have difficulty offering ample opportunities for what's commonly viewed as a well-rounded education. Think about it. To offer adequate coursework, a high school must employ certified subject-area teachers. Supporting an algebra II class of 6 costs just about as much as supporting a class of 28. Regardless of class size, the course requires a teacher and a classroom. Small high schools face similar constraints in offering extracurricular opportunities. It may be difficult to offer French club, debate team, football and basketball teams, and orchestra.

Hiring and retaining qualified teachers in small or large rural schools is a significant problem, even though the schools may be community oriented centers in safe, scenic places. However, the benefits that may accompany a rural area such as ready access to recreation and natural beauty may outweigh any perceived drawbacks.

SUBURBAN SCHOOLS

Suburban schools most often serve students who live in single-family homes with grassy yards in areas dotted with shopping centers, places of worship, and recreational facilities. Apartment complexes and townhouses are scattered among the well-lit paved streets. Every few miles or so, there's a school.

Many people who live in the suburbs are likely to be in the middle-class to affluent socioeconomic spectrum. Their communities are basically safe places with adequate public services that provide a generally comfortable lifestyle. The schools, even in tight state budget situations, generally continue to operate at acceptable levels with tolerable class sizes, textbooks for each child in most subjects, and satisfactory building maintenance. Within suburban schools

Points of Reflection 2.9

Did you live in a rural area, a suburb, or an urban setting? How would you describe the setting(s) of your PreK–12 experiences? If you had the opportunity to live in more than one setting, what do you recall about the differences?

Points of Reflection 2.10

When you graduate with teacher certification, would you consider moving to an isolated rural area where you may be needed, but where there are no shopping malls, no theaters, and few single people under age 50? Does this lifestyle appeal to you? If so, why?

students generally experience organization and order, extracurricular opportunities, and some degree of community participation and approval. These factors don't necessarily mean that students are learning at optimal levels, but there are some obvious advantages.

Many families choose to live in the suburbs and in small- to medium-size towns primarily because of what the schools offer their children. Real estate agents have long known that the public school options for specific residential areas have much to do with property appeal. Families desire stability and a satisfactory free education. If they can afford it, they buy homes in locations that will fulfill these desires. Do they get what they pay for? Most would probably say yes.

URBAN SCHOOLS

Most **urban** school settings are in sharp contrast to those of suburban schools. The facilities tend to be older, part of the fabric of downtowns that may or may not continue to be vibrant community areas. While architecturally appealing, the older buildings are generally more expensive and difficult to maintain and may be in a state of disrepair more often than suburban school buildings.

Urban schools are likely to serve many students who live in low-income settings. Although funding differences certainly exist between some urban and suburban areas, as poignantly related by Jonathan Kozol in *Savage Inequalities* (1991), some urban schools actually receive more funding per student than do suburban schools. One reason for this is that the federal government has programs that provide extra money for schools with

Points of Reflection 2.11

Did you grow up in a suburban area? Do you enjoy the conveniences these areas generally afford? Is this type of location where you want to spend your teaching career? If so, why? If not, why not?

A few miles can make a significant difference in the school experience of students. At Wells High School in San Francisco, students look out the window to see Alamo Hill and the city skyline. Just 30 miles north of the city, students look out the window of Bolinas-Stinson Elementary at sea lions in Bolinas Lagoon.

TABLE 2.4 Comparison of schools in rural, suburban, and urban settings

Setting	Definition of Setting	Percentage of All Public Schools	Advantages	Challenges
Rural	Designated area with fewer than 2,500 people	31%	Smaller schools; community ownership	Inadequate tax base for funding; difficulty hiring qualified teachers; geographic isolation
Suburban	Neighborhoods and small- to medium-size towns located on the fringes of large cities	44%	Families with higher socioeconomic status; relative ease of hiring qualified teachers	Satisfying various factions in the community; making continuous improvements
Urban	Cities that have large downtowns and a dense population	25%	Possibility of making large gains in student learning	Low socioeconomic status of many families; problems associated with low expectations; low levels of parental/family education

Source: National Elementary and Secondary School Enrollment Model, National Center for Education Statistics, 2003.

Points of Reflection 2.12

Is this the kind of challenge you might want to tackle? Can you see yourself nurturing and guiding students who may depend on you for encouragement to see beyond their current circumstances?

student populations living below certain economic levels. Research supports the assertion that students from low-income families require more resources to perform at the same levels as students from middle-income families.

Many urban school settings present some unique challenges. The students in urban schools more often come to school with greater needs than can be met by the curriculum alone (Scherer, 2005).

Table 2.4 illustrates some of the general distinctions among rural, suburban, and urban schools. Keep in mind that there are exceptions in every setting and that schools in every setting can make effective teaching and learning connections.

What Is an Effective School?

Effective schools meet the learning needs of the students who attend them. What are the characteristics of an effective school? Theorists and practitioners have attempted to measure schools' effectiveness for decades. Grappling with what elements characterize effective schools keeps the conversation alive. The minute we say, "Okay. This is it. If a school does this list of things in these ways, it is effective," we will box in our thinking and become stagnant. Still, although characteristics may vary in many ways, we need a picture of what effective schools may look like and what students and teachers do in them.

CHARACTERISTICS OF EFFECTIVE SCHOOLS

The Equal Educational Opportunity Survey in 1966, commonly referred to as the **Coleman Report,** concluded that family and community factors, such as poverty and parental levels of education, prevented some children from learning; that no matter what schools did, some children would not be successful. Appalled by this assertion, many in the education community adopted the mantra "All children can learn." President Lyndon B. Johnson responded in the late 1960s with landmark legislation, the Elementary and Secondary Education Act, which, among other things, provided extra funding for schools with high numbers of children from low-income homes, called **Title I funding**. In the 1970s, President Gerald Ford expanded equal educational opportunity by signing **Public Law 94-142,** making special education services a right, not a privilege.

In the 1970s, the **Effective Schools Movement** was initiated based on the belief that all children can learn. This movement was designed to locate schools deemed effective for all children and to identify common characteristics among these schools. The basic tenets of these identified schools included the following:

- All children can learn.
- Schools control enough of the variables to make it happen.
- Schools should be accountable for measuring achievement to be certain that all children, regardless of gender, race, ethnicity, or socioeconomic status, are learning.
- All schools require qualified and capable people to ensure that all children learn.

Effective Schools research, led primarily by Ronald Edmonds and Lawrence Lezotte, concluded that there are seven elements relating to effective schools. These elements, or correlates, listed in Figure 2.7, are all associated with improved student learning. Examining schools in light of these elements reveals areas of needed improvement.

In 2010 the Bill and Melinda Gates Foundation accepted the challenge to determine what characteristics effective teachers possess that translate into effective schools. Designating six large school districts across the United States for participation in the study, the Gates Foundation pledged over $500 million to the task. Educators and the general public await the results of this largest study to date on teacher and school effectiveness.

Effective schools may be found in rural, suburban, and urban areas. They may be early childhood, elementary, middle, or high schools. They serve any range of colors, classes, and ethnicities of students. School effectiveness exists where students are learning and experiencing positive personal growth, facilitated by teachers who make a difference.

WE MAKE A DIFFERENCE

We make a difference when we ask ourselves and one another "And how are the children?" in conjunction with our best efforts to facilitate learning. According to Kati Haycock, director of The Education Trust, what schools do makes a huge difference in whether students learn. She asserts that what matters most is good teaching (Haycock, 2003). Quality teachers

Figure 2.7 The seven correlates of effective schools

1. *Clear and focused mission.* The school staff shares a commitment to instructional goals, priorities, and accountability, and they accept responsibility for students learning their curricular goals.
2. *High expectations for success.* The school staff believes, and demonstrates that belief, that all students can master essential content and skills.
3. *Instructional leadership.* The principal is the instructional leader who persistently communicates the school mission to staff, students, and parents.
4. *Frequent monitoring of student progress.* Student academic progress is measured frequently in a variety of ways. The results are used to improve instruction and student performance.
5. *Opportunity to learn and student time on task.* Students are engaged in learning essential content and skills for a significant amount of the school day.
6. *Safe and orderly environment.* Schools are orderly, purposeful, and free from threat of physical harm. The climate is conducive to learning.
7. *Positive home-school relations.* Parents understand and support the school's mission and have opportunities to play important roles in helping to achieve the school's mission.

Source: Lezotte, L. W. (1991). *Correlates of effective schools: The first and second generation.* Okemos, MI: Effective Schools Products.

for every student will enhance a school's effectiveness. The education of quality teachers, the hiring and retention of quality teachers, and the continuing professional growth of quality teachers are key elements of effective schools, where a balance exists between students' academic achievement and personal development.

CONCLUDING THOUGHTS

George Albano, 25-year veteran principal of Lincoln Elementary School in Mount Vernon, New York, can answer "And how are the children? Are they all well?" by stating that 99% of his school's fourth graders made it over the New York state achievement bar in English, math, and science even though more than 50% are eligible for free or reduced-price lunch and 60% are African American or Hispanic. He leads an effective school where the achievement gap is nonexistent, and students are in the care of competent teachers who make them feel valued. Albano puts it this way, "Success comes down to hard work; great and dedicated teachers; an integrated curriculum; lots of art, music, and physical education; the willingness to bend and break rules occasionally; and the complete refusal to let any child fail to learn" (Merrow, 2004, p. 456).

Your challenge is clear. Be the generation of teachers who figures it out—the teachers who bring us closer to quality, effective education for all students.

After reading the *Chapter in Review,* interact with Brandi Wade in this chapter's *Developing Professional Competence*.

Chapter in Review

What are the purposes of public schools in the United States?

- Although often used interchangeably, there are distinctions between education and schooling. Education happens continually through all of life's experiences, whereas schooling is the formal structure of teaching and learning.

- Transmitting and reconstructing society are two complementary purposes of U.S. schooling.

- Teaching students how to participate positively in society while facilitating academic learning are two complementary purposes of U.S. schooling.

- There is no conflict between meeting individual student needs and collective student needs.

- Although schooling in the United States sustains students for today, it also prepares them for tomorrow.

What is the culture of a school?

- The culture of a school is the context of the learning experiences, as well as adult and student behaviors and attitudes.

- A school's culture can be a positive force for learning, or a negative influence that interferes with learning, and all shades in between.

- Teachers have an enormous impact on a school's culture.

How do school venues differ?

- There is a great variety of schools in the United States, from the traditional neighborhood public school to the ultimate private school, the home.

- Traditional public schools have education programs that suit most students.

- Full-service schools attend to the academic, health, and social service needs of students and families, and, in many cases, of the community.

- A magnet school is a public school with a specific theme or focus.

- A charter school is a public school that operates under a contract negotiated between the initiator of the school and an oversight agency to which the school is accountable. Charter schools are free from many of the regulations that apply to other public schools.

- Alternative schools are schools designed to meet the needs of students who are not successful in traditional schools.

- Private schools may or may not be affiliated with a religious organization.

- Single-gender schools, almost all of which are private, are schools for boys only or for girls only.

- Homeschooling is a growing trend in the United States.

- For-profit schools are run by management companies. The concept is controversial when applied to public schools.
- School choice plans provide students and parents with options in both the public and private sectors.

What is school like at different levels?

- Early childhood education spans birth through age 8, or roughly through third grade.
- Elementary education may include a variety of grade levels, with K–5 or 6 as the most common. Early childhood and elementary overlap on the low end; elementary and middle overlap on the high end.
- Middle school education usually includes grades 6 to 8.
- High school education includes grades 9 to 12.

What are the three principal settings of U.S. schools?

- Urban settings are cities with large downtowns and a dense population. Urban schools are likely to have a high percentage of minority students from low-income homes.
- Suburban settings are distinct locations that include neighborhoods and small- to medium-size towns that have grown up on the fringe of cities. Suburban schools are likely to have a lower percentage of minorities, with most students coming from middle- or upper-income homes.
- Rural settings are areas with population under 2,500 and few retail stores and services. Rural schools may be all white, all minority, or integrated to some extent, depending on the area.

What is an effective school?

- Effective schools are those that meet the learning needs of the students who attend them.
- Effective schools may have a variety of characteristics, with quality teaching as the most important common element.

Developing Professional Competence

Visit the Developing Professional Competence section on Chapter 2 of the MyEducationLab for this text to answer the following questions and begin your preparation for licensure exams.

You first met Brandi Wade in **Meet the Focus Teachers and Students**. Then in the beginning of this chapter you learned more about Brandi and Summit Primary School.

Brandi enjoys the fact that as a kindergarten teacher she benefits from having all the other district kindergarten teachers in her building. Recall that as a K–2 school, Summit Primary houses all the kindergarten, first grade, and second grade classes in the Licking Heights, Ohio, school district. However, as the district grows and diversifies, community members and individuals on the school board are talking about creating neighborhood schools, five for grades K to 5, three for grades 6 to 8, and two high schools for grades 9 to 12.

Think about this dilemma from the perspectives of a variety of **stakeholders,** or those who have legitimate involvement and stand to gain or lose from the situation. Answer the following multiple-choice questions:

1. Brandi and the other kindergarten teachers think their teaching is more effective because of their collective expertise. They want to stay together. All of the following support the teachers' desire to stay together except
   a. They can share ideas among nine teachers, rather than two or three that would result from structure changes.
   b. If there is a problem student, they have more options for classrooms for him or her.
   c. New programs are easier to implement because they can help each other.
   d. Materials are easier to manage.

2. Teachers of grades 3 to 6 in the intermediate school next door see the value of smaller schools that would be created if the county divides into school zones and also moves grade 6 to the middle school. With

four grade levels, they have over 1,000 children in one building, with projected growth to 1,300 by next fall if nothing changes. Which rationale is the least important to their desire to see the district change grade-level configurations?

   a. There is no place large enough to gather all the students for special events.

   b. Research shows there is more violence and bad behavior in large schools than in small schools.

   c. Research shows that children feel a greater sense of belonging in a small school than in a large school, regardless of class size.

   d. Having grades K to 5 in one building may lend to more family stability, especially for those with several children in the grade range.

3. Teachers in the current middle school that now includes grades 7 and 8 think that participation in after-school activities would increase if kids lived closer to the school they attend. It's very difficult to have after-school clubs and sports when most students are bused to school from all across the county. From a student's standpoint, which of the following would be the least important reason for creating schools that are physically more accessible to all students who attend?

   a. A school with fewer students, based on a smaller geographic area, will allow students more opportunities to be involved in a variety of activities.

   b. The schools would be more ecologically friendly because more students could walk to them.

   c. Students could go to school with others in their immediate vicinity, making it more likely that their friends live close enough to socialize on weekends or after school.

   d. In smaller schools students tend to know each other and their teachers better.

4. Many community members, including parents, believe that smaller schools with wider grade bands located throughout the county will be best for the Licking Heights district. In the plan, Summit High School, which is now a full-service school with a health clinic and adult education classes, would be divided into two smaller schools. Why might two high schools, strategically located in the county, benefit students and their families more?

   a. High school sports teams would have competition within the district, allowing for more playing time for athletes.

   b. Competition between the two high schools would increase enthusiasm in the community.

   c. Research has shown that higher percentages of students in small schools get involved in activities more than students in larger schools.

   d. A full-service school with a health clinic in a central location at the large school has not proven to be useful.

5. Some parents and alums are opposed to breaking up Summit High School into two schools. Which of the following may explain some of their reasons?

   a. A large county high school has a better chance of having an excellent record of athletic championships.

   b. A larger school provides more curricular opportunities for students.

   c. Both a and b.

   d. Neither a nor b.

Now it's time for you to respond to two short essay items involving the scenario. In your responses, be sure to address all the dilemmas and questions posed in each item. Each response should be between one half and one double-spaced page.

6. Brandi and several other kindergarten teachers plan to present their case for keeping the district schools in their current configuration at a school board meeting. What do you think their three strongest arguments will be?

7. Do you predict the district will reconfigure the schools? If so, explain why. If not, explain your reasons for thinking the schools will remain in their current configuration.

Where
DO I Stand NOW ?

In the beginning of this chapter you completed an inventory that gauged your interest in teaching students in a particualr level, the teaching setting you prefer, and your preference for either public or private schools. Now that you have read the chapter, completed exercises related to the content, engaged in class discussions, and so on, answer the following questions in your course notebook.

1. What have you learned about the four levels of school that has affected your choice of students with whom you want to work? Did you learn something that confirmed your original choice? If so, what? Did you learn something that has made you change your preference or at least consider another level? If so, explain.

2. With which setting are you most familiar? What did you learn through this chapter about rural education? How about suburban schools? What did you learn about urban schools? Has your original preference changed? If so, how?

3. If you originally had a preference for either public or private schools, have your experiences through this chapter confirmed your preference or changed your mind? Explain.

MyEducationLab

The MyEducationLab for this course can help you solidify your comprehension of Chapter 2 concepts.

- Explore the classrooms of the teachers and students you've met in this chapter in the Teaching in Focus section.
- Prepare for licensure exams as you deepen your understanding of chapter concepts in the Developing Professional Competence section.

- Gauge and further develop your understanding of chapter concepts by taking the quizzes and examining the enrichment materials on the Chapter 2 Study Plan.
- Visit Topic 2, Schools and Society, to watch ABC videos, explore Assignments and Activities, and practice essential teaching skills with the Building Teaching Skills and Dispositions unit.

3

Student Similarities and Differences

In this chapter we explore the student population in the United States by looking at aspects of similarity as well as aspects of diversity. Here are some questions we focus on in Chapter 3:

✦ How are we similar?

✦ How are gender differences manifested in schools?

✦ How are cultural and language diversity manifested in schools?

✦ What is the impact on students of family structure, religion, and socioeconomic status?

✦ How are learning differences manifested in schools?

✦ Who are students with exceptionalities, and how do we serve them?

This is not an exhaustive list of ways that diversity may be exhibited in your classroom, but it's a good start. These differences and more exist in early childhood, elementary, middle, and high school settings. Before we discuss how we are similar and how we are different, explore your own views about student development and diversity in this chapter's *Where Do I Stand?*

Where DO I Stand?

This inventory addresses two broad issues. One issue deals with your prior knowledge of diversity among PreK–12 students, and the other gauges the extent of your personal experiences with diversity. After reading an item, indicate your level of agreement by choosing a number and placing it in the blank before the statement. Following the inventory are directions for how to organize your responses and what they may indicate in terms of where you stand.

4 I strongly agree
3 I agree
2 I don't have an opinion
1 I disagree
0 I strongly disagree

_____ **1.** Some students have higher IQs than their teachers.

_____ **2.** The white student population is increasing at about the same rate as the Hispanic student population.

_____ **3.** I grew up in a home where I felt secure.

_____ **4.** Girls tend to use their emotions more aggressively than boys.

_____ **5.** Both those with disabilities and those with academic gifts are considered to be students with exceptionalities in public schools.

_____ **6.** I was in what were considered regular classes or advanced classes in PreK–12 school.

_____ **7.** Learning disabilities account for about 20% of those students receiving special services.

_____ **8.** Gender stereotyping occurs when perceived differences in attitudes, interests, and actions based on gender are assumed for all people.

_____ **9.** More people are designating themselves as multiracial now than ever before in the United States.

_____ **10.** I have very few acquaintances that are of a different race than me.

_____ **11.** It is possible for individuals to be smart in a variety of ways.

_____ **12.** Christianity is the religion with which I most relate.

_____ **13.** Studies reveal that about 5% of children in U.S. classrooms have attention deficit hyperactivity disorder (ADHD).

_____ **14.** Teachers tend to call on girls more often than boys.

_____ **15.** Girls are more likely to be inducted into the National Honor Society than boys.

_____ **16.** A diagnosis of ADHD qualifies a student for special education services.

_____ **17.** I don't know many people for whom English is not their first language.

_____ **18.** Immigrant students are spread evenly across the United States.

_____ **19.** About 1 of every 20 children in U.S. schools is an English-language learner.

_____ **20.** A person's ethnicity often reveals more about him or her than race.

_____ **21.** I spent all or much of my childhood in a two-parent home.

_____ **22.** Race is based primarily on a person's place of birth.

_____ **23.** In my K–12 school years, very few, if any, of my classmates were of races other than my own.

_____ **24.** Church services and church friends played a big role in my childhood.

_____ **25.** Boys tend to blame failure on lack of skill rather than lack of effort.

_____ **26.** About half of the people in the United States say their religion is based on Christianity.

_____ **27.** Most children in U.S. public schools who do not speak English fluently were born in the United States.

_____ **28.** I did not personally know students who received special education services when I was in PreK–12 school.

_____ **29.** Federal law states that all students with disabilities have a right to a free education in a regular classroom setting if parents decide it's appropriate.

_____ **30.** Race is based on physical characteristics people have from birth.

_____ **31.** Most of my friends had a mom, a dad, and siblings living together.

_____ **32.** I grew up knowing very few students who spoke a language other than English in their homes.

_____ **33.** Intelligence is a fixed attribute that can be accurately measured.

_____ **34.** My family had enough money for my needs, and most of my wants, to be fulfilled.

_____ **35.** When IQ is used to determine gifted status, the threshold number is about 125.

_____ **36.** Most children will only respond adequately to instruction after their need for security is met.

This inventory has addressed two broad issues:

- _To what extent do my personal experiences reflect exposure to diversity?_

- _How much do I know about diversity among PreK–12 students?_

To answer these questions, record your responses in three columns as indicated.

ITEM #	MY RESPONSE	ITEM #	MY RESPONSE	ITEM #	MY RESPONSE
3		1		2	
6		4		7	
10		5		13	
12		8		14	
17		9		16	
21		11		18	
23		15		19	
24		20		22	
28		27		25	
31		30		26	
32		35		29	
34		36		33	
Sum A		Sum B		Sum C	

To what extent do my personal experiences reflect exposure to diversity?

The closer your column A responses are to 4, the fewer experiences you have had with diversity. Divide Sum A by 12. If your mean is 3 to 4, you have not had significant experiences with diversity; if your mean is 0 to 2, you have had significant experiences with diversity.

How much do I know about diversity among PreK–12 students?

The closer your column B responses are to 4, the more you know about diversity among PreK–12 students. Divide Sum B by 12. If your mean is 3 to 4, you have significant knowledge of diversity among PreK–12 students.

The closer your column C responses are to 0, the more you know about diversity among PreK–12 students. Divide Sum C by 12. If your mean is 0 to 2, you have significant knowledge of diversity among PreK–12 students.

Take a few minutes to think about your responses and what you have learned from this exploration. Share your scores if directed by your instructor.

Teaching in Focus

As Craig Cleveland looks around his classroom at Roosevelt High School in Fresno, California, while his second-period U.S. History students are making their way to their seats, he sees 32 adolescents—7 sophomores, 21 juniors, and 4 seniors. They are chatting as they make themselves comfortable in the crowded second-floor room. Their primary languages tell much of their ethnic stories—15 speak Spanish, 10 Hmong, 6 English, and 1 Laotian. Thirteen of the 32 speak very little English and write even less.

All 32 students qualify for free or reduced-price meals. Craig knows that students from low-income families struggle more to achieve academically. When measured by standardized tests, over half are considered below basic, or far below basic, in both English language arts and math. In addition, 19 of the 32 have impairments of some kind that are recognized by the school and require special accommodations by teachers.

Craig's challenge today is to pique every student's interest in the question, "Is separate ever really equal?" To do this, Craig must find a way to define the issues, present background information and make it relevant to his heterogeneous class, and then facilitate an activity that engages every student.

The students in Craig's class are alike in many ways: They are all adolescents, most are from low-income homes in the same geographic area, and they have all gone through similar developmental stages to become 15-, 16-, 17-, and 18-year-olds. They also have many differences: Some are male, and some are female; some were born in the United States, whereas others are recent immigrants; some are Catholic, some Protestant, some Buddhist. When viewed as a group, Craig's students are a wonderful but challenging example of diversity in the American classroom.

Watch a segment of Craig's lesson, as well as his interview and room tour, in the Teaching in Focus section for Chapter 3 in MyEducationLab for this course.

How Are We Similar?

In the time it takes you to read about three pages of this text, a whole classroom of students will be born. That's right—statistically, every 8 minutes 30 babies are born in the United States. Your entire future kindergarten class, third grade class, middle school social studies class, or high school algebra class may be coming into the world right now.

Statistically, we can predict that of these 30 future students, 14 will be considered a racial minority, 8 will be born into poverty, and 9 will be born out of wedlock. Of these 30 children, 17 will have parents who divorce before the students graduate from high school, 5 will serve jail sentences, 5 will be victims of violence, 4 will commit a violent crime before age 16, and almost half will drop out before finishing high school (National Center for Education Statistics [NCES], 2004; U.S. Census Bureau, 2008). "And how are the children?"

Chances are your classroom won't mirror the statistics you just read. Classroom populations vary from little cultural or socioeconomic diversity to a challenging mix. You may teach in a school with students whose families are financially well off or one with families that move when the rent comes due. You may teach in a stable rural community with conservative values and lifestyles, or you may teach in a suburban area that affords a great variety of opportunities and educational options but where students tend to move often.

The 30 new lives that have begun in this 8-minute time frame may appear to be diverse, but they are actually more similar than they are dissimilar. They are individual beings with unique attributes and a variety of needs. But the most important thing to remember is that they are children, all worthy of our best efforts. Mark Twain said that every day children are born who could change the world. We just don't know who they are yet.

NATURE AND NURTURE

There has been much debate on the question of what has the greater influence in determining who we are—nature or nurture. These two concepts are generally presented as oppositional: nature *versus* nurture. **Nature** refers to genetically inherited influences. Not only are certain physical characteristics, such as eye color, skin tone, and adult height,

Figure 3.1 Maslow's hierarchy of needs

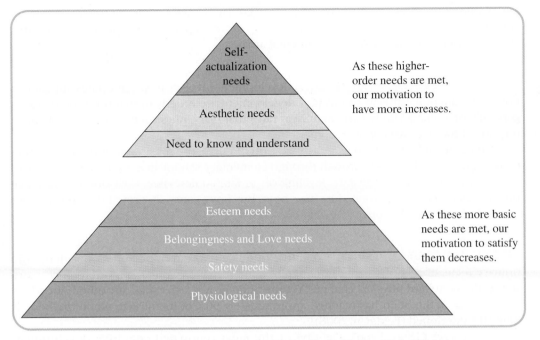

As these higher-order needs are met, our motivation to have more increases.

As these more basic needs are met, our motivation to satisfy them decreases.

Source: Maslow, A. H. (1999). *Toward a psychology of being* (3rd ed.). New York: Wiley.

determined by nature, but some aspects of our intelligence and personalities are established genetically as well. **Nurture** refers to the influences of our environment, encompassing everything that cannot be accounted for genetically. For instance, the people we meet, the schools we attend, and our economic status are all part of nurture.

Each child arrives in the world with predispositions, or tendencies, accounted for by nature and over which we have no control. Teachers do have some influence, however, over nurture. That's why we create classroom environments that stimulate growth—physical, intellectual, emotional, social, and moral. To more fully realize why we need to create this environment, let's examine the importance and relative priority of human needs that we all share.

MASLOW'S HIERARCHY OF NEEDS

Psychologist Abraham Maslow (1908–1970) proposed that human beings experience the same needs. Figure 3.1 shows his classic **hierarchy of needs,** which is widely accepted as an accurate depiction of the order, from bottom to top, in which needs have to be met for healthy and full human development.

Maslow proposed that basic needs for survival and safety must be met first. Once these needs are satisfied, humans are motivated to move up the pyramid toward higher-order needs. Makes sense, doesn't it? If students don't have food and shelter, or if they feel physically threatened, it's unlikely they will be concerned about understanding the Pythagorean theorem. Providing opportunities and support for needs fulfillment and promoting positive student development will help them ascend Maslow's pyramid and develop in positive ways.

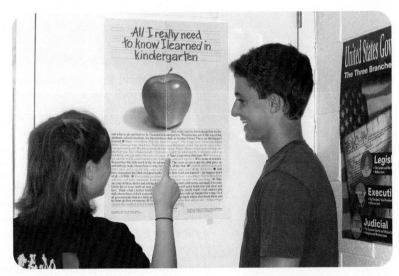

Many older students agree that what they learned during the rapid brain growth period before first grade continues to influence them.

STUDENT DEVELOPMENT

Most children progress through predictable age-related stages of development. The more we know about these developmental stages, the more empathy and support we can offer. Here we briefly consider five developmental areas.

Watch David McBeath's interview, including his mom, in the Teaching in Focus section for Chapter 3 in MyEducationLab for this course. You will see that David's physical development appears to have outpaced his other areas of development.

PHYSICAL DEVELOPMENT. Physical development involves how our bodies appear and how they function. Patterns of physical development are orderly in that the progression is generally predictable. Body parts mature at rates that make physical development the most obvious of the five areas of development.

Although each child follows a distinct growth curve, the most rapid growth occurs in early childhood, with steady growth through elementary school. In early adolescence there may be an explosive growth rate, leveling off in late adolescence. Girls often experience puberty as much as 2 years earlier than boys, but boys generally grow taller and heavier than girls by late adolescence (McDevitt & Ormrod, 2010).

COGNITIVE DEVELOPMENT. Cognitive (intellectual) development is considered the primary focus of school. Changes in cognition are just as profound, but often much more subtle, than outward physical changes. Yet the brain grows faster than any other part of the body. By age 5, the brain has reached approximately 90% of its full size while the body is only 30% developed (Feldman, 2008).

Jean Piaget (1896–1980) was one of the most renowned cognitive development theorists. Piaget recognized distinct differences in children's and adolescents' responses to questions that directly correlated to their chronological ages. This was the beginning of his research into the four **stages of cognitive development** encapsulated in Figure 3.2.

Although Piaget's work is still held in very high esteem, researchers have concluded that he based much of his theory on children's deficits rather than on their strengths. Children may be more capable at younger ages than Piaget believed. Teachers benefit from knowing about Piaget's stages but should never use them to limit how and when the intellectual capabilities of students are stretched.

Figure 3.2 Piaget's model of cognitive development

Sensorimotor intelligence (birth to 2 years of age)

Children primarily learn through their senses as their motor capabilities develop. Children in this stage don't actually "think" conceptually.

Preoperational thought (2–7 years of age)

Children begin to use symbols and their grasp of concepts develops rapidly. They begin to think about things and people outside their observable environment. Their viewpoint is generally limited because they have little ability to see things from different perspectives.

Concrete operations (7–11 years of age)

Children begin to think logically. They understand the concept of conservation, that quantities don't change because they are moved. Through manipulation of concrete objects they understand concepts such as number, space, and causality. They begin to see things from varied perspectives and draw conclusions.

Formal operations (11 years of age and on)

Adolescents progress from concrete thinking to the capability of thinking abstractly. They are able to make predictions, experience metacognition (thinking about thinking), and appreciate and use the structure and subtleties of language.

Source: McDevitt, T. M., & Ormrod, J. E. (2010). *Child development and education.* Upper Saddle River, NJ: Merrill/Pearson Education.

Rather than looking at deficiencies, noted Russian psychologist Lev Vygotsky (1896–1934) advocated determining children's intellectual abilities and then providing opportunities for intellectual growth. He proposed that a child's cognitive development increases through exposure to new information and that learning takes place within the individual's **zone of proximal development**. This zone is the level at which a child can almost, but not completely, grasp a concept or perform a task successfully. As learning takes place, the zone widens. This theory is akin to **scaffolding,** a concept widely accepted within education that takes its name from the construction term for temporary supports placed around a structure to allow work to be completed. Vygotsky viewed learning scaffolding as the support given to children to help them move through progressive levels of learning.

Additionally, Vygotsky believed that children's learning is shaped by the culture and society around them. The more interactions, the greater the learning, as a child moves forward within an ever-expanding zone of proximal development (Feldman, 2008).

High school students' sense of identity develops during adolescence.

EMOTIONAL DEVELOPMENT. Human experiences are given meaning through emotions. Both our emotions and our responses to them become more complicated with time. Children and adolescents experience a wide array of emotions, including happiness, anxiety, anger, fear, sadness, shame, and pride. For young adolescents, all these emotions and more may be experienced in one class period. Teachers need to be able to identity emotions as well as know how and when to respond to them.

In 1995 Daniel Goleman wrote *Emotional Intelligence: Why It Can Matter More Than IQ,* in which he proposed that a person's **emotional intelligence quotient (EQ)** may be the best indicator of future success in life. Emotional intelligence quotient involves a set of skills that accompany the expression, evaluation, and regulation of emotions. A high-level emotional quotient indicates an ability to understand others' as well as one's own feelings, respond appropriately to them, and, in general, get along.

SOCIAL DEVELOPMENT. Learning to get along with others is a process that begins when young children sit next to each other in **parallel play,** agreeably sharing the same space but not communicating. When children begin to share toys and verbally communicate, they are engaged in **associative play**. Progressing to **cooperative play,** children actively coordinate ways to keep the interaction going. When you think about it, these stages of socialization describe how we relate to others regardless of our age. Relating to others and thinking about them (and ourselves) is called **social cognition.** Whether we are simply coexisting (parallel play), communicating when necessary (associative play), or actively engaging with others (cooperative play), we are social creatures.

Relationships matter to us; adolescents are, at times, consumed with them. Relationships are part of America's youth culture, much of which revolves around groups that inevitably form as adolescents search for their identities. It's quite easy to see which youth subcultures appear to fit most easily into the traditional school setting—generally it's the "cool kids," the "jocks," and the "preppies." Other students may exhibit different developmental patterns and be labeled "nerds," "stoners," "eggheads," "loners," "goths," and so on. The names may change, but subgroups live on. As teachers our challenge is to connect with all our students and let them know we care about them, regardless of their social affiliations. Helping students develop positive and productive relationships within society is a major aspect of what teachers do.

Watch Sherlonda Francis's interview, including her mom and dad, in the Teaching in Focus section for Chapter 3 in MyEducationLab for this course. You will hear Sherlonda's parents talk about her very social nature. Her teacher, Renee Ayers, says that Sherlonda's social nature may be a source of difficulty in achieving academic success.

Teaching in Focus

Tim Mendenhall, grades 3–5, multiage classroom, Rees Elementary School, Utah. *In his own words. . . .*

I would first encourage you to follow your heart. Trust yourself and do what you feel needs to be done for your students. Education is messy. You will try things and fail. That's how we learn.

Second, more than reading and math, teaching your students to be lifelong learners is your ultimate goal. Make your classroom fun. If you don't like a book or an activity, why do you think they will? Love what you are doing, and they will learn to love learning.

Finally, stay at teaching long enough to get the REAL pay. This could be a child bringing you a Cherry Coke (instead of an apple) every Friday. Or a former student running off the football field to talk with you when he is quarterback and supposed to be leading a play. Or a parent coming back and telling you that you are still their child's favorite teacher (even after all the years and they are now graduating from high school). The pay is great; you just have to wait for it sometimes.

Read focus teacher Tim Mendenhall's words about forming relationships, adjusting what we do in the classroom based on who our students are, and about making our classrooms fun in *Teaching in Focus*.

CHARACTER DEVELOPMENT. A discussion of character, or moral, development can easily become value laden, depending on particular religious or ethical beliefs. Even so, certain character traits are considered positive by almost everyone, including honesty, trustworthiness, fairness, caring, and citizenship (Gathercoal & Crowell, 2000).

Noted developmental psychologist Lawrence Kohlberg contends that people pass through **stages of moral reasoning** as illustrated in Figure 3.3. Kohlberg's stages are based primarily on observations of males in Western culture and have been criticized for not being more universal or sensitive to gender differences. A psychologist and colleague of Kohlberg, Carol Gilligan (1982) suggests that differences in the way girls and boys are raised (nurture) can lead to differences in how they view moral dilemmas. According to Gilligan, boys tend to view morality in terms of broad principles of justice, whereas girls tend to view morality in terms of responsibility to individuals. We look more closely at gender differences in the next section.

A brief summary of development stages is in Table 3.1. Now that we've established some of the ways we are the same, let's think about ways we may be different.

Figure 3.3 Kohlberg's stages of moral reasoning

Stage 1: A rule is a rule, and people obey rules to avoid punishment.

Stage 2: Rules are followed or disobeyed based on rewards.

Stage 3: People obey rules because it's what others expect of them.

Stage 4: Society's rules are what's right, and people conform to expectations.

Stage 5: People follow rules out of obligation to what is agreed upon behavior in their society. Laws and rules can be changed if society sees a compelling need.

Stage 6: People follow rules that agree with universal ethics. If a law doesn't, they feel free to disobey it.

Source: Adapted from Kohlberg, L. (1984). *The psychology of moral development: Essays on moral development.* San Francisco: Harper & Row.

TABLE 3.1 Developmental characteristics by level

	Early Childhood	Elementary	Middle	High
PHYSICAL	-Dramatic changes in appearance and abilities -Boundless energy -Rapid brain growth -Healthiest time of life	-Coordination increases -Dexterity improves -Steady growth -Significant differences in size among children	-Onset of puberty -Sudden growth spurts may change appearance -Specialized gross and fine motor skills develop -Some risk-taking behaviors exhibited	-Sexual/reproductive maturity is reached -Girls complete growth spurt; boys continue to grow -High level of physical risk-taking activities exhibited
COGNITIVE	-Piaget's preoperational stage -Very intense brain activity -Increased ability to: speak with coherence, understand organization and patterns, learn prerequisites for reading	-Piaget's concrete operational stage -Increased ability to think logically, apply learning strategies, view multiple perspectives, decode phonetically, read aloud	-Beginning of Piaget's formal operational stage -Often self-absorbed -Increased ability to: reason, solve complex problems, use varied learning strategies	-Capacity for adult-like thought -Increased ability to: reason abstractly, make decisions with more realism, discern which learning strategies are effective
EMOTIONAL	-Self-concept develops and is influenced by family and society -self-conscious emotions such as guilt and pride develop	-Self-concept becomes more complex and differentiated -Coping skills develop -Emotional ties beyond family develop	-May be emotionally volatile -Drop in self-esteem -Strong emotional ties with friends develop -Frequent mood changes -Begin to establish a sense of identity	-Sense of being invulnerable -May be prone to depression -Seek independence and a sense of control -Sense of identity develops
SOCIAL	-Relationships with adults centered on direction, care, and protection -First friendships are developed -Types of play change from individual to cooperative -Become aware of other people's feelings	-Increasingly concerned with making and keeping friends -Becoming more assertive -Groups are generally same-gender -Capable of empathy -Awareness of social conventions and rules	-Conflicts with parents and other adults likely -Peers become more influential than adults -Popularity, or lack of it, becomes very important -Awareness develops of sexuality and gender-related relationships	-Identity crisis may lead to social dysfunction -Mixed-gender groups -Conformity with others decreases -Desire for self-reliance -Often overwhelmed with demands of relationships
CHARACTER	-Rules are rigid -Begins to understand intentionality -Aggression declines as language develops -Beginning awareness that actions may cause others harm	-Rules come from shared knowledge -Increased awareness of others' problems -Experience guilt and shame over moral wrong doing	-Strong sense of fairness -Desire to help those less fortunate -May value social approval over moral conviction	-Understand the need for rules to promote society -Increased concern about fulfilling duty to benefit others

Sources: Feldman (2008); Gallahue and Ozmun (2006); Goleman (1995); McDevitt and Ormrod (2010); Powell (2011); Richardson and Norman (2000).

How Are Gender Differences Manifested in Schools?

"It's a boy!" "It's a girl!" These are the exclamations heard in every delivery room in the United States. The anatomical differences between males and females determine sex; **gender** is the sense of being one sex or the other. Boys and girls, men and women—the differences are undeniable and are as fundamental as life itself. By age 2, children understand that they are either boys or girls, and they label others as well (Campbell, Shirley, & Candy, 2004).

It is common in U.S. households for girls to be encouraged to engage in what are considered gender-appropriate activities, such as playing with dolls and cooking on make-believe stoves; boys are encouraged to play with cars and throw balls. Household chores are often assigned by gender, with girls asked to wash dishes and boys asked to cut the grass. Boys and girls sense very quickly that there are expectations based on gender. **Gender stereotyping** occurs when perceived gender differences are assumed for all people, as in assuming that the play and chores described are always appropriate for one gender or the other. Generalizations about gender differences appropriately begin with phrases such as *tend to.* These two words indicate generalizing, as opposed to stereotyping. **Gender bias** is the favoring of one gender over the other in specific circumstances.

The federal government recognized gender bias in schools in 1972 when Congress passed Title IX of the Education Amendments Act, which states, "No person in the United States shall, on the basis of sex, be excluded from participation in, be denied the benefits of, or be subjected to discrimination under, any education program or activity receiving Federal financial assistance." Title IX has helped correct inequitable treatment of males and females in schools, most notably in athletic programs involving teams.

SOCIAL ASPECTS OF GENDER

During early childhood, children are friends with whoever is convenient, at day care, in preschool, or in the neighborhood. During the elementary school years children begin choosing friends of the same gender who have similar interests. With the advent of puberty, friends of the opposite gender begin to be included, and this trend continues through high school.

Boys tend to base their play on activities, whereas girls tend to base their play on talking. In group play, boys tend to play in more adventurous ways, such as acting out battles and physically challenging each other, whereas girls tend to take on roles that are calm, such as playing house or school. Research shows that boys tend to be more aggressive than girls, at least in physical ways. Boys most often show what researchers call **instrumental aggression,** or aggression based on attempting to meet a specific goal, such as grabbing a toy or establishing dominance in an activity. Girls may be as aggressive, but they usually learn to be so in more subtle ways that may be more emotional than physical. This type of aggression is known as **relational aggression** and may include name-calling, gossiping, or saying mean things just to be hurtful (Underwood, 2003).

ACHIEVEMENT AND GENDER

In general, researchers have found that boys tend to set higher goals than girls (Bandura, Barbaranelli, Caprara, & Pastorelli, 2001) and attribute their achievement to ability. When they fail, they tend to attribute their failure to lack of effort. In contrast, when girls meet their goals, they tend to attribute their success to effort. When they fail, they tend to attribute their failure to lack of ability (Vermeer, Boekaerts, & Seeger, 2000). This generalization, illustrated in Table 3.2, is significant for teachers to understand. It indicates that one gender may be conditioned to view failure as the result of a lack of effort, which is easily corrected. The other gender may see failure as the result of a lack of ability, which is not easily corrected.

Until recently it was generally held that boys scored higher than girls in almost every area tested. This academic gender gap has been closing in the last 20 years. Although girls

TABLE 3.2 Boys' and girls' perceived reasons for success and failure		
Perceived reason for	Boys	Girls
Success	High ability	High effort
Failure	Low effort	Low ability

Source: Vermeer, H. J., Bodkaert, M., & Seeger, G. (2000). Motivational and gender differences: Sixth-grade students' mathematical problem-solving behavior. *Journal of Educational Psychology, 92,* 308–315.

Boys in Crisis

This *World News Tonight* report raises the question of whether boys are really in crisis. Headlines are presented that seem to tell us that we need to pay particular attention to the plight of boys. A Harvard researcher says there is something inherently "sad" about boys and tells us that boys are much more likely to attempt suicide than girls and are not as enthusiastic about attending college. After examining test data, however, another researcher says that boys are fine. The Harvard researcher says there's more to the "sadness" of boys, elements that don't show up in test scores. In an interview of recent male high school graduates, we hear one young man say that boys simply don't feel as comfortable seeking help with the various stresses they may face.

To view this video, go to Chapter 3 in MyEducationLab for this course, click on In the News.

1. What do you think the researcher means when he says there is a "sadness" in boys? Do you agree with his characterization? If so, give an example of why. If not, why not?

2. Do you think boys are less inclined than girls to seek help with an emotional or social problem? On what do you base your opinion?

3. As a teacher, what could you do to help your male students not be "in crisis," as the headlines presented at the beginning of the video seem to indiate they are?

---

as a group may lag behind boys in some areas of science and upper-level math, they are outpacing boys in reading and writing, more likely to be inducted into the National Honor Society, and more likely to attend college (Glazer, 2005).

In classrooms many teachers call on boys more often than girls, allow boys to call out answers while scolding girls for doing so, give boys more encouragement to attempt difficult tasks, and generally have higher expectations for boys than for girls. This subtle discrimination is almost always unintentional, but it nevertheless has an effect on classroom participation (Gober & Mewborn, 2001).

This chapter's *In the News* addresses the perception that boys are in crisis. Some who study gender differences contend that boys have unique and previously unacknowledged problems dealing with school and achievement.

SEXUAL ORIENTATION

The sex to which a person is romantically or socially attracted determines a person's **sexual orientation**. Estimates of the percentage of Americans who are gay or lesbian (attracted to the same sex) range from 5% to 10%. It is reasonable to assume that these estimates apply to the American student population as well. Although it has achieved a measure of acceptance, homosexuality remains in many instances the basis of discrimination and focus of hateful attitudes and actions. The two places that we like to think of as safe and supportive—home and school—are often the very places where the most hurtful slurs and overt rejection of gay and lesbian students occur.

> Sexual harassment is addressed in Chapters 9 and 10.

GENDER DIVERSITY: IMPLICATIONS FOR TEACHERS

As of January 2010, 91 of the 547 public schools offering single-sex education opportunities were completely either all-boy or all-girl settings. Note that when schools and classes are discussed by the National Association for Single-Sex Public Education, the label goes from *gender* to *sex*. The word *sex* is used rather than gender because it is a more readily definable attribute. When the National Association for Single-Sex Public Education (NASSPE) was founded in 2002, there were fewer than 20 single-sex education opportunities (NASSPE, 2010). You can see this is a growing trend. For more information, including a list of schools by state offering single-sex options, visit www.singlesexschools.org/home-introduction.htm.

We can't deny that girls and boys are different in some ways, whether the differences stem from nature, from nurture, or from the inevitable combination. With awareness we can diminish gender-biased behaviors and attitudes in our schools. The most important contribution we can make toward alleviating gender bias in our classrooms is to treat our students as individuals, realizing that each is unique. In modeling this behavior we will help promote it in our students.

Our goal in creating **gender equity,** the fair and balanced treatment of boys and girls, is to provide learning environments where all students are free from limitations that might accompany gender stereotyping of what they can or should accomplish. Addressing the following questions will help foster gender equity in the classroom:

Points of Reflection 3.1

Have you ever felt discrimination based on gender? If so, explain. Are you aware of discrimination in a school setting based on sexual orientation? If so, explain. Have you considered teaching in an all-boy or all-girl setting?

- Do I use examples of males and females in all roles and occupations?
- Do I encourage girls as well as boys to explore science and math?
- Do I encourage boys as well as girls to read for pleasure and to participate in poetry writing and drama?
- Am I careful to include historical contributions of both males and females?
- Do I have a way of assuring that I call on boys and girls in equal numbers during class discussions?

How Are Cultural and Language Diversity Manifested in Schools?

Classrooms that were once populated with white students, black students, and perhaps a few students with other cultural identities are now filled with students of many races and ethnicities. Along with this diversity come more and more students whose first language is not English. Figure 3.4 shows projections for the changing student population ages 5 to 19 and represents more than 63 million children and adolescents in 2010. Note the trend of white students comprising diminishing percentages, with black and Asian percentages remaining relatively stable and the Hispanic percentage steadily increasing.

Figure 3.4 Projections of U.S. population, ages 5–19

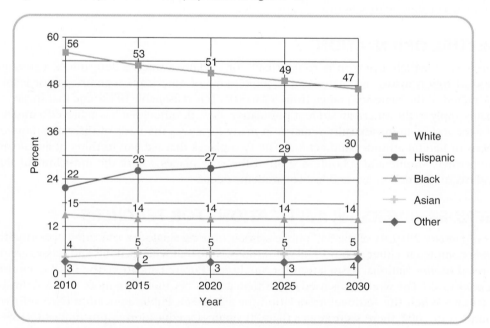

Source: U.S. Census Bureau, http://www.census.gov/population/www/projection/summarytables.html; 2000 census; 2008 prediction.

Teachers in the United States are overwhelmingly white, with only about 5% black, and 5% Hispanic, Asian, and other races. Add this information to the fact that by 2025 less than half of children and adolescents in the United States will be white, and you can see that appreciating, acknowledging, and altering our curriculum and instruction to be responsive to the students in our classrooms will be increasingly challenging. Knowing our students well is imperative.

Teacher characteristics are discussed in Chapter 1.

CULTURAL DIVERSITY

A widely accepted definition of **culture** states that it is a "dynamic system of social values, cognitive codes, behavioral standards, world views, and beliefs used to give order and meaning to our own lives as well as the lives of others" (Delgado-Gaitan & Trueba, 1991). Culture, and the complex combination of elements that compose it, should have a prominent place in any discussion of American education. Geneva Gay (2000) tells us that "culture is at the heart of all we do in the name of education" (p. 8).

Recent research suggests that culture affects perceptions of the characteristics of intelligence. In the study "Who Are the Bright Children? The Cultural Context of Being and Acting Intelligent," Sternberg (2007) tells us that "different cultures have different views of intelligence, so which children are considered intelligent may vary from one culture to another" (p. 148). He contends that teachers' acceptance and understanding of the differences can affect how well students learn. Intriguing idea, isn't it?

Gollnick and Chinn (2009) contend that culture has three primary characteristics. First, culture is *learned*. The language, the ways we behave, the social rules, the expectations, the roles—all these aspects of a culture are learned from family and others who influence our daily lives. The second primary characteristic of culture is that it is sustained and strengthened because it is *shared*. To learn how to "be" in a culture requires mentors, those who share the culture and, in doing so, perpetuate the culture. Third, a culture is *adaptive* to its environment. The culture of a large group of people changes, or adapts, over time in response to many variables.

The characteristics that apply to cultures of groups also apply to cultures of individuals. Each of us has a cultural identity.

CULTURAL IDENTITY. The interactions of many factors, including language, religion, gender, socioeconomic status, age, values, beliefs, race, and ethnicity, form a person's **cultural identity**. This identity is adapted throughout a person's life in response to his or her experiences.

The words *race, ethnicity,* and *culture* are often used interchangeably, but they do not have the same meaning. As teachers, we need to understand the meanings of the terms to better navigate the complexities of our students' lives. Although the color of our skin (race) and the country of our origin (ethnicity) may contribute strongly to our cultural identity, neither encompasses the total concept of culture. Let's consider race and ethnicity separately.

Racial Component of Culture. The word **race,** when applied to a group of people, simply categorizes them according to the physical characteristics they have at birth, such as skin color and facial features. Characterization by race is a social, political, economic, and psychological reality (Mukhopadhyay & Henze, 2003). Some researchers say there are actually as few as three races, whereas others claim there are more than 300 (Gollnick & Chinn, 2009). Not a very precise way to categorize people, is it?

The federal government uses race to categorize people in the United States. For census taking, five races are designated: white, Hispanic, black, Asian/Pacific Islander, and American Indian/Eskimo/Aleut. We still refer to races other than white as minorities. Table 3.3 lists the minority student populations by state. Note the wide range, with Maine at 4% and the District of Columbia at 96%.

Categories of race are indistinct, without consideration of family or country of origin. Beginning in 2000, the census form allowed people to check more than one race. Because race is based solely on physical characteristics, what box would a person check whose mother is Chinese and father is Cuban? Half of Asian immigrants' children marry non-Asians,

TABLE 3.3 Percentage of nonwhite (minority) students in public schools by state

State	Total Students	Minority Students	Percentage of Minority Students	State	Total Students	Minority Students	Percentage of Minority Students
				Tennessee	936,681	269,541	29
District of Columbia	78,057	74,690	96	Rhode Island	159,375	45,475	29
Hawaii	183,609	146,540	80	Washington	1,021,349	291,137	29
New Mexico	323,066	217,243	67	Michigan	1,757,604	478,955	27
California	6,413,862	4,166,409	65	Massachusetts	980,459	249,148	25
Texas	4,331,751	2,653,701	61	Pennsylvania	1,821,146	431,511	24
Mississippi	493,540	260,269	52	Kansas	470,490	109,208	23
Louisiana	727,709	375,099	52	Missouri	905,941	201,670	22
Arizona	1,012,068	514,413	51	Oregon	551,273	126,668	23
Maryland	869,133	430,663	50	Wisconsin	880,031	186,264	21
Florida	2,587,628	1,260,936	49	Ohio	1,845,428	372,406	20
Georgia	1,552,611	729,218	47	Nebraska	285,542	58,499	20
Nevada	385,401	189,721	49	Minnesota	842,854	166,950	20
New York	2,864,775	1,321,845	46	Indiana	1,011,130	186,754	18
South Carolina	699,198	318,812	46	Utah	495,981	81,922	17
Illinois	2,100,961	895,179	43	Idaho	252,120	40,160	16
New Jersey	1,380,753	581,591	42	Montana	148,356	22,062	15
Delaware	117,668	50,252	43	South Dakota	125,537	18,899	15
North Carolina	1,360,209	567,168	42	Wyoming	87,462	12,277	14
Alaska	133,933	55,052	41	Kentucky	663,885	82,314	12
Alabama	731,220	293,015	40	North Dakota	102,233	12,271	12
Virginia	1,192,092	453,961	38	Iowa	481,226	56,885	12
Oklahoma	626,160	241,311	39	West Virginia	281,215	16,563	6
Colorado	757,693	268,351	35	New Hampshire	207,417	11,938	6
Connecticut	577,203	182,036	32	Vermont	99,103	4,090	4
Arkansas	454,523	136,647	30	Maine	202,084	8,472	4

Source: National Center for Education Statistics (2006). Common Core of Data (CCD), "Public Elementary/Secondary School Universe Survey," 2003–04, and "State Nonfiscal Survey of Public Elementary/Secondary Education," 2003–2004.

Khammany, one of our focus students at Roosevelt High School, is Laotian, while most of the Asian students at the school are Hmong or Cambodian. Cultural differences exist among Asian students that are important for teachers to understand. Watch her interview, including her mom, in the Teaching in Focus *section for Chapter 3 in MyEducationLab for this course.*

and 35% of Latino immigrants marry members of other races (Diversity Data, 2000). According to the 2000 census, about 7 million people indicated they were multiracial by marking more than one of the five races listed.

Ethnic Component of Culture. We will use the word **ethnicity** to mean simply an individual's country of origin (Gollnick & Chinn, 2009). Even if families are two, three, or more generations removed from their ancestral country they may still strongly identify with both the country and the people who share their ethnicity. The category of ethnicity often reveals much more about our students than race. Knowing that a student is Hispanic (race) doesn't necessarily tell us much, but knowing that the child is of Cuban, Chilean, or Mexican heritage may be much more revealing and much more personalized (Hodgkinson, 2001).

CULTURAL PLURALISM. We often hear the United States referred to as a *melting pot*, a metaphor that conjures up visions of a big caldron into which we all jump, are warmed to the melting point, and stirred with a big spoon that blends us together until we lose unique and characteristic traits. This pretty much describes **assimilation**, the process of bringing persons of all races and ethnicities into the mainstream by having them behave in ways that align with the dominant culture. Some assimilation is inevitable, and even productive, but the notion that to be successful we all must look, think, and act in similar ways is unhealthy in a nation that values individualism and human rights.

Cultural pluralism involves the recognition that our nation is populated by a rich variety of people of varying races and ethnicities, and thus cultures, all with potential to positively contribute to our common goal of a productive, free society. So what would a school that purposefully promotes cultural pluralism look like? Such a school would teach a curriculum that includes the history and contributions of a variety of cultures; encourage the expression of cultural traditions in the school setting; work toward closing achievement gaps that exist among racial, ethnic, and cultural groups; and assure that no student is excluded from participation in school activities based on race, ethnicity, or any other aspect of culture.

Points of Reflection 3.2

What is your race? What is your ethnicity? How would you define your cultural identity?

CULTURAL DIVERSITY: IMPLICATIONS FOR TEACHERS

Three broad concepts have implications for effective teaching and learning with regard to cultural diversity.

GLOBAL AWARENESS AND 21ST-CENTURY SKILLS. One of the themes of the Partnership for 21st Century Skills (P21) is global awareness, not just for inclusion in what we teach students but as a vital component for teachers themselves. **Global awareness** involves understanding environmental, societal, cultural, political, and economical concepts and issues that impact our world. We must know what's happening on our planet and understand, as well as respect, the fact that there are many worldviews and perspectives among people (Partnership for 21st Century Skills, 2009). Not being globally aware is a disservice to our students.

MULTICULTURAL EDUCATION. The response of many U.S. educators to the fast-paced growth of diversity is **multicultural education,** an approach that celebrates diversity and promotes equal educational opportunities. James Banks (2004), an expert in the field, tells us that multicultural education has several goals, including

- the creation of equal opportunities for students of all cultures
- the development of knowledge, attitudes, and skills needed to function successfully in a diverse society
- the promotion of communication and interaction among groups that work for the common good

Unfortunately, many teachers attempt to include multicultural education by simply observing February as Black History Month or including a social studies unit on Native Americans. Chances are these lessons have little impact on the day-to-day lives of students. Some people actually oppose any attempt to address cultural diversity, fearing that multicultural education will divert attention from more important curriculum or weaken the sense of continuity and tradition in a school. According to Banks, those who promote the inclusion of multicultural education neither approve of shallow inclusion of concepts nor intend for it to in any way weaken U.S. schools.

Sonia Nieto (2003), a leading author on the topic of multicultural education, is concerned about the simplistic ways in which multicultural education is taught in schools. She proposes that multicultural education permeate all areas of schooling. Nieto says that if we ask ourselves the following four questions and then spend our careers as educators answering them, facing the answers, and making continual corrections, we will take multicultural education where it needs to go.

- "Who's taking calculus?" (student population in challenging courses)
- "Which classes meet in the basement?" (distribution of the best resources and facilities)

- "Who's teaching the children?" (distribution of the most effective teachers in our profession)
- "How much are the children worth?" (issue of funding—where the money for education goes and why) (pp. 8–10)

CULTURAL RESPONSIVENESS. To make multicultural education a reality in the classroom requires culturally responsive teaching. A culturally responsive teacher is sensitive to diversity and regularly asks questions such as these:

- Do I know the culture of each of my students beyond their obvious race and ethnicity?
- In what ways might I help my students see their similarities as clearly as their differences?
- How can I help validate the cultures represented in my classroom?
- How can I promote communication among all students?
- How can I assure equal opportunities for learning for all students?

LANGUAGE DIVERSITY

We have looked at race and ethnicity as major contributors to our cultural identity. These two factors are largely based on nature and can't be changed. Our language, however, is rooted in nurture and can be changed. **Language** is our primary means of communication and, through it, we transmit knowledge. Assimilation in terms of language, with all students becoming proficient in English, has benefits because most public school classrooms are conducted in English. Few would argue with the notion that communicating proficiently in English is a major factor for academic success in the United States. The dilemma, however, is how to ensure this for all students.

Not all immigrants are non-English proficient, but for most, English is not their first language. Some immigrant students arrive in the United States with strong records of academic achievement in their native languages, but most do not. Some students may have mastered conversational English in that they can speak and understand it, but they lack the ability to use English to keep up with grade-level coursework (Short & Fitzsimmons, 2007). School settings require **Standard English,** a composite of the language spoken by educated middle-class people in the United States. There are two forms of Standard English: one that's spoken in our everyday lives and a more formal version that is written and considered grammatically correct (Gollnick & Chinn, 2009).

Focus students Guillermo, from Mexico, and Khammany, from Laos, are part of the rich fabric of diversity at Roosevelt High School in Fresno, California.

But even within the English language there are variations. In the United States there are at least 11 regional **dialects,** or deviations from standard language rules used by identifiable groups of people. You may have been the brunt of jokes when you traveled outside your region, or you may have poked fun at someone in your college dorm who spoke with a regional dialect unlike your own. Black English, sometimes referred to as **Ebonics,** is one of the best known and most controversial dialects in the United States. In most school settings, Black English, along with Hawaiian Pidgin and Appalachian English, is associated with lower levels of both intelligence and social class (Gollnick & Chinn, 2009).

ENGLISH-LANGUAGE LEARNERS. Students with **limited English proficiency (LEP)** may speak and understand some English but not enough to be successful in classes taught in English without additional assistance. Non-English speakers and students with LEP are referred to as **English-language learners (ELLs)**. So LEPs are ELLs. We serve them through TESOL, ESOL, ESL, SEI, and any number of bilingual education program configurations. Confused? If your answer is yes, you are more than justified. The dilemma faced by students who do not speak English well enough to learn at adequate levels in a timely fashion in U.S. schools is both recent and rapidly growing. Not only are we unsure about how best to serve this population, our vocabulary pertaining to this situation hasn't solidified either, with overlapping and indistinct definitions.

Whether in the mall or filling out a job application, the value of fluency in English is obvious to students who are ELLs. Children in immigrant families often believe that continuing to speak their native language will hurt them in school settings where often language is the most obvious characteristic that sets them apart. Another phrase used to refer to students whose native language is other than English, regardless of their current level of English proficiency, is **language minority students**. Figure 3.5 is a snapshot of language minority students. An interesting fact to consider is that in 1910, 97% of immigrants to the United States were from Europe or Canada. One hundred years later, only about 10% of the immigrants to the United States are from these parts of the world (Rance-Roney, 2009).

Craig Cleveland's class roll in Table 3.4 mirrors the ethnic mix at Roosevelt High School, California. Although Craig is fluent in Spanish and that's very helpful, notice that most of the designated LEP students are of Asian ethnicity. To meet this challenge head on, Craig involves all his students by

- giving them as many curricular and instructional choices as possible
- having them talk to each other in their native languages about class content
- using role-playing (read more about role playing as an instructional strategy in Chapter 4) to reinforce concepts
- reading picture books that make concepts more transparent
- using written materials in students' native languages when available

Hector Mancia, one of our Rees Elementary focus students, is fluent in English, but in his home, Spanish is the predominant language. Watch Hector's interview, including his mom, in the Teaching in Focus section for Chapter 3 in MyEducationLab for this course.

Role-play is discussed in Chapter 4.

Figure 3.5 Snapshot of language minority students

There are more than 14 million language minority students in K–12 schools.

Children from immigrant families comprise most of the language minority students.

About 1 in 5 children ages 5 to 17 in the United States are from immigrant families.

The population of children in immigrant families is growing faster than any other group of children in the nation.

Almost 80% of children from immigrant families were born in the United States, making them U.S. citizens.

Immigrant families continue to be concentrated in California, Texas, New York, Florida, Illinois, and New Jersey, but many states are now experiencing sharp increases.

English-language learners in the United States speak more than 350 languages, with more than 75% speaking Spanish.

Language minority students are more likely than native-English-speaking students to come from low-income families.

Language minority students tend to be more transient than native speakers, with families trying out different housing options or moving to build closer family connections.

English-language learners with fluently bilingual and culturally responsive teachers tend to perform better in school than those without such teachers.

Source: August and Shanahan (2006); Capps, Fix, Murray, Ost, Passel, and Herwantoro (2005); Garcia and Cuellar (2006); Hernandez, Denton, and Macartney (2008); Rance-Roney (2009).

TABLE 3.4 Craig Cleveland's second period class roll

Name	Gr.	Primary Lang.
1. Acevez, Miguel*	12	Spanish
2. Avelar, Margarita	11	Spanish
3. Chavez, Jennah	11	English
4. Conriquez-Reyes, Dan	11	Spanish
5. Douangsavanh, Khammany	12	Laotian
6. Esqueda, Meagan	12	English
7. Garcia, Alberto	11	Spanish
8. Garcia, Diana	11	Spanish
9. Garcia, Guadalupe	11	Spanish
10. Hurtado, Cassandra	11	Spanish
11. Lopez, Crystal	12	Spanish
12. Maldonado, Sarah	11	English
13. Martinez, Andrew Jame	11	Spanish
14. Perez, Yvonne	10	Spanish
15. Rodarte, Silvia	10	Spanish
16. Rodriguez, Antonio	11	Spanish
17. Rodriguez, Daniel	12	Spanish
18. Romero, Norma	11	Spanish
19. Sanchez, Javier*	11	Spanish
20. Sepulveda, Elizabeth	11	English
21. Toscano, Guillermo	11	English
22. Valles, Leanna Marie	10	English
23. Vang, Doug*	10	Hmong
24. Vang, Ka Yeng*	11	Hmong
25. Vang, Mong Her*	11	Hmong
26. Vang, Pa*	11	Hmong
27. Vang, Sandda*	11	Hmong
28. Vang, Xoua*	11	Hmong
29. Vang, Zoua*	11	Hmong
30. Yang, Don*	11	Hmong
31. Yang, Gloria*	10	Hmong
32. Yang, Tom*	11	Hmong

* Considered limited English proficient (LEP).

You don't have to be in an urban area to have ELLs in your classroom. One of our focus schools, Summit Primary, Ohio, has gone from a mostly white, all English-speaking school to one with the 17 languages listed in Figure 3.6.

Figure 3.6 Native languages at Summit Primary School, Ohio

English	Russian	French
Somali	Macedonian	Creole
Ohomo	Serbo-Croatian	Korean
Bosnian/Albanian	Spanish	Japanese
Sierra Leone/Creole	German	Tagalog/Filipino
Chinese/Cantonese	Croatian	

SERVICES ADDRESSING ELL. The acronyms mentioned earlier indicate the variety of ways we attempt to meet the needs of English-language learners. Let's look briefly at three approaches to delivering ELL services to students: bilingual education, English as a second language (ESL), and structured English immersion (SEI).

Bilingual Education. One of the primary responses of public education to the needs of English-language learners is **bilingual education,** the delivery of instruction in two languages. Attempts are made to preserve native language abilities as students acquire skills in English. Perhaps the greatest barrier to bilingual education programs is the lack of teachers who speak both English and another language fluently. In addition to speaking two languages fluently, however, teachers in bilingual programs must also be qualified to teach math, science, social studies, reading, writing, and other subjects. Angelica Reynosa, one of our focus teachers at Roosevelt High School in Fresno, California, teaches bilingual classes. In her lesson she switches between Spanish and English as she engages her students in their own learning.

Watch Angelica's lesson in the Teaching in Focus section for Chapter 3 in MyEducationLab for this course.

English as a Second Language. In **English as a second language (ESL)** programs, students receive individualized assistance once or twice a week for about an hour each session. Unlike bilingual education, ESL services are delivered only in English. With ESL, little or no emphasis is placed on preserving native language or culture, and ESL teachers do not need to speak another language. ESL programs are far less expensive than bilingual programs for school districts to implement if they have limited numbers of students to serve.

Structured English Immersion. In response to observations that we may be teaching *in* English, but possibly not *teaching* English, **structured English immersion** (SEI) was developed. This approach includes significant amounts of the school day dedicated to the explicit teaching of the English language, with other content supporting instruction, but not as the primary focus (Clark, 2009). In SEI students and teachers speak, read, and write in English. Teachers treat English as a foreign language and apply instructional methods of teachers of foreign languages. Students are expected to transition out of SEI programs on a specified timetable with the skills necessary to be successful in English-only classes.

As of 2009, three states, California, Arizona, and Massachusetts, had passed laws requiring the development of SEI programs to replace many of the existing bilingual programs. SEI is perhaps the least understood of the three approaches. States and districts are creating SEI programs, given their student populations and resources available (Clark, 2009). Figure 3.7 is a schedule for students in the SEI program at George Washington Elementary School in Madera, California, which enrolls more than 500 English-language learners in grades K to 6.

Points of Reflection 3.3

Is English your primary language? If not, what is? Has language ever been a barrier to you? Do you know people who are English-language learners?

Figure 3.7 Structured English immersion sample schedule

Emphasis/Activity	Time Allotted
Pronunciation and listening skills	20 minutes
Vocabulary	30 minutes
Verb tense instruction	20 minutes
Sentence structure	20 minutes
Integrated grammar skills application	20 minutes
English reading and writing	60 minutes
Math (specially designed academic instruction in English)	40 minutes
Science, social science, P.E.	40 minutes

Source: Clark, C. (2009). The case for structured English immersion. *Educational Leadership, 66*(7), 45.

LANGUAGE DIVERSITY: IMPLICATIONS FOR TEACHERS

Language diversity presents a major challenge for educators in the United States. As we welcome increasing numbers of English-language learners to U.S. schools, both teaching and learning are affected. Here are some questions to keep in mind as you consider teaching in a language-diverse classroom:

- How can I make my classroom an academically, emotionally, and socially safe place for students who are ELLs?
- How can I include the cultures of students who are ELLs in my classroom?
- What resources will I need to communicate subject-area concepts to all students?
- How will I communicate with families who are ELLs?
- What community services might benefit students who are ELLs and their families?

Hugo Martinez, one of our Roosevelt High School focus students, is an English-language learner and his parents speak little or no English. Watch Hugo's interview, including his parents, in the Teaching in Focus *section for Chapter 3 in MyEducationLab for this course.*

The influx of diverse cultures with varied languages can be a source of richness for the United States rather than a phenomenon that is feared or avoided. Striking a balance between preserving native cultures while helping students adjust to life in a basically English-speaking environment is a worthy goal.

Before we turn our attention to diversity in family structure, religion, and socioeconomic status, respond to this chapter's ***Diversity Dialogue*** focusing on language diversity in an early childhood setting.

DIVERSITY DIALOGUE

Principal Laura Hill has detected that the teachers at one of our focus schools, Summit Primary, have become increasingly concerned about the children in their K–2 classrooms. Until about 2002 the community was rural, with farms and small businesses scattered throughout. Summit students were primarily white, living in middle to lower income homes. The change to today's student population was rapid, taking many educators by surprise. They are sensing a lack of preparation and a feeling of inadequacy. Laura called them all together to discuss what she knows is a hot topic in the teachers' lounge. Here are two teacher comments.

Brandi: "My morning kindergarten class this year consists of 12 kids whose families are long-time residents of the county. Then I have four children who speak little or no English. Two are twins from Somalia, and the other two are children of migrant farm workers from Mexico. Here we have three families where English isn't spoken in the home."

Melissa: "What good is 2 hours a week in an ESL class? It's not enough time to do any good and, besides, the kids are sometimes taken out of my class when we are doing something they actually understand how to do."

Think about what you have learned so far and respond to these items by writing one well-developed paragraph for each.

1. Melissa's concerns about ESL are understandable, but are there other options? Given what you know about Summit Primary, would bilingual education or structured English immersion be better options, or even possible? What would you recommend and why?

2. Our focus teacher Brandi and her colleague Melissa both teach kindergarten, along with seven other teachers. They each have two to four language minority students representing three different languages. How might they work together to help ELLs become proficient in English?

What Is the Impact on Students of Diversity in Family Structure, Religion, and Socioeconomic Status?

FAMILY DIVERSITY

The 1970s *Brady Bunch* television situation comedy introduced many Americans to the concept of the blended family. Today, blended families come in a variety of configurations. Many students live with people other than their biological parents. With the divorce rate over 50%, single-parent homes have increased more than 300% since 1980 (U.S. Census Bureau, 2008).

The increasing mobility of American families also adds to the instability of students' home lives. Consider, for example, the increasing influx of both documented (legal) and undocumented (illegal) immigrants and the rapidly growing migrant population. These families may move two to four times a year, with children changing schools, enrolling and withdrawing from the same school multiple times, or simply not going to school (NCES, 2004). Not only is all this mobility potentially harmful for students, but it can also wreak havoc on classroom teaching and learning.

FAMILY DIVERSITY: IMPLICATIONS FOR TEACHERS. Knowing with whom our students live can give teachers insight into behavior and achievement patterns. Ideally, families are our partners in educating children and adolescents. If this is going to be a reality in classrooms, our tactics for gaining and maintaining family support must be sensitive and flexible. Here are some questions to consider for your classroom:

- How can I restructure volunteer opportunities to include evenings and weekends?
- Are options available for child care that might lead to greater parental participation?
- Can the school provide easily accessible transportation to boost family involvement?
- Can I be more inclusive by practicing simple tactics such as addressing correspondence with "Dear family" rather than "Dear parents"?

In Chapter 9 we look more closely at societal issues as they relate to families, and in Chapter 12 we discuss teachers' responsibilities toward students' families.

RELIGIOUS DIVERSITY

Religion and faith have considerable daily influence on many of our lives. Over 230 million people, or about 4 of 5 of us, affiliate with a religious group. About 96% of Americans who practice a religion align with Christianity. However, religious diversity exists in urban, suburban, and rural areas in every state, and among Americans who align with a religion, about 1.4% are Jewish and about 0.5% align with each of Islam, Hinduism, and Buddhism (Pew Forum, 2010). Freedom to practice a religion, or not, is central to our common political, social, and cultural heritage. This chapter's *Letter to the Editor* addresses both cultural and religious expression in our schools.

Letter to the Editor

This letter appeared in the Ogden, Utah, newspaper, *The Standard-Examiner*. It was written by a citizen responding to recent local controversy over an expression of cultural and religious diversity.

NOVEMBER 4, 2009

STUDENT AND NOSE STUD

Recently Bountiful Junior High School has been in a tizzy over little 12-year-old Suzannah Singh for wearing a tiny jeweled stud in the nub of her nose (Oct. 28, "Nose-piercing Indian girl readmitted to class").

Is it just me or is there something wrong with this picture? What's even harder to believe is that after Suzannah had worn the accessory for about two weeks (reportedly, according to the Standard's account, even admired by some of her teachers), her stud was "spotted" by none other than a reading teacher. Oh my, spies are everywhere!

(continued)

And here's the best-worst part, all of this time I was led to believe that reading was the greatest opportunity to explore and expand our horizons about religious, cultural and social mores and traditions.

While this is not meant to cast a dim light on the many good citizens of Bountiful, I wish to remind anyone who might have temporarily forgotten, there are plenty of folks in this wide world of ours who possess diverse religious and cultural persuasions, be they Sikh or Sunni, Mormon or Muslim, Episcopalian or Evangelical, Jewish or Jehovah's Witnesses, Buddhist, Baptist, or Bahai, who care for the spiritual and cultural lives of themselves and their loved ones as much as the next guy. And for that reason, I seriously question why this young girl was immediately sent to detention by the school administration and then asked to stay home until her gracious parents agreed on a compromise, of a clear, presumably inoffensive, stud.

The jeweled stud Suzannah had worn had meant something special to her. Isn't that what we wish for our young daughters and sons? A special identity?

What is wrong with this picture? It's cliché. There are much more important issues. Some of us need to learn to pick our battles. Time is too precious. Can we just enjoy it and not make mountains out of tiny nose studs?

Liz Shaner

Now it's your turn. Write a letter to the editor from the perspective of a future teacher expressing your views about this incident and any broader issues you feel it invokes. You may comment on any, or all, of the writer's expressed opinions. The following questions may help you frame your thinking, but should not limit nor determine what you write.

1. Are you surprised that a small nose stud would cause any kind of friction among community members?

2. Is it important that symbolic expressions that appear to be outside a community's comfort zone be cultural or religious to be allowed?

3. Do you think Suzannah's nose stud was disruptive to the education process?

4. Is it the school's responsibility to allow or disallow items of clothing, jewelry, and other accessories deemed disruptive?

5. Do you agree or disagree with the letter writer about the relative importance of the issue? Is there a larger issue here that needs to be addressed?

Write your letter in understandable terminology, remembering that readers of newspaper Letters to the Editor are citizens who may have limited knowledge of school practices and policies. Remember to refer to the letter assessment rubric in Chapter 1.

Private schools are often established to cater to and promote a particular religion. Public schools are open to all and are obligated to serve all. Although separation of church and state is the official stance, religion has considerable influence on what we do in schools. Most of the issues teachers face in terms of religious diversity can be dealt with positively simply through awareness.

RELIGIOUS DIVERSITY: IMPLICATIONS FOR TEACHERS. Our response to religious diversity must be within legal bounds and delivered with sensitivity. Here are some questions classroom teachers should consider concerning religious diversity:

- How do I make sure tolerance is modeled in my classroom?
- How can I guard against being offensive to students of varying faiths?
- How should holidays be observed?
- How can I best respond to the community in which I live and teach?

The last question will be very important to you. While singing "Jesus Loves Me" at nap time in a southern kindergarten might be not only tolerated, but encouraged, singing the same song in a kindergarten in suburban Denver might be seen as offensive and grounds for dismissal.

SOCIOECONOMIC DIVERSITY

One area of diversity that transcends differences in gender, culture, language, family, and religion, and has widespread impact on student success in school, is **socioeconomic status** (SES). The gap between the haves and the have-nots is wider in the United States than in most other industrialized nations. We might call this a **privilege gap**. Approximately 11% of the U.S. population lives below the poverty line. A family of four—two parents and two children—that earns less than about $20,000 a year is considered to be in poverty.

Points of Reflection 3.4

What do you remember about family support, or lack of it, in your own K–12 experience? How did your religious affiliation and beliefs impact you and your school experiences?

A family can be above the poverty line but still qualify for free or reduced-price school meals. Of all the states, New Hampshire, at 15%, has the lowest percentage of students who qualify for free or reduced-price meals, and Kentucky, at 69%, has the highest percentage (U.S. Census Bureau, 2006).

CHALLENGES OF LOW SES. The federal government acknowledges there are unique challenges in teaching students living in low-income settings. Title I funding, additional money given to public schools when more than 50% of the students qualify for free or reduced-price meals, is the government's attempt to make school experiences equitable. These funds are intended to help educators better meet the needs of students in low-income settings who often are students with histories of low achievement.

The following are some generalizations about students from low-income settings. As you read them, keep in mind that they are not true of all students from low-income settings, and they may not be true of those in your classroom. Students from low-SES settings

- may enter first grade having been read to about 25 hours, compared to 1,000 hours in middle-class homes (Neumann, 1999)
- may have been exposed to 30 million fewer words by the age of 4 than children from high-SES settings (Neumann, 2003)
- may be disorganized, lose assignments, not do homework, have many excuses (Payne, 2005)
- may perform poorly on class and standardized tests (Payne, 2005)
- may dislike authority, talk back to adults, not monitor their own behavior, not use middle-class courtesies (Payne, 2005)
- may be physically aggressive (Payne, 2005)
- very often attend schools with inadequate facilities and less effective teachers (Payne, 2005)

SES DIVERSITY: IMPLICATIONS FOR TEACHERS. Ruby Payne (2008) tells us that teachers are in a position to support students and families in poverty by attending to their resource needs, which include

- emotional resources—the stamina to withstand difficult and uncomfortable emotional situations
- mental resources—the ability to learn; to read, write, and compute
- spiritual resources—belief that help is available through a higher power that alleviates hopelessness
- physical resources—having a healthy body
- support systems—knowing who to turn to for everyday and future needs and information
- relationships/role models—having people around who demonstrate appropriate relationships and successful living
- knowledge of unspoken rules—knowing how to get along in a particular group (pp. 17–18).

How Are Learning Differences Manifested in Schools?

The revered **intelligence quotient (IQ)** affixes a number to intelligence that, in one single freeze-frame, labels us for life. Scores on IQ tests may provide useful information, but they are no longer considered the final answer in determining a child's intellectual capacity. We have moved beyond the notion that intelligence is a fixed attribute. Researchers now believe that **intelligence,** a capacity for knowing and learning, can change and is manifested in various ways, as illustrated in Figure 3.8.

Points of Reflection 3.5

How has your own SES affected your school experiences? Were you aware of socioeconomic differences among your classmates? Did this affect how you viewed your own circumstances or the circumstances of other students?

We discuss families and SES in Chapter 9 and religion in Chapter 10.

Figure 3.8 How our views of intelligence have changed

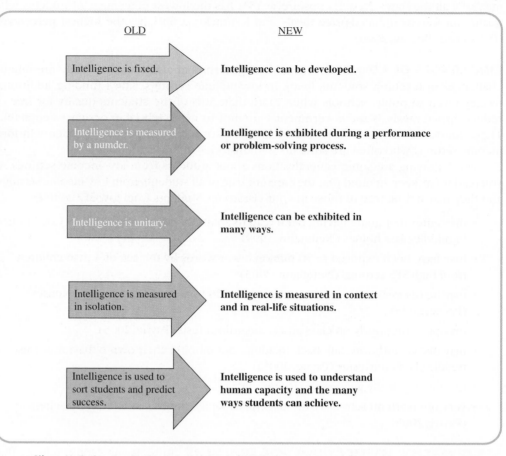

Source: Silver, H. F., Strong, R. W., & Perini, M. J. (2000). *So each may learn: Integrating learning styles and multiple intelligences.* Alexandria, VA: Association for Supervision and Curriculum Development.

MULTIPLE INTELLIGENCES THEORY

Harvard psychologist Howard Gardner added an "s" to the word *intelligence* and revolutionized how we view the concept. In 1983 he theorized that intelligence is multidimensional, that individual brains work in ways that give each of us our own personal intelligences. He called this **multiple intelligences (MI) theory**. The implication of multiple intelligences is that we learn differently.

Gardner (1999) proposed distinct intelligences that can be activated and connected in very individual ways. Table 3.5 lists the nine intelligences he proposed and suggests ways to address the intelligences when planning for instruction.

LEARNING STYLES

Whereas Gardner's theory of multiple intelligences helps explain different forms of intelligence with implications for how we learn, theories of **learning styles** give us more explicit insight into the variety of ways the learning process happens. Perhaps the simplest way to characterize learning styles is through the four commonly accepted **learning modalities,** or preferences: auditory (hearing), visual (seeing), tactile (touching), and kinesthetic (moving). We use all four in the process of learning, but each individual tends to favor one or two over the others. Traditional classrooms rely most heavily on auditory and visual modalities, such as lectures and visual supports, especially in the upper grades, while active learning techniques, such as hands-on manipulatives and

TABLE 3.5 Multiple intelligences and planning for instruction

Disposition/Intelligence	Plan Lessons That Include:
Verbal-Linguistic Intelligence	Speaking, writing, listening, reading, communicating
Logical Mathematical Intelligence	Finding patterns; making calculations; formulating hypotheses; recognizing cause and effect; working with numbers and reasoning
Spatial Intelligence	Representing ideas visually; creating mental images; noticing details; drawing; working puzzles; using colors and shapes
Bodily-Kinesthetic Intelligence	Activities requiring touch, movement, strength, speed, flexibility, hand-eye coordination, balance, and physical expression
Musical Intelligence	Listening, singing, and playing an instrument; using tone, beat, tempo, melody, pitch, and sound to create music
Interpersonal Intelligence	Working with others; understanding body language, moods, and feelings
Intrapersonal Intelligence	Setting goals; assessing personal abilities; reflecting on one's own strengths and weaknesses
Naturalist Intelligence	Identifying and classifying living things and natural objects; analyzing ecological and natural situations; learning from living things; working in natural settings
Existentialist Intelligence	Considering the big picture; imagining very large or very small quantities; seeking answers to seemingly unanswerable questions

Source: Silver, H. F., Strong, R. W., & Perini, M. J. (2000). *So each may learn: Integrating learning styles and multiple intelligences.* Alexandria, VA: Association for Supervision and Curriculum Development.

group work, activate tactile and kinesthetic modalities and may engage students more effectively. Figure 3.9 helps us understand students who learn best through hearing, seeing, touching, or moving.

Figure 3.9 Learning styles and learner preferences

Auditory learners tend to. . .
   Enjoy reading and being read to.
   Be able to explain concepts and scenarios verbally.
   Like music and hum to themselves.
   Enjoy both talking and listening.
Visual learners tend to. . .
   Have good spelling, note-taking, and organizational skills.
   Notice details and prefer neatness.
   Learn more if illustrations and charts accompany reading.
   Prefer quiet, serene surroundings.
Kinesthetic learners tend to. . .
   Be demonstrative, animated, and outgoing.
   Enjoy physical movement and manipulatives.
   Be willing to try new things.
   Be messy in habits and surroundings.
Tactile learners tend to. . .
   Prefer manipulatives when being introduced to a topic.
   Literally translate events and phenomena.
   Tolerate clutter.
   Be artistic in nature.

Source: From *Introduction to Middle School* (p. 59), by S. D. Powell, 2011, Boston: Allyn & Bacon. Copyright 2011 by Allyn & Bacon.

DIFFERENCES IN HOW WE LEARN: IMPLICATIONS FOR TEACHERS

Incorporating what we know about multiple intelligences and learning styles into our plans for instruction helps meet the learning needs of more students. Here are some questions to keep in mind when considering these challenges:

- Do I view the students in my classroom as a collection of individuals, each with unique ways of being smart?
- Do I continually seek to understand the ways in which my students learn best?
- Do I plan some experiences that address and incorporate each of the multiple intelligences?
- Does my awareness of my students' various learning styles change how I teach?

Acknowledging there are many ways to learn leads us to understand that some students have particular difficulties learning, while others learn more quickly and perhaps more deeply. These are students with exceptionalities.

Who Are Students with Exceptionalities and How Do We Serve Them?

Learners with abilities or disabilities that set them apart from other learners are often referred to as **students with exceptionalities**. Heward (2006) tells us that exceptional children

> differ from the norm (either below or above) to such an extent that they require an additional program of special education and related services to fully benefit from education. . . . Thus, exceptional children . . . refers to children with learning and/or behavior problems, children with physical or sensory impairments, and children who are intellectually gifted or have a special talent. (p. 10)

Some exceptionalities are the result of nature; others may be the result of injury or illness, aspects of nurture. Two factors are especially important when we consider the education of students with exceptionalities:

- Identification: Deciding who has what exceptionality and to what degree
- Intervention: Determining how best to meet their educational needs

STUDENTS WITH DISABILITIES

The categories of student exceptionalities considered disabilities, along with the percentage of all disabilities they represent, are shown in Table 3.6. Considering all the categories, about 12% of American students receive **special education services,** services provided by schools to help students function and learn in ways optimal to the individual (Goldstein, 2003).

Many disabilities, especially those that impair daily functioning, such as orthopedic disabilities and hearing, sight, and disease-related impairments, are diagnosed before children enter school. However, disabilities that are more subtle, and perhaps academic, are often officially identified through a team of educators equipped with expertise and diagnostic tools.

A designation of **learning disabled (LD),** which accounts for almost half the students receiving special education services, includes a general category of students with disorders involving problems understanding or using language that results in significant differences between learning potential and achievement (Turnbull, Turnbull, & Wehmeyer, 2010). Misdiagnosis or the absence of diagnosis is problematic. Many students develop coping strategies that mask their learning problems for years and very possibly for life. Students with LD may

- have difficulties with word recognition and text comprehension
- feel overwhelmed by the idea of getting started

TABLE 3.6 Categories of disabilities and percentages of students served

Disability	Percentage of Total Students Receiving Special Services
Specific learning disabilities	47.2
Speech or language impairments	18.8
Mental retardation	9.6
Emotional disturbance	8.1
Multiple disabilities	2.2
Hearing impairments	1.2
Orthopedic impairments	1.1
Other health impairments	7.5
Autism	2.3
Visual impairments	.4
Traumatic brain injury	.4
Developmental delay	1.1
Deaf-blindness	.1

Source: U.S. Department of Education. (2009). *Building the legacy: IDEA 2004.*

- struggle to organize and use the mechanics of writing
- have difficulty differentiating numbers or copying shapes
- have difficulty identifying, using, and monitoring problem-solving strategies (Turnbull et al., 2010)

Intervention for students with LD may include time each day with a special education teacher, often referred to as a **resource teacher,** who will help them develop strategies for school success.

Identification of **attention deficit hyperactivity disorder (ADHD)** may be as problematic as identification of learning disabilities. Students with ADHD demonstrate three defining characteristics: inattention, hyperactivity, and impulsivity. ADHD is defined by the American Psychological Association (APA, 2000) as the frequent existence of these three characteristics in a persistent pattern that is more severe than in others of the same age. The APA estimates that 3% to 7% of students in an average class have ADHD, which falls within the "other health impairments" category of Table 3.6. The intervention for students with ADHD may include specific strategies to help modify behavior or medication. They receive services through special education only if they qualify through impairments other than ADHD (Turnbull et al., 2010).

LEGAL SUPPORT FOR STUDENTS WITH DISABILITIES

Until recently, students with disabilities were often isolated in a room at the end of a hallway—out of sight, out of mind—unless they happened to be seen walking as a group or boarding one of those short buses designed to hold that "special" group of kids. Prior to 1975, most students with disabilities, designated as special education students, weren't even in the same facilities as other students; there were no provisions for them to attend public schools. In 1975 the landmark legislation **Public Law 94-142 (PL 94-142)** changed all that.

Today special education is viewed as a service rather than a place to send children (Jackson & Harper, 2002). The **Education for All Handicapped Children Act (PL 94-142)** opened all public schools to students with disabilities and mandated that students with disabilities be given the opportunity to benefit from special education services at no cost to families. The law established six governing principles, listed in Figure 3.10, that apply to the education of students with disabilities.

In 1990 PL 94-142 was amended and renamed the **Individuals with Disabilities Education Act (IDEA)**. Students with autism and traumatic brain injury were added to those entitled to services under PL 94-142. A change in attitude and philosophy was also evident in the law when the language changed from "disabled individuals" to "individuals

Figure 3.10 Six principles governing the education of students with disabilities

1. **Zero reject:** A rule against excluding any student.

2. **Nondiscriminatory evaluation:** Requires schools to evaluate students fairly to determine if they have a disability and, if so, what kind and how extensive.

3. **Appropriate education:** Requires schools to provide individualized education programs for each student based on evaluation and augmented by related services and supplementary aids and services.

4. **Least restrictive environment:** Requires schools to educate students with disabilities alongside students without disabilities to the maximum extent appropriate for the students with disabilities.

5. **Procedural due process:** Provides safeguards for students against schools' actions, including a right to sue in court.

6. **Parental and student participation:** Requires schools to collaborate with parents and adolescent students in designing and carrying out special education programs.

Source: Turnbull, R., Turnbull, A., & Wehmeyer, M. (2010). *Exceptional lives: Special education in today's schools* (6th ed.). Upper Saddle River, NJ: Merrill/Prentice Hall.

with disabilities." The person comes first, with the disability secondary. In 2004 IDEA was reauthorized as the **Individuals with Disabilities Education Improvement Act**. This latest reauthorization is the most comprehensive yet, including all U.S. laws affecting children with disabilities in one statute (Heward, 2006).

INDIVIDUALIZED EDUCATIONAL PROGRAMS

Serving students with disabilities (ages 3 to 21), regardless of the setting or combination of settings, requires an **individualized educational program (IEP)** as prescribed by Principle 3 of PL 94-142. An IEP is developed by educators, the family, and others as appropriate and involves a detailed plan to reach specific goals. A student's IEP must be revisited annually and student progress evaluated. Although IEP formats may vary, the required elements are listed in Figure 3.11.

An important part of an IEP is the designation of where and with whom students with disabilities will spend their school time. Principle 4 of PL 94–142 explicitly states that students with disabilities will be in the **least restrictive environment (LRE)** possible. The LRE is generally a setting with students who do not have disabilities that also meets the educational needs of the students with disabilities. This is often the regular education classroom.

INCLUSION

Whether you are interested in teaching students with disabilities or not, you may be doing exactly that in a regular inclusive classroom setting if a student's IEP designates it as the LRE. **Inclusion** means that "students attend their home school with their age and grade appropriate

Figure 3.11 Components of an IEP

An IEP must include a statement of:

1. student's present level of academic achievement and functional level
2. measurable academic and functional annual goals
3. how the student's progress toward meeting the annual goals will be measured
4. special education and related services to be provided to the student
5. extent to which the student will not participate with nondisabled students and the regular classroom
6. accommodations necessary to measure the student's achievement on state assessments
7. date of beginning services
8. postsecondary goals and transition services at age 16

Source: Turnbull, R., Turnbull, A., & Wehmeyer, M. (2010). *Exceptional lives: Special education in today's schools.* Upper Saddle River, NJ: Merrill/Prentice Hall.

peers, participate in extracurricular activities, and receive special education and support services, to the maximum extent possible, in the general education classroom" (Rosenberg, O'Shea, & O'Shea, 2006, p. 14). If inclusion is not appropriate, chances are a student with disabilities is served in a self-contained setting with other students with disabilities for much of the day and served by teachers with specific training to work with students with disabilities.

Simply placing students with disabilities in a regular classroom does not mean inclusive practices are in place or that a rigorous learning environment will be maintained. Teachers still must effectively focus on individualized objectives for every student, facilitate interactions and cooperative learning among students at every learning level, and maintain collaborative relationships with students, parents, and special educators. Given this approach, inclusion can be a healthy and positive experience for students without disabilities as well (Heward, 2006). There is a growing trend toward co-teaching, involving a regular classroom teacher and a special educator in a single classroom.

Inclusive classrooms provide opportunities for students with and without disabilities to learn and work together.

Inclusion is not embraced by all. Some parents believe their students with disabilities are better served in smaller, special education classrooms where they are more likely to receive one-on-one attention from teachers specifically trained to work with them. Some regular education teachers are wary of having a student with disabilities placed in their classrooms, an understandable hesitation if they receive little or no training in meeting the emotional, social, and cognitive needs of the student. Although the **Council for Exceptional Children** (CEC), the professional organization of special education, endorses inclusion, the official stance is support of a continuum of services with inclusion as a desirable goal, but not the only appropriate option for all students with disabilities.

ASSISTIVE TECHNOLOGY

The Technology-Related Assistance to Individuals with Disabilities Act of 1988 authorized funding for **assistive technology** devices and services. These devices and services benefit students with disabilities by helping them communicate, increasing their mobility, and aiding in multiple ways that enhance their capacity to learn. The range of assistive technology includes wheelchairs, voice-activated and touch-screen word processors, sound-augmenting devices, and closed-captioned television (Turnbull et al., 2010). Technology is making it possible for students with disabilities to function and learn at levels unimaginable only a decade ago.

STUDENTS DESIGNATED AS GIFTED AND TALENTED

Characteristics of students who are **gifted and talented** include phrases such as

- evidence of high performance capabilities
- intellectual, creative, artistic, or leadership ability well beyond average
- excelling in specific academic fields

Identification of students who are gifted and talented can be objective or quite subjective, depending on the criteria accepted by a particular school district. When IQ is used for identification, the threshold number is 125 to 130, achieved by only about 2% to 3% of the general student population. However, evaluating creativity along with IQ testing allows more students to benefit from gifted and talented services.

Services for students who are gifted and talented vary significantly and include pull-out programs, with students working on projects or an accelerated curriculum. In-school options, such as grade skipping, concurrent enrollment in two levels of schooling, curriculum compacting (faster pace), and advanced placement courses (rigorous high school courses with possible college credit for completion), enhance the opportunities of students designated as gifted and talented. There are also specifically designed magnet schools for them.

Differentiated instruction is discussed in Chapter 4.

Were you diagnosed with a disability while in PreK–12 school? If so, explain. Did you know students who were diagnosed with a disability while in PreK–12 school? If so, describe one.

Were you designated as gifted and talented? If so, what do you remember about being set apart from other kids?

When students who are gifted and talented are in regular classrooms, and most are, we can better meet their needs by

- being flexible
- accepting unusual ideas and encouraging alternative solutions to problems
- not being intimidated by the intellectual and creative capabilities of students who have IQs that exceed our own
- differentiating instruction often (more about this in Chapter 4)

STUDENTS WITH EXCEPTIONALITIES: IMPLICATIONS FOR TEACHERS

The most important aspect of teaching students with exceptionalities is to recognize that each student is an individual with learning potential and at least part of his or her mind "amply equipped to thrive" (Levine, 2003, p. 13). Seeing and seeking strengths before, or

GETTING TO KNOW TRISTA

Trista Kutcher is one of our focus students. She is a very special young lady. Her happy life and remarkable accomplishments are evidence of what dedicated parents and sensitive, knowledgeable education professionals can do to help children, even those with disabilities, realize their potential. Trista has Down syndrome.

Trista's mom, Rebecca, teaches eighth grade English language arts at Cario Middle School in Mount Pleasant, South Carolina, and Trista's dad, Joe, teaches math at Wando High School, where Trista is a freshman. Trista has two younger sisters, Suzanna, age 12, and Samantha, age 4. As a member of the 2003 USA Special Olympics gymnastics team, Trista won five medals at the Dublin, Ireland, games. She is a cheerleader at Wando High and is included in many regular education classes.

After reading Trista's story, watch the interview of Trista and her family and friends in the Choosing Your Teaching Path section of MyEducationLab. Click on Cario Middle School, and then on Trista.

Rebecca has written about many of her experiences as Trista's mom. Here's an abridged version of one of her pieces, entitled "We Danced."

We Danced

Joe and I had the perfect life. . . . We dated in high school and married right out of college. Life was grand! We got pregnant and things were sailing along as we **danced** through life. People would often ask, "What do you want—a boy or a girl?" I never said more than my prayer that the baby would be healthy! Joe's response was that we just wished for "10 fingers and 10 toes." Deep down, however, I really wanted a little girl with blond hair and blue eyes who would **dance** in a recital, **dance** on the beach, and **dance** into everyone's heart!

The pregnancy was perfect, as was the delivery. Joe and I held Trista Sue and cooed over her late into the night.

A few hours later the music stopped. The doctors told us our little blond-haired, blue-eyed Trista Sue had Down syndrome. Joe and I no longer felt like **dancing**.

Knowing breastfeeding was important for her in many ways, I wanted to continue her feeding schedule, even though she was still in the hospital. I would wake up during the night at 1:00 and 5:00 and travel to the hospital to nurse her. I would waltz around the room with her in my arms. How wonderful those **dances** were . . . just us, loving each other.

I decided I was going to get Trista involved in activities that every "normal" girl does. At age two I took her to Tapios School of Dance and Gymnastics. I asked the owner if Trista could enroll in her tap and ballet classes. She welcomed her with open arms and taught her to dance with grace and poise.

Around this time Trista's sister, Suzanna, was born. How proud she was to be a big sister! Oh, the mischief they could get into together. Eventually, Trista and Suzanna were in a dance recital together, Trista 6 and Suzanna 3. Suzanna was amazed at the lights and people in the audience. She completely forgot her dance. Big sister to the rescue! Trista decided this was unacceptable and took matters into her own hands. Trista marched across the stage, positioned herself behind Suzanna, and proceeded to move her arms and legs for her. The audience roared with laughter while Trista made Suzanna **dance**.

When Trista started school, we decided she should be included in the regular classroom. Speech was definitely a concern and having her with the other kids would be great modeling. Each of her accomplishments was celebrated by kids in the class and by teachers who were initially worried about how they would teach her.

concurrently with, acknowledging limitations helps us embrace possibilities for each individual, whether in an inclusive classroom or in a special education setting.

Including students with exceptionalities in the classroom is beneficial to all students because instruction is delivered in a variety of ways to engage diverse learners. To do so successfully, teachers need support and time for planning, as well as an appropriate curriculum, materials, and resources. Ongoing professional development is essential.

Here are some questions teachers of inclusive classrooms need to ask:

- Do I take the time to get to know each student as an individual?
- Do I look for the strengths and abilities of all my students?
- Is cooperative learning used frequently in my classroom?
- Do I continually diagnose the progress of my students and adjust my instruction appropriately?

During your field experiences, look closely for evidence of inclusion. Ask teachers to help you understand more about students with exceptionalities.

Watch Trista Kutcher's interview, which includes her family, as well as teachers and students who know her, in the Teaching in Focus section for Chapter 3 in MyEducationLab for this course.

Through elementary and middle school Trista thrived, making friends and showing all of us what she could do, rather than what she couldn't do. In high school she eats, drinks, and sleeps cheering during the fall and, like her gymnastics, loves it dearly. The other girls could not be more accepting and supportive of her.

Poem written by Trista's sister

Trista-
Famous, idol,
Likes to run, jump, and play,
Annoys me when she says she is right when she is wrong.
She can do cartwheels—I wish I could.
She wishes she could play basketball like me.
I do not like to go to the same parties as she does
Because then I feel like I have to look after her
and I cannot have fun.
It amazes me when she does flips and is not scared.
It makes me sad when she says hi to someone
and they do not respond back to her.
I am proud to tell my friends about all the gold medals she has.
I like when she smiles and her nose crunches up . . . it is so cute.
She has Down syndrome.
She is my sister!

By Suzanna Kutcher
12 years old

Along with regular gymnastics competitions, Trista competed in Special Olympics gymnastics. She was the state champion from the age of 8. Being involved provided many opportunities for independence and pride. During the summer of 2002, she received another very important letter. It asked her to be a part of the Special Olympics team USA for the 2003 World Games. As she opened that letter she beamed from ear to ear. This adventure was one of meeting the governor and the mayor, being featured in a commercial, being on the news and in the newspaper regularly, and having an official day in Mt. Pleasant proclaimed by the mayor as Trista Kutcher Day! Everywhere we went people knew her. Suzanna began to make a joke about all of us being her entourage! Never did we think we would be **dancing in her shadow!** She was leading us on the adventure of a lifetime!

The competition in Ireland was tough but she was ready! She won five medals, two of which were gold! As she stood on the podium, she cried and told me later that she was so proud because "She did it"! After the awards ceremony, the audience flooded the gym floor, joined hands, and **danced the Irish jig**. What a celebration!

The **dance** has been wonderful. The music has played nonstop for 15 years! Our dance began with three people on the floor . . . and ended with **a whole community kicking up its heels!**

CONCLUDING THOUGHTS

Now that we have looked at how students are similar and how they are different, perhaps the concept that all students can learn seems elusive to you. How, indeed, do we make "all children can learn" a reality given the circumstances that pervade some children's lives?

Understanding the uniqueness of each of us calls for an absolute commitment to individuality. Thomas Jefferson expressed the thought that there is nothing so unequal as the equal treatment of unequals. All children are equal in terms of their right to fulfill their own promise, but certainly children are unequal in the many ways we have discussed. The spirit of inclusion draws them all in; the unwavering determination to meet their needs requires attention and action based on each individual.

Yes, all children can learn. These complex questions logically follow this statement:

What can they learn?

When can they learn it?

In what ways will they learn it best?

As always, "And how are the children?" should be the center of our focus.

After reading the *Chapter in Review*, interact with Craig Cleveland in this chapter's *Developing Professional Competence*.

Chapter in Review

How are we similar?

- As human beings, we are more similar than dissimilar.
- Nature (genetics) influences human traits we are born with.
- Nurture (environment) influences who we are through every aspect of our lives that nature does not determine.
- Human beings share the same basic hierarchy of needs.
- We all experience physical, cognitive, emotional, social, and character development.

How are gender differences manifested?

- Anatomical differences between males and females determine sex, whereas gender is the sense of being male or female.
- Gender determines many of the choices we make and the expectations others have for us.
- Homosexuality is often the basis of discrimination.

How are cultural and language diversity manifested in schools?

- Race, although a social, political, economical, and psychological reality, is based solely on physical characteristics.
- Racism is a form of prejudice stemming from a belief that one race is superior to another.
- Ethnicity refers to a person's country of origin.

- Culture has many components and is learned, shared, and adaptive.
- Cultural identity relies on many factors, such as race, ethnicity, language, gender, religion, income level, values, and beliefs.
- Multiculturalism involves beliefs concerning the value of looking at the world through the eyes of people who are different from us.
- To be most effective, multicultural education needs to permeate all areas of schooling.
- Language is an aspect of cultural identity that can be augmented and enhanced.
- Bilingual education involves instruction delivered in two languages.
- English as a second language (ESL) is a pull-out program assisting English-language learners in English only.
- Structured English immersion (SEI) includes significant amounts of the school day dedicated to the explicit teaching of the English language, with other content secondary.

What is the impact on students of diversity in family structure, religion, and socioeconomic status?

- Blended families and family structures other than two biological parents and children are becoming more prevalent.
- The increasing mobility of American families potentially harms students and wreaks havoc on classrooms.

- Religion and faith have considerable influence on lifestyles and choices.
- The religious beliefs of families and communities influence decisions that relate to school issues.
- The gap between the haves and have-nots is wider in the United States than in most other nations.
- Low-income settings contribute to many at-risk situations and behaviors.

How are learning differences manifested in schools?

- There are many different ways to be smart and to exhibit intelligence.
- We all have learning style preferences.

Who are students with exceptionalities and how do we serve them?

- Students with exceptionalities include those with disabilities and those considered gifted and talented.
- A designation of learning disabled accounts for about half of students receiving special services.
- The concept of least restrictive environment means that students with disabilities are to be placed in the highest-functioning setting possible, usually the regular education classroom.
- Students considered gifted and talented are most likely to be included in the regular education classroom and pulled out for special classes for brief periods of time.

Developing Professional Competence

Visit the Developing Professional Competence section on Chapter 3 of the MyEducationLab for this text to answer the following questions and begin your preparation for licensure exams.

You met Craig Cleveland in **Meet the Teachers and Students**. In this chapter we learned about one of Craig's classes. Craig has a student teacher this semester. Jenny Langley grew up in the suburbs of Fresno and attends Fresno State. Jenny never attended a Title I school and her PreK–12 school experiences were ideal by most standards, complete with advanced placement classes, a stable group of friends, and extracurricular activities that rounded out her high school years. In a conversation several weeks before her student teaching semester began, Craig discovered that Jenny's peer group had little diversity, although Jenny told him she had lots of experience with diversity because she was in the International Baccalaureate program and she knew two exchange students, one from Japan and one from Russia. Craig smiled to himself as she talked about her open-minded approach with those who are different from herself, knowing she was about to begin one of the most turbulent experiences of her young life.

Think through this scenario and answer the following multiple-choice questions:

1. Guillermo, one of our focus students, is a really good-hearted young man with acceptable English skills and a desire to help other people. Before and after class,

Jenny might be able to best learn more about students with LEP by
   a. asking Guillermo to help her talk more easily with students whose primary language is Spanish
   b. staying close to Guillermo and listening to his casual conversations in both English and Spanish
   c. talking with Guillermo about what he knows about students who are ELLs
   d. watching Guillermo's easy demeanor with other students and trying to develop the same persona

2. Craig explains Khammany's situation to Jenny by telling her that Khammany, Mom, and younger brother moved into a project apartment with only two rooms and the difficulties they face since Dad died last year. Khammany, one of our focus students, has to work at least 30 hours a week to help support the family. Which of the following benefits of longer blocks of time (the four-block model) will Craig probably say is most important to Khammany?
   a. During the 100-minute class, Khammany has more time to concentrate on history.
   b. The longer blocks afford more time for a variety of participation activities.
   c. The block allows for time to begin homework assignments with Craig available to assist.
   d. Khammany can earn eight credits per year.

3. Remember Craig's class list? Which is the least important reason that longer blocks of class time benefit ELLs?
   a. They get to spend more concentrated time on one subject with one teacher.
   b. There is more time to fully develop a concept, using a variety of communication methods from the standards.
   c. There are fewer subjects to learn at a time.
   d. Fewer passing periods limit opportunities to be involved in turf issues among diverse groups of students.

4. What do you think will be the best way for Jenny to begin to acclimate to her student teaching situation?
   a. study the culture of the students she will encounter at Roosevelt
   b. spend at least 5 days simply shadowing Craig
   c. jump in and begin working with students
   d. spend the month before student teaching brushing up on her Spanish-language skills from taking 2 years of Spanish in high school

5. Jenny has started her 16-week student teaching experience with enthusiasm based on the fact that she had 2 years of Spanish in high school. Which reason most likely causes her enthusiasm to quickly dim?
   a. She can read and write in Spanish to a moderate degree, but conversational Spanish is another story.
   b. There aren't many written resources in Craig's classroom that are in Spanish.
   c. Most of the students with LEP are Hmong.
   d. Craig's class is not desigated as a bilingual class.

Now it's time for you to respond to three short essay items. In your responses, be sure to address all the dilemmas and questions posed in each item. Each response should be between one half and one double-spaced page. As you consider your responses, think about how these standards may apply.

NCATE Standard 4 on Diversity: The new professional teachers should be able to apply effective methods of teaching students that are at different developmental stages, have different learning styles, and come from diverse backgrounds.

NBPTS, Proposition 1: Accomplished teachers recognize that in a multicultural nation students bring to schools a plethora of abilities and attitudes and aptitudes that are valued differently by the community, the school, and the family.

INTASC Principle #2: The teacher understands how children learn and develop, and can provide learning opportunities that support their intellectual, social, and personal development.

INTASC Principle #3: The teacher understands how students differ in their approaches to learning and creates instructional opportunities that are adapted to diverse learners.

INTASC Principle #6: The teacher uses knowledge of effective verbal, nonverbal, and media communication techniques to foster active inquiry, collaboration, and supportive interaction in the classroom.

6. Jenny is walking into a world that is foreign to her. Explain two reasons why she may be apprehensive or even fearful.

7. As a suburbanite from a middle-income family, Jenny is now experiencing adolescents who live in poverty. What characteristics might the students display that will require Jenny to adjust her attitudes and expectations to meet their needs effectively?

8. Given what we know about the students at Roosevelt, which of the three methods for serving their language needs (bilingual education, ESL, SEI) would you recommend and why?

Where DO I Stand NOW?

In the beginning of this chapter you completed an inventory that gauged your prior knowledge of diversity among PreK–12 students. You also had the opportunity to respond to items that addressed your experiences with diversity. Now that you have read the chapter, completed exercises related to the content, engaged in class discussions, and so on, answer the following questions in your course notebook.

1. Has reading the chapter triggered memories about experiences with diversity that perhaps you had forgotten? If so, explain.

2. Explain one aspect of gender diversity you find surprising or interesting.

3. Explain one aspect of cultural and language diversity you find surprising or interesting.

4. Explain one aspect of family and religious diversity you find surprising or interesting.

5. Explain one aspect of socioeconomic diversity you find surprising or interesting.

6. Write briefly about one person you remember in your PreK–12 school experiences who received special education services. If you received services, write about your own experiences.

MyEducationLab

The MyEducationLab for this course can help you solidify your comprehension of Chapter 3 concepts.

- Explore the classrooms of the teachers and students you've met in this chapter in the Teaching in Focus section.
- Prepare for licensure exams as you deepen your understanding of chapter concepts in the Developing Professional Competence section.

- Gauge and further develop your understanding of chapter concepts by taking the quizzes and examining the enrichment materials on the Chapter 3 Study Plan.
- Visit Topic 2, Student Diversity, to watch ABC videos, explore Assignments and Activities, and practice essential teaching skills with the Building Teaching Skills and Dispositions unit.

4

Curriculum and Instruction

In this chapter we explore what is taught in U.S. schools, along with a variety of teaching and learning strategies. Here are the questions we focus on in Chapter 4:

✦ What is the formal curriculum?

✦ What other curricula do we teach in U.S. schools?

✦ How is instruction implemented in U.S. schools?

✦ How do teachers match instruction to school levels?

It's time to move from the "who" of school—the students and teachers—to the "what" and "how." **Curriculum** is the educational term for what students experience in schools, and **instruction** encompasses the strategies used to convey the curriculum and achieve the desired end result of student learning. Curriculum and instruction are interdependent in the sense that content (curriculum) is meaningless without methods (instruction) to convey it, and those methods are useless without the content of the curriculum. Explore your stance on curriculum and instruction by completing this chapter's *Where Do I Stand?*

Where DO I Stand?

The purpose of this inventory is to determine where you stand concerning what is taught and how it is taught in PreK–12 schools. After reading an item, indicate your level of agreement by choosing a number and placing it in the blank before the statement. Following the inventory are directions for how to organize your responses and what they may indicate in terms of where you stand.

4   I strongly agree
3   I agree
2   I don't have an opinion
1   I disagree
0   I strongly disagree

_____ **1.** What students learn in school is basically what the school plans for them to learn.

_____ **2.** Teaching in ways that meet the needs of students with differing aptitudes is important.

_____ **3.** Much of what is learned in schools is unintentional on the part of teachers.

_____ **4.** Most of what is taught in school should be stable and not swayed by society.

_____ **5.** If only English language arts, math, science, and social studies were taught, schools would still fulfill their primary purposes of educating children and adolescents.

_____ **6.** Basing learning on real-world situations is an excellent way to teach.

_____ **7.** Projects provide ideal learning opportunities.

_____ **8.** Teacher-led class discussion is one of the most effective teaching strategies.

_____ **9.** The expectations of society should guide what is taught in schools.

_____ **10.** Although interesting, classes that don't directly address English language arts, math, science, and social studies are not important in fulfilling the primary purposes of U.S. schools.

_____ **11.** After-school clubs and organizations are important to the education of students.

_____ **12.** The teacher should be the focus of attention in the classroom.

_____ **13.** We teach who we are in the classroom.

_____ **14.** Our vision of the future should heavily influence what is taught in U.S. schools.

_____ **15.** Some students should be allowed to go through some topics more quickly than other students.

_____ **16.** Music, visual arts, and dance should be part of a public school education.

_____ **17.** Teaching reading and writing is the responsibility of all teachers at all levels.

_____ **18.** Concentrating on one subject at a time is best for student learning.

_____ **19.** What is taught in schools should not be impacted by cultural diversity.

_____ **20.** Lecture is a preferable way to teach for maximum learning.

_____ **21.** There are benefits associated with student collaboration.

_____ **22.** It is more important to master the basic subjects than to learn how to think critically.

_____ **23.** There is a core of knowledge that should dominate what is taught in PreK–12 school.

_____ **24.** Student learning opportunities depend on what teachers teach.

Now let's analyze your responses. Remember, there are no wrong answers. Find six sums, A to F, based on your responses to the numbered items as indicated.

ITEM #	MY VIEW	ITEM #	MY VIEW	ITEM #	MY VIEW	ITEM #	MY VIEW	ITEM #	MY VIEW	ITEM #	MY VIEW
1		3		2		8		4		6	
5		11		7		12		19		9	
10		13		15		20		23		14	
18		16		21		24		sum E		sum F	
22		17		sum C		sum D					
sum A		sum B									

If sum A is larger than sum B, you believe there is a basic group of subjects that should dominate what is taught. The learning experiences are carefully planned and little is left to spontaneity. Courses or experiences other than what are planned are secondary.

If sum B is larger than sum A, you believe in a broader scope of what should be part of student experiences. Teacher personality and demeanor figure into student learning, as do classes not considered basic and after-school activities.

If sum C is larger than sum D, your preferred approach to teaching and learning is student centered. **If sum D is larger than sum C,** your preferred approach to teaching and learning is teacher centered.

If sum E is larger than sum F, you believe that what is taught in schools should be stable and not altered based on societal changes.

If sum F is larger than sum E, you believe that at least some of what is taught in schools should be responsive to societal changes.

Now that you have explored your opinions, let's discuss curriculum and instruction in the United States, beginning with what we call the formal curriculum. You will recognize the statements and ideas in Where Do I Stand? as you read.

Teaching in Focus

Chris Roberts is an adventurer. He travels extensively, climbs mountains, and rafts in white water. He could do lots of things with his life—and he does. But his career choice is teaching 9-, 10-, and 11-year-olds at Rees Elementary School, Utah.

It takes only a few minutes in Chris's multiage classroom to recognize how his energy and wide range of interests influence how he interacts with students. He teaches all the core elementary subjects, as well as the dance component of the arts emphasis at Rees. When asked what he gets out of teaching, Chris says, "I like to play, I love these kids, and learning is the most exciting thing in the world."

You won't find references to the fascinating displays in Chris's classroom in his lesson plans. Nor will you find "Tell the kids about my last dive off the Yucatan" or "Let my students know that life is a wonderful adventure." When Chris infuses his hobbies, interests, and travel into his classroom, he is teaching what we define later as the informal curriculum—lessons that aren't in a curriculum guide. The cartoons with philosophical messages, the inspirational stories and poems, the giant topographical map of Utah, the newspaper and magazine clippings about people who triumphed over unimaginably difficult circumstances, and the personal family photographs—all of it speaks to who Chris is and what he values.

As you look around his classroom during the room tour in the Teaching in Focus section for Chapter 4 in MyEducationLab for this course, Chris Roberts's personality, interests, and philosophy of life are evident.

What Is the Formal Curriculum?

The **formal curriculum** encompasses what is intentionally taught within the stated goals for student learning. The formal curriculum, sometimes referred to as the **explicit curriculum,** is what teachers are expected to teach, what students are expected to learn, and what society expects of schools. The formal curriculum is based on three foundations: the needs of the subject, the needs of students, and the needs of society (Gunter, Estes, & Mintz, 2007). These three needs align with what John Dewey conveyed in two of his most important books, *School and Society* (1900) and *The Child and the Curriculum* (1902). The titles speak volumes, as does the text, about the interconnectedness of society, students, and the subject matter itself. Dewey (1938) also emphasized that formal curriculum is dynamic, meaning that it is continually changing and evolving. Later in the chapter we explore three other kinds of curricula that contribute to the experiences of students in schools: informal, extra, and null.

As we consider the formal curriculum, we must acknowledge the guiding contributions of Ralph Tyler (1949), one of Dewey's students. Tyler developed what is now called the **Tyler Rationale,** proposing four questions that should be asked throughout the stages of curriculum development. Each question is examined in this text as indicated.

1. What educational purposes should the school seek to attain? (Chapter 2)
2. What educational experiences can be provided that are likely to attain these purposes? (Chapter 4)
3. How can these educational experiences be effectively organized? (Chapter 4)
4. How can we determine whether these purposes are being attained? (Chapter 5)

More information on John Dewey and Ralph Tyler is in Chapter 7.

Before about 1990, broad guidelines for what to teach were developed primarily by state planning committees and were based largely on textbook content, federal educational goals, and a "this is the way it's always been" attitude. Individual schools and teachers refined the state or school district guidelines to suit their particular circumstances. However, in 1989 curriculum development moved abruptly into what might be called the **era of standards** when the National Council of Teachers of Mathematics (NCTM) published math standards for grades K to 12, the first official set of standards written for a core subject area (NCTM, 2000).

STANDARDS INFLUENCE WHAT WE TEACH

Very simply put, **content standards** define what students should know and be able to do relative to subject areas at specific grade levels. Standards help organize and guide teaching and learning in the classroom.

Following NCTM's lead, the professional organizations of other core subject areas developed subject-specific content standards. Each professional organization is quick to say that its standards are not the curriculum but should be used to develop a cohesive plan for what is taught. When we discuss the individual subjects of the formal curriculum, we'll learn more about professional organizations and the standards that guide what teachers teach and students learn within specific disciplines.

Two other types of standards influence curriculum. **Performance standards,** or **benchmarks,** designate the level of the knowledge or skill that's considered acceptable within a particular grade level. Some standards documents also include **process standards** that support content learning by explaining both how the content might best be learned and how to use the content once it is acquired. For example, the five broad areas of NCTM content standards—number and operations, algebra, geometry, measurement, data analysis/probability—are accompanied by five process standards: problem solving, reasoning and proof, communication, connections, and representation.

STATE STANDARDS. Because the Constitution does not specifically address education, what is taught and learned in U.S. schools is largely left up to individual states. By the beginning of the 21st century, virtually every state had content standards in place, leading to what may some call the **standards-based reform movement,** another way of expressing the era of standards.

We examine the involvement of various levels of government in schools in Chapter 11.

Although most state standards are based on professional organization standards, there are variations among them. When the 2001 reauthorization of the Elementary and Secondary Education Act, the No Child Left Behind Act, required accountability, state standards and the associated standards-based testing became key to meeting this mandate. The pressure was on to show student achievement and improvement. The competitive nature of states, with their test results stacked up against one another, inevitably lead to comparisons between state-determined results and results from the National Assessment of Educational Progress (NAEP). This comparison revealed major discrepancies, indicating that some state standards and tests are not as rigorous as others. Some states report high levels of proficiency among their students only to have NAEP results imply that the state's students are not measuring up. In other words, it's easier to look good with regard to test results when standards are lower and tests are easier.

Accountability and NAEP are discussed in Chapter 5.

In part because some states appear unwilling to raise standards even in light of their apparent lack of rigor, there is increasing momentum to adopt common standards to which all states adhere.

NATIONAL STANDARDS. In this second decade of the 21st century, efforts aimed at the adoption of national standards are in full swing. Interestingly, the push for national standards, which would mean in a practical sense a national common curriculum, comes from two organizations that are made up of representatives from all of the states: the **National Governors Association** (NGA) and the **Council of Chief State School Officers** (CCSSO). These organizations have joined together to work on the **Common Core State Standards Initiative**.

With mounting research indicating state-to-state differences in standards and testing, the federal government is putting funding on the line. President Obama and Secretary of Education Arne Duncan are spearheading **Race to the Top,** an initiative that challenges states to make bold efforts to improve teaching and learning. Over $4 billion in federal money was awarded to 11 states in 2010, with one of the four required specific areas of improvement for individual states linked directly to alignment with common, internationally competitive standards and testing.

The debate over whether content standards should be state specific or uniform for the entire United States, and, if so, what those standards should be, will no doubt continue for a number of years. As we more closely examine the issues, objections to the standards currently in place in individual states surface.

OBJECTIONS TO STANDARDS. Although grade-level-specific, subject-based standards have brought unprecedented organization to what is taught and when, they are not perfect documents. Some of the most noted flaws of state content standards include:

- excessive coverage—the sheer volume of standards in any content area may be overwhelmingly impractical
- fragmentation of learning—isolated bits and pieces of knowledge and skills may not be connected and therefore lose context and meaning
- details that obscure major ideas—too many details may keep students and teachers from "seeing the forest for the trees"
- broad concepts that are too nebulous—standards written in broad generalities can be open to many interpretations
- lack of consistency—state standards, and subsequent standards-based testing, are uneven with some more demanding than others
- a less flexible way of teaching—many experienced teachers find adherence to sets of standards inhibiting when compared to a curriculum that gives more choices
- high-stakes accountability—standards lead to testing, the results of which determine student grade-level retention, school status, teachers' jobs, and availability of funds, among other major consequences
- decisions influenced by disagreeing factions—liberals and conservatives, religious and nonreligious all battle for inclusion and exclusion of content, making standards "political footballs"

All of these objections and more are to be expected because any reform measure that changes the way teachers teach and students learn is bound to be controversial. The debate is healthy and keeps the process alive and dynamic. Regardless of the controversy, standards give teachers information about what students should have learned in the past and must learn in the future. Using grade-level-specific standards for planning helps teachers fit their expectations into the bigger picture of student learning over time. Along with standards, another major factor impacts what is taught on a daily basis: the textbook.

TEXTBOOKS

One of the most influential determiners of what we teach has historically been the *textbook*. Now that adherence to standards in the content areas is mandated by states, textbooks may have lost a little of their power to shape curriculum. However, if a textbook publisher responds to the standards movement by aligning content and skills with state standards, textbooks are likely to guide teaching on a daily basis.

TEXTBOOKS IN THE CLASSROOM. Quality textbooks help organize and sequence course content. They provide a logical progression of topics, with content and skills that build on prior understanding and skill mastery. For instance, a social studies text will be organized chronologically so learners see how events impact subsequent events. A math textbook helps learners build on prior knowledge and skills in logical ways as they move, for instance, from recognition of geometric shapes to finding perimeter and then area in elementary geometry.

Teachers base up to 90% of classroom assignments and homework on textbooks and the accompanying supplements (Jones, 2000). Supplementary materials may provide options for enrichment, remediation, extension, application, and practice of skills, as well as lesson plans to guide teachers, online assistance, workbooks, tests, and a variety of other resources for both students and parents. These options allow teachers to more easily tailor content to student needs and readiness.

HOW TEXTBOOKS ARE SELECTED. About half the states have a statewide textbook adoption process, meaning that a committee at the state level chooses several books for each subject/level from which school districts may choose particular texts for use in local schools. In other states, school districts choose their texts directly. Whatever the process or at whatever level of governance, citizens are generally invited to give input. Teachers, as citizens, are encouraged to provide input, but few choose to do so, either indicating a level of trust in those who ultimately make the choices or a lack of time to become familiar with possible books.

Textbook publishing is big business. It would not be economically feasible for publishers to tailor textbooks to every state's standards. Textbook publishers often customize content to more closely align with the content standards of large states with a statewide adoption process such as Texas, California, Florida, and North Carolina.

LIMITATIONS OF TEXTBOOKS. We should be aware that while textbooks can be powerful, and generally positive, influences on what we teach and students learn, they may also pose the following problems:

- Textbook content may not match standards.
- Textbooks may include too many topics and few in adequate depth.
- There may be readability issues as the textbooks attempt to be readable for a range of abilities.
- Textbook authors may avoid interesting but controversial topics to please constituent groups.
- Textbooks may lack content or be of poor quality, problems perhaps masked by concentration on making the books colorful and appealing.
- Textbooks may exhibit bias related to conservative or liberal ideology, culture, race, gender, and the like, either overtly or by omission.

Points of Reflection 4.2

What do you remember about using textbooks in your PreK–12 experiences? Were they major determiners of what was taught and learned? Were they interesting to read? Did they help increase your understanding and skills?

You probably will not have much choice when it comes to textbooks available for your use. Be conscious of both their value and their limitations, knowing that textbooks have a significant impact on what we teach and what students learn in the subject areas of the formal curriculum. But although standards and textbooks have considerable influence on what we teach, the various levels of government also have influence because our public schools are precisely that—public.

GOVERNMENT INFLUENCES WHAT WE TEACH

Because most everyone in the United States has attended school, most of us think we know a lot about what should be taught, as well as how to teach it. This attitude, in part, leads to influence of levels of government on education.

Local government generally has little to do with standards and textbooks, but involved local citizens serve on school boards and, as such, have some say in how schools function. The state level of government, however, exerts a good deal of influence because most standards and other curricular decisions are made at the state level. Governors, legislators, and officials within state departments of education influence what is taught and learned in public schools.

In Chapter 11 we explore school governance and the impact of federal, state, and local government on how schools operate.

The federal government, although not directly dictating standards, has significant influence on how schools educate students through laws that have been passed, most notably since the Russian launch of *Sputnik* in 1957 that created a sense of urgency in terms of improving U.S. education in a competitive world. Once the National Defense Education Act of 1958 created math, science, and foreign language priorities, other federal legislation was passed in rapid succession that continues to influence what we teach and how we teach it, including the following:

- Economic Opportunity Act of 1964 made vocational training a priority.
- Civil Rights Act of 1964 prohibited discrimination, with the stated goal of equal access to quality education.
- Elementary and Secondary Education Act of 1965 established Title I status, intended to increase funding in schools with large populations of economically disadvantaged children.

- Bilingual Education Act of 1968 ensured the teaching of the curriculum in native languages as students learned English.
- Title IX legislation of 1972 provided for more girls to participate in athletics.
- Individuals with Disabilities Education Act of 1975 made participation in public education of students with disabilities a right rather than a privilege.
- No Child Left Behind Act of 2001, one of several reauthorizations of the Elementary and Secondary Education Act of 1965, required states to maintain curricular standards, test all students on the standards' knowledge and skills, and report on student achievement in disaggregated ways (separating various groups so their scores may be compared).

ADDITIONAL INFLUENCES ON CURRICULUM

In addition to those we have discussed, other groups and ideologies influence the formal curriculum.

PARENTS AND THE COMMUNITY. Every community has a unique identity by virtue of the citizens who live within it, including parents who send their children to public schools. While the inclusion of core subject areas in the curriculum is rarely questioned, some of the topics addressed within the core subjects may be. Even more community impact may be exerted on topics addressed in related arts subject areas. What gets the attention of the community is often a controversial issue that strikes a dissonant chord among community members. What may be considered mainstream in Miami, Florida, could be controversial in Boise, Idaho. What is taught in school seems only to grab community and parental attention when it is considered objectionable.

Parental and community involvement in schools is discussed in Chapter 12.

Parents and community members can exert influence on curriculum in a variety of ways including voicing opinions to school personnel and school board members or local media, refusing to allow children to participate in certain activities, suggesting alternative curricular approaches, and serving on textbook adoption committees.

PARTNERSHIP FOR 21ST CENTURY SKILLS. As we have already discussed, the knowledge and skills made explicit in the P21 documents are not necessarily new, but when packaged in this organization's format they make a compelling case for inclusion in the curriculum. The states that have officially become partners are all working toward including the P21 framework of knowledge and skills in their state standards. Even with the development of national curriculum standards, the Partnership for 21st Century Skills will likely continue to impact what is taught and learned in U.S. schools.

CORE KNOWLEDGE. The organization **Core Knowledge** proposes that there is a body of lasting knowledge that should determine the curriculum in PreK–8 schools. Proponents of Core Knowledge believe that this body of knowledge, sometimes referred to as cultural literacy, motivates students to learn more about topics because they grasp foundations of subjects. (Note that in this case, *cultural* refers to what some consider a culture unique to the United States.) For schools and school districts, those who align with Core Knowledge believe their prescribed curriculum provides a coherent, sequential plan for learning that isn't swayed by current events and technology innovations. Core Knowledge doesn't necessarily discount the value of current events and technology in the curriculum but rather sees them as add-ons to a base that remains relatively stable from year to year (Core Knowledge, 2009).

The educational philosophies of perennialism and essentialism align closely with elements of Core Knowledge and are discussed in Chapter 8.

A stable core of knowledge is certainly not something new or innovative in the history of curriculum in U.S. schools. However, as with P21, the very fact that an organization has formed to promote a common core of knowledge in schools leads to a greater impact on curriculum.

COLLEGES AND UNIVERSITIES. Students enter the doors of colleges and universities with knowledge and skills determined by the PreK–12 curriculum. Simultaneously, colleges and universities affect the direction of what is taught and learned in schools primarily through the preparation of teachers, research conducted by faculty, and faculty involvement in standards development. Because of this, higher education is in the unique position of being both a recipient and a molder of curriculum.

SUBJECTS OF THE FORMAL CURRICULUM

We generally consider English language arts, math, science, and social studies as the core subject areas. In early childhood and elementary settings, classes outside the core curriculum are built into the day either within the individual classroom or in special classes that meet perhaps weekly. Most middle and high schools require students to take a specific number of courses that are not part of the core. These courses, known as **related arts, exploratory,** or **encore,** are valuable components that enhance the formal curriculum and include physical education, technology, world languages, music, home arts, theater, and more.

Points of Reflection 4.3

Before reading further, think about your own experiences with English language arts, math, science, and social studies. Which content area appealed to you most? How did the teacher's level of enthusiasm and teaching strategies influence the appeal of the subject for you?

CORE SUBJECT AREAS. The subjects designated as core have basically been the same for over a century. Of course much of the content has changed, but English language arts (ELA), math, science, and social studies are consistently taught in early childhood, elementary, middle, and high schools. The emphasis in early childhood and elementary is on ELA and math, with the degree of attention given to science and social studies sometimes dependent on the teacher's level of knowledge about, and interest in, these subject areas. All four core subject areas are prominent in the curriculum of middle and high school.

English Language Arts. The National Council of Teachers of English (NCTE) and the International Reading Association (IRA) tell us that language development includes reading, writing, speaking, listening, viewing, and study of media. In early childhood, elementary, and middle school, much of the ELA curriculum focuses on skills, including reading, grammar, spelling, mechanics of punctuation and capitalization, editing, and basic research. Reading consists mainly of fiction (short stories and simple books) through fourth grade. In middle school, the focus begins to shift toward a variety of literary forms and writing. High school ELA is primarily literature based, with continued emphasis on writing skills and research. Communication skills such as oral presentation and persuasive speech have figured more prominently in ELA classes at most levels in recent years.

Mathematics. According to the National Council of Teachers of Mathematics (NCTM, 2000), the need to understand and use math in everyday life has never been greater. From making purchasing decisions to interpreting tables and graphs, math is a vital part of the present and will be increasingly important in a more complex future. Children in early childhood settings now explore concepts of algebra, geometry, and data analysis. Elementary and middle school students are asked to write about problem-solving strategies involving scenarios with multiple variables. An increasing number of high school students are taking advantage of advanced placement math courses for college credit.

By viewing math as something students do and connect to real life, NCTM standards ushered in a shift in math education from memorizing procedures to understanding concepts, and from emphasizing isolated mechanical ways of finding solutions to problem solving (NCTM, 2000).

Science. The vision of the National Science Teachers Association (NSTA) is for all students to regularly experience science that revolves around unifying themes such as order, organization, models, change, measurement, and function. To do this, teachers emphasize that science is a process involving observation, inference, and experimentation. This is a major shift from content-specific facts to understanding concepts through process and inquiry (more on inquiry later in this chapter). For instance, when science is taught through themes, young children learn what it means to measure and how to use measurement tools. In middle and high school, they examine how and why measurement is important in every aspect of science (NSTA, 2005).

Social Studies. The National Council for the Social Studies (NCSS) tells us that the "primary purpose of social studies is to help young people develop the ability to make informed and reasoned decisions for the public good as citizens of a culturally and demographically

Science comes alive for students like Amanda at Rees Elementary when they are encouraged to observe and experiment.

diverse society in an interdependent world" (2005, p. 1). This is a definite shift from the way social studies was approached for much of the last century. Before the influence of NCSS and the curricular changes prompted by standards, social studies was dominated by names and dates to be memorized, with little or no application of concepts to local, national, or international dilemmas.

The NCSS standards are based on 10 themes that are addressed in all school levels but approached differently based on the developmental level of the students. For instance, for standard 1 (culture), students in early childhood and elementary settings may explore food, clothing, and shelter in places that represent the ethnicities of students in a class. In middle grades a unit on the culture of a country may involve examining the lifestyles of the people and the environment and completing comparative writing exercises. A high school social studies class may address culture through a unit on religious expression in schools in which students consider different faiths, examine relevant case studies, argue opposing views, freely voice opinions, and develop supporting rationales (NCSS, 2005).

RELATED ARTS. Related arts courses complement and enhance the core curriculum. Let's take a look at some that are frequently offered.

Technology. The International Society for Technology in Education (ISTE) is a professional organization whose mission is to provide "leadership and service to improve teaching and learning by advancing the effective use of technology in education" (ISTE, 2005). The standards for technology are organized into categories such as basic operations, communication tools, and ethical issues. Almost all schools have computer labs used for classes in **information literacy,** a broad phrase involving recognition of when information is needed, knowing how to access information, and judging information credibility. In these labs, designated technology teachers teach whole classes of students at a time.

Foreign Language. The statement of philosophy of the American Council for the Teaching of Foreign Language (ACTFL) tells us that "the United States must educate students who are linguistically and culturally equipped to communicate successfully in a pluralistic American society and abroad" (2005, p. 2). To accomplish this mission, high schools and most middle schools offer courses in a variety of world languages, most commonly Spanish and French. Because of the recognition that young children acquire a second language more readily than do young adults, many early childhood and elementary schools offer opportunities to learn a second language.

The Standards for Foreign Language Learning are organized according to five goals that ACTFL calls the "Five C's of Foreign Language Education": communication, cultures, connections, comparisons, and communities (ACTFL, 2005, p. 2).

Physical Education and Health. Leaders of physical education (PE) and health education strongly advocate for more time spent in physical activity and health-related instruction. Supporting standards are provided by the National Association for Sport and Physical Education (NASPE) and the American Association for Health Education (AAHE).

In early childhood and elementary schools PE may be unorganized play time, often the responsibility of the classroom teacher, or there may be a designated PE teacher who conducts whole class sessions two or three times a week for each grade level. In middle school PE and health are likely to be rotated courses, perhaps covering 9 weeks each year, with health taught by the PE or science teacher. In high school, students are usually required to take only one or two courses in PE and even fewer in health. Given the health risk factors associated with adolescence in society today, implementation of the NASPE and AAHE standards is especially important for teenagers.

In Chapter 9 we look at how societal health issues add urgency to the uniform implementation of PE and health standards.

Arts. The National Standards for Arts Education define what students should know and be able to do in the four arts disciplines: music, dance, theater, and the visual arts. Essentially, the standards state that by the end of high school students should be able to communicate at a basic level in the four disciplines and be proficient in at least one art form. The availability of art experiences in music, dance, theater, and visual arts in PreK–12 schools varies tremendously. In early childhood and elementary schools, the classroom teacher may be responsible for the art curriculum or the school may have an art specialist. In middle and high schools, students usually have a variety of arts classes from which to choose and perhaps a limited number of arts activities.

It is an unfortunate fact that when the budget is tight in schools and districts, the arts are often the first to go. After all, standardized tests don't even mention forms of dance, genres of paintings, composers and their works, or elements of drama.

Career and Tech-Prep Courses. Career and tech-prep cover a broad category of courses usually offered in high school. Some courses are of general interest, such as basic industrial or home arts classes, while some are career oriented, such as auto mechanics and cosmetology. The federal government supports a program called **School-to-Work,** initiated to bring real-world work-related skills and understanding to students through courses that introduce them to career possibilities.

Before discussing the remaining types of curricula, let's look briefly at three aspects of the formal curriculum that cross subject-area boundaries: integrated curriculum, culturally responsive curriculum, and arts-infused curriculum.

IMPORTANT CONCEPTS THAT ADD VALUE TO CURRICULUM

There are some important concepts to consider as we explore curriculum. If we think of the formal curriculum as a cloth that covers the school day with learning opportunities, these concepts may be thought of as threads that weave in and out of the subjects and add value, as illustrated in Figure 4.1.

INTEGRATED CURRICULUM. Continuing the cloth analogy, the strength of cloth comes from weaving the threads in different directions so the cloth holds together. When teachers include content and skills from a variety of subjects in lessons, and weave them together in meaningful ways they are incorporating **integrated,** or **interdisciplinary,** curriculum. An integrated curriculum basically involves approaching a concept from different perspectives to create learning opportunities based on connections. This is often accomplished through the use of a unifying topic or theme. Early childhood and elementary teachers do it all the time. Second grade teachers may weave a study of farm life throughout the year, aligning core and related arts subjects with the theme whenever possible. Math problems may deal with farming scenarios and science may revolve around light, rain, and soil, along with zoology. The history of farming and literature about farming and farmers may be taught.

Figure 4.1 Integrated curriculum

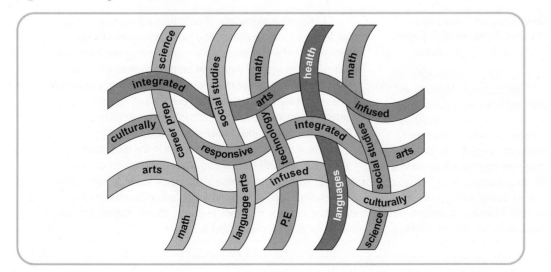

Points of Reflection 4.4

What do you remember about related arts classes? Which ones did you particularly enjoy and why? Were there related arts classes you did not want to take? If so, which ones and why? Did related arts classes impact how you spend your time now? If so, how?

In middle school, teams of teachers may weave whole days, or even weeks, around a theme that brings together research of real-world events and phenomena. Curriculum integration is least common in high school. Although high school teachers are usually organized into subject-area departments, this in no way prevents an ELA teacher from teaching about literature through short stories, poems, and novels that reflect a topic addressed in the social studies curriculum for the grade level. For instance, if U.S. history is a course taken by most sophomores, the sophomore ELA teachers could incorporate period literature that coincides with the progressive history of the United States as taught by the history department faculty.

Connecting subjects of the formal curriculum can occur at a variety of levels of complexity. From merely mentioning in a geometry lesson that the word *symmetry* is also important in art, then showing a painting that exhibits the concept, to a well-planned series of lessons with subject-area boundaries blurred by real-world context, our efforts to make connections within the curriculum pay big dividends in terms of student interest and learning.

CULTURALLY RESPONSIVE CURRICULUM. As diversity in U.S. schools increases, the importance of, and demand for, a culturally responsive perspective grows. When we approach curriculum in **culturally responsive** ways, we incorporate a **multicultural curriculum** that purposefully includes contributions and viewpoints from the perspectives of different cultures, ethnicities, races, genders, socioeconomic levels, or any other way we may differ. At its best, a multicultural curriculum is accurate, timely, and sensitive while avoiding tokenism or a sense of forced inclusion (Banks, 2003).

The methods used to demonstrate cultural responsiveness and infuse a classroom with a multicultural curriculum will depend on the grade level and subject area. In early childhood and elementary settings, celebrating historical events and holidays of a variety of cultures helps create awareness of values and traditions within various cultures. In middle and high school, making a variety of perspectives part of your classroom discussions, and asking students to research and report on issues of interest to them that include various perspectives, can help forge an understanding of people of different cultures. One of the most effective tools for including a variety of perspectives is an emphasis on current events.

Considering our cloth analogy, think of culturally responsive curriculum as adding texture to the cloth, and perhaps a tapestry effect, as connections are made among subject

Points of Reflection 4.5

What do you recall about your teachers' efforts to connect subject areas? Did you experience thematic units of study? If so, describe what you remember.

We explore student diversity and multicultural curriculum in Chapter 3.

Teaching in Focus

Derek Boucher, History and Reading, Roosevelt High School, California. *In his own words. . . .*

After 12 years working in an urban, public high school in the Central Valley of California, I still firmly believe that teaching is a noble profession. Allow me to share the components that have made the biggest difference in my life as a teacher.

Love your content area. Engage in reading, writing, research, discussions, and even travel in your content area. The passion these activities generate comes across to students and changes lives.

Developing a philosophy of education will serve you better than learning multiple strategies. From a rich philosophy, great strategies emerge. Strategies apart from a philosophy come and go. In 1995 my teacher education program pushed me to think deeply about my philosophy of teaching and learning. For example, I believe that curriculum should be relevant and meaningful to students as often as possible. Humans are innately curious. I believe that faith in the learner is imperative.

Go to graduate school. After 5 years in the profession, I enrolled in graduate school and studied in the area of reading/language arts. This experience changed my life as a professional and benefited me infinitely more than school district training has ever done. Find the most progressive graduate program around and go for it! You'll never regret it.

areas. Read focus teacher Derek Boucher's philosophy about a teacher's relationship to the curriculum, making curriculum relevant, and furthering our knowledge and skills in *Teaching in Focus*.

ARTS-INFUSED CURRICULUM.

Including arts in the curriculum requires awareness of opportunities, along with purposeful determination to include music, theater, dance, and the visual arts when possible. You don't need to be an artist or musician to display art or play music in the classroom. Encouraging students to create their own works of art to enhance a project takes exactly that—encouragement.

"The arts are the great equalizer in education. Regardless of native language, ability or disability, music, art, and drama are accessible to all" (Gregoire & Lupinetti, 2005, p. 159). As an equalizer, the arts can provide both expression and success for all students, regardless of the diversity they may display. Consider these four reasons for integrating the arts:

- Arts provide a natural view into the contributions and perspectives of other cultures.
- Arts are primary means of communication.
- Arts provide opportunities for achievement that may not otherwise be available.
- Arts may focus on alternative ways to assess and evaluate (Cornett, 2003).

Brenda Beyal, the multiage teacher at Rees Elementary in Utah who infuses both visual arts and drama into the curriculum, encourages her students to express themselves in unique ways through what she calls a squiggle, a randomly drawn curvy line that forms the basis for artistic expression. Each student is given a piece of paper with the same squiggle on it and is asked to use imagination and creativity to fashion a drawing around the basic structure. While they work on their masterpieces, music plays in the classroom. Does this activity distract from the formal curriculum? Brenda views experiences such as the squiggle as enriching her classroom by creating a sense of ownership on the part of her students that ties them more closely to the formal curriculum they will encounter during the day.

Although it's hard to imagine objections to infusing arts into the curriculum, there are groups who oppose arts on the grounds that their inclusion detracts from the core subjects. Controversy and curriculum are never far apart.

CONTROVERSY AND CURRICULUM

In a society that values opposing views and encourages diversity, the curriculum is sure to be debated. The dynamic nature of debate is healthy, but it can also be frustrating at times for educators. Religious beliefs, censorship for a variety of reasons, and philosophical differences all influence what's included in the formal curriculum. Here are a few examples of issues that are controversial in some school districts and states with regard to what is taught in public schools.

- There is an ongoing debate over the exclusive teaching of evolution to explain the origin of human beings. **Intelligent design,** proposed by some parents and community members who practice Christianity and oppose the teaching of evolution, includes a belief that certain features of the universe and of living things are best explained by an intelligent being (God), not by the process of natural selection espoused by evolution. Some people argue for an evolution-only curriculum; others argue for intelligent design only. Still others propose the teaching of both as theories, incurring the disapproval of many in the scientific community, including most colleges and universities, where evolution is considered factually based.
- Earlier we discussed multicultural curriculum, or the purposeful inclusion of contributions of persons of diversity and traditions that are not considered

What do you remember about your teachers' efforts to be culturally responsive? Were various holidays acknowledged or did you study contributions of a variety of people of different races and ethnicities? If so, what do you recall? How did you experience the arts as part of your PreK–12 experiences?

To see some of the multiple ways the arts are infused at Rees Elementary, view Mike Larsen's school tour and Brenda Beyal's room tour by visiting the Teaching in Focus *section for Chapter 4 in the MyEducationLab for this course.*

mainstream America (a loosely conceived concept). One of the arguments for more cultural responsiveness is that U.S. curriculum is too **Eurocentric,** meaning that contributions and traditions that do not originate in Europe are underrepresented. For instance, in 2010 there was ongoing debate in the Texas legislature about whether or not Hispanics should be added as historic characters to the public school curriculum now that about 40% of the Texas population is Hispanic. Some proponents of a core knowledge curriculum argue there is enough to learn about basic ideas, classic literature, scientific knowledge, and so on, without efforts to be culturally responsive that may take away valuable classroom time.

Societal circumstances and pressures that may affect curricula, including health and sex education, are discussed in Chapter 9.

- Whether schools should teach sex education, and, if so, what should be taught, and when should topics be introduced, are questions about which many in the United States feel strongly. The whole issue of sex education is value laden and emotionally charged. Many believe that the responsibility to teach children and adolescents about sex falls squarely on the home and religious organizations, while others contend that the school is the appropriate venue because it impacts the most students over a long period of development. With the goal of reducing teen pregnancies and sexually transmitted diseases, courts generally uphold the rights of schools to provide sex education. But the mere legality of a controversial issue such as this does not equate with widespread benign acceptance, nor does it alleviate the burden of deciding what to teach and when to teach it. This chapter's *Letter to the Editor* addresses the issue of sex education.

Letter to the Editor

This letter appeared in the Fort Wayne, Indiana, newspaper, *The Journal Gazette*. It was written by a citizen responding to recent local controversy over sex education in schools.

SEPTEMBER 10, 2009

There have been several letters lately from concerned parents who have embraced their right and responsibility to educate their children about sexuality. They are all adamant that schools should not be teaching sex ed. But what about the millions of children who obviously aren't getting "the talk" at home? What happens to them? They are the ones who will go out, have babies, ready or not, and continue the cycle of failing families. Don't those children deserve to be educated about the consequences of sexual activity?

It would be great if all parents would accept the responsibility for the education of their own children. But clearly they are not doing so. If we really want to do something about teen pregnancy and reduce the spread of sexually transmitted diseases, we have to educate as many children as possible. This self-congratulatory attitude of "I'll educate my own and to heck with everyone else" only perpetuates the problem. Biological

facts can and should be taught in schools. The preaching and moralizing can be done somewhere else.

Brad Huff

Now it's your turn. Write a letter to the editor from the perspective of a future teacher expressing your views about the role of schools in sex education. The following questions may help you frame your thinking, but should not limit nor determine what you write.

1. Who has responsibility for teaching children and adolescents about sex-related issues? Why? Are there multiple parties, or is responsibility limited to a specific group?

2. If sex education is appropriate in schools, who should decide which topics and issues should be taught in a classroom setting?

3. If sex education is appropriate in schools, who should teach it and why?

4. At what point in the PreK–12 curriculum might some form of sex education be appropriate?

Write your letter in understandable terminology, remembering that readers of newspaper letters to the editor are citizens who may have limited knowledge of school practices and policies. Remember to refer to the letter assessment rubric in Chapter 1.

What Other Curricula Do We Teach in U.S. Schools?

We've learned what goes into creating the formal curriculum for U.S. schools. Now let's look at other kinds of curricula that are part of what teachers do. Although not as obvious in many ways, and certainly not as regulated by standards and policies, the informal, extra, and null curricula nonetheless impact teachers and students.

INFORMAL CURRICULUM

The **informal curriculum** is what teachers and schools teach and what students learn that is not part of a lesson plan, a curriculum guide, or standards. It encompasses what is learned by students through attitudes, values, and various types of informal teaching situations, such as in the hall between classes, at recess, and on field trips when conversations are casual. This informal learning may be positive or negative and is sometimes unintentional. When the formal curriculum is referred to as the explicit curriculum, the informal curriculum may be called the **implicit curriculum,** meaning that often it is implied and subtle. You may also hear informal curriculum and **hidden curriculum** used interchangeably. There is a distinction, however, because the informal curriculum has positive connotations, while the hidden curriculum has more of a negative sense, implying there may be teacher motivations that are somehow less than positive.

Another phrase equated with the informal curriculum is **wayside teaching**. John Lounsbury (1991), a noted middle-level educator and advocate for young adolescents, tells us that wayside teaching is the teaching we do inside and outside the classroom through our attitudes, values, habits, interests, and creation of classroom climate. Regardless of what students learn in terms of content and skills through the formal curriculum, they learn *us*. They watch us, listen to us, and notice their surroundings; they learn more than we imagine. If we are positive, caring, excited about learning, fair, and organized, students learn that

- optimism is more productive than pessimism
- cooperation and empathy matter
- structure and enthusiasm enhance learning
- responsibility is personal and valuable (Powell, 2010)

On the other hand, if we are negative, lack interest in students and subjects, and exhibit a general disdain for our work, students are likely to mirror these qualities. If our classrooms are a mess, if the school building is dilapidated, and if the community is unsupportive, students learn that they may not matter very much.

The informal curriculum is all about relationships. Purposefully using wayside teaching involves taking advantage of teachable moments, accepting students for who they are rather than what they do, teaching to student strengths, and building a sense of belonging among students (Powell, 2010). When students sense they are valued, they are more willing to cooperate and engage in the classroom (Jensen, 2005). Students who sense they belong have more inner resources to use to be successful (Osterman, 2002). Nel Noddings, a highly respected teacher and researcher, tells us that caring about students leads to their sense of belonging. Moreover, Noddings (1992, p. 27) maintains that "Care is the bedrock of all successful education." In this very important way, the informal curriculum complements the formal curriculum. Building relationships leads to increased student engagement and achievement (Stipek, 2006).

A middle school science teacher wrestling with the "What should I teach?" question decided to ask her former students what they remembered about her class and what they believed were the most important lessons. She developed a survey and received responses

Renee Ayers at Summit Primary develops caring relationships with her students. Here she and Sherlonda share secrets in the positive environment Renee maintains for her students.

from students she taught in each of her 9 years in the classroom. These responses included the following:

> "The most important things I learned from you weren't in class, but during the Science Olympiad . . ."

> "The [finest] things I learned from you have nothing to do with science."

> "The most important thing I learned from you would have to be the ability to be nice to people even if you feel like screaming. . . . The way you acted toward our class and the compassion you showed to our class [taught me this]."

> "Self-confidence and how important it is."

> "How important science is to society."

> "How you encouraged everyone to do their best."

Points of Reflection 4.7

Think about how the informal curriculum affected you. What did teachers say and do that impacted you most? What attitudes did they display that spoke volumes to you as a learner? What informal lessons do you remember most from grades PreK–12?

Several students responded that the books she read aloud to them (in science class!) changed their opinions on diversity (Little, 2001, pp. 62–63). What a powerful example of positively teaching the informal curriculum!

EXTRACURRICULUM

Activities sponsored by the school but outside the limits of the formal curriculum are considered extracurricular. Although some elementary schools offer extracurricular activities, such as jump rope and craft clubs, most extracurricular opportunities begin in middle school and expand in high school.

Extracurricular activities provide opportunities for active involvement for students, and for sponsorship and coaching for teachers. Examples include

- Odyssey of the Mind, math and book clubs
- debate, chess, and photography clubs
- band and choral activities
- athletics of all kinds, including cheerleading
- school newspaper, student government, and honor society

Points of Reflection 4.8

In what extracurricular activities did you participate? What did participation mean to you? In which activities did you want to be involved but for some reason were not?

Recently there has been renewed interest in the factors that contribute to **school connectedness,** or student bonding and engagement. Lack of school connectedness may lead to disruptive behavior, substance abuse, emotional distress, absenteeism, and dropping out. The importance of doing what it takes to foster connectedness is magnified when we consider that approximately half of all high school students, whether urban, suburban, or rural, feel "chronically disengaged" from school (Klem & Connell, 2004, p. 262). A major factor that influences school connectedness is participation in extracurricular activities (Blum, 2005). Researchers have found that extracurricular activities "provide all students—including at-risk and gifted students—an academic safety net" (Holloway, 2000, p. 88). This chapter's *Diversity Dialogue* addresses connecting students to school in culturally responsive ways, with extracurricular possibilities.

Watch Angelica's interview in the Teaching in Focus section for Chapter 4 in MyEducationLab for this course.

One of our focus teachers, Angelica Reynosa, has taught Folkloria as one of her five classes each year for 5 years. Through her section of Folkloria students explore their genealogical roots and the history of Hispanic cultures. Students at Angelica's school may register for one section of Folkloria each semester as their related arts choice. Other Folkloria classes concentrate on visual and craft art of Hispanic origin, or music and dance of Hispanic cultures. When it is announced that the Folkloria program will no longer be offered during the school day, Angelica is quite distressed.

Angelica sees the reasons given for discontinuing Folkloria as a credit-bearing experience as reasonable but only if the students aren't considered. The school budget is tight and the teachers who have Folkloria as part of their teaching loads are needed to teach core subject areas now that there is a hiring freeze (no one can be hired for a period of time). Angelica would be happy to pick up an additional World History class, but she also feels strongly that the Folkloria program meets needs that the regular classes do not. Her fear is that if Folkloria is completely eliminated at her school, aspects of the Hispanic culture will be relegated to the null curriculum that she has read about in education journals.

Think about Angelica's beliefs concerning Folkloria. Respond to these items by writing one well-developed paragraph for each.

1. What is a possible way Angelica can continue offering a program similar to Folkloria at her high school? What would be involved? What are two possible benefits?

2. From what we know about Angelica, what strengths does she bring to Folkloria?

NULL CURRICULUM

The **null curriculum** is what *isn't* taught—those concepts and skills that perhaps simply haven't been considered or are not considered important enough. The way certain subjects are taught is simply based on tradition. "We teach what we teach largely out of habit" (Eisner, 2002, p. 103). The null curriculum also includes topics considered controversial, including almost anything dealing with religion, abortion, homosexuality, and other topics that are controversial in some areas but not in others.

The null curriculum may not be as important as the formal curriculum, the informal curriculum, and the extra curriculum, but it is certainly worth thinking about. What's *not* part of the school curriculum may never be considered by students and therefore may have little to do with their futures. For instance, if we neglect to incorporate a culturally responsive curriculum, failing to acknowledge and celebrate differences may contribute to prejudice and exclusionary attitudes in students.

The Partnership for 21st Century Skills promotes the teaching of some concepts that are not currently in most curricular plans. On the P21 Web site we are told that the challenge is to purposefully incorporate the broad literacies they support. A **literacy** involves the ability to analyze and apply knowledge and skills necessary to solve problems within a discipline. The Partnership recommends that schools promote financial, economic, business, entrepreneurial, civic, health, wellness, information, and communication literacies. In many schools these broad disciplines are not addressed

The poster behind Mayra and Roosevelt Assistant Principal John Lael lists some of the extracurricular possibilities at RHS.

Points of Reflection 4.9

Did you gain insight concerning any of Wolk's missing curricular pieces when you were in PreK–12 school? If so, through what part of the curriculum? What do you wish would have been included in your PreK–12 experiences?

and are part of the null curriculum. When schools incorporate them, they will become part of the formal curriculum.

Wolk (2007) tells us there are important concepts typically missing from school curriculum, thereby relegated to the null curriculum. He contends that students and society as a whole would benefit from the inclusion of, and emphasis on, knowledge of self; love of learning; caring and empathy; environmental literacy; social responsibility; global awareness; and money, family, food, and happiness.

How Is Instruction Implemented in U.S. Schools?

Just as curriculum is the *what* of teaching, instruction is the *how.* Without effective instruction that meets the needs of learners, "the most elegant curriculum in the world . . . would fall short of its promise" (Tomlinson & McTighe, 2006). We know there is not one single approach to instruction that works for every student in every subject all the time. Differing student intelligences, learning styles, abilities, societal contexts, and so on, make using a variety of instructional approaches necessary to meet students' needs. Therefore, building a repertoire of instructional strategies is vital. No need to worry—instructional possibilities are practically limitless.

A teacher provides learning opportunities that fall within a spectrum from teacher centered to student centered, depending on the topic or skill, the level of students, the time frame in which instruction must occur, and the teacher's instructional style. There are circumstances when lecture (perhaps the most teacher centered of all strategies) is appropriate, and other circumstances when student exploration with guidance works best. You may hear the phrases *sage on the stage* and *guide on the side* as you continue your teacher preparation. When a teacher is a *sage on the stage*, there is a lot of telling and demonstrating going on. Strategies such as lectures and **mini-lectures** (shortened, focused versions of the lecture) and teacher demonstrations are examples of *sage on the stage* teaching. These can be effective strategies as part of a teacher's broader repertoire of teaching techniques. When a teacher is a *guide on the side,* the teacher is setting expectations, providing instructions, and serving as a resource while students do the work and exploration that lead to learning. Guiding, or facilitating, student learning leads to increased active engagement.

BIG IDEAS OF INSTRUCTION

Now let's explore some of the big ideas of instruction, along with some supporting instructional strategies that allow teachers to apply the big ideas in their classrooms. Each of the big ideas of instruction deserves, and indeed has had, entire books written about it. What you read here is an overview so you will be aware of some of the ideas that will likely be emphasized during your teacher preparation program.

PROMOTING CRITICAL THINKING. **Critical thinking** involves observing, comparing and contrasting, interpreting, analyzing, seeing issues from a variety of perspectives, weighing variables, and then making decisions and solving problems based on these thinking skills. Can we really teach children and adolescents to think critically as they learn the standards of the formal curriculum? The answer is *yes.* Teaching critical thinking and **problem solving** is not an addition to the curriculum but rather a way of approaching the knowledge and skills we teach.

Benjamin Bloom and others at the University of Chicago first published what is now referred to as **Bloom's taxonomy** of thinking skills in 1956. Simply put, **thinking skills** are those skills that aid in processing information. These skills grow in complexity and sophistication as they progress from level I to level VI of the taxonomy that has become a tool used by teachers as they plan and organize learning experiences. All the levels, as

TABLE 4.1 Bloom's taxonomy

Categories	Key Verbs		Question Stems
Knowledge (Remembering)	Recognize Identify Recall Memorize	Retrieve List Define Duplicate	When did _____? Who was _____? Where is _____? Why did _____? Can you list four _____?
Comprehension (Understanding)	Interpret Summarize Infer Illustrate	Classify Compare Explain	How would you compare _____ to _____? What is the main idea of _____? What is meant by _____?
Apply	Implement Use Operate	Dramatize Illustrate Solve	How would you use _____ to _____? What approach would you use to _____? Can you _____ by _____?
Analyze	Organize Integrate Focus	Categorize Differentiate Examine Test	What evidence can you find to conclude that _____? What does _____ have to do with _____?
Evaluate	Check Critique Judge	Monitor Defend Support	How would you change _____ to form _____? Can you propose a different way to _____? How would you design _____ to _____?
Synthesis (Creating)	Generate Plan Design	Construct Produce Develop	What is your opinion of _____? How valuable is _____ for _____? Why would you recommend _____?

Source: From *Introduction to Middle School*, 2e (p. 206), by S.D. Powell, 2011, Boston: Allyn & Bacon. Copyright 2011 by Pearson Education, Inc.

illustrated in Table 4.1, are necessary, and none should be neglected. Designing learning experiences that call only for knowledge and comprehension is cheating the minds of students who need to apply and analyze what they know, synthesize or create something new, and evaluate ideas and events. When planning lessons and assessments, teachers should use Bloom's taxonomy and the action verbs associated with each level. Questioning, as an important strategy to promote student thinking, is enhanced by using the question stems, or question beginnings, in Table 4.1. In 2001 Anderson and Krathwohl revised Bloom's taxonomy by, among other things, using different words to describe some of the levels and designating synthesis (creating) as a higher thinking level than evaluation.

TEACHING THROUGH INQUIRY. When students pursue answers to questions posed by others or developed on their own, they are involved in **inquiry learning**. Observation, questioning, hypothesizing, and predicting are all part of inquiry-based learning, which requires students to move beyond rote memorization to become independent thinkers and problem solvers. Teaching and learning through inquiry may involve real-world contexts and discovery, and it can be accomplished in such simple ways as providing scenarios for students to explore or objects for students to manipulate.

Inquiry-based instruction is not new. All discoveries have come about as the result of questioning and answer seeking. Before students can formulate questions on their own or search for answers, they need knowledge and skills as building blocks. Once these building blocks are in place, then students are ready to inquire and look for answers. Inquiry-based instruction is an effective way of teaching and learning because the ideas we create ourselves are the ones we tend to retain (Renzulli, Gentry, & Reis, 2004).

A common way of implementing inquiry-based teaching is to design experiences that require students to engage, explore, explain, elaborate, and evaluate. This is commonly called the **5-E lesson plan**. For instance, an elementary teacher can tell third graders the conditions necessary for bean plants to sprout and grow. The students can be tested and many will be able to recite the conditions, at least for the test. Using the 5-E plan, here's how the teacher might guide children through a cycle of inquiry learning:

- Take students outdoors and ask them to observe the plants in the schoolyard (engage and explore).
- Have students discuss with each other what they observed as the conditions for plants to grow and thrive (explain).
- Talk with students about the possibility of an experiment involving some beans given the conditions the students think are needed for plants to thrive, as well as other beans deprived of the conditions (elaborate).
- Assist students as they work together to create the desirable and undesirable conditions using real beans (elaborate).
- Guide students as they observe and record bean growth and come to conclusions about what contributes to bean plants thriving, and whether their predictions were correct (evaluate).

An important element of inquiry learning is the thinking skill of questioning. Asking students appropriate questions helps them examine concepts and phenomena in in-depth ways. When a teacher asks thoughtful questions, students also learn how to frame questions that lead to meaningful learning.

DIFFERENTIATING INSTRUCTION. Approaching instruction in a variety of ways provides multiple paths for students to learn the knowledge and develop the skills of the curriculum. In 1999 Carol Ann Tomlinson gave this philosophy and practice a name: **differentiation of instruction**. Tomlinson tells us that teachers who differentiate instruction strive to do whatever it takes to diagnose student strengths and weaknesses in terms of readiness, interests, and learning profiles. Then they provide an array of content, a variety of processes, and choices of products when possible. The *content* is what the students should know, understand, and be able to do. *Process* consists of the ways students make sense of content, typically through activities and practice. A *product* shows what students know and are able to do; it may be, for example, a project, demonstration, test, or display.

Tomlinson wisely cautions against trying to differentiate too much, too quickly. She advises us to start slowly by recognizing one need in our classroom, changing one part of a lesson (content, process, or product), and implementing this differentiated strategy followed by reflection on the results. As our comfort level grows with diagnosing the readiness, interests, and learning profiles of our students, we can incorporate more and more instructional practices to meet their needs. Tackling too many differentiated strategies too soon in a career can lead to doing activities for activity's sake and the sacrifice of solid, well-designed teaching (Tomlinson, 1999). Great advice.

Taking Tomlinson's advice and starting small may involve simply incorporating **manipulatives,** or objects, to represent numbers or concepts into a lesson on fractions. Differentiating may involve letting pairs of students complete an assignment together, allowing students to teach each other. Or perhaps differentiation will be giving students choices about how they want to work on the week's vocabulary words, with some individually writing definitions and others quizzing each other quietly in a corner of the room. In Figure 4.2 you'll read Tomlinson's view, in general terms, of what teachers do in differentiated classrooms.

INCORPORATING STUDENT COLLABORATION. When students collaborate in a learning environment there are benefits. Students may share responsibility for a project, discuss a question or prompt given by a teacher, tutor each other, help each other study for a quiz, or participate in a planned group activity. Most often student collaboration in schools is referred to as cooperative learning.

Figure 4.2 Differentiation of instruction

When teachers differentiate instruction they . . .

- begin where students are
- accept and build upon the premise that learners differ
- engage students through different learning modalities
- ensure that a student competes against himself more than he competes against other students
- believe that students should be held to high standards
- ensure that each student realizes that success is likely to follow hard work
- use time flexibly
- are diagnosticians who prescribe the best instruction for their students

Source: Tomlinson, C. A. (1999). *The differentiated classroom: Responding to the needs of all learners.* Alexandria, VA: Association for Supervision and Curriculum Development.

Loosely defined, **cooperative learning** refers to any instance of students working together. It was, however, more strictly defined in the 1980s when Roger and David Johnson designed the following cooperative grouping patterns:

- informal groups that meet together for a variety of tasks as needed
- formal groups that complete designated, often long-term, tasks
- base groups whose members support one another with remembering and completing assignments, studying, and sharing resources (Johnson & Johnson, 1999)

The Johnson brothers devised five requirements for effective student grouping practices:

1. Positive interdependence—setting group goals for which all members must work to achieve; shared rewards; roles for each member including facilitator, recorder, materials gatherer, timekeeper, and encourager
2. Face-to-face interaction—students work together to explain, complete assignments, solve problems, and so on
3. Individual accountability—students must complete individual tasks that contribute to the group
4. Interpersonal skills—students learn to work together in socially acceptable ways
5. Group processing—students reflect on how well they worked together and how effectively they accomplished their goals; students give teacher feedback on group functioning (Johnson & Johnson, 1999)

Cooperative learning is a big idea of instruction that can be successfully implemented in early childhood, elementary, middle, and high school. It's likely that you have been a member of many cooperative groups during your school experiences. Table 4.2 contains some ways teachers group and regroup students for learning.

USING TECHNOLOGY. Today's students are referred to as the "Media Generation," digital learners in "techno-drenched atmospheres" that are "gizmo-intensive" (McHugh, 2005, p. 33). "No generation has ever had to wait so little to get so much information" (Renard, 2005, p. 44). Using technology in instruction that enhances learning is imperative. **Educational technology** is any technology-based device that assists teachers in teaching and students in learning. As educators we have the responsibility to guide students in ways that will help them excel in our technology-rich society.

The International Society for Technology in Education (ISTE) provides detailed descriptions of the knowledge and skills related to technology use appropriate for children and adolescents. Virtually all major subject-area organizations join ISTE in promoting technology use in the classroom, as do professional organizations representing the various levels of PreK–12 education.

Points of Reflection 4.10

Think about the cooperative learning experiences that were productive and pleasant for you in school (including college), as well as those that either failed or were not enjoyable. What made them successful? What contributed to problems with group functioning?

TABLE 4.2 Cooperative learning strategies

Strategies	Description
Think-Pair-Share (T-P-S)	T-P-S involves all students in nonthreatening ways. Teachers expose students to information, give a prompt, ask a question, or provide an experience and then challenge them to think about it in a particular way and perhaps record their thoughts on paper (T). Students then choose a partner (P) and share their thoughts with another student (S).
	Pyramid T-P-S involves multiple pairs of students discussing the question/prompt.
Jigsaw	This strategy involves students becoming experts on particular topics within *expert groups* and then teaching those topics to the other students in their *base groups*. Jigsaw is a powerful tool that actively involves students both in their own and other people's learning.
Role play	Getting students up and moving as they dramatize a scenario can make a point or prompt students to think in divergent ways. Role playing becomes more effective with practice.
Tableau	Similar to role play, tableau involves students assuming a freeze-frame position that illustrates an event in a short story, book, or historical event. While students pose, another student in the tableau group reads a narrative that is being dramatized.

In looking at technology available in schools, the two broad categories to consider are teaching tools and tools for teachers. Technology *teaching tools* are resources that enhance curriculum, instruction, and assessment when used by teachers to teach and by students to learn. Some of the available technology teaching tools are in Table 4.3. Technology *tools for teachers* are those that expedite and/or enhance the work of teachers and, consequently, curriculum, instruction, and assessment in the classroom. Examples include software that helps with lesson planning and electronic gradebooks. Many technologies accommodate both categories.

Handheld computers may be used to share information commonly referred to as *beaming.*

INTEGRATING READING AND WRITING ACROSS THE CURRICULUM. Reading and writing are vital skills, without which life is difficult and limited in many ways. Regardless of the subject or grade level, all teachers need to be teachers of reading and writing. Infusing the curriculum with reading and writing is often referred to as *reading across the curriculum* and *writing across the curriculum.*

Reading. An old adage says that children learn to read through third grade and read to learn from then on. If only that were true. Emphasis is placed on emergent literacy (getting ready to read) and beginning reading (letter/word recognition, story patterns) in early grades when teachers expect to be teachers of reading, and often their efforts are supported by reading specialists whose sole responsibility is teaching children to read.

Many students are not proficient readers by the end of third grade. Even if they are proficient, reading expectations become more stringent and complex, creating the need for specific literacy instruction beyond third grade. In middle and high school there is a devastating

TABLE 4.3 Technology teaching tools

Technology Tool	Value in the Classroom
Word processor	Built-in support for writing and publishing
PowerPoint	Popular presentation program used by teachers in their classrooms to deliver instruction and by students to demonstrate skills and display project products
Streaming video	Allows students to view video that is either stored on a site, or live, as it downloads on the computer
Instructional software	Used to learn about concepts and/or practice skills; five categorizes of instructional software: drill-and-practice, tutorial, simulation, instructional games, and problem solving (Roblyer, 2006)
Handheld computers	Pocket-sized computers with small folding keyboards give teachers and students flexibility to move around while using them; class sets are easily mobile; information and products may be shared simply by pointing one computer at another, commonly referred to as "beaming"
Internet	Most widely used network: World Wide Web (WWW)
Podcast	Like creating a radio program and then distributing it on the Internet; virtual publishing
Electronic books	e-media; iBooks
Distance learning	Acquisition of knowledge and skills through instruction delivered using technology; learning is not place based
Digital games	Attention getting and interactive; simulations

lack of reading proficiency. More than half of the ninth graders in the 35 largest cities in the United States read at the sixth grade level or below (Vacca, 2002). The average student in a high school classroom is reading below the level of content-area texts (Allington, 2002), and 25% of adults are functionally illiterate (Moats, 2001). Some ideas for promoting reading skills are in Figure 4.3.

Access to books, recreational reading, and silent reading all lead to improved skills in both decoding and comprehension (Krashen, 2002). Fluent readers have the skills to be fluent writers. Conversely, students who struggle to read will struggle to write as well.

Writing. Techniques for effective writing in multiple genres have not received as much attention or classroom time as reading instruction. Writing can be meaningfully integrated into all subjects at all grade levels and may be descriptive, creative, factual/informative, or expository. Teaching students to write involves many components, including sentence formation, punctuation, capitalization, word usage, style, and spelling.

Figure 4.3 Ways to promote reading skills

- Give students access to student-friendly, inviting, content-rich reading materials (books, magazines, newspapers, etc.).
- Read aloud to students at all grade levels to show them how to navigate through difficult text.
- Provide opportunities for silent, oral, and recreational reading.
- Use appropriate before (explain vocabulary, predict), during (graphic organizers, note taking, integrating prior and new knowledge), and after (summarizing, checking for understanding) reading strategies.
- Take a "textbook journey" as a class to help students understand the way the pages are set up, the purposes of the illustrations and data representations, the length and structure of the lessons and sections, the activities and exercises that follow sections, the glossary, and so on.

Students may benefit from keeping notebooks or journals in any subject in which they take notes, record questions about content, reflect on their learning, and so on. Writing essays, biographical sketches, descriptions of events, stories, poetry, and answers to prompts fit naturally into ELA and social studies classes. Writing narrative explanations of science and math procedures deepens and extends understanding.

Now that we have considered some big ideas of instruction and some strategies that bring the big ideas to life in the classroom, we are ready to explore how teachers plan for instruction.

PLANNING FOR INSTRUCTION

We discuss assessment in depth in Chapter 5.

In the beginning of the chapter we established that curriculum and instruction are interdependent, that curriculum is meaningless without instruction to convey it and instruction is useless without curriculum. **Assessment,** the gathering of evidence of student learning, is a third component of teaching and learning that is interdependent with curriculum and instruction. All three components are vital in planning learning experiences for children and adolescents.

BACKWARD DESIGN. In their 1998 book, *Understanding by Design*, Wiggins and McTighe introduced educators to a concept that links curriculum, instruction, and assessment in meaningful and interconnected ways. The approach to planning for teaching and learning to accomplish understanding is called **backward design**. The word *backward* is used because the approach is in contrast to the way many teachers approach planning, which is to think of activities before considering the desired results of using those activities. Backward design starts with deciding on the desired learning results (curriculum), then identifying how to collect the evidence necessary to know if the results have been achieved (assessment), and finally proceeding to choosing how to help students acquire the desired knowledge and skills (instruction). These three stages, as illustrated in Figure 4.4, constitute backward design. Although some teachers view backward design as revolutionary, others call the concept just plain common sense and say they have used some version of it to plan their work for years.

In addition to introducing the concept of backwards design and expanding our view of understanding, Wiggins and McTighe (2005) contend there is too much for teachers to teach and for students to thoroughly understand in state content standards. They advise us to prioritize the standards within three categories. The most vital knowledge and skills are in the first category and are referred to as the big ideas and core tasks, defined as those that give "meaning and connection to discrete facts and skills" (p. 5). The next category consists of the knowledge and skills that are important to know and be able to do. The third category, and the one where some content may simply be mentioned or possibly eliminated altogether, consists of the knowledge and skills that may be worthy of being familiar with but don't rise to the category of being important to know and do. This is good advice.

LEVELS OF PLANNING. In early childhood and elementary classrooms, a daily **lesson plan** may mean planning experiences involving reading and math, with perhaps some social

Figure 4.4 Stages of backward design

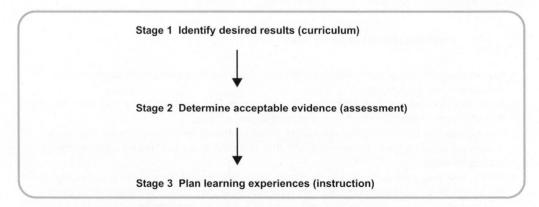

Source: Wiggins, G. P., & McTighe, J. (2005). *Understanding by design* (2nd ed.) (p. 18). Alexandria, VA: Association for Supervision and Curriculum Development.

studies and science, a little art and maybe some music and physical activity. In middle and high school, a daily lesson plan may mean planning for two English classes and two literature classes. Daily lesson planning is the planning that links teaching and learning every day in U.S. schools.

A daily lesson plan should build on the lessons of previous days in cohesive ways. To assure this, daily lesson plans should be conceived within weekly plans or unit plans. A weekly lesson plan is just that, 5 days of sequential lessons. A **unit of study** usually involves a theme, with daily plans within the unit addressing aspects of the theme. Weekly and unit plans should be conceived within **long-range plans** that may encompass a 9-week time frame, a semester, or a year. The best way to plan is with the entire school year's worth of standards in focus. Many schools and school districts provide **pacing guides** that outline what should be taught and when it should be taught, designating the order of concepts and skills. There are online resources to assist in all levels of planning. Figure 4.5 lists helpful Web sites.

COMPONENTS OF A LESSON. There are many lesson plan formats, with a common one shown in Figure 4.6. Subject-area organizations recommend specific components and particular formats that you will learn about as part of your teacher preparation program. Regardless of the lesson format, there are lesson components that are usually considered necessary for effective instruction. Keep in mind that not every lesson will include each component, but over the course of a week, teachers generally incorporate the components in Figure 4.6 in some way.

Here is a brief explanation of each of the lesson components in Figure 4.6.

- Standards—As we have discussed, standards basically set the curriculum and determine what teachers teach and students learn.

- **Objectives**—This is a concise statement about what students are expected to learn and be able to do as a result of the lesson.

- Lesson opening—The lesson should begin in a way that captures students' attention and creates interest. The opening can be a time to figure out what students already

Figure 4.5 Internet sources to assist with lesson planning

- Education World
  www.education-world.com/
  Includes many subjects, professional development,
  technology integration, multiple resources

© Copyright EducationWorld .com, reprinted with permission.

- Eisenhower National Clearinghouse
  www.enc.org
  Multiple math and science resources for all grade levels

- Lesson Planet
  www.lessonplanet.com
  Resources, tools, lessons in many subjects

- Ed Helper
  www.edhelper.com/
  All grades, seasonal lessons, includes special education

- Teachers.net Lesson Bank
  http://teachers.net/lessons/
  Allows you to search, submit, or request lessons;
  covers multiple subject areas and grade levels

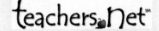

- A to Z Teacher Stuff
  http://atozteacherstuff.com/
  Lesson plans, thematic units, teacher tips,
  discussion forums for teachers, downloadable
  teaching materials

- The Educator's Reference Desk
  www.eduref.org/
  Resource guides Lesson plans in all subject areas,
  including foreign language and vocational

Figure 4.6 Sample lesson plan format

Standard(s) to be addressed:
Lesson objective(s):
Lesson opening:
Procedures:
Plan for differentiation:
Opportunities for guided practice with feedback:
Independent practice:
Assessment of learning:
Closure of lesson:
Materials and resources:

know about the lesson content (their prior knowledge). The information teachers gather requires them to be flexible as they adapt the lesson based on student knowledge and skill.

- Procedures—This is the step-by-step plan for how students will learn/explore a topic and/or skill. Procedures may include a variety of models including cooperative learning, inquiry-based instruction, technology integration, and more, with combinations of strategies that include reading and writing and contribute to project- and problem-based learning. Class discussion, questioning, note taking, demonstration, and so on, are traditional teaching genres that may be part of the lesson procedures.

- Plan for differentiation—All of the ways previously discussed for differentiating instruction and more provide choices for meeting the needs of students.

- Opportunities for **guided practice** with feedback—It's important for students to have opportunities to work independently on applying knowledge in a nonthreatening setting (without being graded). Feedback from the teacher (or as part of an online program) as to whether the student is on the right track will prevent students from practicing incorrectly.

- Independent practice—This can be in or out of class and often takes the form of **homework**.

- Assessment of learning—How do we know if students have learned what we have articulated in the lesson objective? There are multiple ways of assessing student learning that we will explore in the next chapter.

- Closure of lesson—Providing a way for students to summarize what has been learned is a good way to close a lesson. The bell should not end the class period; there should be a plan to logically draw the class session to a close.

- Materials and resources—Planning a lesson includes gathering everything necessary for the lesson to proceed.

Planning for instruction is a vital part of what teachers do. Knowing our students and their developmental levels allows us to plan our teaching appropriately to facilitate their learning.

How Do Teachers Match Instruction to School Levels?

Not every instructional strategy is appropriate for every grade level. Early childhood is not the place for note taking, and high school is not the place for graphing solely with pictures. Some strategies, however, are appropriate for all levels of school. For instance, demonstration and cooperative learning can be used effectively in early childhood, elementary, middle, and high schools.

Each of our focus teachers uses instructional strategies that are level appropriate. As we discuss the strategies of the teachers, note that concepts we have discussed are in italics.

To watch sample lesson segments in the classrooms of Brandi, Brenda, Traci, and Craig, go to Chapter 4 in MyEducationLab for this course.

EARLY CHILDHOOD INSTRUCTION

Active engagement is absolutely necessary in early childhood classrooms. Early childhood teachers need to be masters of engaging children in meaningful activities and providing an environment for creative and cooperative play. In PreK, children learn prereading strategies and the meaning of numbers, among other basic concepts. In kindergarten through third grade, children *learn to read* and perform basic *problem solving.*

In Brandi Wade's kindergarten class at Summit Primary, Ohio, the lesson *objective* is for students to make judgments about the concepts of less than, greater than, and equal to as they manipulate objects. Because Brandi works with the children every day, she knows that their *prior knowledge* includes awareness of the symbolism involved with the concepts and how to count to at least 20 by assigning a number to an object (one-to-one correspondence). Brandi uses what the students already know to engage them in an activity. Here are some strategies Brandi uses in her lesson:

- *demonstrates* counting, sorting, writing numbers, choosing correct symbols
- uses *manipulatives* (M&Ms)
- encourages children to work at tables where they can observe and help each other (*cooperative learning*)

Brandi uses the natural social nature of children to encourage them to work together with real objects to accomplish the lesson objective.

ELEMENTARY INSTRUCTION

For students in elementary classrooms, reading takes on new purposes beyond learning to decode words and reading fiction. Reading becomes a tool for acquiring new knowledge in language arts, math, social studies, science, and other subjects. Although *active engagement* remains vital, elementary children can be expected to read, study, and complete assignments with some measure of independence for brief periods of time.

In Brenda Beyal's multiage class at Rees Elementary, Utah, the students experience *tableaus*, discussed earlier in Table 4.2. Here are some strategies Brenda uses to support the tableau lesson:

- delivers *mini-lecture* on author Eve Bunting
- *reads aloud* portions of *Smoky Night*
- uses a graphic organizer to explain what a *tableau* involves
- incorporates *cooperative group work* as a vital part of the tableau
- *facilitates* work of groups

Brenda knows that her students would have been able to read *Smoky Night* silently and answer questions about its content. However, she wanted her students to be more deeply involved with the book and, among other things, understand the author's motivations, become knowledgeable about the period of history in which the story takes place, understand the societal implications of the story, and experience some of the emotions of the characters. She chose the tableau strategy to accomplish her instructional *objectives.*

MIDDLE-LEVEL INSTRUCTION

Young adolescents typically respond positively to *active learning* opportunities. They are eager to be involved in meaningful experiences that require *inquiry* and creative *problem solving.* They also respond to more traditional strategies such as *mini-lectures* and *note taking* if they have been taught to actively listen, record, and organize what they learn. Variety and frequent shifts in strategies are key to engaging middle-level students.

In Traci Peters's seventh grade math classroom at Cario Middle School, South Carolina, the students are reviewing topics. They complete a worksheet and are both responding to *teacher questions* and *taking notes.* The new learning in this lesson involves students discovering the sum of the measures of the angles of a triangle, then writing generalizations about what they have learned. Here are some strategies Traci uses to support the day's lesson:

- begins class with checking *independent practice (homework)* to support and review concepts
- *demonstrates* and *questions* using overhead projector
- uses *manipulatives* to discover concept
- facilitates *cooperative learning* to check for understanding
- requires *written explanation* of learning
- *facilitates* small group work

Traci knows the value of *inquiry-based learning.* She knows that if her young adolescents *discover* the sum of the angles of a triangle they will understand the concept and remember what they learn.

HIGH SCHOOL INSTRUCTION

Students in high school respond to *active learning* opportunities. They work best when the content interests them and when they interact with the subject or topic in ways that require them to be *problem solvers.*

Craig Cleveland's U.S. History class at Roosevelt High School, California, engages in thought-provoking class discussion after he reads a picture book to them about discrimination. The students then read a series of Jim Crow laws, with the purpose of developing role plays that illustrate a particular law. The students act out their role-play scenarios, and then the class discusses what they have seen. This kind of active involvement is excellent for promoting *critical thinking.* Here are some of the strategies Craig uses in his lesson:

- *reads aloud* to students
- facilitates *class discussion*
- delivers *mini-lecture*
- uses quotation to provoke *critical thinking*
- assigns *role play*
- incorporates *cooperative groups*

Craig knows his students well. He understands that the study of discrimination through Jim Crow laws will appeal to them because of the *real-world context.* He also knows that language barriers in his classroom may be partially bridged through *role play.*

CONCLUDING THOUGHTS

John Goodlad, following his landmark study of American high schools, wrote that the typical classroom is a site where "boredom is a disease of epidemic proportion" (1984, p. 9). What a devastating indictment.

Can you picture a classroom full of students deeply immersed in learning rather than entrenched in boredom? Asking, "And how are the children? Are they all well?" leads us to make engaging teaching that leads to optimum student learning our ultimate goal. Now that you know more about curriculum—what it is and where it comes from—you understand the importance of both knowing content and being enthusiastic about it. Now that you know more about instruction—its limitless variety and potential—your ability to envision student engagement has increased.

We began this chapter by considering Chris Roberts and his classroom at Rees Elementary in Utah. Now as the chapter comes to an end, we join Chris as he uses his knowledge of curriculum and instruction to support multiage grouping. Read through *Chapter in Review* to help refresh your memory of what we have discussed. Then interact with Chris as he confronts a challenge in *Developing Professional Competence*.

Points of Reflection 4.11

Can you imagine being the teacher in Brandi's classroom? Brenda's classroom? Traci's classroom? Craig's classroom? Which lesson and style appeal to you most?

To watch Chris Roberts's interview, visit the Teaching in Focus section for Chapter 4 in the MyEducationLab for this course.

Chapter in Review

What is the formal curriculum?

- The formal curriculum is what is intentionally taught and stated as student learning goals.
- Standards, defined as what students should know and be able to do, serve as the framework for much of the formal curriculum.
- Textbooks have a great deal of influence on the school and classroom curriculum.
- Various levels of government influence the formal curriculum.
- The formal curriculum includes both core and related arts subjects.
- An integrated curriculum involves linking curricular areas as their contents complement one another.
- A culturally responsive curriculum includes contributions and ways of viewing the world from perspectives of different cultures, ethnicities, races, genders, and socioeconomic levels.
- Infusing arts (music, theater, dance, visual arts) into the curriculum provides opportunities for expression that motivate and engage students.
- There are multiple points of controversy related to curriculum.

What other curricula do we teach in U.S. schools?

- The informal curriculum is what teachers teach and students learn that is not part of the planned curriculum or standards.

- The extra curriculum consists of activities that are sponsored by the school but outside the formal curriculum.
- The null curriculum is what isn't taught.

How is instruction implemented in U.S. schools?

- Backward design is an approach to planning for teaching and learning that starts with deciding on the desired learning results, then identifies how to collect the evidence, and concludes with choosing appropriate instructional strategies.
- Content priorities include first, vital knowledge and core tasks; then, what is important to know and do; and finally, what is worth being familiar with.
- There are big ideas of instruction that serve to ground and provide a framework for teaching and learning.
- Multiple strategies of instruction allow for variety in how the curriculum is taught.
- Thoughtfully planning for instruction is vital for effective teaching and optimal student learning.

How do teachers match instruction to school levels?

- Some instructional strategies are appropriate for students of all levels.
- Choosing instructional strategies for each of the four levels of school requires thoughtful consideration.

Developing Professional Competence

Visit the Developing Professional Competence section in Chapter 4 of the MyEducationLab for this text to answer the following questions and begin your preparation for licensure exams.

The district school board where Chris Roberts teaches is considering doing away with multiage classrooms. We read about multiage classrooms in Chapter 2 as we explored a variety of configurations for teaching and learning in U.S. schools. We also know from the interviews with Chris and his teammates Brenda and Tim that they have successfully taught for years in classrooms occupied

by third, fourth, and fifth graders. We hear Chris admit in his interview, however, that he doubts he gets to all the content standards of the three grade levels as he teaches in a multiage setting each year.

Chris believes strongly in exposing students to the world through a variety of means. His extensive travels, his love of the arts, and his selection of books for the classroom provide opportunities for him to infuse teaching and learning with real-world context. Through this context Chris knows that his students are learning valuable lessons.

It will be difficult to defend multiage grouping to the school board, but Chris is convinced the configuration works for his teaching team.

Think through this scenario and answer the following multiple-choice questions:

1. Chris states that he probably doesn't get to all the state standards in his classroom. He may be able to clarify which, if any, of the standards he doesn't address by
   a. reading summaries of the standards provided in the state document
   b. matching the textbooks he uses to the standards
   c. taking the time to look very closely at the standards for each grade level and create one document that sequences the standards
   d. asking someone from the state to observe his classroom

2. Chris knows that he will be questioned about the range of ages in his classroom. Which of the following statements is least appropriate for making a case for multiage grouping?
   a. My teaching style work because kids will learn what interests them.
   b. Chronological age does not necessarily determine learning readiness.
   c. Sometimes students learn much from each other and the age disparities often work in favor of peer teaching.
   d. In multiage classrooms teachers can guide learning over a 3-year period to make sure there is consistency and continual progress.

3. All of the following will likely be helpful to Chris as he prepares to make his case before the school board except for which one?
   a. Brenda and Tim
   b. parents of students in his class
   c. Mike Larsen, the principal
   d. Utah Superintendent of Education

4. What information might be most convincing if he had time to research it?
   a. the number of other schools using multiage grouping
   b. a comparison of the success of the students in multiage grades 3–5 settings in sixth grade and the students in self-contained classes in grades 3 to 5
   c. a survey of parents of children in grades K to 2 to see how many will request a multiage setting when their children reach third grade
   d. a comparison of how Utah fares relative to other states on the NAEP exam

5. Which combination of big ideas of instruction should Chris emphasize as the most powerful justification

for having third, fourth, and fifth graders in one classroom?
   a. promoting critical thinking and differentiating instruction
   b. incorporating student collaboration and promoting critical thinking
   c. differentiating instruction and incorporating student collaboration
   d. teaching through inquiry and using technology

Now it's time for you to respond to two short essay items involving the scenario. In your responses, be sure to address all the dilemmas and questions posed in each item. Your responses should each be between one half and one double-spaced page.

6. Chris has decided that he will attend the next school board meeting and present his reasons for continuing multiage grouping. This item is about his preparation. Who should he speak with to help him prepare to do this? What elements of his classroom practice should he emphasize? About what should he be very knowledgeable before addressing the board? Consider the following INTASC Standards and how Chris might use them as he prepares to address the school board:

Principle #2: The teacher understands how children learn and develop, and can provide learning opportunities that support their intellectual, social and personal development.

Principle #3: The teacher understands how students differ in their approaches to learning and creates instructional opportunities that are adapted to diverse learners.

Principle #4: The teacher understands and uses a variety of instructional strategies to encourage students' development of critical thinking, problem solving, and performance skills.

Principle #5: The teacher uses an understanding of individual and group motivation and behavior to create a learning environment that encourages positive social interaction, active engagement in learning, and self-motivation.

Principle #7: The teacher plans instruction based on knowledge of subject matter, students, the community, and curriculum goals.

Principle #9: The teacher is a reflective practitioner who continually evaluates the effects of his or her choices on others and who actively seeks out opportunities to grow professionally.

7. Chris knows how important his introduction is in terms of getting the board to listen to him and find him credible. What should he say in his opening remarks?

Where
DO I Stand NOW?

In the beginning of this chapter you completed an inventory that gauged where you stood on a variety of issues. Now that you have read the chapter, completed exercises related to the content, engaged in class discussions, and so on, answer the following questions in your course notebook.

1. If you discovered through this chapter's inventory that you favored a basic curriculum of ELA, math, science, and social studies to one that encompasses related arts while acknowledging the power of the informal curriculum and extracurricular activities before considering the chapter's content, have you changed your mind? If so, how?

   If, on the other hand, you began the chapter favoring a broad curriculum and now prefer a more basic curriculum, what changed your stance?

2. If you discovered that you prefer to approach instruction in a teacher-centered manner but now are leaning toward a more student-centered approach, what changed your mind?

   If, however, you now prefer a teacher-centered approach given what you have read, what convinced you that a teacher-centered approach will work better for you?

3. The debate involving a stable, not easily changed curriculum versus a curriculum that responds to societal circumstances is one that has existed for centuries. If you began this chapter with the opinion that curriculum should be a stable body of knowledge and skills but now think that societal changes should affect what is taught and learned, what altered your opinion?

   If, however, you began the chapter with the opinion that societal circumstances should influence teaching and learning but now believe that the curriculum should not be swayed by what's happening in the world, what changed your mind?

My Education Lab

The MyEducationLab for this course can help you solidify your comprehension of Chapter 4 concepts.

- Explore the classrooms of the teachers and students you've met in this chapter in the Teaching in Focus section.

- Prepare for licensure exams as you deepen your understanding of chapter concepts in the Developing Professional Competence section.

- Gauge and further develop your understanding of chapter concepts by taking the quizzes and examining the enrichment materials on the Chapter 4 Study Plan.

- Visit Topic 10, "Curriculum and Instruction," to watch ABC videos, explore Assignments and Activities, and practice essential teaching skills with the Building Teaching Skills and Dispositions unit.

5

Assessment and Accountability

Effectively determining what students know and are able to do involves *assessment.* Considering who bears the responsibility for student learning involves *accountability.* Here are some of the questions we consider in Chapter 5:

✦ What is involved in classroom assessment?

✦ How do teachers evaluate student learning and assign grades?

✦ What are standardized tests, and how are their results used?

✦ Who is accountable for student learning?

Before we discuss assessment and accountability, explore your own views in this chapter's *Where Do I Stand?*

Where DO I Stand ?

This inventory addresses your general perceptions of classroom and standardized assessment in K–12 school. It also gauges your preference with regard to two broad categories of test formats. After reading an item, indicate your level of agreement by choosing a number 0 to 4 and placing it in the blank before the statement. Following the inventory are directions for how to organize your responses and what they may indicate in terms of where you stand.

4   I strongly agree
3   I agree
2   I don't have an opinion
1   I disagree
0   I strongly disagree

_____ **1.** My experiences with assessment had a kind of "gotcha" feel to me.

_____ **2.** Standardized tests made me uncomfortably nervous.

_____ **3.** My teachers only monitored my learning through tests.

_____ **4.** I preferred tests that asked me to choose the right answer.

_____ **5.** I enjoyed projects more than tests to show what I knew and could do.

_____ **6.** Being compared with other students on standardized tests seemed unfair to me.

_____ **7.** The grades I received were not an accurate representation of my knowledge and skills.

_____ **8.** My end-of-course grades did not show how much I really learned.

_____ **9.** Oral reports allowed me to shine as I showed what I knew and could do.

_____ **10.** Too much emphasis was placed on standardized tests and their results.

_____ **11.** My teachers didn't reteach material that students didn't seem to get on a test.

_____ **12.** My teachers rarely gave feedback on assessments that helped me learn from my mistakes.

_____ **13.** I had trouble understanding assignments and following directions.

_____ **14.** I preferred essay tests over other forms of assessment with single right answers.

_____ **15.** Multiple-choice tests gave me a chance to accurately show what I knew.

_____ **16.** I had a hard time understanding how teachers arrived at my grades.

_____ **17.** When I had a test, I felt more nervous and anxious than most of my friends.

_____ **18.** I preferred true-false tests and did well on them.

_____ **19.** I experienced obvious test preparation tactics that seemed to detract from real learning.

_____ **20.** If I had one or two bad days, my overall grade suffered.

_____ **21.** Results of standardized tests didn't show how much I knew.

_____ **22.** I liked opportunities to be creative in how I demonstrated what I knew.

_____ **23.** I liked multiple-choice tests.

Record your responses to the following items, then divide by 15 to get an average (round to nearest tenth).

ITEM	RESPONSE
1	
2	
3	
6	
7	
8	
10	
11	
12	
13	
16	
17	
19	
20	
21	
Sum A	
Average A (divide by 15)	

Now plot Average A on this number line. The closer to zero, the more positive your experiences were with classroom and standardized assessment in K–12 school.

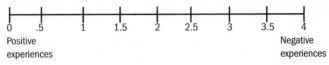

| 0 | .5 | 1 | 1.5 | 2 | 2.5 | 3 | 3.5 | 4 |

Positive experiences — Negative experiences

You will learn in this chapter about forced-choice assessment with only one possible answer on a paper-and-pencil test. Assessment that may have a variety of answers or may be experiential is considered open ended and/or performance based. Your responses to the designated items will indicate your preference when you find average responses to the items as indicated by dividing Sum B by 4 and Sum C by 4.

ITEM	RESPONSE	ITEM	RESPONSE
4		5	
15		9	
18		14	
23		22	
Sum B		Sum C	
Average B		Average C	

Now plot your averages and compare your preference for forced-choice assessment and open-ended, performance-based assessment.

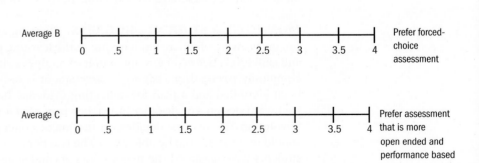

Average B

| 0 | .5 | 1 | 1.5 | 2 | 2.5 | 3 | 3.5 | 4 |

Prefer forced-choice assessment

Average C

| 0 | .5 | 1 | 1.5 | 2 | 2.5 | 3 | 3.5 | 4 |

Prefer assessment that is more open ended and performance based

Teaching in Focus

Renee Ayers believes that ongoing assessment is vital to her teaching. The progress her second graders are making at Summit Primary, Ohio, is recorded and analyzed in multiple ways. She even finds ways for her students to view their own progress.

One of Renee's favorite uses of student self-assessment involves writing. She asks her second graders to write their best about any topic they choose during the first week of school. She then tucks these little masterpieces away until the last week of second grade when the students again choose a topic and write about it. Renee surprises her students by giving them their first week's writing to compare. She says it's one of the most joyous celebrations a 7- or 8-year-old can experience. The looks on their faces and their obvious pride in recognizing their progress are priceless!

Renee keeps anecdotal records on her students in two distinct and user-friendly ways. One method involves a clipboard and note cards. She tapes the first card to the board so the bottom of the card and the bottom of the clipboard are even. She writes a student's name on the bottom of the card. Then she tapes another card so that its lower edge lines up just above the name on the first card and writes another student's name on the bottom of that card.

She continues this process, taping cards up the board to the clip. She carries this board around as she talks with students about their reading or math or a project they may be working on. In doing so she is practicing teacher observation with the added benefit of recorded notes.

Renee uses another clipboard to hold pages of sticky-back labels. She writes students' names, the date, and her observations about student learning on the labels. Later she simply puts the labels in a notebook on pages designated for each student. This is a quick way to record informal assessments all day and then easily organize them.

Of course Renee also does more formal assessments similar to what most early childhood teachers do. But she feels that her informal assessments help her develop the kind of rapport with her students she values and give her clear insights concerning their learning.

Renee models both attitudes and techniques that promote the use of assessment as an integral part of classroom practice. She takes seriously her responsibility to understand her students' strengths and weaknesses, to know their learning profiles, and to monitor their continual progress. Her innovative approach contains ideas you can adapt to your own classrooms.

Watch an interview with Renee in the Teaching in Focus section for Chapter 5 in MyEducationLab for this course. You'll recognize her twin sister, Tara, a high school physics teacher, from a photo in Chapter 1.

What Is Involved in Classroom Assessment?

Classroom assessment encompasses all the possible ways teachers determine what students know and can do measured against standards or other learning goals. The assessments developed and used by individual teachers are **criterion referenced,** meaning that student results indicate levels of mastery of a subject and do not depend on how other students score. In its many forms, classroom assessment serves multiple purposes that are appropriate for the variety of curricula and instructional strategies used in U.S. schools.

PURPOSES OF CLASSROOM ASSESSMENT

Determining student achievement and reporting grades are the most commonly understood reasons for classroom assessment, but these are not the only purposes. The National Council of Teachers of Mathematics (NCTM) broadened our view of the purposes of assessment. Figure 5.1 illustrates NCTM's four purposes of assessment.

MONITORING STUDENT PROGRESS. Ongoing assessment allows teachers to be continuously aware of where students are in the learning process. Assessing student knowledge and skill levels before beginning a unit of study is called **diagnostic assessment** or, more commonly, **pretesting**. Diagnostic assessment is only possible when desired results have been identified and a plan for collecting evidence has been made, the first two stages of backward design. For instance, a teacher may plan a unit of study based on the Industrial Revolution. The teacher decides on the major concepts (content) and skills the students should understand and be able to do. The teacher then decides how to determine when the students have mastered the major concepts and skills. A diagnostic assessment is then formulated that will diagnose what the students may already know about the topic.

Figure 5.1 NCTM's four purposes of assessment

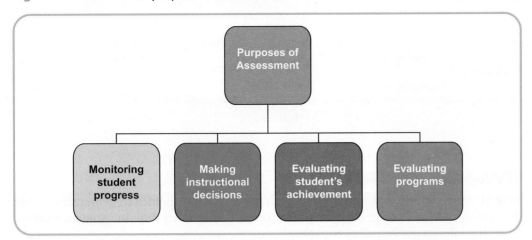

Source: National Council of Teachers of Mathematics. (1995). *Assessment standards for school mathematics.* Reston, VA: Author.

The results of diagnostic assessment should be used to plan the daily lessons of the unit, including multiple **formative assessments** in a variety of formats that gauge student progress toward learning objectives. Feedback is the key to making formative assessment effective. Feedback needs to be timely and specific enough to make students aware of not only where they are in the learning process but also what they need to do to move forward.

MAKING INSTRUCTIONAL DECISIONS. Assessment can be a waste of time and effort if it does not influence the content, the instructional strategies, and the pacing or sequencing of classroom experiences. Effective monitoring of student progress provides the information and insight to make instructional decisions that promote student growth. These decisions may involve reteaching or teaching differently to help more students master the unit content and skills.

A teacher's instructional decisions should be guided by the results of ongoing monitoring of student progress through formative assessment and not by what materials are available, how last year's class responded, or the fact that a favorite topic already has complete detailed lesson plans.

EVALUATING STUDENT ACHIEVEMENT. Assessment allows teachers to measure if, and how much, students learn. Formative assessments and their results may have a part in the measurement, but **summative assessment** is most often used to evaluate student achievement. A summative assessment is typically more formal than a formative assessment and involves judging the success of a process or product. Summative assessments most often occur at the end of a unit of study. Paper-and-pencil tests are traditional summative assessments, but they need not be the only format used. Students should be given opportunities to demonstrate what they know and are able to do in a variety of ways, such as completion of a project or performance of an authentic task. When students succeed, teachers can and should recognize accomplishments.

Look closely at Figure 5.2. Notice the flow from diagnostic to formative to summative assessment. The double arrows between formative assessment and instruction indicate that formative assessment helps teachers make decisions about instruction. There is fluidity between ongoing formative assessment and what is planned in the classroom. Summative assessment occurs at the end of the formative assessment/instruction ebb and flow.

EVALUATING PROGRAMS. The fourth purpose of assessment may extend beyond the classroom. Instructional materials and formalized programs such as Scholastic 180, the literacy program used by Deirdre at Cario Middle School, South Carolina, are purchased by schools and districts. The components of these programs are monitored for effectiveness, and decisions are made regarding their value based on results of various forms of assessments.

Figure 5.2 Diagnostic, formative, and summative assessment in the classroom

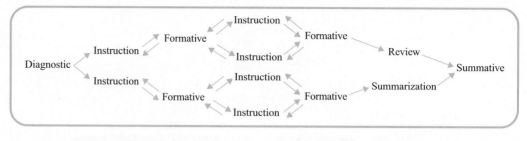

FORMS OF ASSESSMENT

Students learn differently and should have a variety of opportunities to demonstrate what they know and can do. Varying assessment format ensures that differing student learning styles and intelligences are accommodated.

Robert Marzano (2000), a researcher with Mid-continent Research for Education and Learning (McREL), formulated the seven basic forms of classroom assessment listed in Table 5.1. Read about each and think about if and how it might serve a diagnostic, formative, and/or summative function.

One of the forms of assessment, teacher observation, is a given. We watch, we listen, and we make mental or written notes about student progress. One of our focus students

Learning styles and multiple intelligences are discussed in Chapter 3.

TABLE 5.1 Seven forms of assessment

Form of Assessment	Characteristics
1. Forced choice	• Multiple choice, matching, true/false, fill-in-the-blank • Can be scored objectively • Most common form of assessment • Choose from among alternatives given
2. Essay	• Good for assessing thinking, reasoning, and expression skills • Opportunity to demonstrate knowledge of relationships • Gives information on how students process knowledge • Scoring can be subjective
3. Short written responses	• Mini-essays • Brief explanations of information or processes • Scoring more objective than for essays
4. Oral reports	• Assess student speaking ability • Similar to essay but more impromptu • Require acute listening skills to score
5. Teacher observation	• Informal • Best for process-oriented and nonachievement factors • Good when linked to interview • Teacher notes used to record observation results
6. Student self-assessment	• Most underused form of assessment • Helps develop higher-order metacognitive skills • Assessment conference allows student to clarify own level of learning
7. Performance tasks	• Require student to construct responses, apply knowledge • Require more than recall of information • Can assess a variety of forms of knowledge and skills • Scoring dependent on task

Source: Marzano, R. J. (2000). *Transforming classroom grading.* Alexandria, VA: Association for Supervision and Curriculum Development.

at Summit Primary School in Ohio is repeating kindergarten, not so much for academic reasons as for social ones. Dylan Todd was a young 5-year-old when he started kindergarten. A bright little boy living in a comfortable socioeconomic status (SES) home with adoring parents, Dylan experienced expected academic growth in his first year at Summit Primary. But, as his teacher observed, he was still quite immature at the end of his initial year in kindergarten. Teacher observation, as we see in Table 5.1, is particularly effective when assessing nonachievement factors. In consultation with Mom and Dad, the decision was made to have Dylan repeat kindergarten, this time in the enrichment class. In this group designed for children who have mastered a set of basic skills, Dylan is thriving.

PERFORMANCE ASSESSMENT.
The last of Marzano's seven forms of assessment involves performance. This simply means that students actually show what they know and can do in ways that do not solely involve paper-and-pencil tests. **Performance assessment** may be a project, a demonstration, a creation, or anything that requires the application of knowledge and skills. You may hear the terms *alternative assessment* and *authentic assessment* used interchangeably with performance assessment. **Alternative assessment** is assessment that doesn't fall within Marzano's first three categories. **Authentic assessment** means that students show what they know and can do in a real-life setting or situation. Performance assessment is alternative assessment and may also be authentic.

Forced choice, essay, and short written responses continue to dominate classroom assessment.

PORTFOLIO ASSESSMENT.
One way to put a variety of assessments together to reflect student learning is to use portfolios. To create a **portfolio,** students or teachers, or both, assemble a cohesive package of representative evidence of student learning. A portfolio may serve as

Watch a video featuring Dylan, his teacher Brandi Wade, and his mom and dad in the Teaching in Focus *section for* Chapter 5 *in MyEducationLab for this course.*

- A compilation of all the work a student does over a period of time. The student may feel a greater sense of accomplishment from reviewing a portfolio than from seeing individual assessments that are quickly discarded.
- A selected collection of work intended to show growth over time.
- A display tool for work samples that showcase the student's best work.

You are likely creating a portfolio, or will be soon, of products related to your education coursework. Your portfolio will show your professional growth. At some point your instructors will evaluate your portfolio and assign a grade that indicates your achievement.

ASSESSMENT OF 21ST-CENTURY KNOWLEDGE AND SKILLS

The Partnership for 21st Century Skills (2009) defines goals for assessment that reflect their philosophy and practical advice you have read about in each of the preceding chapters. They endorse assessment that

- Promotes balance, including both standardized assessment and classroom formative and summative assessment.
- Emphasizes the role of feedback as part of learning.
- Uses technology and measures student mastery of 21st-century skills.
- Includes development of portfolios.

Teaching in Focus

Brenda Beyal, Grades 3–5 Multiage Classroom, Rees Elementary School, Utah. *In her own words....*

What a wonderful, scary, exhilarating, confusing, demanding profession you have chosen. Wonderful because you spend it with children. Scary because you have to teach them to become literate, capable human beings. Exhilarating because your creative juices have a place to flourish. Confusing when students come with baggage and with very little room for instruction, practice, and evaluation. And, finally, demanding because it takes hard work, perseverance, and commitment. To help with your journey, I offer the following five bits of advice.

1. Be present in your classroom. Be intellectually, emotionally, and socially present in your room. Pay attention to the students, what they are saying and doing. Keep yourself present.

2. Search out colleagues who will nourish you and your profession. Find the teachers who aren't protective and territorial over their teaching. Search out the ones who share, don't compete, and have a philosophy similar to yours.

3. Continue learning, read education journals, subscribe to a professional publication, and read for pleasure.

4. Focus on student learning and not on your teaching. Teach to see students grasp ideas and come up with their own ideas. You may have delivered a lesson that was outstanding, uses all the bells and whistles and the correct language you have been taught, and still not reach a child. Focus on student learning.

5. Live a rich life. Children need teachers who experience, explore, and discover. Take vacations, learn to knit, do it.

Given all the possible ways to assess what students know and can do, it is important to create a balanced assessment plan for the classroom. Each assessment method has appropriate uses and each has limitations. Paying close attention to which assessment is appropriate and when will help ensure assessments align with curriculum, instructional strategies, and the needs of students. In *Teaching in Focus,* Brenda Beyal, one of our three focus teachers at Rees Elementary School in Utah, gives valuable advice about balance in teaching and the merits of focusing on student learning.

Points of Reflection 5.1

What forms of assessment do you remember from your K–12 experiences? Did you have preferences? If so, what aspects of the different assessments did you prefer? Why?

How Do Teachers Evaluate Student Learning and Assign Grades?

Now that we have discussed the purposes and forms of assessment, let's look at how we use assessment to evaluate student learning and, ultimately, assign grades. Recall that evaluating student achievement is one of the four purposes of assessment.

EVALUATION

The words *evaluation* and *assessment* are often used interchangeably, but they are not the same. Assessment is gathering evidence of student learning. **Evaluation** makes judgments about, and assigns values to, the results of assessments. For example, a student writes an essay about the effects of rail travel on the gold rush of the 1800s. The teacher uses the essay as an assessment of what the student learned in a unit on the events leading to the statehood of California. The assessment provides the evidence to evaluate the quality of student learning.

It is not necessary, or advisable, to evaluate all evidence of student learning. In our previous example, the teacher may assess the note-taking skills of the student by checking on the completeness of note cards the student filled out during research in the library (first formative assessment). This assessment and teacher feedback help the student make corrections in the research process and move forward with the project. The teacher may simply record a check in the grade book to indicate that student progress was assessed through an examination of note cards. There's no need to make an evaluation at this point. When the student submits an outline for approval, a second formative assessment occurs. Later the teacher may read through the essay rough draft and give feedback on it (third formative assessment), yet still not record an evaluation. In this scenario there are three formative assessments without evaluation. When the student turns in the completed essay, the teacher will use a rubric to do a summative assessment of this student's alternative performance, and then record an evaluation.

RUBRICS

One of the most productive innovations in assessment is the **rubric,** an assessment tool that makes explicit what is being assessed, lists characteristics of degrees of quality, and provides a rating scale to differentiate among these degrees. Rubrics add consistency to subjective evaluation and serve several distinct, yet related, purposes:

- Rubrics provide clear expectations for assignments. Therefore, they are instructional tools as well as assessment tools.
- Rubrics allow teachers to differentiate consistently among performance levels.
- Rubrics provide guidelines for student improvement.
- Rubrics make grading more transparent and consistent.

There are two basic types of rubrics. A **holistic rubric** uses one scale for an entire project. In Table 5.2 you can see that a student may receive a score of 0 to 5 according to the descriptor that most closely matches the work being assessed.

An **analytic rubric** specifies separate parts of an assessment task, product, or performance and the characteristics of various levels of success for each. An analytic rubric gives much more information than a holistic rubric. The sample analytic rubric in Table 5.3 could be used to evaluate a demonstration lesson you may create and deliver in a teacher preparation class.

Along with numbers for scoring, most rubrics include descriptors of what the numbers mean. For instance, on a 0 to 5 scale, the numbers may be interpreted as follows:

5 – Advanced		5 – Highly accomplished
4 – Proficient		4 – Developed
3 – Adequate	or	3 – Developing
2 – Basic		2 – Emerging
1 – Below basic		1 – Preparing to begin
0 – Not attempted		0 – Not attempted

TABLE 5.2 Sample holistic rubric

Score	Descriptor
5	Student clearly understands the assessment task and the product fulfills all the requirements accurately and completely.
4	Student understands most of the assessment task and the product fulfills the requirements.
3	Student understands just enough of the assessment task to fulfill most of the requirements.
2	Student has little understanding of the assessment task and fulfills a minimum of the requirements.
1	Student does not understand the assessment task and fulfills none of the requirements.
0	Student does not attempt the assessment task.

TABLE 5.3 Sample analytic rubric

Criterion	4	3	2	1	0
Topic choice	Relevant, interesting	Appropriate	Shallow, lacks interest	Very limited	Not appropriate
Planned assessment	Creative, matches instruction	Adequate and appropriate	Only addresses part of topic content/skills	Does not address topic	Not included
Standard(s) objective(s)	Appropriate, well written	Appropriate	Improperly written	Not appropriate	Not included
Lesson procedures	Clear, detailed, could be easily implemented by others	Clear and adequately detailed	Not detailed enough to be implemented by others	Unclear	Not included
Handout for class	Professional, detailed, few mechanical errors	Adequate detail, useful, few mechanical errors	Not enough detail, distracting mechanical errors	Not useful	Not included

Many Internet sites provide templates for the creation of rubrics for multiple content areas and performance tasks. To take advantage of all the benefits of using rubrics to evaluate classroom assessment tasks, products, and performances, teachers should

1. create rubrics for as many tasks as appropriate
2. explicitly teach students how to read and use rubrics
3. distribute rubrics when the task is explained or assigned
4. refer to the rubric when giving directions, answering questions, guiding students, and so on
5. provide samples of work (sometimes called anchors or **exemplars**) that fit the various criteria for scoring so that students actually see what a product that earns a particular number looks like
6. inform families about the use and benefits of rubrics as assessment tools so they will understand the evaluation criteria and know how to help guide their students

ASSIGNING GRADES

A **grade** is a judgment of assessment quality, or an evaluation, with a number attached to it. A student may receive a grade on an individual assignment, assessed using a rubric, as well as a grade at the end of what is sometimes called a grading period, for instance, a 9-week or semester time frame.

The wisdom of assigning grades has been questioned for decades by many who have viewed grades as harmful to student self-esteem and detrimental to progress (Powell, 2011). Even so, Marzano (2000) states that "Americans have a basic trust in the message that grades convey—so much so that grades have gone without challenge and are, in fact, highly resistant to challenge" (p. 1).

REASONS FOR GRADES. Perhaps the most compelling reason for grades is that they are expected by students, families, administrators, and the public in general. In *How to Grade for Learning*, O'Connor (2002) summarizes reasons for grading as follows:

1. Instructional uses: Clarify learning goals, pinpoint strengths and weaknesses, motivate
2. Communication uses: Inform students and parents about achievement

3. Administrative uses: Promotion, graduation, honors, eligibility
4. Guidance uses: Help students and parents make educational and vocational plans

GUIDELINES FOR GRADING. There are guidelines that assist teachers in making grades fair and accurate depictions of student learning, including:

1. Relate grading procedures to learning goals.
2. Relate grades to an individual's achievement on learning goals, not an individual's relative achievement to other students.
3. Grade individual achievement only.
4. Include a sampling of student work, not all work, in a student grade.
5. Update grades to reflect how much learning occurs by the end of the grading period, not a compilation of scores when topics were new.
6. Carefully arrive at a final grade by considering the method of averaging to be used and the significance of zeros.
7. Base all grades on quality assessments.
8. Involve students in the grading process whenever possible and appropriate. (O'Connor, 2002, pp. 243–244)

As you consider implementing classroom assessment, remember this mantra: "Teach what you test; test what you teach." Return often to the four purposes of assessment discussed earlier in this chapter.

What Are Standardized Tests, and How Are Their Results Used?

A **standardized test** is one that is given to multiple groups of students, designed for specific grade levels, and typically repeated annually. These tests are administered and scored under controlled conditions, and their exact content is unknown to everyone except the test makers before they are administered.

Let's begin by comparing standardized tests and standards-based tests. A **standards-based test** is one that is devised according to the content of a specific set of standards. For instance, state standardized tests are also standards based because state content standards are addressed in the writing of the test items. But to say a test is standardized doesn't necessarily mean it's standards based. The content may be derived from textbooks or various curriculum guides but not necessarily from a specific set of standards.

In the previous section we discussed ongoing classroom assessment in varied formats that provides a broad view of learning over time. In contrast, standardized tests and their results tend to be more isolated snapshots of learning. These are often termed **high-stakes tests**—standardized tests that have far-reaching consequences, sometimes referred to as high-stakes consequences. A single test administered in one format once a year is very different from ongoing classroom assessment.

STANDARDIZED TESTS IN THE UNITED STATES

Standardized tests are given in some form in every public school in the United States. Let's explore four broad categories.

TRENDS IN INTERNATIONAL MATHEMATICS AND SCIENCE STUDY. As the only international test that compares students worldwide, the **Trends in International**

Mathematics and Science Study (TIMSS) has been administered every 4 years since 1995. In general, the TIMSS test

- provides achievement data to show trends in performance over time
- fosters public accountability
- allows achievement comparisons among countries

In 2007, 36 countries administered the TIMSS test to sample populations of fourth graders and 48 countries administered the TIMSS test to sample populations of eighth graders. Note that the conditions under which the TIMSS exams are given are not tightly regulated. Some nations do not follow the appropriate guidelines for randomly selecting students. Here are some highlights from the most recent administration of the test.

- The average mathematics score of U.S. fourth graders was higher than those in 23 of the 35 other countries.
- The average mathematics score of U.S. eighth graders was higher than those in 37 of the 47 other countries.
- The average U.S. fourth grade science score was higher than those in 25 of the 35 other countries.
- The average U.S. eighth grade science score was higher than those in 35 of the 47 other countries.
- Both U.S. fourth and eighth graders improved in mathematics in 2007 compared to 1995.
- Neither U.S. fourth nor eighth graders showed any detectable change in science achievement in 2007 compared to 1995.
- All of the countries scoring higher than U.S. students in both fourth and eighth grade were Asian or European. (National Center for Education Statistics [NCES], 2010)

NATIONAL ASSESSMENT OF EDUCATIONAL PROGRESS. Often called the nation's report card, the **National Assessment of Educational Progress (NAEP)** is the only standardized test systematically administered to a sampling of students across the United States. The NAEP is administered to fourth, eighth, and twelfth graders in math, reading, writing, science, history, economics, geography, civics, foreign language, and a variety of the arts. The grade levels and subjects are rotated so that not every subject is assessed in every grade each year. The results are not reported by student, school, or district but only by race, grade level, and state. The NAEP

- allows for the achievement tracking of students at specific grade levels over time, both nationally and by individual states
- provides a basis for state-to-state comparisons
- allows for results tracking for a particular subject area and for comparisons among subject areas

Scores on the NAEP are divided into three categories: basic (partial mastery), proficient (solid performance on grade-level content/skills), and advanced (superior). Unfortunately, many students do not even achieve at the basic level. With a few exceptions, scores on the NAEP have remained about the same over the years. One exception occurred in 2005, when fourth and eighth grade math scores were the highest since NAEP testing began in 1969. However, in all subject areas except reading, the percentage of twelfth graders at the proficient and advanced levels is consistently lower than the corresponding percentage for fourth and eighth graders. Over the years, scores at all grade levels in social science subjects such as history, civics, and geography have been lower than the scores in other areas. In all subjects, significant gaps remain between the scores of white students and those of African American, Hispanic, and Native American students (NCES, 2006).

GENERAL STANDARDIZED TESTS. Mandatory testing of students using standardized tests has existed for decades. The most frequently administered general standardized tests include the California Achievement Test (CAT), the Comprehensive Test of Basic Skills (CTBS), the Iowa Test of Basic Skills (ITBS), the Metropolitan Achievement Test (MAT), and the Stanford Achievement Test (SAT). Chances are, you've taken one or more of these tests multiple times.

Many nationally published standardized tests provide detailed score reports for individual students that serve diagnostic purposes when studied by teachers. If given annually, it's possible to track a student's progress in a variety of content and skill areas within a subject.

A major thrust of national standardized tests involves comparing students, both individually and in groups. Comparison is possible because the tests are **norm referenced,** meaning that they are administered to a group of students selected because they represent a cross section of students. The scores of these representative students become the norm against which all other students are compared. Students receive percentile rankings. For instance, if Enrique's reading comprehension performance on the MAT is 78%, this means that 78% of students in his grade-level norm group scored lower than he did, and 22% scored higher.

Two important concepts of standardized assessment are validity and reliability. **Validity** means that an assessment measures what it is intended to measure. Think about how backward design has the potential to increase validity. If desired learning results are known by the test makers, the assessment will likely measure what it's supposed to measure. **Reliability** means that an assessment yields a pattern of results that is repeated and consistent over time. Makers of standardized tests expend much effort to ensure validity and reliability and to assure the users of the tests that both of these critical components are in place.

STATE STANDARDS-BASED STANDARDIZED TESTS. The newest category of standardized tests in the United States is the standards-based test, with items based on state standards. All 50 states now have their own tests based on specific state standards and usually administered at a minimum to students in third through eighth grade. This widespread use of standards-based tests resulted from the No Child Left Behind Act of 2001, a reauthorization of the Elementary and Secondary Education Act. In the first decade of the 21st century, NCLB dramatically changed the public education landscape in the United States in a number of ways, notably in the area of assessment.

Test results in some states are not reported in ways that are useful to teachers as they make instructional decisions. For instance, many state tests simply place students in one of four categories, such as below basic, basic, proficient, and advanced. These types of results do not provide information about performance within a particular subject area. In science, for example, the tests do not reveal whether students lack understanding in earth science, biological science, or both. In other words, the results are evaluative and summative, not educative. "Educative feedback is immediate, relevant, and useful, and it promotes student learning" (Reeves, 2004, p. 9). Teachers and other educators have expressed disappointment that many state standards-based tests do not provide educative feedback.

State standards-based assessments are high-stakes tests because there may be drastic consequences associated with inadequate results. For instance, the results are used to make decisions about funding and human resources, which students are promoted or held back, and who graduates and who doesn't (Stiggins, 2001). States threaten (and sometimes follow through) to close schools, dismiss principals and teachers, and then reopen schools with new staffing and perhaps new programs. This chapter's *In the News* examines the high-stakes consequences in Florida, where large numbers of children and adolescents are repeating grade levels or not graduating from high school because of low scores on the Florida Comprehensive Assessment Test (FCAT).

This chapter's *Letter to the Editor* revolves around the CSAP, the Colorado Student Assessment Program. The principal of a middle school made the decision to have two assemblies before the test was administered, one for eighth graders and one for sixth and seventh graders. Not so unusual, except that all the students in the assemblies were African American. The African American students of Morey Middle School make up about 25% of the total population. An article addressing the assemblies appeared in the *Denver Post* and is shown in Figure 5.3. Read the article carefully before reading the Letter to the Editor. Then respond with your own letter, using the questions to help guide your writing.

In the News abc NEWS

The Test

High-stakes testing has become a way of life for students in U.S. schools. The state of Florida, during the governorship of Jeb Bush, has taken the consequences of this testing to extremes, as explained in this ABC video. Large numbers of students are being required to repeat grade levels or do not graduate from high school based on the results of a snapshot of their learning taken through the lens of the Florida Comprehensive Assessment Test, the FCAT. We hear proponents of the strict use of test results acknowledge that the test won't fix the ills in the schools but will clarify how bad the problems actually are.

To view this video, go to the In the News section of Chapter 5 on MyEducationLab for this text and watch the clip *The Test*. Think about our discussion of standardized testing, and then respond to these questions.

1. We hear a parent say of students that the FCAT and subsequent use of the results "takes the wind out of their sails." And then we hear a counselor say that the tests are "deflating." What do they mean by these statements?

2. In the Little Havana section of Miami, 98% of the children are on free or reduced lunch. Most live in homes where English is not the primary language spoken. How might these facts skew the percentages of students who are not promoted based on FCAT results?

3. We hear Marie talk about the fact that she works hard in school to earn a 2.8 grade point average and yet cannot graduate because of her FCAT scores. What is your opinion of this situation?

4. Stephanie asks a pertinent question in the video. She wants to know whether the large number of students failing the FCAT might indicate there is something wrong with the schools and the curriculum, not just a lack of student achievement. How would you answer Stephanie's question?

5. Governor Bush says there are some positive results of this stricter use of test results and that students who couldn't read before are now doing so. The state is providing multiple opportunities for students to get extra help and retake the tests. What suggestions do you have for how to turn what appears to be primarily a negative issue into one with promise and hope for success?

Figure 5.3 Article in the *Denver Post*

Pep talk for black students raises eyebrows

By Allison Sherry
Denver Post Staff Writer
March 20, 2007

Before students at Morey Middle School took CSAP tests this year, school administrators pulled all the African-American students into two assemblies and told them that, as a whole, they were not performing as well as their peers at the school. The sixth-, seventh- and eighth-graders were told that the school's principal and assistant principal care about them and that they wanted to hear from them about what they could do to help.

This has sparked controversy at the Denver middle school, where some parents say the achievement gap is so dramatic that drastic conversations such as this must take place. Others, though, decry the assemblies as inappropriate and insensitive because they unfairly single out students by their skin color. "The students were made to feel like they were worse than the white kids," said Stacey DeKraker, whose daughter was at the assembly. "If even one of the students got that message, was it worth it?"

Morey principal Dori Claunch, who has spoken with DeKraker about her concerns, said she decided to call the assembly after winter break because she noticed that black students were lagging behind other ethnic groups at the school.

College fair also broached

Fifty-three percent of African-American sixth-graders at the school are proficient readers. Among white sixth-graders, that number is 89 percent. "The idea of the assembly wasn't just to talk about how African-American kids aren't performing well," Claunch said. "We wanted to talk to our

African-American students to let them know we care about them and to let them know they have the best opportunity at Morey." She said she also talked to the eighth-graders about attending a college fair.

Of the roughly 773 students at the school, 24 percent are African-American, and 51 percent are white. Twenty percent of the students are Latino.

"I think it's necessary"

Claunch said several Morey children—in all ethnic groups—are not meeting the school's student-achievement expectations and that the school has interventions for these students. These include "DPS Success," a tutoring program offered before the Colorado Student Assessment Program tests, as well as giving students who are below grade level in reading and math a double dose of those core subjects during the school day.

Claunch, and her assistant principal, Gwen Victor, didn't pull out students from other ethnic groups for an assembly. And that is fine, said Tracey Peters, who has two children at Morey. "I think it's necessary. I'm sorry if our students are being targeted, but when a large group of our students fails to achieve, then drastic measures must be taken," said Peters, who is a member of the school's African-American parent-advisory council. "We can't ignore the problem because it makes us feel uncomfortable."

Must be explained well

Lawrence Borom, head of Denver Public Schools' Black Education Advisory Council, said pulling students out based on race isn't wrong, but it must be explained well. "If you don't let people know what you're doing, if you don't explain it to people, it can be misinterpreted," Borom said. "You have to make sure parents know what's going on, and the message is correct."

DeKraker said she wished she would have known about the assemblies in advance because she would have pulled her daughter out of school that day. "She struggles in school," DeKraker said. "Does she need to be reminded of that in an assembly?"

Source: Reprinted with permission of the *Denver Post.*

Letter to the Editor

This letter appeared in the *Denver Post*. It was written by Dr. Thomas D. Russell, a professor of law at the University of Denver. He is responding to the article reprinted in Figure 5.3 about the assemblies for African American students at Morey Middle School in Denver.

PRINCIPAL'S CSAP PEP TALK FOR BLACK STUDENTS

Re: "Pep talk for black students raises eyebrows," March 20 news story.

However well-intentioned Morey Middle School principal Dori Claunch may have been, her decision to segregate her African-American students in order to deliver a CSAP pep talk may have had an effect exactly opposite to what she intended.

Some years ago, Stanford psychologist Claude Steele discovered that when subjected to racial stereotyping, students perform less well on standardized tests. In one experiment, Professor Steele separated white *male Stanford undergraduates into two groups. He told one group that the exam would compare their math skills to Asian students. He said no such thing to the other group. After testing, those white students who had been subjected to the racial stereotype in advance of testing scored lower than the other group. He found the same results with other racial groups including African-Americans.*

The performance gap between students of different races, ethnicities or genders is not attributable solely to such stereotyping, of course. Nonetheless, my prediction would be that Ms. Claunch's pep talk had the unintended effect of lowering the CSAP scores of Morey's African-American students.

Thomas D. Russell, Denver

Now it's your turn. The information about the assemblies and the various perspectives expressed in the *Denver Post* article provide the context for Dr. Russell's letter. Consider this information along with these questions as you formulate your own letter.

(continued)

1. Dr. Russell talks about research that he feels applies to this incident. Does his conclusion make sense to you? Why or why not?

2. The principal knew the history of the performance of many African American students on the CSAP test. She wanted the students to know that she and the staff cared about them and their success. Do you think this justifies the assemblies? Why or why not?

3. The article does not reveal that both assemblies were actually led by African Americans, one by a teacher and one by the assistant principal. What, if any, influence does this fact have on your opinion of the assemblies? Do you think this knowledge might have influenced the letter writer's stance?

Your letter to the editor should be in response to the *Denver Post* letter—supporting it, adding information, or refuting it. Write your letter in understandable terminology, remembering that readers of newspaper letters to the editor are citizens who may have limited knowledge of school practices and policies. Remember to refer to the letter assessment rubric in Chapter 1.

THE GOOD, THE BAD, AND THE UGLY OF STANDARDIZED TESTING

Many educators, parents, concerned citizens, and others loudly criticize standardized testing, particularly state standards-based standardized testing practices. Among the most well-known critics are James Popham, Susan Ohanion, Alfie Kohn, Anne Lewis, Richard Stiggins, and David Sadker. Critics of current standardized testing practices are not against assessments that are well-constructed tools for improving instruction. Their criticisms are directed at certain current practices. We hear them say, in essence, "You can't fatten cattle by weighing them," meaning that testing alone won't result in more learning. Alfie Kohn's (2000) criticism is graphically portrayed when he likens standardized testing to a horror movie monster that swells and mutates and threatens to swallow schools whole (p. 60).

In a series of focus groups in 2003, Public Agenda, an education watchdog organization, asked questions about accountability issues. The groups of teachers, parents, students, employers, and professors all overwhelmingly responded that using one test to judge what and how much is learned has questionable merit. They agreed that basing high-stakes consequences on the results of a single test is not appropriate (Johnson & Duffet, 2003). High-stakes consequences for those accountable for learning are attached to the results of most standardized tests, even while the tests are considered by many to be narrow measures of learning.

There's an adage that says, "What we measure, we do." This means that assessment often drives progress—and the curriculum. With test-based accountability and high-stakes consequences, this is probably inevitable. As long as assessments address a solid standards-based curriculum, it may be acceptable for testing to drive the curriculum. However, this approach has some problems. Often what gets tested gets taught, and little else. For instance, announcements of which subjects will be tested at which grade levels influence how teachers allocate time, often leading them to exclude valuable curricular components for the sake of test preparation. In elementary schools in states where only math and language arts are tested, social studies and science are often relegated to 30 minutes or less in late afternoon. This practice leaves obvious holes in the curriculum to which students are exposed. The consequences of ignoring standards that are not tested show up in later grades when students lack prior knowledge upon which the curriculum may depend. Do you recall the discussion of the null curriculum in Chapter 4? What *isn't* taught can have far-reaching consequences.

Figure 5.4 contains statements about the good and the bad of standardized testing. Of course, the statements don't apply to all tests, just as the statements don't paint a complete picture. The issues are much too complex to be examined adequately in a chart. For our purposes, however, Figure 5.4 serves as an overview.

Figure 5.4 Pros and cons of standardized testing

Standardized testing is a *positive* component of public education in the United States because

- many tests align with acknowledged learning goals (standards) and measure progress toward those goals
- administering the same test to large numbers of students allows for comparisons to be made and resources to be allotted where they are most needed
- standardized tests are cost effective because they are administered and scored uniformly
- without testing on a grand scale there is no way to make sure schools and teachers are doing the jobs they are assigned

Standardized testing is a *negative* component of public education in the United States because

- the results are often misused, with consequences that are out of line with the relative importance or meaningfulness of the scores
- the tests are often poorly constructed, with items that are not grade-level or subject-area appropriate
- standardized testing often reduces the curriculum by requiring teachers to concentrate on what is tested and eliminate what is not
- inadequate evidence is available to show a correlation between raising scores on state standardized tests and learning as reflected on the NAEP, ACT, SAT, or other nationally published standardized tests
- test-taking skills have an undetermined effect on raising scores, making increased learning a questionable result of better scores
- low-income, mostly minority, students predictably score below students with higher socioeconomic status, validating the opinion that the tests may actually test what's learned, or not, outside school
- teachers generally support standards, but undue pressure from high-stakes standardized tests can undermine productivity
- standardized tests don't measure important concepts such as cooperation, creativity, and flexibility

The purpose of considering the good and bad, or the pros and cons, of standardized testing is to develop a sense of balance. Standardized tests serve several positive purposes, as we have seen. Do they serve these purposes adequately? Maybe not. Can we "fatten cattle simply by weighing them"? No. But used reasonably and as one of several indicators, standardized tests can inform us about instruction that is successful, as well as where improvement is needed. Once again, balance is the best approach.

Now that we've looked at the good and the bad, let's briefly touch on some of the ugly aspects of standardized testing. This will give you perspective on the fact that, as with any widespread program, abuses can occur unless management at all levels is both vigilant and consistent. Susan Ohanion, an often published outspoken critic of standardized testing, refers to the following examples as "weirder and more vicious" than anything she could make up (2003, p. 739).

- Tenth graders in one state take a math exam required for high school graduation that consists of items too tough for graduate engineering students.
- In one state, a third grade teacher complained about how difficult certain items were for her students, and then she discovered the items were subsequently moved to the seventh grade test.
- Parents in one state were told that only 6 of 90,000 students tested received top marks in writing. Is it possible that the other 89,994 students somehow missed out on writing instruction that would lead them to achieve high scores on an appropriately leveled test?
- In one school, teachers were pulled out of their regular classroom to drill low-scoring students full time while the other students were left with aides, deprived of their teachers.

Points of Reflection 5.2

Did you approach standardized tests in grades K–12 with confidence? Or did you feel anxious and intimidated on test days? Recalling your own reactions to high-stakes testing will help you approach this fact of life with understanding in your own classroom.

- In one state where tests are given in October, teachers stay with their students from the previous year until tests are completed, rather than beginning a new school year in August with a new group of students.
- Some states find ways to actually push students out of school on their 16th birthday if they perform poorly on tests so they won't adversely affect school scores.

Standardized testing is not going away. Recognizing that reality, and making classrooms positive places in spite of testing pressures, is the challenge facing us in this age of accountability. Classroom teachers can take the reality of standardized testing and use it in beneficial ways by

- modeling mature and reasoned responses to the assessments
- encouraging positive attitudes in colleagues and students
- teaching students that life is full of challenges we may not like or agree with, but that we must meet head on with our best efforts

TEST-TAKING PREPARATION

"Teaching to the test" is a phrase almost always viewed negatively. Stop and think for a moment. If the test is a good one that aligns with standards and contains reasonable questions, then teaching to it is a positive thing. "Teaching to the test" means emphasizing particular content and format. There's nothing inherently wrong with this if the practice doesn't limit the curriculum more narrowly than the standards or inhibit the implementation of a variety of engaging instructional practices. However, these are big ifs and may constitute pitfalls in the name of accountability.

Test preparation is an expectation. However, "many teachers . . . experience a disconnect between their vision of a challenging and rewarding career and the day-to-day grind of test preparation" (Renzulli, Gentry, & Reis, 2004). It doesn't have to be this way. Creative teachers are able to weave test-preparation strategies throughout a rich curriculum and engaging instruction in ways that benefit students and expand their learning. Here are some examples of appropriate strategies.

- Practicing the format of a standardized test increases students' chances of success. If students are familiar with the way the test looks and the way answer choices are arranged on the answer sheet, the possibility of non-content-related errors is reduced, and the test itself becomes a more accurate assessment of student knowledge and skills. For instance, if students are accustomed to listening to directions and working in silence, test day will not seem quite so extraordinary.
- If an anticipated test is in multiple-choice format, it's a good idea to occasionally provide classroom assessments in multiple-choice format.
- If short written response items are anticipated, teaching students to compose succinct, logical answers to prompts should be part of a teacher's instructional strategies.
- Almost every state provides practice materials that supposedly align with their state tests. Districts and individual schools often purchase commercially produced materials designed to prepare students for standardized tests and make them available to teachers, or even mandate that they be used. If used on a limited basis, this practice is acceptable.

Focus teacher Deirdre McGrew has difficulty accepting the impact of standardized testing on students in the Cario Middle School CARE program. Read about her dilemma in *Diversity Dialogue*.

DIVERSITY DIALOGUE

You met Deirdre Huger-McGrew in *Meet the Focus Teachers and Students.* She teaches language arts and social studies for 3 hours a day to a special group of students who generally work below grade level. As one of two teachers in the Cario Middle School Academic Recovery and Enrichment program (CARE) in Mt. Pleasant, South Carolina, Deirdre has some major concerns about how standardized assessment impacts her students in the CARE program. Deirdre's students have not experienced academic success in school. Most have at some point been diagnosed with a learning disability or have been designated as low achievers. These are the kids on the low end of the academic diversity spectrum. In Deirdre's interview she tells us that her goal is for her students to work at grade level.

Deirdre believes her students are capable of much more than annual standardized tests reveal. When she works one on one with them she sees understanding and conceptual knowledge that multiple-choice questions don't adequately measure. But the students must take the annual state standardized tests just the same. Almost without exception they score in the below basic category in all subjects. Deirdre knows that part of her job is to prepare the CARE students for the annual tests. She doesn't believe in constant drill and practice but knows the students need to be exposed to as much of the content of the standards as possible.

Respond to these items by writing one well-developed paragraph for each.

1. Why is it especially important for Deirdre to know the standards inside and out? With what you know about planning for instruction, how might she link language arts and social studies in meaningful ways for her students?

2. What test preparation strategies do you recommend for the students in the CARE program? Explain your choices.

3. What role might Deirdre's belief in the abilities of the CARE students play in their level of success on standardized assessment?

Who Is Accountable for Student Learning?

When *A Nation at Risk* was published in 1983 by the National Commission on Excellence in Education (a commission appointed by President Reagan), America's public schools were painted as inadequate. Too many students were dropping out or graduating without basic literacy and math skills. People began asking who should be held responsible for student learning or the lack of it. Who should ask, "And how are the children? Are they all well?" and accept responsibility for the answer?

Students have the choice of listening, participating, behaving, and learning—or not. Given the finest and most equitable opportunities and full support from home, students should be held **accountable** for their own learning. And they are. Teachers grade them, and much of their future success rests on their school accomplishments. But students have very different starting positions when it comes to learning. Some have built-in family and community support and advantages, but others do not.

Parents and families bear a share of the accountability burden. If students are not supported in terms of adequate shelter and food, encouragement to value education, and physical and emotional surroundings conducive to studying, then families are not doing their part to promote student learning.

The adults who spend the most time with students outside the home are their teachers. Few teachers would ever deny that they are accountable, but most will be quick to add they are not alone in their accountability. They expect their principals to support their efforts in every way possible, as well as the other adults in the lives of students. Teacher evaluations often include their students' score reports from year to year. The days of assuming a teacher is effective based on pleasant personality or self-declaration of competency are over. It has become absolutely necessary for teachers to follow a curriculum that is standards based. If student scores on state standards-based standardized tests are not acceptable, or at least improving, then teachers do not meet expectations.

Local school districts and school boards are also accountable for student learning because they make financial, programmatic, and personnel decisions that affect schools and classrooms.

Communities are accountable for student learning. If financial support of schools and a fundamental respect for education are not present, then communities are failing to accept their portion of accountability. Elected representatives of communities—legislators, members of city councils, mayors, governors—all play roles in accountability because they are responsible for policies that either promote or thwart student learning.

State and federal governments share in accountability for student learning. Both levels of government pass laws and deliver mandates that directly affect schools.

So we see that "Who's accountable?" may be answered, "All of us." In other words, "And how are the children? Are they all well?" should be asked and answered over and over by everyone in the United States.

Levels of school governance and education funding are addressed in Chapter 11.

Points of Reflection 5.3

Who bears the heaviest load of accountability for student learning? If you do not believe only one group is totally responsible, explain your view of balance with regard to accountability.

CONCLUDING THOUGHTS

In today's educational and political environment, accountability for student learning falls most heavily on teachers and schools. Whether student learning occurs, and to what degree, may be gauged by classroom tests. For the sake of coordination of state and national goals, a standardized system is necessary. Both classroom and standardized assessment results should guide the decisions teachers make every day in terms of curriculum and instruction. It is important to see the big picture of teaching and learning that involves the interconnectedness of assessment, curriculum, and instruction. Given that, a great deal of work is required to create a fair and equitable system that does not stifle imaginative teaching and learning and that yields results teachers can use to make the very best instructional decisions.

We began this chapter by looking at assessment through the practices of Renee Ayers at Summit Primary School in Ohio. Now as the chapter comes to an end we join Renee as she decides to use portfolio assessment in her second grade class. Read through *Chapter in Review* to help refresh your memory of what we have discussed, and then interact with Renee as she plans for portfolio assessment in *Developing Professional Competence*.

To hear about and see Renee's classroom organizational scheme, go to her room tour in Teaching in Focus for Chapter 5 in MyEducationLab for this course.

Chapter in Review

What is involved in classroom assessment?

- The four major purposes of classroom assessment are to monitor student progress, make instructional decisions, evaluate student achievement, and evaluate programs.

- The three major kinds of assessment are diagnostic, formative, and summative.

- The seven basic forms of assessment are forced choice, essays, short written responses, oral reports, performance tasks, teacher observation, and student self-assessment.

- Both performance and portfolio assessment provide information on what students know and can do.

- 21st-century assessment promotes balance, includes feedback, uses technology, and encourages portfolio development.

How do teachers evaluate student learning and assign grades?

- To evaluate is to make judgments about quality and quantity.

- Rubrics are instructional and assessment tools that make expectations explicit.
- A grade is an evaluation with a number attached to it.

What are standardized tests, and how are their results used?

- Most standardized tests are high-stakes tests.
- The Trends in International Mathematics and Science Study compares student achievement among countries.
- The National Assessment of Educational Progress is called the nation's report card because it allows comparisons to be made among states.

- State standardized tests are also standards based.
- There are both benefits and drawbacks to standardized testing.
- There are appropriate ways to prepare students for standardized tests in addition to providing a rigorous and standards-based curriculum.

Who is accountable for student learning?

- Teachers, principals, and schools bear much of the burden of accountability.
- Families, the government, and local and state administration are often viewed as less accountable for student learning.

Developing Professional Competence

Visit the Developing Professional Competence section in Chapter 5 of the MyEducationLab for this text to answer the following questions and begin your preparation for licensure exams.

In the Teaching in Focus opening segment of this chapter you read about Renee Ayers's focus on using assessment as an avenue for growth for her second grade students. She understands the value of keeping track of growth over time. In her classroom, Renee has a filing system that allows her to conference conveniently with parents about their child's progress. With all these measures in place, Renee is ready to employ portfolio assessment in more formal ways with her students at Summit Primary School in Ohio.

Think through this scenario and answer the following multiple-choice questions:

1. Renee is most likely planning to use portfolios to
   a. Display each student's best products
   b. Substitute for traditional report card grades
   c. Primarily teach students how to be organized
   d. Show student growth over time

2. Knowing Renee as we do leads us to predict that compiling work will be done by
   a. Students alone to teach organizational skills
   b. Renee and students working together
   c. Renee alone because she knows which pieces best accomplish the purposes of portfolio assessment
   d. Renee, in conjunction with Principal Laura Hill

3. Given what you know about Summit Primary School, how will Principal Laura Hill get the word out to all the other second grade teachers in the district if Renee's experiment with portfolio assessment is successful?
   a. Ask Renee to explain what she experienced and her perceptions of results in a faculty meeting
   b. Report Renee's success in a district principal's meeting
   c. Invite all the district second grade teachers to a special portfolio showcase event at Summit Primary
   d. Ask Renee to write about her experiences for the district educator newsletter

Now it's time for you to respond to two short essay items involving Renee and portfolio assessment. Your responses should each be between one half and one double-spaced page.

4. Given what you know about Renee and her classroom practices, why is portfolio assessment the next logical step for her?

5. Consider the NBPTS Core Proposition 3, which says "Accomplished teachers . . . employ multiple methods for measuring student growth and understanding and can clearly explain student performance to parents." Explain how Renee's plan addresses this standard.

Where
DO I Stand NOW?

In the beginning of this chapter you completed an inventory that gauged where you stood concerning assessment. Now that you have read the chapter, completed exercises related to the content, engaged in class discussions, and so on, answer the following questions in your course notebook.

1. What have you learned that will make assessment in your future classroom more fair and accurate than what you experienced in K–12 school? Briefly explain.

2. How will you establish assessment balance in your classroom? What assessment strategies appeal to you most? Which of these strategies did you experience in K–12 school?

MyEducationLab

The MyEducationLab for this course can help you solidify your comprehension of Chapter 5 concepts.

- Explore the classrooms of the teachers and students you've met in this chapter in the Teaching in Focus section.

- Prepare for licensure exams as you deepen your understanding of chapter concepts in the Developing Professional Competence section.

- Gauge and further develop your understanding of chapter concepts by taking the quizzes and examining the enrichment materials on the Chapter 5 Study Plan.

- Visit Topic 8, "Assessment, Standards and Accountability," to watch ABC videos, explore Assignments and Activities, and practice essential teaching skills with the Building Teaching Skills and Dispositions unit.

6 Creating and Maintaining a Positive and Productive Learning Environment

It's not too soon to begin thinking about the learning environment you want to create in your future classroom as you continue your journey toward becoming a teacher. In this chapter we explore answers to these questions:

✦ How do teachers create a positive learning environment?

✦ What routines contribute to maintaining a productive classroom environment?

✦ How do teachers establish expectations, incentives, and consequences?

✦ How can I develop a classroom management plan?

Before beginning our discussion, explore your experiences with the learning environment and your opinions about creating and maintaining a positive and productive classroom by completing the inventory *Where Do I Stand?*

Where DO I Stand?

This inventory will help you think about your own experiences in K–12 school regarding the learning environment. As you consider each item, you may have memories from most of your years in grades K to 12 that align with the statement or you may have never experienced what is described, and various shades in between. Use the 0 to 4 scale to indicate the frequency of your experiences. There are no wrong answers, just differing experiences. *Following the inventory are directions for how to organize your responses and what they may indicate in terms of where you stand.*

4 Most or all of my experiences
3 Many of my experiences
2 Maybe half of my experiences
1 Only a few of my experiences
0 I don't recall this as part of my experiences

_____ **1.** My classrooms were pleasant environments.

_____ **2.** My teachers attempted to decorate my classrooms in appealing ways.

_____ **3.** I remember classrooms with couches or chairs that students were allowed to use for reading or working together.

_____ **4.** My teachers had plants and/or small animals in my classrooms.

_____ **5.** Seating arrangements were flexible and changed to match what was planned in the classroom.

_____ **6.** There were interesting things displayed in my classrooms.

_____ **7.** There were colorful and appealing posters and displays.

_____ **8.** Student work was displayed in the classroom.

_____ **9.** It was obvious that teachers were caring individuals.

_____ **10.** My teachers made a point to develop relationships with students.

_____ **11.** Teachers talked informally with students before, during, and after class.

_____ **12.** Teachers knew and used student names.

_____ **13.** I felt a sense of trust among teachers and students.

_____ **14.** Teachers appeared glad to see students.

_____ **15.** Teachers accepted students for who they were rather than what they did.

_____ **16.** Teachers seemed to have "eyes in the back of their heads" in the classroom.

_____ **17.** Teachers used time wisely in classes.

_____ **18.** Classroom routines were in place.

_____ **19.** Materials were readily available in classrooms.

_____ **20.** Transitions between classes were relatively orderly.

_____ **21.** Rest room and water passes worked smoothly.

_____ **22.** I understood behavior guidelines in my classrooms.

_____ **23.** My teachers kept off-task behaviors from interrupting learning.

_____ **24.** My teachers were able to prevent cheating.

_____ 25. Fighting and violence among students was minimal and not disruptive.

_____ 26. Students and teachers treated each other with respect.

_____ 27. My classrooms were places where order ruled.

_____ 28. Teachers were the authorities in my classrooms.

_____ 29. My teachers used praise wisely to motivate students.

_____ 30. My teachers provided appropriate incentives for students to behave.

_____ 31. My teachers gave incentives that led to productive behavior.

_____ 32. My teachers were fair as they accomplished classroom management.

_____ 33. Teachers handled discipline problems without administrative intervention.

_____ 34. School property was treated respectfully.

_____ 35. My teachers were consistent and impartial when dealing with behavior problems.

_____ 36. My teachers followed through with discipline procedures rather than just making idle threats.

Now add all your responses and divide by 36 to get an average.

_____ sum

_____ sum divided by 36

If your average is between 3 and 4, your K–12 experiences with the learning environment were positive and productive.

If your average is 2.5 to 3, your K–12 experiences with the learning environment were mostly positive.

If your average is 1.5 to 2.5, your K–12 experiences with the learning environment were less than positive overall.

If your average is less than 1.5, you have very little experience with a positive, productive learning environment.

What memories did this inventory bring back to you? Look at the items you marked with 2, 1, or 0. Do you see a pattern of teacher actions or circumstances that did not promote positive and productive classrooms? Explain.

Teaching in Focus

When Jeff walked into Tim Mendenhall's multiage classroom at Rees Elementary School, Utah, in late September, he had one of those "I don't want to be here" looks. His entrance was more of a shuffle than a walk, and his demeanor was obvious to other students as well as to Mr. Mendenhall. Jeff had just moved to Spanish Fork from Los Angeles. He was 12 and entering fifth grade for the second time. Tim sensed that Jeff would prove to be quite a challenge. When it was time for the third, fourth, and fifth graders in Tim's multiage class to go out for recess, Tim asked Jeff to spend the time with him so they could get to know each other. Jeff's first words were "Why do I have to be in here with all these babies?"

Fortunately for Jeff he had come to a school and a homeroom with structure, and a teacher with a classroom management philosophy that responds to students as individuals. Tim applies a theory that might be called game therapy. He believes in playing with kids—on the field and in the classroom. He tells us, "If you earn the kids' respect by being respectful, consistent, and fun, there are few problems. If you make learning enjoyable and meaningful, then students stay on task and want to be with you. Wanting to learn, wanting to be with you, and wanting to do whatever you have planned is motivation enough to behave."

Tim had his work cut out for him. Jeff had no intention of joining in. The first week or so he sat silently and sullenly. He resisted any kind of group work and refused to take part in classroom and outside games until Tim tossed a basketball his way. He threw it back. Tim shot at the basket and missed. Jeff picked up the ball, made the basket, and grinned. That's all Tim needed to plan his strategy. Back in the classroom he placed a three-ring binder filled with basketball player cards on Jeff's table.

Jeff had the potential to be very disruptive to the classroom community Tim had so carefully built. By being sensitive and purposeful, Tim was able to avoid power struggles and give Jeff a behavioral comfort level. Although behavior didn't become a problem, Jeff continues to struggle academically. That's the challenge Tim faces daily. However, Tim has cleared a major hurdle because he has won Jeff's respect and Jeff wants to be with him.

Watch an interview with Tim Mendenhall and a lesson in his classroom in the Teaching in Focus section for Chapter 6 in MyEducationLab for this course.

How Do Teachers Create a Positive Learning Environment?

Creating and maintaining a positive and productive learning environment is complex and compelling—complex because there are multiple variables to consider, and compelling because without a positive and productive learning environment, teaching has little effect. New and experienced teachers alike are often puzzled by the whole process. They sometimes think of the learning environment in narrow terms of student cooperation and student misbehavior. But the learning environment is so much more. When teachers expand their view to include the elements discussed in this chapter, it becomes clear that creating and maintaining a positive and productive learning environment is indeed a puzzle, one with many interlocking pieces that depend on one another to form a complete, stable picture. Some of the most important pieces of the puzzle are shown in Figure 6.1. A positive and productive learning environment that includes these vital components doesn't just happen. It takes planning, continuous effort, and a watchful eye.

PHYSICAL SPACE

A welcoming, well-organized, student-friendly environment goes a long way toward helping accomplish both learning and affective goals. John Dewey's wisdom concerning the physical surroundings of learning includes his statement that "any environment is a chance environment so far as its educative influence is concerned unless it has been deliberately regulated with reference to its educative effect" (1944, p. 19). This statement tells us that our classrooms themselves matter. The learning environment can actually enhance teaching and learning when we deliberately and thoughtfully arrange and decorate with student well-being in mind.

Teachers seldom have much to say about which classroom they are assigned or the general condition of the school building. You may have gone to school in well kept, relatively modern buildings; in older stately surroundings; or in dilapidated structures beset with never-ending maintenance problems. Your teachers may have had clean, comfortable spaces

Figure 6.1 A positive and productive learning environment

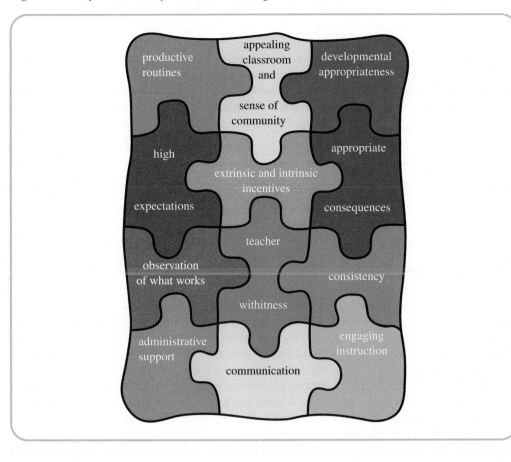

to decorate, or they may have fought off bugs and fungus in a dingy, poorly lit room plagued with a leaky roof. Teachers are responsible for making the most of room assignments. Even under dismal circumstances, designing a classroom can be both challenging and fun. Do it for your students, and do it for yourself. The classroom truly is "home away from home."

Watch Deirdre Huger-McGrew's room tour in the Teaching in Focus *section for Chapter 6 in MyEducationLab for this course.*

HOME AWAY FROM HOME. As a teacher you will spend 8 to 9 hours a day for almost 200 days every year in your classroom. Early childhood and elementary students will spend almost all of their days in the classroom with you, whereas middle and high school students will generally spend about a sixth of their school time in any one classroom. The classroom atmosphere is important for all students, but it is particularly influential for students who may, through circumstances beyond their control, find that school and their classrooms are the cleanest, most welcoming environments in their lives.

If space allows, adding a comfortable couch, chairs, lamps, rugs, plants, curtains, and other homey items does wonders for inviting students in to learn. Focus teacher Deirdre Huger-McGrew of Cario Middle School, South Carolina, created a reading center in her classroom with a couch, chairs, tables, and lamps, as you can see in her room tour.

Deirdre's classroom at Cario Middle School takes on a home-like appearance with the addition of furniture other than desks.

SEATING ARRANGEMENT. The arrangement of desks and tables in a classroom depends on a number of variables, including the level of the school, the subject(s) taught, and available floor space and furniture. Traditional rows of desks are fine for whole group instruction, whereas clusters of desks or students sitting together at tables work well for group work. Ideally, the arrangement will be flexible so seating can accommodate various instructional strategies.

PROXIMITY. Whatever the seating arrangement, one vital element to keep in mind is **proximity,** the accessibility of teacher to students. The teacher needs to be able to approach each student quickly and easily, without having to negotiate narrow pathways that could lead to stumbling or a complex maze that makes it difficult to work one-on-one with students. Students also need to have visual access to boards and screens.

Tour the classrooms of Brenda Beyal, Angelica Reynosa, Chris Roberts, and Derek Boucher in the Teaching in Focus section for Chapter 6 in MyEducationLab for this course.

WALL SPACE AND INTEREST CENTERS. Creative teachers often find ways to entice students to come into the classroom and browse. Walls and tables offer tremendous opportunities to create spaces that students will want to explore just to see what's up. Brenda Beyal (Rees Elementary, Utah) uses part of her classroom to display artifacts from her Native American culture; Angelica Reynosa (Roosevelt High School, California) displays Hispanic cultural items; Chris Roberts at Rees Elementary displays objects from his worldwide travels, along with inspirational pieces that are meaningful to him; and Derek Boucher at Roosevelt High School has an extensive classroom library.

A simple yet potentially powerful use of wall space is the organized display of student work. Preprinted posters may be appropriate on classroom walls, but they should not be used to the exclusion of regularly updated student work. Displaying student work fosters student ownership of the classroom. Some teachers only display exemplary work, such as tests that received As or perfectly colored maps. This practice stops short of being optimally effective if half or more of the students never see their work displayed because their achievement on traditional assignments never rises to the top of the class. Ingenious teachers who know students well incorporate creative assignments that give average and even below-average achievers opportunities to excel. It is well worth the time to arrange physical classroom space thoughtfully, which in many ways shapes the interactions of the people who inhabit the classroom and contributes to building classroom community.

Points of Reflection 6.1

Think about the classrooms in your PreK–12 experiences. Were they inviting and conducive to learning? Why or why not? How do you envision your future classroom's appearance?

BUILDING COMMUNITY

The concept of classroom climate is introduced in Chapter 1.

A **classroom community** is not just a place but also a way of actively learning together. Dewey (1944) expands on this thought by telling us that people in a community are "like-minded," that they have common beliefs, understandings, and aims (p. 4). Maintaining what Dewey calls like-mindedness can be thought of as maintaining **classroom climate,** the everyday environment in which teachers and students work together.

Let's look at four ways teachers can maintain a classroom climate that builds community among themselves and their students:

1. Demonstrate care
2. Develop trust
3. Teach unconditionally
4. Embrace social media

DEMONSTRATE CARE. A teacher must care about curriculum, instruction, assessment, society, the past, the present, the future, and, most of all, about students. Nel Noddings, noted educator and author, believes strongly that care is the vital foundation for building community. She tells us, "Caring is the very bedrock of all successful education" (1992, p. 27). As Angela Lumpkin writes, "When students know that their teachers genuinely care, they respond by exerting greater effort to reach their potential" (2007, p. 158).

A caring classroom centers on relationships—between teacher and students and among the students themselves. Taking a personal interest in students is the first step in developing caring relationships. Linda Darling-Hammond (1997) states, "Environments that attend to students as individuals also help heighten the probability that school relationships

Figure 6.2 Ways to develop student-teacher relationships

- talking informally with students before, during, and after class about their interests
- greeting students outside of school, such as at extracurricular events or at stores
- singling out a few students each day in the lunchroom, and talking to them
- being aware of and commenting on important events in students' lives, such as participation in sports, drama, or other extracurricular activities
- complimenting students on important achievements in and outside of school
- including students in the process of planning classroom activities, soliciting their ideas and considering their interests
- meeting students at the door as they come into class and saying hello to each child, making sure to use each student's name

Source: Marzano, R. J. (2003). *What works in schools: Translating research into action* (pp. 100–101). Alexandria, VA: Association for Supervision and Curriculum Development.

will be characterized by respect and caring rather than by demeaning interactions, threats, and sanctions" (p. 137).

So how do we get to know individual students? Early childhood and elementary classrooms of 15 to 30 students allow teachers to know students and their families well. The numbers are manageable, and teachers have most of the day, every day, to develop relationships. Middle and high school teachers are challenged by both numbers and time because they may have 60 to 120 students a year in their classes for only a small portion of each school day. Marzano (2003b) suggests a number of ways teachers can get to know students, shown in Figure 6.2.

DEVELOP TRUST. For a classroom community of learners to function optimally, trust is an absolute necessity: trust between teacher and students, and among students. A safe environment—academically, emotionally, and physically—is necessary. Maslow's hierarchy of needs indicates that physiological needs, safety, love, and belongingness form the basis for meeting higher-order needs. All of these needs must be met by a classroom characterized by trust.

> Maslow's hierarchy of needs is discussed in Chapter 3.

In a trust-filled classroom, students are more comfortable with the environment and willing to take risks that lead to learning. They know that if they attempt a task and don't succeed, they will be encouraged to try again and given tools that increase the likelihood of success. They are more willing to answer questions and to pose them as well, knowing they won't be ridiculed or demeaned in any way. Trust fosters learning. In ***Teaching in Focus***, Craig Cleveland at Roosevelt High School, California, tells us that teacher-student relationships characterized by trust and respect encourage students to take more risks that lead to learning.

Teaching in Focus

Craig Cleveland, history, Roosevelt High School, Fresno, California. *In his own words....*

Educators first teach who they are. Their dispositions, views of life, and how they perceive their students is picked up on and learned by the students before the first quiz. The opportunity for excellent student performance in the classroom is directly related to how the teacher interacts with the students. I believe that teachers must be fair, have no favorites, and be liberal in providing needed help. Kindness is the fundamental rule for communication between student and teacher. Kindness is hopeful, encourages students to do better, and shows respect for others. Both Guillermo and Khamanny *[two of our focus students]* come from supportive families where they are loved. They thrive in a classroom environment where their ideas are listened to and respected. I believe that students are more willing to take risks in class when they know that their contribution will be appreciated.

TEACH UNCONDITIONALLY. When we practice **unconditional teaching** we accept students for who they are, not for what they do. It's an attitude that conveys clearly to students that they matter to us, no matter how many times they may fail to achieve or misbehave. Unconditional teaching requires that we allow students to begin fresh, that we don't take their misbehavior or lack of effort personally. We are adults who do what we can to help students grow. Alfie Kohn (2005) tells us that unconditional teaching involves

- showing students we are glad to see them
- showing students we trust and respect them
- displaying an appealing informality
- spending time with students even when we don't have to
- asking about students' lives outside school and remembering their answers
- finding something appealing about each student

EMBRACE SOCIAL MEDIA. It has been estimated that in approximately 1 minute, 42,000 people will update their Facebook status, 36,000 tweets will be sent, and 15 hours of video will be uploaded to YouTube (Ray, 2010). Social media are part of our lives, whether we choose to recognize it or not. In addition to Facebook, Twitter, and YouTube, outside of school social media tools such as Ning communities, Google Groups, EtherPad, Wordle, and VoiceThread, to name a few, are connecting both adults and students.

So what does all of this have to do with the learning environment? Plenty, says Marc Prensky, author and founder of Games2train. Prensky (2010) tells us that when we think that virtual relationships, or those that exist online, are somehow less real or important than face-to-face ones, we are barriers to our students' progress by limiting their relationships and harming the learning community. Computers, to be of optimal value, must be personalized so they become extensions of the students' personal self and brain, customized to be tools of expression—communication tools.

Checking technology tools at the door of the school or telling students to keep cell phones turned off while in the school building is not going to stop texting and other technology-enhanced communications from happening. Cell phone communication is the new form of note passing. Try as we might, for the last two and a half centuries of American public education, note passing persists, just in ever-changing formats. To fight it is to lose.

School-provided technology, typically classroom computers, have filters in place with the purpose of protecting students from admittedly dangerous situations. But once students leave school, the filters are gone and they face the perils alone. Steve Johnson (in Ray, 2010) advises teachers to teach students about the devastating possibilities of **cyberbullying,** for instance, by teaching them **cybercitizenship**. Using an abstinence stance when it comes to social media cheats our students of wisdom we could convey.

Johnson (in Ray, 2010) urges us to stop ignoring and blocking and to start embracing and amplifying social media. He tells us to be open and willing to learn as we explore possibilities. The use of social media can help build community in creative and ever-expanding ways.

KOUNIN'S PHILOSOPHY

As a result of observation and analysis, Jacob Kounin (1970) described what effective classroom managers do. To create and maintain a positive and productive learning environment, teachers must practice **withitness**. This term refers to a teacher's awareness of what's going on in the whole classroom, which enables the teacher to step in when needed to keep the environment positive. Teacher withitness often surprises students because they perceive the teacher must have eyes in the back of his or her head. Withitness allows teachers to do what Kounin calls **overlapping,** which means multitasking, or taking care of several things at once. A teacher who has withitness and the ability to overlap can help a small group with an assignment, see a student pestering another student, and give a "cut-it-out" look while answering a question and checking the clock to see how much time remains in the class period.

In addition, Kounin says effective classroom managers understand the **ripple effect,** an effect that occurs when one action directly affects another. He tells us that the cut-it-out look given to one student may help deter another student from the same off-task behavior. This is a positive ripple effect. Similarly, but with negative results, if the teacher interrupts the whole class, loudly saying, "Jeremy, stop that right now. You do nothing but continually disturb," other students may perceive that the teacher overreacted and begin to display the same pestering behaviors (Lemlech, 2010).

Kounin's research has yielded the commonsense view that teachers who know what's going on, who can switch from one activity to another smoothly, and who can maintain positive momentum will be successful in maintaining a productive classroom environment. As you continue reading this chapter, keep withitness, overlapping, and the ripple effect in mind.

Points of Reflection 6.2

Do you recall teachers who appeared to have withitness? Describe one of these teachers and why you believe withitness was part of his or her style.

USING TIME WISELY

One constant in schools is time; how we spend that time is variable. Although some communities have increased the length of the school day, and even the number of days in a school year, most have 180 school days a year, and about 7 hours a day, for impacting students. This 180/7 configuration is based on tradition and not necessarily on what we know about teaching and learning. The length of the school year and the hours in a school day are often political pawns and are not likely to change before you enter your first classroom as a teacher.

Our challenge is to maximize the time we have with students. Early childhood and elementary teachers may have 7 hours a day with students, but that doesn't mean they have 7 hours of **instructional time,** the time available for teaching and learning. Middle and high school teachers may have 65 minutes in each class period, but that doesn't mean they have 65 minutes in which to actually implement instruction. If we are not careful, too much time is spent in nonproductive ways or at least in ways that do not promote academic learning. Given administrative demands such as collecting lunch money, taking attendance, responding to interruptions, getting students where they need to be throughout the day, we often sense that the amount of time available for instruction is limited. Recess, transitions from class to class, lunch, and so on—all legitimate uses of time—further limit instructional time.

One study yields some fairly shocking results concerning the breakdown of the time allotted for the school day. The minimum school day in most elementary schools consists of 6 hours, or 360 minutes. After subtracting time for recess, lunch, and transitions, the time left for academics is about 4.5 hours, or 270 minutes. In the schools studied, researchers found that teachers actually used about 3 hours, or 180 minutes, for actual instruction. Of these 180 minutes, only about 120 resulted in productive learning time, or **time on task** (Weinstein, Romano, & Mignano, 2011). What this amounts to is about 2 hours a day, out of 6, spent on meaningful application of the formal curriculum. This is not acceptable. But before we view this finding too negatively, keep in mind that the informal curriculum is also very important. Interaction time between a teacher and students has positive effects on student learning in terms of relationship building and motivation, two concepts we know make a positive difference in student learning. However, a teacher's goal must be to spend more than a third of a school day in meaningful teaching and learning. Be very conscious of our responsibility to maximize the valuable commodity of time in the classroom.

The formal curriculum and the informal curriculum are discussed in Chapter 4.

What Routines Contribute to Maintaining a Productive Classroom Environment?

A **routine,** sometimes referred to as a procedure, is an expected action that occurs in a given circumstance to accomplish a task efficiently. When routines are in place in the classroom, teachers have more time to teach, and students have more time to learn.

PRACTICING ROUTINES

It is important to practice routines in the first weeks of school. In this way, the routines become habits. Three important reasons for routines that help preserve instructional time are getting student attention, responding to interruptions, and transitioning from one activity to another.

STUDENT ATTENTION. When students are engaged in class activities, and the teacher wants to make an announcement, give directions, or remind students of the time, an attention getter is necessary. Some teachers turn the classroom lights off and on or simply speak loudly enough to be heard. An excellent method for getting attention involves the teacher raising a hand and students doing likewise. Students know to stop talking as their hands go up. Once there is silence, the teacher talks while students listen. If rehearsed repeatedly during the first weeks of school, this method (and a variety of others you'll observe in field experiences) will become automatic. Having one method, practicing it, and consistently using it will return big dividends.

RESPONDING TO INTERRUPTIONS. Class interruptions constitute a real frustration for teachers. The most frequent culprit is often the public address (PA) system. The routine of students instantly "freezing" will allow the announcement to be heard and any necessary action to be taken quickly.

At all levels students have legitimate reasons for leaving a particular class to go somewhere else in the building. Perhaps it's a resource class, a special counseling group, a remedial reading class, or a gifted and talented program. The students involved need to practice the routine of watching the clock and leaving when it is time or watching the doorway for someone who may arrive to escort them. These comings and goings should not be allowed to interrupt the whole class. Students occasionally need to go to the restroom or get a drink of water during class time. Teachers should establish routines for these occasions as well.

When a visitor (an administrator, teacher, student, or parent) enters the classroom, the routine of students noticing and working more quietly will allow the teacher to respond without interference. This routine will not come naturally for students; it must be practiced.

TRANSITIONS. When students change activities or locations they are in **transition,** the time when most classroom disruptions happen (Boynton & Boynton, 2005). In early childhood and elementary schools children may transition between learning activities three or four times before going to recess or a special area class such as music or physical education. Then it's back to the classroom until lunch, perhaps followed by another recess, then back to class. Teachers typically have routines for all these transitions.

In middle and high schools the transitions between classes provide opportunities for misbehavior. Students may be in crowded, rushed circumstances, where social dilemmas can easily surface. A routine for *teachers* that can decrease the likelihood of misbehavior involves merely standing outside their classroom doors during transitions.

ROUTINES IN THE FOUR LEVELS OF SCHOOL

The nature and number of classroom routines vary depending on the school level. Early childhood and elementary classrooms have many more elements to which routines apply than middle school classrooms, and high school classrooms have even fewer. But there are some elements at all four levels that call for routines. For instance, attendance must be taken one or more times daily. Distribution of materials and entering and leaving the classroom also occur daily. Let's take a look at some of the routines of our focus teachers.

EARLY CHILDHOOD. Brandi Wade and Renee Ayers, teachers at Summit Primary, Ohio, implement routines in their classrooms for activities such as

- paying attention
- gathering supplies

- moving about the room
- working in groups
- playing with, and putting away, games and toys
- reacting to interruptions
- going to the rest room
- lining up and moving through the building
- sharpening pencils
- keeping desks in order
- filing and retrieving folders

Brandi and Renee provide a personal routine for each student in the form of classroom jobs that help develop responsibility. These routines/jobs make life in the classroom run more smoothly and increase instructional time. Some of the jobs include board eraser, floor patrol (uses small broom and dust pan), computer helper (turns off computers at the end of the day), and gardener (waters plants).

Renee tells us that her classroom space is limited and she needs to use every inch of it in optimal ways. Routines and classroom jobs for her students maximize efficiency. Each morning Renee follows a routine that organizes her students. She uses a pocket chart (plastic hanging chart with clear pockets) to display her daily classroom schedule in terms second graders can read. She changes the activities as needed so the students know ahead of time what to expect. A sample of the contents of Renee's pocket chart is shown in Figure 6.3.

Tour Renee's classroom in the Teaching in Focus *section for Chapter 6 in MyEducationLab for this course.*

ELEMENTARY. Many elementary teachers deal with classroom elements that require routines similar to those found in early childhood classrooms. Students in grades 3 through 5, however, are developmentally able to adhere to more complicated routines and to do them without direct prompting from the teacher. Chris Roberts, Tim Mendenhall, and Brenda Beyal work as a team at Rees Elementary, Utah. They have established similar routines because they share students throughout the day. Chris, Tim, and Brenda expect their students to come and go between classrooms and throughout the school responsibly. Within each classroom the routines vary, but basically, they deal with these activities:

Watch Tim Mendenhall's room tour in the Teaching in Focus *section for Chapter 6 in MyEducationLab for this course.*

- gathering/using materials
- turning in homework assignments
- borrowing library books
- dismissal procedures for walkers, bus riders, and car riders

Figure 6.3 Second grade pocket chart schedule

9:30 Welcome/Morning Work
Calendar/Morning Message
Self-Selected Reading
Working with Words
Rest Room Break/Snack
Writing
11:55 Music
12:35 Lunch
1:05 Recess
Guided Reading
Rest Room Break
Math
Science/Social Studies
4:00 Dismissal

Source: From Renee Ayer's classroom at Summit Primary School in Ohio.

Early childhood and elementary classrooms should be cheerful and organized for learning. This one includes clusters of desks and supplies for group work, a cubby and coat hook for each student, plants to care for, a word wall, and more.

Tim has a schedule on a bulletin board in his classroom. He tells us his students look at it every day and, if he doesn't keep it current, they readily remind him. Tim not only thinks a schedule is important but also organization of the classroom. He makes it easy for routines to be followed by providing resources and everyday supplies in bins that are clearly labeled. His students know where to go to get what they need, and how to do so in an orderly way.

MIDDLE SCHOOL. Because Deirdre Huger-McGrew at Cario Middle School, South Carolina, has one small group of students half a day and another small group for the other half, she finds it relatively easy to get the students to follow routines that make the classroom run smoothly. These routines revolve around the following activities:

- computer use
- gathering and returning materials
- rest room and water breaks

Traci Peters, seventh grade math teacher at Cario, believes in the value of structure. The routines she establishes include

- passing in and handing back papers
- borrowing supplies from the bins in the room
- obtaining rest room passes, used only during the first and last 5 minutes of class

Traci is extremely organized. Each desk has a number; each critical math resource has a number. A student in Traci's class knows that his seat number must match his calculator, protractor, and ruler number. There is a chart on Traci's wall assigning students to write a summary of the day on a "What did I miss?" board to which absent students go when they return. These routines save valuable instructional time in Traci's classroom.

 *Watch Traci Peters's room tour in the* Teaching in Focus *section for Chapter 6 in MyEducationLab for this course.*

HIGH SCHOOL. Students in high school can be expected to understand routines. There are generally fewer to deal with, but they are no less important than in the earlier grades. Craig Cleveland, Derek Boucher, and Angelica Reynosa, teachers at Roosevelt High School, California, have routines addressing these activities:

- entering and leaving class
- paying attention
- working in groups
- checking out and returning materials
- responding to class interruptions, such as announcements, hand-delivered messages, and visitors

Craig's classroom routines revolve around group work and his classroom library. Students practice working together in the beginning of the school year, learning to collaborate and cooperate. Craig teaches them. Then for the rest of the school year the students know the routine and follow it. They also know where to go in Craig's classroom to get the reading material that interests them or that is assigned. There are books on every wall in the classroom. Craig uses house gutters mounted on the wall to serve as book shelves, making book and magazine covers visible to attract students.

Watch Craig Cleveland's room tour in the Teaching in Focus *section for Chapter 6 in MyEducationLab for this course.*

Establishing developmentally appropriate routines, teaching and practicing them, increases the effectiveness and efficiency of the classroom. Also necessary for classroom effectiveness and efficiency are developmentally appropriate expectations, incentives, and consequences.

How Do Teachers Establish Expectations, Incentives, and Consequences?

When you read the title of this chapter you may have thought it was just a fancy way to refer to a chapter on **classroom management,** the establishment and enforcement of rules and disciplinary actions. You should now see that creating and maintaining a positive, productive learning environment encompasses much more than the traditional notion of classroom management. There is no single recipe for effective classroom management that works all the time in every classroom. Teachers have always struggled with this part of their work.

Expectations, a word with positive connotations, will be used in place of *rules*, a word with negative connotations. **Incentives** will be used in place of the overused and value-laden word *rewards.* **Consequences** imply more natural ramifications for wrongdoing than does the word *punishment,* which can be arbitrary. The three concepts of expectations, incentives, and consequences are interdependent. However, for the sake of organization and clarity, they are addressed separately here.

Before discussing expectations, incentives, and consequences, think about the concepts of prevention and intervention. When it comes to student misbehavior, teachers have only two options: *They can prevent it, or they will need to intervene.* Obviously, prevention is more desirable. Remember that the best way to prevent behavior problems in the classroom is through engaging instruction.

Engaging instructional practices are discussed in Chapter 4.

EXPECTATIONS

Teacher expectations impact students in significant ways as they affect students' academic performance and behavior. Teacher expectations may become self-fulfilling prophesies for some students. Therefore, it is vital to set and communicate high expectations.

ESTABLISHING BEHAVIORAL EXPECTATIONS. How do teachers establish expectations that are foundational, including physical norms for preserving the health and safety of students, moral norms pertaining to respect for others, and societal norms for politeness and individual responsibility? The answer, in large measure, depends on the developmental stages of the students. With young children, most expectations have to be made very explicit, for example, "Don't bother classmates," "Share materials," "Don't tease one another." For older children and adolescents, many expectations can be summed up with statements such as "Treat one another with respect."

Establishing behavioral expectations is generally a teacher task. However, proponents of what is sometimes called a **democratic classroom,** one that promotes choice, community, authentic learning, and relevant, creative curriculum (Wolk, 2003), encourage student participation in the establishment of behavioral expectations. Other influences affect the task, including expectations previously established by the school district and those held by the grade level or the whole school staff. There are few circumstances in which an individual teacher should set expectations less

This teacher should establish behavioral expectations to help maintain productive routines such as class transitions.

stringent than grade-level, team, or whole-school expectations. However, teachers can certainly add to, or make more stringent, their own classroom expectations. For instance, if school expectations include a "no gum" rule, then a teacher cannot allow gum chewing in the classroom. But if there is no school-wide rule against gum chewing, a teacher may nonetheless establish the expectation that students will not chew gum in a particular classroom.

Here are some examples of behavior, some mild, some moderate, and some severe, that fall short of most teachers' behavioral expectations:

- talking or moving around the classroom at inappropriate times
- disturbing others (of course, there are thousands of ways students might do this!)
- tardiness and excessive absences
- off-task behaviors (missing materials, working on an assignment that is not the current task, daydreaming, sleeping)
- leaving the classroom without permission
- cheating, lying
- using obscene or vulgar language
- defacing property
- verbal or physical noncompliance (refusing to do what is asked)
- theft and vandalism
- fighting or inflicting violence
- being under the influence of illegal substances

Points of Reflection 6.3

What classroom expectations, or rules, do you remember in your K–12 experiences? Were they clear and rational, or were they ambiguous and nonsensical? On what do you base your opinion? What is the most important expectation for your future classroom?

SAMPLE EXPECTATIONS. Some teachers choose to keep their lists of expectations short and general, as illustrated in Figure 6.4. Notice that none of the sample lists of expectations mentions cheating, lying, vulgar language, vandalism, theft, substance abuse, or violence. As stated earlier, most teachers lump all of these negative actions under the word *respect*, assuming that if students show respect, they won't engage in any of these behaviors.

In this chapter's *Diversity Dialogue*, we read about experiences of focus teacher Derek Boucher at Roosevelt High School in California concerning behavioral expectations.

Why would students choose to live up to classroom expectations? Many do so because they are accustomed to living up to expectations at home or in other settings. Some students require specific incentives to comply with expectations. Most students fall somewhere in between.

Figure 6.4 Sample lists of classroom expectations

1. Pay attention.
2. Listen when others talk.
3. Treat each other with courtesy.

1. Work all class period.
2. Complete all assignments.
3. Stay in the area you are assigned.
4. Show respect at all times.

1. Respect each other and the teacher at all times.
2. Talk quietly so as not to disturb others.
3. Ask for help by raising your hand.
4. Follow all classroom procedures.

1. Arrive on time for class every day.
2. Have all materials needed to participate fully.
3. Maintain a respectful attitude.

1. Respect yourself.
2. Respect others.
3. Respect property.

Focus teacher Derek Boucher at Roosevelt High School in Fresno, California, understands the value of shared expectations and routines. He agrees with the general rules and regulations published in the handbook by the Roosevelt administrators. Teachers are reasonably free to set their own classroom guidelines, and Derek has done so in two morning classes, American History and Language Arts/Reading. Each class is 90 minutes long and he has the same 9th and 10th grade students in both. This is a purposeful configuration that Principal Maria Romero approved. The students are all Hispanic, some first generation in the United States and others second or third. In all cases, Spanish is the primary language spoken at home, and all the students have a history of low academic achievement with at least one incident of being retained in a grade level. They began the year as poor readers and most had little interest in reading. Derek sees potential and hope for all the students and values his 3-hour morning with them.

Derek involved his students in setting the behavioral expectations for this group. He has received criticism from a couple of the teachers in his area because he has not followed some of the traditional guidelines. For instance, he does not stick with the passing period guidelines because he has the students for 3 hours in class and a 10-minute transition between the two classes. Rather than his students milling around for 10 minutes between bells, they all agreed that they could have bathroom and water breaks at times that fit their instructional schedule, not the bell schedule. This means his students may individually or in small groups be in the halls at random times. Derek also allows students to bring food and drinks into class as long as it's not disruptive. Although there are no school-wide rules against this, most teachers do not allow it.

In terms of electronic items, Derek actually encourages this group of students to share using text messaging, and he makes use of student-created podcasts for history projects. Students use streaming video in their presentations and download pictures they take with their cell phones. The rule at Roosevelt is that cell phones and iPods may be carried but must be off during instructional time. However, when the kids hit the door of Derek's classroom, all electronics come to life. He sees social media as a way to reach these students.

Think about what you have learned about Derek Boucher and his style at Roosevelt High School. Respond to these items by writing one well-developed paragraph each.

1. What about Derek's morning group constitutes diversity? Compared to the general population of Roosevelt High, why would Derek want to set special behavioral expectations for them?

2. The teachers at Roosevelt respect Derek's passion for students and, in particular, his training to teach reading to high school students. They tend to give him leeway in some areas because they have faith in his judgment. However, when their students see Derek's students in the hall, often carrying a can of soda or texting, they understandably question these privileges. What might Derek do to prevent other teachers from resenting the behavioral expectations he and his students use? How might he explain the rationale for how students interact in his class?

INCENTIVES

An incentive is a reason for doing something. For instance, a first grade student may stay in line while walking to music class (expectation) because the teacher told the class if everyone stayed in line, the music teacher would be pleased (incentive). Keep in mind that incentives that motivate one individual may have little effect on another. If the first grade student doesn't like music or the music teacher, pleasing that teacher would not serve as an incentive. Teachers are responsible for understanding their students well enough to provide the bases for incentives that will motivate students in terms of behavior, academics, and personal growth.

The two basic kinds of incentives are extrinsic and intrinsic. **Extrinsic incentives** are those that are imposed or that originate outside the individual. **Intrinsic incentives** are those that come from within and result from students' natural drives.

EXTRINSIC INCENTIVES. Most theorists (and indeed probably most of your professors) downplay the value of extrinsic incentives in the classroom. And they are right. Extrinsic incentives are less desirable than intrinsic incentives. Extrinsic incentives depend on people other than the student. For instance, if a fourth grade teacher offers a popcorn party on Friday if the class has fewer than five names recorded for misbehavior during the week, then students depend on one another to behave and on the teacher to keep his or her word. They apply peer pressure, again external, to achieve the Friday incentive. Do you think the students will be just as motivated to behave acceptably the next week without the promise of a popcorn party? Probably not. When extrinsic incentives are taken away, positive results are less likely to be reinforced. When teachers employ extrinsic motivation, they are taking on the full responsibility for motivating their students (Erwin, 2003). Even so, extrinsic incentives are common in all levels of school.

In early childhood and elementary classrooms extrinsic incentives may include

- extended time for recess
- a movie at the end of the day or week
- special food treats
- free time for students to explore classroom centers on their own
- music to accompany an activity
- more time to engage in a favorite activity
- stickers, certificates

At some point in your field experiences you will likely encounter extrinsic incentives in the form of a **token economy,** a system of distributing symbolic rewards (tokens) for appropriate behavior and withholding or taking away rewards for inappropriate behavior. At a designated time, students can exchange their tokens for something they value. Principal Susan McCloud at T.C. Cherry Elementary School in Bowling Green, Kentucky, reports that the culture of Cherry changed remarkably when her teachers began concentrating on positive behavior and incentives rather than negative behaviors and punishment. One major aspect of the change was the establishment of a token economy, in which students accumulated Cherry Pit Points that they could later "spend" at the Cherry Pit Store. Principal McCloud says this token system gives the students a sense of power and control when they think, "'Hey, I can behave and if I do, I get things that I want'" (2005, p. 49).

A primary influence for young adolescents revolves around friends. Many middle-level teachers capitalize on this developmental trait by promising socializing time at the end of a class period or at the end of a week in exchange for appropriate behavior. High school teachers take advantage of adolescent tendencies in the same way. In middle and high school, extrinsic incentives tend to be less tangible and more social in nature, such as the use of praise as a motivator.

> Young adolescents and peer influence are discussed in Chapter 3.

Praise. Praise may be a powerful extrinsic motivator for some students. It is extrinsic because it depends on someone else, the praiser. There are important guidelines for optimizing the value of praise. Specific praise is more effective than general praise. For instance, saying to a student, "Your participation in today's activity helped your whole group stay on task. Thanks, Marcus," is more valuable than simply saying, "Nice work" as Marcus's group leaves the classroom. Using the student's name is important. Whether to praise in private or in public depends in large measure on the developmental level of the students. Most early childhood and elementary students enjoy being praised in front of their classmates. Young adolescents and high school students are often embarrassed by public praise. A compliment in private is generally more motivational and increases the likelihood of the desired behavior being repeated.

Logic of Extrinsic Incentives. In a perfect world, extrinsic incentives would not be necessary. We would all behave appropriately because it's the right thing to do. We would all work hard to reach our potential and to benefit others. Real teachers in real school settings understand the theories that reject extrinsic incentives; they also understand that much of society runs as smoothly as it does because of extrinsic motivation. Ask how many people who work in service industries (fast-food restaurants, dry cleaners, etc.) actually get out of bed and go to work because they are internally motivated to do their jobs. How they do their jobs—their attitude, attention to quality, drive to be successful—may indeed be intrinsically motivated. But chances are, most go to work to earn money.

Ideally, students complete assignments and behave appropriately because they want to (intrinsic motivation). But there are tasks (drill and practice, assignments with no readily apparent value) and behaviors (walking in a straight line, being quiet when a visitor enters) that simply may not be internally motivating for some students in some settings. When it comes to extrinsic and intrinsic incentives, most teachers use a mixture to meet the real needs in their real classrooms.

INTRINSIC INCENTIVES. For lasting results, intrinsic incentives, such as the satisfaction of completing an assignment that is challenging or behaving appropriately in an assembly, have the most value. Helping students understand why a particular behavior is desirable builds an internal "want to" that is motivating. When an individual behaves appropriately because of intrinsic motivation, chances are the desired behavior not only lasts but spreads to other aspects of life with positive results.

The best classroom management involves **student self-monitoring**. This is the ultimate in intrinsic incentives because when students assume control of their own behavior, they develop a sense of ownership. Sounds good, doesn't it? We all want this for our students and our classrooms. However, helping students move toward this ideal when they may be used to being told what to do, when to do it, and how to do it, with the promise of rewards for compliance, is a difficult task. Teaching for obedience is much easier than teaching for responsibility. Methods of accomplishing student self-monitoring are beyond the scope of this text, but this discussion may plant the seed that will give you the intrinsic motivation to think about, read about, and plan for a classroom full of self-monitoring students.

Akin to intrinsic motivation is the concept that when student needs are met, misbehavior is less of an issue. When student needs are met, students behave appropriately because (1) they want to, and (2) there's little need to do otherwise. Glasser's *Choice Theory* (1998) says that five basic needs constitute the source of all intrinsic motivation: survival, love and belonging, power, freedom, and fun. Glasser contends that giving students what they need will get teachers what they want: student responsibility and more appropriate behavior. Erwin (2003) tells us that when teachers understand these needs, it is possible to "transform your classroom into a place where students . . . behave in respectful, responsible ways" (p. 21). Figure 6.5 includes ways in which teachers can address Glasser's five basic needs.

As with other aspects of teaching, teachers must remember that their classrooms are likely to include diverse groups of students. What is valued and what is motivating may be quite different classroom to classroom, and student to student. Knowing students well— their cultures, their home settings, their disabilities, and more—is vital in understanding how to help them behave in respectful and responsible ways. We'll look more closely at this issue later in the chapter.

Now let's turn our attention to what takes place when students do not respond favorably to incentives.

CONSEQUENCES

Proactive prevention strategies, coupled with a system of incentives that helps students self-monitor their behavior, is the best approach to classroom management. But when expectations are not met, and prevention isn't enough, teachers must intervene. Intervention usually involves consequences. There are two guidelines teachers should follow to help ensure that consequences are reasonable, fairly applied, and not overly reactive, punitive, or exclusionary. First, *consequences should match the inappropriate behavior.* Second, *consequences should focus on the behavior, not on the person,* thus preserving both the student's dignity and the teacher-student relationship.

Figure 6.5 Addressing Glasser's five basic needs

Survival
- provide opportunities to get food, water, fresh air
- maintain behavior guidelines that promote safety and respect
- develop routines that add a sense of order and security

Love and Belonging
- learn names and personal information quickly
- greet students as they enter the classroom
- let students know you personally
- teach cooperation
- engage students in ways that show them they are valued

Power
- give students a voice in the classroom
- be conscious of a variety of learning styles
- teach personal responsibility
- allow for second and third chances to demonstrate learning

Freedom
- give choices
- use a variety of instructional strategies

Fun
- use games in instruction
- engage students in brain teaser activities

Source: Erwin, J. C. (2003). Giving students what they need. *Educational Leadership, 61*(1), 21–23.

Points of Reflection 6.4

What do you remember about consequences in your K–12 experiences? Which appeared to be effective and why? What kinds of consequences make sense to you?

MATCHING CONSEQUENCES TO MISBEHAVIOR. Consequences should match misbehavior both in appropriateness and in severity. Although it would be impossible to design a distinct consequence for every type of misbehavior, teachers should attempt to match consequences whenever possible. For instance, if a student writes on desks or lockers, an appropriate consequence would involve cleaning during a school-required detention. If a student wastes class time, spending free time making up class work would be appropriate. If teasing and hurt feelings are involved, perhaps an apology and reading a short story about how hurtful teasing can be may be effective. Most schools have a standard list of consequences ranging from mild to severe. As with expectations, these consequences need to be applied in the classroom. Teachers can go beyond school-wide agreed-upon consequences by developing and implementing consequences tailored to the misbehavior of their own students.

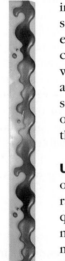

What Mr. White expects of you:

I expect you to....

1. Take responsibility for your work and grade.
2. Respect your teachers, peers, and surroundings.
3. Follow ALL directions.
4. Raise hand before speaking.
5. Come in quietly and ready to learn.

What you can expect from Mr. White:

(Positive Consequence)

You can expect....
1.) a smile.
2.) verbal praise.
3.) a positive call home.
4.) tangible rewards (candy, pencils, etc).

OR

(Negative Consequence)

You can expect....
1.) a warning.
2.) a minor referral for lunch or after school detention
3.) a negative call home.
4.) a major referral.

Setting expectations and consequences, and then making them public and explicit, helps bring order and civility to the classroom.

Unobtrusive Interventions. The variability of both students and misbehavior dictates a wide range of consequences, beginning with consequences that do not disrupt instruction. There are nonverbal and verbal ways to address relatively minor behavior problems such as student inattention; minor off-task behaviors like daydreaming, doing something other than what is expected, and not using proper materials; leaving a designated area; pestering another student; and many others. Nonverbal interventions include moving closer (proximity) to the offending student, giving a disapproving look, stopping mid-sentence for a moment to gain student attention, and making an established gesture. To be effective, nonverbal interventions take thought and proactive behavior on the part of the teacher. The best way to learn about nonverbal interventions is to watch experienced teachers make them work. You'll have opportunities to do this during field experiences in your teacher preparation program. Watch and listen carefully to learn from experienced teachers.

Verbal interventions can resolve minor problems if delivered quickly, calmly, and in ways that match the offense. From saying, "Everyone needs to listen," to using the offending student's name in a classroom scenario, to a class discussion about why a particular behavior is inappropriate, teachers' words can make a difference. Whatever is said should purposefully lead students back to focus on instruction or learning activities.

Simply asking a student to move to another part of the classroom temporarily, or permanently, may solve some minor misbehavior problems. Withdrawing privileges is another tactic some teachers use successfully.

Teacher-Prescribed Consequences. Teachers must move beyond unobtrusive nonverbal and verbal intervention when misbehavior warrants. The timing of this escalation depends on a number of variables, including school level, student needs, and assessment of possible damage or danger involved with the behavior.

Time-out is a consequence often used in early childhood and elementary classrooms. Students are isolated, usually within the classroom, and not allowed to participate in whatever is going on. Time-out works well as a consequence if not overused and if classroom instruction and activities are engaging, making isolation undesirable.

Detention is a consequence often used at all grade levels. It is most effective when it involves isolation and requires the student to give up time he or she would rather spend elsewhere. Some teachers, teams of teachers, and whole schools find that lunch detention works well. Students assigned to lunch detention are separated from others and required to eat lunch alone in silence. After-school detention is typically used for completion of assignments or for school-related chores such as cleaning or helping in some way. Weekend detention, sometimes called Saturday school, is generally reserved for more serious or repeated offenses.

Boynton and Boynton (2005) describe the concept of sending a student out of the classroom with the purpose of reflection and planning for better choices as **processing**. Students may be sent to another classroom, the hallway, the library, or a designated room, sometimes called a behavior improvement room (BIR). An important part of processing is what Marzano (2003a) refers to as "written self-analysis" (p. 84). He recommends that students analyze what part they played in the misbehavior, how others contributed, how it should be resolved, and what might prevent it from happening again. Processing is appropriate for minor misbehavior that occurs repeatedly or student disruptions that aren't resolved through unobtrusive nonverbal or verbal interventions.

Serious Consequences. Some misbehavior calls for consequences beyond what an individual teacher may assign. Misbehavior involving physical violence, loud or threatening verbal abuse, vandalism, theft, and possession of illegal substances or weapons dictates the involvement of building-level administrators who may elect to involve law enforcement. Such serious misbehavior often results in suspension, either in school or out of school, or expulsion. Classroom teachers should not attempt to handle such misbehavior alone. A supportive and decisive administrator can be one of the most valuable assets to teachers and the classroom management process.

Chances are most in America would be surprised to know that **corporal,** or physical, **punishment** is still practiced in 22 states today (Farrell, 2010). Interestingly, the perceived need for such punishment dates back to the early days of the United States. Figure 6.6 provides a portion of a teacher's journal dated 1776 that describes a "bad boy" and the philosophy of the day about "curing" the student. Most teachers will recognize at least some of the traits described by Master Lovell in at least a few of the students they have known. Considering the history of educational practices provides a perspective showing the struggles that teachers face in today's classrooms are not necessarily new.

The first state to ban corporal punishment was New Jersey in 1867. Many large cities in the Northeast banned corporal punishment before their states. Notably, New York City

Figure 6.6 Master Lovell's journal

> A Bad Boy is undutiful to his father and mother, disobedient and stubborn to his master, and ill natured to all his playmates. He hates his books and takes no pleasure in improving himself. . . .
>
> He is always in mischief, and when he has done a wrong, will tell twenty lies to clear himself. He hates to have anyone give him good advice, and when they are out of sight, will laugh at them. He swears and wrangles and quarrels with his companions, and is always in some dispute or other. . . .
>
> He is frequently out of humor, and sullen and obstinate, so that he will neither do what he is asked, nor answer any question put to him. In short, he neglects everything that he should learn, and minds nothing but play and mischief. He grows up a confirmed blockhead, incapable of anything but wickedness and folly. . . . [T]o make a bad boy into a good one, he should be thrashed daily for some reason or other, and locked securely in a closet. There he can meditate upon his sins and thus avoid his fate.

Source: Loeper, J. L. (1973). *Going to school in 1776.* New York: Macmillan.

banned the practice in 1870, whereas the state of New York did not ban it until 1985. Educators may use paddling, the most common form of corporal punishment, in all the southern states, plus others. The last state to ban the practice was Ohio in 2009. Of the remaining states, paddling takes place most often in Texas, Mississippi, Tennessee, Arkansas, and Alabama. The total number of incidents has decreased sharply from about 3% of the student population experiencing some form of corporal punishment in 1976 to only 0.5% of students in 2003 (Farrell, 2010). Even though the use of corporal punishment is steadily declining, the writer of this chapter's *Letter to the Editor* is in favor of the practice.

Letter to the Editor

This letter was posted by a local teacher in *The Community Voice*, the online version of the Nashville newspaper, *The Tennessean.*

JUNE 11, 2005

As a Metro public school teacher, I deplore the elimination of corporal punishment in the elementary schools. The past three years have resulted in an increase in bullying, intimidation, and threats not only to other children but to staff itself. My school (K–4) has had teachers assaulted by 5 year olds this year! The fear of not having good ADA—average daily attendance—has paralyzed administration into ignoring repeat offenses until they often turn into zero tolerance issues. If teachers aren't given tools to keep order in class, this already bad situation will worsen. . . . We have a new generation of parents who have no respect for schools, teachers, the law or anybody. And their children are entering school now! Sugarcoat it all you want; I see it every day. Teachers spend more time keeping order than actually teaching. Visit your child's school and get involved! Demand discipline and good order! It's worse now than you think.

Now it's your turn. This chapter has given you information about possible consequences for misbehavior as well as insight into the controversial nature of corporal punishment. These questions will help you formulate your own letter.

1. Do you think there are ever instances that justify corporal punishment? If not, why not? If so, what might those instances be?
2. If you support the writer, what justification do you propose? If you do not support the writer, what would you say to an experienced teacher who believes in administering corporal punishment?
3. If you do not agree with corporal punishment, what alternative can you suggest? If you do agree with corporal punishment, how would you explain the need for it in a public forum?

Your letter to the editor should be in response to the *Community Voice* of the *Tennessean* letter—supporting it, adding information, or refuting it. Write your letter in understandable terminology, remembering that readers of newspaper letters to the editor are citizens who may have limited knowledge of school practices and policies. Remember to refer to the letter assessment rubric in Chapter 1.

School districts that practice corporal punishment must follow guidelines governing its use that have resulted from court cases. These guidelines include giving specific warnings that a behavior may result in physical punishment, having more than one adult present, and ensuring that the punishment is reasonable and humane (Dunklee & Shoop, 2002). Although corporal punishment has vocal critics and its practice has fallen out of favor with most districts and educators, some people still believe it is warranted.

FOCUS ON THE BEHAVIOR, NOT THE PERSON. Children and adolescents are developing and growing. Their misbehavior often results from fleeting moods, spontaneous impulses, and poor decision making linked to immaturity.

Constructive Correcting. Assigning consequences in ways that serve as student learning experiences is both productive and constructive—productive in that students sense that they are viewed as individuals, and constructive in that students may use the experience to build their understanding of why certain behaviors are unacceptable. Correcting students in constructive ways can turn something negative into a growth experience. For instance, a consequence for using the word *retard* in a joking manner may be viewing a video about children with Down syndrome that explains their mental retardation and the coping strategies they are taught. The disrespect shown by using *retard* as a slang word will hopefully be corrected with increased understanding.

Boynton and Boynton (2005) tell us that the goal of correcting students should be to have them reflect on their actions, be sorry for their misbehavior, and determine to make better choices next time. How teachers correct students makes a difference. If done constructively, the chances of a student walking away hating the teacher and planning to misbehave again, but not get caught, are diminished. Steps to use when correcting a student and assigning a consequence are listed in Figure 6.7.

Starting Fresh. When focus is placed on the misbehavior, not on the student, it is possible for the student to see beyond the incident and consequence to the possibility of a fresh start. Chris Stevenson (2002), noted expert on middle-level education, advises us to have an attitude that says to students, "Redemption is always close, not closed" (p. 219). In other words, when a student misbehaves and a consequence is assigned, the student deserves to be given a fresh start. This helps students build **resilience,** the ability to bounce back and meet life's challenges.

Family Communication. When communicating with the family of a student who misbehaves, it is vital to focus on the misbehavior, not the person. In essence, if a student is maligned rather than the misbehavior, then the family is maligned, with a negative effect on the family-school relationship. A wise teacher emphasizes the positive and the potential before discussing the misbehavior.

If a teacher has already had a positive family communication, such as a complimentary note sent home or a pleasant meeting at Back-to-School Night, then a phone call about a behavior problem may work wonders. For some students, just the threat of a call is enough.

We look more closely at family conferences in Chapter 12.

Figure 6.7 Steps to use when correcting students

1. Review what happened.
2. Identify and accept student's feelings.
3. Review alternative actions.
4. Explain the building policy as it applies to the situation.
5. Let the student know that all students are treated the same.
6. Invoke an immediate and meaningful consequence.
7. Let the student know you are disappointed that you have to invoke a consequence to his or her action.
8. Communicate an expectation that the student will do better in the future.

Source: Boynton, M., & Boynton, C. (2005). *The educator's guide to preventing and solving discipline problems.* Alexandria, VA: Association for Supervision and Curriculum Development.

Points of Reflection 6.5

Were you ever involved in a teacher-initiated family conference because of behavior issues? If so, how did you feel about it? Did your behavior improve? If so, in what ways? Do you have friends or siblings who were involved in such a conference? Do you remember their reactions?

For other students, a call home is meaningless. For instance, parents may not be available for a call (and students know this) or parents may have received many such calls and may not care or may feel helpless to remedy the situation.

Parent or family conferences can be effective if they are handled professionally and result in an agreed-upon, enforceable plan to correct the problem.

Now that we have considered ways to create a positive learning environment, how routines contribute to a productive learning environment, and some of the basics of expectations, incentives, and consequences, we are ready to explore developing a classroom management plan.

How Can I Develop a Classroom Management Plan?

Considering elements that contribute to a successful classroom management plan will create an awareness of what to look for in field experiences throughout your teacher preparation program as you observe teachers dealing daily with learning environment issues.

This section looks briefly at what selected theorists and researchers have to say about classroom management; the necessity of considering students' special needs, societal context, and developmental stages; and some general guidelines for planning and implementing classroom management.

PROMINENT THEORIES OF CLASSROOM MANAGEMENT

If you presented a classroom management scenario to a room full of teachers and asked them how they would respond, you'd no doubt hear as many solutions as there were teachers. A foolproof recipe for classroom management doesn't exist. Many new teachers are dismayed to hear this because a recipe or formula would make life much easier. But take heart! Teachers can take advantage of what experienced theorists like those in Table 6.1 have to say, as well as research-based strategies, to garner ideas to consider in developing personalized classroom management plans.

CONSIDER THE STUDENTS

We have already discussed the importance of considering all aspects of students' lives when planning for curriculum, instruction, and assessment. This outlook is equally important in planning for the learning environment.

An important part of a classroom management plan involves teaching students to follow directions.

TABLE 6.1 Overview of selected theories of classroom management

Theorist	Model	Basic Beliefs
Skinner	Behavior modification	Teachers use positive and negative reinforcements or rewards and punishments to modify or shape students' behavior.
Glasser	Choice therapy and quality schools	Schools help satisfy students' psychological needs and add quality to their lives. Teachers teach, manage, provide caring environments, and conduct class meetings in a way that adds quality to students' lives.
Gordon	Teacher effectiveness training	Teachers teach self-discipline, demonstrate active listening, send "I-messages" rather than "you-messages," and teach a six-step conflict resolution program.
Canter	Assertive discipline	Teachers and students have rights in the classroom. Teachers insist upon responsible behavior and use a hierarchical list of consequences to manage behavior.
Kounin	Instructional management	Teachers use effective instructional behaviors (teaching techniques, movement management, and group focus) to influence student behaviors.
Curwin and Mendler	Discipline with dignity	Teachers protect the dignity of students. Teachers are fair and consider individual situations (as opposed to rigid rules), list rules that make sense to students, and model appropriate behaviors.
Gathercoal	Judicious discipline	Teachers provide behavioral guidelines for property loss and damage, threats to health and safety, and serious disruptions of the educational process. They also demonstrate professional ethics and build a democratic classroom.

Source: Manning, M. L., & Bucher, K. T. (2007). *Classroom management: Models, applications, and cases* (pp. 12–14). Upper Saddle River, NJ: Merrill/Prentice Hall.

SPECIAL NEEDS. Students with special needs, those requiring unique services to optimize their learning potential, usually also require specific guidelines for classroom management. The best way to find out what the guidelines are for a student with special needs is to talk with the person in your school who has oversight responsibility for the student's education, most often one of the special educators in your building. You will be referred to the student's Individualized Education Program, which will contain information about any variances from what are considered normal, reasonable incentive-and-consequence systems necessitated by the student's disability. The Individuals with Disabilities Education Act (IDEA) includes provisions for the development of a management plan through a team of educators using a process known as **functional behavioral assessment (FBA)**. FBA looks for events and actions that may lead to misbehavior and devises strategies to help students abide by classroom expectations.

In Chapter 3 we discuss students with special needs, related services, and IEPs.

SOCIETAL CONTEXT. Students don't leave their home lives on the schoolhouse steps at 8 A.M., to be picked up again at 3:30 P.M. as they leave the classroom. The societal context in which they are growing up colors their attitudes, aptitudes, and reactions. You name it, they bring it with them into the classroom. The answer to the familiar questions, "And how are the children? Are they all well?" should guide the development and implementation of a classroom management plan.

What motivates one child to follow routines and expectations may be meaningless to another. Student perceptions, regardless of whether the source may be culturally or socioeconomically based, influence their reactions to expectations, incentives, and consequences.

Some of the everyday areas about which perceptions may differ include eye contact, physical closeness to others, competition, and receiving attention (Manning & Bucher, 2007).

To understand this issue of differing perspectives, examine what experienced educators and sociologists have to say about sensitivity and insightful management options. Some of the best sources of information, including Ruby Payne, Lisa Delpit, Alfie Kohn, and Jonathan Kozol, remind us that diversity exists within specific groups, as well as among groups. This diversity and resulting issues may impact the day-to-day functioning of classrooms as teachers strive to match their classroom management systems to students' developmental levels.

> In Chapter 3 we discuss student diversity, and in Chapter 10 we examine the societal context of our students and schools.

DEVELOPMENTAL APPROPRIATENESS. Understanding human development is absolutely essential when writing and implementing a classroom management plan. Let's take a look at how some of our 10 focus teachers maintain learning environments through classroom management plans that match their personal styles and respond to the developmental stages of their students.

Early Childhood. Brandi Wade at Summit Primary, Ohio, works to create a safe, loving, consistent environment for kindergartners. She attempts to match misbehavior with logical consequences. For instance, if during group time on the classroom carpet a child is disruptive, the child must go back to his or her desk, continuing to listen, but not sitting with the rest of the children.

Brandi uses a system that is theme related, and her expectations for behavior increase as the year progresses. For instance, her expectation in September may be for students not to argue as they form lines to leave the room. If students "earn" 15 apples in their class apple basket for meeting this expectation, they may enjoy an apple-tasting party.

Elementary. Chris Roberts, multiage teacher at Rees Elementary School, Utah, has a classroom management/learning environment philosophy best related in his own words.

> Maintaining a positive environment really boils down to a quote I follow by Ron Miller, "Our work is not about curriculum or a teaching method. It is about nurturing the human spirit with love." I do my best to have unconditional love for my students. I think my students feel that and do their best to work hard and learn all they can. We don't have "rules," but we do have "agreements." I believe that language change is important. Kids are smothered in rules. We meet together a lot in the beginning of the year and do experiential activities to build teamwork. We talk about how we want our village to be. We write down our discussions and sign an agreement that we will do our best to show respect for ourselves, others, and property. We continually assess how we are doing all year long. I write a lot of letters to my students telling them I appreciate the positive things they are doing. (From e-mail communication with Chris Roberts, November 11, 2005)

In the opening scenario of this chapter you read about Tim Mendenhall and a new student who came into his classroom with a history of misbehavior and poor academic performance. Tim applied his classroom management plan to help Jeff acclimate to Rees Elementary and make behavioral progress, a necessary step toward academic success. The general guidelines of Tim's management plan are presented in Figure 6.8.

Figure 6.8 Tim Mendenhall's guidelines for classroom management

1. Build trust from the moment students walk through the door.
2. Protect trust all year long.
3. Play with students on the field and in the classroom (sports, checkers, educational games, etc.).
4. Don't send students away to be disciplined unless absolutely necessary. If you do, you give away their respect for you and your role.
5. Don't ever be degrading. This ruins your relationship with students.
6. Set up clear expectations with consequences that apply when students make bad choices.
7. Make students take responsibility. Keep their problems, their problems.
8. Be sympathetic but firm, fair, and consistent.

Source: From e-mail communication with Tim Mendenhall, November 12, 2005.

Figure 6.9 Cario Middle School student expectations

1. Conduct yourself in an orderly manner.
2. Be on task.
3. Respect yourself and others.
4. Take care of all property.
5. Promote safety in everything you do.

Middle School. Focus teacher Traci Peters at Cario Middle School, South Carolina, invests a lot of time in getting to know her students and attending school events to support their participation. Building relationships is foundational to Traci's classroom management plan.

Traci and her students abide by the five basic behavior guidelines agreed on by the entire staff of Cario Middle School and listed in Figure 6.9. The Charleston County School District requires teachers to give conduct grades for each student in every 9-week grading period. Employing a system commonly found in many schools, Traci gives demerits for misbehavior. She has a system for converting demerits into letter grades. She also uses a "three strikes, you're out" policy, meaning that after three demerits in her classroom in a quarter, a student goes outside her classroom management plan and talks with a building-level administrator. Traci says, "Basically, I give kids a chance to be kids, but at the same time I expect them to respect me and those around them." She tells us that parent communication is a major help in managing a middle school classroom.

High School. A high school administrative team and staff with expectations for respect and consistent consequences can generally run a positive and productive campus. Most high school students understand behavioral expectations and the rationale behind them. If adolescents ages 15 through 19 are disruptive in the classroom, they know exactly what they're doing and, in some cases, do it because they know they can get away with it or perhaps because they want to be suspended. Students who are disruptive in high school are often sent out of the classroom, instructed to see an administrator, and may be given **suspension,** or sent off school grounds, for a specified length of time. This severe consequence should be reserved for extreme cases.

Roosevelt High School, California, publishes school rules as well as its Student Code of Conduct in a student handbook. The school rules on which Roosevelt teachers build their classroom expectations are shown in Figure 6.10. The Code of Conduct covers expectations for a safe environment, closed-campus rules and exceptions, the necessity of ID tags, absences, the use of electronics, and a sexual harassment policy. In addition, the Fresno Unified School District maintains a zero-tolerance policy for possession of firearms, weapons of any kind, explosives, controlled substances, and attempted or actual harm to another person. Immediate suspension occurs for violations, many times resulting in **expulsion,** or permanent removal from school.

Our three focus teachers at Roosevelt High, Craig Cleveland, Derek Boucher, and Angelica Reynosa, seldom have misbehavior in their classrooms that a certain look or a private word won't remedy. They are instead often faced with the dilemma of students not engaging in learning. So rather than overt misbehavior, a lack of desire or enthusiasm for the whole educative process often challenges them. This can be an even more perplexing problem than dealing with students who are disruptive.

INCORPORATE 21ST-CENTURY SKILLS

We have discussed the Partnership for 21st Century Skills (P21) in the context of curriculum, instruction, and assessment while addressing the first three 21st-century outcome categories: core subjects; learning and innovation skills; and information, media, and

Points of Reflection 6.6

Do the behavior and classroom management dilemmas of early childhood sound like something you might find intriguing? If so, in what ways?

Can you envision yourself managing an elementary classroom? If so, what appeals to you about this age group?

Does managing a classroom of unpredictable, yet wonderful young adolescents appeal to you? If so, why?

Do you have the desire to establish caring relationships with maturing adolescents who wish to be treated as adults but who may not have the self-control or self-motivation to match? If so, explain.

When planning for classroom management, always consider your students and their developmental needs.

Figure 6.10 Roosevelt High School behavior guidelines

Roosevelt High School students are required to conduct themselves in an appropriate, acceptable manner at all times when present in school, in classrooms and hallways, on school grounds, and at school-sponsored events. Students are to:

1. Treat others with consideration and dignity.
2. Respect the property of others.
3. Be punctual and prepared for class.
4. Follow the direction of all staff.

Figure 6.11 21st-century life skills

- Flexibility and adaptability
- Initiative and self-direction
- Social and cross-cultural skills
- Productivity and accountability
- Leadership and responsibility

technology skills. P21's philosophy is that mastering the first three outcome categories is not enough to be successful in life. The fourth outcome category is *Life and Career Skills*. The five major components of Life and Career Skills are listed in Figure 6.11. Let's briefly examine each component.

FLEXIBILITY AND ADAPTABILITY. Being flexible and adaptable doesn't mean passively going with the flow. P21 suggests that we teach students to respond to change in ways that make growth a priority and to use feedback constructively. This means that students need to develop resilience that helps them deal with both praise and criticism. Teaching students to be adaptable involves giving them experiences in different roles, responsibilities, and schedules.

Although we can control many elements in the classroom, it is inevitable that something will interrupt the flow of teaching and learning. For instance, in an elementary classroom a teacher may purposefully orchestrate a disruption in an event students helped plan, like an afternoon outdoors looking for plant samples. The teacher might lead the students to plan the event on a day when she knows the field is scheduled to be mowed. When she tells the students about the mowing the morning of their planned outing, they will be disappointed. She can have the students get into small groups and brainstorm how they might be flexible and adaptable and still accomplish their goals. Then students should share and discuss their possible alternatives. This is a life skill that is very much a part of a productive classroom environment.

INITIATIVE AND SELF-DIRECTION. The components addressed in these life and career skills include managing goals and time, working independently, and being self-directed learners. All of these components play major roles in maintaining a positive and productive learning environment. Independent, self-directed learners will be able to manage time as they accomplish their goals. Helping students become this ultimate vision of who we want them to be isn't necessarily something that becomes part of daily lesson plans. It is a teacher attitude that weaves in and out of every formal and informal encounter we have with students. For instance, a high school civics teacher may plan for students to complete a semester-long project. Many steps are built into the project, beginning with a whole-class activity of brainstorming, followed by small group work for those with similar interests. Then the individual student, armed with skills from working with two different size groups, sets off independently to work through the assignment step by step at his or her own pace. The teacher is deliberately creating experiences that lead to independence and self-direction.

SOCIAL AND CROSS-CULTURAL SKILLS. This area is all about relationships and communication, two vital aspects of a classroom community. Showing respect in a variety of circumstances and with a broad spectrum of people, based on age, gender, ethnicity, abilities, political persuasions, religion, and all the ways we may differ, is key. Every day in the classroom teachers have the responsibility to model acceptance and respectful communication. They model when to speak and when to listen, when to be open minded, and then when to stand on reasoned ground.

One way to foster social and cross-cultural skills is purposefully grouping and regrouping students in ways that expose them to all the diversity a particular setting can offer. Some demographics are rich in diversity; others are not. Even where race and socioeconomic circumstances are similar, students display diversity in learning styles, abilities, motivation, and achievement. Teachers need to look beyond the obvious and into the subtle, and then group students, teaching them how to communicate and work together in positive and productive ways.

In Chapter 3, we discuss student diversity.

PRODUCTIVITY AND ACCOUNTABILITY. Producing results and fulfilling responsibilities, or being accountable, are vital attributes of success. When students experience success through being productive and accountable, success will likely lead to more success. It's a cycle we often have to orchestrate the first or second time around until students experience what it's like to actually be productive. We certainly have to be close guides for younger students to first succeed, and then recognize success in the form of productivity so they understand the cycle and will want to replicate it. But adolescents often need this close guidance as well. Our hovering will have to take different forms to be effective, but that's part of understanding the development of our students. If adolescents have little experience with productivity and accountability, we have to make the elements obvious, actually *plan* for them to succeed, and then help them reflect on the big picture of the relationship between hard work and success.

LEADERSHIP AND RESPONSIBILITY. There's a reason why social studies standards begin with the study of self and family in kindergarten, neighborhoods and community in first grade, and then progress to an overview of local, state, and national dimensions before concentrating on U.S. History in fifth grade. From there, a broad view of history is tackled, followed by in-depth study of how our world works regarding people, geography, politics, and so on. Children and adolescents develop from a narrow perspective on life and their world, to an understanding of interdependence, built in large measure through the guidance of their teachers.

Integrity and ethical behavior, two attributes we hope will be part of all aspects of leadership, don't necessarily happen naturally. Pointing out moral dilemmas and then prompting students to make choices and act in responsible ways is a positive and healthy part of the informal curriculum. For instance, when a dispute arises on the playground, and it most certainly will, rather than assigning a consequence based on what appears to be a rule infraction or just a child being mean, a teacher might plan a class debriefing of the situation with students asking questions of the kids involved in the dispute, attempting to get at the cause of the problem. In this way, students begin to think through situations, look at possible causes and solutions, recognize volatile circumstances, and learn to take responsibility and lead others in that direction as well. Although this all sounds quite straightforward and simple, it takes incident after incident, solution seeking over and over again, to internalize the lessons. As adults this is a lifelong learning task, and for children we can't start too soon to help them develop leadership and responsibility skills.

We discuss appreciation for moral dilemmas in Chapter 1 and the informal curriculum in Chapter 4.

GENERAL GUIDELINES FOR DEVELOPING A CLASSROOM MANAGEMENT PLAN

We have discussed some of the most important elements of developing and implementing a classroom management plan. Figure 6.12 presents Boynton and Boynton's (2005) concise version of the crucial components of an effective system.

Figure 6.12 Components of an effective classroom management system

Five components that, when implemented correctly, are crucial for establishing an effective classroom discipline system include

1. Positive teacher-student relationships
2. Strong content instruction
3. Clearly defined parameters of acceptable student behaviors
4. Use of effective monitoring skills
5. Appropriate consequences

Source: Boynton, M., & Boynton, C. (2005). *The educator's guide to preventing and solving discipline problems* (p. v). Alexandria, VA: Association for Supervision and Curriculum Development.

Certain guidelines are nonnegotiable when establishing a classroom management plan. Although it is impossible to address all of them within the scope of this book, here are several important ones:

- *Always stay within school and district policies and guidelines.*

- *Use positive rather than negative statements when establishing expectations.* Students need to know what they *should* do, not just what they *shouldn't* do. For instance, the expectation "We will show respect for others when working together or apart" is more likely to gain compliance than "We will not be disrespectful of others when working together or apart." Plant positive thoughts in students' minds to promote productive habits of appropriate behavior.

- *Consistently apply expectations and consequences.* Some teachers set an expectation and have different consequences based on the number of times a student's behavior is outside the expectation. This sort of consequence layering in no way undermines the consistency of consequences.

- *Explore conflict resolution and peer mediation.* This approach involves students trained as go-betweens to help other students work through their differences and agree to disagree amicably. Look for such programs as you observe and interact in schools.

- *Communicate and document.* Once established, a teacher's classroom management plan should be explicitly taught to students, the building administrators should receive a written plan, and parents and families should be informed of it. An aspect of communication often neglected by teachers is documentation, or record keeping. When a consequence is applied, document it.

- *Ask for help.* There are some behavior issues that classroom teachers should not handle alone. Physical violence, overt bullying, and verbal abuse of students or adults cannot be tolerated in a classroom setting. Episodes of this nature must be dealt with immediately by administrators.

DON'T BE PART OF THE PROBLEM

Think back to your days in prekindergarten through 12th grade. Can you remember a classroom behavior problem actually getting worse because of something a teacher did or didn't do? Were you ever in a class when student misbehavior escalated so that it was almost out of control even as the teacher yelled for attention? How about out-of-control behavior in the presence of a teacher who repeatedly used "shhhh" to ask for silence? Neither approach works.

Purposefully embarrassing students should never be a teacher tactic. The result may be serious psychological damage to the student. Another likely result is the student's loss of respect for the teacher who has displayed his or her own version of misbehavior.

Avoid making threats without following through. This practice can have disastrous results in a classroom. A teacher repeatedly saying, "If you don't stop that I'll . . ." may cause the immediate misbehavior to escalate, and it guarantees future problems because students won't believe the teacher will follow through.

Teachers should never allow a classroom confrontation to escalate into a power struggle. When a student loses control of his or her temper and directs remarks at a teacher, and the teacher reacts in kind, the opportunity to be a mature, reasonable role model is lost. No one wins. Giving a student time to calm down and gracefully save face will provide a chance for student and teacher to talk about the situation. In some exaggerated cases, avoiding a power struggle prevents physical violence and gives time for administrators to get involved in a resolution.

CONCLUDING THOUGHTS

Students learn much more than academic subjects in our classrooms. They learn how to exist in society. They learn limits of what they can and can't do in terms of behavior. A positive and productive learning environment is safe—physically, emotionally, and academically. When students feel safe they are more likely to participate, learn, and grow.

Creating and maintaining a positive and productive learning environment is hard work. Teachers can learn how to cultivate appropriate relationships with students, how to establish routines that foster productivity, and how to thoughtfully develop classroom management plans that are effective. With diligence and consistent monitoring, a positive and productive learning environment can be maintained.

Well-managed classrooms are marked by civility. Some students come to school without a clear idea of what civility looks like because they don't live in the midst of it. Teachers must model civility, orchestrate an environment that fosters it, and then expect nothing less of students.

After reading the ***Chapter in Review,*** interact with Tim Mendenhall as he struggles to mentor a new teacher in this chapter's ***Developing Professional Competence.***

Chapter in Review

How do teachers create a positive learning environment?

- The physical layout, appearance, usefulness, and overall appeal of the classroom either enhance the learning environment or detract from it.
- Care and trust help teachers and students build a sense of community.
- Teacher awareness, ability to multitask, and recognition that one action directly affects another are valuable assets in creating a positive learning environment.
- Time is a constant in schools that should be used wisely to promote learning.

What routines contribute to maintaining a productive classroom environment?

- The types of routines needed vary by school level, but their importance at all levels cannot be overemphasized.
- Students need to practice routines so they become productive habits.

How do teachers establish expectations, incentives, and consequences?

- Successful classroom management is a prerequisite for successful teaching and learning.
- The best prevention of behavioral problems is engaging instruction.
- Many issues and situations require teachers to establish behavioral expectations, incentives for achieving these expectations, and consequences for not fulfilling them.

How can I develop a classroom management plan?

- Prominent theories and classroom observations provide background and strategies for new teachers to use to formulate management plans.
- Teachers should consider student needs and development when formulating a plan.
- Classroom management plans are most effective when expectations are stated positively, when expectations, incentives, and consequences are applied consistently, and when teachers model appropriate behavior.

Developing Professional Competence

Visit the Developing Professional Competence section in Chapter 6 of the MyEducationLab for this text to answer the following questions and begin your preparation for licensure exams.

You met Tim Mendenhall in the beginning of this text when all the focus teachers, students, and schools were introduced. Then as this chapter began we learned about Tim and his relationship with a new student. We also read about his classroom expectations. He is an experienced teacher who values relationships with students and has confidence in his classroom management procedures.

Tim was asked by Principal Mike Larsen to mentor a new teacher. She came to Rees with a very strong academic record that included graduating with a 4.0 GPA and a master's degree in teaching reading. Mr. Larsen was very excited to give her an opportunity to teach a self-contained fourth grade class as her first teaching assignment. Tim was happy to be her mentor, but when Elizabeth arrived at Rees she wasn't keen on the idea of someone actually assigned to help her be successful, and she let others know it.

Tim was friendly and offered to help her set up her room and to go through the fourth grade curriculum and materials she would use. She politely listened but showed little interest. For classroom management she posted pre-printed posters with rules and warnings. Tim explained that Rees has basic expectations that involve respect and that she may want to meet with her students to talk about what respect might look like in the classrooms and allow the kids to have some input. To that she said no, and told Tim that her training was as a Skinnerian behaviorist.

One afternoon in October, after hearing repeatedly from students that Elizabeth's kids were not happy and several parents had complained to Mr. Larsen, Tim overheard a conversation in the hallway. Elizabeth told Marcus that she was at the limit of her patience, that he was nothing but trouble, that she now knew how to treat him for the rest of the year, and that his parents would be very disappointed in him. Tim knew it was time to talk with Elizabeth even though she had resisted his attempts before.

Think through this scenario and answer the following multiple-choice questions:

1. Which guideline for developing positive teacher-student relationships do you think Elizabeth most likely violated in her encounter with Marcus?
   a. strong content instruction
   b. clearly defined parameters of acceptable student behaviors
   c. use of effective monitoring skills
   d. appropriate consequences

2. Elizabeth told Tim that she is a Skinnerian behaviorist. This means that
   a. She must have studied Skinner and believes that children will behave if they understand what's right.
   b. In her study of Skinner she learned that rewards and punishment will shape student behavior.
   c. In graduate school she learned that B. F. Skinner believed in verbally reprimanding students and humiliating them to gain obedience.
   d. She is a trained specialist in behavior management.

3. Based on what he heard in the hall, Tim is afraid that Elizabeth's style of classroom management will possibly destroy which quality he believes in building?
   a. Resilience
   b. Self-determination
   c. Students' love of learning
   d. A healthy sense of competition among students

Now it's time for you to respond to three short essay items involving the scenario. In your responses, be sure to address all the dilemmas and questions posed in each item. Your responses should each be between one half and one double-spaced page.

4. Refer to Tim's guidelines for classroom management in Figure 6.8. Name two guidelines for which it is likely too late for Elizabeth and this year's fourth graders. Name two guidelines that Elizabeth may have in place, given what you know from this scenario. Explain why you selected each of the four guidelines.

5. What problems does Elizabeth invite for the rest of the year by telling Marcus that she knows how she will treat him? Explain.

6. How might Tim use INTASC Knowledge Principle 5 as he tries to explain to Elizabeth the responsibilities he sees she is missing when it comes to the learning environment? How does this standard differ from her proclaimed Skinnerian approach?

INTASC Knowledge Principle 5
The teacher uses an understanding of individual and group motivation and behavior to create a learning environment that encourages positive social interaction, active engagement in learning, and self-motivation.

Where
DO I Stand NOW?

In the beginning of this chapter you completed an inventory that gauged your experiences with the learning environment in K–12 school. Now that you have read the chapter, completed exercises related to the content, and engaged in class discussions and so on, answer the following questions in your course notebook.

1. Reading this chapter has likely triggered memories of at least a few aspects of your K–12 learning environment that were not positive. What is an example of a less-than-positive experience, and what do you now see that your teacher could have done to improve the situation?

2. Has your view of what constitutes a positive, productive learning environment changed as a result of reading this chapter? If so, in what way(s)?

3. Considering your own experiences and what you have learned, what aspect of the learning environment do you predict will be most challenging for you to manage: the physical environment, relationships with students, setting expectations, matching consequences to infractions, another aspect? Explain.

MyEducationLab

The MyEducationLab for this course can help you solidify your comprehension of Chapter 6 concepts.

- Explore the classrooms of the teachers and students you've met in this chapter in the Teaching in Focus section.
- Prepare for licensure exams as you deepen your understanding of chapter concepts in the Developing Professional Competence section.

- Gauge and further develop your understanding of chapter concepts by taking the quizzes and examining the enrichment materials in the Chapter 6 Study Plan.
- Visit Topic 9, "Managing the Classroom," to watch ABC videos, explore Assignments and Activities, and practice essential teaching skills with the Building Teaching Skills and Dispositions unit.

7

History of Education in the United States

Knowing the major influences, issues, ideologies, and individuals in the history of education will give you some perspective as you explore education in the United States. The major questions guiding this chapter include:

✦ What were the major influences, issues, ideologies, and individuals in 17th-century American education?

✦ What were the major influences, issues, ideologies, and individuals in 18th-century American education?

✦ What were the major influences, issues, ideologies, and individuals in 19th-century American education?

✦ What were the major influences, issues, ideologies, and individuals in 20th-century American education?

✦ What major influences, issues, ideologies, and individuals are we experiencing in 21st-century American education?

✦ How are U.S. schools addressing racial and ethnic diversity in the 21st century?

✦ How can I be aware of education history in the making?

History is not dull or dry. Real people in real places used problem-solving techniques to address and solve real issues as they arose and made history in the process.

Before we discuss the history of education in the United States, see how much you already know in this chapter's *Where Do I Stand?*

Where DO I Stand?

This chapter's inventory consists of statements about both the history of our country and the history of education in America. All of the topics in the inventory are addressed in the chapter.

Rather than a 0 to 4 scale asking for agreement or opinion, this inventory is in true/false format. The purpose is to activate your prior knowledge, not to assign a grade to what you know or don't know.

In 17th-century America...

_____ **1.** colonization began in New York about 1650.

_____ **2.** the first settlers valued children's play.

_____ **3.** colonial schools were established for religious reasons.

_____ **4.** schools were primarily for both white girls and boys.

_____ **5.** the first elementary schools were known as dame schools.

_____ **6.** schools were very different based on where children lived.

_____ **7.** the first high school was the Latin Grammar School.

_____ **8.** the Old Deluder Satan Act established the requirement that communities have churches.

_____ **9.** educational opportunities in southern colonies were based on social class.

_____ **10.** teacher preparation schools flourished.

In 18th-century America...

_____ **1.** Ben Franklin introduced the idea of a variety of courses.

_____ **2.** town schools met intellectual and economic needs.

_____ **3.** Thomas Jefferson was primarily concerned with intellectual pursuits in schools.

_____ **4.** the University of Virginia was founded and shaped by Thomas Jefferson.

_____ **5.** the Quakers established a school for elementary students that included girls, African Americans, and Native Americans.

_____ **6.** Noah Webster believed that education of women was an absolute necessity.

_____ **7.** the Northwest Land Ordinance of 1787 required the building of schools.

_____ **8.** the Bill of Rights included education.

_____ **9.** education began to emerge as a priority.

_____ **10.** the Declaration of Independence almost immediately followed the Constitution.

In 19th-century America...

_____ **1.** almost 30 states were added to our country.

_____ **2.** the war between the North and South erupted at the end of the century.

_____ **3.** schools were consistent and evenly distributed.

_____ **4.** McGuffey was considered the father of education.

_____ **5.** common schools were community-supported elementary schools for all children.

_____ **6.** kindergartens were developed after elementary and high schools.

_____ **7.** normal schools prepared teachers.

_____ **8.** mental disabilities were addressed.

_____ **9.** most schooling of Native American children was provided by missionaries.

_____ **10.** the education of African American children faced legal objection by state or federal governments.

In 20th-century America...

_____ **1.** progressivism involved letting student interests guide learning.

_____ **2.** Maria Montessori founded progressive education.

_____ **3.** junior highs were established.

_____ **4.** middle schools became a popular alternative to junior highs by 1950.

_____ **5.** *Brown* v. *Board of Education* dictated that schools for African American students must meet the same standards as schools for white students.

6. _____ **6.** the election of John F. Kennedy gave rise to a sense of idealism.

_____ **7.** the *Elementary and Secondary Education Act* (ESEA) of 1965 provided extra money for school districts with low-income families.

_____ **8.** the Education for All Handicapped Children Act made provisions for children with disabilities to be educated in their own special schools.

_____ **9.** *A Nation at Risk* stated that public education in the U.S. was mediocre at best.

_____ **10.** tests were designed to determine whether students had met standards.

In 21st-century America...

_____ **1.** trust of government and business prevail.

_____ **2.** the defining legislation of the first decade was the No Child Left Behind Act of 2001.

_____ **3.** it would be difficult to recognize how schools have changed since the 1990s.

_____ **4.** the Partnership for 21st Century Skills (P21) has little impact on state goal setting.

_____ **5.** a major challenge to the viability of NCLB is that individual states have to abide by the same standards and testing.

_____ **6.** virtual education is becoming more widespread.

_____ **7.** overall U.S. schools are more segregated now than before the Court ruling.

_____ **8.** there are over 45 million Hispanic people living in the United States.

_____ **9.** the Asian population is rapidly growing.

_____ **10.** more Middle Eastern Americans align with Christianity than with Islam.

Now use the key and score each century's items. Shade this bar graph to indicate the number of items you got correct in each century.

# correct	17th	18th	19th	20th	21st
10					
9					
8					
7					
6					
5					
4					
3					
2					
1					

Key

	17TH	18TH	19TH	20TH	21ST
1	F	T	T	T	F
2	F	T	F	F	T
3	T	F	F	T	T
4	F	T	F	F	F
5	T	T	T	F	F
6	T	T	T	T	T
7	T	T	T	T	T
8	F	F	F	F	T
9	T	T	T	T	F
10	F	F	T	T	T

*According to **Where Do I Stand?**, which century do you know most about? Which century do you know least about?*

Teaching in Focus

Angelica Reynosa, a world history teacher at Roosevelt High School, California, knows that her task of helping sophomores understand historic events and their impact on today's world is a complex one. Most of the 31 students in Angelica's lesson are new to the United States. Some of them may have picked up English through classes at Roosevelt or simply from living in Fresno. Many live in homes where only Spanish is spoken. These students haven't grown up steeped in the U.S. social studies curriculum and reciting the Pledge of Allegiance each morning since they were 5 years old. As a second-generation American herself, Angelica understands at least some of her students' challenges.

Angelica has always loved to study history. She views the subject she teaches as a living, breathing entity that's filled with problem-solving scenarios and intrigue. Her teaching philosophy dictates that she engage her students, not merely give reading assignments. The objective of the lesson in the video is "Students will participate in an activity that will help them grasp the reasons for the rise of Marxist theory. They will experience the 'haves' and 'have-nots' of the capitalist system and critically evaluate the benefits and drawbacks of capitalism and socialism." That's an ambitious objective, one that takes lots of thought and planning.

Many of Angelica's students fall into the have-nots, similar to the people Angelica describes in her lesson. They may be in the United States illegally, crowded into the homes of extended family while their parents look for work or hold low-paying jobs. There's so much Angelica wants them to understand about the world.

Watch Angelica's lesson in the Teaching in Focus *section for Chapter 7 in MyEducationLab for this course.*

What Were the Major Influences, Issues, Ideologies, and Individuals in 17th-Century American Education?

Schools in the 17th century were established by the Europeans who settled along the east coast of what would become the United States of America.

CONTEXT FOR CHANGE

The founding of Jamestown, Virginia, in 1607 by roughly 100 men is used to mark the formal beginning of America's colonization. Previous voyages to the New World were mostly prompted by the hope of finding riches. The English Puritan religious sect who settled in Plymouth, Massachusetts, 23 years later included men, women, and children. Families came to begin new lives in a place where they hoped to be free to worship their God in their chosen ways. Culturally, the first colonists had their roots in England; religiously, the first colonists opposed the Church of England because it lacked tolerance for any doctrine other than its own. The Church of England in the 17th century was an extension of the English government. To escape being forced to abide by the Church of England's doctrine, the Puritans, who held that the Bible in its literal (or pure) form is the source of all wisdom, sought to establish English-style colonies with their own biblical interpretations to guide them. However, they were not particularly more tolerant than the Church of England they had escaped. For instance, because Roger Williams, one of the prominent Puritans of the 17th century, espoused separation of church and state, he was banished from the Massachusetts Bay Colony to what is now Rhode Island.

The Puritans believed that people were basically sinful and children would remain so if they could not ward off Satan by reading the Bible and faithfully upholding its principles. To the Puritans, children were merely small adults who needed to learn scripture. Play was considered a waste of time, and discipline was stern (Pulliam & Van Patten, 2007). This attitude carried over into early American schools.

Some of the events of the 17th century, and those of the centuries since, are depicted on the timeline in Figure 7.1. Notice that selected events of American history are depicted alongside momentous events in U.S. public education to provide context for what you read in this chapter. Refer to Figure 7.1 often as you progress through the centuries.

17TH-CENTURY AMERICAN SCHOOLS

The early colonists recognized the need to provide schooling for their children, at least for their male children. They also knew that learning a trade was perhaps best accomplished by working with an expert artisan. Later, as colonies flourished in New England, the middle Atlantic area, and the South, more formal types of schools grew in both number and variety.

EARLY COLONIAL SCHOOLS. Having left England and suffered the hardships of the transatlantic voyage to the New World, the Puritans established an early type of schooling influenced both by European theorists, some of whom are listed in Table 7.1 (p. 186), and by Puritan religious beliefs and social customs. Although the first colonial schools were established for religious purposes, they helped the secular aspects of society develop and prosper as well by teaching students to read and write. These students, overwhelmingly white boys, then had the skills to participate in commerce.

The earliest Puritan settlers educated their children within their own homes, but **dame schools** soon became common. Dames were respected women who, usually without formal schooling, had learned to read and write, and who turned their homes into schools where parents paid to have their children educated. Some children went from a dame school, which was essentially the first American elementary school, or from no schooling at all, to an apprenticeship that required them (virtually all boys) to move into the home of a master. The master taught them a trade and often also taught them basic literacy skills. Girls usually stayed home and learned homemaking skills from their mothers.

As education moved from individual homes into schools throughout colonial America, notable differences in education emerged among colonies in different geographic areas. Figure 7.2 is a map of colonial America showing the three basic geographic areas we discuss next.

SCHOOLS IN THE NEW ENGLAND COLONIES. In 1630 the Massachusetts Bay Colony was established, followed by Rhode Island, Connecticut, and New Hampshire. These four colonies made up early New England. Their inhabitants tended to be very much alike, sharing the Puritan faith and English roots. They tended to settle in towns that made formal education a relatively easy endeavor. Dame schools were commonplace for New England children, who learned basic reading, writing, and arithmetic skills, all within a religious context. Girls in New England were allowed to attend the dame schools, although their curriculum was different and focused primarily on homemaking. The elementary education of a dame school was generally the extent of what girls received in terms of formal schooling for much of the colonial period.

In 1635 the first **Latin grammar school** was established in Boston for boys whose families could afford education beyond the dame school. The word *grammar* is associated with elementary school today but was a term for secondary schools in the 17th century. Students learned higher levels of reading, writing, and arithmetic, along with classical literature. The Latin grammar schools were considered the forerunners of modern high schools and specifically prepared boys to attend Harvard University, established in 1636 (Tehie, 2007).

Only the wealthiest New Englanders went beyond dame schools. Schooling opportunities and apprenticeships for white boys from poorer families were either less desirable or nonexistent. Girls, African Americans, and Native Americans had even fewer opportunities for educational advancement.

Some Puritan leaders recognized the benefits of educating all children, at least all white children. The **Massachusetts Act of 1642** was the first **compulsory education law** in the New World. Although the law required all white children to attend school, it did not specify how or where children would get an education. Nor did the law provide funding, making it the first **unfunded mandate,** a legally enforceable law without provision for monetary support. Five years later, the Massachusetts Act of 1647, also known as the **Old Deluder Satan Act** because education was considered the best way to fight the devil, established that every town of 50 or more households must provide a school. Again, no funding was attached, and either parents or the whole community contributed to supporting a

Figure 7.1 U.S. education in historical perspective

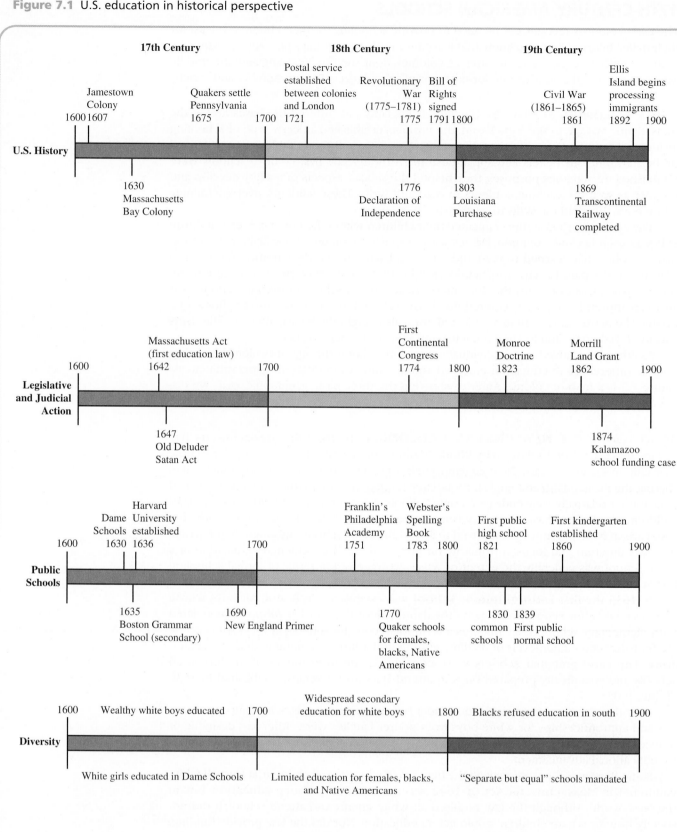

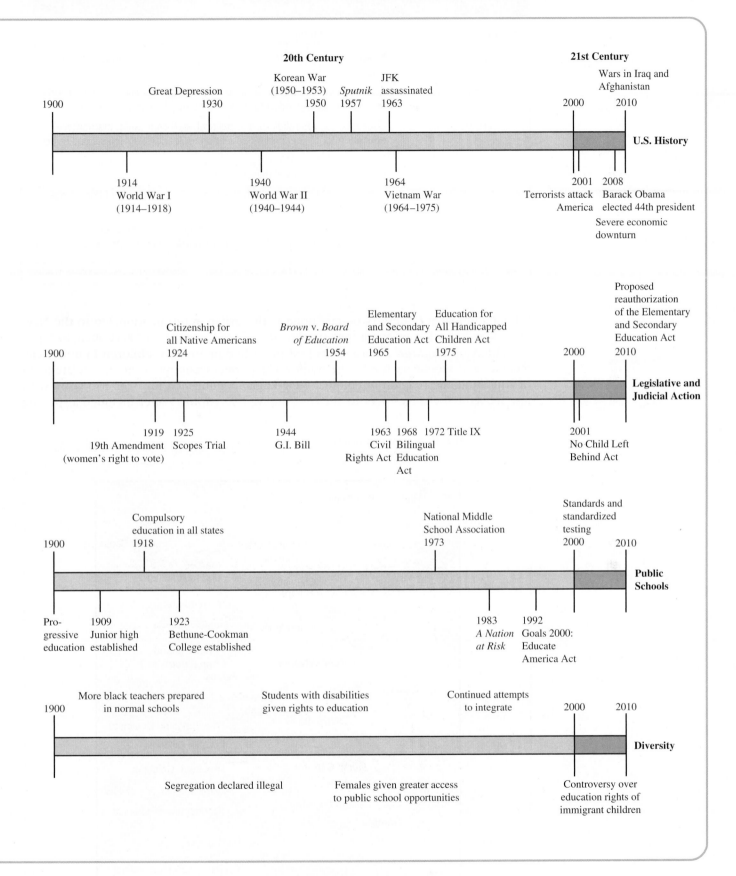

20th Century

Great Depression
1930

Korean War
(1950–1953)
1950

Sputnik
1957

JFK
assassinated
1963

21st Century

Wars in Iraq and
Afghanistan

1900   2000   2010

U.S. History

1914
World War I
(1914–1918)

1940
World War II
(1940–1944)

1964
Vietnam War
(1964–1975)

2001
Terrorists attack
America

2008
Barack Obama
elected 44th president

Severe economic
downturn

Citizenship for
all Native Americans
1924

Brown v. *Board
of Education*
1954

Elementary
and Secondary
Education Act
1965

Education for
All Handicapped
Children Act
1975

Proposed
reauthorization
of the Elementary
and Secondary
Education Act

1900   2000   2010

**Legislative and
Judicial Action**

1919
19th Amendment
(women's right to vote)

1925
Scopes Trial

1944
G.I. Bill

1963
Civil
Rights Act

1968
Bilingual
Education
Act

1972 Title IX

2001
No Child Left
Behind Act

Compulsory
education in all states
1918

National Middle
School Association
1973

Standards and
standardized
testing
2000

1900   2010

**Public
Schools**

Pro-
gressive
education

1909
Junior high
established

1923
Bethune-Cookman
College established

1983
*A Nation
at Risk*

1992
Goals 2000:
Educate
America Act

More black teachers prepared
in normal schools

Students with disabilities
given rights to education

Continued attempts
to integrate

1900   2000   2010

Diversity

Segregation declared illegal

Females given greater access
to public school opportunities

Controversy over
education rights of
immigrant children

TABLE 7.1 Influence of major theorists on early American education

Theorist	Summary of Influence
Erasmus (1466–1536)	Need for systematic training of teachers; liberal arts education includes classics
Luther (1483–1546)	Education necessary for religious instruction; education should include vocational training; need for free and compulsory education
Calvin (1509–1564)	Education serves religious and political establishments; elementary education for all; secondary education for leaders; emphasis on literacy
Bacon (1561–1626)	Education should advance scientific inquiry; provide rationale for development of critical thinking skills
Comenius (1592–1670)	Learning must come through the senses; general body of knowledge (*paideia*) should be possessed by all
Locke (1632–1704)	Goal of education is to promote the development of reason and morality to enable men to participate in the governing process

Source: Webb, L. D., Metha, A., & Jordan, K. F. (2010). *Foundations of American education* (6th ed.). Upper Saddle River, NJ: Pearson/Merrill.

school and teacher. These two acts, along with Puritan determination, led to the New England colonies having about the same literacy rate as England by 1700 (Cohen, 1974).

The ***New England Primer*** was first published in 1690 for children in upper elementary and secondary levels. The book was a perfect example of the interrelatedness of education and religion in colonial New England. Published for over 150 years with few substantial changes over its lifetime, the *New England Primer* included a spelling

Figure 7.2 The 13 original colonies

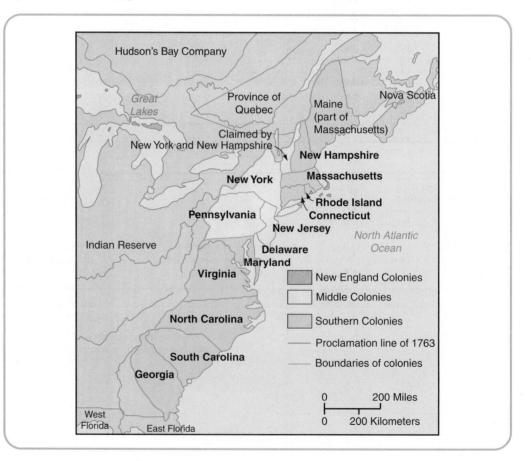

Figure 7.3 New England Primer

guide based on the alphabet denoted in brief rhymes and pictures. The *New England Primer* also included the Lord's Prayer, the Apostles' Creed, the Ten Commandments, a list of the books of the Bible, and the numbers 1 to 100. Figure 7.3 contains a sample from the *New England Primer.*

SCHOOLS IN THE MIDDLE COLONIES. New York, New Jersey, Pennsylvania, and Delaware made up the middle colonies. Their population was much less homogeneous than that of New England. Settlers came from Sweden, the Netherlands, Germany, France, and other parts of Europe, along with people of the Quaker faith who primarily settled in Pennsylvania.

No one kind of school could satisfy the diversity of the middle colonists. Each religious sect established its own brand of schooling: Lutherans, Presbyterians, Jews, Mennonites, Catholics, Quakers, Baptists, Huguenots, and so on. The colonies attempted to license schools but did not provide financing. The middle colony schools were mostly private, or *parochial,* a term typically associated with religion. These parochial schools often taught a greater variety of subjects than the New England schools and included topics such as business, bookkeeping, and navigation.

> Parochial schools are discussed in Chapter 2.

SCHOOLS IN THE SOUTHERN COLONIES. Like the middle colonies, the southern colonies were settled by diverse groups, but the settlers were even more widespread geographically. In Virginia, Maryland, Georgia, and the Carolinas, more so than in New England or the middle colonies, opportunities for education were based almost exclusively on social class. Children of plantation owners and wealthy merchants either attended private schools or were taught at home by tutors. These privileged students went from elementary to secondary schools either in the South or in Europe. Children who lived on small farms or children of laborers experienced whatever education was available through charity schools run by people who believed education should be more widely available, apprentice programs, or church schools. The children of slaves received no formal education in the southern colonies during the 17th century.

Points of Reflection 7.1

What evidence are you aware of that leads you to believe that where students live today affects their educational opportunities?

TEACHERS IN COLONIAL AMERICA

During the 17th century there was no formal system of teacher preparation. The closest parallel would have been apprentices assigned to Quaker teachers, who themselves lacked formal training in the education of both children and teachers. In dame schools the teachers were widows or housewives who could read and write to some unspecified degree of proficiency. Men who taught in the first elementary schools often did so for very short periods of time before beginning official training for the ministry or law.

Many teachers were indentured servants who taught in exchange for passage to the New World. Often people were teachers because they were not successful in other occupations; some were even of questionable character or conduct (Pulliam & Van Patten, 2007).

Teachers in the secondary schools (Latin grammar schools) enjoyed more status than those in elementary-level schools. They often had more education themselves, and many had college training (Ornstein & Levine, 2006).

Many teachers in both the 17th and 18th centuries participated in the curious custom of boarding 'round. To save lodging money, towns required teachers to live with the families of their students for 1 week at a time. This practice did nothing for the dignity of the teacher or the profession. Pay was low, about what farmhands made, and without permanent homes, teachers often thought of themselves as expendable part-time employees.

What Were the Major Influences, Issues, Ideologies, and Individuals in 18th-Century American Education?

The first half of the 18th century was one of geographic expansion on American soil and the maturation of economic and political climate. In perspective, it was relatively calm in terms of history and schools when compared to the second half.

CONTEXT FOR CHANGE

Representatives to the First Continental Congress (1774) in Philadelphia met originally to discuss how to claim their rights as British citizens in America. However, the Declaration of Independence soon followed, as did the writing of the Constitution, and then the Bill of Rights. The United States of America was rapidly taking shape (Boyer & Stuckey, 2005).

Future leaders, such as Benjamin Franklin (1706–1790) and Thomas Jefferson (1743–1826), were born and grew up not only to pave the way for the new nation, but also to influence the direction in which 18th-century education was heading.

18TH-CENTURY AMERICAN SCHOOLS

In 1751 Benjamin Franklin established the Franklin Academy, a school that was oriented toward real-world, useful learning. The Franklin Academy offered mathematics, astronomy, navigation, accounting, bookkeeping, French, and Spanish. One significant contribution of the Franklin Academy was its provision for students to choose some courses, the forerunner of today's electives.

Private **academies** sprang up across America. These schools were designed to teach content intended to prepare students to participate in business and trade. They met not only intellectual needs but also economic needs. In addition to these academies, **town schools** were established for whole communities. Although some schools still limited curriculum to reading, writing, and the classics, specialized schools in the form of academies became popular.

Thomas Jefferson had political, practical, and intellectual motives for his interest in and attention to education. He believed that education

Benjamin Franklin (1706–1790)

A pudgy, bookish man with long curly hair and little square glasses, flying a kite in the middle of a thunderstorm, is the image most have of Ben Franklin. Inventor and philosopher extraordinaire, Franklin contributed to American education in many valuable ways. In the mid-18th century he espoused educating America's youth in the practical and useful arts and trades. In addition to the traditional study of reading and math, he was the first to propose the study of history that included not just past politics and wars but also customs and commerce. He founded the Library Company of Philadelphia in 1731 to promote reading by subscription to help tradesmen and farmers become as intelligent as gentlemen of other countries. In his *Proposals Relating to the Youth of Pennsylvania* (1749), Franklin said that wise men view the education of youth as "the surest foundation of. . . happiness" (Franklin, 1931, p. 151).

Franklin (1749/1931); Good (1964).

was essential to the maintenance of a viable republic. Education, in Jefferson's view, would increase production and preserve health. In 1779 he proposed the Virginia Bill for the More General Diffusion of Knowledge that provided for broader availability of education for more children. Jefferson's bill did not pass the Virginia legislature, but it raised awareness of the need and potential value of education among both lawmakers and the public (Good, 1964).

In the 18th century many Quakers came to America. They believed that education should be all-inclusive. In Philadelphia in 1770 Quakers established a school for elementary students that included girls, African Americans, and Native Americans. In the South, however, formal education for African and Native Americans was nonexistent, despite a high literacy rate for white men and women. In Virginia, for example, 9 of 10 white men, and 2 of 3 white women were able to read (Button & Provenzo, 1989).

Noah Webster (1758–1843) had a profound influence on 18th-century American schools, particularly because of his writing. His most important work was the *American Spelling Book*, published in 1783. Some scholars say Webster had more influence on American education than anyone else in the 18th century and have referred to him as "Schoolmaster of the Republic" (Webb, Metha, & Jordan, 2010).

Several colleges were established in the colonies prior to the American Revolution, among them Yale University in 1701, the University of Pennsylvania in 1753, Brown University in 1764, and Dartmouth College in 1769. At first, theology was the most popular degree; later, other majors, such as law, medicine, and commerce, increased in popularity (Cohen, 1974).

18TH-CENTURY TEACHERS

As was true in the 17th century, teachers in the 18th century continued to be undervalued in most of colonial America. Figure 7.4 contains a description of the life circumstances of an itinerant teacher who, while enjoying a stellar reputation, found that employment was both uncertain and difficult. The second excerpt is from the journal of a female teacher who lived with her students' families and found teaching to be a very exasperating job.

EDUCATION AS A PRIORITY

Education received a boost in priority with the passage of the **Northwest Land Ordinance of 1787,** which divided federally owned wilderness land into townships and required the building of schools. Article Three of the Ordinance proclaimed "Religion, morality, and knowledge being necessary to good government and the happiness of mankind, schools and the means of education shall be forever encouraged."

Education is not directly mentioned in the U.S. Constitution ratified in 1788. However, the Tenth Amendment in the Bill of Rights states, "The powers not delegated to the United States by the

Thomas Jefferson (1743–1826)

As author of the Declaration of Independence and the third president of the United States (1801-1809), Thomas Jefferson believed that only through education could people preserve freedom and promote their own happiness. Historian S. Alexander Rippa (1997) said of Jefferson that "none has so consistently viewed public education as the indispensable cornerstone of freedom" (p. 55). Jefferson believed that government must be by the consent of the governed, and he wanted those governed to read. In fact, he suggested to President John Adams that anyone who was given the opportunity to learn to read but didn't, should not be allowed to vote. President Adams disagreed with this idea.

Disappointed by the Virginia House of Burgess's refusal to pass his Bill for the More General Diffusion of Knowledge, Jefferson spent the years following his presidency establishing the University of Virginia (UVA). It was truly his university in the beginning. He designed both the curriculum and the buildings, bought the trees and designed the landscaping, purchased the library books, chose the faculty, and admitted the first class of students. Thomas Jefferson died on July 4, 1826, 1 year after UVA opened and exactly 50 years following the adoption of the Declaration of Independence.

Good (1964); Rippa (1997).

Noah Webster (1758–1843)

More than any other education statesman of the late 18th and early 19th centuries, Noah Webster reshaped the English language and literature into America's own. He was intensely patriotic and believed that America needed not only political independence from Europe but also cultural independence. The enormous success of Webster's *American Spelling Book*, which included moral stories, lists of words, and a pronunciation guide, put an end to the importing of English books to be used as textbooks. Webster believed in free education for all American boys and girls. Interestingly, he saw the education of women as an absolute necessity because they are the first teachers of children. A Yale graduate, member of the Massachusetts legislature, lawyer, writer, scholar, and businessman, Noah Webster had a tremendous impact on American education.

Good (1964); Gutek (2005); Webb et al. (2010).

Figure 7.4 Teachers in the 18th century

About Silas Crocker.
Mr. Crocker is an itinerant schoolteacher, going from village to village in search of employment. During the summer months he earns a living plowing, mowing, and carting manure. In the winter, he teaches school. Having the reputation as the greatest 'arithmeticker' in the county, he is a respected schoolmaster. Most of the schoolrooms in the area are familiar with this tall, gaunt master.

 From Mistress Robbins' Journal.
 My name is Elizabeth Robbins, and I am in my seventeenth year. I have been engaged to teach at Litchfield. A committee of the subscribers examined me and asked that I read passages from the Old Testament. They seemed pleased when I did not stumble over the big words....I was hired for a period of five months, at four dollars a month.

 I find a wretched schoolhouse, in the road, as it were, with a tiny fireplace. At first, it was easy, as the older scholars stayed away. When the school is full, however, it is very difficult to teach. The older boys make threats against me. They are generally lawless, and in the habit of using profane language. I have to resort to using severe corporal punishment to maintain order.

Source: Loeper, J. L. (1973). *Going to school in 1776.* New York: Macmillan.

Constitution, nor prohibited by it to the states, are reserved to the States respectively, or to the people." Thus, from the inception of the United States to the present, except for the occasional federal mandate, states have grappled independently with educational issues.

As the new nation of the United States of America approached the 19th century, a surge of energy was directed toward education. Leaders and policies emerged that would place American education squarely in the foreground of thought and action.

What Were the Major Influences, Issues, Ideologies, and Individuals in 19th-Century American Education?

The 19th century was one of unprecedented growth, both geographically and governmentally.

CONTEXT FOR CHANGE

In 1800 American geography lessons included maps showing 17 states. By the end of the century maps of America boasted 45 states. During this century the United States established a functioning and flourishing economy, endured a protracted test of the strength of its union (the Civil War), and matured into a stable, respected political entity.

With the election of President Andrew Jackson in 1828, the birth of the Democratic Party brought changes to American politics, turning a nation governed largely by an aristocratic society to one based in greater measure on government of, by, and for the people. Westward expansion propelled by the continuing desire for individual independence and opportunity took the growing nation all the way to the Pacific Ocean.

Cultural and economic differences between an increasingly industrialized North and an agrarian South grew and festered in the 19th century. The rift erupted into the Civil War in 1861 as southern states seceded from the Union and formed the Confederacy.

Although the most commonly perceived reason for the Civil War is slavery, other actual issues surrounding the onset of hostilities revolved around states' rights and economics. Over 600,000 Americans on both sides lost their lives before the North and South were reunited in 1865.

Of all the issues facing the American population as the 19th century drew to a close, the most significant were associated with the Industrial Revolution. Poverty-level wages, a workforce that would soon include too many children, unchecked immigration, and abysmal working conditions all reflected poorly on the country's ability to cope with the abuses actually brought about by its wonderful spirit of inventiveness. Each of these issues would have to be faced and solved, and the educational system revamped to meet the needs of the more commerce- and industry-based society that was on the horizon.

19TH-CENTURY AMERICAN SCHOOLS

The 19th century in the United States was characterized by a wide variety of schools. There were town schools, primarily in the northern states; charity schools, run by churches and philanthropic groups; and widely varying dame schools serving as small venues for local education. Religious schools grew as families banded together with others of the same denomination and country of origin. Academies of all descriptions, some prestigious and some humble, flourished in the first half of the 19th century. In the South most educational opportunities still belonged to the wealthy; in the West most frontier children did not attend school. The obvious lack of consistency and opportunity did not mirror the ideals of America's founders, who saw education as a means to accomplish the goal stated in the Preamble of the U.S. Constitution to "promote the general Welfare."

On the post–Civil War education front, one fact was crystal clear: Both the classical educational system popular in the Northeast and the one-room schoolhouse approach adopted during western frontier days were increasingly incapable of meeting the needs of the country. Let's look at some of the categories of schools developed in 19th-century America.

Horace Mann and the common school movement made it possible for some black children to be educated in public schools.

COMMON SCHOOLS. The system of free public schools that exists today had its beginnings in the common schools movement, first established about 1830. **Common schools** were community-supported elementary schools for *all* children established in response to a variety of economic, social, and political factors. This was a radical departure from previous schooling that catered primarily to wealthy males. Think about it…*all* children. Because free public education for all children was a new concept, common schools were debated, with many citizens seeing their value and others remaining skeptical, as illustrated in Table 7.2. Horace Mann was the champion of common schools. In fact, he was widely regarded as a champion of children in general and of the basic American ideal of opportunity for all.

TABLE 7.2 Merits of and objections to the common school from various viewpoints	
Group	**Merits**
From the viewpoint of...	Common schools provided...
the working class	avenues for social and economic mobility
some in business and industry	an increase in the supply of literate and trained workers
social groups	means of controlling crime and social unrest
people of the frontier	symbols of civilization and ways to keep literacy and citizenship alive in the wilderness
Group	**Objections**
From the viewpoint of...	Common schools were objectionable because...
private school proponents	free schools meant fewer private school students
some in business and industry	they decreased the workforce of children who opted for school instead of jobs
some political leaders	of their apprehensions that an overeducated citizenry might question authority

Points of Reflection 7.2

How would you compare the views of businesspeople and politicians today concerning public schools to the views held by businesspeople and politicians in the 19th century concerning common schools, the first public schools?

Horace Mann (1796–1859)

Widely known as the Father of American Education, Horace Mann had a profound influence not only on early American schools but also on modern schools. He believed that regular attendance in schools with quality teachers would serve to equalize opportunities for poor, African American, and disabled children. He vigorously advocated for common schools.

As attorney and state legislator turned education advocate, Mann established the first **normal school** in 1839 in Lexington, Massachusetts. Normal schools proved to be incredibly important as 2-year colleges specifically designed to prepare teachers. Mann was not afraid of controversy as he pushed for separation of church and schools, not a popular stance in 19th-century America. Even as an avowed religious man, he was often criticized from church pulpits. As the first secretary of education for the Massachusetts Board of Education, which he helped establish in 1837, and throughout his life, Horace Mann spoke eloquently and worked tirelessly as a champion of schools and students.

Not only was Horace Mann an advocate for free quality education, but he also worked for the abolition of slavery and the limiting of alcohol as a social problem and was a vocal supporter of women's rights.

Chartock (2004)

More court cases are discussed in Chapter 10.

Early childhood education is discussed in Chapter 2.

W. H. McGuffey (1800–1873)

Far from the overly pious and drab books that painted a dreary picture of the worth of children and first appeared in American schools, W. H. McGuffey's six-volume set of *McGuffey's Readers* included stories and poetry that appealed to the interests of students. The volumes were geared to specific levels and paved the way to the separation of elementary school into grade levels. The volumes sold over 1 million copies between 1836 and 1906 and helped students learn to read and study while instilling in them virtues such as patriotism, morality, and a work ethic. McGuffey, as a minister, professor, and college president, indelibly left his mark on American education.

McNergney and McNergney (2009); Webb et al. (2010).

In common schools, and most other schools of the 19th century, the works of William Holmes McGuffey had the most significant impact on what children learned. McGuffey's books differed from the unimaginative literature of previous centuries and included stories that promoted truth, honesty, and hard work.

As common schools increased in number, their inconsistencies became more and more apparent. Some were housed in acceptable buildings with adequate supplies and appropriate heating and lighting. Other common schools were housed in dilapidated, poorly heated and lit, filthy surroundings.

SECONDARY SCHOOLS. When the English Classical School opened for young men in Boston in 1821, it marked the beginning of the public high school. In 1824 the school's name was changed to the Boston English High School. In 1838 a coeducational high school opened in Philadelphia. This school offered three tracks: a classical (Latin) curriculum (4 years), a modern language curriculum (4 years), and an English curriculum (2 years) (Webb et al., 2010).

Before the Civil War, high schools were almost exclusively found in the North and always in cities. Because children could learn to read in common schools, and reading was considered sufficient education by many citizens, high schools were slow to grow in number.

In the aftermath of the Civil War, with Reconstruction and rapidly growing industrialization, economic growth spurred the establishment of more schools—not just common schools, but also secondary schools. High schools began to flourish about 1850 and by 1870 had replaced academies as the dominant secondary school. In 1874 a case in the Michigan Supreme Court called the **Kalamazoo case** established that the legislature could tax for support of both common and secondary schools, propelling public high schools into school systems in every state (Ornstein & Levine, 2006).

KINDERGARTEN. Early childhood education in the United States developed after elementary (common schools) and high schools (secondary schools). In Europe, Swiss educator Johann Pestalozzi (1746–1827) developed the theory of child-centered education and the concept of individual differences among children. German educator Friedrich Froebel (1782–1852) agreed with Pestalozzi, but he took child-centered education further. Froebel was a proponent of an activity-based curriculum in an early childhood setting, where children are encouraged to be creative and expressive. This setting was called a kindergarten, or "children's garden." The first kindergarten in the United States was established in 1860 in Boston. By 1873 kindergartens had become part of many public school systems (Chartock, 2004).

With the establishment of kindergarten, common school, and high school, the need for specially prepared teachers grew.

TEACHER PREPARATION

Before Horace Mann's proposal that teachers receive special training, few completed any form of secondary education. Teachers were inadequately and inconsistently prepared. Notable exceptions were the teachers prepared at the Troy Female Seminary, the first institution of higher learning for women in the United States, established in Troy, New York, in 1821 by Emma Willard (1787–1870).

The first normal school, a publicly funded institution dedicated exclusively to preparing teachers, was established 18 years later, in 1839 in Lexington, Massachusetts. Catherine Beecher (1800–1878), along with Horace Mann, was instrumental in making teacher preparation a priority in normal schools.

As these first specially prepared teachers entered their classrooms, they seldom encountered children with disabilities, children of color, or children of poor immigrants. This situation would change with time.

19TH-CENTURY EDUCATION FOR CHILDREN WITH DISABILITIES, MINORITIES, AND IMMIGRANTS

The 19th century was marked by meager, yet important, advances in education for children with disabilities, children of color, and children of poor immigrants.

CHILDREN WITH DISABILITIES. Social mores of the day demanded that any educational opportunities for children with disabilities be separate from those for children without disabilities. A few innovative schools were established in the 19th century for students with certain disabilities. In 1817 Thomas Gallaudet established the first school for the deaf in Hartford, Connecticut. In the mid-19th century, physician Samuel Howe was influential in the establishment of the first school for blind children, the Perkins School for the Blind in Watertown, Massachusetts (Cubberly, 1934). Mental and behavioral disabilities were not addressed in 19th-century schools.

NATIVE AMERICAN CHILDREN. In 1824 the U.S. government established the Bureau of Indian Affairs and began placing whole tribes of Native Americans on reservations. Most of what little formal schooling Native American children received was provided by missionaries, whose efforts were fueled by a desire to convert the children to Christianity. The missionary schools were not consistently organized or maintained (Chartock, 2004).

A further goal of most efforts to educate Native American children in the 19th century was **assimilation,** that is, making the children more like white children, the dominant culture, or, in the terms of the time, "civilizing" them. The

Friedrich Froebel (1782–1852)

When the first English-speaking kindergarten in the United States opened in Boston in 1860, it was the direct result of the work of Friedrich Froebel, widely viewed as the father of the kindergarten or "children's garden." Froebel thought of young children as flowers that would blossom into healthy adults if given the opportunity to be creative in an active curriculum. His emphasis on self-development and self-expression is the theoretical basis for early childhood education.

Johnson, Musial, Hall, Golnick, and Dupuis (2005).

Emma Willard (1787–1870)

While boarding schools were teaching girls how to be polite, proper wives who could serve tea and make gentile conversation, Emma Willard was formulating plans for a school to teach girls and women useful, solid skills in homemaking as well as content and pedagogy to enable them to be teachers or to enter other professions. In 1821 she established the Troy Female Seminary, the first institution of higher learning for girls. Before the first normal school was established in 1839 by Horace Mann and others, the Troy Seminary had prepared over 200 teachers. Emma Willard is also credited with the establishment of home economics as a legitimate subject area. Willard wrote textbooks, traveled extensively, and was a lifelong activist for women's rights.

Chartock (2004); Good (1964); Webb et al. (2010).

Catherine Beecher (1800–1878)

Although Catherine Beecher's sister, Harriet Beecher Stowe, author of *Uncle Tom's Cabin*, may have more name recognition, Catherine had a great impact on the establishment of teacher training schools, or normal schools. In 1832 she established the Western Institute for Women, partially because she saw a need for better educated teachers. The institute was not publicly funded and did not prepare teachers exclusively, but it spawned other institutions of higher learning for women. In 1839 Beecher, along with Horace Mann and others, started the first publicly supported normal school for teacher preparation.

Holmes and Weiss (1995).

Prudence Crandall (1803–1889)

Way ahead of her time, and incredibly courageous, Prudence Crandall believed strongly in the rights of African American students to an education. Her Quaker roots and her own education under a noted abolitionist, Moses Brown, helped shape her steadfast belief in equal opportunity. In 1830 Crandall founded a school for neighborhood girls in Canterbury, Connecticut. When she admitted an African American girl, Sarah Harris, Crandall and her school became the target for vandalism and ostracism. White parents withdrew their daughters. When Crandall established a school populated entirely by African American girls, it was destroyed by outraged whites. Sarah Harris went on to teach many years in Louisiana, thus carrying on Prudence Crandall's legacy.

Pulliam and Van Patten (2007).

American government built boarding schools in the latter part of the 19th century and forced thousands of Native American children to leave their homes and live in these boarding schools where attempts were made to diminish their culture in favor of English-speaking, white social norms of the time. The boarding schools proved to be complete failures with Native American students running away or returning to their reservations immediately after graduation (Webb et al., 2010).

MEXICAN AMERICAN CHILDREN. At the end of the Mexican American War in 1848, vast territories comprising what are now Arizona, California, Colorado, Nevada, New Mexico, and Utah came under U.S. control. The Mexican families who stayed in these territories after the United States took over suffered discrimination much like the Native Americans. Like Native Americans, Mexican Americans were targets of efforts at assimilation. For much of the 19th century most Mexican American children had few, if any, educational options. When they did attend school, teachers generally tried to Americanize them, or assimilate them into the dominant culture by insisting they learn and use English and give up some of their customs (Webb et al., 2010).

AFRICAN AMERICAN CHILDREN. Although the education of Native American and Mexican American children was far from ideal and was inconsistently implemented, at least it didn't face legal objection by state or federal governments. The education of African American children in the 19th century did. For example, when Prudence Crandall admitted an African American student, Sarah Harris, to the school she founded in Connecticut in 1830, the school was forced to close. Crandall reopened the school for girls and enrolled 15 African American students from other states. The Connecticut legislature subsequently passed the **Black Law,** a law that specifically forbade a school intended to educate African Americans from other states without the permission of local authorities.

Prior to the Civil War, **Black Codes** were enacted, predominantly in the South, prohibiting the education of slaves. Some white people feared that educating slaves would give the slaves a sense of self-importance and they might begin to think they were created equal and had certain inalienable rights as stated in the Declaration of Independence. In 1850, with increasing numbers of free African Americans in the North desiring education, the Massachusetts Supreme Court upheld the decision in *Roberts* v. *City of Boston* that separate-but-equal schools did not violate the rights of African American children. This ruling solidified the practice of separate but equal, meaning that separate schools for black and white children supposedly offered the same opportunities for children. This assumption proved to be false, with schools for black children receiving less funding and housed in inferior facilities (Kaplan & Owings, 2011). At the end of the 19th century, the practice was reinforced by the ruling in a similar case, *Plessy* v. *Ferguson.*

The doctrine of separate but equal was evident in schooling in the United States until well past the middle of the 20th century.

Following the Civil War, the Bureau of Refugees, Freedmen, and Abandoned Lands, more commonly referred to as the Freedmen Bureau, made efforts to help African Americans find ways of making a living and settle into a free lifestyle. The Freedman's Bureau opened 3,000 schools in the South to educate African American children. By 1869 about 114,000 African American students were being educated in these schools. Along with typical school subjects, these new schools added industrial training in an effort to prepare African American students for employment (Gutek, 2005). In addition, many ex-slaves formed their own education associations that sponsored schools exclusively for black children, staffed exclusively by African American teachers. By 1870 southern African Americans had established over 500 of these schools, resembling the earlier common schools movement (Kaplan & Owings, 2011). Hampton Institute, founded in 1868, was an institution of higher education that emphasized industrial skills and teacher preparation for African Americans.

The most famous graduate of the Hampton Institute was Booker T. Washington. Following graduation he became Hampton's first African American teacher. Washington was a major supporter of vocational education for African Americans. He viewed learning practical skills as a way of advancing socially and economically in the United States. In 1881 Washington founded the Tuskegee Institute in rural Alabama. By 1890 Tuskegee had 88 faculty members and more than 1,200 students, making it one of the larger colleges in the South (McNergney & McNergney, 2009).

ASIAN AMERICAN CHILDREN. Although their numbers were smaller than immigrants from Mexico, there were children of Asian parents in U.S. schools in the 19th century. Most were Chinese, who began to arrive midcentury and filled a need for laborers in an increasingly industrialized America. The Immigration Act of 1882 slowed the arrival of people from China. In the latter part of the century traders from India began arriving, mostly on the East Coast of the United States. Until 1886 people from Japan could not leave their country. Once the restriction was lifted, Japanese (mostly men) moved to the United States and began to fill the void for inexpensive labor created by the Chinese government's crackdown on emigration (Note that to *emigrate* means to leave one's country. When people emigrate, they become *immigrants* in their destination country.)

CHILDREN OF POOR IMMIGRANTS. The United States is a nation of immigrants. The country's motto, *E Pluribus Unum*, means "from many, one." The issue of how to educate the *many* and have a strong *one* is not new. From 1870 to 1900, the United States experienced an influx of almost 2 million immigrants, many from Mexico, Asia, and Eastern Europe, and many whose primary language was not English (Boyer & Stuckey, 2005).

Many immigrants were very poor, but their skills were needed in the rapid industrialization of the United States. As the economy grew, so did the tax base for supporting free elementary schools and high schools. The number of free public schools increased dramatically as the country attempted to cope with its industrial growth and with the many coming to its shores to become one nation (Gutek, 2005; Takaki, 1993).

Most poor immigrants in the 19th century had no means of providing for their families when they first arrived in the United States, generally in the already heavily populated cities of New York and Chicago. **Settlement houses**

Booker T. Washington (1856–1915)

As a steadfast believer that education was the way to advance socially and economically, Booker T. Washington spent his life furthering educational opportunities for African American students. First graduating from, and then teaching at, the Hampton Institute, Washington later founded the Tuskegee Institute in Alabama in 1881. Throughout his career, Washington promoted his message that African Americans needed vocational skills to get and keep good jobs. Washington led the Tuskegee Institute until his death in 1915.

Chartock (2004); McNergney and McNergney (2009).

Jane Addams (1860–1935)

Raised in a wealthy home with an abolitionist Quaker father, Jane Addams set her sights on becoming a doctor. However, because of back problems, she quit her studies and determined to dedicate her life to helping the urban poor. She founded Hull House in an old, rundown Chicago mansion. Located in the middle of an immigrant neighborhood, Hull House provided education for both children and adults.

Addams recruited college-educated young women to work at Hull House. Many later used what they learned there to propel them to make major contributions to social reform. For years Hull House served as a model for other successful settlement houses, which numbered almost 100 by 1900.

Addams tirelessly promoted women's suffrage (right to vote) and was president of the Women's International League for Peace and Freedom from 1919 until her death in 1935. In 1931 she received the Nobel Peace Prize.

Boyer and Stuckey (2005).

Letter to the Editor

This letter appeared in the Waco, Texas, newspaper, the *Waco Tribune Herald*. It was written by a citizen advocating for a way for immigrant children to achieve citizenship.

APRIL 30, 2010 PATH TO CITIZENSHIP

In 1982, the U.S. Supreme Court struck down a Texas state law prohibiting undocumented children from attending public school. Justice William Brennan, writing for the majority, said the law was unjust toward children who were "not accountable for their disabling status."

In 2005, there were roughly 1.8 million undocumented children attending U.S. schools from kindergarten through high school. About 65,000 undocumented students graduated from high school in 2009, and about 13,000 enrolled in college nationwide. However, these ambitious, bright students have no way to become tax-paying, legal residents after they graduate.

If passed, the DREAM Act—which stands for the Development, Relief and Education for Alien Minors Act—would allow undocumented students a pathway to citizenship after attending college.

Comprehensive immigration reform will be a slow and arduous process. In the meantime, we have an obligation to protect the rights of these children, many of whom had no choice in immigrating to the United States with their families.

Support the DREAM Act in 2011 by writing your state and national lawmakers. For more information, go to dreamact.info.

Elena Solano
Austin

Now it's your turn. Write a letter to the editor from the perspective of a future teacher expressing your views about children who come to America through little or no choice of their own. Consider if the DREAM Act would be good for America, for the children involved, or for U.S. public schools. The following questions may help you frame your thinking but should not limit nor determine what you write.

1. What is your response to Justice Brennan's characterization of immigrant children as "not accountable for their disabling status"? Do you consider children who are immigrants to be disabled in some way?

2. What do you believe the economic impact might be of college graduates who are not citizens? If employers can't legally hire them and, if they do, cannot take federal and state taxes from their pay, what effects might this have?

3. The DREAM Act has been in the works since 2009. Knowing what you do from this letter, does it sound like something you want to support?

4. Do you think the DREAM Act might encourage more families to come to America illegally because it provides hope to their children? In your opinion, would this be positive or negative?

Write your letter in understandable terminology, remembering that readers of newspaper Letters to the Editor are citizens who may have limited knowledge of school practices and policies. Remember to refer to the letter assessment rubric in Chapter 1.

were established by reformers to address the problems of urban poverty. These were community service centers that provided educational opportunities, skills training, and cultural events. Jane Addams (1860–1935), raised in a wealthy Quaker home, established the most famous of the settlement houses, Hull House, in Chicago in 1889.

In this chapter's ***Letter to the Editor*** we see that the United States remains a nation with many immigrants. The dilemmas involving immigration are complex and, for many in America, emotionally charged.

HIGHER EDUCATION

In 1862 President Lincoln signed a congressional bill called the **Morrill Act.** Through this act the government granted states 30,000 acres of land for every senator and representative it had in Congress in 1860. The income the states could generate from this land was to be used to support at least one college. The Second Morrill Act of 1890 further stipulated that no grants would be given to states where college admission was denied because of race unless the state provided a separate-but-equal institution. As a result of the Morrill legislation, 65 land-grant colleges were established, including the universities of Maine (1865), Illinois (1867), and California (1868); Purdue University (1869); and Texas A&M (1871) (Rippa, 1997).

As colleges flourished, more progressive ways of educating children and adolescents also began to grow. The discussion of 20th-century education begins with progressive education, first introduced at the close of the 19th century.

What Were the Major Influences, Issues, Ideologies, and Individuals in 20th-Century American Education?

Varying population patterns, American inventiveness, wars, and technology made the 20th century one of extremes.

CONTEXT FOR CHANGE

In the 20th century, America survived two world wars, numerous regional conflicts in Korea, Vietnam, and elsewhere, and a protracted period of dire economic stress. It also thrived in years of unprecedented economic prosperity. The populace of the United States grew increasingly aware of its own diversity. Periods of rampant racial tension necessitated healing and both legal and educational responses on a national level.

Technological advances took us to the moon and beyond, enhanced communication of all sorts, and brought about global awareness unimagined in other centuries. In schools, the beginning of the century ushered more of the components of John Dewey's progressive education into classrooms.

PROGRESSIVE EDUCATION

There's more information about progressivism in Chapter 8.

In 1896 John Dewey established the first laboratory school at the University of Chicago to test the principles of **progressive education.** The progressive method was very different from the traditional 19th-century approach to education. What started with students learning in cooperative groups and letting their interests guide what they learned about traditional subjects grew into a major movement with far-reaching implications. The influence of John Dewey was tremendous as the United States moved from the 19th to the 20th century.

The progressive movement gained momentum during the first quarter of the 20th century and flourished until the end of World War II. The influences of progressivism are still evident in the 21st century. The basic principles of progressive education are summarized in Figure 7.5. These principles show the sharp contrast between the philosophy of progressivism and the established ways of doing school discussed earlier. John Dewey's primary focus was the implementation of schooling as a means of social reform and the improvement of life for Americans.

JUNIOR HIGH AND MIDDLE SCHOOL

The need for a bridge between elementary and high school became apparent as the high school developed into a 4-year institution and the courses taught there became more standardized in content. Educators began to delineate the kinds of preparation necessary for high school

John Dewey (1859–1952)

Think about all the things that happened in the United States during John Dewey's life, from the Civil War to the Korean War. He lived and wrote a very long time. In terms of education, many consider Dewey the most influential American of the 20th century. He was a professor of philosophy and pedagogy at the University of Chicago and at Columbia University. In Chicago, Dewey's son attended a school run by an ardent follower of Pestalozzi and Froebel. Dewey was so impressed with the approach of the school that he began researching, thinking, and writing about it. What we know today as progressive education was given an intellectual foundation by Dewey.

Dewey wrote more than 500 articles and 40 books, among which *The School and Society* (1900) and *The Child and the Curriculum* (1902) had perhaps the greatest impact on American education. In his laboratory school at the University of Chicago, he implemented progressive education and introduced projects such as carpentry, weaving, sewing, and cooking into the curriculum. Dewey believed that education should be experiential and child centered, rather than subject driven. He proposed that education is best served when the whole child is considered, including all the aspects of development.

John Dewey believed that democracy should be practiced not only in the governance of the United States but also in the day-to-day life of a school. Children should be free to question, investigate, and make changes in their environments. Learning the principles of democracy early in life would serve them well later as adults.

Dewey (1956); Rippa (1997).

Figure 7.5 Basic principles of progressive education

1. Education is life, not just preparation for life.
2. Learning should be directly related to the interests of the child.
3. Learning through problem solving should be emphasized more than rote memorization of subject matter.
4. The role of the teacher is to facilitate learning more so than to direct it.
5. Cooperation among students should be emphasized more than competition.
6. Democracy should be practiced to encourage the free interplay of ideas that leads to growth.

Source: Kneller, G. F. (1971). *Introduction to the philosophy of education.* New York: Wiley.

success. High school teachers and administrators asked for basic preparation in algebra and English before high school. Writers such as G. Stanley Hall began recognizing a period of life called adolescence and acknowledging that adolescence was different from childhood. This new viewpoint led to a change in the configuration of schools; elementary schools shifted from eight grades to five or six, and the remaining two or three grades became junior high schools. Later in the century, junior high most frequently encompassed grades 7 through 9.

In the 1960s, another concept of schooling was formed to meet the unique needs of young adolescents: the middle school. Rather than viewing grades 5 to 8 or 6 to 8 as merely a time of preparation for high school, middle school philosophy called for recognition of the unique developmental qualities of young adolescents and use of developmental appropriateness in the school, in both curriculum and instruction.

Maria Montessori (1870–1952)

A compassionate medical doctor, Maria Montessori established a children's house, a kind of school within a house, for poor children in early 20th-century Italy. As people recognized transformation in these children they began studying Montessori's methodology and opening other children's houses, later referred to as Montessori schools. As Maria Montessori herself said, "The task of the child is to construct a man [or woman] oriented to his environment, adapted to his time, place, and culture" (1967, p. xiv). She believed that children are capable of integrating aspects of the world around them through the use of their senses. Children ages 3 to 6 are the ideal participants in the Montessori method. Montessori insisted that children's environments be carefully constructed to allow them to sense their learning with materials, such as letters made of sandpaper and colored objects to count.

Chartock (2004); Good (1964); Montessori (1967).

Montessori philosophy is discussed in Chapter 2.

MONTESSORI METHOD

Although Maria Montessori (1870–1952) was developing a philosophy of early childhood education in Italy and other parts of Europe in the beginning of the 20th century, the Montessori method was not widely implemented in the United States until the 1950s. Today many Montessori principles can be found in early childhood settings across the United States.

W. E. B. Du Bois (1868–1963)

As a champion for equality of Africans and African Americans, W. E. B. Du Bois spent his life as a scholar, a writer, and a reformer. In 1895 he was the first African American to earn a doctorate from Harvard. From 1895 through the 1950s he was a college professor and a civil rights activist. He organized worldwide conferences of black leaders. Du Bois considered Africa the homeland of all black people and wrote about the dual citizenry of black people who had left Africa in his 1903 book, *The Souls of Black Folks.* In 1907 he cofounded the National Association for the Advancement of Colored People (NAACP). Disillusioned by lack of progress for people of African descent in the United States, Du Bois embraced socialism. At age 93, he joined the Communist Party and moved to Ghana, where he died at age 95.

Boyer and Stuckey (2005).

INFLUENTIAL AFRICAN AMERICAN LEADERS

W. E. B. Du Bois believed that African Americans should pursue higher education to become leaders in politics and education. He sharply disagreed with Booker T. Washington's philosophy that African Americans would best serve themselves and their race by pursuing vocational arts and skills to prepare them to compete in the workplace with white people.

Mary McLeod Bethune was influential in both education and government policy. Her long career as a teacher, as well as college instructor and founder, took her from her home in South Carolina to college experiences in Chicago, to Florida, where she founded Bethune-Cookman College, and all the way to Washington, D.C., where she served as an adviser to President Franklin D. Roosevelt in the 1930s (Chartock, 2004).

THE LAST FIVE DECADES OF THE 20TH CENTURY

1950S. The *Leave It to Beaver* white-bread world of Ward and June Cleaver and their two sons was experienced by many families in the United States and was considered a desirable social paradigm during the period of unprecedented economic growth and prosperity following World War II. In 1957, however, the "all's right with the world" syndrome was shaken by the Soviet launch of *Sputnik*, the first satellite to venture into space. The **National Defense Education Act of 1958** called for strengthening of science, math, and foreign language programs. Teachers were given training in the use of new methods and materials in hopes of bringing American student learning up to, and beyond, the levels of learning in other countries.

Another major factor in the American schools of the 1950s was the increasing pressure to desegregate. After all the years of separate-but-equal schools, the Supreme Court upheld the complaints of the National Association for the Advancement of Colored People (NAACP) made on behalf of a Kansas family in the now famous ***Brown v. Board of Education*** ruling of 1954. Chief Justice Earl Warren declared that segregating children based solely on race was wrong and illegal. Some schools integrated peacefully, but others did not. Still other segregated schools made little or no attempt to change at all.

While the launching of *Sputnik* triggered immediate changes in American education, and desegregation came to the forefront as an ongoing issue with significant moral implications, another, quieter, yet very important change was also taking place in the 1950s. Educators began to examine curriculum more carefully as a result of the thinking of Ralph Tyler (1902–1994). Tyler proposed that data concerning the needs of the learner, the needs of society, and the needs of the subject area should all be considered in the process of developing curricula. Tyler believed that learning should have both specific objectives and appropriate assessments.

Another influential person in American education, Benjamin Bloom (1913–1999), headed a group that composed what has become known as Bloom's taxonomy of learning objectives. The taxonomy was introduced in 1956 and continues to influence how educators think about and write learning objectives today.

1960S. The 1960s were characterized by a more outspoken U.S. citizenry. The election of a young, vibrant president, John F. Kennedy, gave rise to a sense of idealism among younger voters. After the assassination of President Kennedy in 1963, Lyndon Johnson attempted to continue in this vein with what he called the War on Poverty and the creation of the Great Society. Both the Kennedy and Johnson administrations allocated large amounts of money to break the

Mary McLeod Bethune (1875–1955)

Born in South Carolina of former slave parents, Mary McLeod Bethune was educated in a Presbyterian mission school and attended Moody Bible Institute in Chicago. The school in her hometown of Mayesville was for whites only. Although Bethune originally wanted to be a missionary to Africa and was often quoted as saying the drums of Africa still beat in her heart, she dedicated her life to educating African American students. She established a school in Florida that became a normal school to train female African American teachers. Later the school evolved into Bethune-Cookman College, a 4-year coeducational college with mostly African American students.

In the midst of her work with education, Bethune became good friends with Eleanor Roosevelt, who drew her into government service, specifically the National Youth Administration (NYA), a branch of the Works Progress Administration (WPA) created by President Franklin D. Roosevelt. In 1935 Bethune founded the National Council of Negro Women, an umbrella group for all organizations working on behalf of African American women.

Boyer and Stuckey (2005).

Ralph Tyler and Benjamin Bloom are discussed in Chapters 4 and 5.

Ralph Tyler (1902–1994)

Upon his death, a news release from the Stanford University News Service called Ralph Tyler "the grand old man of educational research." Ralph Tyler's contributions to education were many, with his impact on curriculum development perhaps the most meaningful. Of the 16 books and over 700 journal articles he wrote, the one with perhaps the most impact was among his first, *Basic Principles of Curriculum and Instruction*, published in 1949.

Tyler's commonsense approach to curriculum development involved

- determining the goals of the school
- selecting learning experiences useful in attaining the goals
- organizing instruction around the experiences
- and then deciding how best to evaluate the learning

Tyler conducted a groundbreaking longitudinal analysis of 30 schools and the careers of their students called the Eight-Year Study (1933–1941). This study focused on the opportunities students had who stayed in school rather than joining the workforce during the depression.

Tyler is also responsible for initiating the National Assessment of Educational Progress (NAEP) test in the 1960s, still the only test that evaluates the U.S. school system rather than the success of the students in it. Ralph Tyler was often heard to make two statements: "I never wanted to be anything but a teacher," and "I never met a child who couldn't learn."

McNeil (1995); Stanford News Service (1994); Tyler (1949).

Benjamin Bloom (1913–1999)

Following the 1948 convention of the American Psychological Association, Benjamin Bloom chaired a team that examined the cognitive, affective, and psychomotor domains of educational activity. From their work came what today is known as Bloom's taxonomy, discussed in Chapter 4. As part of his work at the University of Chicago, Bloom observed that about 95% of all classroom questions were at the knowledge (recall) level. The taxonomy provides a way to structure both activities and questions that run the gamut of intellectual processing.

Bloom also did extensive work in the area of assessment. He was influenced by Ralph Tyler and recognized that comparing students wasn't as important in terms of assessment as helping students master the learning.

Benjamin Bloom's work has been both condensed and expanded over the years by scholars and practitioners. His contributions to education are meaningful and enduring.

Bloom (1956); Eisner (2000).

cycle of poverty in the United States (Boyer & Stuckey, 2005). For example, the **Vocational Education Act of 1963** quadrupled the amount of money allocated for vocational education.

The following year, the **Civil Rights Act of 1964** stipulated that if schools discriminated based on race, color, or national origin, they would not be eligible for federal funding. Similarly, in a series of court battles, the Supreme Court continued to strike down school segregation.

In 1965 Congress passed the Elementary and Secondary Education Act (ESEA), which provided extra money for school districts with low-income families. Project Head Start was also established to boost the early learning of children ages 3 to 6 from low-income homes. The **Bilingual Education Act of 1968** (Title VII of the ESEA of 1965) validated children's native language and provided funds to assist non-English-speaking students who were dropping out of high school at a rate of about 70%. The dramatic increases in numbers of Mexican and Mexican American children in the schools as a result of both legal and illegal immigration have created an ongoing challenge for educators that the Bilingual Education Act only partially addresses.

Immigration is discussed in more detail in Chapter 9.

1970S. During the first half of the decade, the country's attention was focused on the Vietnam conflict and the administration of President Richard Nixon. Public trust in establishment institutions was repeatedly shaken, resulting in a general lack of confidence in schools and teachers. The number of students in public schools decreased during the 1970s while private schools and homeschooling grew. Public school students' test scores dropped. Many perceived the need to implement a back-to-basics curriculum, and demands for accountability increased.

At the same time, some good things happened in 1970s education. Title IX of the Education Amendment Acts, which prohibited sexual discrimination in any education program receiving federal funding, took effect in 1972. Additionally, in 1979 President Carter elevated the federal office of education to a department, making its secretary a member of his cabinet.

PL94-142 and Title IX are discussed in Chapter 3.

PL 94–142, the Education for All Handicapped Children Act, passed in 1975. This important legislation granted children with disabilities the right to an education that meets their needs in the least restrictive environment.

It wasn't until the 1970s that the U.S. policy changed from one of assimilation to fostering self-determination, encouraging Native Americans to take charge of their own education, whether on reservations or in other public schools. Today, even though there are more Native Americans under age 20, proportionally speaking, than in the general white population, a smaller percentage of Native Americans participate in formal education (Ornstein & Levine, 2006). In other words, in the whole Native American population, there is a greater percentage of people under the age of 20 when compared to the white population. Yet there is a smaller percentage of these young people in school when compared to white young people.

1980S. During the 8 years of Ronald Reagan's presidency (1981–1989) federal funding for elementary and secondary education declined by 17%. Even so, the quality of education received renewed attention for two basic reasons. The first reason was concern over economic competition with Japan. Many Americans believed that the United States had begun to compare unfavorably with Japan, in part because of inferior schools.

The second reason for the renewed attention to education was the release in 1983 of a report commissioned by President Reagan called *A Nation at Risk: The Imperative for*

Educational Reform. The language of the report was strong, referring to public education in the United States as a "rising tide of mediocrity." In response, various proposals for reform and improvement surfaced. The *Paideia Proposal* (1982) by Mortimer Adler called for a core curriculum based on Great Books. The 1989 Carnegie Council on Adolescent Development report, *Turning Points: Preparing American Youth for the 21st Century,* validated the middle-level philosophy of the National Middle School Association, which called for small learning communities, the elimination of tracking, and careful guidance.

Restructuring became a buzzword in education. Some of the efforts included year-round schools, longer school days, longer school years, and more funding for technology.

1990S. The 1990s might be labeled as the era of standards. Along with the standards came tests designed to determine whether students had met the standards. The emphasis shifted from the input of education (what teachers do, funding, support) to the output of education (student learning). President Bill Clinton brought increased attention to education as he promised to be an effective "education president." He formalized Goals 2000, an initiative begun by his predecessor, George H. W. Bush (1988–1992). Although the goals were admirably lofty, they were also unrealistically high and have, for the most part, been unfulfilled.

> Standards are discussed in detail in Chapter 4.

In the 1990s, teachers began taking on leadership roles in schools and in school districts. There was more collaboration among parents, the community, students, administrators, and teachers. Record enrollments resulted in a teacher shortage. President Clinton, in addition to providing federal support for the recruitment of 100,000 new teachers, joined policy makers in asking states to raise teacher standards (Webb et al., 2010).

What Major Influences, Issues, Ideologies, and Individuals Are We Experiencing in 21st-Century American Education?

One full decade of this new century has passed. Our nation has experienced turbulence on every front.

CONTEXT FOR CHANGE

The new century was ushered in with fears that proved to be unfounded as we anticipated what was called Y2K, or Year 2000. Many gathered around televisions to watch as the year 2000 dawned in countries around the globe, complete with celebrations and massive displays of fireworks—and an eerie sense of anxiety about events such as worldwide computer blackouts and destruction of all sorts that were prophesized but never materialized.

Less than 2 years later, our worst fears did materialize in the form of the disastrous day now simply known as 9/11. When terrorists killed thousands of Americans on American soil, our way of life changed, both politically and practically. The subsequent conflicts and political unrest in Iraq and Afghanistan continued to take their toll. The administration of George W. Bush (2000–2008) was one of turmoil and strong disagreements in terms of war, economics, and governmental controls. The economic downturn that began during the Bush years strangled American prosperity and perpetuated a downward spiral of failed businesses and unemployment that made life very difficult for many in the first decade of the 21st century. Rampant mistrust and suspicion plagued America.

The election in 2008 of America's first African American president, Barack Obama, brought jubilation for some and a newly expressed animosity for others. The abrupt change from a conservative Republican administration to what many viewed as a liberal Democrat occupant in the White House put American's political tolerance for bipartisan decision making and action to the test.

NO CHILD LEFT BEHIND

NCLB is discussed in more detail in Chapter 4.

The defining legislation of the first decade of the 21st century was the No Child Left Behind Act of 2001 (NCLB). The act was the reauthorization of the Elementary and Secondary Education Act (1965) and called for accountability of schools and school districts to states, and of states to the federal government. No Child Left Behind was formulated as a response to evidence that students were being promoted without mastering concepts and were graduating without basic literacy skills.

21ST-CENTURY KNOWLEDGE AND SKILLS

As noted in previous chapters, the Partnership for 21st Century Skills (P21) exerts considerable and growing influence in schools across the country. But it's not just an organization that is influencing what we teach and learn; it's the concept that our world is changing and schools need to change as well.

In Context for Change we get a sense for the complexity of life in the United States and around the world. The goal of teachers and schools should be to provide educational experiences that reflect this complexity as we equip students to live productively and positively. The present, and therefore history as well, is shaped by human responses to dilemmas. It's all about problem solving, a 21st-century skill that is more relevant than ever before.

In the 21st century, information will continue to grow at exponential rates. Teaching students how to figure out what they need to know, where and how to access it, and then how to use it effectively, should be emphasized in teaching and learning. Then wrapping this package in appreciation for, and the ability to accomplish, collaboration will help students thrive in the 21st century.

21ST-CENTURY SCHOOLS

In most schools in the United States it would be difficult to recognize change between the 1990s and the first decade of the 21st century. In some schools the classrooms may not have changed physically or in terms of learning experiences since long before 1990. Yet in others innovative technology such as SMART Boards, laptop computers, LCD projectors, and more tell the story of mushrooming technological advances.

Virtual education is becoming more widespread as educators use technology to deliver and reinforce teaching and learning. Books of all kind are available electronically, and communication with classrooms around the globe changes the way we view instruction. Although teaching is still viewed as place based in a classroom for most educators, the possibilities of using whole communities and cyberspace as learning environments are taking education into uncharted dimensions. What an exciting time to become a teacher!

How Are U.S. Schools Addressing Racial and Ethnic Diversity in the 21st Century?

The short answer to this question is "Not very well," and certainly not with consistency. For instance, research shows that 55 years after the Supreme Court declared that separate is not equal in *Brown* v. *Board of Education,* U.S. schools are more segregated now than before the Court ruling (Orfield, 2009). Of the defining issues in American education, perhaps none is so challenging as finding ways to address racial and ethnic diversity. Table 7.3 shows the percentage of students by race and ethnicity in regions of the United States.

Although American public schools have been relatively successful in educating immigrants from Europe and Asia and helping them achieve at least middle-class status in the United States, our schools have been much less successful in doing so for those students from nonwhite communities—African Americans and Hispanics (Orfield, 2009).

AFRICAN AMERICAN STUDENTS

Laws have been passed and policies have been made with the intent of fully integrating U.S. schools. In our history, African American students were not treated as benignly as Native and

TABLE 7.3 Public school student enrollment percentages by region and race/ethnicity (2006–2007)

Region	White	Black	Latino/ Hispanic	Asian	Native American and Other
West	44.6	6.4	38.7	8.3	2
South	48.9	26.5	21.5	2.6	.5
Northeast	64	15.4	14.9	5.3	.3
National	56.5	17.1	20.5	4.7	1.2

Source: Orfield, G. (2009). *Reviving the goal of an integrated society: A 21st century challenge.* Los Angeles: The Civil Rights Project/Proyecto Derechos Civiles at UCLA.

Mexican Americans or any other racial/ethnic group. They have suffered outright and purposeful discrimination, including laws that forbade their education. Today there are no such laws, and yet in some locations and in some circumstances we still find differences in opportunities for black students, compared with white students (Banks & Banks, 2009).

One of our focus students at Cario Middle School, Patrick Sutton, is an excellent student with what appears to be an intact sense of confidence. For Patrick, as a black student, the doors of opportunity seem to be open wide. His positive experiences at Cario are what we should desire for all students, regardless of their race or ethnicity.

> *To watch an interview with Patrick and his mom, go to the Teaching in Focus section for Chapter 7 in MyEducationLab for this course.*

HISPANIC AMERICAN STUDENTS

At the end of the first decade of the 21st century there were over 45 million Hispanic people living in the United States. Some families have been in America for centuries, and the vast majority has come here to escape some form of oppression. They have come from many countries, and thus have a variety of ethnicities, as illustrated in Figure 7.6.

> The differences between race and ethnicity are discussed in Chapter 3.

Figure 7.6 Hispanic subgroups in the United States

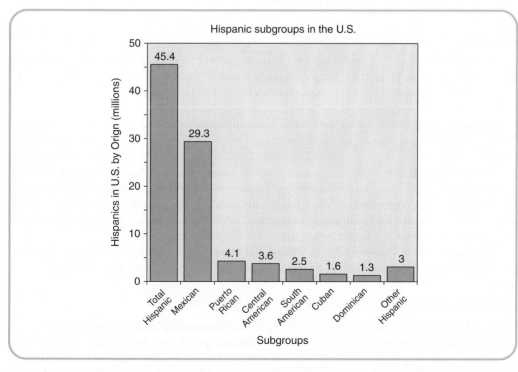

Source: U.S. Census Bureau. (2008). *American Factfinder: BO3001. Hispanic or Latino origin by specific origin.* Retrieved May 22, 2010, from http://factfinder.census.gov/servlet/DTTable?_bm=y&-geo_id=01000US&-ds_name=ACS_2008_3YR_G00_&-mt_name=ACS_2008_3YR_G2000_B03001.

Teaching in Focus

Angelica Reynosa, World History, Roosevelt High School, California. *In her own words . . . .*

I can't imagine being anywhere else professionally than in a school. My husband and I are both teachers. It is a wonderful life!

I teach in a school where minority populations are the majority. Most of my students, and indeed most of the students at Roosevelt, are Latino Americans. Some were born in America; others have been here for only a few weeks. Some have families with established careers; others have families who are undocumented workers. Regardless, they are the faces of an ever-growing Latino presence in America. Some of my students, like Hugo, have secure, loving homes headed by parents who risked their lives to come to America. Hugo will be successful. He knows it's his legacy. He attends school regularly, and he is learning English quickly.

I see my job as not only a teacher of a course for high school credit but also as an advocate for the well-being of my students, most of whom are in bilingual classes so they can learn their subjects while learning to be fluent in English. As a Spanish speaker, I am able to teach both history and coping skills in English communication. Find your special niche in education. You have unique talents and gifts that will be valuable to students. Search for those talents and develop them for the sake of the students.

Dilemmas of English-language learners are addressed in more detail in Chapters 3 and 9.

The dilemmas for schools regarding the rapid increase of Hispanic students are complex. Perhaps the dilemma with the most impact on schools is that of language diversity. How do we teach the standards to children who can't understand what we say or write? Currently our schools attempt to answer this question through three basic programs: English as a Second Language (ESL), bilingual education, and Structured English Immersion (SEI). Our efforts are inadequate, particularly for any child raised in a non-English-speaking home. Read what focus teacher, Angelica Reynosa, has to say about her role as an advocate for Hispanic students in *Teaching in Focus*.

ASIAN AMERICAN STUDENTS

About half of the world's population falls into the broad category of Asian. They may live in China, Japan, India, Pakistan, Vietnam, Korea, Samoa, and many more countries. Asian Americans have vastly different experiences both before emigrating and when in the United States either legally or illegally (U.S. Census Bureau, 2009).

Students from China, Japan, and India generally achieve at high levels in U.S. schools, while students from Southeast Asian countries such as Vietnam and Cambodia tend to struggle. Many children who come to America from war-torn, trauma-filled areas find their problems within U.S. education exacerbated, or made worse, by their life experiences. Again, language is a major barrier to success. In large cities and small towns across America, teachers who speak only English work daily with children who speak a great variety of languages in their homes and struggle to communicate in English in order to learn even small bits and pieces of our curricular standards.

To review principal Romero's interview, go to Maria Romero in the Teaching in Focus section for Chapter 7 in MyEducationLab for this course.

The principal of Roosevelt High School, California, discusses her school that is populated primarily by Hispanic and Asian students in this chapter's *Diversity Dialogue*.

MIDDLE EASTERN AMERICAN STUDENTS

So often targets of prejudice in our post-9/11 world, students of Middle Eastern descent are entering our schools in increasing, yet still relatively small, numbers. They may be from countries including Egypt, Jordan, Iraq, Iran, Syria, Lebanon, and Saudi Arabia. Many are linked to Islam, the religion of people referred to as Muslim. But in reality, more Middle Eastern Americans align with Christianity than with Islam.

Maria Romero, principal of Roosevelt High School in Fresno, California, is acutely aware of the diversity in her school. She has been there in some capacity since 1986. Roosevelt students are primarily of Hispanic and Asian ancestry. But she is quick to tell us that this doesn't mean that all the Hispanics are alike; nor are all the Asians alike. Within the Hispanic population there are students whose families have lived in the United States for generations, and others who crossed the Mexican border illegally only weeks before coming to Roosevelt. Some speak fluent English, and little or no Spanish, and others who understand and speak practically no English at all. Within the Asian population, students may be Hmong, Cambodian, Laotian, and more, with very few from China, Japan, or India. They speak different languages and have a variety of dialects of each language. Most of the students at Roosevelt qualify for free or reduced-price lunch, revealing their socioeconomic status.

When asked by students if she is Mexican, Mrs. Romero replies that she is American, a U.S. citizen with Mexican ancestry. She tells students it is important to keep their first language, and that it is imperative for them to be fluent in English to be successful in the United States. She and her teachers have lots of lessons they want to pass on to the students at Roosevelt. Respond to the following items by writing one well-developed paragraph for each.

1. According to Mrs. Romero, why is it important for Roosevelt teachers to inspire students to believe they can be more than they thought they could be? Why is this more of a challenge at Roosevelt than in some other schools? What are two ways teachers might accomplish this given what we know about Roosevelt students?

2. Mrs. Romero tells us that unlike in many schools, Roosevelt parents put students completely in the hands of the adults in the school. They want their children to succeed, but most haven't been educated themselves. In what ways might Roosevelt teachers involve parents in the education of their children, given their parental reluctance?

Cultural norms of Middle Eastern American students are often noticeably different from the mainstream. They may talk more loudly with what sounds like an odd intonation, hold hands with same-sex friends, not consider being late a sign of disrespect, not hold females in as high regard as males, and so forth. Because these norms are counter to what we generally expect in U.S. schools, life in school may be more difficult for some. Even so, students of Middle Eastern heritage tend to do quite well in school, go to college at a higher than average rate, and live productive lives in the United States (Banks & Banks, 2009).

> Muslim American students and Ramadan are discussed in **Diversity Dialogue** in Chapter 10.

How Can I Be Aware of Education History in the Making?

Time gives us perspective. We can look at the history of American education and determine which of the various influences, issues, ideologies, and individuals have most affected the course of schools, teachers, and students. What is less than obvious is which of these influences, issues, ideologies, and individuals are making a difference or initiating significant change now. Fifty or 100 years from now, it will likely be evident.

Education issues come and go, often in predictable cycles. The notable individuals involved in education at any given point are numerous. Sifting through them to determine who has significant and long-term influence generally only happens with time. The danger of listing contemporary movers and shakers in any field is the inevitable omission of names. Given that risk, Table 7.4 is an attempt to provide a partial list of individuals and their contributions that are currently influencing American education. You will no doubt hear and read about these people as you pursue a degree in teaching.

Reading professional journals, continuing to take courses, attending conferences, having conversations with colleagues—all of these activities will help you stay abreast of the

Points of Reflection 7.4

Do you anticipate a diverse classroom with a sense of excitement or a nagging dread? Explain your answer. Is there anything in your background that uniquely prepares you for a diverse classroom? If so, explain.

TABLE 7.4 History in the making

Individual	Theory, Field of Research, Written Works
Mortimer Adler	Paideia Proposal; core curriculum based on Great Books
James Banks	Multicultural education
David Berliner	Educational researcher; teacher effectiveness
Marva Collins	Tireless advocate for all children; founder of Westside Preparatory School
James Comer	Comer Model; emphasis on social context of teaching and learning
Larry Cuban	Expert on change in education
Linda Darling-Hammond	*The Right to Learn*; teacher quality and preparation
Marian Wright Edelman	Children's Defense Fund; advocate for all children
Elliot Eisner	Arts education; curriculum reform
Jaime Escalante	Outstanding high school math teacher in urban Los Angeles
Paulo Freire	*Pedagogy of the Oppressed*; education gives power to the poor
Howard Gardner	Multiple intelligences theory
William Glasser	Choice theory of human behavior
John Goodlad	*A Place Called School*; democracy and education; teacher education
Maxine Greene	Existentialism; *Landscapes of Learning*
E. D. Hirsch	*Cultural Literacy: What Every American Needs to Know*
Ivan Illich	Social reconstructionism; *Deschooling America*
Herbert Kohl	*36 Children*; the value of teachers and teaching differentiated instruction
Jacob Kounin	Classroom management
Jonathan Kozol	*Savage Inequalities: Children in America's Schools*; study of urban children
Sonia Nieto	Multicultural and bilingual education
Nel Noddings	Caring in the classroom; teacher reflection
Theodore Sizer	Coalition of Essential Schools; necessity of community in school environment; *Horace's Compromise*
Robert Slavin	Success for All program; early intervention
Kay Toliver	Outstanding teacher in urban New York City
Carol Ann Tomlinson	Differentiated instruction
Grant Wiggins/Jay McTighe	*Understanding by Design*; development of curriculum, instruction, and assessment

Points of Reflection 7.5

Which educators in your school experiences have had the most positive impact on you? Explain their impact.

individuals in the forefront of our work as teachers. History is in the making all around us. In classrooms across the United States, excellent teachers are the real heroes of education. If you decide to be a teacher, then the history of American education has been changed, perhaps not in ways that will make it into history books but in ways that influence the lives of the hundreds, maybe thousands of students in your future classroom.

CONCLUDING THOUGHTS

This brief look at the history of education in the United States has been written from a majority culture viewpoint (white, middle class) primarily using sources having the same lens. Encapsulating 400 years into one brief chapter involves choices that have inherent limitations. Be aware of this when you consider any aspect of history. Understand that there's always more to the story.

American education has been more reactionary than trailblazing, more foundational than earthshaking. In an ideal world educators would be ahead of dilemmas, and the teaching and learning in U.S. schools would lead the way toward solutions to our country's problems. And indeed this is true, but in a subtle way. The adage "Teachers make all other professions possible" elevates teachers to indispensable heroes, although they are largely unheralded as such.

The history of education in the United States parallels the history of the country. Although once relatively simple and perceived as manageable, education in the United States is now incredibly complex and often unwieldy, with issues to match. In spite of the lessons to be learned from studying the history of American education, there remain unacceptable conditions for learning in some schools, unequal opportunities for children based on such factors as socioeconomic status and race, and international test results that show mediocre performances by U.S. students. Together we will face many challenges as we strive to effectively build on the past to do a better job of educating in, and for, the future, asking, "And how are the children? Are they all well?"

We began this chapter by considering Angelica Reynosa's classroom and teaching responsibilities at Roosevelt High School in Fresno, California. As she teaches world history, she is often reminded that the plight of many of her students resembles some in history who have suffered hardships but who also possess hope for a better life. Now as the chapter comes to an end, we join Angelica as she considers ways to make history relevant for her students. Read through *Chapter in Review* to help refresh your memory of what we have discussed, then interact with Angelica as she plans learning experiences for her students in *Developing Professional Competence*.

You watched Angelica's lesson in Chapter 3, but review it now to help you respond to these items. The lesson may be accessed in the Teaching in Focus section for Chapter 7 in the MyEducationLab for this course.

Chapter in Review

What were the major influences, issues, ideologies, and individuals in 17th-century American education?

- Many of the original colonists came to America seeking religious freedom and established schools to bolster their beliefs.
- Colonial schools primarily served white males.
- Education differed greatly among the New England, middle, and southern colonies.

What were the major influences, issues, ideologies, and individuals in 18th-century American education?

- Private academies served as secondary schools that went beyond what was taught in dame schools and town schools.
- Influential leaders, such as Benjamin Franklin, Thomas Jefferson, and Noah Webster, contributed to the expansion of educational opportunities.
- Education became a state responsibility by virtue of not being addressed in the Constitution.

What were the major influences, issues, ideologies, and individuals in 19th-century American education?

- Common schools were the first public, free American elementary schools.
- Following the Civil War, the first high schools began to flourish to meet the new economic demands of an increasingly industrialized United States.

- Kindergarten, with an activity-based curriculum, became common by the end of the 19th century.
- Teacher preparation institutions called normal schools were created to respond to the need for more teachers with increased and consistent preparation.
- Few educational opportunities existed for children with disabilities, children of color, or children of poor immigrant parents.
- Land-grant colleges were established as a result of the Morrill Acts.

What were the major influences, issues, ideologies, and individuals in 20th-century American education?

- John Dewey and the philosophy of progressive education fostered more active student participation in a school system based on democratic principles.
- Junior highs, and then middle schools, bridged the gap between elementary and high schools.
- Interest in science and math education increased following the launch of *Sputnik*.
- During the 1970s, the Education for All Handicapped Children Act and Title IX increased educational opportunities for all children.
- *A Nation at Risk* served as a wake-up call for education in the United States.
- Curriculum standards emerged in the 1990s as the defining criteria for the quality of teaching and learning.

What major influences, issues, ideologies, and individuals are we experiencing in 21st-century American education?

- The first decade of the 21st century in America was filled with turmoil.
- The No Child Left Behind Act of 2001 called for increased accountability on local and state levels and emphasized the need for all children to learn.
- The Partnership for 21st Century Skills (P21) exerts considerable and growing influence in schools across the country.
- Some schools have remained virtually unchanged for decades; others reflect the technology and strategies available for teaching and learning in the 21st century.

How are U.S. schools addressing racial and ethnic diversity in the 21st century?

- Although some strides have been made in a quest to provide equal opportunities for learning to all children in the United States, there is still much to do.
- African American students are more segregated now than they were at the time of *Brown* v. *Board of Education* when *separate but equal* was designated as unlawful.
- The Hispanic student population is rapidly growing, but our ability to improve their learning and their language skills is not keeping up with their need.
- Students from China, Japan, and India generally appear to be achieving at high levels in U.S. schools, while students from Southeast Asian countries such as Vietnam and Cambodia struggle.
- Cultural norms of Middle Eastern American students are often noticeably different from mainstream Americans, necessitating an even greater need for understanding on the part of teachers.

How can I be aware of education history in the making?

- Teachers should assume the responsibility of staying current with major shifts in educational concepts and trends. Time provides perspective. As history unfolds, those most influential will emerge in prominence.

Developing Professional Competence

Visit the Developing Professional Competence section on Chapter 7 of the MyEducationLab for this text to answer the following questions and begin your preparation for licensure exams.

Angelica Reynosa wants her students to see the big picture included in the world history curriculum and help them grasp the significance of how various forms of government enhance or inhibit people's lives. She wants them to understand how knowledge of history is meaningful for their futures and how it can give them perspective about their roots and cultural struggles.

Think about Angelica and her students as you answer the following multiple-choice questions:

1. Why is the establishment of the United States in the 17th century relevant to many of Angelica's students?
   a. The people who came to the United States from Europe did so to find refuge from a government that they found to be oppressive.
   b. It's been 400 years and we now have perspective on the early days of the United States.
   c. Many Hispanics came to America then as they do now.
   d. Mexico was experiencing a similar fight for independence in the 17th century.

2. Why is it important for Angelica's students to understand how various people throughout history have suffered oppression?
   a. They need to see that they are not alone.
   b. They will be encouraged to see how people have overcome difficulties.
   c. They need to understand it so they won't perpetuate it.
   d. It is vital to understand that history repeats itself.

3. In the lesson you observed, what purpose does the candy serve?
   a. The candy randomly given and taken shows students that they actually have very little control over their lives.

b. They are learning to cleverly hoard candy and keep it from being taken away, much as they will need to do in a capitalistic country.

c. The candy is an incentive to participate fully in the rock-paper-scissors activity.

d. The candy is randomly given and taken away, showing that in governments without freedom there is little control over one's destiny.

Now it's time for you to respond to two short essay items involving Angelica and her students. In your responses, be sure to address all the dilemmas and questions posed in each item. Your responses should each be between one half and one double-spaced page.

4. The class you observed is bilingual. How did Angelica approach the lesson to both teach the content and the English language? Why is Angelica's own ethnicity important to the teaching and learning process in her classroom?

5. As Angelica considers her students and her responsibilities, she reflects on these two NBPTS and INTASC standards. Why is each especially important to her, given that she teaches in a bilingual classroom?

NBPTS Standard 5 *Teachers are members of learning communities.*

INTASC Standard 9 Professional Commitment and Responsibilities *The teacher is a reflective practitioner who continually evaluates the effects of his/her actions on others and who actively seeks out opportunities to grow professionally.*

Where DO I Stand NOW?

In the beginning of this chapter you completed an inventory that gauged your knowledge of history of the United States and history of U.S. education. Now that you have read the chapter, completed exercises related to the content, engaged in class discussions, and so on, answer these two questions in your course notebook.

1. Explain one lesson America appears to have learned from the past and how that lesson is evident in education today.

2. Explain one lesson America appears *not* to have learned from the past. What evidence do you have that the lesson has not changed how public education functions today?

MyEducationLab

The MyEducationLab for this course can help you solidify your comprehension of Chapter 7 concepts.

- Explore the classrooms of the teachers and students you've met in this chapter in the Teaching in Focus section.

- Prepare for licensure exams as you deepen your understanding of chapter concepts in the Developing Professional Competence section.

- Gauge and further develop your understanding of chapter concepts by taking the quizzes and examining the enrichment materials on the Chapter 7 Study Plan.

- Visit Topic 7, "History and Philosophy of Education," to watch ABC videos, explore Assignments and Activities, and practice essential teaching skills with the Building Teaching Skills and Dispositions unit.

8

Philosophical
Foundations of Education in the United States

Some people spend their entire careers studying philosophy. This chapter provides only a very brief survey of some of the components of philosophy that apply to education. These are the major questions addressed in Chapter 8:

✦ What is a philosophy of education?

✦ What are four branches of philosophy?

✦ How do five prominent philosophies of education affect teaching and learning?

✦ How do I begin to develop my personal philosophy of education?

Every time we make a decision, form an opinion, or take an action, we are expressing a philosophy. A philosophy of education is a living, dynamic part of who we are in the classroom. It's healthy and productive for teachers to teach according to combinations of philosophies. This creates balance and produces commonsense decisions in the classroom.

Where DO I Stand?

Before we discuss philosophies of education and how they look in the classroom, think through these items that prompt you to consider your own views. There are no wrong answers, just differing viewpoints. *After reading an item, indicate your level of agreement by choosing a number and placing it in the blank before the statement. Following the inventory are directions for how to organize your responses and what they may indicate in terms of where you stand.*

4	I strongly agree
3	I agree
2	I don't have an opinion
1	I disagree
0	I strongly disagree

_____ **1.** It is vital that we teach personal responsibility in school.

_____ **2.** Students must be disciplined hard workers in order to learn.

_____ **3.** The classroom should be a model of democracy.

_____ **4.** Memorization is a learning strategy that should be employed frequently in classrooms.

_____ **5.** Schools should use intense study of the classics to strive for excellence in students.

_____ **6.** Making a lesson interesting to students is important to their learning.

_____ **7.** Learning is worthwhile only if it increases a student's sense of self.

_____ **8.** The school and teachers should determine what is learned, without regard for student interests.

_____ **9.** A major goal of public education is positive social change.

_____ **10.** Choices and electives have no place in the curriculum.

_____ **11.** A teacher should be a facilitator of learning.

_____ **12.** Rules are very important in the classroom and must be adhered to at all times.

_____ **13.** Teachers teach the whole child, not just the intellectual aspects.

_____ **14.** An important part of teaching involves instilling students with a sense of responsibility for humanity.

_____ **15.** Part of the responsibility of a teacher is to be an intellectual and moral role model.

_____ **16.** Active engagement is important for learning.

_____ **17.** Curriculum should be established that does not easily or often change, but may shift because of changes in society.

_____ **18.** Cooperative learning is an instructional tool that should be used often in the classroom.

_____ **19.** There is a set curriculum of basic core knowledge that all Americans should know.

_____ **20.** Individualism and freedom of choice are paramount in successful classrooms.

_____ **21.** Teachers are primarily dispensers of knowledge.

_____ **22.** Learning takes place through experiences.

_____ **23.** The wisdom students need may be obtained through study of the writings of great thinkers down through history.

_____ **24.** Standards and testing are of the utmost importance in schools.

_____ **25.** Traditional teaching methods, primarily those that are teacher directed, work best.

_____ **26.** Choices in what and how to learn are important.

_____ **27.** Curriculum should be established that does not change regardless of shifts in society.

_____ **28.** Standardization, tracking, and testing should have a minor role, if any, in the classroom.

_____ **29.** Student differences are not important when determining what and how to teach.

_____ **30.** Exploration and discovery are major factors in student learning.

What you have just experienced sets the stage for our discussion of five philosophies of education. This exercise has accessed your prior knowledge and experiences and has "set the hook" for further exploration, as we discussed in Chapter 4. You may sense a need to alter some of your responses as you learn more, and that's a very healthy thing to do. The more we know and understand, the more we grow.

Place the number you chose representing your level of agreement beside each of the following item numbers. Then find the sum of each column.

ITEM	MY #	ITEM	MY #
2		1	
4		3	
5		6	
8		7	
10		9	
12		11	
15		13	
17		14	
19		16	
21		18	
23		20	
24		22	
25		26	
27		28	
29		30	
Sum A		Sum B	

- *If Sum A is larger than Sum B, your views of schools and teaching tend to be more teacher centered. If this is the case, continue your analysis by adding the numbers you chose for items 17 and 19. If this sum is greater than the sum of items 23 and 27, your philosophy resembles essentialism. If not, you tend more toward perennialism. You'll read about these philosophies in the chapter.*

- *If Sum B is larger than Sum A, your views of schools and teaching tend to be more student centered. Most teachers who are student centered fall into a broad philosophical category of progressivism, a philosophy we will discuss. A distinction can be drawn between two other student-centered philosophies, social reconstructionism and existentialism. If you are more student centered, continue your analysis by adding the numbers you chose for items 9 and 14. If this sum is greater than the sum of items 7 and 28, your philosophy more resembles social reconstructionism than existentialism. If not, you tend more toward existentialism. You'll read about these philosophies in the chapter.*

Don't dismiss the contents of this chapter on the philosophical foundations of education as irrelevant theory. On the contrary, consider the concepts seriously and internalize them. This won't happen with a quick read-through and a glance at the figures. The chapter is relatively brief, allowing time to read it twice or even three times, purposefully reflecting on the content to make it personally meaningful.

According to the inventory, I am more _____centered than _____ centered. (either "teacher centered" or "student centered" in each blank)

If I am more teacher centered, I tend more toward _____ than _____. (either "essentialism" or "perennialism" in each blank)

If I am more student centered, I tend more toward _____ than _____. (either "social reconstructionism" or "existentialism" in each blank)

Teaching in Focus

Brenda Beyal's passionate approach to teaching is evident in every aspect of her work—curriculum choices, teaching methods, relationships with students, interactions with colleagues, and the learning environment she has created in her classroom. In her interview, Brenda tells us she considers her choice to teach a "calling." She had planned to be an engineer until she took a course that addressed the needs of children with disabilities. That's when she knew teaching would be her life's work. She has taught for over 20 years, most of them spent in a multiage classroom at Rees Elementary, south of Salt Lake City, Utah.

Brenda's classroom is very student friendly, with tables and a couch rather than desks in rows; a large classroom library with books for all reading levels on a wide range of topics; multiple cabinets of art supplies; display boards of student work; and an area filled with Native American art, posters, and artifacts that have personal meaning to Brenda because of her Native American heritage.

Brenda was one of the originators of the multiage concept at Rees Elementary. She wanted to have longer term relationships with individual students. She saw the benefits of children at different stages of maturation being together for several years. She also liked the idea of collaborating with other teachers in creative ways. With colleagues Chris and Tim, Brenda maintains an arts-infused curriculum by teaching all three classes of multiage students an art form. Brenda's specialty is visual arts, evident by the amount of artwork in her classroom.

Each day is filled with opportunities, according to Brenda, who finds purpose and beauty all around her as she fulfills her calling. Later in the chapter we'll translate what we know about Brenda into a philosophy of education.

Watch Brenda's interview in the Teaching in Focus section for Chapter 8 in MyEducationLab for this course.

What Is a Philosophy of Education?

Let's begin by taking a look at the word *philosophy*. The Greek *philo* means "love," and *sophos* means "wisdom." **Philosophy,** then, means "love of wisdom." Philosophy is a means of answering fundamental questions. It is not a boring, stuffy subject but rather a vibrant way of discovering and expressing ways of being and behaving.

If you've ever considered questions such as "Who am I?" or "What's my purpose in life?" you have engaged in philosophical thought. Every attitude and action is determined by some deeper basic beliefs, conscious or unconscious. To bring a philosophy to the surface of your consciousness requires consideration of your values and views about life. It necessitates reflection on circumstances, reactions, assumptions, intentions, and so on.

Few people have a formally defined philosophy. If asked, most may shrug and say, "I've never thought about it," or, "I don't have time for that kind of stuff." But if you study a person's attitudes and actions over a relatively brief period of time, you can probably make some statements about the person's basic philosophy. This is particularly true for teachers and the work they do. A teacher's **philosophy of education,** whether written or not, is the teacher's love of wisdom regarding teaching that expresses itself in attitudes and actions every day in the classroom.

WHY IS A PHILOSOPHY OF EDUCATION IMPORTANT?

A teacher's philosophy of education affects every decision made in the classroom. Allan C. Ornstein (2003) expresses the far-reaching impact of a philosophy of education when he writes,

> Philosophy enters into every important decision about curriculum, teaching, instruction, and testing. . . . The methods and materials a teacher chooses to use in a classroom reflect a professional judgment, which reflects philosophy. When a teacher decides to increase the homework load or assign a particular author, he or she is acting on the basis of philosophy. In short, choices reflect philosophy—and whether we recognize our own philosophy in education, it is out there and it influences our behavior and attitudes in classrooms and schools. Philosophy then operates overtly and covertly, whether we know that it is operating or not. (p. 17)

Figure 8.1 Karen Heath, 2005 Vermont Teacher of the Year

One of the ubiquitous rites of passage for preservice teachers is the completion of a philosophy of education. When I was a senior in college 22 years ago, having just completed my student teaching, one of the final requirements before being certified was to complete such a document. I was still a student, and much of what I thought about and wrote was largely theoretical. I wrote about the need for children's differences to be recognized, the importance of process in education, and freedom within a structured environment. "A Personal Philosophy of Education," as it was titled, went subsequently into a box in an attic while I ventured across the country and, a few years later, settled into a home in Vermont where the box was moved to a new attic, gathering dust with other college relics.

Last year when I was nominated to be Teacher of the Year, I was called upon once again to produce a philosophy of education. I sat down one weekend and wrote about what I believe to be the most important aspect of education—the heart. Years of experience have taught me that in order to be an effective teacher, my heart must be in it fully, from devotion to subject matter, to striving to keep up with best practices, and, most importantly, to having a heart connection to the children, as that is the only sure avenue to effective student learning.

It took a bit of digging, but I found the old college box, and at the very bottom of it lay my original philosophy of education. I took it like a treasure into the afternoon sun in our yard and carefully read not just a philosophy, but also the mind-set of an idealistic 21-year-old. Surprisingly, I still agreed with everything I had written, but there was a distinct lack of mention of anything having to do with relationships. I guess that is the aspect of teaching that I have truly learned over time.

Though my first written document sat untouched for 23 years and my newest one was just composed, I have always carried with me a philosophy of education. It brings stability to my work as initiatives and programs come and go. From a fairly benign population of children in a wealthy college town to an inner-city Boston high school, my philosophy is the backbone of what I do as a teacher. It directs what and how I teach and, most importantly, how I interact with my students. It is the core of who I am as a teacher.

Source: E-mail communication with Karen Heath, January 18, 2007.

Because teacher preparation puts you in a position to think about decisions relative to teaching, prospective teachers are usually asked to write a philosophy of education. This means you will look closely at established philosophical viewpoints, you will analyze what these viewpoints mean to teachers and their work, and then you will either state with which philosophy you agree or with which combination you most closely align. The philosophy of education you write before entering the classroom as a teacher will be based on limited experience and will be a work in progress. But it's a start and an important one.

An educational philosophy should not be a static document that you write because you have to and then never look at again. People change and grow, often in response to personal experiences. Your philosophy will change and grow. In Figure 8.1, read about Karen Heath's experience of writing an initial philosophy of education as a college assignment and her subsequent experiences leading her to revisit her philosophy.

What Are Four Branches of Philosophy?

There are branches of philosophy just as there are branches of medicine (e.g., cardiology, oncology, dermatology) and branches of law (e.g., civil, criminal, tax), each having its own definition. Because the study of philosophy is based on questions and the pursuit of answers, four commonly held basic branches of philosophy are best explored through the questions addressed in each. Metaphysics, epistemology, axiology, and logic each has its own unique category of questions that will aid in understanding its primary content and purposes. As you read this section, think about how the philosophical questions may apply in early childhood, elementary, middle, and high school classrooms.

METAPHYSICS

Metaphysics addresses the search for reality and purpose (Jacobsen, 2003). The word *metaphysics* means "beyond the material or the physical." Those who study metaphysics look for answers that go beyond scientific experiments. To understand more about metaphysics, first read the questions associated with this branch of philosophy, and then read about how metaphysics may be manifested in the classroom.

- What is reality?
- What is a human being in the grand scheme of things?
- Do cause-and-effect relationships exist?
- Does reality change, making the search for truth meaningless?
- What is the meaning of life?
- Are people born either good or evil?
- Does life have a purpose?

METAPHYSICS IN THE CLASSROOM. Curriculum is based on what we know about reality. Those who make decisions about what to teach are expressing a view of reality. When teachers attempt to inspire students to look to the future and find reasons for studying and learning, they are expressing metaphysics-related beliefs that life has purpose and that people can make decisions that affect the future. For instance, in a middle school career exploration class, a teacher may ask students to think about what they consider important in life. The teacher may then ask how aspects of a career in business management, for example, might help the students and others affected by a particular business to concentrate on what is considered important.

EPISTEMOLOGY

Epistemology addresses the dilemma of determining truth and ways of acquiring knowledge. The skeptic says it's impossible to know what the truth is, whereas the agnostic says there is no truth and therefore no need to look for it. Some people who are skeptics or agnostics in one area of their lives may believe that truth exists and can be determined in other areas. Consider the questions posed in the study of epistemology, and then read how epistemology may look in a classroom.

- What is truth?
- Does truth depend on circumstances or on the person seeking it?
- How do we acquire knowledge?
- What are the limits of knowledge?
- Is knowledge changing or fixed?

EPISTEMOLOGY IN THE CLASSROOM. Curriculum standards are stated as truths. When teachers consider there are absolute truths in the curriculum that students need to know, they must then deal with epistemological questions.

There are commonly held beliefs about where knowledge comes from and how it is acquired. Teachers tend to organize instruction or to use some instructional strategies more than others depending on their own views. For instance, believing that students learn best when they discover knowledge themselves will lead a teacher to practice inquiry-based strategies

Once teachers have determined what is true about their content area (or have accepted the curriculum standards as truths), they are ready to consider how they want students to know or discover these truths. Consider the following sources of knowing, based loosely on Eisner (1985):

1. We know based on *authority*. This belief puts the teacher, the textbook, and other sources of information squarely in the forefront of instruction.

2. We know based on *experience.* This belief leads to active learning involving the students' senses and the gathering of data.

3. We know based on *reasoning and logic.* This belief says that we think through situations and problems and draw conclusions.

4. We know based on *intuition.* This belief bases truth on a feeling about the answers.

5. We know based on *divine revelation.* This belief is in the power of the supernatural to reveal knowledge or truth.

The first three ways of knowing are the ones most often employed in the classroom. Knowing based on authority leads to reading assignments, lectures, review of the appropriate literature, and many traditional ways of teaching. Knowing based on experiences would lead to the use of manipulatives in math, survey research in social studies, and experiments in science. Knowing based on reasoning is what most teachers promote in the classroom. Learning to use higher-order thinking skills and moving through Bloom's taxonomy are part of knowing based on reasoning.

AXIOLOGY

Axiology addresses values, both in ethics and aesthetics. **Ethics** is the determination of what's right and what's wrong. **Aesthetics** is the determination of what is beautiful and artistic. Both ethics and aesthetics require judgments. Consider the questions posed in the study of axiology, and then read about how axiology may look in the classroom.

- What is valuable?
- What values should a person possess?
- What is right, and what is wrong?
- What is just, and what is unjust?
- How should life be lived?
- How should we judge the quality of what we see, hear, and touch?
- What is the quality of an artistic expression?
- What is beauty?

AXIOLOGY IN THE CLASSROOM. Teachers contend daily in their classrooms with questions of axiology. Ethics deals with how students treat one another, how they respect property, and how they make decisions about right and wrong in the classroom community. When a school adopts a character education program to help students establish attitudes about respect, it is acknowledging that ethics matter.

Deciding what is aesthetically pleasing also involves axiology. Part of what teachers do is help students recognize and appreciate beauty in any form. For instance, a math teacher who encourages students to explore geometry in nature and to discover the artistry of the geometric structures is prompting them to expand their definition of what is beautiful.

School itself expresses a value. Requiring children to attend school suggests the belief that it is right to give students the opportunity to learn (Nelson, Carlson, & Palonsky, 2000). Also, teachers are expected to possess certain values and to behave in ethical ways. Focus teacher Chris Roberts tells us that teachers teach who they are, making an internalized philosophy of education even more important. Read what Chris has to say in *Teaching in Focus*.

LOGIC

Logic is reasoning that avoids vagueness and contradictions. Simply put, people use logic when they think to understand a situation, solve a problem, or draw a conclusion. Two basic kinds of reasoning, or logic, are commonly addressed in school. **Deductive reasoning** is a process that begins with a general statement, from which more specific statements are assumed to be true. **Inductive reasoning** works the other way: Given

Teaching in Focus

Chris Roberts, Grades 3–5 Multiage Classroom, Rees Elementary School, Utah. *In his own words. . . .*

I heard or read somewhere that "you teach who you are." I know, after teaching 29 years, that there is a lot of truth in those five words. I've had students return to visit me years after they've been in my class and I get invited to many of their weddings. As we catch up on the years that have passed, none of them talk about their reading or math; they tell me about me. Their memories don't focus on the great unit I taught on Native Americans, but rather on the time I told them about a trip I went on or a belief I have about life. I don't think you can be an excellent teacher if your own life is boring or "unexamined," as Henry David Thoreau would caution. Children will naturally be less interested in learning from someone they find uninteresting. Don't let the classroom, and pressures you will surely face, rule your life. Live a full life. Share with your students what you learn and experience on your amazing path.

some specific statements, a general conclusion may be assumed. Figure 8.2 illustrates these two types of logic. Consider the questions posed in the study of logic and then read how logic may look in the classroom.

- What makes sense?
- Is an idea or conclusion valid?
- How can we get from point A to point B in a way that makes sense?
- Is there a foundation for a particular argument?

LOGIC IN THE CLASSROOM. Teaching thinking skills—teaching the use of logic—is a major emphasis in many subject areas. An essay question that asks students to judge the

Figure 8.2 Deductive and inductive reasoning

General to specific

DEDUCTIVE

Example

Generalization:
The day is sunny and dry.

Specifics:
We will go outside for recess.
The children will have opportunities to use their energy.

Specific to general

INDUCTIVE

Example

Specifics:
Children are usually hungry in the morning.
Many of our children do not live in homes where breakfast is served.
A good breakfast promotes concentration/learning.

Generalization:
A school breakfast program will increase our children's capacity for learning.

TABLE 8.1 Four branches of philosophy

Branch of Philosophy	Defining Questions
Metaphysics	What is reality?
	Does life have a purpose?
Epistemology	What is truth?
	How do we acquire knowledge?
Axiology	What is right, and what is wrong?
	What is beauty?
Logic	What makes sense?
	Is there a foundation for a particular argument?

outcome of a government program as good or bad (axiology) is asking them to use inductive reasoning as they look at individual results and draw a conclusion. A test that asks students to explain how to apply a theorem to particular variables is prompting them to use deductive reasoning. A teacher who intervenes in a student squabble and says, "Now stop and think about this" is asking students to think clearly, using logic and reasoning.

Review the four branches of philosophy and their defining questions in Table 8.1. The basic questions can be applied to the five schools of philosophical thought expressed as philosophies of education in the following section.

How Do Five Prominent Philosophies of Education Affect Teaching and Learning?

Just as knowing about individual branches helps lay the groundwork for understanding what philosophy encompasses, exploring prominent philosophies will provide a framework for understanding what they mean for teaching and learning. The five philosophies featured in this section are not the only ones that directly impact the work of teachers. A few others are discussed briefly at the end of this section.

We have explored teacher-centered and student-centered curricula and instruction. The five philosophies discussed here fall neatly into these two categories. Essentialism and perennialism are teacher-centered approaches, whereas progressivism, social reconstructionism, and existentialism are more student centered, as illustrated in Figure 8.3. Keep this

> Teacher-centered and student-centered curricula and instruction are discussed in Chapter 4.

Figure 8.3 Teacher- and student-centered approaches

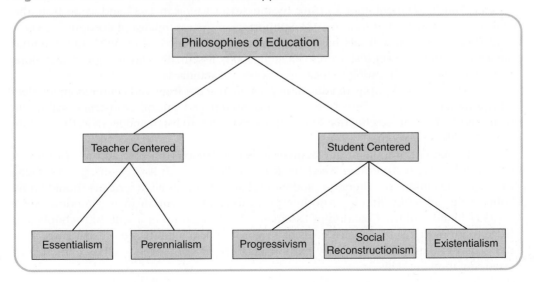

in mind as you read about the five philosophies. Also remember to think about early childhood, elementary, middle, and high school classrooms as you consider each philosophy of education.

PHILOSOPHY TREES

The discussion of each philosophy is accompanied by a diagram of a tree. The analogy of a philosophy of education to a tree is appropriate in many ways. The tree trunk represents teaching. The root system is a particular philosophy of education, or a combination of philosophies, providing the strength and foundation of the tree: The philosophy literally grounds the tree. The branches of the tree represent the work of teachers. Each trunk-attached branch supports smaller branches with plentiful leaves that represent teaching and learning.

Many aspects of a tree's growth are directly analogous to teaching and learning. Do you recall seeing a cross section of a tree trunk? Elementary students learn that you can count the rings to determine the age of a tree because each year of growth not only takes a tree skyward but also wraps another layer of life around it. So it is with teaching experience. Each year, previous experiences aren't shed but rather are wrapped in new experiences.

Trees have two kinds of roots: anchor roots, which grow deeper with time and hold the tree upright against most winds, and feeder roots, which shoot out in all directions and draw in nourishment. Have you ever noticed a makeshift fence or stakes with colored tape around the base of a tree when construction is nearby? The purpose of this barrier is to let workers know that digging closer would likely damage the tree. Although a tree can survive the loss of some feeder roots, the diameter of the feeder and anchor root system is generally the same as the diameter of the canopy of the tree's branches and leaves. Cutting away feeder roots will diminish the canopy in like proportion. The size and stability of the philosophical root system determine the effectiveness of the teaching and learning canopy. Your anchor matters; your philosophy of education affects all aspects of your success as a teacher.

ESSENTIALISM

Essentialism is a philosophy of education based on the belief that a core curriculum exists that everyone in the United States should learn. This core can shift in response to societal changes but should always be basic, organized, and rigorous. When you hear someone praise the concept of "back to basics," chances are that person is an essentialist.

Progressivism, *A Nation at Risk,* and *Sputnik* are discussed in Chapter 7.

Essentialism is an ancient philosophy, but in the 20th century it grew as a backlash to progressivism, the educational philosophy begun by John Dewey. Whereas progressivism puts student interests at the center of curriculum and instruction, essentialism puts little stock in what students want in terms of what and how they learn. Essentialism gained impetus from the launching of *Sputnik* by the Soviet Union in 1957 and again from the publication of *A Nation at Risk* in 1983. Supporters of the essentialist philosophy are vocal about their view that schools have dumbed down the curriculum with nonessential courses, resulting in lower test scores (Ravitch, 2000). Essentialists favor high expectations for students, along with testing to measure mastery of standards.

An essentialist philosophy of education puts the teacher front and center as an intellectual and moral role model. Direct instruction is encouraged, but other instructional methods are used if they prove effective. Students are expected to listen and learn as they follow the rules of the classroom.

One prominent proponent of essentialism is E. D. Hirsch (b. 1928), author of *Cultural Literacy: What Every American Needs to Know* (1987). Hirsch lists events, people, facts, discoveries, inventions, art, literature, and more that he believes all Americans should know about to be culturally literate. Another proponent of essentialism is Theodore Sizer (b. 1932), founder of the Coalition of Essential Schools, a group of about 200 schools that pledge to promote the essentialist goals of a rigorous curriculum based on standards. Sizer (1985) insists that students clearly exhibit mastery of content as well as evidence of developing thinking skills.

Figure 8.4 Essentialism tree

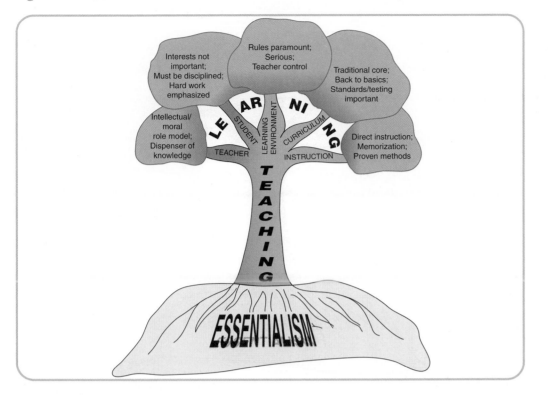

Take a few minutes to study the essentialism tree in Figure 8.4. Visualizing how teachers might translate the elements of essentialism into their classrooms will help you understand this philosophy of education.

PERENNIALISM

Perennialism is a philosophy of education based on a core curriculum, and in that regard it is similar to essentialism. The difference lies in what constitutes the core. The word *perennial* means "everlasting" and is often used when talking about plants. A perennial flower blooms in season, is dormant for a time, and then blooms again, year after year. A flower that is not a perennial is an annual that must be replanted each year. Perennialism, as a philosophy of education, says there is a curriculum with themes and questions that endure, that are everlasting. In contrast, the curriculum of essentialism is considered basic and core, but its components may change as society changes and, as such, the essentialist curriculum is more comparable to an annual.

Perennialists believe that even as life changes and times change, the real substance and truths of life remain the same. The wisdom students need may be obtained through the study of **Great Books,** the writings of those considered to be the great thinkers through the history of Western civilization, such as Homer, Shakespeare, Melville, Einstein, and many others. Perennialists do not endorse choices in the curriculum or elective courses, and they ascribe to a rigid curriculum for elementary, middle, and high schools.

Teachers who practice perennialism as a philosophy of education want to be in control of the classroom. They dispense knowledge and lead discussions of classics that require rigorous, logical thought by students. Differences in students are rarely considered, as all are expected to learn from the classics (Webb, Metha, & Jordan, 2010).

Mortimer Adler (1902-2001), author of the *Paideia Proposal* (1982), is perhaps the best known recent proponent of perennialism as a philosophy of education. The word *paideia* refers to a state of human excellence. Adler said that schools should use intense study of the classics to strive for excellence in students (Pulliam & Van Patten, 2007). Adler

Points of Reflection 8.1

Do you identify with some of the elements of essentialism? If so, which ones? Do some of the aspects of essentialism in the classroom, illustrated in Figure 8.4, appeal to you as a prospective teacher? Are there some aspects that do not appeal to you? If so, which ones?

Figure 8.5 Perennialism tree

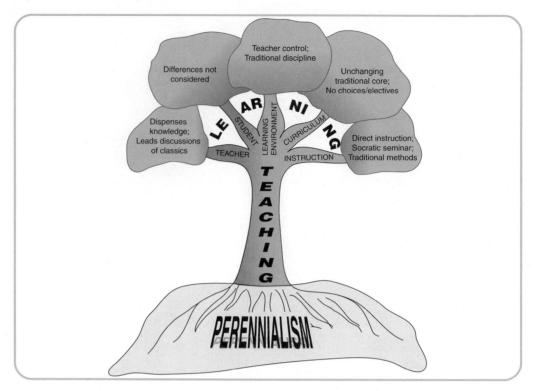

Points of Reflection 8.2

Do you identify with some of the elements of perennialism? If so, which ones? Do some of the aspects of perennialism in the classroom, illustrated in Figure 8.5, appeal to you as a prospective teacher? Are there some aspects that do not appeal to you? If so, which ones?

founded the Great Books of the Western World program at the University of Chicago in 1930 (Adler, 1982).

Take a few minutes to study the perennialism tree in Figure 8.5. Visualizing how teachers might translate the elements of perennialism into their classrooms will help you understand this philosophy of education.

PROGRESSIVISM

Progressivism is a student-centered philosophy of education that focuses on a curriculum of interest to students. To progressivists, education is more than preparation for the future: It is life itself. The progressive philosophy of education endorses experiential learning full of opportunities for student discovery and problem solving.

Constructivism and pragmatism are philosophies of education that fall within the broader philosophy of progressivism. Constructivism, an inquiry-based way of approaching instruction, builds on progressivism because students are challenged to construct, or discover, knowledge about their environments. Process is valued in progressivism, often more than product. The theory is that students who learn through the processes of construction, discovery, and problem solving will be better able to adapt to a changing world. Another philosophy, **pragmatism,** says that student-centered perspectives integrated with first-hand experiences are the most effective (Chartock, 2004).

Teachers who ascribe to progressivism act primarily as facilitators of learning, serving as resources and guides to students who explore, gather evidence, and draw conclusions. Real-world problem solving is intended to promote individual student development (Gutek, 2005).

John Dewey (1859–1952) was the most prominent of all the proponents of progressivism, beginning in the late 19th century and continuing well into the 20th century. Dewey supported a balance between valuing established content with structured learning activities and planning experiences that interest, motivate, and actively involve students. Although progressivism fell out of favor in a call for more rigor in the late 1950s, many tenets of the philosophy continue to be part of today's most widely used instructional strategies.

Take a few minutes to study the progressivism tree in Figure 8.6. Visualizing how teachers might translate the elements of progressivism into their classrooms will help you understand this philosophy of education.

SOCIAL RECONSTRUCTIONISM

More than any other philosophy of education, **social reconstructionism** looks to education to change society, rather than just teach about it. Social reconstructionism as a philosophy of education calls on schools to educate students in ways that will help society move beyond all forms of discrimination to the benefit of everyone worldwide. This philosophy addresses such topics as racial equality, women's rights, sexism, environmental pollution, poverty, substance abuse, homophobia, and AIDS. Proponents of other educational philosophies often avoid such topics, thus relegating the topics to the null curriculum.

Encouraging students to engage in learning and express themselves is part of the philosophy of progressivism.

According to some educators, Theodore Brameld (1904–1987) founded the philosophy of social reconstructionism following World War II. Brameld (1956) based the philosophy on two premises: (1) people now have the capacity to destroy civilization, and (2) people have the potential to create a civilization marked by health and humanity. The basic tenets of social reconstructionism, however, go back to the early Greeks and, more recently, to Karl Marx, who called for a social revolution that would bring about equity among all people (Jacobsen, 2003).

The null curriculum is discussed in Chapter 4.

Teachers who ascribe to social reconstructionism promote active student involvement in societal problems. They plan experiences for students to explore issues and possible

Points of Reflection 8.3

Do you identify with some of the elements of progressivism? If so, which ones? Do some of the aspects of progressivism in the classroom, illustrated in Figure 8.6, appeal to you as a prospective teacher? Are there some aspects that do not appeal to you? If so, which ones?

Figure 8.6 Progressivism tree

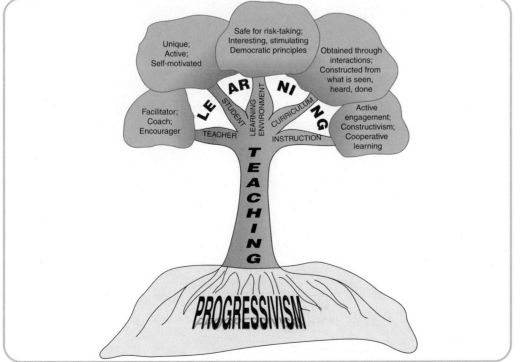

solutions, but avoid moralizing. They promote democracy and freedom to make choices while helping students discover the consequences of particular lines of reasoning and action. All of this occurs within an educational context that focuses on reading comprehension, research techniques, analysis and evaluation skills, and writing as a form of persuasive communication.

Major proponents of social reconstructionism as a philosophy of education include George Counts (1907–1974), Paulo Friere (1922–1987), and Ivan Illich (1926–2002). In his book *Dare the School Build a New Social Order?* (1932), Counts wrote about his view that schools should equip students to deal with world problems. Friere, in *Pedagogy of the Oppressed* (1970), wrote about his personal experiences in working with poor illiterate peasants that led him to the philosophy that education is the key to empowering the poor to control and improve their lives. In his book *Deschooling Society* (1971), Illich promoted a radical view. He wrote that schools as we know them should be eliminated because they do nothing to decrease poverty. He contended that schools actually prevent what he saw as real education, a process he viewed as happening in more informal ways. While "deschooling" American society will likely not happen, the social reconstructionist views of Illich have prompted important questions about the role of public education (Chartock, 2004).

Take a few minutes to study the social reconstructionism tree in Figure 8.7. Visualizing how teachers might translate the elements of social reconstructionism into their classrooms will help you understand this philosophy of education.

Points of Reflection 8.4

Do you identify with some of the elements of social reconstructionism? If so, which ones? Do some of the aspects of social reconstructionism in the classroom, illustrated in Figure 8.7, appeal to you as a prospective teacher? Are there some aspects that do not appeal to you? If so, which ones?

EXISTENTIALISM

The primary emphasis of **existentialism** is on the individual. As a philosophy of education, existentialism contends that teachers teach the whole person, not just math, reading, science, or any other particular subject. Each student searches for personal meaning and personal understanding. If learning about a subject increases a student's sense of self, then it's worthwhile. Practices such as standardization, tracking, and testing do not fit into an existentialist viewpoint. Because meaning is personal, each student has the freedom and the subsequent responsibility to make his or her own choices. Existentialism rejects traditional

Figure 8.7 Social reconstructionism tree

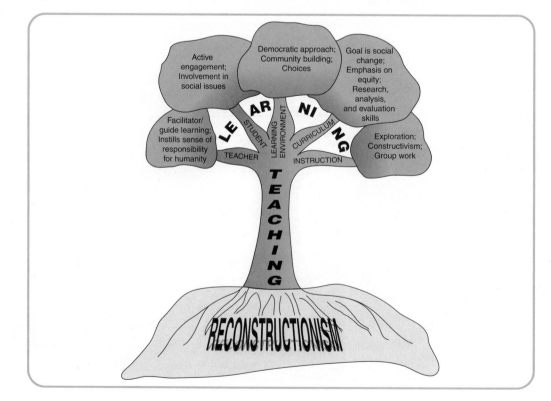

education. Few schools practice existentialism as an educational philosophy, and most that do are private. However, there are teachers in both public and private classrooms who practice some elements of existentialism.

The existentialist teacher honors individual students by arranging for learning experiences from which each student may choose. The classroom atmosphere is supposed to be stimulating and full of choices. The student's job is to make choices and then take responsibility for those choices. Teachers and students have a great deal of individual contact, participating in learning that is self-paced and self-directed (Greene, 1978). A teacher who follows existentialism as a philosophy of education teaches best by being a role model and demonstrates the importance of a discipline by pursuing academic goals related to the subject area.

A. S. Neill (1883–1973) was one of the most influential proponents of existentialism. He founded the Summerhill School in England following World War I. Learning by discovery was the primary feature of Summerhill. The student as an individual was emphasized and exploration for the sake of learning had few restrictions (Neill, 1960).

Maxine Greene (b. 1917) is the most well-known proponent of existentialism. She refers to a heightened level of personal awareness as "wide-awakeness." Greene refutes critics of existentialism who say that the philosophy in practice allows children to run free and out of control. She maintains that freedom has rules that allow others to be free as well (Greene, 1995).

Take a few minutes to study the existentialism tree in Figure 8.8. Visualizing how teachers might translate the elements of existentialism into their classrooms will help you understand this philosophy of education.

Although focus teacher Craig Cleveland does not completely fit the existentialist profile, we see that many of the ways Craig approaches his teaching responsibilities mirror an existentialist philosophy. Read more about Craig as you consider this chapter's ***Diversity Dialogue***.

As we established early in this chapter, we all have philosophies. They may be consciously held, or they may just be "how we are" or "what we think." But one thing's for sure, our philosophies become evident when an issue arises. In this chapter's ***Letter to the Editor,*** a citizen expresses his philosophy concerning the current state of public schools.

Points of Reflection 8.5

Do you identify with some of the elements of existentialism? If so, which ones? Do some of the aspects of existentialism in the classroom, illustrated in Figure 8.8, appeal to you as a prospective teacher? Are there some aspects that do not appeal to you? If so, which ones?

Figure 8.8 Existentialism tree

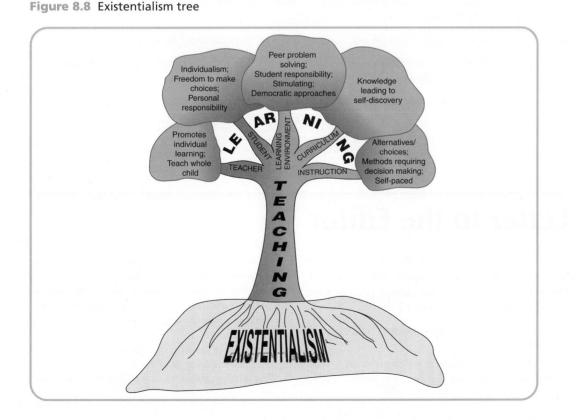

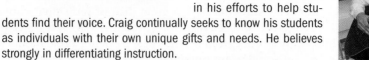

Craig Cleveland's philosophy of education is evident in everything he does at Roosevelt High School. He is intense and focused in his efforts to help students find their voice. Craig continually seeks to know his students as individuals with their own unique gifts and needs. He believes strongly in differentiating instruction.

For Craig to address diversity and emphasize the value of each individual, he must have competency in the subject he teaches. He abides by this INTASC standard:

INTASC Knowledge Principle 1
The teacher understands major concepts, assumptions, debates, processes of inquiry, and ways of knowing that are central to the discipline(s) s/he teaches.

"Ways of knowing" is a defining piece of epistemology. Teachers deal with this every day, whether consciously or unconsciously. Craig is very conscious of the more complex nature of history and its implications than many other teachers. He knows his subject: the major concepts, assumptions, debates, and processes of inquiry. He also believes that many of these aspects change as society changes, although the basic historical events may not.

Another standard that resonates with Craig is part of the principles of the National Board of Professional Teaching Standards (NBPTS) that says,

Accomplished teachers are models of educated persons . . . and the capacities that are prerequisites for intellectual growth: the ability to reason and take multiple perspectives, to be creative and take risks, and to adapt to an experimental and problem solving orientation.

One issue Craig is determined to help change is that in most arenas of the United States, white voices are more likely to be heard than those of minorities. As he looks around his classroom, and as we saw from his class role in Chapter 2, Craig sees few white faces. To him, his mission is clear: help empower all his students to find and express their values and beliefs, to speak in their own voices and be heard.

1. What are two ways Craig encourages his students to find and express their voices in his classroom? Explain each.

2. How does Craig inform his own opinions and grow professionally? Explain.

3. With regard to how Craig views the subject he teaches, with which philosophy of education would he closely align? Why?

4. With regard to instruction, with which philosophy of education would he closely align? Why?

You watched Craig's interview, room tour, and lesson in Chapter 3. Reviewing all three brief videos will help you think more clearly about Craig and the questions concerning how his philosophy is manifested in his classroom. The videos are in the Teaching in Focus *section for Chapter 8 in MyEducationLab for this course.*

Letter to the Editor

This letter appeared in the Greensboro, North Carolina, newspaper, the *News & Record.* The writer is expressing a philosophy about the purposes of school.

AUGUST 1, 2010 SCHOOLS' FIRST PRIORITY SHOULD BE ON ACADEMICS

In the last 57 years, reading, writing and arithmetic have become collateral damage in a public school system increasingly devoted to solving social problems ranging from hunger to teen pregnancy.

Providing security for students and teachers on the same campus with at-risk populations warehoused until they become dropouts strains local police and school administration resources.

This is not a racial issue. This is not a socioeconomic issue. The issue is about the priority placed on reading, writing and arithmetic in a public system that

(Continued)

is broken. We can continue to bus children to achieve racial diversity. We can continue to let school boards tell parents what's best for their children. If we cannot find another venue to deal with social problems, we will be having this same harangue 57 years from now, probably in Chinese.

Joe Exum
Snow Hill

Now it's your turn. Write a letter to the editor from the perspective of a future teacher expressing your philosophy about the purposes of school. The following questions may help you frame your thinking but should not limit nor determine what you write.

1. Which of the five philosophies of education is the letter writer expressing in the first sentence? Which philosophy do you think he is definitely opposed to? How does what he's expressing fit with what you believe? Is there a happy medium you might express?

2. Mr. Exum is expressing his belief that some students are too at risk to be in regular school settings, that they require excessive effort on the part of administration and police. Does he have a valid point? As a teacher, what comment would you make to address this point?

3. Mr. Exum expresses that the public education system is broken. Do you agree? If not, what might you write to express to the public that education in America is *not* broken?

4. Mr. Exum seems to think that finding solutions to social problems outside the school system is the only way to save life as we know it in America. Is this a justified concern or an exaggeration?

Write your letter in understandable terminology, remembering that readers of newspaper Letters to the Editor are citizens who may have limited knowledge of school practices and policies. Remember to refer to the letter assessment rubric in Chapter 1.

OTHER PHILOSOPHIES

Other "isms" may impact educational philosophy. Let's look briefly at some of them.

Idealism is a philosophy based on the belief that ideas are the only reliable form of reality. Idealists believe that because the physical world changes continually, ideas are what should be taught. Taking the opposite stance, **realism** is based on the belief that some facts are absolutes whether recognized by all or not. Realists contend that the only way to know these absolutes is to study the material world.

Romanticism, or naturalism, as a philosophy of education contends that the needs of the individual are more important than the needs of society. Many early childhood and elementary educators incorporate into their classrooms the tenets of romanticism that say young children are born good, pure, and full of curiosity and that their individual interests should be validated with opportunities to explore and manipulate elements of their environment.

Postmodernism grew out of a sense that those in power control those who don't have power. Postmodernists believe this control is manifested through major institutions such as schools. The decades of the 1960s and 1970s were times of unprecedented outcry for justice and equality through the civil rights movement, the feminist movement, and a renewed concern for the poor. Postmodernist philosophy grew as a response to these cultural stirrings. The postmodern curriculum includes perspectives on history and literature by a variety of authors representing different lifestyles. Proponents of postmodernism contend they are attempting to strike a balance of power among all people and that intellectual growth from multiple perspectives is one avenue for doing so. Critics of postmodernism contend that the philosophy seeks to promote political purposes rather than intellectual purposes (Ozmon & Craver, 2008).

You will likely encounter other philosophies as you participate in future teacher preparation courses. The ones you have read about so far provide many choices for you to consider as you begin the process of writing your own philosophy of education.

How Do I Begin to Develop My Personal Philosophy of Education?

When it comes to developing a philosophy of education, balance is important. If you found yourself aligning with parts of one and parts of another as you read about the prominent philosophies of education, and thinking, "How will I weigh all this and decide?" you are

Figure 8.9 Brenda's philosophy tree

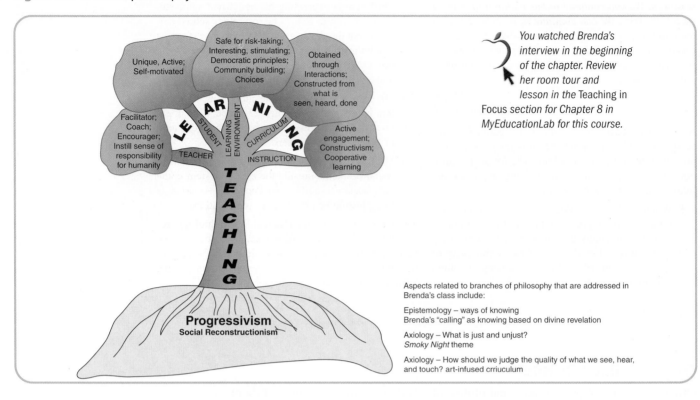

Brenda, one of the focus teachers at Rees Elementary, demonstrates her skills during a field trip with her students.

certainly not alone. Very few educators can place themselves squarely in one camp or another. Picking and choosing from among the components of several philosophies is referred to as taking an *eclectic approach*. This entails balance. It's natural for teachers to lean toward one philosophy or approach more than another, but prescribing to only one philosophy will not serve the needs of all children. Chartock (2004) states, "For every belief there is an equal and opposite belief and data to support both. That's why the field of education is never dull" (p. 136). Never dull, indeed.

Reread the opening scenario of this chapter about Brenda Beyal. The philosophy tree in Figure 8.9 represents Brenda's philosophy. As you examine the tree, think about evidence, given what you know about Brenda, to support the elements on the tree.

YOUR TURN

Now it's your turn to grow a philosophy tree. The root system will consist of an anchor philosophy, the philosophy with which you most closely align. There's no need to ascribe to every tenet of this anchor philosophy, but it should express most of your current beliefs about teaching and learning. Other philosophies may be part of the feeder root system. The branches and leaves of the tree's canopy will be a mix of what you believe about the roles of teacher, students, the learning environment, the curriculum, and instruction. Keep in mind that the deeper and wider the philosophy root system, the stronger and more stable the trunk will grow and the richer and more extensive the canopy will be.

Figure 8.10 is a tree waiting for you to make it your own. Your philosophy tree can be a valuable component of the teaching portfolio you will no doubt develop as part of your teacher preparation.

One approach to begin examining your own philosophy is to study the content of Table 8.2 carefully. Considering the responses to the questions in the table that relate

Figure 8.10 My philosophy tree

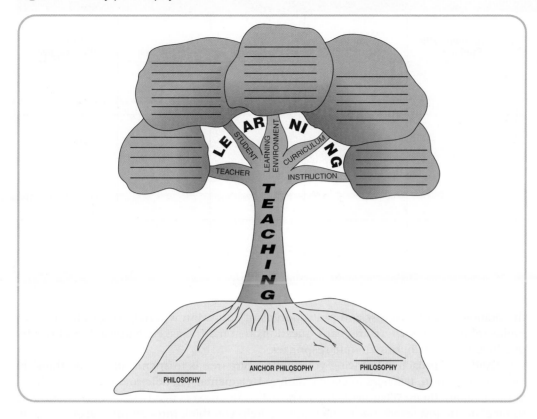

TABLE 8.2 Sample questions and philosophical responses					
Question (Branch)	Essentialism	Perennialism	Progressivism	Reconstructionism	Existentialism
What is real? (metaphysics)	Elements of core curriculum; may change	Elements of core curriculum; unchanging	What can be verified through the senses	What can be verified through research and analysis	Based entirely on the individual's perspective and experience
How do we acquire knowledge? (epistemology)	From a combination of the classics and science	From the never-changing classics	From individual experiences and discovery	From individual and group searches for meaning and justice	Through individual quests; making choices
What is valuable? (axiology)	Core of knowledge that responds to some societal shifts	Changeless core of knowledge	Determined by individual interacting with own culture	Whatever makes society more just and equitable	Whatever leads to greater self-knowledge
What makes sense? (logic)	Classics provide generalizations; specifics are deduced; observation and analysis of specifics may lead to generalization	Deductive reasoning from truths of classics	Discovered through problem solving	Weighed against potential benefit or harm to society	Whatever enhances individual freedom and increases personal responsibility

TABLE 8.3 My favorite teachers' philosophical bents

Teacher's Name	Teacher's Role	Interactions with Students	Learning Environment	Curriculum	Instruction	Aligned with Which Philosophy?

the branches of philosophy and philosophies of education will help you examine your philosophical views. There are many questions that may be asked, with each philosophy of education contributing unique responses.

Another approach to growing your philosophy tree is to spend some time thinking about your favorite teachers in early childhood, elementary, middle, and high school. Why did you admire them? What made them special? Your answers need to go beyond "She was so nice" or "He just stands out in my mind." To help you think through the reasons particular teachers had positive effects on you, put a special teacher's name on the chart in Table 8.3. Then think about how this person appeared to view his or her roles as a teacher, including relationships with students, the creation of the learning environment, and approaches to curriculum and instruction. Table 8.3 will help organize your recollections.

A sincere, honest start to the development of a philosophy of education will help grow you into the teaching profession. Having opportunities to talk about your philosophy and listen to your classmates, your instructor, and teachers in the field will make you more comfortable articulating your stance. The more you think, talk, and listen, the more confident you will become that you are grounded in your reasons for how you approach your role, your students, the learning environment, curriculum, and instruction.

CONCLUDING THOUGHTS

Chances are that a philosophy of education is not something you've ever seriously considered. Now you have some background about major branches of philosophy, as well as philosophies of education. You have been prompted to think about, and tentatively declare, which philosophy represents your primary beliefs about teaching and learning. You also know that an eclectic approach is not only natural but will actually benefit the diverse groups of students you will no doubt encounter.

Thoughtful teachers are not necessarily swayed by gimmicks and fads, they have basic beliefs about teaching and learning that guide their practice, and they can articulate the bases for decisions. These are teachers who will positively affect student learning throughout their careers. This applies to early childhood, elementary, middle, and high school teachers equally. A carefully considered philosophy of education provides a solid foundation for professionals in the classroom.

After reading the *Chapter in Review,* read more about Brenda and respond to items in this chapter's *Developing Professional Competence*.

Chapter in Review

What is a philosophy of education?

- We all have philosophies that guide our decisions, attitudes, and actions.
- A teacher's philosophy of education affects every decision about teaching.

What are four branches of philosophy?

- Metaphysics addresses the search for reality and purpose.
- Epistemology addresses the dilemma of determining truth and ways of acquiring knowledge.
- Axiology addresses values, in both ethics and aesthetics.
- Logic is reasoning that avoids vagueness and contradiction.

How do five prominent philosophies of education affect teaching and learning?

- Essentialism is a philosophy of education based on the belief that there is a core curriculum that is responsive to the times and that every American should know.
- Perennialism is a philosophy of education based on the belief that there is a changeless core curriculum that every American should know.
- Progressivism is a philosophy of education that focuses on a curriculum of interest to students and experiential learning.
- Social reconstructionism is a philosophy of education that endorses a curriculum that benefits society by promoting equity.
- Existentialism is a philosophy of education that focuses on the individual's search for meaning.

How do I begin to develop my personal philosophy of education?

- Incorporating components of more than one philosophy of education into your personal philosophy is an eclectic approach.
- Growing an effective philosophy tree requires a strong root system with philosophical grounding to enhance both teaching and learning.

Developing Professional Competence

Visit the Developing Professional Competence section on Chapter 8 of the MyEducationLab for this text to answer the following questions and begin your preparation for licensure exams.

Brenda ascribes to a very student-centered philosophy of education, as we have seen in her interview, room tour, lesson, philosophy tree in Figure 8.9, and what we have read in *Teaching in Focus*. She knows the content she teaches and works very hard to be the best teacher she can be. The one thing that continually bothers Brenda is the fact that we are in an era of standards, where curriculum is prescribed and teaching is on a fast-paced schedule. Add to this the week of standardized tests she must monitor every spring, and we find Brenda seeking balance for her students and innovative ways to accomplish what is expected of her while paying attention to individual student needs.

One of Brenda's favorite authors is Vito Perrone (1991). Here is an excerpt that is particularly poignant for her.

> To engage students constructively, the school day needs more continuities, not more fragmentation. Work that can truly be valued takes time, sometimes hours and days. It is hardly reasonable to expect a child to complete a fine piece of artwork in ten- or twenty-minute intervals, twice a week, or produce a well-organized, thoughtful description, a poetic or narrative story within ten minutes. Teachers know this but claim that in this current basic skills, testing, "academic" environment, they don't have the time any more for work of that quality. (p. 33)

Given what we know about Brenda, answer these multiple-choice questions.

1. What do you think Brenda considers a source of fragmentation of her teaching day?
   a. District administrative guidelines that outline the time to be spent each day on language arts, reading, math, science, and social studies.
   b. Her students go to dance/movement class with Chris Roberts in the morning and to music/theater class with Tim Mendenhall in the afternoon.
   c. She has an early lunch time with her class.
   d. Rees incorporates two recess times a day.

2. Brenda attributes her agreement with Perrone's point about what's valuable to her Native American heritage. What might be the best of these four options for Brenda to let students know about her opinion?
   a. She could teach the students some of the soothing chants and tunes Native American mothers sing to their children.
   b. She could share artifacts and talk with students about how they are preserved.
   c. She could tell them stories about patience and perseverance from Native American folklore.

   d. She could explain to students the meaningfulness of the sundial and how Native Americans have historically honored the sun.

Now it's time for you to respond to three short essay items involving Brenda. In your responses, be sure to address all the dilemmas and questions posed in each item. Your responses should each be between one half and one double-spaced page.

3. Which do Brenda and Vito Perrone appear to value more: progress of a group or progress of the individual? Explain your response.

4. Perrone writes about "continuities." What kinds of activities do you think Brenda would put in this category? Explain two continuities you would expect to see in her classroom.

5. How might Brenda incorporate balance into the day as she teaches the standards while valuing quality and creativity?

Where DO I Stand NOW?

In the beginning of this chapter you completed an inventory that helped you discover your own philosophy of education. Now that you have read the chapter, completed exercises related to the content, engaged in class discussions, and so on, answer the following questions in your course notebook.

1. If you fell into the teacher-centered philosophy in **Where Do I Stand?** do you still think that essentialism and perennialism are the philosophies that most closely align with you and your beliefs? Why or why not? What has strengthened or weakened your alignment with a teacher-centered philosophy?

2. If you fell into the student-centered philosophy in **Where Do I Stand?** do you still think that progressivism, social

reconstructionism, and existentialism are the philosophies that most closely align with you and your beliefs? Why or why not? What has strengthened or weakened your alignment with a student-centered philosophy?

3. What is one aspect of education philosophy that has surprised you or had an impact on you in large measure, and why?

MyEducationLab

The MyEducationLab for this course can help you solidify your comprehension of Chapter 8 concepts.

- Explore the classrooms of the teachers and students you've met in this chapter in the Teaching in Focus section.

- Prepare for licensure exams as you deepen your understanding of chapter concepts in the Developing Professional Competence section.

- Gauge and further develop your understanding of chapter concepts by taking the quizzes and examining the enrichment materials on the Chapter 8 Study Plan.

- Visit Topic 7, "History and Philosophy of Education," to watch ABC videos, explore Assignments and Activities, and practice essential teaching skills with the Building Teaching Skills and Dispositions unit.

9

The Societal
Context of Schooling in the United States

This chapter examines elements that make up the complex societal context in which schooling occurs, including responses to these questions:

- ✦ How do family, community, and society impact students in the United States?

- ✦ How does socioeconomic status affect students in the United States?

- ✦ How do health issues affect students in the United States?

- ✦ How does race affect students in the United States?

- ✦ What are the effects of bullying, theft, and violence on students and schools in the United States?

- ✦ How do truancy and dropping out affect youth in the United States?

The issues in this chapter do not affect all students or all schools, but they do reach into all settings—urban, suburban, and rural. They affect all races and all ethnicities in both affluent neighborhoods and impoverished ones. And they affect both U.S. citizens and noncitizens.

Where DO I Stand?

This inventory gauges your awareness of the societal context of education in the United States. The inventory is in true/false format. As tempting as it may be, try the inventory without peeking at the answers! The purpose of this exercise is to activate your prior knowledge, not to assign a grade to what you know or don't know. Think about what we have discussed about the instructional purposes of diagnostic assessment.

All of the topics in the inventory are addressed in the chapter. After you respond to the items as true or false, you are instructed how to score the inventory.

_____ **1.** The U.S. graduation rate is about 65%; 1 in 3 kids in the United States drop out.

_____ **2.** Boys are much more likely to complete the act of suicide than girls.

_____ **3.** Approximately 50% of 12th graders have used illegal drugs.

_____ **4.** The teen pregnancy rate is lower now than in the past five decades.

_____ **5.** Child neglect is a form of abuse resulting from the failure to act in the best interest of the child.

_____ **6.** Weight issues are likely to affect the longevity of the lives of today's children.

_____ **7.** Frequent school transfers are the most significant barrier to the academic success of homeless students.

_____ **8.** About 7,000 students drop out of school every single day.

_____ **9.** Ninety percent of African American children will at some point live in households that use food stamps.

_____ **10.** About 2,000 youth ages 10 to 19 die by suicide each year.

_____ **11.** Some forms of neglect, and sexual and emotional abuse, are not recognizable to a casual observer.

_____ **12.** In 2009 there were over 1.35 million homeless children in America.

_____ **13.** Over half of all adolescents who suffer from depression eventually attempt suicide.

_____ **14.** One of every three students in U.S. classrooms is overweight or obese.

_____ **15.** There are about 50 school-associated violent deaths a year.

_____ **16.** Pregnancy among girls ages 10 to 14 occurs about once in a thousand girls.

_____ **17.** Children and adolescents who smoke cigarettes are more vulnerable to alcohol and drug addiction.

_____ **18.** Seriously overweight children are twice as likely to be in special education and remedial classes from an early age.

_____ **19.** Children and adolescents of color make up about 40% of students in American public schools.

_____ **20.** About 1 in every 70 students experiences some form of theft in school during the year.

_____ **21.** About 1 million teenage girls in the United States get pregnant annually.

_____ **22.** Suicide is the third leading cause of death among teens, trailing only accidents and homicide.

_____ **23.** Mothers and fathers acting alone, or together, account for about 75% of child abuse and neglect.

_____ **24.** About 60% of all teen deaths in car accidents are alcohol or drug related.

_____ **25.** On any given day, about 5% of students are absent from U.S. schools.

_____ **26.** About half of African American, Hispanic, and Native American students drop out of school.

_____ **27.** Recent evidence confirms that homelessness among families is increasing.

_____ **28.** One in every five students has an immigrant parent.

_____ **29.** School is a relatively safe place to be.

_____ **30.** Almost 90% of the reported fatalities due to child abuse are children under the age of 8.

_____ **31.** Over 1 million children are abused each year.

_____ **32.** The government takes responsibility for providing transportation for homeless students to go to the schools they attended before becoming homeless.

_____ **33.** Rates of substance abuse—specifically of alcohol, legal and illegal drugs, and tobacco—are not rising.

_____ **34.** What used to be considered adult health problems are now serious health problems for adolescents and children because of weight issues.

_____ **35.** Dropouts typically earn an average of $9,000 less a year than graduates.

_____ **36.** It's illegal to discriminate by race in American public schools.

_____ **37.** Weight issues may result in the current generation of children living shorter lives than this generation of adults.

_____ **38.** Random drug testing in public schools may be applied to those who voluntarily participate in activities such as cheerleading, band, debate, and so on.

_____ **39.** The average boy takes his first drink at age 11; the average girl, at age 13.

_____ **40.** Half of all children in America live in households that make use of food stamps at some time in their first 18 years of life.

Scoring this inventory is easy. All of the statements are true. This chapter contains information that isn't pleasant to read. The societal context of education in America is filled with elements that put kids at risk of failure. However, each category of challenge is accompanied by suggestions for how teachers can help. We are in positions to make a difference, sometimes one student at a time. We will not make a difference, however, if we are not aware of the difficulties faced by our students or, and this is unacceptable, are not willing to put effort into helping change the life circumstances that inhibit growth of the students with whom we are entrusted.

As you look back at the items you marked false in **Where Do I Stand?**, which three items surprise you most and why?

Teaching in Focus

After reading the title of this chapter, you may be asking why this opening scenario would be about Brandi Wade, a kindergarten teacher. The answer is actually simple: Social issues do not suddenly appear in the lives of adolescents. The societal context of students' lives surrounds them from birth. By the time children are in kindergarten, many influences have already shaped them.

Brandi is very aware of the fact that her students enter kindergarten with individual histories as well as present circumstances. They do not come to her, as educators once proposed, as blank slates. Many already have strikes against them not of their own making, such as poverty or a family that doesn't value education. Brandi understands the saying, "There's nothing so unequal as the equal treatment of unequals." Think about this.

Her 14 years in the classroom have allowed Brandi to see her first group graduate from high school, or not. She has watched her students progress through primary, elementary, middle, and high school. She has seen some cope and thrive, and others become involved in destructive lifestyles. One thing she knows for sure is that success is more likely for some than for others. Thus she continually adjusts and differentiates.

In early December Brandi decided that she needed to change some of her routines and instructional strategies. She had lived with her kindergartners 5 days a week for more than 3 months, and she knew some of them were not yet thriving. Her experience had taught her that treating these 5- and 6-year-olds equally was not going to meet their needs.

Brandi's decision to make some general changes in her classroom, including a new seating arrangement, a new rule-and-consequence system, a heavier reliance on one-on-one instructional strategies, and a buddy plan, came as a result of her consideration of the students in her class.

Brandi's realistic view that some of her students will struggle more than others lowers neither her hopes nor her expectations for all her students. Regardless of the strikes against them, Brandi maintains that her children can and will learn. She knows that the challenges for children may come in many forms. Students raised in poverty face particular challenges. Children who are minorities face other challenges. Children who live in relative wealth, but with few restraints or little structure, are challenged in other ways. All of Brandi's students need academic and interpersonal skills, along with self-confidence and the ability to make reasoned decisions. All are, or will be, at risk in some way.

Watch Brandi Wade's interview and room tour in the Teaching in Focus section for Chapter 9 in MyEducationLab for this course.

How Do Family, Community, and Society Impact Students in the United States?

The most basic societal unit of humankind is the family. Families exist within communities, and communities make up the larger building blocks of any society. This relationship, as illustrated in Figure 9.1, creates a pattern of influence that is undeniable. When children are very young, the family has the most direct influence. As they grow, the community plays a bigger role in children's lives. The influence of society grows immensely stronger with age.

For some children, family life is idyllic and supportive; for others it is not. Some children's families live in communities that are peaceful and caring; others live in the midst of destruction and violence. Although they all live within the same society, some children in the United States are shielded from negative influences by family and community, and others are not.

FAMILY

Family diversity and child abuse are discussed in Chapter 3.

Family is a source of diversity. Regardless of what a family may look like or the societal pressures the family may experience, members of families can support student success—or thwart it.

Many children and adolescents are victims of abuse and neglect, which places them squarely in the at-risk category. **Child abuse** is any act that results in death, serious harm, or exploitation; **child neglect** is a form of abuse resulting from the failure to act in the best interest of the child. Child abuse is reported on average every 10 seconds in the United States, and three children die each day as a result of abuse (Tenneyson Center for Children, 2006).

Information from the National Child Abuse and Neglect Data System (NCANDS), as part of the U.S. Department of Health and Human Services, indicates that approximately

Figure 9.1 Individual, family, community, society

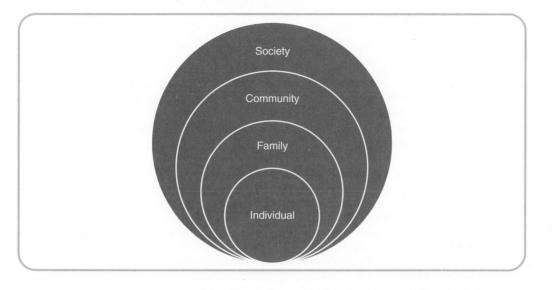

760,000 children were victims of child abuse or neglect in 2008. While this number is disturbing, NCANDS reports that it represents only the tip of the iceberg. For a case of abuse or neglect to be included in government statistics, it must be reported, meet the established definition, and be investigated. Some forms of neglect and sexual and emotional abuse have few recognizable symptoms to a casual observer. The maltreatment can remain undiscovered for an entire childhood. The recorded cases could actually represent millions of victimized children and adolescents. It is also appalling to realize that almost 90% of the approximately 1,740 reported fatalities due to child abuse in 2008 were predominantly those most vulnerable, children under the age of 8. And by some estimates, as many as 60% of deaths by abuse are not reported as abuse cases (U.S. Department of Health and Human Services [DHHS], 2010).

It is difficult to determine the scope of the toll that child abuse takes on children and adolescents in the United States. For many, it's hard to imagine the reasons or the results of such cruelty. Even harder to imagine is that over 90% of the abuse and neglect is at the hands of parents and caregivers; less than 10% is perpetrated by strangers. Mothers and fathers acting alone, or together, account for over 75% of child abuse and neglect (U.S. DHHS, 2010). For some students, teachers and school personnel are their most trusted adults.

WHAT CAN SCHOOLS AND TEACHERS DO? School personnel are among those required to report suspected abuse. Also included are social workers, health-care workers, mental health professionals, child-care providers, medical examiners or coroners, and law enforcement officers. Teachers should report suspicions to administrators or guidance counselors. As citizens, teachers may also report suspicions of abuse to any Child Protection Services agency or to Childhelp at 800-4-A-CHILD (800-422-4453).

As a teacher, you may be the adult who comes between a child and a lifetime of suffering or, worse, death. Knowing the signs of neglect and abuse is an important first step. Figure 9.2 lists the signs provided by Child Welfare Information Gateway (2006). Read how focus teacher Tim Mendenhall sees his impact on families in *Teaching in Focus*.

COMMUNITY AND SOCIETY

Previous chapters have discussed the concept of community as it refers to relationships in a classroom or school. In this section, **community** refers to the neighborhood, town, city, or county in which a student lives. The members of a community are those who live within a specific geographic vicinity, those with whom students may come in contact through everyday activities like shopping or when seeking services.

Most towns, cities, and counties provide services such as medical facilities, utilities (electric, gas, water), welfare and Medicaid, some form of counseling or assistance, law

Points of Reflection 9.1

How familiar are you with child and adolescent abuse and neglect? Do you have personal experiences with abuse or neglect? Do you know people who were victims of abuse? Briefly explain.

Figure 9.2 Recognizing child abuse

The following signs may signal the presence of child abuse or neglect.

In general, the child:

    Shows sudden changes in behavior or school performance.
    Has not received help for physical or medical problems brought to the parents' attention.
    Has learning problems (or difficulty concentrating) that cannot be attributed to specific physical or psychological causes.
    Is always watchful, as though preparing for something bad to happen.
    Lacks adult supervision.
    Is overly compliant, passive, or withdrawn.
    Comes to school or other activities early, stays late, and does not want to go home.

In general, the parent:

    Shows little concern for the child.
    Denies the existence of—or blames the child for—the child's problems in school or at home.
    Asks teachers or other caretakers to use harsh physical discipline if the child misbehaves.
    Sees the child as entirely bad, worthless, or burdensome.
    Demands a level of physical or academic performance the child cannot achieve.
    Looks primarily to the child for care, attention, and satisfaction of emotional needs.

In general, the parent and child:

    Rarely touch or look at each other.
    Consider their relationship entirely negative.
    State that they do not like each other.

Here are the signs of child physical, sexual, and emotional abuse, as well as the signs of neglect.

Signs of Physical Abuse

Consider the possibility of physical abuse when the **child:**

    Has unexplained burns, bites, bruises, broken bones, or black eyes.
    Has fading bruises or other marks noticeable after an absence from school.
    Seems frightened of the parents and protests or cries when it is time to go home.
    Shrinks at the approach of adults.
    Reports injury by a parent or another adult caregiver.

Consider the possibility of physical abuse when the **parent or other adult caregiver:**

    Offers conflicting, unconvincing, or no explanation for the child's injury.
    Describes the child as "evil," or in some other very negative way.
    Uses harsh physical discipline with the child.
    Has a history of abuse as a child.

Signs of Sexual Abuse

Consider the possibility of sexual abuse when the **child:**

    Has difficulty walking or sitting.
    Suddenly refuses to change for gym or to participate in physical activities.
    Reports nightmares or bed wetting.
    Experiences a sudden change in appetite.
    Demonstrates bizarre, sophisticated, or unusual sexual knowledge or behavior.
    Becomes pregnant or contracts a venereal disease, particularly if under age 14.
    Runs away.
    Reports sexual abuse by a parent or another adult caregiver.

Consider the possibility of sexual abuse when the **parent or other adult caregiver:**

    Is unduly protective of the child or severely limits the child's contact with other children, especially of the opposite sex.
    Is secretive and isolated.
    Is jealous or controlling with family members.

Signs of Emotional Abuse

Consider the possibility of emotional abuse when the **child:**

Shows extremes in behavior, such as overly compliant or demanding behavior, extreme passivity, or aggression.

Is either inappropriately adult (parenting other children, for example) or inappropriately infantile (frequently rocking or head-banging, for example).

Is delayed in physical or emotional development.

Has attempted suicide.

Reports a lack of attachment to the parent.

Consider the possibility of emotional abuse when the **parent or other adult caregiver:**

Constantly blames, belittles, or berates the child.

Is unconcerned about the child and refuses to consider offers of help for the child's problems.

Overtly rejects the child.

Signs of Neglect

Consider the possibility of neglect when the **child:**

Is frequently absent from school.

Begs or steals food or money.

Lacks needed medical or dental care, immunizations, or glasses.

Is consistently dirty and has severe body odor.

Lacks sufficient clothing for the weather.

Abuses alcohol or other drugs.

States that there is no one at home to provide care.

Consider the possibility of neglect when the **parent or other adult caregiver:**

Appears to be indifferent to the child.

Seems apathetic or depressed.

Behaves irrationally or in a bizarre manner.

Is abusing alcohol or other drugs.

Source: Child Welfare Information Gateway. (2006). *Recognizing child abuse and neglect: signs and symptoms.* Retrieved April 22, 2007, from http://www.childwelfare.gov/pubs/factsheets/signs.cfm

enforcement, recreation opportunities, and schools. The available services vary. Some students and their families live in communities that support healthy lifestyles. In these communities traditional measures of success—economic stability, nonviolent approaches to problem solving, education—are valued and promoted.

Unfortunately, many students live in communities that are not only nonsupportive but may actually be harmful to them. Some neighborhoods and communities are filled with

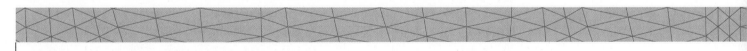

Teaching in Focus

Tim Mendenhall, Grades 3–5 Multiage Classroom, Rees Elementary School, Utah. *In his own words. . . .*

I have found that my influence goes beyond the classroom. It overflows into the home as well. My relationships with students are built before and after school and in the hallways. Their siblings look forward to being in my classroom. I get to know parents through my students, at parent-teacher conferences, and while working with parent volunteers. I take the time to build relationships with parents. I have found that students and their families become fiercely loyal to teachers who care. It hit me when one of my student's parents said, "I feel I can come to you anytime with a problem with my child and you listen." Education is a partnership, and the more bridges we build, the more it benefits our students.

Teachers are obligated by law to report suspected child abuse. Some symptoms are more noticeable than others.

violence and drugs, where children and adolescents are exposed to unhealthy lifestyles. For many children, negative influences of society will be mitigated by positive forces, such as supportive families, higher socioeconomic status, or membership in the majority race. Other children will suffer proportionately more from negative societal influences due, at least in part, to poverty.

WHAT CAN SCHOOLS AND TEACHERS DO? Regardless of the community in which a student lives, there are havens that provide private and government services. Teachers need to be knowledgeable about the services available to students and their families and provide them with information about how they can use the services to improve their lives.

How Does Socioeconomic Status Affect Students in the United States?

We may think we know what "poor" looks like: the house, the car, the neighborhood, the need for a warm coat and school supplies, hunger and meals through Title I free breakfast and lunch programs. But Richard Rothstein (2008), a researcher who analyzes effects of poverty, tells us to look more deeply to see the multitude of effects that may accompany poverty. If two groups of students, one distinctly disadvantaged in terms of socioeconomic status (SES), attend the same quality school, the group with low SES will achieve at lower levels. This is true not only according to Rothstein but also according to statistics in almost every school setting. Why is this so? Rothstein lists some of the reasons, stating that children in low-SES settings may have:

- no routine medical and dental care, leading to more absences
- increased likelihood of asthma, often resulting in sleeplessness, irritability, lack of exercise
- lower birthweight, resulting in many possible health issues
- lead poisoning and iron-deficiency anemia, each leading to cognitive and behavioral difficulties
- more mobility when the rent comes due, resulting in less school continuity
- greater family stress due to employment uncertainty, often resulting in arbitrary discipline
- fewer adult role models with professional careers
- more likelihood of living in single-parent homes
- fewer family vacations, trips to museums and zoos
- fewer opportunities for dance lessons, music instruction, organized sports teams, cultural awareness, and other activities that build confidence

"Each of these disadvantages makes only a small contribution to the achievement gap, but cumulatively, they explain a lot" (Rothstein, 2008, p. 8). Some say that emphasis on the disadvantages of poor children gives educators excuses for why these children don't learn at the levels of other children. Excuses are unacceptable; understanding is invaluable. Awareness of these and other disadvantages provides teachers a more realistic view of what our mission involves.

Mark Rank, researcher in the area of poverty and children, tells us that half of all children in America will live in households that make use of food stamps at some time in their first 18 years of life. Even more startling is the fact that nearly 90% of African American children will have this experience. "Taken as a whole, the negative impact of poverty on children's overall health status is reflected in the fact that it has been estimated that poverty among American children raises the direct expenditures on health care by approximately $22 billion per year" (Rank & Hirschl, 2009, p. 998).

Points of Reflection 9.2

Think about the community in which you spent a portion of your childhood. Was it a supportive community with people and services that contributed to your overall well-being? Or did you encounter situations that made it more difficult to grow and learn? Briefly explain.

HOMELESS CHILDREN AND YOUTH

Perhaps the most devastating impact of poverty is homelessness. The federal government defines homeless children and youth as those who lack a fixed, regular, and adequate nighttime residence. The children and youth may share overcrowded temporary housing or live in motels, hotels, trailer parks, camping grounds, or emergency or transitional shelters due to lack of alternative adequate accommodations. Or they may spend nights in cars, parks, public spaces, abandoned buildings, substandard housing, bus or train stations, or similar settings. Just reading this definition is troubling; imagine what life must be like for the children it describes.

In 2009 there were over 1.35 million homeless children in America, from 600,000 families. In fact, 41% of the entire homeless population is composed of families. Of these homeless families, 87% cited a lack of affordable housing as the primary cause of their homelessness. The severe economic downturn of 2008 made things even worse for those struggling to maintain adequate housing. Many families that had homes in 2008 or 2009 lost them and became homeless. Therefore, the reported 1.35 million homeless children is likely a low estimate. Causes of homelessness among children fall into three interrelated categories: family problems, economic problems, and residential instability. Regardless of the cause, recent evidence confirms that homelessness among families is increasing (National Coalition for the Homeless, 2009).

The McKinney-Vento Act of 1986 is part of the federal government's response to homelessness. The act addresses the problems homeless children and youth face in enrolling, attending, and succeeding in school (National Coalition for the Homeless, 2006). Because of this act, homeless students are assured of:

- equal access to the same free, appropriate public education
- a public preschool education
- comparable educational services, including transportation and meals
- a mainstream school environment, free from being stigmatized in any way

Homelessness is a devastating experience for families, disrupting every aspect of family life, causing physical and emotional damage, interfering with children's education and development, and often resulting in the separation of children from parents. Figure 9.3 lists

Figure 9.3 Impact of homelessness on families

Homeless parents and their children are more likely to have experienced violence and to be separated from each other.

- Domestic violence is the second most frequently stated cause of homelessness for families.
- One out of three homeless teens has witnessed a stabbing, shooting, rape, or murder in their community.
- Homelessness is the most important predictor of the separation of mothers from their children.
- 34% of school-aged homeless children have lived apart from their families.
- 62% of children placed in foster care come from formerly homeless families.

Homeless children have less of a chance of succeeding in school.

- Homeless children are more likely than housed children to be held back a grade.
- Homeless children have higher rates of school mobility and grade retention than low-income housed children.
- Frequent school transfers are the most significant barrier to the academic success of homeless students.

Homeless parents suffer various impacts of homelessness.

- Over two thirds of homeless parents are unemployed.
- 53% of homeless mothers do not have a high school diploma.
- Over 50% of all homeless mothers have a lifelong mental health problem.
- Homeless adults in family shelters, when compared to the general adult population, have three times the rate of tuberculosis and eight times more HIV diagnoses.

Source: Institute for Children and Poverty. (2009). *Quick facts: National data on family homelessness.* Retrieved June 8, 2010, at http://www.icpny.org/index.asp?CID=7

In the News

A Teacher's Mission

Elementary teacher Kayla Brown thought hunger was something she saw in developing countries on TV until she found herself staring it in the face as one of her students picked up his lunch plate and licked it voraciously. She discovered that his lack of energy and enthusiasm could be traced to one factor: He was hungry. Kayla's life changed that day.

This *ABC News* video features Backpack Buddies, a program developed by Kayla Brown and volunteers from her church to help families that struggle because of low-paying jobs and lack of opportunity often associated with limited education and from a myriad of misfortunes that beset many people in the United States. Food is donated, organized, and distributed in backpacks so that children who eat breakfast and lunch free at school 5 days a week will also have food for dinner and snacks.

To view this video, go to the *In the News* section of Chapter 9 on MyEducationLab for this text and watch the clip *A Teacher's Mission*. Then respond to these items.

1. Teachers are responsible for students during the school day. Children from low-income homes can eat breakfast and lunch for free during the school week. Given these facts, what would drive a teacher to do what Kayla Brown did?

2. Kayla's school has seen a recent rise in standardized test scores. The counselor and others credit Backpack Buddies for the increase. On what might they base their claim?

3. The concept of a full-service school was discussed in Chapter 2. Should schools attempt to address social problems? Or should only other government agencies work directly with social issues such as poverty and hunger?

Points of Reflection 9.3

With what socioeconomic status (SES) group(s) are you most familiar? How did your own SES affect your school days?

generalizations about the conditions in which homeless children live and the effects of homelessness on their parents.

Although generalizations may be useful for understanding children and planning learning experiences, it is important not to lump all low-income or homeless students together as a group and design programs based on one element of their lives—their socioeconomic status (Landsman, 2006). This kind of categorizing flies in the face of all we know about student learning differences and the value of getting to know students individually. The teacher in this chapter's *In the News* suddenly recognized poverty and its effects in the lives of some of her students. Kayla Brown develops a proactive response to the shocking realization that some of her students simply didn't have enough to eat in *A Teacher's Mission*.

WHAT CAN SCHOOLS AND TEACHERS DO? Figure 9.4 lists strategies for teaching students who live in low socioeconomic conditions. "Teachers need to see assets and possibility where conventional eyes often see a dead end" (Landsman, 2006, p. 32). What excellent advice.

Landsman (2006) advises us to have "a practical awareness of the students' physical needs coupled with a passion for teaching" (p. 28). She gives examples of educators who fit this description as they recognize the pervasive negative effects of poverty.

- Doug is a middle school science teacher who keeps granola bars in his desk drawer for students who are so hungry that they fall asleep in his class. He also goes to the cafeteria for free breakfast with students who are hungry but may be embarrassed to go in alone.

- George is a high school teacher who collaborates with social workers to get clothes for students who need them and allows homeless students to leave school materials with him.

- Mary is principal of a middle school where local businesses contribute classroom supplies instead of asking students and parents to provide them. For Christmas the staff gave bags to homeless students filled with practical items and gift certificates to grocery stores. They report that the toughest students soften and begin to trust the adults at school.

Figure 9.4 Strategies for teaching economically struggling students

- Assume that all students can learn complex and creative material
- Create a classroom that gives students as much control as possible while maintaining safety and structure. Let students' interests drive the curriculum.
- Do not assume common behaviors or states of mind for all low-income students or parents.
- Focus on the assets that students bring to the classroom: resiliency, perseverance, flexibility, compassion, and hope.
- Understand that you cannot change the world but you can work within your classroom and community to effect change. Advocate for small class size.
- Build a network of colleagues who are finding ways to challenge low-income students. Meet in the media center on Fridays to talk about "what went right this week."
- Maintain your "other life" so that you can go into the classroom ready to meet kids whole-heartedly and without resentment.
- Find ways to provide the necessities, such as winter coats, art materials, and a place to wash clothes. Look in the community for resources—for example, a place for students to do homework.
- Find respectful ways to survey students about their home situations. Make yourself available for students to talk with you. Refer them for help when they share serious problems or speak of a lack of basic needs at home.
- Ask students to do jobs for you to help them feel important and in control of something in their lives.
- Do not single out kids or indicate in front of others that you know they are homeless or poor.
- "Cut deals" with students, helping them find realistic ways to meet work requirements.
- Convince students that "I believe you can learn and I will listen to you and give you meaningful work to do."

Source: Landsman, J. (2006). Bearers of hope. *Educational Leadership, 63*(5), 26–32.

There is little we can do about the societal conditions of poverty that plague the current generation of students in our classrooms. But think about it: What we do in our classrooms to promote learning may indeed affect the future conditions of the students we teach and, ultimately, their children, the next generation of students. In a very real way, we *can* affect the economic conditions in which children grow.

How Do Health Issues Affect Students in the United States?

Some health issues pose immediate and obvious dangers to children and adolescents. Underage alcohol consumption and abuse of both legal and illegal drugs alter mental states and lead to overt behavioral changes. Other health issues are just as insidious, but their effects are incremental; their negative consequences occur gradually and are generally not accompanied by alarm. For instance, tobacco use and obesity among children and adolescents rarely push adult panic buttons, but they can lead to deadly consequences.

Rates of substance abuse—specifically of alcohol, legal and illegal drugs, and tobacco—are not rising. Early sexual experiences are declining, with a teen pregnancy rate that has remained relatively steady for several years. However, some health professionals say that the overall health of children and adolescents is worsening because of dramatic increases in obesity rates.

SUBSTANCE ABUSE

Substance abuse is a pattern of alcohol or drug use that can lead to detrimental and habitual consumption, impaired functioning at school and work, and legal difficulties (Schlozman, 2002). The guarded good news is that substance abuse among children and adolescents did not appear to be escalating when the most recent 5-year study

(2002–2007) was released by the U.S. Substance Abuse and Mental Health Services Administration (2009). Since the beginning of the 21st century, abuse has increased for only three categories of substances: sedatives, OxyContin, and inhalants, with inhalants the drug of choice, or the one most available, for 12- and 13-year-olds. The bad news continues to be that substance abuse is extremely dangerous and can be deadly. Even if the statistics show leveling or a decline, one child or adolescent harmed by substance abuse is one too many.

When do children and adolescents begin drinking alcohol and using drugs? Although most research studies begin with eighth graders, elementary teachers and principals know that experimentation with alcohol, drugs, and tobacco begins even earlier. The average boy takes his first drink at age 11; the average girl, at age 13 (Alcoholism Information and Resources, 2010). Despite recent lower rates of consumption, alcohol usage remains widespread, with about 72% of high school seniors and 39% of eighth graders consuming more than just a trial taste. Binge drinking, defined as five drinks in a row at least once in 2 weeks, is reported for about 25% of seniors and 8% of eighth graders. Approximately 21% of eighth graders, 38% of tenth graders, and 50% of twelfth graders have used illegal drugs (Century Council, 2009).

The heartbreaking stories of automobile accidents involving intoxicated or high adolescents at the wheel spur groups like Mothers Against Drunk Driving (MADD) and Students Against Destructive Decisions (formerly Drunk Driving; SADD) to continue their awareness campaigns. Teenage drunk driving kills about eight teens a day. In fact, 60% of all teen deaths in car accidents are related to alcohol or drugs. Statistics show that a teenage boy with a blood alcohol level of 0.05, below the level to be considered legally drunk, is 18 times more likely to be in a single car accident than nonimpaired boys. For girls the number is even worse. A girl with a blood alcohol level of 0.05 is 54 times more likely to cause a single-car crash (Alcoholism Information and Resources, 2010). Staggering statistics.

Both cigarettes and smokeless tobacco pose health dangers for children and adolescents. Smokeless tobacco use appears to be increasing, although slightly fewer teenagers smoke cigarettes now than in the 1990s (U.S. Substance Abuse and Mental Health Services Administration, 2009). Eighty percent of adult smokers begin the habit before the age of 18. Nicotine in tobacco affects the structural and chemical changes in developing brains of children and adolescents, making those who smoke more vulnerable to alcohol and drug addiction, as well as mental illness. In fact, research by the National Center on Addiction and Substance Abuse (CASA) at Columbia University tells us that teens who smoke cigarettes are five times more likely to drink, 13 times more likely to use marijuana, and 10 times more likely to develop alcohol and drug dependencies. Although we have known for a long time that smoking causes deadly cancers and cardiovascular and respiratory diseases, we now have a better idea of the long-term damage nicotine can have on brains that are still developing (National Center on Addiction and Substance Abuse, 2007).

Children and adolescents often have an unfounded sense of immortality. Do you remember thinking, "Well, sure. Some people are hurt by this, but it won't happen to me"? The students in your future classrooms will likely often have this attitude. They grossly underestimate the serious consequences of abusing alcohol, drugs, and tobacco.

It is a heartbreaking fact that thousands of adolescents die each year as a result of underage drinking and driving.

WHAT CAN SCHOOLS AND TEACHERS DO? In 1995 the Supreme Court ruled that schools can arrange to randomly test student athletes for drugs. In 2002 another ruling included those who voluntarily participate in activities such as cheerleading, band, debate, and so on. In 2006 the government reported that about 600 of the approximately 15,000 school districts in the United States had implemented random drug testing. Some people believe that just the threat of testing is a deterrent (Sullivan, 2006).

Research published by Rutgers University shows that when teenagers first get their driver's license, they perceive the risk of drinking and driving to be high. With driving experience, the perceived risk decreases and illegal behaviors of drinking and/or using drugs while driving increase (McCarthy & Brown, 2004). In other words, the longer they have a license, the more teenagers engage in dangerous activity. This implies that safe driving education needs to continue throughout high school, not just as a prerequisite for obtaining a license.

Teachers need to be informed about the warning signs—often sudden, negative changes in behavior and academic performance—of alcohol and drug abuse. We need to be articulate when it comes to describing the consequences of substance abuse of all kinds. We must take the problem seriously. Here are some suggestions for positively influencing students:

1. Develop strong relationships with students and understand their perceptions concerning substance abuse, some of which are listed in Table 9.1.

2. Become a trusted mentor for individual students at risk for using alcohol, drugs, and tobacco.

3. Don't just give statistics. Expose students to graphic video of the consequences of risky behavior, introduce them to families that have suffered the consequences of substance abuse, have students with recovery stories speak with your class, and so on.

4. Promote honest discussions about real-world issues, including substance abuse.

5. Use active instructional techniques such as role playing to teach refusal skills.

6. Make information available about community services related to prevention and intervention of substance abuse.

TABLE 9.1 Harmfulness of drugs as perceived by 8th, 10th, and 12th graders (2005)

How much do you think people risk harming themselves (physically or in other ways), if they	Percentage Saying "Great Risk"		
	8th graders	10th graders	12th graders
Try marijuana once or twice	31.4	22.3	16.1
Smoke marijuana regularly	73.9	65.5	25.8
Try inhalants once or twice	37.5	45.7	
Try inhalants regularly	64.1	71.2	
Try crack once or twice	49.6	57.0	48.4
Try crack occasionally	69.4	76.9	63.8
Try one or two drinks of an alcoholic beverage (beer, wine, liquor)	13.9	11.5	8.5
Take one or two drinks nearly every day	31.4	32.6	23.7
Have five or more drinks once or twice each weekend	57.2	53.3	45.0
Smoke one or more packs of cigarettes per day	61.5	68.1	76.5
Use smokeless tobacco regularly	40.8	46.1	43.6

Source: Johnston, L. D., O'Malley, P. M., Bachman, J. G., & Schulenberg, J. E. (2005). *Monitoring the future: National results on adolescent drug use.* Bethesda, MD: U.S. Department of Health and Human Services. Retrieved April 15, 2006, from http://monitoring_the_future.org/pubs/ monographs/overview2005.pdf

SEXUALITY-RELATED CONCERNS

Fewer never-married 15- to-19-year-olds are having sexual experiences now than did in the 1990s. From 49% of girls and 55% of boys in 1995, the percentage in 2002 was down to 46% for both girls and boys. By racial subgroups within the 9th through 12th grade population, 42% of whites, 51% of Hispanics, and 67% of African Americans have had sexual intercourse. Condom use has increased slightly for sexually active adolescents, but there remains significant cause for concern regarding the spread of sexually transmitted diseases (STDs) and of the HIV virus that leads to AIDS (Education Vital Signs, 2006). In one widespread survey, about 90% of high school students reported that they had been taught about HIV/AIDS in schools (NCES, 2005).

TEEN BIRTHRATE. Although pregnancy among girls ages 10 to 14 is especially tragic, only about 1 in every 1,000 girls in this age group becomes pregnant (Infoplease, 2009). As illustrated in Figure 9.5, except for the first half of the 1990s, the teen birthrate for 15- to 19-year-olds has declined since 1960, with slight increases in 2006 and 2007. A decrease in sexual intercourse among adolescents has contributed to the decline (Centers for Disease Control and Prevention, 2009). Also contributing to lower pregnancy rates is a more informed student population of sexually active teens concerning the use of contraceptives (Healthcommunities.com, 2010). Even with the incidences of teen births decreasing, the United States still has the highest teenage birthrate among developed countries. About 1 million teenage girls get pregnant annually, resulting in over 400,000 births. More than 4 of 5 teen mothers are unmarried, putting them and their babies at greater risk of living in poverty (Infoplease, 2004).

There are, of course, many consequences of teenage pregnancy, including:

- Eighty percent of teen mothers must rely on welfare at some point.
- Teenage mothers are more likely to drop out of school, with only about a third of teen mothers obtaining a high school diploma.
- Teenage pregnancies are linked to increased rates of alcohol and substance abuse.

Figure 9.5 Pregnancy rates per 1,000 teens, ages 15 to 19

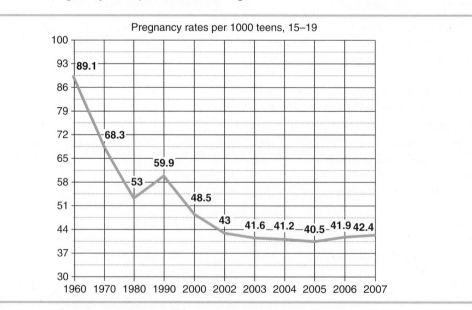

Source: Infoplease. (2009). Teen birth rates in the U.S. Retrieved June 2, 2010, from http://www.inforplease.com/ipa/A0193727; Healthcommunities.com. (2010). Consequences of teenage pregnancy. Retrieved June 4, 2010, from http://www.infoplease.com/ipa/A0193727 .html

- Both teen mothers and teen fathers have lower educational levels and reduced earning potential.
- The annual cost in the United States of teen pregnancies from lost tax revenues, public assistance, child health care, foster care, and involvement with the criminal justice system is estimated to be about $7 billion (Healthcommunities.com, 2010).

HOMOSEXUALITY. Sexual orientation is an issue that evokes strong sentiments that spill over onto school grounds. "Tragically, public schools have become front lines in the culture war over homosexuality—and the biggest losers are the kids caught in the cross-fire of incendiary rhetoric and bitter lawsuits" (Haynes, 2006, p. 3). In an effort to find a process that will allow educators and students alike to civilly discuss issues of sexual orientation, a document entitled "Public Schools and Sexual Orientation: A First Amendment Framework for Finding Common Ground" was endorsed in 2006 by organizations including the American Association of School Administrators and the Association for Supervision and Curriculum Development (First Amendment Center, 2006). Will documents such as this end teasing and harassment aimed at adolescents who are, or are perceived to be, homosexual? Perhaps eventually official documents will help. However, the effects will not come quickly enough to spare many hurt feelings and prevent acts of violence toward individuals.

Homosexuality is discussed in Chapter 3.

WHAT CAN SCHOOLS AND TEACHERS DO? Schools should provide health education courses for at least middle and high school students that include open and honest information concerning matters of sexuality, with a forum for asking and answering questions. Teachers should show informed sensitivity to students grappling with sexuality-related issues. As with substance abuse, refusal skills are important, and they are more likely to be demonstrated by students who perceive a sense of control over their lives. The physical and emotional dangers of early sexual activity, STDs and HIV/AIDS, and teen pregnancy can be communicated in nongraphic and noncontroversial ways, often couched in terms of self-respect.

In the classroom, treating all students with respect is vital. Not allowing students to use derogatory language about sexual orientation will help keep a respectful atmosphere. Among upper elementary and middle school students, saying, "That's so gay" is a sign of disapproval. Students often use the phrase lightly, but its implications can deeply hurt students who perceive themselves to be homosexual. Simply saying, "We don't use that phrase in this classroom or this school" and then sticking to it is an example of creating a more respectful atmosphere.

Some schools have established sex education programs and clinics that provide access to birth control information and devices; others primarily advise abstinence. Both programs are controversial. Many districts support special schools for pregnant students and new mothers. These schools help young women stay in school and graduate. Teenagers should be assisted in the development of skills in communication and sexual decision making so that sex does not just "happen." As teachers, we can help make teens aware of the consequences of sexually risky behaviors.

CHILDHOOD OBESITY

Americans rank obesity as a health problem second only to cancer. The number of children who are obese has tripled since 1975 (Haskins, Paxson, & Donahue, 2006). In 2007, 16.4% of children in America qualified as obese, and a total of over 30% were considered overweight (Singh, Kogan, & van Dyck, 2010). Preliminary research in 2009 tells us that the percentage of obese children has leveled off, but having 1 of every 3 students in U.S. classrooms overweight or obese is unacceptable (Education Vital Signs, 2009). The commonly held definition of **obesity** involves the body mass index (BMI), a measure of how

Points of Reflection 9.4

Did you receive sexuality-related information in middle or high school? Was it presented in concise, helpful ways? Do you agree with including sexuality-related information in the curriculum? Why or why not?

Josie Ford is one of our focus students at Rees Elementary. As you watch Josie's interview with teacher Brenda Beyal and Mom in the Teaching in Focus section for Chapter 9 in MyEducationLab for this course, consider whether Josie should receive sex education as a fifth grader.

TABLE 9.2 Computing body mass index (BMI)	
BMI	**Status**
Below 18.5	Underweight
18.5–24.9	Normal
25.0–29.9	Overweight
30.0–39.9	Obese
40 and above	Morbidly obese

Note: BMI = (weight in pounds × 703) ÷ [(height in inches) × (height in inches)].

Source: Craig, G. J., & Dunn, W. L. (2007). *Understanding human development* (p. 248). Upper Saddle River, NJ: Prentice Hall.

Points of Reflection 9.5

Use the BMI formula to determine your own weight status. Are you surprised by what you discover about yourself? Do you think it's wise to make children and adolescents face the reality of where they are on the scale? Why or why not? What difference might this knowledge make to them?

much a person weighs relative to height, as illustrated in Table 9.2 (Paxson, Donahue, Orleans, & Grisso, 2006).

First Lady Michelle Obama (2010) has chosen childhood obesity as a cause to champion. Her program *Let's Move* is a nationwide campaign with the goal of solving the problem of childhood obesity in a generation and empowering children born today to reach adulthood at a healthy weight. Mrs. Obama is traveling the country promoting healthy habits in schools, communities, and families. She is asking school food services to cut calories and offer more fresh produce. It is estimated that as many as half of school-age children eat about half their daily calories at school; what is served in the cafeteria matters.

What's considered normal weight for children and adolescents varies with their age. But take a look at a line of children walking down an elementary hallway or adolescents gathered around the school commons. It is obvious which students are grossly overweight or on their way to becoming so.

Researchers are studying the causes and consequences of childhood obesity. Figure 9.6 lists seven factors that contribute to what the authors of the study cited call an "epidemic of childhood obesity" (Paxson et al., 2006).

The consequences of childhood obesity include serious health issues such as type 2 diabetes, heart disease, sleep disorders, asthma, joint dysfunction, and mental health problems. What used to be considered adult health problems are now serious health problems for adolescents and even children. As a result of weight issues, today's children may live shorter and less healthy lives than their parents (Paxson et al., 2006).

Serious social and psychological problems are also consequences of childhood and adolescent obesity. Being teased, loneliness, low self-esteem, and other consequences result from being a severely overweight child or teenager (DeAngelis, 2004).

Figure 9.6 Factors contributing to childhood obesity

1. increases in television and computer game use that have led to a new generation of "couch potatoes"
2. the explosive proliferation of fast-food restaurants, many of which market their products to children through media campaigns that tout tie-ins to children's movies and TV shows
3. increases in sugary and fat-laden foods displayed at children's eye level in supermarkets and advertised on TV
4. schools that offer children junk food and soda while scaling back physical education classes and recess
5. working parents who are unable to find the time or energy to cook nutritious meals or supervise outdoor playtime
6. the exodus of grocery stores from urban centers, sharply reducing access to affordable fresh fruits and vegetables
7. suburban sprawl and urban crime, both of which keep children away from outdoor activities

Source: Paxson, C., Donahue, E., Orleans, T., & Grisso, J. A. (2006). Introducing the issue. *The Future of Children, 16*(1), 3–18.

While researchers are not saying that obesity causes lower academic performance, the link between obesity and lower achievement may reveal serious academic consequences. Seriously overweight children are twice as likely to be in special education and remedial classes from an early age. A study of approximately 11,000 kindergartners found that overweight children had significantly lower reading and math scores when compared to children in the normal weight range. These academic difficulties continued through first grade (Story, Kaphingst, & French, 2006).

Mrs. Obama is quick to point out that childhood obesity is not the fault of the children themselves. The kids don't choose what's offered in the school cafeteria for breakfast and lunch. They are not responsible for foods loaded with sugar and fat or super-sized portions, nor do they determine how much time is allotted for recess and physical education. Yes, they may choose to watch TV and play video games or surf the Internet instead of running around outside, but it's the adults who make all of the alternatives available (Obama, 2010).

Physical activity, healthy food choices, and lessons relating to the dangers of obesity may help curb the alarming trend of childhood obesity.

WHAT CAN SCHOOLS AND TEACHERS DO? In 2004 Congress passed the Child Nutrition Reauthorization Act, mandating that all schools participating in the federal school meal program develop comprehensive wellness policies focusing on the following:

1. What children and adolescents eat in school
   - provide more nutritious school breakfasts and lunches
   - limit à la carte items to healthier foods
   - reduce or eliminate vending machines or stock only nutritious foods
2. How physically active students are in school
   - provide daily physical education (PE) in elementary and middle school
   - increase high school PE requirements and provide more extracurricular physical activity options
3. In-school health and nutrition education

Teachers can encourage all of the elements of a wellness policy by serving as role models for healthy living. Eating nutritious, balanced meals and snacks in school and showing evidence of an active lifestyle that includes exercise will go a long way toward influencing students. Teachers can help prevent childhood and adolescent obesity by being vocal advocates for students' health. Chris Roberts, the focus teacher at Rees Elementary School in Utah in charge of dance and movement for the multiage team, regularly gets kids up and moving. Not only does he live a very active life, he also requires his third, fourth, and fifth graders to participate in movement to music and to the beating of drums.

Watch Chris Roberts and his multiage class as they participate in movement and dance at Rees Elementary in Chris's lesson in the Teaching in Focus *section for Chapter 9 in MyEducationLab for this course.*

SUICIDE

The ultimate health issue and absolute tragedy for young adolescents (ages 10 to 14) and adolescents (ages 15 to 19) is suicide. Although teen suicide has decreased by 25% since 1990, it remains the third leading cause of death among teens, trailing only accidents and homicide. In 2006 about 1,800 youth ages 10 to 19 died as a result of suicide. For every suicide there are an estimated 100 to 200 attempts. Girls are much more likely to attempt suicide than boys, but boys complete the act of suicide four times as often as girls (American Association of Suicidology, 2009).

Depression is a mental illness characterized by a deep sense of sadness and a loss of interest or pleasure in activities. Students who are depressed are 14 times more likely to make a first suicide attempt. In fact, over half of all adolescents who suffer from depression

Figure 9.7 Signs and symptoms of suicidal feelings

- change in eating and sleeping habits
- withdrawal from friends, family, and regular activities
- violent actions, rebellious behavior, or running away
- drug and alcohol use
- unusual neglect of personal appearance
- marked personality change
- persistent boredom, difficulty concentrating, or a decline in the quality of schoolwork
- frequent complaints about physical symptoms, often related to emotions, such as stomachaches, headaches, fatigue, etc.
- loss of interest in pleasurable activities
- not tolerating praise or rewards

A teenager who is planning to commit suicide may also:

- complain of being a bad person or feeling rotten inside
- give verbal hints with statements such as I won't be a problem for you much longer, nothing matters, it's no use, and I won't see you again
- put his or her affairs in order, for example, give away favorite possessions, clean his or her room, throw away important belongings, etc.
- become suddenly cheerful after a period of depression
- have signs of psychosis (hallucinations or bizarre thoughts)

Source: American Academy of Child and Adolescent Psychiatry. (2009). *Facts for families: Teen suicide.* Retrieved June 3, 2010, from http://www.aacap.org/cs/root/facts_for_families/teen_suicide

eventually attempt suicide (American Psychiatric Association, 2005). Depression is one of the factors contributing to suicide attempts, as shown in Figure 9.7. One or more of the factors listed are usually present when an adolescent attempts suicide, but it is possible that none of them are evident. The American Psychiatric Association (2005a) tells us that "Teenagers who are planning to commit suicide might 'clean house' by giving away favorite possessions, . . . they may also become suddenly cheerful because they think that by deciding to end their lives they have found the solution" (p. 2).

Points of Reflection 9.6

Has suicide touched your life? If so, in what way(s)?

WHAT CAN SCHOOLS AND TEACHERS DO? The American Psychiatric Association (2005a) advises that simply taking time to talk with troubled adolescents about their emotions and problems can prevent what they call the "senseless tragedy of teen suicide" (p. 2). Here are some guidelines for dealing with adolescents at risk for suicide attempts.

- Understand and recognize factors that may indicate suicidal tendencies such as those in Figure 9.7.
- If you suspect suicidal tendencies, always notify others such as a mental health professional or a school counselor who may, in turn, contact family members.
- Be willing to listen, rather than lecture.
- Find ways to involve students in service learning that takes them "outside" themselves.
- Reassure adolescents that depression and suicidal tendencies are treatable.

How Does Racism Affect Students in the United States?

Even though race has been discredited as a legitimate, precise way to categorize people, "race and racism profoundly structure who we are, how we are treated, how we treat others, and our access to resources and rights" (Mukhopadhyay & Henze, 2003, p. 669). **Racism** is a form of prejudice that stems from a belief that one race is superior to another. Racism may be perpetuated by individuals or even governmental policies (Gollnick & Chinn, 2009).

DISCRIMINATION

It's illegal to discriminate by race in American public schools. So that should be the end of the discussion, right? You will never find a public school policy that says, "If you are a racial minority, you must attend schools with peeling paint and inadequate, poorly maintained bathrooms," or, "If you are a child of color you may not experience advanced classes or be in gifted programs." No, this would be against the law.

However, official policies of nondiscrimination often do little to remedy discrimination in the day-to-day realities of children and adolescents of color who make up about 40% of students in American public schools. Even in classrooms where a rich racial diversity exists, subtle forms of racism may be at play. The most subtle may be silence, with no ill intent on the part of the teacher. Polite and Saenger (2003) tell us that "the most pernicious and pervasive silence in . . . school classrooms is the silence surrounding the subject of race" (p. 275). Children are aware of physical differences of race at a very early age. Avoiding the subject doesn't make children's questions go away; they simply go unasked and unanswered. If children are not given opportunities to explore their own identities, as well as those of others around them, they will move from elementary to middle to high school carrying increasingly "complex feelings about race and racial issues, including pride, ignorance, anger, shame, ambivalence, and alienation" (Lewis-Charp, 2003).

Another subtle form of discrimination in schools is what has become known as the *soft bigotry of low expectations.* Whether these expectations are the result of an assumption about abilities and intelligence, of previous experiences with students of various races, or of some other factor, low expectations for some students amount to racism. Landsman (2006) says, "I believe that a true test of any country's morality is whether it gives all children a fair and equal chance to achieve their potential as human beings" (p. 29).

Statistics about the racial make-up of U.S. schools are in Chapter 3.

Points of Reflection 9.7

What is your racial identity? How has this identity affected you as a student? How does your own racial identity impact your beliefs about, and attitudes toward, those with racial identities other than your own?

IMMIGRATION AND CLASSROOM SUCCESS

The presence of immigrant children and adolescents in our classrooms helps all students understand that people view the world differently. They contribute to our classrooms by increasing our knowledge and appreciation of diversity and by providing our classrooms with richer learning experiences.

One in every five students has an immigrant parent. A quarter of these children were born outside the United States. By some estimates, immigration will account for 96% of the future increase in the school-age population over the next 50 years (U.S. Census Bureau, 2008). This is a societal fact that will affect, if it doesn't already, every teacher. Deb Perryman, an advocate for immigrant students, tells us about her experiences in Figure 9.8.

Teachers often need to make an extra effort to understand how immigrant children may respond to many aspects of school in the United States. Without sensitivity to differences, racism may become part of their classroom experiences. Ariza (2002) gives us some examples of differences that may be manifested in a classroom with children who are immigrants or the children of immigrants.

- Manes is a student from Haiti whose parents have gone to great lengths and considerable risk to ensure an education for their children. In Haiti, teachers rarely send communications home with students. Weeks after sending home notes that required parental attention and signatures, a frustrated teacher assumes Manes's parents don't care. However, they simply didn't know to look in Manes's book bag for notes and papers requiring their attention.

- Hong, a student from Southeast Asia, has had a cold and sore throat. A common ethnic remedy in her country of origin is to rub a coin up and down on an area that is causing illness to draw out the pain. When Hong arrives at school with what appear to be bruises on her neck, the teacher suspects child abuse.

- Mohammad, a son of recent immigrants from the Middle East, is Muslim. Normally an active, cheerful child, he became withdrawn and wanted to change his name following the 9/11 tragedy in 2001 so that no one would associate him with his religion or with terrorists.

Figure 9.8 Deb Perryman, 2004 Illinois Teacher of the Year

I teach the very fine students of Elgin High School in Illinois. EHS is an urban school serving 2,200 students speaking 56 languages. Official records show that 50% of our kids are living at or below the poverty level. However, we know that percentage is much higher due to our large immigrant population. These families do not yet qualify for government assistance.

I remember the stories my grandparents told me of the hard times they had coming to the United States from Ireland. They faced name calling and worked dangerous jobs for low wages. I am thankful for all of the risks they took because I have so many opportunities. I remember my great grandpa yelling at the top of his lungs during dinner. He wasn't mad but nearly deaf after many years working as a boiler maker. That is the first time I can remember thinking to myself, "I will never treat another person the way my grandparents have been treated."

The immigration process is very complicated. As of May 2005 Illinois has a law (HB 60) that is providing possibilities for thousands of students. It buys time for those students seeking citizenship to actually complete the process while continuing their education. It gives me hope and, best of all, gives hope to students who are children of immigrants.

I have a set of twins I am working with now. When they entered the United States from Mexico 10 years ago, their parents went to the Immigration and Naturalization Service and began their road to citizenship. They have diligently tried to meet every stipulation and deadline, only to find themselves basically still on square one because of the bureaucracy involved, along with our overloaded, and understaffed, naturalization system. Now the boys are ready for college and the family is threatened with deportation.

I will continue to champion the cause of protecting immigrant children from arbitrary harm. I will ask the hard questions. When will we accept the next wave of immigrants without prejudice? When will we realize that every generation before us has come to the land of opportunity to get/create jobs and live productively?

Source: From e-mail communication with Deb Perryman, January 13, 2007.

- Maria, a 7-year-old whose family is from Colombia, routinely carries a baby bottle filled with milk in her lunch box. Her classmates teased her, and her teacher asked if she had mistakenly put her baby brother's bottle in her lunch. She was humiliated. The teacher later discovered that it is both proper and commonplace in some areas of Colombia for primary children to drink from bottles.

Immigration and the laws addressing it continue to be a major source of contention and animosity in the United States. Regardless of the political infighting and social stigmas, the immigrant children and adolescents in our classrooms are just that—children and adolescents. They deserve the same care and consideration teachers give to all students.

WHAT CAN SCHOOLS AND TEACHERS DO? The authors of *Black Men Emerging* (1999), Joseph White and James Cones, tell us there are three basic steps to confronting racism.

1. **Explore the issue of racism intellectually.** Read about racism and minority groups and discuss what you read with other teachers. Attend sessions at conferences that explore issues of racism and how to combat it in the classroom.

2. **Engage in dialogue about racism.** Start conversations with families, students, and the community about racial issues. Be open to frank talk and serious exchange of ideas.

3. **Immerse yourself in other cultures.** If you are white, attend a black church service or a Kwanza celebration where you can join in and begin to understand

Watch an interview with *Carol Bartlett* in the *Teaching in Focus section for Chapter 9 in MyEducationLab for this course.*

DIVERSITY DIALOGUE

While teachers know and are concerned about their students, principals are in the position to have an overview of the whole school—all the teachers, students, families—as well as the community and the district leadership. Carol Bartlett is very aware of all of these elements that impact Cario Middle School in South Carolina. Cario is located in a large and lovely upscale neighborhood where many of the middle school's students live. Other students within the attendance boundary attend the school and make up about 25% of the student population. Most live within a couple of miles of the school but in very different settings. Just outside the immediate neighborhood is a rural community established many years ago by African American families with pre–Civil War roots. Carol knows that the socioeconomic differences between these two neighborhoods creates issues that impact her school.

The CARE program is discussed in the Chapter 5 *Diversity Dialogue.*

The Cario faculty is relatively young, mostly white, and from backgrounds more similar to the neighborhood than to the outlying rural setting. After attending the National Middle School Association conference and participating in an intense workshop on the school-related impact of poverty, Carol is determined to uncover how socioeconomic status affects what happens in her school. She finds that of the 37 students in the CARE program, only two live in the neighborhood. While teams of teachers handle almost all discipline issues because Cario follows the middle school philosophy, the office referrals that the assistant principal addresses reflect a disproportionate amount from the rural area. Carol looks at the students designated as special needs and finds the same disparity. Cario has a strong, active program for students designated as Gifted and Talented (GT), and of the 92 students who participate in the GT pullout program (meets 90 minutes a day by grade level), only 4 are from outside the neighborhood.

Respond to these items by writing one well-developed paragraph for each.

1. Carol is overwhelmed as she puts all the information together about how Cario fits the profile of an unexamined school of young adolescents from very different settings. She sees that her school fits the profile she learned about that discriminates, although not intentionally, against poor and minority students. What is one step Carol should take in efforts to help remedy the situation?

2. Principals and teachers can't change the home settings or race of children, all of whom have strengths that have not been cultivated. How might the Cario faculty begin looking for strengths and address the disparities in the various programs at their school?

traditions and perceptions. If you are Jewish, attend a Christian service. If you are non-Hispanic, join in Cinco de Mayo festivities.

In our classrooms we need to be sensitive to each and every student, listen to interactions and guard against racial slurs of any kind, hold high expectations for all students, and continually seek to understand and appreciate differences that may accompany race. Read about a racial issue Principal Carol Bartlett faces at Cario Middle School in this chapter's *Diversity Dialogue.*

What Are the Effects of Bullying, Theft, and Violence on Students and Schools in the United States?

School is a relatively safe place to be. Considering that more than 55 million students attend school each day, the chances of one of them being a victim of a violent act are small. Even though the occurrence of violence and theft in schools has decreased since the mid-1990s, widespread crimes against students by other students continue to be problematic (Dinkes, Kemp, & Baum, 2009).

Recent data indicate that school-age students are victims of all kinds of minor crimes about as often at school as away from school. However, with serious violent crimes, such as rape and murder, the difference between in-school and out-of-school victimization is dramatic, with school the least likely place for harm (Dinkes et al., 2009).

Physical threat is not the only aspect of victimization to consider. The insidious nature of bullying causes real harm to students who are bullied, to those who perpetrate the bullying, and even to the bystanders who see it happening and do nothing to help.

BULLYING

In the aftermath of the 1999 Columbine High School tragedy, people across the United States asked, "How could something like this happen?" Psychologists, counselors, principals, teachers, and parents, as well as the print and electronic media, began to speculate about what might have led Dylan Klebold and Eric Harris to kill their schoolmates and a teacher and then turn the guns on themselves. From conversations with people who knew Dylan and Eric, the conclusion was drawn that they were adolescents who felt alienated from other students and from school.

Although the extreme violence of Columbine cannot be entirely explained by examining student relationships, interest in interactions among students has grown. Bullying, often considered just "what kids do," has become a topic of concern. **Bullying,** or relationally aggressive behavior, is "a type of emotional violence where individuals use relationships to harm others. Examples include exclusion from a group and rumor spreading" (Ophelia Project, 2005, p. 3). In addition, bullying may involve physical aggression, such as shoving, tripping, and taking personal items. "Bullying is a weapon of people driven by the need for power. Bullying can be a single interaction—verbal, physical, or emotional—but it is always crafted to cause fear and to exert power" (White-Hood, 2006, p. 30). Bullying may be linked to current and future psychological and behavioral difficulties, including depression, dropping out of school, substance abuse, risky sexual behavior, abnormal eating habits, delinquency, and suicide. Figure 9.9 gives an overview of the most frequent forms of bullying, as reported by students. One in three of these students said they had been bullied.

Almost everyone has been teased or called names at some point, and most people have teased others or been guilty of name-calling. When teasing becomes malicious and repetitive, when its intent is to embarrass, hurt, or isolate, it crosses the line into bullying. When rumors are intentionally spread to destroy the reputation of another, gossip becomes bullying. Most teachers can identify students who bully, as well as those who seem to be magnets for taunts and subtle forms of relational aggression. This chapter's *Letter to the Editor* recounts the harm done through bullying for one woman.

Points of Reflection 9.8

Do you recall being bullied? If so, how did it happen? Did you know students who were relentlessly bullied in school? Did you know students who bullied others? How did you feel toward those who bullied others? How about toward those who were bullied?

WHAT CAN SCHOOLS AND TEACHERS DO? In 2004 Congress amended the Safe and Drug Free Schools Act to include bullying and harassment. This addition requires all schools that receive federal funding to actively prevent bullying and to respond to all instances of it. School districts are developing policies and mandating antibullying programs. Books

Figure 9.9 Forms of bullying

Being made fun of: 21%
Being the subject of rumors: 18%
Pushed, shoved, tripped, or spit on: 11%
Threatened with harm: 6%
Excluded from activities on purpose: 5%
Coerced to do something they did not want to do: 4%

Source: Dinkes, R., Kemp, J., & Baum, K. (2009). *Indicators of school crime and safety: 2009* (NCES 2010–012/NCJ 228478). Washington, DC: National Center for Education Statistics, Institute of Education Sciences, U.S. Department of Education, and Bureau of Justice Statistics, Office of Justice Programs, U.S. Department of Justice.

Letter to the Editor

This letter appeared in the Minneapolis, Minnesota, newspaper, the *Star Tribune*. It was written by a woman who is responding to an article in the newspaper that she perceived as trivializing the role of teachers in the impact of bullying.

AUGUST 14, 2009 HARASSMENT AT SCHOOL

I was maddened to learn about Alex Merritt's story this week. . . . I was sexually harassed just like Alex for all of seventh grade. The students said I stuff my bra, they told me I liked girls, they told me I was a transvestite. Sometimes teachers would join in and laugh. When I finally got up the nerve to tell someone, I had actually started believing I was a lesbian. The school counselor told the bullies to say that they were sorry. I didn't forgive them and on telling them that, one of the bullies told me that "God wouldn't accept me into Heaven." I was sexually confused for two years after that, not sure if I was gay or straight, not sure if I could ever be loved. I still have self-confidence issues to this day, and sometimes the taunting still comes back to me. Not to mention my faith was down the toilet after the last comment. . . . I hope these stories cause more teachers to stand up for students and not join in because it is very traumatic and you will never forget it when it happens to you.

Hannah D.
Plymouth

Now it's your turn. Write a letter to the editor from the perspective of a future teacher expressing your views about bullying and the role teachers should play. You may comment on any, or all, of the writer's expressed opinions. The following questions may help you frame your thinking but should not limit nor determine what you write.

1. In the account you just read, do you think kids are "just being kids"? If so, why? If not, why not?

2. What part might peer pressure play in the scenario described? What do we know about seventh graders that may be relevant?

3. Have you ever been in a situation where teachers did, as Hannah says, and joined in and laughed at something hurtful? Briefly explain.

4. What do we know about young adolescent development that would lead to Hannah starting to believe the taunts might be true?

5. Do you have memories of being teased or bullied, perhaps not as dramatic as Hannah's, that have stayed with you? How might someone deal with these memories to lessen their effects?

6. What should teachers do to combat bullying?

Write your letter in understandable terminology, remembering that readers of newspaper Letters to the Editor are citizens who may have limited knowledge of school practices and policies. Remember to refer to the letter assessment rubric in Chapter 1.

---

such as *Odd Girl Out: The Hidden Culture of Aggression in Girls* (Simmons, 2002) and *Best Friends, Worst Enemies: Understanding the Social Lives of Children* (Thompson & Grace, 2001) shed new light on the ramifications of relational aggression for both the aggressor and the victim. Books like these and established anti-bullying programs indicate that many times bullies were themselves bullied at some point or perhaps abused in some way by family members. Most scenarios are complex. Even when teachers don't understand all the circumstances and are not trained to work through the psychological maze of causes for episodes of bullying, they can take steps to help prevent bullying in classrooms and schools. These steps include the following:

1. Watch for bullying and take it seriously.

2. Be an obvious presence. Early childhood and elementary teachers should monitor the playground. Middle and high school teachers should be visible and vigilant in the hallways, at lunchtime, at bus drop-off areas, at extracurricular events, and so on.

Bullying in middle school is a growing threat to the physical and psychological well-being of young adolescents.

3. Do everything possible to help students develop genuine self-esteem that will prevent bullying driven by lack of confidence. An intact self-esteem will also prompt victims of bullying to better withstand the torment and to seek assistance.

4. Incorporate lessons, formally or informally, that help students internalize the belief that bullying and relational aggression in all forms are harmful and absolutely wrong.

5. Implement prescribed anti-bullying programs with sincerity and purpose.

Research indicates that bullying may be the last significant step before the bully or the victim turns to more physically dangerous behavior, such as physical violence against other students.

THEFT AND VIOLENCE IN SCHOOLS

The most common forms of violence in schools are physical fights, with about equal fault among fighters, and simple assault involving a perpetrator and a victim. Both forms of violence involve boys about twice as often as girls. A larger percentage of black and Hispanic students (17% each) report being in fights than Asian students (13%) and white students (10%). Fighting is reported more often in urban settings than in suburban and rural settings (NCES, 2005a). The information in Figure 9.10 provides a perspective on violence and theft in U.S. schools in 2007–2008. In that school year, about 55.7 million students were enrolled in prekindergarten through grade 12.

Points of Reflection 9.9

Have you experienced theft or violence as a student? Have you seen any of these activities take place in school? What consequences did the perpetrators face? What was your reaction to these crimes?

WHAT CAN SCHOOLS AND TEACHERS DO? To help ensure the safety of students from early childhood through high school settings, schools have formulated a variety of plans and policies, ranging from programs that foster respect among students to overt ways of increasing security, such as installing surveillance cameras and metal detectors, requiring ID badges, locking school entrances during school hours, and using drug-detection dogs in random sweeps. Some school districts have adopted **zero tolerance** policies, meaning there are nonnegotiable consequences for certain infractions. For instance, the consequence for fighting may be automatic suspension for 3 days. Possession of a weapon may result in automatic expulsion.

Figure 9.10 Violence and theft in U.S. schools, 2007–2008

- There were 43 school-associated violent deaths, compared to about 6 per 100,000 total in the United States. This means that a person is 77 *times more likely* to die a violent death away from school as on school grounds. In the same time frame, a person is *847 times more likely* to die a violent death in our nation's capital than on school grounds. Shocking statistic, isn't it?
- About 800,000 thefts occurred. This includes incidents such as purse-snatching and pick-pocketing (not involving violence and use of force). About 1 in every 70 students experienced some form of theft during the year.
- About 700,000 violent crimes occurred, including simple assault, rape, sexual assault, robbery that included force, and aggravated assault. This means that about 1 in every 80 students experienced some victimization, with most involved in some sort of student-on-student fight.
- Approximately 5% of students reported that they were afraid of attack or harm at school.
- About 85% of public schools recorded that at least one violent crime, theft, or other crime occurred at their school.

Source: Dinkes, R., Kemp, J., & Baum, K. (2009). *Indicators of school crime and safety: 2009* (NCES 2010–012/NCJ 228478). Washington, DC: National Center for Education Statistics, Institute of Education Sciences, U.S. Department of Education, and Bureau of Justice Statistics, Office of Justice Programs, U.S. Department of Justice; *Homicide rate (per 100,000), 1950–2007* by Pearson, 2010, published as Infoplease. Retrieved June 6, 2010, from http://www.infoplease.com/ipa/A0873729.html; Snyder, T. D., Dillow, S. A., & Hoffman, C. W. (2009). *Digest of Education Statistics 2008* (NCES 2009-020). Washington, DC: National Center for Education Statistics, Institute of Education Sciences, U.S. Department of Education. Washington, DC: National Center for Education Statistics, Institute of Education Sciences, U.S. Department of Education.

Between the horrific events at Columbine in 1999 and the 2007–2008 school year, many schools responded to the threat of violence. Controlled access to the building during school hours went from 75% to 90%; the requirement that students wear badges or picture IDs went from 4% to 8%; the use of security cameras went from 19% to 55%; the provision of telephones in most classrooms went from 45% to 72%; and the requirement that students wear uniforms went from 12% to 18% (Dinkes et al., 2009).

Individual teachers may be able to have the greatest effect on school safety and security by being aware and watchful. Although they may occur, violent episodes are relatively infrequent. When students take weapons to school or there is a student fatality on school grounds, it is often front-page news, probably because it doesn't happen very often and, when it does, most people are appalled by it. Rather than being frightened day in and day out, think through how you would respond to a variety of scenarios, primarily how you would get help from nearby teachers, administrators, counselors, school security officers, and the like. Most schools have plans in place to address violence when it occurs.

Bullying and violence don't have a single source or cause. They originate from complex situations that didn't begin in an instant and won't be fixed quickly or with one solution. A multifaceted approach is needed that emphasizes civility, tolerance, and respect for dignity and life, as well as the inclusion of commonsense security measures.

How Do Truancy and Dropping Out Affect Youth in the United States?

Dropping out of school has been called "the silent epidemic" by researchers at the Bill and Melinda Gates Foundation—"silent" because it has been covered up and ignored for decades, and "epidemic" because the problem has reached near panic proportions (Bridgeland, Dilulio, & Morison, 2006). One of the most accurate predictors of dropping out is truancy.

TRUANCY

Nonattendance of compulsory education, not including excused absences generally granted for health reasons, is called **truancy** (Focus Adolescent Services, 2006), often referred to as cutting class or skipping school. Not only does truancy indicate who is most at risk for dropping out, but it also correlates strongly with juvenile delinquency, according to the Los Angeles Office of Education. In Van Nuys, California, a 3-week sweep of the city for truant middle and high school students correlated with a 60% drop in shoplifting arrests. School officials concluded that when they're not in school, there's a likelihood truant-prone students are committing crimes (Focus Adolescent Services, 2006).

On any given day, about 5% of students are absent from U.S. schools. At some schools, however, the rate may be closer to 20%. Absenteeism for any reason causes students to fall behind. With too many absences, students may feel lost in class, resulting in low self-esteem and a sense of resignation. According to a 2005 poll of 467 ethnically and racially diverse students who dropped out of public high school in urban, suburban, and rural areas, 43% said they missed too many days of school and could not catch up (Focus Adolescent Services, 2006). Families suffer the consequences of truancy as they watch someone they love drift toward academic failure. Communities suffer, not just because of crime, but because of the possible loss of productive, self-sufficient citizens.

According to a study by the Center for Social Organization of Schools at Johns Hopkins University, when truant students were asked why they skipped school, about half said they just didn't want to go to school, about a fourth said they felt pushed out or bullied, and the remaining fourth reported external problems, many of them family related. The researchers found this information encouraging because they contend that 75% of the truancies, or all except those attributed to external problems, can be altered by school actions that give students reason to be in school as well as safe environments free of bullying (MacDonald, 2004).

WHAT CAN SCHOOLS AND TEACHERS DO? Schools need to maintain accurate attendance records and communicate all absences to families. Although it sounds obvious, many schools do not pay attention to absences and do not call students' homes to ask about students who don't show up. Often parents and guardians don't know there's an attendance problem until it appears insurmountable.

Because student engagement is key to boosting attendance, some schools are establishing after-school programs that motivate students with a wide range of activities. The Los Angeles School District, reeling from the loss of millions of dollars of federal funding because of poor attendance, now has a program called Count Me In, giving tangible incentives, such as tickets to professional sports events, to students who improve attendance (MacDonald, 2004).

Teachers must develop relationships with students that let them know they matter. Engaging, relevant instruction and a "we miss you when you're gone" attitude go a long way toward doing away with the "I just didn't want to go" syndrome expressed by so many truant students. Catching the problem in the truant stage will help prevent the travesty of dropping out.

DROPPING OUT

When President Obama delivered his first major address to Congress, he said he envisions a country where dropping out is no longer an option. He made an explicit link between high school graduation rates and the nation's ability to recover economically, as well as to restore the world's opinion of the United States as a leader among nations. In early 2010 the president allocated an additional $900 million toward dropout prevention (Paulson, 2010). Former Secretary of State General Colin Powell annouced the formation of a new movement in 2010 called GradNation through America's Promise Alliance in an effort to mobilize communities around finding solutions to the dropout epidemic (America's Promise Alliance, 2009). The reality is that each year over a million students who begin ninth grade with their peer group will not walk across the stage at graduation 4 years later. About 7,000 students drop out of school every single day. The graduation completion rate hovers at around 65% (Alliance for Excellent Education, 2009a).

The dropout rate hasn't necessarily dramatically increased in the last few decades, but the alarming news of just how drastic the problem is made its way to the surface in 2005 when all 50 governors agreed on a definition of a dropout and how the data would be collected (Jerald, 2006). Prior to 2005, students who left school but indicated that they would seek a GED certificate or who simply never returned to school after numerous absences were not considered dropouts. For decades states reported grossly inflated high school completion numbers, with most percentages above 80% and many above 90%. The desire to portray success is understandable. However, honestly acknowledging how many students **drop out,** or do not graduate from high school in 4 years (and most will leave high school if they don't graduate in 4 years), is the first step to fixing the problem. And there definitely is a problem.

The U.S. Department of Education defines **high school completion,** or **graduation rate,** as the "percentage of students, measured from the beginning of high school, who graduate from a high school with a regular diploma in the standard number of years" (Hall, 2005, p. 4). Graduation rates by state, from New Jersey with the highest to Nevada with the lowest, are listed in Table 9.3.

While the overall U.S. graduation rate of 67% is low, only about half of our African American, Hispanic, and Native American students graduate. In addition, a student living in the highest quartile of family income is about seven times as likely to have completed high school as a student living in the lowest quartile (Alliance for Excellent Education, 2009a). Figure 9.11 illustrates graduation rates by race.

Why do students drop out of school? The reasons are complex and often overlapping. Figure 9.12 lists the top eight reasons given by dropouts in a survey conducted by Bridgeland, Dilulio, and Morison. You can mix and match the reasons to form plausible scenarios. For instance, boredom in a particular class may lead a group of students to identify with one another and to ditch school occasionally; skipped classes may then lead to

TABLE 9.3 Graduation rates by state

State	Graduation Rate, %	State	Graduation Rate, %
New Jersey	86	West Virginia	73
Iowa	85	Kentucky	72
Minnesota	85	Oregon	71
Nebraska	82	Colorado	70
South Dakota	82	Indiana	70
Wisconsin	81	Delaware	70
Vermont	80	Washington	69
Montana	79	Virginia	68
Arkansas	79	Arizona	68
North Dakota	79	Hawaii	68
Pennsylvania	79	Michigan	67
Utah	79	Tennessee	67
Idaho	79	California	66
New Hampshire	79	North Carolina	65
Connecticut	77	New York	64
Missouri	77	Texas	64
Kansas	77	Alaska	62
Maine	76	New Mexico	62
Illinois	75	Alabama	62
Oklahoma	75	Mississippi	61
Massachusetts	75	Louisiana	58
Wyoming	75	South Carolina	57
Ohio	74	Georgia	56
Maryland	74	Florida	54
Rhode Island	73	Nevada	51
		United States	**67**

Source: National Center for Higher Education Management Systems. (2006). Public high school graduation rates—2006. Retrieved June 4, 2010, from http://www.higheredinfo.org/dbrowser/index.php?measure=23

academic problems, more absences, and finally dropping out. There is actually good news in Figure 9.12. The most cited reasons for dropping out are largely within our control; they are school related. Although we can't change much of the societal context of our students, we can change what happens within the walls of our classrooms. In the section "What Can Schools and Teachers Do?" there are steps to take to increase graduation rates and, in doing so, have tremendous impact on the lives of students, as well as the economic viability of our nation.

Dropping out often results from a slow process of disengagement, with costly ramifications that may last a lifetime. The negative consequences included in Figure 9.13 are primarily economic. However, the cognitive, social, emotional, physical, and moral impact of dropping out is often devastating for individuals, families, communities, and our country.

One of our focus students at Roosevelt High School in Fresno, California, is absent too often. Mayra Reyes's homeroom teacher, Derek Boucher, is concerned about her. She seems to have a very active social life with many friends and cousins, but her home life with her mom and mom's boyfriend is volatile. Mayra is a U.S. citizen and is a second-generation American. As such she can attend community college using government grants. Derek encourages her to think about her future as a way to keep her interested in school.

Watch Mayra Reyes in the Teaching in Focus *section for Chapter 9 in MyEducationLab for this course.*

The Societal Context of Schooling in the United States   **259**

Figure 9.11 Graduation rates by race, 2008

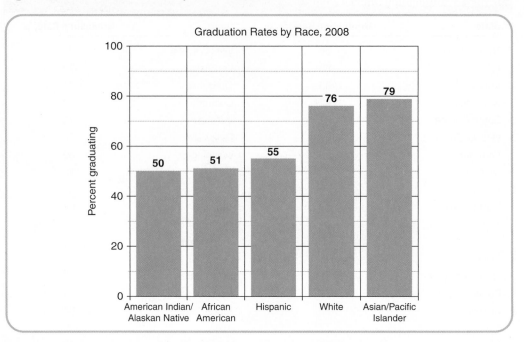

Source: Alliance for Excellent Education. (2009a). Understanding high school graduation rates in the United States. Retrieved June 4, 2010, from http://www.all4ed.org/files/National_wc.pdf

He knows that truancy often results in dropping out and that nationally the dropout rate for Hispanic students is close to 50%.

Dropping out of high school today is to a student's social health what smoking is to his or her physical health—an indicator of a host of poor outcomes to follow, from low lifetime earnings to high incarceration rates to the likelihood that the dropout's children will also drop out of high school and start the cycle anew (Thornburgh, 2006).

WHAT CAN SCHOOLS AND TEACHERS DO? There are no simple solutions to the problem of students dropping out of school. But much of the dilemma is solvable with purposeful effort that focuses on the whole child. Addressing an isolated problem area will likely not be enough, but addressing several areas of concern may produce the desired result of keeping students in school.

In most instances, the students who drop out are capable of succeeding academically: Most are passing when they drop out, and 70% are confident they could complete the program of

Figure 9.12 Top reasons dropouts identify for leaving school

High school dropouts say they . . .

- were not motivated or inspired to work hard (69%)
- found classes to be uninteresting (47%)
- were failing in school (35%)
- started high school poorly prepared (35%)
- would have been required to repeat a grade to graduate (32%)
- had to get a job and make money (32%)
- became a parent (26%)
- had to care for a family member (22%)

Source: Bridgeland, J. M., Dilulio, J. J., & Morison, K. B. (2006). *The silent epidemic: Perspective of high school dropouts.* Retrieved April 8, 2006, from http://www.civicenterprises.net/pdfs/thesilentepidemic3-06.pdf.

Figure 9.13 Negative consequences of dropping out

- Nearly half of dropouts ages 16 to 24 are unemployed (Thornburgh, 2006).
- Dropouts typically earn less than graduates: The average earnings difference is estimated to be $9,000 a year and $260,000 over the course of a lifetime (Dynarski, Clarke, Cobb, Finn, & Rumberger, 2008).
- Dropouts in 2008 will cost the United States almost $319 billion in lost wages over their lifetimes (Alliance for Excellent Education, 2009).
- Dropouts contribute only about half as much in taxes as do high school graduates (Dynarski et al., 2008).
- If U.S. high schools and colleges raise the graduation rates of Hispanic, African American, and Native American students to the levels of white students by 2020, the potential increase in personal income would add more than $310 billion to the U.S. economy (Alliance for Excellent Education, 2009a).
- Increasing the graduation rate and college matriculation of male students in the United States by just 5% could lead to combined savings and revenue of almost $8 billion each year by reducing crime-related costs (Alliance for Excellent Education, 2009).
- Dropouts draw larger government subsidies in the form of food stamps, housing assistance, and welfare payments (Dynarski et al, 2008).
- Dropouts constitute a disproportionate percentage of all prisoners and of prisoners on death row; 67% of the latter did not complete high school (Thornburgh, 2006).
- Dropouts have worse health outcomes and lower life expectancies than high school completers (Dynarski et al., 2008).

Source: Alliance for Excellent Education. (2009). *High school dropouts in America.* Retrieved June 7, 2010, from http://all4ed.org/files/GraduationRates_FactSheet.pdf; Dynarski, M., Clarke, L., Cobb, B., Finn, B., & Rumberger, R. (2008). *Dropout prevention.* Retrieved June 8, 2010, from http://ies.ed.gov/ncee/wwc/pdf/practiceguides/dp_pg_090308.pdf; Thornburgh, N. (2006, April). Dropout nation. *Time,* pp. 30–40.

study (Education Vital Signs [EVS], 2006a). Educators don't need to dumb down the curriculum. Efforts to retain students should center on some or all of the following suggestions:

1. Know the warning signs. For instance, sixth graders who don't attend school regularly, receive poor marks for behavior, or fail math or English for any reason have only a 10% chance of graduating (EVS, 2006a). So even a group of sixth graders can be targeted for intervention.

2. Establish ninth grade academies. Many schools have found success in separating ninth graders and providing them with extra counseling and support.

3. Consistently provide engaging curricula and instruction.

4. Maintain a safe environment and a welcoming climate.

5. Ensure an adult advocate for every student at every grade level. This person may be a classroom teacher, counselor, mentor, or administrator who has a specific responsibility to stay connected to the student.

6. Improve home and school communication.

7. Provide flexible, and alternative where needed, school configurations.

CONCLUDING THOUGHTS

There's a saying "We cannot control the wind, but we can adjust our sails." The societal issues that negatively affect students are complex and multidimensional. They don't begin with us, and most won't be completely resolved through us. However, with that reality in view, we can begin to focus on positive steps to prevent or halt risky behaviors and their impact on children and adolescents. Controlling the wind may not be within our reach as teachers, but adjusting our own and our students' sails is indeed possible.

After reading the *Chapter in Review,* read about Brandi's dilemma involving child neglect and respond to items in this chapter's *Developing Professional Competence.*

Points of Reflection 9.10

What experiences have you had with dropping out? Do you know students who dropped out? What have their experiences been?

Chapter in Review

How do family, community, and society impact students in the United States?

- Families, communities, and society in general can support student success or thwart it.
- Children and adolescents who are victims of child abuse or neglect are at risk physically, emotionally, socially, and academically.
- Communities can provide vital services for students and their families.

How does socioeconomic status affect students in the United States?

- The privilege gap between the haves and have-nots is a societal dilemma with far-reaching ramifications for children and adolescents.
- Children in low-income settings have many disadvantages that affect achievement in school.
- The most devastating impact of poverty is homelessness.

How do health issues affect students in the United States?

- The rates of most forms of substance abuse have recently decreased, yet even one child or adolescent harmed by it is too many.
- Children and adolescents often have an unfounded sense of immortality, which makes them feel they will not be harmed if they use substances such as inhalants, alcohol, legal and illegal drugs, and tobacco.
- Risky sexuality-related behavior can result in emotional distress, sexually transmitted diseases, and unplanned pregnancy.
- Teasing and harassment about homosexuality can be the root of distress for students in and out of school.

- Childhood obesity is near epidemic proportions and has long-term negative effects on students and society.
- Suicide is the third leading cause of adolescent deaths, with contributing factors that may be recognizable, leading to intervention.

How does race affect students in the United States?

- Racism is a form of prejudice stemming from the belief that one race is superior to another.
- Racism may take the form of inaction through silence or of low expectations for certain students.
- Immigrants and their children require special attention to ensure success in school.

What are the effects of bullying, theft, and violence on schools and students in the United States?

- Bullying can be verbal, physical, or emotional and is intended to exert power and cause harm.
- Violent acts in school include simple assault (usually fighting), sexual assault, and aggravated assault (definite perpetrator and victim) and occur most frequently in urban areas and among high school students.

How do truancy and dropping out affect youth in the United States?

- Truancy is a reliable predictor of dropping out.
- The dropout rate in the United States is over 30%, with long-term negative effects for students, families, communities, and the country.
- Reasons for dropping out are many and complex, with financial, self-esteem, and crime-related consequences.

Developing Professional Competence

Visit the Developing Professional Competence section on Chapter 9 of the MyEducationLab for this text to answer the following questions and begin your preparation for licensure exams.

One thing Principal Laura Hill at Summit Primary School is adamant about is making sure there is a visible adult at home when her kindergarten, first, and second graders are dropped by the bus after school. The drivers are instructed to bring children back to school if an adult does not appear in the yard or doorway. Consistently, an adult welcomes Caroline each afternoon.

Caroline is in Brandi Wade's kindergarten class. She is quiet and shy. As you read in the beginning of the chapter, in December Brandi rearranged physical aspects and instructional strategies in her class based on her observations of the children. During the first couple of months of the year her concern for Caroline grew. Although her mom came to Back-to-School Night and raised no red flags for Brandi, she sees some indications that all may not be well at Caroline's house.

In her 12 years as a classroom teacher she has seen bruises and burn marks on children and has reported them to the principal, who took appropriate action. After the fact she has known of sexual abuse of her students, but she has never had suspicions. Brandi sees no obvious signs of abuse with Caroline but rather subtle hints of something wrong. On the playground, there are times when she notices that Caroline appears to be sore when she walks. Brandi has also noticed that when a man is around, Caroline clings to her. One day during free drawing time, Caroline drew a picture of a man that was anatomically pretty accurate.

Think through this scenario and answer the following multiple-choice questions:

1. Because there are no overt signs of neglect, Brandi should
   a. continue to watch Caroline and document what she notices.
   b. talk with Principal Hill about her observations and leave it to her to pursue the situation.
   c. try to get Caroline to confide in her.
   d. ask a family in Caroline's neighborhood if they notice anything suspicious about the family.

2. One day Caroline mentions that her mother has a boyfriend who lives with them. Brandi's response to this should be to
   a. tell Principal Hill immediately.
   b. ask Caroline if she likes him.
   c. call Caroline's mom and ask for a parent conference.
   d. wait and see what else happens.

3. The children like to post their drawings on a large bulletin board in Brandi's classroom. She encourages them to do so. On the day she sees Caroline's drawing, how might she avoid having the picture of the man posted?
   a. She could ask the children to put their drawings in their desks and then take Caroline's after the children leave for the day.
   b. She could say she will choose drawings for the day that will be posted.
   c. She could post all the drawings in an effort to let Caroline know she has done nothing wrong.
   d. She could say they don't have time to post at the moment and she would just like to keep the children's drawings for now.

Now it's time for you to respond to two short essay items involving the scenario. In your responses, be sure to address all the dilemmas and questions posed in each item. Your responses should each be between one half and one double-spaced page.

4. There is always a danger that stepping into a domestic problem will actually make it worse. Perhaps nothing wrong is taking place. Given this, should Brandi share her concerns about Caroline as the holidays approach or wait until the children return after winter break? Explain your response.

5. Brandi takes the portion of INTASC Principle 10 that follows very seriously. She always tries to understand the context of her students' lives. This particular situation with Caroline, however, is a new challenge and one that makes her feel inadequate to handle. What might Brandi do to help Caroline feel safe in school and not to fear the men who are part of the school environment?

INTASC Knowledge, Principle 10
The teacher understands how factors in the students' environment outside of school (e.g., family circumstances, community environments, health and economic conditions) may influence students' life and learning.

Where DO I Stand NOW?

In the beginning of this chapter you completed an inventory that gauged your prior knowledge of the societal context of students in the United States. Now that you have read the chapter, completed exercises related to the content, engaged in class discussions, and so on, respond to the following items in your course notebook.

Before you begin this exercise, take a minute to think about the fact that issues in life typically aren't just black or white. When it comes to societal issues, there's a lot of gray, a lot of room for understanding and moderation. The scenarios in the following three items paint pictures of students with complex lives. Write at least a half page to describe your thoughts about what a teacher could do to help each student grow and succeed.

1. Juan is in third grade. He came to the United States less than a year ago with his mom, dad, and two older sisters. His teacher has seen him take small things from other students. What issues are likely at play in Juan's life? How could she approach this situation in a way that will teach Juan and avoid punishment or humiliation?

2. Heather is a seventh grader with a weight problem. She's not just overweight; she's obese. Her teacher has heard her blurt out hurtful things to other kids on occasion, and she typically has a sneer on her face. Since school started she has been absent 12 times and it's only November. Her teacher is justifiably concerned. What could he do to help Heather? What other information would be helpful to know?

3. Marvin lives with his aunt and five cousins in the low-income government housing that's part of his high school's attendance area. Most of the students at his school are from wealthier parts of town. Marvin's teacher knows that he is under pressure to earn enough money to pay for his room and food. He has a job after school at McDonald's and often falls asleep in class. She is afraid he will drop out during his sophomore year now that he is 16. Marvin has never achieved what he's capable of and his teacher knows it. What could she do to encourage him to stay in school?

MyEducationLab

The MyEducationLab for this course can help you solidify your comprehension of Chapter 9 concepts.

- Explore the classrooms of the teachers and students you've met in this chapter in the Teaching in Focus section.
- Prepare for licensure exams as you deepen your understanding of chapter concepts in the Developing Professional Competence section.

- Gauge and further develop your understanding of chapter concepts by taking the quizzes and examining the enrichment materials on the Chapter 9 Study Plan.
- Visit Topic 3, "School and Society," to watch ABC videos, explore Assignments and Activities, and practice essential teaching skills with the Building Teaching Skills and Dispositions unit.

Ethical **and Legal** Issues in U.S. Schools

This chapter explores ethical values involved in being a teacher. It examines how teacher and student rights and responsibilities are granted and enforced by law, as well as the nature of the relationship between ethics and laws. These are the questions we consider:

✦ What does it mean to be an ethical teacher?

✦ How do laws affect schools, teachers, and students?

✦ What are the legal rights of teachers?

✦ What are the legal responsibilities of teachers?

✦ How does the law impact the relationship between school and religion?

✦ What are the legal rights of students?

The United States has laws for a reason—they make it possible for people to live together as a nation. They prompt civility in neighborhoods, towns, cities, states, and across the country. It is important to read about actual people and events that have helped shape the fabric of laws that affect education. In doing so we gain perspective and more fully understand how laws affect the daily work of teachers. The cases in this chapter are not fictional. They are true. Read carefully and think about the implications for your future career in an early childhood, elementary, middle, or high school classroom.

What do you believe about the legal rights and responsibilities of teachers and students? Do your opinions agree with laws that have been established in U.S courts? Explore your stance on issues that have been legally challenged by completing *Where Do I Stand?*

Where DO I Stand?

This inventory will help you explore your perceptions regarding the legal rights and responsibilities of teachers and students before reading the chapter. After reading an item, indicate your level of agreement by choosing a number and placing it in the blank before the statement. Following the inventory are directions for how to organize your responses and what they may indicate in terms of where you stand.

> 4   I strongly agree
> 3   I agree
> 2   I don't have an opinion
> 1   I disagree
> 0   I strongly disagree

_____ **1.** Teachers should not exclude a student from an activity based on race, color, or national origin.

_____ **2.** All students with disabilities have the right to a free education.

_____ **3.** A district should be able to fire a teacher for health reasons (e.g., obesity, disabilities, AIDS, mental disability), if a link is shown between the health problem and impaired function in the classroom.

_____ **4.** A teacher should be dismissed if he or she engages in illegal activities.

_____ **5.** Teachers should be able to go on strike and remove themselves from the classroom while teacher unions negotiate with district administration.

_____ **6.** A teacher should be fired for conceiving a child out of wedlock.

_____ **7.** Material on the Internet must not be copied without citing its source.

_____ **8.** Teachers should be fired for using obscene language when speaking with students.

_____ **9.** Having a sexual relationship with a student should permit districts to begin immediate procedures toward dismissal.

_____ **10.** Students should be allowed to wear armbands or other symbols to school to protest a war (e.g., in Iraq or Afghanistan).

_____ **11.** A teacher should be fired for encouraging others to lie.

_____ **12.** Teachers must not make copies of textbooks or workbooks.

_____ **13.** A teacher should be able to openly debate questions, even involving school policies, without fear of retaliatory dismissal.

_____ **14.** A teacher should be dismissed for assigning material that includes offensive language about which parents complain.

_____ **15.** On a field trip to a public place, teachers should be held accountable for any injury that occurs to students.

_____ **16.** Teachers should be fired for what the community regards as immoral behavior.

_____ **17.** Administrators should be able to search a student's locker if there are reasonable suspicions of contraband.

_____ **18.** Teachers should serve in the place of parents when students are in their care.

_____ **19.** Students should be allowed to refuse to recite the Pledge of Allegiance.

_____ **20.** Teachers and administrators should have the right to exercise editorial control over student newspapers.

_____ **21.** When a teacher's students are on the playground, he or she should make sure there is appropriate adult supervision.

_____ **22.** Parents should be able to refuse to allow their children to be immunized.

_____ 23. Schools should excuse individual students from lessons that are objectionable to the student or the students' parents on religious or other conscientious grounds.

_____ 24. A teacher should be fired for having sexual relations with an underage child, even if the child has never been his or her student.

_____ 25. Students should be entitled to question and appeal a decision when punishment is imposed that will become part of a student's permanent record.

_____ 26. Public schools that impose uniform policies should provide an opt-out clause for parents who don't want their children to participate.

_____ 27. Students who are married, are parents, or are divorced should be allowed to attend the same public schools as those who are not.

_____ 28. Who a teacher lives with should not have any impact on his or her right to remain in a teaching position.

_____ 29. A teacher who has a reasonable suspicion of child abuse or neglect must report it to a school counselor or administrator.

_____ 30. Drug testing should be permissible for all students who participate in extracurricular activities, with no distinction between basketball and debate teams.

_____ 31. Students with HIV/AIDS should be allowed to attend public schools.

_____ 32. Students should be allowed to refuse to dance, even when it is part of the physical education curriculum.

_____ 33. Students should be allowed to opt out of sex education if they, and/or their parents, object to the content.

_____ 34. School officials should not be able to mandate or organize prayer at any public school sponsored event or graduation.

_____ 35. Teachers and school administrators, when acting in those capacities, should be prohibited from encouraging religious activity and from participating in such activity with students.

_____ 36. Schools should not single out religion-related messages and symbols to prohibit on clothing.

_____ 37. Asking students to empty their pockets and take off coats should be allowed if there is reasonable cause to believe there may be concealed contraband.

_____ 38. Educators should be held liable if they do not respond to complaints of sexual harassment.

_____ 39. Students should be allowed to pray individually or in a group as long as they are not disruptive.

_____ 40. Student homework, artwork, and other written and oral assignments should be allowed to contain religious content and have it graded according to the standards of the lesson.

Now add all of your responses and divide by 40. The closer your mean response is to 4, the more in agreement you are with established laws concerning teacher and student rights and responsibilities. Where do you stand?

4 I strongly agree with established laws regarding education.

3 I agree with most laws, but perhaps I have doubts about some.

0–2 I need to know more about how and why the laws were made and perhaps I will find more areas with which I agree.

As you continue reading the chapter you'll see that most of the responsibilities we've discussed so far in this book are guided by the abilities we hone as classroom teachers and not by laws. However, laws are important in that they protect the basic rights of teachers and students and outline the responsibilities of adults who teach and administer within public schools. Before discussing laws, we'll consider what it means to be an ethical teacher. Laws don't address many of the most important aspects of teaching. A teacher's personal belief system about right and wrong and what constitutes obligation, along with ethical codes provided by professional organizations, guide teaching practices in areas where no laws have been established.

Teaching in Focus

Derek Boucher teaches modern world history and U.S. history at Roosevelt High School in Fresno, California. He is also the reading intervention teacher for sophomores and juniors, many of whom are English-language learners. It is in this capacity that Derek feels a keen sense of responsibility toward building his students' literacy skills. He tirelessly searches for ways to engage his students in reading.

Derek believes that to transform students into readers, it is important to make reading both satisfying and focused on meaning. The nature of the content is what pulls students into the process. Consequently, Derek continually builds his classroom library. He selects books and magazines that will capture student imagination. He engages students in literature by selecting topics and sources that capture student interest yet contain embedded skills instruction. In his lesson Derek uses a newspaper article that gives examples of sexual stereotyping to draw students in.

Derek's passion for teaching compels him to grow professionally. He tells us, "Professional literature has changed my life as a teacher. That's why I'm an avid reader of books and journals that push me to think more deeply and conceptually about teaching and pedagogy." Derek regularly expresses his views on curricula and reading instruction by writing letters to the editor and opinion pieces for newspapers and magazines. He extends his influence in this way because he sees it as the right thing to do.

To watch Derek's classroom lesson, room tour, and interview, go to the Teaching in Focus *section for Chapter 10 in MyEducationLab for this course.*

What Does It Mean to Be an Ethical Teacher?

Laws tell us what we can and can't do. Ethics tell us what we should and shouldn't do. Ethics are standards of conduct based on moral judgments. Because ethics are grounded in personal belief systems, what is ethical in one person's view might not be ethical from another's perspective. Although most of the time what is lawful is also ethical, and what is ethical is also lawful, this is not always the case from everyone's viewpoint. For instance, abortion is legal in the United States, but many U.S. citizens consider it unethical. For some people with strong antiabortion beliefs, acting on personal ethics may mean becoming involved in unlawful forms of protest against a legal activity.

PROFESSIONAL ETHICS

Most professions have codes of ethics. The largest teacher organization, the National Education Association (NEA), has a code of ethics (see Figure 10.1). The NEA Code of Ethics is divided into two sections, teacher commitment to students and teacher commitment to the profession. Take a few minutes to read the code. Notice that most of the points begin with the words *shall not*.

It is important for teachers to understand what they "shall not" do because these kinds of guidelines can be helpful in keeping us out of ethical trouble. However, there are also many "shalls" involved in practicing ethical teaching, as we have discussed throughout this entire text. If these positive elements are internalized, practicing ethical teaching becomes habitual. Ethical teachers *shall*

- purposefully serve as positive role models for their students
- put students' best interests ahead of other considerations
- involve families often and positively
- support colleagues and work collaboratively
- create and maintain a productive learning environment
- diversify instruction to address student differences

Figure 10.1 National Education Association Code of Ethics

Preamble

The educator, believing in the worth and dignity of each human being, recognizes the supreme importance of the pursuit of truth, devotion to excellence, and the nurture of the democratic principles. Essential to these goals is the protection of freedom to learn and to teach and the guarantee of equal educational opportunity for all. The educator accepts the responsibility to adhere to the highest ethical standards.

The educator recognizes the magnitude of the responsibility inherent in the teaching process. The desire for the respect and confidence of one's colleagues, of students, of parents, and of the members of the community provides the incentive to attain and maintain the highest possible degree of ethical conduct. The Code of Ethics of the Education Profession indicates the aspiration of all educators and provides standards by which to judge conduct.

The remedies specified by the NEA and/or its affiliates for the violation of any provision of this Code shall be exclusive and no such provision shall be enforceable in any form other than the one specifically designated by the NEA or its affiliates.

PRINCIPLE I

Commitment to the Student

The educator strives to help each student realize his or her potential as a worthy and effective member of society. The educator therefore works to stimulate the spirit of inquiry, the acquisition of knowledge and understanding, and the thoughtful formulation of worthy goals.

In fulfillment of the obligation to the student, the educator—

1. Shall not unreasonably restrain the student from independent action in the pursuit of learning.
2. Shall not unreasonably deny the student's access to varying points of view.
3. Shall not deliberately suppress or distort subject matter relevant to the student's progress.
4. Shall make reasonable effort to protect the student from conditions harmful to learning or to health and safety.
5. Shall not intentionally expose the student to embarrassment or disparagement.
6. Shall not on the basis of race, color, creed, sex, national origin, marital status, political or religious beliefs, family, social or cultural background, or sexual orientation, unfairly—
   a. Exclude any student from participation in any program
   b. Deny benefits to any student
   c. Grant any advantage to any student
7. Shall not use professional relationships with students for private advantage.
8. Shall not disclose information about students obtained in the course of professional service unless disclosure serves a compelling professional purpose or is required by law.

PRINCIPLE II

Commitment to the Profession

The education profession is vested by the public with a trust and responsibility requiring the highest ideals of professional service. In the belief that the quality of the services of the education profession directly influences the nation and its citizens, the educator shall exert every effort to raise professional standards, to promote a climate that encourages the exercise of professional judgment, to achieve conditions that attract persons worthy of the trust to careers in education, and to assist in preventing the practice of the profession by unqualified persons.

In fulfillment of the obligation to the profession, the educator—

1. Shall not in an application for a professional position deliberately make a false statement or fail to disclose a material fact related to competency and qualifications.
2. Shall not misrepresent his/her professional qualifications.
3. Shall not assist any entry into the profession of a person known to be unqualified in respect to character, education, or other relevant attribute.
4. Shall not knowingly make a false statement concerning the qualifications of a candidate for a professional position.
5. Shall not assist a noneducator in the unauthorized practice of teaching.
6. Shall not disclose information about colleagues obtained in the course of professional service unless disclosure serves a compelling professional purpose or is required by law.
7. Shall not knowingly make false or malicious statements about a colleague.
8. Shall not accept any gratuity, gift, or favor that might impair or appear to influence professional decisions or action.

Source: National Education Association. Retrieved May 27, 2005, from http://www.nea.org/aboutnea/code.html?mode=print.

Laws do not dictate these actions; ethical attitudes and beliefs call for them. Similarly, Derek Boucher's attitudes and actions—both in and outside the classroom—with regard to the teaching profession stem from his ethics.

Let's bring these concepts into the reality of the classroom by examining what it means to be an ethical teacher. Regardless of what our students learn, they learn *us*. We either represent, or *mis*represent, ethical behavior in the classroom.

ETHICS FOR TEACHERS

An ethical teacher is guided by a set of beliefs that leads to attitudes and actions focused on what's best for students. Being ethical means taking the high road and behaving professionally in the midst of big issues as well as in everyday decision making in the classroom.

Howe (1996) tells us that six characteristics form a conceptual basis for making ethical decisions. The first characteristic, appreciation for moral deliberation, means understanding that situations are complex and part of our obligation is to ensure that the rights of all involved are protected. The second characteristic, empathy, refers to the ability to put oneself mentally in the place of others to appreciate a variety of perspectives. Knowledge, the third characteristic, is necessary to have a clear view of the dilemma at hand. Dealing with knowledge requires reasoning, the fourth characteristic, and courage, the fifth characteristic, is needed to act on that reasoning. Finally, the sixth characteristic, interpersonal skills, allows teachers to communicate effectively with others about their ethical deliberations. These six characteristics are described in Figure 10.2. Characteristics 2 through 6 are self-explanatory. This doesn't diminish their value, but we more often know what they look like in practice than characteristic number 1.

Cultivating an "appreciation for moral deliberation," as Howe puts it, is a career-long area of growth for teachers. When we have big decisions to make, we generally see the right and wrong sides pretty clearly. We know there are consequences for our choices and we usually recognize many of them. This is a good thing. But what about the seemingly little decisions and actions, the things we do, or don't do, on a regular basis? Is it possible that these less-than-life-changing situations have "complex moral dimensions" and require that we have a "realization that care is needed to protect the rights of all parties"? Bringing higher-order thinking and problem-solving skills to bear on dilemmas, big and small, is what teachers must do.

In Table 10.1 you'll find some sample attitudes and decisions leading to actions, along with questions a teacher might consider. Could a teacher be dismissed because of these? Maybe, but probably not. Would a teacher's reputation suffer in the eyes of some? Maybe, and probably so. Every teacher could name similar, as well as very different, scenarios from personal experience if prompted to think about it. Perhaps there's the dilemma: *if prompted to think about it*. When our actions go unexamined, we are less likely to consider moral deliberation and therefore not be the ethical teachers we might otherwise become.

When we habitually apply ethical thinking and actions (the "shalls" referred to earlier) to situations, we are contributing to the development of students who ideally will do the same. As we model morally sound decision making, it is helpful to have a vision of desirable

Figure 10.2 Six desirable characteristics for teachers as they make ethical judgments

1. Appreciation for Moral Deliberation—ability to see complex moral dimensions of a problem and realization that care is needed to protect the rights of all parties
2. Empathy—ability to "get inside the skin of another"
3. Knowledge—facts to enable us to put issues in context
4. Reasoning—reflecting systematically on an issue and moving step by step to a conclusion
5. Courage—the willpower to act in what we perceive to be the right way, rather than just the comfortable way
6. Interpersonal Skills—communicating about issues sensitively and tactfully

Source: Howe, K. R. (1996, May/June). A conceptual basis for ethics in teacher education. *Journal of Teacher Education, 37,* 6.

TABLE 10.1 Recognizing ethical dilemmas

Attitudes/Decisions/Actions	Thinking It Through
With a wink, I say to a few students that I think I'm coming down with something. I return 48 hours later with an obvious skier's sunburn.	Is it OK to indicate to students that I am going to call in sick when I'm really planning to go on a ski trip? What lesson are they learning from me about responsibility and honesty?
A spelling bee competition is planned for tomorrow in which all the students in each class must participate. I have three students who are English language learners. I really want to win this bee since I am a candidate for my school's Teacher of the Year award. I casually mention to the three students that tomorrow would be a great day to stay home and enjoy the new fallen snow since it's Friday and they won't miss much.	Have I let my desire to look good get in the way of doing what's right for my students? Without these three students, my fifth grade class has the best chance of winning our grade-level bee. Winning will be a big boost for my students. So am I justified in encouraging these three students to stay home? After all, it's Friday before winter vacation and not much will go on that's academic in nature besides the spelling bee. They won't miss much . . . or will they?
On a field trip to a local museum I decide to buy each student a cold drink from a vending machine. I drop in two quarters and out pops not just one soda, but three. I laugh and say this must be my lucky day.	It's only a dollar loss for the vending company, but am I setting a good example for students? If I think that cheating the system makes me lucky, what message am I giving my students?
I just started a landscaping business that hopefully will occupy my weekends and give me extra income. I have developed an advertising flyer that I will distribute in the community. Because I haven't made much money yet, I decide to use the school copier one late afternoon to make a thousand flyers.	The students will likely never know I did this. But if another teacher walks into the workroom and sees what I'm doing, will my reputation be somewhat affected?
A parent generously donated $200 for me to buy a classroom set of a novel to use in spring semester. She determined the donation amount by going to a local bookstore. Knowing that I would get a 10% teacher discount, she gave me a check rather than buying the books herself. I go online and find the books for $150 and order them. I decide that it was my ingenuity that resulted in the discount and decide to keep the extra $50 for my trouble.	It's unlikely that anyone will ever know about this, so why should I care? After all, I work very hard as a teacher and this is just a small perk. Is $50 worth living with a small voice inside that says I should have spent the money on something for my classroom?
It's time for the first-quarter grades to be submitted just as football season has become very exciting. Our team is looking promising as a contender for the district championship. Mike has a 68% in my class, making him ineligible to play in a big rivalry game Friday night. He's had a lot to do with practice every afternoon and he's a really good guy. I decide to make his grade a C– instead of a D.	I didn't make this adjustment for several other students who struggled, or maybe didn't struggle enough, to make a C–. Because I insist that all my students keep up with their grade averages, Mike will know that I changed his grade. What message am I sending him about doing just enough to get by and then receiving "gifts"? If he brags about this, what about the other students, both those who didn't get the extra boost and others who do fine in my class but will know that I fudged on Mike's grade? Will some parent discover what I have done and complain to my principal?
It's time once again to promote the sale of wrapping paper to earn money for school projects. I send a letter home encouraging parents to join in. I e-mail parents each day reminding them to help their students sell the paper. I promise the students a party, but only for those who bring in orders for $100 of paper. The students feel the pressure, as do the parents.	Because my class is composed of kids from a wide range of socioeconomic-level homes, am I unduly putting pressure on some families who don't know many people with discretionary money to spend on fancy wrapping paper? If I still like the party idea, how might I design the party incentive so that particular students would not be ostracized?
Because fund-raising efforts have been disappointing in recent years, and our school improvement team wants to landscape the courtyard, our principal decides to give each student who brings a $20 donation 10 points to be used on any test in any class during the quarter.	At first I buy into this plan, not considering the fairness or morality of it. Then a student comes to me and complains that being able to give $20 will be difficult. Suddenly I see this initiative as very unfair and fundamentally misguided. Should I express this to my principal? Should I tell my students that I won't honor the 10-point bonus?

traits we want to promote in those we profoundly influence through ethical teaching. In writing about her vision of young adolescents, Donna Marie San Antonio (2006, p. 7) simply and eloquently describes some desirable traits. We want students to be

- smart but not arrogant
- flexible but not easily deterred from their hopes and dreams
- compassionate toward others but not overly accommodating
- self-confident but not too preoccupied with themselves
- proud but not exclusive

Points of Reflection 10.1

What are your memories of teachers who promoted ethical behavior? Describe a scenario from your PreK–12 school experiences.

What are your memories of teachers who displayed unethical attitudes and actions? Describe a scenario from your PreK–12 school experiences.

Helping students build these traits is a tall order and one we must fulfill with ethical attitudes, decisions, and actions. The results will be positive and cumulative.

Now that you have considered what it means to be an ethical teacher and some of the ways ethics guide classroom practice, it's time to look at more concrete guidelines that determine actions.

How Do Laws Affect Schools, Teachers, and Students?

The U.S. government, its legal system, and the laws that affect schools, teachers, and students are based on a balance of rights and responsibilities. The government and legal system achieve a viable balance of power through the interaction of the three branches of government: executive, legislative, and judicial. Since the founding of the United States of America, four basic sources of law have directly impacted the everyday work of all teachers: the U.S. Constitution, federal laws, state and local laws and policies, and case law.

U.S. CONSTITUTION

The Constitution does not specifically mention education. However, certain amendments directly impact teachers and schools.

FIRST AMENDMENT. The First Amendment to the Constitution, shown in Figure 10.3, guarantees, among other things, freedom of speech and religion and prohibits government (i.e., public school) advancement of religion. The relationship between law and religion is discussed later in this chapter.

Freedom of speech, as guaranteed in the First Amendment, applies to schools. As you read this chapter you'll recognize how often the First Amendment is cited as a guide in decision making on educational issues. The Association for Supervision and Curriculum Development (ASCD) established The First Amendment center to help educators better understand how to apply the tenets of this amendment in schools. The Web site www.firstamendmentschools.org is designed to provide resources to assist schools in implementing the guiding principles of the First Amendment.

FOURTH AMENDMENT. The Fourth Amendment protects citizens from unreasonable search and seizure and, in doing so, protects the basic privacy and security of all people, including students' rights to privacy. For instance, do students have the right to keep whatever they want in a locker assigned to them? Under what circumstances can adults examine the locker contents? This topic is discussed later in the chapter.

Figure 10.3 First Amendment

Congress shall make no law respecting an establishment of religion, or prohibiting the free exercise thereof; or abridging the freedom of speech, or the press; or the right of the people peaceably to assemble, and to petition the government for a redress of grievances.

FOURTEENTH AMENDMENT. The Fourteenth Amendment protects the rights of due process and guarantees equal protection to all citizens. For teachers, this amendment pertains to job security and the right to be heard if charges are made against them. Later in the chapter we examine how this amendment affects both teachers and students.

The general guidelines of the U.S. Constitution, specifically the First, Fourth, and Fourteenth Amendments, provide the framework for the federal laws that affect schools, teachers, and students.

FEDERAL LAWS

The federal statutes written and passed by Congress (the legislative branch of the U.S. government) have a major impact on the daily work of teachers and the operation of schools.

Here are examples of federal laws impacting education:

> We briefly discuss some of these federal laws in Chapter 4.

- The National Defense Education Act (1958) established curricular priorities, placing math, science, and foreign language at the top.
- The Civil Rights Act (1964) officially ended more than 50 years of overt racial segregation in public schools by declaring, "No person in the United States shall on the grounds of race, color, or national origin, be excluded from participation in or be denied the benefits of, or be subjected to discrimination under any program or activity receiving federal financial assistance." Unfortunately, however, segregation still exists in public schools in many areas.
- The Elementary and Secondary Education Act (1965) was originated to benefit children in low socioeconomic settings. This act created Title I funding and has been reauthorized several times.
- The Bilingual Education Act (1968) proposed that students be taught in their native languages while they learned English.
- Federal Title IX legislation (1972) opened many doors, specifically to girls, by prohibiting discrimination based on gender.
- The Individuals with Disabilities Education Act (1975, 1990, 2004) guarantees the rights of students with disabilities to a free education in the least restrictive environment.

Another federal law you've read about many times throughout this text is the 2001 reauthorization of the Elementary and Secondary Education Act, known from 2001 through 2010 as No Child Left Behind. The federal law has significantly impacted schools so far in the 21st century.

STATE AND LOCAL LAWS AND POLICIES

The U.S. Constitution stipulates that anything not specifically addressed by it becomes a state issue. Consequently, laws and policies affecting education vary from state to state, and from district to district within each state. Some of the issues addressed by state and local laws and policies include curriculum standards and assessment mandates, as well as funding and governance. The guidelines for teacher certification are left up to states, with some federal stipulations.

CASE LAW

Many legal decisions concerning education are based on precedence—what has been done in the past and what the judicial system has decided with regard to specific rights and responsibilities. The cases brought before the courts are deliberated and settled based on what the U.S. Constitution says, what federal law dictates, and what state and local governing bodies have established. All of these aspects are considered, ideally with heaping doses of common sense, as decisions are made by the courts.

Case law is based on the doctrine of *stare decisis,* a Latin phrase meaning "let the decision stand." This means that once a decision is made in a court of law, that decision sets a

Figure 10.4 Relationship of law and ethics

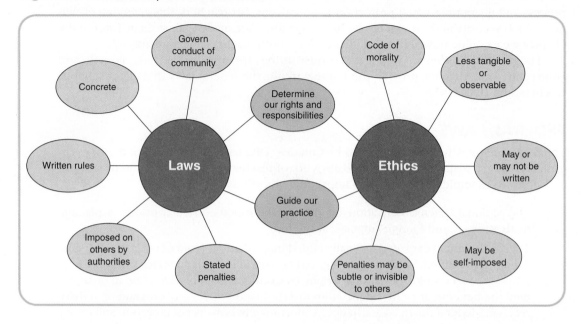

precedent for future cases of a similar nature until challenged or overturned. There is a large body of federal case law on which state and local cases rely for precedence. A decision made by the U.S. Supreme Court establishes case law until either the Supreme Court changes the ruling or an amendment to the Constitution alters the decision. Unfortunately, many school and local government officials have not abided by this principle. Because the Supreme Court doesn't have an enforcement arm, continued court action is sometimes necessary to bring school districts into compliance. For instance, the famous *Brown* v. *Board of Education* (1954) court decision ruled that separate schools are not equal and opened many schoolhouse doors for African Americans. Occasionally during the last 50 years, however, decisions have been made that do not comply with the *Brown* results, and more court action has been needed (LaMorte, 2008).

Throughout this chapter, discussions of the legal rights and responsibilities of teachers, the rights of students, and the relationship between schools and religion will cite sample case law. Read these highlighted cases carefully.

Before addressing the rights and responsibilities of teachers and students, consider the relationship between laws and ethics. Take a few minutes to examine Figure 10.4 that shows how laws and ethics differ in a number of ways, yet still share some qualities.

What Are the Legal Rights of Teachers?

Teachers in the United States are entitled to the same rights as other Americans. However, some rights are occasionally tempered by the opinions of either the community or the court when there is concern that teachers' individual rights may impact classroom effectiveness. In addition, certain legal rights apply specifically to the teaching profession. Most teachers will never find themselves in positions where their legal rights are threatened in any way. The day-to-day realities of teaching rarely involve legal challenges.

EMPLOYMENT LEGALITIES

Being employed by a school district entails understanding your rights and responsibilities. You will sign a contract, possibly have tenure in your future, and have procedures for filing grievances if things go wrong or if dismissal is threatened.

TEACHING CONTRACTS. A **contract** is an agreement between parties that states the rights and responsibilities of each. A teacher signs an initial contract and then signs again each year to continue in the same position. Teaching contracts typically include a formal offer of employment, the salary, and a description of the position. When you sign a teaching contract, you state that you will abide by district policies. It is very important to carefully read and understand the policies and the contract. Both are extensive and may be written in complex language. Don't hesitate to ask for an explanation.

Contracts are binding on both parties. If you sign a contract and then back out or take a different job, or if the district backs out, you or the district can be sued for damages involving **breach of contract.**

TENURE. Continuing contract status is known as **tenure.** A teacher with tenure is entitled to a contract each year unless the district has reason not to renew it or the teacher decides to go elsewhere. In most states tenure doesn't guarantee a particular position in a particular school, but it does guarantee employment in the district.

Some object to the concept of tenure because it requires more steps to dismiss an ineffective teacher who has it. However, even teachers with tenure cannot keep their jobs if they are shown to be incompetent, display immoral behaviors, are insubordinate, or are involved in any of a wide array of behaviors considered unprofessional conduct.

DISMISSAL. Teachers have been dismissed for many reasons, some of which sound outrageous to us today. Historically, teachers have been dismissed for not attending a particular church, for wearing pants in public (a female teacher), for marrying or becoming pregnant during the school year, and even for moving to a neighboring town. More recently the courts have ruled for dismissal due to, among others, the following reasons:

- insubordination
- neglect of duty
- conduct unbecoming a teacher
- incompetence
- physical or mental health problems
- engaging in illegal activities
- causing or encouraging disruptions

The general direction of court cases that consider dismissal tends today more toward a teacher's personal liberty than in the past. Here are two overriding questions asked when considering dismissal:

- Is the educational process significantly disrupted by the action?
- Is the teacher's credibility significantly harmed among students, colleagues, families, and the community?

Some teacher offenses are considered by the courts to be remediable, meaning that given assistance and time, a teacher may be able to correct the problem and be effective in the classroom. For instance, if a district begins dismissal procedures because a tenured teacher's classroom management skills are considered very poor, the court will likely say the teacher has a right to try to remediate those skills. On the other hand, some actions are considered irremediable in that they are so unprofessional that a district is not obligated to provide assistance. Conviction in a criminal case and having a sexual relationship with a student are two examples of actions for which districts may begin immediate procedures toward dismissal.

Most districts require teachers to serve successfully for about 3 years before offering them a continuing contract, or tenure. During these first 3 years or so, teachers can be dismissed for suspected incompetence or because of a general **reduction in force** of the district teacher population. Such a reduction may result from lower student numbers, budget cuts, or program cancellation. Reduction in force (rif) may also apply to tenured teachers. However, the general rule of "riffing" is that the last hired are the first to go.

DUE PROCESS. When a tenured teacher is threatened with dismissal, the steps the district must take to pursue the charges against the teacher are called **due process.** Due process is an important principle that requires guidelines to be followed to ensure that individuals are protected from arbitrary or capricious treatment by those in authority. The procedures of due process vary by state, but generally a teacher must be

1. notified of the proposed charges
2. given reasonable time to examine evidence
3. told who will be called as witnesses and given the right to legal representation
4. provided with a hearing before an impartial jury, panel, and/or judge
5. given the opportunity to call witnesses and cross-examine the district's witnesses
6. afforded a decision based on evidence
7. provided a transcript of the proceedings
8. given the right to appeal

Even though due process has been in force for many years and will likely continue to be part of the profession, outcomes of hearings based on due process may vary by location and according to the times (LaMorte, 2008). For instance, until the 1970s, if an unmarried teacher lived with someone of the opposite sex, the teacher could go through due process procedures and be dismissed. Today, it would be very rare for a teacher's living arrangements to serve as grounds for dismissal.

Points of Reflection 10.2

How do you feel about teachers going on strike and removing themselves from the classroom for a period of time during which collective bargaining takes place? Should teachers be allowed to strike because of grievances about their work environment (salary, hours, class size, etc.) if it means closing schools during the process? Why or why not?

UNIONS AND COLLECTIVE BARGAINING. Although not exclusively related to getting and keeping a job, collective bargaining is a right practiced in most states by teacher unions. States often allow unions to negotiate with school boards concerning elements of teacher contracts and working conditions. The two major teacher organizations that act as unions are the National Education Association (NEA) and the American Federation of Teachers (AFT). States have their own affiliates of NEA or AFT to represent teachers in more local ways. Individual teachers and groups of teachers can file **grievances,** or formal complaints against a district. NEA and AFT, or their state affiliates, often represent teachers who file grievances. NEA and AFT, as unions, can also call for teacher strikes when collective bargaining does not result in changes that satisfy the large groups of teachers who affiliate with the unions.

Teachers affiliated with unions may go on strike when collective bargaining does not result in satisfactory changes.

FREEDOM OF EXPRESSION

There are many ways to express opinions and beliefs, including symbolic, written, and verbal expression. Symbolic expression generally involves making a statement by what is worn—a style of clothing, a political button, particular colors, an armband, a ribbon. Some symbolic statements are socially acceptable, even desirable. For instance, ribbons showing support for breast cancer research or bracelets commemorating important days in history are considered appropriate. However, wearing an armband to protest an ongoing war or a shirt with inflammatory or offensive words or pictures may be legal outside school but ruled unacceptable in school and can serve as possible grounds for dismissal. For teachers, freedom of symbolic expression has limits, especially if it disrupts the school or classroom.

As with symbolic expression, written and spoken expression must not interrupt the education process. Teachers have the right to express themselves through letters to the editor, written articles, conversations, speeches, and debates. Since the often-quoted case of

Pickering v. *Board of Education,* 1968, the courts have generally ruled on the side of teachers' rights to freedom of spoken and written expression, even when that expression involves harsh criticism of a school, district, or personnel connected to education. In *Pickering,* an Illinois teacher wrote a sarcastic letter to the editor criticizing the school superintendent and school board for funding practices. The board fired Pickering, and the state supreme court upheld the dismissal. Pickering appealed to the U.S. Supreme Court. Justice Thurgood Marshall stated that the problem was one of balance between personal rights of the teacher and the district's right to promote efficient public service through its employees. The court ruled in favor of Pickering and his right to openly debate questions without fear of retaliatory dismissal.

If a teacher's expression is intended to incite unprofessional behavior, the courts may rule against the teacher. John Stroman was fired for encouraging teachers to call in sick as a form of protest against some administrative decisions. In *Stroman* v. *Colleton County School District,* 1992, the Supreme Court ruled in favor of the school district on grounds that encouraging others to lie is unprofessional.

ACADEMIC FREEDOM

Academic freedom is a form of expression that allows teachers to use their judgment in making decisions such as what to discuss, what to assign as readings, and what teaching strategies to employ. Like the other freedoms, academic freedom has limits that courts have upheld in many cases.

One recurring issue involves the courts' attempts to balance the right of academic freedom with a district's desire for students to learn a specific curriculum. Districts and states set the curriculum teachers must teach. When teachers exercise academic freedom and go beyond or eliminate parts of this curriculum, problems occur because either (1) including the additional topics does not leave time for the prescribed curriculum, or (2) the nonprescribed topics are controversial and may be deemed inappropriate.

In this era of standards and high-stakes testing, failing to teach the prescribed curriculum is likely to become evident, but it may take time. The line between what is appropriate in the classroom, and what is not, is the most common cause of disagreements between districts and teachers with regard to academic freedom. Some of the topics deemed inappropriate in the public school classroom when they are not part of the curriculum include sexuality-related issues, gun control, abortion, some political issues, and any topic involving offensive language. For instance, in *Keefe* v. *Geanakos,* 1969, a Massachusetts high school English teacher assigned an article from the *Atlantic Monthly* that contained offensive language. He was fired because he would not agree never to give the assignment again. A court decision gave Keefe his job back and stated that because some of the school's library books contained the same words and students would likely not be shocked by them, parental complaints about the words did not dictate what was proper in the classroom.

Some teaching methods may be deemed inappropriate if a teacher cannot substantiate the approach using professional opinions and research. In *Murray* v. *Pittsburgh Board of Education,* 1996, a teacher used a motivational technique called "Learnball" with at-risk high school students involving dividing the class into teams. Competition between teams involved rewards, such as listening to the radio and shooting baskets with foam balls. The school board ordered the teacher not to use the method. Murray sued the board but lost. The courts determined that the school board had the right to set policy against particular teaching methodologies.

Summaries of the four cases in this section concerning freedom of expression, plus two others of interest, are in Figure 10.5.

TEACHERS' PERSONAL LIVES

A teacher has a right to a personal life. However, the notion that teachers are role models entails some limits that have been upheld in courts. As late as the 1960s, teachers were quickly and without challenge fired for adultery, drunkenness, homosexual conduct, illegal drug use, cohabitation with the opposite sex, or becoming pregnant while single. To lend

Points of Reflection 10.3

Are there issues about which teachers should not talk or write about if it means the community will be aware of his or her views? If not, justify your answer. If so, what is one issue and why?

If you felt strongly about teaching a particular topic in an advanced high school class, but the district said that you should not spend time on the topic even though it was not offensive, how would you respond?

Figure 10.5 Case law: Freedom of expression

***Pickering* v. *Board of Education* (1968)**
Teacher kept job after publicly criticizing school board.

***Keefe* v. *Geanakos* (1969)**
Teacher keeps job after assigning controversial readings.

***Kingsville Independent School District* v. *Cooper* (1980)**
Teacher uses role play to teach about racial relations
A teacher was dismissed when she refused to stop using role-play simulations to teach about post–Civil War American history. Parents complained that the activity caused racially charged sentiments in their children. The Court of Appeals reinstated the teacher, with back pay. The court determined that the district violated the teacher's First Amendment rights.

***Krizek* v. *Cicero-Stickney Township High School* (1989)**
Teacher showing R-rated movie
A teacher was dismissed for showing an R-rated movie to her class as a modern-day parallel to *Our Town* by Thornton Wilder. She apparently told her students they would be excused if their parents objected, but she did not communicate directly with parents. The court upheld Ms. Krizek's dismissal saying the movie was a planned event, and not an inadvertent mistake, and that her methodology was problematic.

***Stroman* v. *Colleton County School District* (1992)**
Teacher fired for encouraging others to lie.

***Murray* v. *Pittsburgh Board of Education* (1996)**
Teacher may not use instructional strategy considered unorthodox by school board.

Sources: Dunklee, D. R., & Shoop, R. J. (2002). *The principal's quick-reference guide to school law: Reducing liability, litigation, and other potential legal tangles.* Thousand Oaks, CA: Corwin Press. LaMorte, M. W. (2008). *School law: cases and concepts* (9th ed.). Fischer, L., Schimmel, D., & Stellman, L. R. (2007). *Teachers and the law* (7th ed.). Boston: Allyn & Bacon.

some perspective to this discussion, take a look at an excerpt from an actual teacher contract from the 1920s, shown in Figure 10.6.

PERSONAL CONDUCT AND JOB PERFORMANCE. The notion that teachers can be automatically fired for what is considered by the community as immoral behavior was rejected by the California Supreme Court in *Morrison* v. *State Board of Education,* 1969. The court found that grounds for dismissal must include evidence that the personal conduct of a teacher adversely affects job performance. The Morrison case involved a teacher who had a brief homosexual relationship with another teacher. When the superintendent found out, Morrison's teaching license was revoked on the grounds that his immoral conduct was contrary to the moral standards of the people of California. However, the court ruled in favor of Morrison and said the term *immoral* was interpreted too broadly. No evidence was found to connect Morrison's personal life and his professional work.

In *Morrison,* the California Supreme Court said it was dangerous to allow the terms *immoral* and *unprofessional* to be interpreted too broadly. The court established that immoral conduct means vastly different things to different people. To some immoral behavior includes laziness, gluttony, selfishness, and cowardice, and unprofessional conduct for teachers may include signing controversial petitions, opposing majority opinions, and drinking alcoholic

Figure 10.6 Excerpt from 1920s teacher contract

I promise to abstain from all dancing, immodest dressing, and any other conduct unbecoming a teacher and a lady. I promise not to go out with any young men except in so far as it may be necessary to stimulate Sunday School work.

I promise not to fall in love, to become engaged, or secretly marry.

I promise to sleep at least eight hours at night [and] to eat carefully . . . in order that I may be better able to render efficient service to my pupils.

Source: Fischer, L., Schimmel, D., & Stellman, L. R. (2007). *Teachers and the law* (7th ed.). Boston: Allyn & Bacon.

beverages. The court ruled that a teacher should not be fired because someone disapproves of the teacher's personal life unless it directly relates to his or her professional work and that today's morals may well be considered absurd in the future (Fischer, Schimmel, & Stellman, 2007). Generally the courts have ruled that teachers have the right to privacy in regard to procreation, marriage, child rearing, and other activities in the home (Underwood & Webb, 2006).

Since 1969 other cases have been brought to courts by teachers who felt they were wrongly dismissed. The courts continue to look for evidence that particular conduct adversely affects job performance. In *Eckmann* v. *Board of Education,* 1986, an Illinois teacher was fired when she became pregnant while unmarried and decided to raise the child as a single parent. The judge found in favor of the teacher and said that she had a due process right to conceive and raise her child, even out of wedlock, and without school board intrusion (Fischer et al., 2007). In contrast, and in what may seem like a frivolous situation, a high school teacher was not rehired because she refused to stop wearing short skirts. In *Tardif* v. *Quinn,* 1976, the court recognized the teacher's constitutional right to choose her grooming but ruled that the right did not extend to wearing whatever she pleased during the school workday.

As with personal conduct, if a district wants to fire a teacher for health reasons (e.g., obesity, disabilities, AIDS), it must show a direct link between the health problem and impaired classroom function. And there is a considerable gray area when it comes to the following situations:

- conviction of a misdemeanor or felony
- possession or use of illegal drugs
- overuse of alcohol

Figure 10.7 summarizes the cases in this section along with several others that concern teachers' personal lives.

Points of Reflection 10.4

Do you think the role of teacher carries with it personal restraints? Would you be willing to alter your lifestyle somewhat to conform with what a particular community considers moral and professional behavior?

Figure 10.7 Case law: Teachers' personal lives

Morrison v. *State Board of Education* (1969)
Teacher keeps position because behavior does not directly affect job performance.

Tardif v. *Quinn* (1976)
Teacher challenges dress code but does not keep job.

Thompson v. *Southwest District* (1980)
Teacher unmarried cohabitation
A female teacher was fired because she lived with her boyfriend. Although she didn't particularly keep the arrangement a secret, when the school board suspended her for immorality, they publicized it. The court ruled that it was unfair to make the issue public in an attempt to gain support. In addition, the court found that living with her boyfriend did not diminish the teacher's classroom effectiveness. The board lost and the teacher kept her job.

Eckmann v. *Board of Education* (1986)
Single teacher raising child keeps job.

Ware v. *Morgan County School District* (1988)
Teacher using obscene language toward students
A Colorado high school music teacher took a misbehaving student outside and used obscene language to tell him he was a disgrace to the band. The teacher was fired and the court sided with the school district.

Elvin v. *City of Waterville* (1990)
A divorced female fourth grade teacher was fired for having sexual relations with her 15-year-old neighbor boy. Although he had never been her student, the court agreed with the school district's decision to fire her saying she had proven herself unfit to teach. The judge added that public awareness of her conduct undermined her ability to deal with students and parents.

Sources: Dunklee, D. R., & Shoop, R. J. (2002). *The principal's quick-reference guide to school law: Reducing liability, litigation, and other potential legal tangles* by D. R. Dunklee and R. J. Shoop, 2002. Thousand Oaks, CA: Corwin Press. LaMorte, J. W. (2008). *School law: Cases and concepts* (9th ed.). Boston: Allyn & Bacon. Fischer, L., Schimmel, D., & Stellman, L. R. (2007). *Teachers and the law* (7th ed.). Boston: Allyn & Bacon.

MISCONDUCT WITH STUDENTS. The most clear-cut decisions involving the firing of teachers on moral grounds involve misconduct with students. When a teacher's personal life or habits intersect a student's in illegal or morally questionable ways, it is relatively easy for a school district to dismiss a teacher for

- sexual relations with students
- profane, abusive language directed at students
- allowing students to drink alcohol
- encouraging students to be dishonest

What Are the Legal Responsibilities of Teachers?

Teachers have many responsibilities, some dictated by laws and others by state, district, or school policies. Some responsibilities are governed by ethical and professional guidelines.

LIABILITY

To be **liable** means to be responsible for. We generally hear the term in a negative sense, for instance, "He was found liable for the accident" or "That will raise my liability insurance premium." In a positive sense, though, liability is what teaching is all about—accepting responsibility for students while they are under our supervision. This is why we study such aspects as child development, subject matter, instructional and assessment strategies, guidelines for health and safety, and school law. However, being held liable when something goes wrong is far from positive. Depending on the severity of the issue, liability for a situation can end a career.

Teachers serve *in loco parentis,* "in place of parents." They are bound by law to care for and protect children in the school setting as a parent would and are held to a standard of reasonableness. Teachers, schools, and districts are frequently sued over issues related to liability. For a school employee to be considered liable for something, the following four components must be proven to be present:

1. The person has a legal duty to protect students.
2. The person fails to act within reason and provide the appropriate standard of care.
3. There is a causal connection between the person's conduct and the result of the injury.
4. Actual damage occurs to the injured person. (LaMorte, 2008)

Focus teacher Chris Roberts believes in teaching through a variety of experiences. He is responsible for student safety when he takes his class on field trips.

In the case of *Mancha* v. *Field Museum of Natural History,* 1971, students ages 12 to 15 went on a field trip with teachers to the Chicago Natural History Museum. The students were allowed to tour the exhibits on their own. One student was beaten up by teenagers from another school. In this case, the teachers had a legal duty to protect students (1), and there was actual damage (4). The court had to decide if the teachers failed to act within reason and provide an appropriate standard of care (2) and if there was a causal connection between the teachers' conduct and the injury (3). The teachers were not held liable for the student's injuries because the court determined there was minimal risk at the museum, and the teachers could not reasonably have been expected to directly supervise them.

In a similar case the same year, an eighth grader sustained a severe eye injury when a student threw rocks during a baseball game. The teacher involved in *Sheehan* v. *St. Peter's*

Catholic School, 1971, had accompanied the students outside but then returned to the building. The courts determined that the teacher left the area and therefore was not properly supervising the students. She was found liable for leaving students alone in a potentially dangerous setting.

Teachers can take some precautions that will lessen the causal connection between their actions and any harm that may come to students. Here are a few to consider:

- Be 100% present when with students. Limit personal distractions and remain focused.
- Think through situations and, if possible, avoid those that have unusual potential for danger.
- Establish routines and rules that make safety a habit among students.
- Remind students of appropriate behavior to help them remain safe.

Accidents happen—in the classroom, the hallway, the cafeteria, the science lab, the gym, on school grounds, and on field trips. Additional cases involving teacher liability are summarized in Figure 10.8. Using good judgment in the *in loco parentis* role will be enough for most teachers. But occasionally students are injured and teacher liability may be questioned. Liability insurance is a good idea. Teacher organizations offer reasonably priced policies that are recommended even for student teachers. These organizations often also provide legal assistance to members who find themselves involved in a school-related lawsuit.

Points of Reflection 10.5

Have you considered the many ways things may go wrong for teachers and students? Were you ever involved in a situation where a teacher's liability was questioned? If so, what were the circumstances?

COPYRIGHT LAWS

Copyright laws provide guidelines for authorized use of someone else's intellectual property and are intended to protect the rights of creators of intellectual property by preventing others from copying or distributing it without permission. Intellectual property includes written material, original audio and visual work, and computer programs.

Copyrighted materials may be used under three conditions: the user has permission from the copyright owner, the work is in the public domain, or the use is considered "fair

Figure 10.8 Case law: Teacher liability

Kaufman **v.** *City of New York* (1961)
Teacher supervising basketball
A boy was seriously injured when he bumped heads with another boy during a basketball game. The court ruled that any amount of supervision could not have prevented the accident and that the school and teacher were not liable.

Morris **v.** *Douglas County School District* (1965)
Teacher's lack of caution on field trip
A first grade teacher took her students on a field trip to the Oregon coast. While students waded in the water, a large wave washed a log onto a student causing serious injury. The court found that the teacher was liable because this kind of injury was not uncommon and the teacher was responsible for the safety of the young children in her care.

Mancha **v.** *Field Museum of Natural History* (1971)
Teacher allowing students to "self-guide" during field trip is not held liable for injury.

Sheehan **v.** *St. Peter's Catholic School* (1971)
Teacher leaving students on field
The teacher had accompanied the students outside but then returned to the building. The courts determined that the teacher left the area and therefore was not properly supervising the students.

Station **v.** *Travelers Insurance Co.* (1974)
Teacher leaving students during class is held liable for student injury.

Sources: LaMorte, J. W. (2008). *School law: Cases and concepts* (9th ed.). Boston: Allyn & Bacon. Fischer, L., Schimmel, D., & Stellman, L. R. (2007). *Teachers and the law* (7th ed.). Boston: Allyn & Bacon.

Figure 10.9 Guidelines for classroom copying

1. A single copy may be made of any of the following for your own scholarly research or use in teaching:
   - a chapter from a book
   - an article from a periodical or newspaper
   - a short story, short essay, or short poem
   - a chart, graph, diagram, drawing, cartoon or picture from a book, periodical, or newspaper.

2. Multiple copies (no more than one per student) may be made for classroom use if each copy gives credit to the copyright holder and passes three tests.
   - The brevity test includes guidelines such as poems of fewer than 200 words and prose of fewer than 2,500 words.
   - The spontaneity test generally says that you are inspired to copy and use material for the sake of teaching effectiveness and there was not time to ask and receive permission.
   - The cumulative effect test generally restricts the length of time copied material is used and how many instances of copying take place in a period of time.

3. Teachers cannot copy individual works and put them together to serve as an anthology.

4. Students cannot be charged for the photocopying of copyrighted works.

Source: Underwood, J., & Webb, L. D. (2006). *School law for teachers: Concepts and applications.* Upper Saddle River, NJ: Merrill/Prentice Hall.

use." A work is in the **public domain** if it is more than 75 years old or is published by a government agency. **Fair use** allows the nonprofit reproduction of certain materials in the classroom without permission of the copyright owner (Underwood & Webb, 2006, p. 87). Generally, fair use stipulates that the material copied must be for educational purposes and that the amount copied must fall within certain guidelines, some of which are listed in Figure 10.9. Teachers may not, however, make copies of consumable products such as textbooks, workbooks, and standardized test materials. If copies could be freely made of these kinds of materials, then their creators and publishers would lose money because the need for them would diminish.

Because teachers often want students to create work using certain computer software, it is important to know that computer software is copyrighted and that fair use guidelines do not apply. Some software publishers allow one backup copy to be made, but more than this is illegal. Additionally, commercially produced videos may not be copied. Copies made of television programs can be kept for 45 days and then must be erased or destroyed.

With the Internet serving as a major research tool in classrooms today, teachers must be aware that what is on the Internet is not in the public domain. Because the Internet is international, laws governing its use are somewhat unclear. Following fair use guidelines is a safe way to use Web resources.

Whether using written works, audiovisual materials, computer software, or information from the Internet, teachers must take copyright laws seriously. School districts have policies based on fair use guidelines. A school's media specialist is often a helpful, knowledgeable source of information about what is lawful and what is not. Teachers should ask if there is any question about how they plan to use any form of intellectual property.

REPORTING SUSPECTED CHILD ABUSE

A teacher who has a reasonable suspicion of child abuse or neglect has a legal obligation to report it to a school counselor or administrator, who in turn will report it to a social services agency or the police. Teachers don't have to be certain that they are correct. They are granted immunity and may not be sued for reporting their suspicions (Fischer et al., 2007).

It is a good idea for teachers to keep lists of signs of abuse and neglect handy for easy reference. Teachers should never become too busy to be observant. Physical abuse may be visually evident and difficult to miss. However, sexual abuse may be more subtle in terms of symptoms, and emotional or mental abuse may be even more difficult to detect. Reviewing the signs periodically, watching for behavioral or emotional changes, and reporting suspicions of abuse or neglect to administrators or school counselors will help protect students. This is a teacher's legal and ethical responsibility—and simply the right thing to do.

We discuss signs of abuse and neglect in Chapter 9, specifically Figure 9.2.

Teacher responsibilities obviously include protecting their students however and whenever they can. Teacher responsibilities also include safeguarding students' rights.

How Does the Law Impact the Relationship Between School and Religion?

The First Amendment makes it clear that the founders of the United States did not want government to have any say in how or whether citizens worship. Because public schools are government entities, they may neither establish religion nor interfere with the free exercise of it. As clearly stated as it is in the Constitution, the issue is anything but clear cut in practice. Few topics are as charged with emotion and passion, and hence with such potential to polarize people, as religion.

Let's establish some basic dos and don'ts for teachers and students with regard to religion and education. In 1998 President Clinton asked Secretary of Education Richard Riley to prepare guidelines based on law and court decisions to help educators determine the rights of students and staff regarding religion and public schools. For easy reference, these guidelines are adapted to question format in Figure 10.10.

Figure 10.10 Guidelines for religious expression in public schools from the U.S. Department of Education

Can students pray in school?
Yes. Students may pray individually or in a group as long as they are nondisruptive. For instance, students may pray before meals or tests to the same extent they may engage in comparable nondisruptive activities.

Can students read religious materials and discuss religion among themselves?
Yes. Students may read and talk about religion to the same extent as they may read and talk about anything else in school.

Can students meet to express their religious beliefs during the school day and on school grounds?
Yes. Students may meet for nondisruptive purposes during their lunch periods or other noninstructional time during the school day, as well as before and after the school day. This includes religion-related meetings.

Is it legal to have organized prayer at sporting events or other school functions?
No. Under current Supreme Court decisions, school officials may not mandate or organize prayer at any school-sponsored event or graduation.

Can teachers participate in religious meetings while at school?
No. Teachers and school administrators, when acting in those capacities, are representatives of the state and are prohibited from soliciting or encouraging religious activity, and from participating in such activity with students.

Can teachers teach about religions in school?
Yes. Teachers may teach *about* religion, including the Bible or other scripture: the history of religion, comparative religion, the Bible (or other scripture)-as-literature, and the role of religion in the history of the United States and other countries. They may also prompt students to consider religious influences on art, music, literature, and social studies.

Can teachers display religious-related holiday items or encourage the celebration of religious holidays in school?
No. Although public schools may teach *about* religious holidays, including their religious aspects, and may celebrate the secular aspects of holidays, schools may not observe holidays as religious events or encourage students to do so.

(continued)

Figure 10.10 Continued

Is it acceptable for students to express religious beliefs in school assignments?
Yes. Students may express their beliefs about religion in the form of homework, artwork, and other written and oral assignments free of discrimination based on the religious content of their work. The assignments should be graded according to the standards the lesson is intended to address.

If a lesson may be considered offensive by a student and/or the student's family, can the student opt not to participate?
Yes. Schools can excuse individual students from lessons that are objectionable to the student or the students' parents on religious or other conscientious grounds.

Can students opt out of a particular dress code or uniform for religious reasons?
Legally, the answer is no. However, schools have discretion to interpret this in ways that make sense in their communities.

Can students wear religious messages or symbols on their clothes?
Yes. The restrictions are the same as for any other comparable messages. Schools can not single out religion-related messages and symbols to prohibit.

Source: Adapted from Riley, R. W. (1998). *Secretary's statement on religious expression.* Retrieved November 12, 2006, from www.ed.gov/inits/religionandschools.

RELIGION AND COMPULSORY EDUCATION

> Private and parochial schools and homeschooling are discussed in Chapter 2.

Compulsory education laws require students to attend school through a certain age. *Pierce v. Society of Sisters,* 1925, established that compulsory education laws could be met through attendance at private or parochial schools. In the 1970s, Amish families asked to be exempt from compulsory education beyond eighth grade on the grounds that attendance in upper grades would have a negative effect on their traditions and way of life. The Supreme Court ruled in their favor in *Wisconsin v. Yoder,* 1972. This ruling is known as the "Amish exception." If non-Amish parents wish to isolate their children from public or private school beyond a particular grade (under age 16), they must show that school will somehow destroy their religion. Homeschooling is a legal option with very few requirements or constraints. Because families aren't required to supply a reason for homeschooling, it is unknown how many families use their right to homeschool their children as a way to avoid compulsory education laws.

Students may pray together on school grounds, as long as it is not disruptive to the education process.

PRAYER IN SCHOOL

Students may pray silently or quietly in small groups in school. But that's it. Legally there may be no school-sponsored public prayer, even nondenominational prayer (Underwood & Webb, 2006). This prohibition includes prayer at gatherings such as graduation ceremonies, football games, and assemblies. In *Santa Fe Independent School District* v. *Doe,* 2000, a Texas school district allowed students to vote on whether to have prayer and who would deliver it before football games. Groups of Mormon and Catholic students, alumni, and parents filed a suit claiming the district was violating the First Amendment. The U.S. Supreme Court ruled against the district, contending that the school would be endorsing a specific religion depending on who delivered the prayer.

Some communities choose to violate the First Amendment principle of separation of church and state by endorsing prayer in school-related settings. If challenged, they would likely lose in court. Some school boards even begin their meetings with prayer, often careful not to use language that would offend Christians or Jews. However, these prayers may offend Muslims,

Buddhists, and other religious groups, as well as atheists. Regardless of who is present, prayer is not legal in public education meetings.

RELIGIOUS ORGANIZATIONS MEETING ON SCHOOL GROUNDS

If a school building is used before or after hours for organizations of any kind, it may also be used for organizations that are religious in nature. In *Good News Club* v. *Milford Central School,* 2001, the Supreme Court ruled that a private Christian organization for children ages 6 to 12 in New York could use a public school for weekly after-school meetings. Although some lower courts have ruled that teachers may be involved in student religious organizations on their own time, generally school employees may not sponsor the groups (Fischer et al., 2007).

RELIGIOUS HOLIDAYS. Observing specific religious holidays in class is not allowed. This is a visible and controversial aspect of mixing school and religion. The longest traditional school breaks or vacations (other than summer) occur during Christian celebrations—December break at Christmas and spring break at Easter. What was once called Christmas break is now generally referred to as the winter holiday. The traditional holiday student presentation once called the Christmas Program is now the choral/band event that may be referred to as the Holiday or Winter Program. Students may sing Christmas songs with religious messages, such as "Silent Night," but these songs may not dominate the program.

Holiday displays that depict Christian or Christmas symbols may be used if they are balanced with other cultural symbols such as a Jewish menorah. The displays must be temporary and help show diversity (Underwood & Webb, 2006). Parents and students may request to be exempt from activities focused on holidays.

RELIGION AND CURRICULUM. Must schools do away with all reference to religion to separate church and state? The answer is no. It is permissible to teach about religion but not with the purpose of convincing students that a particular belief should be followed. Use of the Bible, Talmud, Koran, and other religious books for teaching literature and history is permissible as long as one is not endorsed over another.

Perhaps the greatest point of tension concerning religion and curriculum is the theory of evolution. In the so-called Scopes Monkey Trial, 1925, a high school teacher was convicted of violating a Tennessee regulation against teaching anything that contradicted the biblical Genesis account of the creation of humans. Although the conviction was overturned on a technicality, controversy over the teaching of evolution in schools has continued. In 1982 Louisiana passed the Balanced Treatment Act, which required the teaching of both creationism and evolution. The U.S. Supreme Court ruled the act illegal because it endorsed creationism, a Christian view, to the exclusion of other views. Some school districts, and even whole states, have attempted to give equal time to what some Christians believe about creation as embodied in the literal translation of the Bible and to evolution. Some districts have attempted to outlaw the teaching of evolution or to require a disclaimer stating that it is only a theory, one of many that tries to explain the origin of humans.

Figure 10.11 summarizes the cases in this section plus two others that affect how religion and schools coexist.

As you can see, the rights and responsibilities of teachers and students often intersect at the delicate point of separation of church and state. In some communities, and at some times of the year, preserving this separation is challenging.

What Are the Legal Rights of Students?

Students do not leave their constitutional rights at the schoolhouse door. You may notice that there isn't a section of this chapter devoted to students' legal responsibilities. If there were, the section would be short. Students have the responsibility to go to school as long as it is compulsory (usually to age 16, but to age 18 in some locations). That's about it in terms of legal responsibilities. Although we hope students take responsibility for their learning

> We discuss controversy and the curriculum in Chapter 4.

Points of Reflection 10.6

Did you or your family ever have religion-based views that conflicted with events at your school? Were your views conservative (opposition to dancing, nonacceptance of evolution theory, nonparticipation when certain movies were shown, etc.)? Were there restrictions imposed that you believed unnecessary?

Figure 10.11 Case law: Religion in schools

Wisconsin **v.** *Yoder* **(1972)**
Amish allowed to end formal education at eighth grade.

Stone **v.** *Graham* **(1980)**
Parents protest posting of Ten Commandments
A Kentucky statute required the posting of the Ten Commandments on the wall of every public school classroom. The plaques were purchased with private funds and had a notation describing them as secular. The posting was declared unconstitutional on the grounds that merely stating that the Ten Commandments (rooted in Judeo-Christian beliefs) were secular did not make it so.

Herdahl **v.** *Pontotoc County School District* **(1996)**
Parent protested prayer in public school
A Mississippi mother sued a K–12 school for having prayers following morning announcements on the intercom. The court ruled that the practice violated separation of church and state because the students are a captive audience. This case was an example of violations of already established law that continue to go through our judicial system.

Santa Fe Independent School District **v.** *Doe* **(2000)**
Public prayer at school events violates the First Amendment because the school would be endorsing a specific religion, depending on who delivered the invocation.

Good News Club **v.** *Milford Central School* **(2001)**
Student Christian group allowed to use school facilities.

Sources: Fischer, L., Schimmel, D., & Stellman, L. R. (2007). *Teachers and the law.* Boston: Allyn & Bacon. McNergney, R. F., & McNergney, J. M. (2009). *Education: The practice and profession of teaching.* Boston: Allyn & Bacon.

and behavior, unless their behavior is deemed illegal or extremely disruptive, there are no other laws binding them.

FREEDOM OF EXPRESSION

Before 1969 students were not recognized as having First Amendment rights to freedom of expression. The U.S. Supreme Court's decision in *Tinker* v. *Des Moines Independent Community School District,* 1969, provided a clear message that a student is entitled to freedom of expression (LaMorte, 2008). The case involved three students who wore armbands to protest the war in Vietnam. They were suspended and subsequently sued the district. In this monumentally important case the U.S. Supreme Court ruled that teachers and students do not "shed their rights to freedom of speech or expression at the schoolhouse gate." The *Tinker* case has been cited repeatedly since 1969.

However, court challenges since *Tinker* have served to balance the rights of students to express themselves and the necessity of limiting personal freedom to ensure the safety and well-being of others. For students, understanding the need for this balance is a lesson in the principles of democracy.

FREEDOM OF SYMBOLIC EXPRESSION. The *Tinker* decision so influenced how students are viewed in relation to freedom of expression that it is known as the *Tinker doctrine*. This doctrine extends to symbolic freedom. As with other rights, students are allowed to express their views symbolically through what they wear as long as it doesn't disrupt the educational process.

Dress Codes. Since the 1960s, numerous lawsuits have been initiated over the restrictions imposed by dress codes, but the U.S. Supreme Court has not ruled on the issue. In 1972 Justice Black wrote that the U.S. Constitution doesn't require the courts to bear the burden of supervising clothing or hairstyles.

However, schools are concerned about immodest dress and unusual hairstyles because they could disrupt the educational atmosphere of the classroom as well as lead to more serious issues. For instance, violence generated by gangs and groups such as the "trench coat mafia" (the students associated with the 1999 Columbine school shootings) has prompted educators to identify and attempt to ban insignia clothing and hats associated with specific groups. LaMorte (2008) lists the following as school concerns:

- T-shirts depicting violence, drugs (e.g., marijuana leaves), racial epithets
- ripped, baggy, or saggy pants or jeans
- colored bandanas
- baseball or other hats
- words shaved into scalps
- brightly colored hair
- exposed underwear
- tattoos, . . . pierced noses
- decorative dental caps (p. 172)

These forms of symbolic expression are not protected by the First Amendment because they may contribute to school unrest. Most dress codes outlaw some or all of the items in LaMorte's list. However, because some of the items are associated with particular cultures, it is difficult for schools to designate them without appearing to be biased. Rules designating shirt length, requiring belts, and prohibiting exposed midriffs are more generic but still hard to enforce.

Students often enjoy expressing personal taste in their choices of clothing and shoes.

Uniforms. Dress codes are often ambiguous, leaving much room for interpretation. They can infringe on learning time if teachers are expected to watch for and report violations. Thus some schools and entire districts choose to impose a uniform policy, giving students several modest, relatively plain choices of clothing. Currently, more than half the states have schools with uniform policies. Some large cities, such as Long Beach, Chicago, and San Antonio, require at least elementary students to wear uniforms. In 2002 Memphis, Tennessee, became the nation's first large public school district to adopt a uniform policy in all of its 175 schools.

Public schools that impose uniform policies must provide an opt-out clause for parents who don't want their children to participate. For instance, some parents may not want their children to wear a uniform because it conflicts with the clothing traditions of their religion. Other parents may request to be exempt simply because their children don't want to wear the uniform and are persistently making that clear. Private schools do not receive government support and, unlike public schools, may impose a uniform policy on all students without allowing them to opt out.

Before we discuss student freedom of speech, consider this chapter's ***Diversity Dialogue*** (p. 288) involving focus teacher Brenda Beyal and a dilemma she faced that began with symbolic freedom. Reflect on the opportunities for Brenda and her students to learn about aspects of culture and a belief system with which they are not familiar.

Points of Reflection 10.7

Did your schools have dress codes or uniforms? What do you remember about them? Did you feel that your freedom of expression was restricted by what the schools said you could and couldn't wear?

As a future teacher, do you like the idea of dress codes or uniforms? Why or why not? Are they more important at particular levels of school?

FREEDOM OF SPEECH. The freedom of speech implied in *Tinker* was challenged in 1986 when a student made a speech containing sexual innuendo in a high school assembly. He was reprimanded and subsequently sued the school, claiming that his freedom of speech was denied. The case, *Bethel School District No. 403* v. *Fraser,* 1986, went to the U.S. Supreme Court, where the adolescent lost. The court ruled that a school does not have to accept indecent or offensive speech.

Although students enjoy free speech, it does have limits. An individual student's freedom of speech, as well as freedom of the press, must be balanced against the school's ability to maintain a safe and civil atmosphere, where all students are shown respect.

FREEDOM OF THE PRESS. School publications have long been fertile ground for disputes about students' rights to express themselves. In attempts to make school newspapers relevant and truly student owned, students tend to write about what's on the minds of classmates, no matter how controversial. However, it is clear from court decisions such as

Brenda Beyal, as a teacher in a multiage classroom, enjoys the fact that her school, colleagues, and students are open minded and accepting of differences. She also enjoys the status of her school as an arts-focused elementary. The arrival of fifth grade twin girls in Benda's classroom 2 weeks after school began proved to be both a challenge and an opportunity.

Amira and Farah were the first children of traditional Muslim parents to attend Brenda's school. These 11-year-old twins walked into Brenda's classroom one Friday morning in September. They wore loose-fitting pants and long tunic tops, along with scarves on their heads that completely covered their hair. Amira and Farah smiled sweetly and took their seats at a table with three other children. Brenda welcomed them and invited the girls to introduce themselves to the class. Amira went first and explained that her name means *princess* in Islam. Then Farah followed suit by saying that her name means *happiness*.

Brenda had been told she would have two new students, but she had not been told that the girls were part of a very traditional Muslim family and that there would be some challenges because of their presence as the first students of Islamic faith. Here are some of the challenges Brenda faced:

- A school rule states that headgear may not be worn in the school building. The girls wore *hijab,* traditional Muslim headwear.

- Amira and Farah arrived in the middle of Ramadan, a Muslim month in which believers fast during daylight hours.

- Amira and Farah are required to pray five times a day, and two of the times fall within the school day.

- The parents of Amira and Farah talked with Principal Larsen and told him they are aware that his school is known for the arts. They have concerns because (in their tradition) dance serves no purpose and needlessly causes girls and boys to come in contact, they find some music offensive, and Muslim children are not allowed to draw human figures.

- Sentiment in the United States is generally unfavorable toward people of the Muslim faith, especially following the events of 9/11. The uncle of one of Brenda's students was killed in the New York City bombing of the World Trade Center.

Think about Brenda's challenges and opportunities to help all her students learn from, and about, each other's similarities and differences. Respond to these items by writing one well-developed paragraph each.

1. Is it legal for Amira and Farah to pause twice each day for prayer and refuse to eat lunch during Ramadan? If not, why? If so, how might Brenda explain this to her students?

2. Should the school rules be relaxed to allow Amira and Farah to wear *hijab*? If not, how should Brenda handle the situation? If so, how might Brenda explain this rule variation to her students?

3. On September 11 of each school year, a tradition at Rees consists of students reading stories written by children about the heroes of 9/11. Laura, the niece of a firefighter who lost his life in the World Trade Center bombing, brings a picture of her uncle each year as part of a memorial. When Amira and Farah arrive at Rees, the commemoration is only a few days away. Brenda anticipates there will be questions from students, perhaps expressed privately to her, about whether the new girls are part of the group responsible for the tragedy. What are three points Brenda should make to her students?

Hazelwood School District v. *Kuhlmeier,* 1988, that teachers and administrators may exercise editorial control over school publications. In this case, two articles written by students for a Missouri high school newspaper were deleted by the principal. The main topics of the articles were teen pregnancy and divorce, and they contained references to sexuality the principal thought inappropriate for younger students. In addition, even though their names were changed, the principal was concerned that students written about in the articles were identifiable. The Supreme Court ruled in favor of the district, stating that educators may exercise substantial control over school-sponsored publications and events.

For all three forms of expression—symbolic, speech, and written—students' rights must be balanced with what is in the best interest of the school population. The adults in charge—school board members, district personnel, administrators, and teachers—must be vigilant and protect student rights while also protecting those who may be adversely affected by the exercise of those rights.

THE RIGHT TO BE PROTECTED

Freedom of expression refers to what students may do. The right to be protected is freedom from actions that may be imposed on students.

SEARCH AND SEIZURE. The Fourth Amendment provides for citizens to be secure from unreasonable search and seizure. This right applies to students in schools—to a point. The courts have attempted to balance the student's right to privacy and the school's need to know. The key term is *reasonableness*. In *New Jersey* v. *T.L.O.*, 1985, two high school girls were accused of smoking in the bathroom. One admitted it, and one (T.L.O.) denied it. In the principal's office T.L.O. was asked to empty her purse. In it were cigarettes, cigarette-rolling paper, marijuana, a pipe, a roll of money, and a list titled "People who owe me money." The student was turned over to juvenile court. She sued the school for invasion of privacy. The U.S. Supreme Court ruled against her and maintained that the search and seizure were reasonable.

In most cases the courts have ruled against schools that arbitrarily and routinely search lockers, use drug-sniffing dogs, and search through students' clothes. Privacy is upheld as a right unless a search is deemed reasonable. But school lockers are part of school property. If there are reasonable suspicions of contraband in lockers, they may be searched.

Drug testing as a form of search of students remains controversial among the general public. However, since about 2000 most court decisions have ruled that drug testing is permissible for all students who participate in extracurricular activities, making no distinction between basketball and debate teams.

If there is reasonable suspicion for a search, the search itself must be reasonably conducted. Age and gender need to be considered. Walking through a metal detector or putting a book bag through a detector is noninvasive and considered reasonable if there have been problems with weapons at the school. Searching lockers, either by hand or using dogs, is more invasive but reasonable if there is suspicion. Asking students to empty their pockets and take off coats may be called for and is reasonable. However, strip searches are very invasive and should only be done if there is probable cause (more stringent than reasonable suspicion) and by proper authorities, not by teachers. The courts have been split on the legality of strip searches. In elementary school strip searches are typically supported by the courts, whereas in middle and high school they are sometimes not supported by court decisions. This kind of intrusive search should not be done by teachers alone under any circumstances.

SEXUAL HARASSMENT. According to the American Association of University Women (AAUW) (2001), **sexual harassment** is behavior with sexual implications that is neither wanted nor welcome. It interferes with a person's life. Sexual harassment may include obvious looks with lewd intent, taunts with sexual innuendo, touching, kissing, groping, and any actions or behaviors that have sexual connotations. The AAUW conducted a survey in 1993, and again in 2001, of eighth and eleventh grade students to gauge the extent of sexual harassment in schools. The survey revealed that 80% in both grade levels experienced sexual harassment. The results served as a wake-up call for schools as sexual harassment came into the public eye. However, a positive change is that in 2001, 69% of respondents, as opposed to only a small percentage in 1990, reported knowing about school policies against sexual harassment and the consequences for harassing. Awareness has increased, but the problem persists.

This chapter's Letter to the Editor highlights an incident of sexual harassment that occurred in 2006 in Mt. Lebanon, Pennsylvania. Excerpts from two articles published in the *Pittsburgh Post-Gazette*, shown in Figure 10.12, set the stage for the letter. Although one or

Points of Reflection 10.8

Did you ever sense that your freedom of speech or press was restricted in some way in high school? Were you on a newspaper staff? Did anyone censor or limit in any way how students could express themselves in the paper? If so, how? What was your reaction?

Points of Reflection 10.9

Did you ever experience any form of search as a student in K–12 schools? What experiences do you recall of teachers or administrators acting on their suspicions of contraband? Have you or has anyone you know been subjected to a locker or clothing search? If so, what were the circumstances and how did you or the other person respond?

Do you think teachers and administrators should be able to conduct random searches?

Figure 10.12 Articles dealing with sexual harassment

Explicit ranking of high school girls sparks outrage in Mt. Lebanon

'Top 25' list details students' looks, bodies

Wednesday, April 26, 2006

By Mary Niederberger and Nikki Schwab, *Pittsburgh Post-Gazette*

The Mt. Lebanon School District and Mt. Lebanon police are investigating the distribution of an anonymous document that features sexually explicit descriptions of 25 girls at the high school.

The document, titled "Top 25 in 2006," ranks the girls in order from one to 25. It includes their names, grade levels and photos.

Each girl is assigned a letter grade for her breasts, buttocks and face, followed by a brief description of each girl in crude and vulgar terms.

There are references to girls performing oral sex and comments about their height and weight. . . . "I think that it's outrageous, the equivalent of a written rape on our daughter," said the father of one girl, who didn't want his name published to protect his daughter's identity.

He and another parent said they are frustrated that the district hasn't disciplined the students who created the publication. . . .

The second father said he has done some investigating and talked to students, including his children, who told him that ballots to choose the "Top 25" were circulated at high school basketball games and that students had been seen reading the list in the school cafeteria.

He said he embarked on his investigation after [the] Mt. Lebanon High School principal . . . told him that the list was not a district matter because none of the activities involved with it took place on school grounds. . . .

Mt. Lebanon Police Chief Thomas A. Ogden Jr. said the "Top 25" list is "in very poor taste," but that his department could not substantiate that any crime had been committed. . . .

[School officials] said the district is examining to see whether the publication violates the district's sexual harassment policy. . . .

Mt. Lebanon suspends student for role in list

'Too little, too late,' one girl's father says

Friday, May 05, 2006

A Mt. Lebanon High School student has been suspended for his involvement with a vulgar "Top 25" list of female students.

School officials wouldn't comment on any action taken, beyond a letter issued yesterday by Superintendent George D. Wilson, which states:

"Those proven to be responsible will receive consequences that include disciplinary action, a requirement for atonement and character education. However, since this is a student disciplinary matter, I am prohibited from releasing any confidential information."

The letter was mailed to high school parents and posted on the district's Web site. . . . Although the disciplinary action wasn't announced, the district must follow procedures set in state law when a student is removed from school.

If a suspension is longer than three school days, the student and parents must be offered an informal hearing within five days of the suspension. Formal hearings are required for expulsions, which by definition are longer than 10 school days.

The fathers of two of the girls whose names were on the list were angry when they read Dr. Wilson's letter.

"Way too little, way too late," said one of the fathers, who repeatedly has criticized the superintendent for not taking immediate action on the list when it was presented to him in early April. . . .

In his letter, Dr. Wilson said he was "appalled" by the actions of any student who participated "in any way." . . .

The superintendent's letter said the district will reinforce with all students "the importance of treating each other with respect and dignity. . . . Schools cannot control popular culture, but, together with the home, we exert a strong influence on how our students conduct themselves." The district has a policy prohibiting sexual harassment.

Letter to the Editor

This *Letter to the Editor* appeared in the Pittsburgh, Pennsylvania, newspaper, the *Post-Gazette*. It was written in response to the situation at Mt. Lebanon High School described in Figure 10.12.

MAY 6, 2006 WOMEN OBJECTIFIED

It is a sad comment on the state of our society that young men from a highly rated school district find nothing wrong in objectifying young women, humiliating them and possibly betraying their trust.

Does it really matter whether the list was compiled on school property? Obviously the school district and the parents of these young men fell down on the job when it came to instilling respect and good values in these young men.

And one has to wonder if the list had been a ranking of male students, teachers, administrators and/or police officers based on parts of their anatomies, whether the uproar and response would have been swifter, with more concern for the victims.

Celia Shapiro

Now it's your turn. These questions will help you write your own Letter to the Editor.

1. Would it be possible to determine if the list was made on school grounds? Even if the list was not written on campus, is it the school's responsibility to investigate and discipline students?

2. Whose responsibility is it, as the writer puts it, to instill respect and values? Who should be held responsible for the actions of the perpetrators? Why?

3. Do you agree that a similar incident with male victims might have received swifter action? Why or why not?

4. The articles refer to due process rights in disciplinary actions. Do you have a sense that these rights will be granted? Why or why not?

5. Are the parents overreacting? Explain your reasoning.

6. The superintendent says there will be a "requirement for atonement." What do you envision this might be?

Your letter should be in response to the *Pittsburgh Post-Gazette* letter: supporting it, adding information, or refuting it. Be prepared to share your letter. Write your letter in understandable terminology, remembering that readers of newspaper Letters to the Editor are citizens who may have limited knowledge of school practices and policies. Remember to refer to the letter assessment rubric in Chapter 1.

---

more high school students described in the articles may have been dismissed by some with the attitude of "Oh, well, boys will be boys," the young women, their families, and the community were clearly outraged by the sexual harassment perpetrated by these students.

When students report incidents that appear to be sexual harassment, teachers must take their complaints seriously. The ruling in *Davis* v. *Monroe County Board of Education,* 1999, determined that educators can be held liable if they do not respond to complaints of sexual harassment. A fifth grade girl in Georgia was groped and verbally harassed by a classmate. She and her parents repeatedly reported it to the school, but it continued. The family filed a lawsuit, and 6 years later the U.S. Supreme Court ruled in a 5-to-4 decision that the school failed to act appropriately to protect the girl.

Teachers must also be conscious of their own behavior with students to prevent it from being misconstrued as harassment. In the 2001 AAUW survey, 7% of the respondents said that teachers sexually harassed them. Teachers must be constantly aware of how students may perceive their actions.

When sexual harassment is detected, the school is likely to take disciplinary action. The range of possibilities, governed by both common sense and lawful procedures, is broad.

DISCIPLINARY ACTION. The U.S. court system has been clear that schools have the right to administer a variety of punishments based on policy. Relatively minor rule infractions call for relatively minor consequences or punishment that may be administered at the classroom or school level. Rule infractions that are more serious require more serious consequences.

CORPORAL PUNISHMENT. Fewer than half of states allow corporal punishment. Individual districts may choose not to allow corporal punishment even if allowed by the

Points of Reflection 10.10

Have you ever experienced sexual harassment? What were the circumstances? Was it addressed by anyone, or did it go unnoticed by everyone but you? How did it make you feel? Have you ever been guilty of sexually harassing someone else?

We discuss corporal punishment in Chapter 7.

Points of Reflection 10.11

Have you ever received corporal punishment in a school setting? If so, how did it make you feel? Have you ever been suspended or expelled? If so, did the exclusionary punishment take care of whatever behavior it was intended to curb?

Are corporal punishment, suspension, and expulsion ever justified? If not, why not? If so, under what circumstances?

state. People who are in favor of corporal punishment say it's necessary and educationally sound, while those who oppose it call it archaic, cruel, inhumane, and unjustifiable (LaMorte, 2008).

In *Ingraham* v. *Wright,* 1977, the Supreme Court found that corporal punishment does not violate the tenets of the Constitution. In this case two boys were paddled, causing bruises that kept them out of school for a few days. The court commented that schools can be held liable for injuries, but that students are not entitled to due process before district- or state-sanctioned corporal punishment is administered. The most common restrictions in states that permit corporal punishment are that only an administrator can spank or paddle a student, and there must be an adult witness. Teachers can lose their jobs if they violate state laws or local policies related to corporal punishment (Fischer et al., 2007).

EXCLUSIONARY PUNISHMENT. Exclusionary discipline, or discipline that takes students out of school, such as suspension and expulsion, carries with it the need for student due process, or steps that protect student rights (Pauken, 2006). Excluding students from school through suspension or expulsion has been ruled a denial of property rights to an education. Suspension is time out of school that may range from 1 day to less than a semester but is usually 10 days or less. Expulsion is more permanent and is generally for a semester or for an indefinite period.

Exclusionary punishment carries possible long-term consequences that may exceed the seriousness of the original offense. Any time away from school can be harmful to students in many ways. For instance, if a brief suspension causes a student to miss an exam, grades will suffer. Being out of school more than 10 days makes it almost impossible for a student to catch up. An expulsion almost always means a grade must be repeated. For some students a lengthy suspension or expulsion may make admission to college difficult or impossible.

Students are entitled to due process when exclusionary punishment is imposed or when the rule infraction and resulting punishment will become part of a student's permanent record. In the case of *Goss* v. *Lopez,* 1975, several Ohio high school students were suspended for up to 10 days without receiving a hearing. The students maintained complete innocence and were never informed of what they were accused of doing. When a federal district court agreed with the boys in their suit against the school, administrators appealed to the U.S. Supreme Court, where the decision went in favor of the students again. The justices wrote that students have a property right in school and that they may not be withdrawn without due process that includes

- written notification of time and place of hearing, along with a description of the procedures to be followed
- list of evidence to be presented and names of witnesses
- description of the substance of witnesses' testimonies
- taped or written record of the proceedings and findings
- notification of the right to appeal (Fischer et al., 2007)

STUDENT RIGHT OF NONPARTICIPATION. Students have a right to refuse to participate in some activities, including these that have been upheld in the courts.

- Students may refuse to recite the Pledge of Allegiance.
- Students may refuse to dance, even when it is part of the physical education curriculum.
- Students may have other literature substituted for the planned curriculum if they object for religious or other reasons.
- Students may opt out of certain courses (usually dealing with sex education) if they and their parents object to content.
- Parents may refuse to follow guidelines that require students to be immunized.

This list will no doubt grow as parents and students have their voices heard in the courts. Administrators and teachers need to be aware of students' rights to nonparticipation, or at least question the legitimacy of insisting on compliance with school policies and traditions.

STUDENT RECORDS: ACCESS AND PRIVACY. The **Family Educational Rights and Privacy Act (FERPA) of 1974,** commonly called the **Buckley Amendment,** allows parents and guardians access to their students' academic records and requires written parental permission for the records to be shared with anyone else. When students turn 18, they have control over who sees their records.

The Buckley Amendment establishes the minimum standards of privacy of records, with some states and districts going beyond to allow students access to their own records. Some items, however, are not subject to student or parent viewing. For instance, teachers' grade books, notes kept by teachers for their own use, and the private notes kept by school law enforcement teams typically remain inaccessible to others.

The extent to which student records must be kept private was tested when an Oklahoma parent challenged the long-standing practice of students grading each others' work in *Owasso Independent School District* v. *Falso,* 2002. The parent sued an Owasso school saying peer grading was embarrassing and often inaccurate. Because of conflicting court actions the case ended up in the U.S. Supreme Court, which ruled unanimously that day-to-day grading is not covered by FERPA.

RIGHT TO NONDISCRIMINATION. Students may not legally be discriminated against by public schools. Discrimination cases that have been tested in U.S. courts have resulted in the following principles:

- Students of any race, religion, or disability may attend U.S. public schools.
- Students who are married, are parents, or are divorced may attend the same public schools as those who are not.
- Students with HIV/AIDS pose no significant risk to others and may attend public schools.

Not only are all students guaranteed the right to attend public schools, but the right has also been extended to extracurricular activities.

Figure 10.13 summarizes the cases in this section plus others that deal with students' rights.

Figure 10.13 Case law: Student rights

Tinker v. *Des Moines Independent Community School District* (1969)
The rights of students to wear arm bands to protest the war in Vietnam was upheld.

Goss v. *Lopez* (1975)
Students suspended without due process. Court ruled that school attendance is a property right.

Ingraham v. *Wright* (1977)
Corporal punishment may be administered without due process in states that allow it.

New Jersey v. *T.L.O.* (1985)
Student's purse searched after she was caught smoking. Court ruled search was reasonable.

Bethel School District No. 403 v. *Fraser* (1986)
Student reprimanded for lewd language. Court said school has the right to censor to avoid school disruption.

Hazelwood School District v. *Kuhlmeier* (1988)
Schools have the right to censure controversial articles in school publications.

(continued)

Sources: Dunklee, D. R. & Shoop, R. J. (2002). *The principal's quick-reference guide to school law: Reducing liability, litigation, and other potential legal tangles.* Thousand Oaks, CA: Corwin Press. LaMorte, M. W. (2008). *School law: Cases and concepts* (9th ed.). Boston: Allyn and Bacon. Fischer, L., Schimmel, D., & Stellman, L. R. (2007). *Teachers and the law* (7th ed.). Boston: Allyn & Bacon.

CONCLUDING THOUGHTS

Controversial issues, such as sex and AIDS education, Internet usage, school choice, high-stakes testing, school uniforms, protection for homosexual students, and funding for public education, continue to emerge and will no doubt prompt legal questions. The courts will interpret the Constitution or rely on case law to settle disputes. Teachers need to stay current on how laws affect what takes place in classrooms and schools.

When you choose to teach you make a commitment to a service profession. You take on the serious responsibility not only to abide by laws but to continually promote what is ethical for students and for yourself in the big issues as well as in the seemingly minor issues that test you every day. You commit to thoughtful and deliberate decision making, the courage to do what's right for students, and the good sense to ask for advice and guidance when needed.

We began this chapter by considering Derek Boucher and his classroom at Roosevelt High School in California. Now as the chapter comes to an end we join Derek as he addresses issues that have come about as he sponsors a newsletter written by students in his reading remediation class. Read through *Chapter in Review* to help refresh your memory of what we have discussed, and then interact with Derek as he confronts challenges in *Developing Professional Competence.*

Chapter in Review

What does it mean to be an ethical teacher?

- Laws tell us what we can and can't do. Ethics tell us what we should and shouldn't do.
- The National Education Association provides a professional code of ethics for educators.
- To be an ethical teacher means to be guided by a set of beliefs that lead to attitudes and actions focused on what's best for students.
- Six characteristics that help teachers make ethical decisions include appreciation for moral deliberation, empathy, knowledge, reasoning, courage, and interpersonal skills.
- Ethical attitudes, decisions, and actions involve both major and seemingly minor issues.

- It is important to have a vision of the characteristics we want to help cultivate in our students.

How do laws affect schools, teachers, and students?

- The laws that affect schools, teachers, and students are based on a balance of rights and responsibilities.
- Four basic sources of law directly impact the work of teachers: the U.S. Constitution, federal laws, state and local laws and policies, and case law.

What are the legal rights of teachers?

- The legalities of employment include contracts, tenure, and dismissal.

- Due process involves a set of guidelines that must be followed to ensure that individuals are protected from arbitrary or capricious treatment by those in authority.
- Teachers enjoy the same rights as other citizens, including freedom of expression, whether symbolic, written, or spoken, but with restraints based on the responsibilities of teaching.
- Academic freedom is a form of expression that allows teachers to use their judgment concerning what and how to teach.
- Teachers have some restrictions on their personal lives that other people do not have because of the nature of the profession.

What are the legal responsibilities of teachers?

- Teachers serve *in loco parentis* and are responsible to care for and protect the students they supervise.
- Among other things, teachers have the legal responsibility to avoid liability, abide by copyright laws, and report suspected child abuse.

How does the law impact the relationship between school and religion?

- The First Amendment says that government (public schools) can neither establish religion nor interfere with the free exercise of it.

- Public prayer is illegal in public school. Religious organizations may meet and pray in school facilities outside regular school hours.
- It is permissible to teach about religion but not with the purpose of persuading students to believe in a particular religion.

What are the legal rights of students?

- Court decisions attempt to balance the rights of students to express themselves and the necessity of limiting personal freedom to ensure the safety and well-being of others.
- Students have freedom of symbolic expression, speech, and the press.
- Student privacy is protected from unreasonable search and seizure.
- Students have the right not to be sexually harassed.
- Students have due process rights when facing serious disciplinary action.
- Students and parents have rights concerning privacy and access to records.
- Students may not legally be discriminated against by public schools.

Developing Professional Competence

Visit the Developing Professional Competence section on Chapter 10 of the MyEducationLab for this text to answer the following questions and begin your preparation for licensure exams.

Derek Boucher's mission to ensure literacy for all his students at Roosevelt High School often leads him to be quite innovative. Because most of the students in his sophomore reading remediation class speak Spanish as their primary language, one of his ideas led to the development of a newsletter written for, and by, Latino students. The purpose of the newsletter is to encourage English-language learners to write articles that the students who are also learning to speak English would enjoy reading.

Derek followed the proper channels to get permission to initiate the newsletter and to use school supplies to publish it twice a month. Things went fine for 3 months, and Derek was quite pleased with how much his students were learning about writing and editing and, as an added bonus,

about expressing themselves in English. Articles ranged from reporting of some school and local issues to movie reviews to opinion pieces. After school every other Thursday when the pieces were due, Derek would read them for content and mechanics, make notes, return them Friday at the beginning of class, and then spend all of the Friday class period helping with rewrites and putting the pieces together in the four-page format in which it would be published.

Although most of the content of the student-written articles proved to be noninflammatory, one Thursday Derek found in the stack of articles two pieces that implicated several students in marijuana possession and sales. No names were given as the authors of the two pieces spoke out against the illicit drug activity, but from what Derek knew about the kids at Roosevelt and what the authors implied, he was fairly certain he could identify the culprits. Although students knew Mr. Boucher had the ultimate responsibility to edit what they wrote, censorship had not yet been a topic of discussion. Now Derek faced a number of serious questions about how he would proceed.

Think through this scenario and answer the following multiple-choice questions:

1. The student newsletter is a good idea for all of these reasons except which one of the following?
   a. Students saw a purpose for writing.
   b. Students learned to communicate better in their native language.
   c. The newsletter helped give Latino students an identity on campus.
   d. Derek was able to build literacy skills in a way that engaged his students.

2. Derek had a right as a teacher to censor the content of the student-generated newsletter because of which of the following case law precedents?
   a. *Pickering v. Board of Education*
   b. *Brown v. Board of Education*
   c. *Tinker v. Des Moines Independent Community School District*
   d. *Hazelwood School District v. Kuhlmeier*

3. Derek knows that if he tells Ms. Romero or Mr. Lael, the principal and assistant principal at Roosevelt, they will have the right to search the lockers of students who are implicated in drug possession and sale. The case that grants school officials the right to search lockers of students if they have reasonable suspicion is
   a. *New Jersey v. T.L.O.*
   b. *Hazelwood School District v. Kuhlmeier*
   c. *Tinker v. Des Moines Independent Community School District*
   d. *Pickering v. Board of Education*

4. The most meaningful reason Derek demonstrates one of the six characteristics of teachers who make ethical judgments, *appreciation for moral dilemma*, is
   a. Derek believes strongly that marijuana use is wrong.
   b. Derek believes that any lengths he may go to in order to encourage reading and writing are justified.
   c. Derek recognizes that this situation is complex and that the rights of everyone involved should be protected.
   d. Derek is concerned that the way he communicates his concerns to the administrators does not imply his students are involved.

Now it's time for you to respond to two short essay items involving the scenario. In your responses, be sure to address all the dilemmas and questions posed in each item. Your responses should each be between one half and one double-spaced page.

5. Is Derek obligated to reveal what he knows to the administration? How is Derek's decision related to his personal code of ethics? If, from an administrator's viewpoint, the newspaper is somehow fueling problems at Roosevelt and Derek is asked to stop publishing it, how might Derek defend the newsletter as a valuable teaching tool?

6. Derek knows that he has to talk with the students in his reading remediation class. When should he approach the subject? What should he say about his right and responsibility to act as a censor of newsletter content? How could he encourage his students to continue to write about relevant issues now that they know he can block items if he sees the need?

Where DO I Stand NOW?

In the beginning of this chapter you completed an inventory that gauged how closely your opinions matched laws regarding education. Now that you have read the chapter, completed exercises related to the content, engaged in class discussions, and so on, complete the following items in your course notebook.

1. List the items in *Where Do I Stand?* on which you indicated 3 rather than 4. Then choose one of the items and explain if your stance has changed from "I agree" to "I strongly agree" or if you still have slight reservations about the statement.

2. List the items in *Where Do I Stand?* on which you indicated 2 rather than 4. Then choose one of the items and explain if your stance has changed from "I don't have an opinion" to "I agree" or "I strongly agree" or if you still don't agree or disagree with the statement.

3. List the items in **Where Do I Stand?** on which you indicated 0 or 1 rather than 4. Then choose one of the items and explain if your stance has changed from "I disagree" or "I strongly disagree" to "I agree" or "I strongly agree" or if you still do not agree with the law.

4. Were you surprised to read about any of the issues and/or laws in this chapter? If so, which ones and why?

MyEducationLab

The MyEducationLab for this course can help you solidify your comprehension of Chapter 10 concepts.

- Explore the classrooms of the teachers and students you've met in this chapter in the Teaching in Focus section.

- Prepare for licensure exams as you deepen your understanding of chapter concepts in the Developing Professional Competence section.

- Gauge and further develop your understanding of chapter concepts by taking the quizzes and examining the enrichment materials on the Chapter 10 Study Plan.

- Visit Topic 4, "Ethical and Legal Issues," to watch ABC videos, explore Assignments and Activities, and practice essential teaching skills with the Building Teaching Skills and Dispositions unit.

11

Governing and Financing Public Schools in the United States

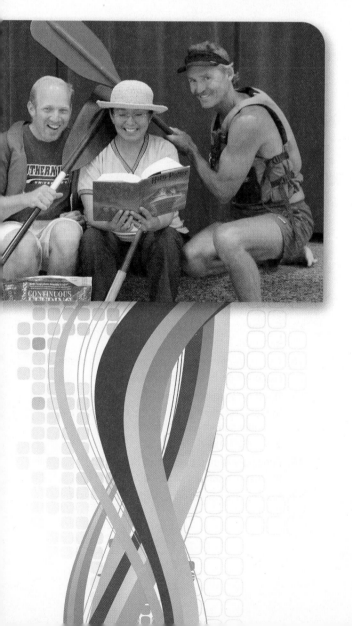

Most teachers get to know the system of public school governance and funding only when a particular issue demands their attention. Developing an overview now will help you put in context what you read in the newspaper or see on TV about issues such as school board proceedings, hiring of administrators, legislative decisions, and test score reports. As we explore the complex array of individuals and groups that have governing and financial authority over public schools in the United States, we consider the following questions:

✦ How does the federal government influence public education in the United States?

✦ What is the state's role in public education?

✦ How do school districts function?

✦ What is the management structure of individual schools?

✦ What other entities impact the governance of public schools in the United States?

✦ How are public schools financed?

✦ How are funds for education spent?

Before we discuss the governance and financing of public schools, explore your own views in this chapter's *Where Do I Stand?*

Where DO I Stand?

This inventory involves your general perceptions about which level of authority would best address a variety of responsibilities. The complexity of governing and financing schools makes both topics controversial. After reading an item, indicate your level of agreement by choosing a number 0 to 4 and placing it in the blank before the statement. Following the inventory are directions for how to organize your responses and what they may mean in terms of where you stand. You'll notice that this inventory frequently uses the word should. Some of what you read in the items actually happens, while other statements don't depict what is typically practiced. But remember that just because something occurs doesn't mean that it should, and, conversely, just because something doesn't occur, it doesn't mean it shouldn't.

4　I strongly agree
3　I agree
2　I don't have an opinion
1　I disagree
0　I strongly disagree

_____ **1.** The federal government should play an increasingly significant role in the functioning of schools.

_____ **2.** The state legislature is the place where most budgetary decisions should be made for schools.

_____ **3.** Decisions about curricula should be made at the district level.

_____ **4.** Principals and teachers are the appropriate people to be in charge of how schools operate and are assessed for effectiveness.

_____ **5.** A governor, as the leader of a state, should have extensive influence on the schools of the state.

_____ **6.** A school district, as an organizational structure of local schools, should be in charge of how schools operate and are assessed for effectiveness.

_____ **7.** School budgets should be handled at the federal level.

_____ **8.** An important leadership role of the president is to guide education in the United States.

_____ **9.** A state department of education is the organization to determine what it takes to qualify for a teaching position.

_____ **10.** School budgets should be handled by principals and teachers.

_____ **11.** District personnel should have extensive influence on local schools.

_____ **12.** A principal is the right person to oversee every aspect of school life.

_____ **13.** School budgets should be handled at the district level.

_____ **14.** A state department of education should make curricular decisions for schools.

_____ **15.** The federal government should have the right to take over the operation of a school, or even an entire school district, that is deemed unsatisfactory.

_____ **16.** Principals should function in the role of instructional leader of schools.

_____ **17.** School district personnel know what's best for local schools.

_____ **18.** The U.S. Congress should have an influence on K–12 education through legislation.

_____ **19.** Decisions about curricula should be made at the state level.

_____ **20.** Principals should determine what it takes to qualify for a teaching position.

_____ **21.** State departments of education personnel know what's best for local schools.

_____ **22.** The U.S. Department of Education is the most logical body to have oversight control over schools.

_____ **23.** Principals should have the authority to dismiss ineffective teachers.

_____ **24.** A district school board should have the authority to close a school.

_____ **25.** The federal government is right to withhold funding from states that choose to not comply with designated programs.

_____ **26.** Decisions about curricula should be made at the local level.

_____ **27.** School districts should have the right to determine the attendance boundaries of schools.

_____ **28.** School budgets should be handled at the state level.

_____ **29.** The U.S. Department of Education is the right organization to determine what it takes to qualify for a teaching position.

_____ **30.** The state superintendent of education should have the authority to dismiss ineffective teachers.

_____ **31.** A principal and his or her teachers should have the right to determine the attendance boundaries of their school.

_____ **32.** School district personnel should have the authority to dismiss ineffective teachers.

_____ **33.** A state department of education should have the right to take over the operation of a school, or even an entire school district, that is deemed unsatisfactory.

_____ **34.** The federal government should have the authority to dismiss ineffective teachers.

_____ **35.** A district school board is the organization to determine what it takes to qualify for a teaching position.

_____ **36.** Principals should be able to hire teachers.

_____ **37.** District authorities should make major decisions concerning the operation of public schools.

_____ **38.** U.S. Department of Education personnel know what's best for local schools.

_____ **39.** Members of a state board of education should make major decisions concerning the operation of public schools.

_____ **40.** Principals and teachers know what's best for local schools.

ITEM	MY #	ITEM	MY #	ITEM	MY #	ITEM	MY #
1		2		3		4	
7		5		6		10	
8		9		11		12	
15		14		13		16	
18		19		17		20	
22		21		24		23	
25		28		27		26	
29		30		32		31	
34		33		35		36	
38		39		37		40	
Sum		Sum		Sum		Sum	
÷ 10	F =	÷ 10	S =	÷ 10	D =	÷ 10	L =

Now plot F for Federal, S for State, D for District, and L for Local on this number line.

A complex system of people and policies make it possible for teachers to teach and students to learn. This number line indicates your opinion concerning which level of governance should have the greatest authority over public schools. The closer each sum is to 4, the more authority you would give the federal, state, district, and local levels.

```
|---+---+---+---+---+---+---+---|
0   .5  1  1.5  2  2.5  3  3.5  4
```

Teaching in Focus

Chris Roberts, Brenda Beyal, and Tim Mendenhall teach in multi-age classrooms of third, fourth, and fifth graders at Rees Elementary, Utah. They function beautifully as a team and enjoy working together as they shape their multiage program. Because multiage education is not the norm, teachers and administrators must have an interest in initiating the concept. Chris, as a former special education teacher, is very aware that students of different ages can actually learn at the same level and rate. Brenda and Tim, teachers who routinely find ways to individualize instruction, know that the learning capabilities of students the same age can vary widely. Experience has taught all three that 8- to 12-year-olds may be able to grasp some concepts at the same time from basically the same experiences, whereas other concepts may come easily or prove more difficult for individual students regardless of age. This knowledge prompted them to establish multiage classrooms.

As accomplished and respected teachers, Chris, Brenda, and Tim had workable plans to go with their idea. They learned a lot about district governance policies as they worked through the approval process, beginning with their principal, then the district director of elementary education, and, finally, the school board and superintendent. After hours of talking and preparing, district authorities approved the idea of multiage education. Although school board approval was almost certain once the district director of elementary education endorsed the plan, Chris, Brenda, and Tim still needed to present their ideas in a formal meeting of the board and superintendent.

To learn more about Chris, Brenda, and Tim's philosophies of teaching, go to the Teaching in Focus section for Chapter 11 in MyEducationLab for this course and watch their interviews.

How are the geographic boundaries that determine who attends your school drawn? If the principal is your boss, who is the principal's boss, and what's the chain of command? Who decides whether your school building gets a new wing and how it is financed? Who decides what standardized tests your students take? Why do you have so many forms to fill out? Who pays for special programs for kids in low socioeconomic settings? These questions, and a myriad more, are all related to the governing and financing of public schools in the United States. Figure 11.1 shows the four basic governing levels of public schools, and this chapter explains at what levels particular decisions are made.

How Does the Federal Government Influence Public Education in the United States?

Because education is not addressed in the Constitution, it has historically been basically a state's responsibility. However, the federal government's involvement in the functioning of schools through the institutions and agencies shown in Figure 11.2 has increased in recent decades.

Figure 11.1 Overview of American public school governance

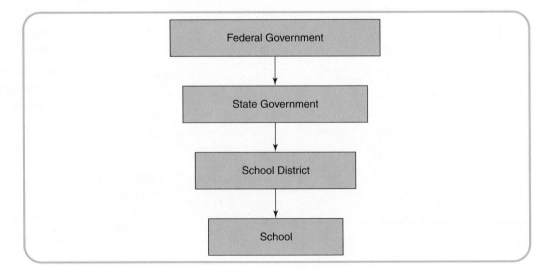

Figure 11.2 Federal government role in American public school governance

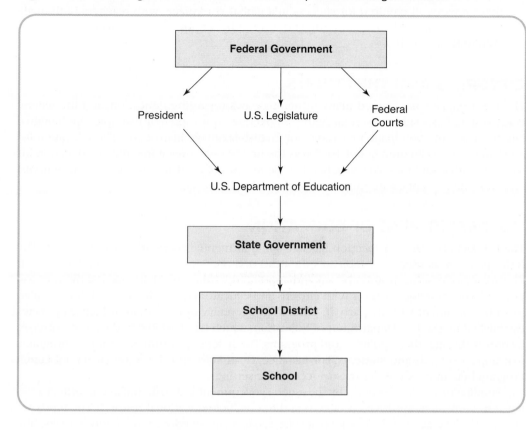

PRESIDENTIAL INFLUENCE

Almost every presidential candidate in the 20th century included education in his or her campaign platform; most had boldly articulated plans and promises. From its establishment in 1857 until 1980, the U.S. Department of Education served in an advisory capacity with little impact on public schools. President Ronald Reagan (1980–1988) was the first president to experience the department as a cabinet-level agency, an impact resulting from President Jimmy Carter's administration in 1979. Since 1980 the influence of the U.S. Department of Education has steadily increased. President Bill Clinton (1992–2000) worked vigorously toward achieving the objectives of *Goals 2000,* an ambitious list of goals for students in U.S. public schools. President George W. Bush's legacy (2000–2008) regarding education is the No Child Left Behind Act of 2001, discussed throughout this text.

President Barack Obama declared his commitment to public education on Inauguration Day 2009. On the official White House (2010) Web site we read,

> Providing a high-quality education for all children is critical to America's economic future. Our nation's economic competitiveness and the path to the American Dream depend on providing every child with an education that will enable them to succeed in a global economy that is predicated on knowledge and innovation. President Obama is committed to providing every child access to a complete and competitive education, from cradle through career.

The American Recovery and Reinvestment Act of 2009 invests heavily in education, both as a way to provide jobs now and to prepare for the future, with almost $100 billion pledged as additional support for public education, including emphasis on teacher effectiveness, early learning programs, programs for children with special needs, and greater achievement in low-performing schools. The Obama administration is working to ensure that teachers are supported as professionals and that they are held accountable for student learning. One means of accomplishing both aims is to provide competitive funding to states with innovative plans to deliver a 21st-century education that prepares all children for success in a global workplace, with teachers both qualified and responsible. This funding is delivered in the form of *Race to the Top* grants (White House, 2010).

CONGRESS AND THE COURTS

Laws affecting education are discussed in Chapters 3 and 10.

The U.S. Congress has passed many influential laws regarding education, and the federal court system has made numerous rulings impacting education. For example, the Bilingual Education Act of 1968 made provisions for English-language instruction. The Education for All Handicapped Children Act of 1975 was the first to guarantee a free public education for students with disabilities. The No Child Left Behind Act of 2001 has impacted K–12 schools, teachers, and students, with mixed and impassioned reviews.

U.S. DEPARTMENT OF EDUCATION

The U.S. Department of Education has had some influential secretaries over the years. The term *secretary* as used here indicates the head of a presidential cabinet-level department. The secretary of education is chosen and appointed by the president, making the position political. The incumbents' favor with citizens and educators rises and falls with the popularity of the president and the party in power. The secretary of education influences policies established by the U.S. Department of Education, which has a sizable budget and exercises its power through these policies and programs. The federal government sponsors programs that impact schools and students. For instance, Head Start and the National School Lunch Program benefit children in low socioeconomic settings.

Funding provided to schools by the federal government is distributed in the form of assistance to implement approved programs and to conduct educational research. The funds are also used as leverage to help ensure that state departments of education comply with specific mandates, such as guidelines and policies related to attempts to equalize educational opportunities for all children, and the use of widespread testing programs. In some cases states may choose whether to comply with U.S. Department of Education policies. However, the federal government withholds funds from states and their schools when they choose not to comply.

What Is the State's Role in Public Education?

Governors, legislators and judges, as well as state boards of education, state departments of education, and state superintendents, have much influence on public schools. Figure 11.3 is an overview of the basic state structure that impacts schools in the United States.

BALANCE OF POWER AT THE STATE LEVEL

States use a balance of power with three major branches of government, similar to what exists at the federal level. Governors have executive authority, legislatures have lawmaking authority, and state courts uphold and interpret laws, as well as establish constitutional guidelines.

GOVERNORS. Governors, as leaders of state governments, potentially have tremendous impact on public schools. A governor's attitude toward education has far-reaching influence on policies and laws. In many states the governor appoints the state's superintendent of education, as well as members of the state board of education. In addition, governors make budgetary recommendations that impact schools.

The National Governors Association (NGA) was founded in 1908 and serves as the collective voice of the nation's governors. The NGA Center for Best Practices is an online clearinghouse that provides governors and the public with information about public education, including such topics as disparities in academic achievement, turning around low-performing schools, and quality of teaching. The organization describes policy options for states, identifies how states cope with dilemmas pertaining to education, helps governors

Figure 11.3 State government role in American public school governance

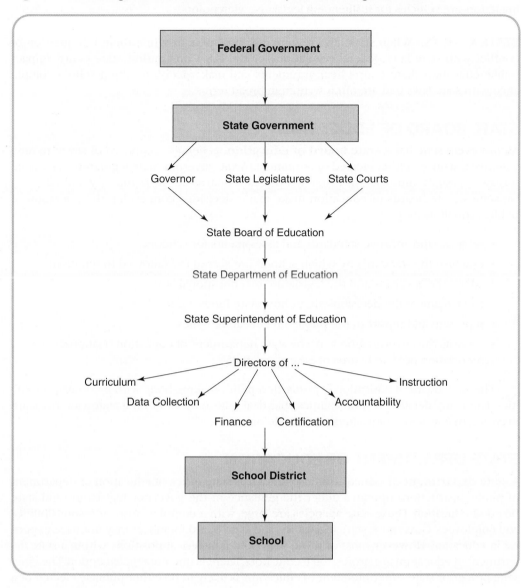

establish and maintain quality education in their states, and counsels them on how to work effectively with state legislatures (National Governors Association [NGA], 2010).

STATE LEGISLATURES. Members of state legislatures have significant influence on public education. State legislators impact schools as they determine

- state laws that affect every aspect of public education
- how state chief officers of education and state school board members are selected
- responsibilities of state-level school officials
- how taxes are used to support schools
- the general direction of the curriculum
- the length of the school day and year
- aspects of teacher employment, including issues involving tenure, retirement, and collective bargaining

There are no requirements in terms of educational background or experience for state legislators. Teachers and school administrators frequently question the wisdom of decisions made in the legislature. Having conversations, inviting legislators to visit schools, and writing letters are vehicles for influencing legislative viewpoints.

STATE COURTS. When state laws require interpretation, or when there is a question of conflict with state laws, federal regulations, or the U.S. Constitution, state courts impact public education. State courts hear arguments and make decisions about school compliance with state laws that are often written in broad terms.

STATE BOARD OF EDUCATION

Almost every state has a **state board of education,** generally composed of seven to nine volunteers who are either elected or appointed by the governor. State legislatures give state boards oversight authority; in other words, state boards act in regulatory and advisory capacities. State boards of education make major decisions concerning the operation of public schools as they

- set goals and approve standards and assessments for schools
- establish the standards by which schools are accredited (allowed to function)
- advise the governor and the legislature on educational issues
- make many of the decisions about how state funds are used
- represent and report to the public on education issues
- serve as the governing body of the state department of education (National Association of State Boards of Education, 2005)

The state board of education is primarily a policy-making body with broad responsibilities. The many detailed responsibilities that deal with education on a statewide basis are overseen by the state's department of education.

STATE DEPARTMENT OF EDUCATION

A **state department of education** (also known as state office of education or department of public instruction) operates under the guidance of the governor, legislature, and state board of education. These state agencies are large, with a complex array of responsibilities and employees. Governors, state legislators, and state board members may not have expertise in education. However, most of those who hold nonclerical positions within a state department of education are professional educators. There is one notable exception. The chief state officer, or state superintendent of education, is likely to be either publicly elected or a political appointee and may not be a professional educator.

STATE SUPERINTENDENT OF EDUCATION. The one person with responsibility for managing the state department of education may be called **state superintendent,** chief state education officer, or commissioner of education. This person may either be elected by the voters or appointed by the governor or state school board, depending on the state's policy (Council of Chief State School Officers, 2006). The state superintendent position is both public and political. The superintendent is in charge of the bureaucracy that is usually centralized in the state's capital city and travels throughout the state as the acknowledged authority on how schools operate and are assessed for effectiveness.

STATE DEPARTMENT OF EDUCATION RESPONSIBILITIES. The state superintendent of education generally has a large staff of individuals with varied expertise. The people who work as department directors are in charge of divisions within the state department that address, among other issues,

- teacher certification (or licensure)
- curriculum standards and accountability
- instruction (usually a director for each content area)

- special education
- school levels (high, middle, elementary, early childhood)
- technology
- charter schools
- teacher professional development
- state budget funds
- communication and public relations
- collection and reporting of school data

Although not commonly done, a state department of education may take over the operation of a school, or even an entire school district, that is deemed unsatisfactory.

How Do School Districts Function?

A **school district** is an organizational structure of local schools defined by geographic boundaries. Figure 11.4 provides an overview of the basic structure that exists in most school districts.

School districts have at least one **feeder system** of schools, early childhood/elementary schools that feed into middle schools that feed into a particular high school. There are

Figure 11.4 School district role in American public school governance

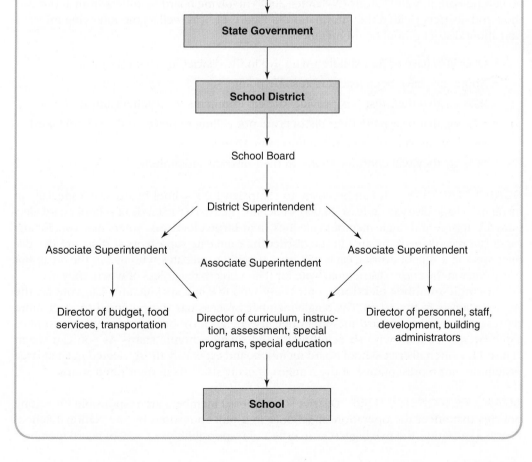

over 15,000 school districts in the United States. In the early to mid-20th century, there were almost 10 times as many. The decrease occurred as officials realized it was more efficient to combine small districts and share services and administration. Interestingly, the entire state of Hawaii is one school district, whereas the state of Texas has more than a thousand separate districts (National Education Association [NEA], 2009).

School districts vary greatly in size, from one building that houses all grade levels, as in Gilpin County School District in Colorado with about 300 students, to New York City public schools, with over 1 million students. Small and large districts each have distinct advantages as well as limitations. Small and medium districts have the advantage of accessibility. Teachers feel as though they can be heard in policy matters, and parents often sense a distinct connection to the schools and faculty. In very large districts teachers may sense that they are far removed from where policy decisions are made. Large districts generally have the advantage of availability of numerous services and specialists to oversee the many aspects of life in schools and classrooms. In small and medium districts, individuals tend to have an array of duties, and fewer curricular and service options are offered. Regardless of size or complexity, each district has a school board and a superintendent who function as leaders of central administration.

Points of Reflection 11.1

Were your K–12 experiences in a small, medium, or large district? What advantages or limitations because of the size of your district were you aware of? Did you attend school from kindergarten through 12th grade in one feeder system, or did you move frequently?

Schools in colonial America are discussed in Chapter 7.

DISTRICT SCHOOL BOARDS

District school boards are unique American institutions composed of elected citizens who volunteer their time. This form of governance originated in the locally controlled schools of the colonies and in the common schools movement. Through one reform effort after another, the basic structure of school boards has not changed. They represent democratization by linking the public to public schools. Many educators find school boards to be flawed in terms of how they govern, but most agree that they serve a worthwhile purpose (Hess, 2010). Because local schools are profoundly affected by district school board decisions, we spend more time discussing them than the other levels of governance.

Most members of public district school boards are noneducators and receive little or no compensation. A 2007 study (Nylander, 2007) involving board members from about two thousand districts yielded the information in Figure 11.5, as well as the following information about district school board members:

- Over 90% have or had children who live in the district in which they serve.
- About 25% have been teachers at some point.
- 96% say that their districts provide safe environments for teachers and students.
- 92% say that parents in their districts are not willing to serve on the school board.
- 88% have lived in their communities more than 5 years.
- 90% say they will continue to live in their districts indefinitely.

BOARD ELECTIONS. It can be costly to campaign for a school board seat, especially in medium to large districts (at least 20,000 students). The two basic kinds of school board elections are at-large and single-member elections. In **at-large elections,** voters may vote for any candidate regardless of the area in the district the candidate represents. If there are five distinct areas in a school district, each will have specific candidates who live in the areas, but *every* voter in the *entire* district may vote for their choices regardless of where they live.

In **single-member elections,** only those who live in a specific area can vote for the representatives in their area. The single-member process has the potential to elect more representative school board members because neighborhoods are more likely to have candidates and voters who share ethnicity and socioeconomic status. As you can see in Figure 11.5, often district school board members, and especially those elected in an at-large system, are not representative of the families of many students in the United States.

BOARD RESPONSIBILITIES. District school board members are responsible for setting policies that affect the operation of schools. In a poll sponsored by the National School Boards Association, the five biggest concerns and responsibilities of school board members

Figure 11.5 Profile of school board members

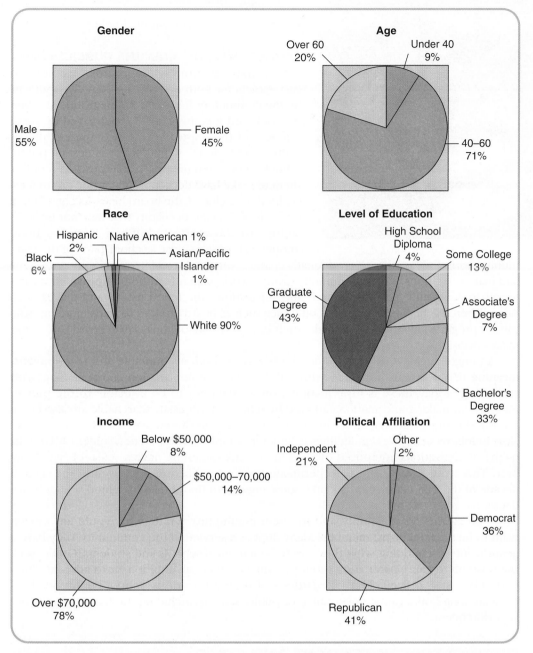

Source: Nylander, A. (2007). National School Board Survey. Accessed at: http://www.oldham.kyschools.
us/files/reports/National_Surveys/National%20School%20Board%20Survey%202007%20Final%20Results_
pdf.pdf

from small, medium, and large districts were funding, student achievement, teacher quality, improving technology, and special education (Hess, 2002). Dealing with these concerns and fulfilling other duties require numerous meetings and research. Among other responsibilities, school board members

- decide how much money will be spent on teacher salaries, facilities improvement, and instructional materials
- hire and fire personnel, both professional and classified (clerical, custodial, etc.)
- approve and evaluate programs that may affect some or all schools, teachers, and students within the district

Teachers, families, and community members voice their questions and opinions at public school board meetings.

- make curricular decisions within state guidelines
- determine organizational policy

SCHOOL BOARDS AND THE PUBLIC. Controversy is never far from school boards. Members are easy targets for both oral and written chastisement by the community. It's a rare moment indeed when school board members are not perceived by some segment of the population as incompetent, downright stupid, or even evil. As trustees of public schools, their often unappreciated position requires them to make hard decisions. When one group feels slighted or excluded, the board hears its complaints, but must still make decisions that may not be satisfactory to those affected. When it makes fiscal (monetary) sense to close a school, parts of the community storm the board with emotionally charged, often valid, objections. The board listens and makes decisions. When community groups work diligently to help improve education for all students and present research and suggestions, the board listens and makes decisions. When teachers take positions on issues such as board choices to transfer administrators, or program alterations, they make their case to the school board. The board listens and makes decisions.

An ongoing challenge for school boards is to be both accountable and **transparent,** meaning that decisions are made with full disclosure of information and reasoning. With technology today, there is little justification for data not to be available to the public. Methods for making information gathered by school boards easily searchable are also possible. But this organizational structure, almost as old as the United States itself, will likely be slow in following any new guidelines calling for complete transparency. Snider (2010) tells us that organizations composed of elected citizens sometime have a sense of "we know best." This attitude may appear to permeate local school boards and, even in the second decade of the 21st century, it may take some digging to find the logic behind school board decisions.

With all this responsibility, and frequent community wrath, why would any citizen want to be a school board member? Many do it as a service to the community. They have a genuine interest in doing what they can to benefit local schools and students. Others seek the position to gain power and visibility, to further political ambition, or to advocate for a particular cause (Mizell, 2010). Regardless of their motivations, school board members dedicate long hours to the governance of public schools, including the hiring of a district superintendent.

Points of Reflection 11.2

Have you observed the functioning of a district school board, either firsthand or through television news or newspapers? What impressions did you have?

DISTRICT SUPERINTENDENT AND STAFF

A **district superintendent** functions as the school district's chief executive officer. The superintendent is hired by the board and serves at its pleasure, which means the board can also dismiss the superintendent. The superintendent is expected to both advise the board and carry out board policies. As largely noneducators, board members often choose an educator as superintendent to keep schools running smoothly on a day-to-day basis. The superintendent serves at the pleasure of the board meaning that the school board has authority over the superintendent and evaluates his or her performance. The relationship between the board and the superintendent can become awkward when school board members go beyond policy making into what is considered the authority of the superintendent. When board members get involved in day-to-day operations, it is often referred to as **micromanagement**. If tensions develop over policies or decisions, a school board may dismiss a superintendent. Generally, before things escalate to this point, the public is involved and meetings are held to discuss the situation. These can be trying times for communities.

In small districts, superintendents may handle all the responsibilities listed in Figure 11.4. The larger the district, the more necessary it is for the superintendent to delegate. Medium to large districts have associate or assistant superintendents who handle specific duties such as supervision of the different levels—early childhood, elementary, middle, and high. They work with district curriculum and instruction directors to coordinate efforts. Larger districts also have associate superintendents in charge of areas such as personnel, facilities, and finance.

People in the community sometimes complain there are too many administrators and non-classroom teachers doing supervisory work rather than directly teaching children. Before making this judgment, citizens should recognize the complexity of operating school districts and individual schools in ways that free teachers to teach and students to learn.

What Is the Management Structure of Individual Schools?

Now we consider individual schools, the places where teachers and students interact. Within the school building, the management structure often depends on both the size and the level of the school. Figure 11.6 lists some of the people who may contribute to the management of local schools, including the one constant person in almost all building-level management structures, the principal.

PRINCIPALS

The **principal** oversees every aspect of school life and is responsible to the district for all that occurs at the school. The principal's role involves oversight of administrative tasks such as facility maintenance, attendance, discipline, parent and community relationships and communication, transportation, and all manner of paperwork. Principals also have the role of instructional leader, with knowledge of, and experience with, the teaching and learning process. Instructional leaders have the ability to make positive suggestions and model practices that enhance student learning (Sergiovani, 2001).

Figure 11.6 Local American public school governance

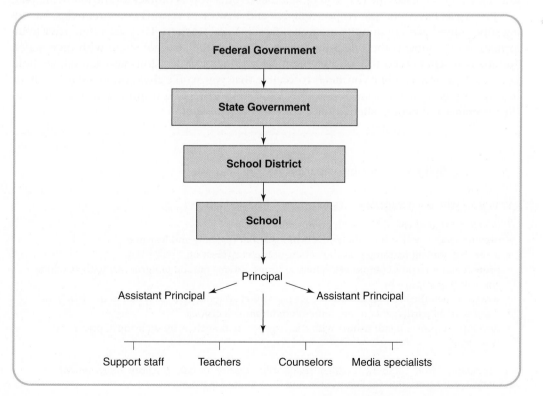

Rees Elementary principal Mike Larsen takes a personal interest in students and their success.

A principal who is an instructional leader focuses teachers on improved learning for all students. Many principals who are confident in their administrative and instructional leadership skills believe in the benefits of sharing leadership with teachers and members of the community.

SITE-BASED MANAGEMENT. In *Leadership Capacity for Lasting School Improvement* by Linda Lambert (2003), we are told that the most effective principals build leadership capacity in teachers and others who are sincerely interested in student learning. Site-based management is a form of local school governance that puts much of the decision-making power regarding curriculum, textbooks, student behavior, staff development, budget, and hiring in the hands of teachers, family members, and the community. Principals who want to share leadership and management of schools employ some or all of the actions listed in Figure 11.7. Serving on a site-based management team gives teachers deeper insight into the role of the principal.

From the list in Figure 11.7, perhaps the most fundamental thing principals do to empower teachers to take responsibility for student learning is the third statement: *insist that student learning is at the center of the conversation*. In other words, students take precedence and empowered teachers do what's best for them. In **Teaching in Focus,** Tim Mendenhall advises teachers to experiment to find what works for their students in their own circumstances.

UNDERSTANDING THE ROLE OF PRINCIPAL. As you beginning your teaching career, your principal will have a major impact on you. Your memories of the principals you have experienced may factor into how you view your first principal when you become a teacher. He or she will select you and ask the school board to hire you, will determine the grade level or subject you teach, will likely assign a teacher mentor for you, will evaluate your teaching performance, and will make the decision of whether to offer you a contract for the following year.

Principals have multiple responsibilities and answer to various constituencies, including superintendents, community members, families, and teachers. They are often privy to information that impacts their decisions, some of which they cannot share with their staffs. Too many teachers tend to pass judgment on a principal's decisions and sometimes hold grudges. As a new teacher you need to realize that you won't always understand why or how decisions are made. Your best path is to be supportive of your principal and helpful to the programs and people aligned with your school's mission.

Figure 11.7 Building leadership capacity

Principals who build leadership capacity in teachers and others . . .

- develop a shared vision based on community values
- organize, focus, and sustain the conversations about teaching and learning
- insist that student learning is at the center of the conversation
- protect and interpret community values, assuring a focus on, and congruence with, teaching and learning approaches
- work through the evaluation and district personnel systems to dismiss ineffective teachers
- work with all participants to implement community decisions
- develop reciprocal relationships with the larger system, such as by securing support and resources

Source: Adapted from Lambert, L. (2003). *Leadership capacity for lasting school improvement.* Alexandria, VA: Association for Supervision and Curriculum Development.

Teaching in Focus

Tim Mendenhall, Grades 3–5 Multiage Classroom, Rees Elementary School, Utah. *In his own words. . . .*

I would first encourage you to follow your heart. Trust yourself and do what you feel needs to be done for your students. Don't follow a program just because it's been adopted. If there is something better for your students, use it, adjust it. Education is messy. You will try things and fail. That's how we learn.

Second, more than reading and math, teaching your students to be lifelong learners is your ultimate goal. Make your classroom fun. If you don't like a book or an activity, why do you think they will? Love what you are doing, and they will learn to love learning.

Finally, stay at teaching long enough to get the REAL pay. This could be a child bringing you a Cherry Coke (instead of an apple) every Friday. Or a former student running off the football field to talk with you when he is quarterback and supposed to be leading a play. Or a parent coming back and telling you that you are still their child's favorite teacher (even after all the years and they are now graduating from high school). The pay is great; you just have to wait for it sometimes.

Figure 11.8 illustrates gender, age, and racial characteristics of school principals at the elementary and secondary (high school/middle school) levels. You will notice that the overwhelming majority of these school leaders are white, and, overall, male and over the age of 45. Just as there is a need for a more diverse teaching force, there is also a need for principals who more closely mirror student gender, racial, and ethnic characteristics. Regardless of their gender or race, most principals in all but small schools (fewer than 400 or so students) generally receive help in fulfilling their administrative and instructional leadership roles from assistant principals.

> Teacher characteristics and the importance of diversity are discussed in Chapter 1.

ASSISTANT PRINCIPALS

The position of assistant principal entails a variety of duties. If there is only one in a school, then the responsibilities may be general and similar to the principal's, or as specific as the principal chooses to make them. When there are multiple assistants, they generally have designated areas of responsibility. For instance, a medium-size elementary school (400 to 700 students) may have a principal and one assistant who may do various aspects of the principal's job, depending on day-to-day needs. A large middle school (more than 1,000 students) may have a principal and three assistants, each responsible for a grade level. A principal of a large high school (more than 1,500 students) may have more than three assistants who specialize in areas such as student discipline, athletics and extracurricular activities, transportation, and materials. Teachers often work with

Points of Reflection 11.3

What do you remember about your schools' principals? Were they accessible or did they seem aloof? Did you view them as disciplinarians to be feared or as friendly adults who were helpful to teachers, parents, and students?

Assistant principals may be perceived as stern in their roles of student disciplinarian and yet be approachable as supporters of teachers.

Figure 11.8 Characteristics of elementary and secondary principals

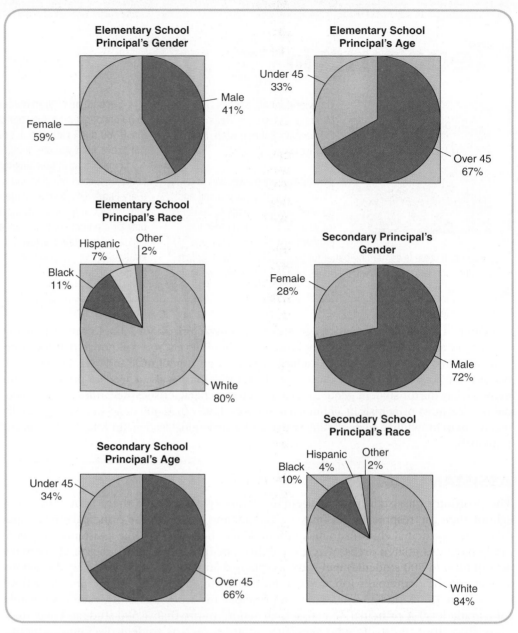

Elementary School
Principal's Gender

Male
41%

Female
59%

Elementary School
Principal's Age

Under 45
33%

Over 45
67%

Elementary School
Principal's Race

Hispanic
7%

Other
2%

Black
11%

White
80%

Secondary Principal's
Gender

Female
28%

Male
72%

Secondary School
Principal's Age

Under 45
34%

Over 45
66%

Secondary School
Principal's Race

Hispanic
4%

Other
2%

Black
10%

White
84%

Source: U.S. Department of Education. (2009). *Characteristics of public, private, and Bureau of Indian Education elementary and secondary school principals in the United States.* Washington, DC: Author.

assistant principals. A teacher in a large school may be more connected with the assistant principal(s) than with the principal.

TEACHER LEADERS

The phrase *teacher leader* has come to mean in many circles that a teacher has taken on additional responsibilities such as chairperson of a grade level of teachers or perhaps a subject area specialist who works with other teachers to help them improve their knowledge and/or skills. But individuals can be leaders in their schools, as well as in their districts and states, simply by being dynamic, well-informed classroom teachers. They don't need official titles to impact other educators around them, their own students and others in their buildings, and their communities. An example of teacher leadership is in this chapter's *Diversity Dialogue,* featuring focus teacher Brandi Wade.

Brandi Wade, our kindergarten focus teacher at Summit Primary School in Ohio, believes in experiential learning. Her years in the classroom have shown her that children become more excited when they are actually involved in their own learning and engaged in activities that capture their imagination. In her classroom she tries to provide experiences that get kids moving and doing, rather than passively listening and watching.

To watch Brandi's lesson, go to the Teaching in Focus section for Chapter 11 in MyEducationLab for this course.

Brandi is researching the Columbus area for possible field trips for her students. She wants her students to experience the Heritage Gardens at the governor's residence in Columbus, the farmers market in both fall and spring, and the Franklin Park Conservatory and Botanical Garden. They'll learn so much on these adventures. But there's a problem. Field trips cost money. Some of the students in Brandi's class come from homes where paying for these trips will not pose a problem; she also knows that for at least 10 of her 24 students, it will be out of the question to ask the families to pay their part of the transportation costs and admission fees. When the children are with Brandi at Summit Primary they sense that they are all valued the same and insulated from the problems of poverty. She knows that economic dilemmas are not just affecting families who have been in low-income circumstances for a long time. With high unemployment, parents of Brandi's students are struggling financially.

Respond to these items by writing one well-developed paragraph for each.

1. A free public education is a wonderful aspect of life in America, even with the occasional fee and the tax burden. Is what Brandi wants to do with her students out of line, considering that schools and school districts may be in tough economic times? If you think her plans are justifiable, explain why. If you think Brandi is using less than optimal judgment, explain why.

2. Do you think it would be a good idea for Brandi, with the principal's approval, of course, to send a letter home to families asking for their help? They might volunteer time, materials, or money. The money could be used for transportation and admission fees for the whole class, rather than asking for specific amounts per child. What might be the benefits of this plan? What might be drawbacks?

A growing number of teachers with specialized training are relieved of some or all of their classroom teaching duties to lead a grade level or be an in-school subject area expert. For instance, a school may have an instructional coach, a teacher who works with individual teachers as they improve or add to their toolboxes of instructional strategies. Another school may have a math specialist who teaches math to all fourth and fifth graders, regardless of their homeroom. These specially designated teacher leaders may become part of the school management team along with the principal and assistant principal(s).

Instructional strategies are discussed in Chapter 6.

What Other Entities Impact the Governance of Public Schools in the United States?

The decisions about policies and laws by the individuals and groups discussed so far in this chapter are influenced by many constituencies. Among them are parents, businesses, universities, and special interest groups.

PARENTS

Parents, including stepparents, foster parents, and guardians, have the potential to be among the most influential players in the education of children. Parents, by virtue of their position, are influential in the lives of their own children and, if they are informed and involved in

Watch an interview with focus student Amanda Wiley that includes her mom, the president of the Rees Elementary PTA, in the Teaching in Focus section for Chapter 11 in MyEducationLab for this course.

Points of Reflection 11.4

In what school activities do you recall parent volunteers participating? Were your parents members of a PTA or other organized school groups? What do you remember about their involvement?

schools, can make a positive difference in the lives of many children in their local schools. One question is "How can they do this?" But perhaps even more important to ask is "Why don't they do it more often?"

One way for parents to be involved in the life of the school is through the Parent Teacher Association (PTA), a national organization with millions of members at thousands of schools across the country. School PTAs have varying degrees of impact. Some groups boast large numbers of members whose only involvement is the payment of small annual dues ($2 to $10). Other groups have very active members who volunteer to help out at school in a variety of ways. Although individual PTAs contribute to school life, rarely do they impact decision-making bodies.

Parents can volunteer to help in schools and classrooms and impact the quality of students' school-related experiences. They also have opportunities to serve on committees that address school issues. In some school districts, parents are encouraged to be part of site-based management groups sometimes called School Improvement Councils (SIC) or Local School Councils (LSC). Being part of an SIC or LSC is a serious responsibility that far too few family members are willing to accept. Parents are usually busy providing for their families and often feel that their time is too limited to commit to membership in a site-based management group. Some parents may be intimidated by the process or may feel they are not qualified to represent families.

BUSINESSES

Businesses have a vested interest in education. Having competent employees is a major key to business success, and these employees are likely to be products of public education. Large businesses and their chief executive officers are increasingly becoming involved in **education summits,** or organized meetings to advocate for school improvement. This is a positive step because business leaders can potentially support schools and students in meaningful ways.

Business leaders can be influential in supporting educational initiatives. Some businesses offer scholarships to promising students. Other businesses, whether locally owned or national franchises, form partnerships with schools to sponsor events, such as science fairs, and contribute resources to enhance school activities. Additionally, some large businesses give employees paid time off to volunteer in schools and may match funds their employees donate to school organizations.

UNIVERSITIES

Schools of education and teacher educators have important influence on schools because most classroom teachers are prepared on university campuses. Future teachers learn about the concepts in this text and more as they go through teacher preparation programs. The more teachers know, the better prepared they are to take active roles in influencing policies and working toward school improvement.

Teacher educators have the knowledge, and ideally the will, to exert influence by expressing their views to school administrators, school board members, and legislators. They can serve on School Improvement Councils, curriculum revision and textbook adoption committees, and, in general, be active in local, state, and national education associations. University faculty also have an impact on schools through research focused on classroom programs and practices and by facilitating staff development. These activities can form the foundation for recommending policy changes and promoting effective practices.

SPECIAL INTEREST GROUPS

When a group of people join together with a common mission and work to have an impact they are often called a **special interest group**. An example would be a group composed of parents of children who have special needs. Informal groups of parents of children with autism or Down syndrome, for example, may band together to help ensure more effective services for their children.

Sometimes community members join forces to form local **watchdog groups,** meaning they keep an eye on school district accountability by examining policies and practices. One such group is the Charleston Education Network (CEN). This group of citizens meets regularly to review happenings in, and policies of, the Charleston County School District in South Carolina, where one of this text's four focus schools, Cario Middle, is located. Members of CEN often fund or conduct research on issues, articulate findings and viewpoints, and lobby school board members and state legislators to bring about change. Groups like CEN offer effective services by asking hard questions and being persistent in their search for answers.

On the national level, groups like the Public Education Network (PEN) tirelessly advocate for children. In addition to activities similar to those of CEN, PEN gathers articles and research results on education issues and distributes them through its Web site to help individuals and organizations stay informed. You can subscribe for free to *PEN Weekly NewsBlast* at http://news.publiceducation.org and receive valuable updates on many education issues.

Now that we have examined governance structures of public schools and those who influence these structures, let's explore how schools are financed and how the money is spent.

How Are Public Schools Financed?

Free public education—think about it. What a remarkable and noble concept. But is it really free? Hardly. It's true that students don't pay tuition. However, their parents often pay fees for specific items, such as science equipment, gym clothes, band instruments, and workbooks, as well as vague charges for grade-level fees. Parents are also asked to supply certain materials each school year. But these expenses barely make a dent in what it costs to provide K–12 education. So where does all the money come from?

SOURCES OF EDUCATION FUNDING

Most of the funding for public education comes from federal, state, and local governments in the proportions shown in Figure 11.9. It's interesting to note how these three major sources of funding have shifted over the years from local funding as the primary source in the early part of the 20th century, to local and state sources currently sharing funding responsibilities at approximately the same levels. Figure 11.10 illustrates these historical shifts in the proportion of funding from each major source. As the number of K–12 students and the cost of educating them have grown, most states have increased both the amount and the percentage of their contributions. Although Figure 11.10 appears to indicate a decrease in local funding, that is not the case; rather, the states' average proportion of total funding has simply increased. The call for equitable funding, regardless of race, socioeconomic status, or geographic location, has led states to increase their portion of funding responsibility (Biddle & Berliner, 2002). States have also come to recognize that the quality of public education has lifestyle and economic implications. As indicated in Figure 11.10, the federal government's contribution to public schools is relatively small, with an increase occurring about the time of the release of the 1983 report *A Nation at Risk* and remaining fairly stable since then.

A Nation at Risk is discussed in Chapter 7.

FEDERAL FUNDING. The federal government budget is supported through income taxes, investments, and various charges for services and goods. Federal government contributions to public education account for only about 2% of the U.S. government budget (U.S. Department of Education, 2006).

The federal government supplies a little less than 10% of the total education budget. Although this doesn't sound like a lot, federal contributions have a major impact on public schools because the money is allocated as **categorical grants,** or funds earmarked for specific purposes. Programs previously discussed like Head Start, Title I, the Bilingual Education Act, and the Education for All Handicapped Children Act are examples of categorical grants. As a group, these and other grants are referred to as **entitlements,** meaning that certain

Figure 11.9 Percentage of revenues received from federal, state, and local sources for public elementary and secondary schools

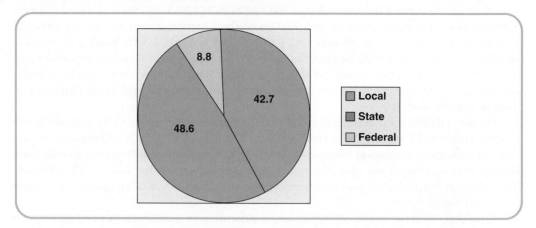

Source: National Education Association. (2009). *Rankings of states 2008 and estimates of school statistics* 2009. Washington, DC: Author. Retrieved June 18, 2010, from http://www.nea.org/assets/docs/09rankings.pdf

segments of the population have specific needs and the federal government deems these individuals as entitled to extra assistance.

The Reagan administration attempted to diminish the influence of the federal government on schools while still funding their efforts. In the 1980s, some federal funding changed from categorical grants to **block grants,** which provide funding with few restrictions for its use. This type of funding allows states and school districts the freedom to use the money in ways that meet their specific needs.

Figure 11.10 Revenues for public schools, by source of funds, 1920–2008

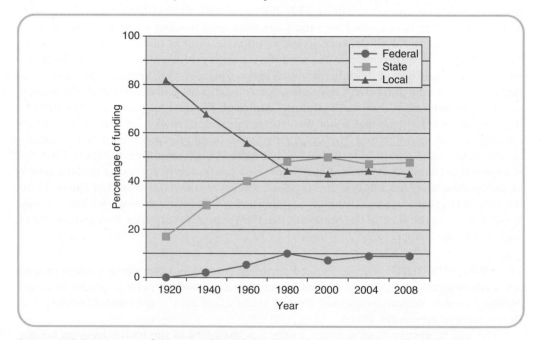

Sources: U.S. Department of Education (2001b). *Statistics of state school systems: Revenues and expenditures for public elementary and secondary education.* Washington, DC: U.S. Department of Education, National Center for Education Statistics. Retrieved August 2, 2006, from http://www.nces.ed.gov. National Education Association. (2009). *Rankings of the states 2008 and estimates of school statistics 2009.* Retrieved June 18, 2010, from http://www.nea.org/assets/docs/09rankings.pdf

The No Child Left Behind Act of 2001, as a reauthorization of the 1965 Elementary and Secondary Education Act, involved federal funds tied to school improvement as prescribed by the act's specific guidelines. Schools were required to meet the mandates of NCLB to receive the funds. In most cases, states attempted to protect federal funding by complying with the mandates.

STATE FUNDING. About half of the funding for public education comes from state sources. State money for schools is basically raised through taxes, such as:

- state income tax based on personal earnings
- state corporate tax based on company earnings
- state sales tax added as a percentage of the cost of goods and services
- **excise tax,** or tax on luxury items such as boats and travel trailers
- **"sin" tax** on items some consider vices, such as alcohol and cigarettes

As of 2010, 44 states had lottery games with portions of the funds specifically earmarked for education (North American Association of State and Provincial Lotteries, 2010). Although lottery-based funding may sound appealing and, indeed, has been used productively in many instances, there are inherent problems. First, gambling through state-run lotteries appears to attract a disproportionate number of low-income people who often have little schooling. Many disagree with the concept of a lottery system for this reason (Brimley & Garfield, 2004). Second, although lottery funding is initially viewed as extra money to supplement other, more stable sources, over time having this easy source of funds often leads to the reduction of more stable funding. In other words, a state's attitude may be "We have all this lottery money so we don't need to give schools as much from the state budget." This is risky business, from both state and local standpoints, considering the uncertainty of a lottery's ability to provide money consistently for schools.

In tough economic times, difficult budgetary decisions must be made at all levels. This often proves especially difficult at the state level. When money is tight, some services and programs must be cut. Because education is such a large part of a state's overall budget, the decision to withdraw funding from schools is both public and painful. In 2010 most states faced shortfalls, including California, where some citizens have gone from passive disapproval to aggressive action. More than 60 individual students and their families, 9 school districts from throughout the state, the California School Boards Association, California State PTA, and the Association of California School Administrators filed a lawsuit against the state based on their view that the current educational finance system is unconstitutional. Through *Robles-Wong* v. *State of California,* the plaintiffs are asking that California's finance system, specifically its funding policies for education, be changed. They are asking that the state determine the cost to adequately fund public education to meet both the state's own program requirements and the needs of the students. The state would then have to develop and implement a new finance system consistent with California constitutional requirements.

Figure 11.11 provides two editorial opinions published in the Santa Rosa *Press Democrat* that reflect the situation in communities all across California. Following the two pieces is this chapter's **Letter to the Editor** written by a citizen in response to the first opinion piece.

LOCAL FUNDING. The source of local funding for schools is primarily **property taxes**. Values of property are determined, and a small percentage of the assessed amount (usually less than 1%) is collected annually and used for local services. Most goes to schools (Brimley & Garfield, 2004). On the surface, using property taxes to finance education seems reasonable. After all, everyone benefits from an educated citizenry.

Figure 11.11 Editorial opinions

Published: Wednesday, May 26, 2010
The Press Democrat, Santa Rosa, CA

Written by Frank Pugh

I'm a local school board member and also the president of the California School Boards Association. In this last capacity, I assisted our organization in filing the historic *Robles-Wong* v. *California* lawsuit against the state of California last week. It has been reported by at least one national newspaper reporter that this lawsuit could be on par with *Brown* v. *Board of Education* for the potential to affect the future of education funding in the state of California.

In short, we argue that California's broken school finance system is unconstitutional. We also believe that California's school finance system is unsound, unstable, insufficient, and erratic. This current system is not aligned with required educational programs or with student needs.

As a result, our students are being denied the opportunity to master the educational programs that the state requires. Education is a fundamental right of every child in California, and our state constitution requires a school system that prepares students to become informed citizens and productive members of society.

The formulas that this state relies upon to fund education date back to the early 1950s. The formulas do not take into account, for example, the costs to implement demanding standards, the requirements of No Child Left Behind, special education, the California High School Exit Exam, the diversity of the children we serve and the avalanche of unfunded mandates required from our state Legislature.

The facts are clear about the staffing ratios in California schools. California is 49th among all states in student-to-teacher ratios. We are 45th in instructional aides. We are 46th in district officials and administrators. We are 48th in total school staff. We are 49th in guidance counselors. We are 50th in librarians.

California spends $2,131 less per pupil than the national average, ranking the state 44th in the country. From a different perspective, California spends less per pupil than each of the largest 10 states in the nation—almost $6,000 less per pupil than New York.

With school funding not being a priority in our state, is it any wonder why we are not as successful as we should be in student achievement? Because of the lack of interest on the part of our lawmakers in solving the school finance problem, we were left with no choice but to file a lawsuit against the state of California.

Published: Wednesday, June 6, 2010
The Press Democrat, Santa Rosa, CA

Editorial Opinion

By practically any measure, financial support for public education in California is discouraging. So is student achievement.

According to statistics compiled from various sources by the *New York Times,* the Golden State is tied for 47th in the nation in fourth-grade reading and tied for 46th in the nation in eighth-grade math.

With districts eliminating school days and increasing class sizes because of budget cuts, California's rankings probably will get even worse, though there isn't much farther to go in this race to the bottom.

So it was hardly surprising when a group of students, parents and school officials filed a lawsuit challenging the state's method of funding education for California's 6 million public school students.

If schools expect a larger share, or a dedicated source of revenue for education, they must accept greater accountability, including data-based evaluation of the performance of teachers, principals, schools and entire districts, as well as open enrollment and other forms of parental choice.

Better resources must be matched by better achievement.

However, as illustrated in Figure 11.12, many people believe an alternative method of funding public education should be imposed. In 1978 California was the first state to put a limit on how high property taxes could go. California's Proposition 13 was a model for other states. Now almost all states impose what is called a **tax cap** on local property taxes, or an upper limit to taxation.

Letter to the Editor

This letter appeared in the Santa Rosa, California, newspaper, *The Press Democrat*. It was written in response to an opinion piece published the week before. The author is expressing frustration over state funding for education.

JUNE 5, 2010 SCHOOL LAWSUIT

[Frank] Pugh has taken action in a situation that has been neglected for so long—the survival of our schools, as we have known them. We have seen the governor make and break promises about funds coming to our schools; they never come. As Pugh so rightly puts it: "Our state constitution requires a school system that prepares students to become informed citizens and productive members of society." I have watched this requirement be ignored, and our students often leave school unprepared to function in our communities, earn a living, and, more important, ready to be informed citizens, as we so vitally need in these rapidly changing times.

Bravo to Pugh for assisting in his role as president of the California School Boards Association in taking action by filing "the historic Robles-Wong v. California lawsuit against the state of California."

Penny Wolfsohn
Santa Rosa

Source: The Press Democrat / Santa Rosa, California.

Now it's your turn. Write a letter to the editor from the perspective of a future teacher expressing your views about funding and education, specifically the situation in California. You may comment on any, or all, of the writer's expressed opinions. The following questions may help you frame your thinking but should not limit or determine what you write.

1. Ms. Wolfsohn obviously agrees with Mr. Pugh's perceptions concerning California state funding for education. She lays at least some blame on Governor Arnold Schwarzenegger. Do you think she is literally talking about the actions of one person?

2. While Mr. Pugh and the author of the editorial that follows agree that funding is a problem, the editorial brings to light specific achievement difficulties. Do you think funding and academic success are necessarily linked? If so, how? If not, why not?

3. Ms. Wolfsohn wrote her letter before the second editorial opinion appeared in *The Press Democrat*. What would you add to her point concerning funding that might make her case stronger in the eyes of a wider audience who may or may not agree that funding and academic success go hand in hand?

4. The second author ends his piece suggesting some specific steps schools should take. Now that you know more about accountability and school choice, do you agree with his suggestions? If so, why? If not, why not?

Write your letter in understandable terminology, remembering that readers of newspaper Letters to the Editor are citizens who may have limited knowledge of school practices and policies. Remember to refer to the letter assessment rubric in Chapter 1.

IMPACT OF RELIANCE ON PROPERTY TAXES. Let's consider what reliance on property taxes for almost half of public school funding might mean for different communities. A district composed of middle-to-upper socioeconomic suburban neighborhoods with prospering retail stores and a couple of thriving industries will likely generate a healthy amount of money with a relatively low percentage of the assessed property value. In this case people who own homes and businesses pay what might be considered reasonable taxes on their property and appear to have adequate funding for schools. Now think about a district in a very rural area, with a lot of land, but few homes, with families who drive out of the area for jobs or who work in the few businesses located in the district. In this case, home and business owners may have to pay a much larger percentage of the assessed value of their property to support schools. There may simply not be enough property value to generate adequate funding. Finally, consider a densely populated urban area, with many people who are renters in high-rise buildings and often living on government subsidies such as welfare. An area such as this may have large numbers of children and few home owners. In some urban areas, business and industry provide an adequate tax base, but in others the base is very low, resulting in inadequate school funding.

Figure 11.12 Sample community responses to property taxes and their use to fund schools

We moved into this home in 1968. We made the last of our monthly mortgage payments the same year we both retired. Our pensions were supposed to give us enough income to stay right here for as long as our health allows. But year after year the value of the house goes up, with all the new stores and shopping centers popping up in the area. Our property taxes have doubled. If they go much higher, we may have to move. We raised our kids, and now they're raising their own. I'm all for good schools, but not if we lose our home.

I have a good job that allows my wife, who used to be a third grade teacher, to homeschool our two kids. We live in an upscale neighborhood and are very happy with our lives. But what we're not happy about is the way our property taxes are skyrocketing. I believe in public education, but we can afford to homeschool while the kids are young, and then they'll go to our church's private 6–12 school. Why should I have to pay exorbitant property taxes for schools I'll never use?

I don't have kids and never plan to. I like my life as it is, with good friends and a job that calls for me to travel to interesting places. I bought a great downtown loft apartment with payments I can afford. However, now that this area of downtown is being revitalized, the value of my place is on the rise, along with escalating property taxes. I understand that most of this money goes for public schools. Well, the school a few blocks away sure doesn't look like much of my money, or anyone else's, is being spent there. If that school represents how this school district is spending my money, I'll vote for any decrease of the spending cap.

Relying on property taxes to provide a substantial portion of support for public education can create a funding gap that further exacerbates socioeconomic differences. And, as we have discussed, where there are socioeconomic gaps, there are almost certainly achievement gaps. In states with tax caps, it may not be possible for communities to raise the percentage of the tax on assessed property value, even when most people believe it should be done to support their schools. They are stuck with the limit, despite what may be unfair and nonproductive funding. If you hear or see an expression such as "Drop the cap, end the gap," you'll now better understand the meaning of this slogan. Read more about the funding gap in Figure 11.13. With all the problems inherent in using property taxes as the primary source of local funding, alternatives are often sought.

LOCAL FUNDING ALTERNATIVES. Some communities are attempting to support public education through an increase in sales tax. For instance, when sales tax is raised from 6% to 7%, an extra penny is collected for every dollar spent on taxable goods. This translates into a sizable amount of money. For a district, such an increase could mean less dependency on property taxes as the source of local funding.

Another way school districts acquire funds is to borrow money through what is called a **bond referendum,** an amount of money stipulated for specific projects. When using a bond referendum, the school board asks voters in their district to approve the borrowing of the money (the bond) that will be repaid over a period of time. Bond referendums can be for hundreds of millions of dollars. In some states, boards are not required to ask voters for permission to borrow money for schools. The request may need only city or county council approval.

PRIVATE DONATIONS. In addition to federal, state, and local funding, many districts and individual schools receive private gifts of either money or goods. These gifts rarely account for more than 3% of the total amount of school funding (Brimley & Garfield, 2004). Individuals and foundations may contribute to a particular program or project and have a

Figure 11.13 The funding gap

> "Closing the achievement gap is a familiar theme these days. But lurking behind the achievement gap is another contentious issue: funding. Excellence in education doesn't come without a price tag." This statement by Amy Azzam, associate editor of *Educational Leadership*, begins her 2005 special report on *The Funding Gap 2004*, a study conducted by the Education Trust.
>
> The study used the financial data from the U.S. Census from each of the more than 14,000 school districts. The focus of the study was on funding disparities by state between high-poverty and low-poverty districts, as well as between high-minority and low minority districts. The results revealed that more than half the states provide less money to high poverty districts than to low poverty districts. This translates into less money for high-minority areas since there tends to be a higher concentration of minorities in high poverty areas.
>
> The disparities become even more glaring when we consider the fact that it costs more for high-poverty districts to meet the same standards as low-poverty districts, by some estimates as much as 40% more. Education Trust found that with this cost adjustment, 36 states provide an average of $1,348 per students less for high-poverty versus low-poverty districts. Some states have disparities as high as $2,500 per student.
>
> Given the study results, Education Trust recommends that states:
>
> - reduce reliance on local property taxes
> - spend extra money to help low-income children
> - do away with funding gaps among individual schools within districts
>
> Azzam closes her report by stating "Closing the achievement gap starts with closing the funding gap. Only by providing the necessary resources can states help ensure quality education for all students."

Source: Azzam, A. M. (2005). The funding gap. *Educational Leadership, 62*(5), 93.

significant impact on that particular segment of school life. However, states, districts, and schools should be cautious about considering private gifts when planning budgets. These sources are often onetime donations or may prove to be unstable.

How Are Funds for Education Spent?

Just as with the ability to generate money varies greatly from state to state and district to district, the amount each state spends on public education varies as well. Rather than totals per state, the number that is most meaningful is the amount of money spent per pupil.

EXPENDITURE PER PUPIL

The average amount of money spent from federal, state, and local sources on an individual student is called the **expenditure per pupil**. A comparison of expenditures per pupil by state is found in Figure 11.14. Keep in mind as you look at this figure that the cost of living, and consequently the cost of education, varies from state to state and region to region. Does almost three times the learning occur in Washington, D.C., where expenditures per pupil are over $20,000, as in Arizona, where per pupil spending is about $6,300? The answer, of course, is *no*. Look back at Figure 11.13, which points out that children of poverty require 40% more spending. Spending more to educate students who need extra services to succeed in school is being responsive to differences that often relate to race, socioeconomic status, and levels of disabilities. There are so many variables to consider, including issues such as the percentage of teachers who are experts in their teaching fields, state-of-the-art or dilapidated facilities, and large or small class size. They all cost money.

The national average expenditure per pupil has continually increased. Everything required to fund education becomes more expensive, as with any large enterprise. When gas prices rise, so does the cost of transportation. When construction costs rise, so does the cost of building new schools. The more diversified student populations become, the more expensive it is to hire personnel to meet their needs. It is understandable that public education is

Figure 11.14 Average expenditures per pupil by state, 2009

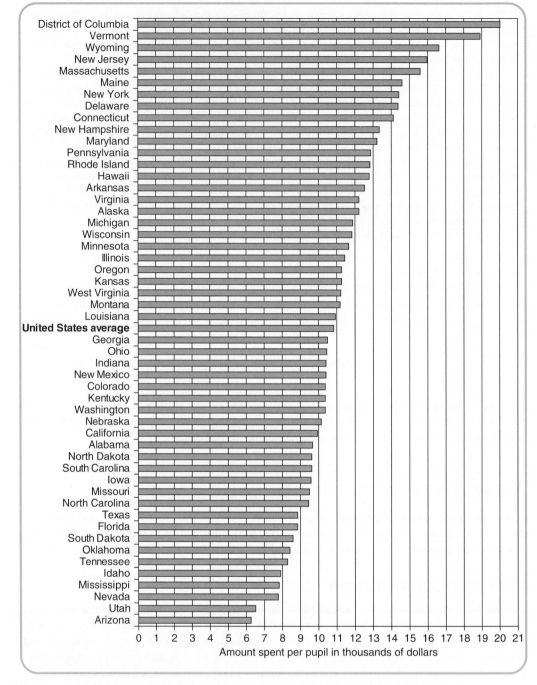

Source: National Education Association. (2009). *Rankings of the states 2008 and estimates of school statistics 2009.* Retrieved June 18, 2010, from http://www.nea.org/assets/docs/09rankings.pdf

Points of Reflection 11.5

What is your view of the connection between spending on education and student achievement? What do you base your opinions on?

criticized for increased spending when there appears to be little progress in terms of test scores. But it is a complicated issue as schools continue to struggle with the connection between spending and levels of learning.

This chapter's *In the News* feature is a story of how private funds and public schools can work together to achieve success, at least cautious success at this point in the tale. The story focuses on the Village Academy in Delray Beach, Florida, and pulls together many of the concepts discussed so far in this book including the achievement gap, segregation and integration, community involvement in schools, class size, and high expectations.

The Power of the Neighborhood School

Village Academy is the first new school to be built in Delray Beach, Florida, in 30 years. Before its establishment many of Delray's children (mostly poor, mostly minority) took long bus rides to get to schools attended primarily by white children from mostly middle- to upper-class families. In this ABC video you see Village Academy as a K–2 school in the beginning. By 2007 it was a K–8 school, with plans to add a grade a year through 12th grade. Village Academy changed not only the length of the bus ride but also the attitudes of an entire community.

To view this video, go to the In the News section of Chapter 11 on MyEducationLab for this text and watch the clip *The Power of the Neighborhood School.* Then respond to these items.

1. In the video you hear that the school has many extras provided through private funding from a philanthropist. Why is this private/public school partnership having the positive results you see at Village Academy?

2. In the video you hear the Village Academy founder say that he has replaced diversity as a goal with the development of the power of community. What does he mean by this?

3. Given what you learned in Chapter 2, what elements of the Village Academy qualify it as a full-service school?

4. Given what you learned about the dropout epidemic in the United States in Chapter 9, what are some plausible reasons for the high dropout rate of minority students bused to other areas from Delray Beach?

ALLOCATION OF EDUCATION FUNDING

With any large endeavor there are administrative and other costs that affect, either directly or indirectly, the cause or people served. So it is with education. It would be wonderful if 90% of an education budget could go directly into the classroom to pay teachers, buy books and supplies, and provide the latest technology. But as you saw earlier in this chapter, support for the work of individual teachers in their classrooms requires (at least as the education system is currently configured) people in district and state positions. Some of the current programs with the greatest impact require national level support as well.

Figure 11.15 shows the average expenses of a school district. Considering there are more than 15,000 school districts, labeling only about 10% of the spending as "Other support services" isn't bad. The allocation of more than 60% directly to instruction is impressive, with most spent on teacher salaries. The rest buys books, classroom supplies, technology, and so on.

- *General administration* includes district-level administrators.
- *Student transportation* mainly involves school buses. The buses must be purchased, maintained, and filled with gas, and drivers must be paid.
- *Instructional staff support* includes curriculum and instruction specialists, teacher training, and teacher assistants.
- *Student support services* include school psychologists, nurses, behavior specialists, home liaisons, and others who work with students with needs, special and otherwise (not including special education teachers).
- *School administration* refers to principals and assistant principals and funds needed to support their positions. Notice that over twice as much is spent at the school level versus the district level.
- *Operation and maintenance* includes anything related to facilities—building repair, custodial staff, lights, water, heat, air-conditioning, and grounds.

Figure 11.15 How funds are spent at the district level

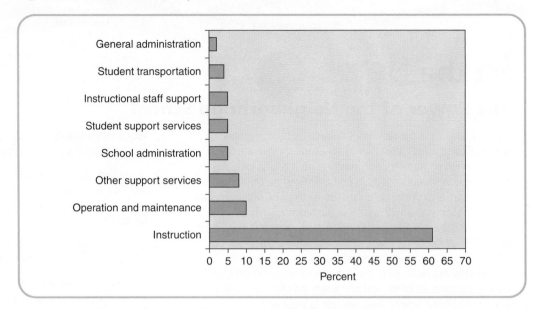

Source: U.S. Census Bureau. (2009). Public education finances. Washington, DC: Author.

CONCLUDING THOUGHTS

The only way teachers can hope to understand and possibly influence the more political aspects of education in the United States—basically what happens outside the individual classroom—is, first of all, to be informed. It's actually very interesting to learn about the support systems that help us do what we do in the classroom. You can be engaged by keeping up with education-related current events at all levels and informed by reading education journals and books. The second step to affecting the bigger picture of education is to have the will to be involved, to step outside the classroom doors and advocate for children in the larger arena of the community, the district, the state, and the nation.

After reading the ***Chapter in Review,*** read about Chris, Brenda, and Tim as they advocate for an after-school arts program at Rees Elementary. Then respond to items in this chapter's ***Developing Professional Competence.***

Chapter in Review

How does the federal government influence public education in the United States?

- The president, the U.S. Congress, and the federal court system endorse specific programs and make and enforce laws that impact schools.
- The U.S. Department of Education initiates programs and mandates the compliance of states using federal money as leverage.

What is the state's role in public education?

- Each state has its own unique governance system.
- State governors, legislatures, and court systems all impact the functioning of education within the state.

- A state board of education is a volunteer policy-making body that has oversight responsibilities.
- A state department of education functions under the leadership of a state superintendent and many administrators who work to support schools and teachers.

How do school districts function?

- A school district is made up of schools defined by geographic boundaries.
- District school boards set policies that affect the operation of schools.
- A district superintendent is the chief executive officer of a school district and may have a staff with specified duties.

What is the management structure of individual schools?

- The principal oversees every aspect of a school and answers to the district for all that occurs.
- Assistant principals and teacher leaders play important roles in school management.

What other entities impact the governance of public schools in the United States?

- Parents and families have the potential to positively impact student success in school.
- Businesses have a vested interest in effective schools that prepare their employees and consumers. Business-school partnerships benefit both.
- Universities and teacher education faculty prepare teachers and impact education.
- Special interest groups are composed of concerned citizens who work for the benefit of specific causes within schools.

How are public schools financed?

- On average, state and local funding share about 92% of the funding burden equally, with federal funds accounting for most of the rest.
- Federal funds are either earmarked for specific purposes in the form of categorical grants or given for states to use at their discretion in the form of block grants.
- State funds are generated primarily through sales taxes and income taxes.
- Most local funds usually come from property taxes, a controversial source.
- Private donations provide boosts to specific programs and efforts but account for a very small percentage of total school funding.

How are funds for education spent?

- The amount spent on each student, the expenditure per pupil, varies greatly from state to state.
- Over half of the money spent on public education goes for expenses related to classroom instruction. The rest is spent on support services, including administration, facilities, and transportation.

Developing Professional Competence

Visit the Developing Professional Competence section on Chapter 11 of the MyEducationLab for this text to answer the following questions and begin your preparation for licensure exams.

The arts emphasis at Rees Elementary School is more extensive than in most elementary schools. Both fine arts and performance arts are part of the everyday world of Rees students. They learn about art and do art during the school day, with evidence of this on display throughout the school. But as their student population begins to shift, and the teachers become aware of more and more students going home to empty houses and remaining there for several hours before their parents get home from long days at work, Chris, Brenda, and Tim decide it's time to take art beyond the 3 P.M. afternoon dismissal bell. To do this will take time and money.

Chris Roberts has a good idea about what's involved in working through the public school governance system, thanks to his experiences with the initiation of multiage classrooms. He has volunteered to take on the task of finding support for the idea of Afternoon Arts and finding funding to make it happen. He understands the meaning and value of these two pertinent standards:

INTASC Principle 10, Knowledge

The teacher understands schools as organizations within the larger community context and understands the operations of the relevant aspects of the system(s) within which s/he works.

NBPTS

Accomplished teachers can evaluate school progress and the allocation of school resources in light of their understanding of state and local educational objectives.

Think through this scenario and answer the following multiple-choice questions:

1. What challenges do you anticipate that may stem from the fact that Rees Elementary is in Utah?
   a. Utah is a rural state and incorporating the arts may be difficult.

b. Utah's per pupil expenditure is comparatively quite low.
   c. There may be resistance among the new families in the Rees attendance zone.
   d. There are few models of arts programs.

2. In what order would Chris want to present the Afternoon Arts program to individuals and groups to gain approval and possible funding?
   a. principal, district arts director, community businesses, families.
   b. families, principal, district arts director, state curriculum director.
   c. principal, community businesses, families, district arts director.
   d. principal, district arts director, state curriculum director, families.

3. Rees has a state arts grant, but this funding will be withdrawn next year, given the tough economic times. Which of the following would *not* be a possible source of funding for Afternoon Arts?

   a. community businesses contributing to the program
   b. district funding designated for at-risk students
   c. federal categorical grant
   d. federal block grant

Now it's time for you to respond to two short essay items involving the scenario. In your responses, be sure to address all the dilemmas and questions posed in each item. Your responses should each be between one half and one double-spaced page.

4. Refer to item 2. In one well-developed sentence for each, describe the kind of support Chris might expect from the people/groups in the response choices.

5. The teachers who believe in the potential of Afternoon Arts will likely want to be part of the program. Should they be paid for the 3 hours a day required, or should the intrinsic value of the program and what it may mean to kids who need it be enough reward for their efforts? Justify your response.

Where DO I Stand NOW?

In the beginning of the chapter you responded to 40 items, indicating your level of agreement with each concerning who and/or what agency should be in charge of which aspects of school. Now that you have read the chapter, completed exercises related to the content, engaged in class discussions and so on, complete the following items in your course notebook.

1. What is one aspect of how the federal government interacts with public education that you think is viable and why? What is one aspect of how the federal government interacts with public education that you do *not* agree with and why?

2. From what you now know about sources of funding for public schools, with which aspect do you agree most (examples: fed-

   eral percentage and use; state percentage and where it comes from; local funding through property taxes; other)?

3. Look back at **Where Do I Stand?** and determine one item on which your opinion varies by least 2 points from what you now know to be reality. Have you changed your opinion? If so, why? If not, why not?

MyEducationLab

The MyEducationLab for this course can help you solidify your comprehension of Chapter 11 concepts.

- Explore the classrooms of the teachers and students you've met in this chapter in the Teaching in Focus section.
- Prepare for licensure exams as you deepen your understanding of chapter concepts in the Developing Professional Competence section.

- Gauge and further develop your understanding of chapter concepts by taking the quizzes and examining the enrichment materials on the Chapter 11 Study Plan.
- Visit Topic 5, "Governance and Finance," to watch ABC videos, explore Assignments and Activities, and practice essential teaching skills with the Building Teaching Skills and Dispositions unit.

12

Developing
Professionalism

This chapter looks at a broad range of professional responsibilities and opportunities. The following questions guide our discussion.

✦ How can I practice professionalism during teacher preparation?

✦ How does professionalism look in the various relationships involved in teaching?

✦ How can I develop as a professional when I am a teacher?

✦ What do I have to offer the teaching profession?

✦ What is my role as a professional in education reform?

Before we discuss professional responsibilities and opportunities, explore your own views in this chapter's *Where Do I Stand?*

Where DO I Stand?

As you think through the following statements that prompt you to consider your own views, indicate your level of agreement by choosing a number and placing it in the blank before the statement. Following the inventory are directions for how to organize your responses and what they may mean in terms of where you stand.

4   I strongly agree
3   I agree
2   I don't have an opinion
1   I disagree
0   I strongly disagree

_____ **1.** Professionalism entails meeting responsibilities head on, as well as taking full advantage of opportunities involving teaching and learning.

_____ **2.** One of the most valuable aspects of a teacher preparation program is the opportunity to spend time in schools.

_____ **3.** Becoming a professional entails reflecting on field experiences in schools.

_____ **4.** Upon graduation, a teacher candidate has time to develop professional attitudes and actions.

_____ **5.** Being positive is a choice. It doesn't mean glossing over difficulties but rather approaching each day with possibilities in focus.

_____ **6.** Core courses, although interesting, have little bearing on teacher preparation.

_____ **7.** It is very important to respect the adults and students in your school.

_____ **8.** Spending time in schools is peripheral to learning to be a teacher.

_____ **9.** Becoming a professional involves field experiences that let you see reality, reflect on what you see, and formulate possible solutions to the dilemmas you observe.

_____ **10.** Learning what not to do as a result of seeing its actual, or potential, damage is powerful.

_____ **11.** Being realistic about schools is counter to being positive about the possibilities of quality education.

_____ **12.** When we fulfill our responsibilities and take advantage of our opportunities involving relationships, we are doing so for the children and adolescents we teach.

_____ **13.** We only learn valuable lessons in professionalism from positive role models.

_____ **14.** Teachers who take responsibility for student learning take no excuses—from students, parents, or themselves.

_____ **15.** Part of professionalism entails teaching the whole child, requiring that we accept students for who they are rather than what they do.

_____ **16.** When conditions outside the classroom are severely impaired, making a positive difference for kids within our classrooms is close to impossible.

_____ **17.** When we take responsibility for teaching all students unconditionally, regardless of the circumstances, we will necessarily have high expectations for them.

_____ **18.** The way schools care about children is reflected in the way schools care about the children's families.

_____ **19.** Parental involvement is actually an interference in many instances.

20. Parental involvement matters to student achievement.

21. Teachers need to grasp the reality of parental concern and tenaciously find ways to involve them.

22. Professional courtesy dictates that teachers not observe one another in their classrooms because of the possibility of being judgmental.

23. Whatever the barriers to parental involvement, teachers need to strive continually to break them down by cultivating an invitational attitude.

24. Part of being a professional teacher is knowing what is available and, along with administrators and counselors, making sure families are aware of how to access community services.

25. Although teachers have responsibility for the welfare of students in their classrooms while in school, they bear little responsibility for their relationships with students' families.

26. Professional growth is an absolute necessity for teacher effectiveness

27. There is always something to be learned when teachers get together, regardless of the perceived quality or relevance of what is formally presented.

28. Teachers have a responsibility to join professional organizations to help build the teaching profession.

29. Classrooms and groups of children benefit from engaging lessons, but this does not promote the professionalism of teaching.

30. When a teacher tries an instructional strategy that works well with a particular topic, or with a specific group of students, sharing the experience with other teachers is an act of professionalism.

Now record your responses in these tables, find the sum of each column, and then divide each sum by 10 to determine A, B, and C.

ITEM#	MY RESPONSE	ITEM#	MY RESPONSE	ITEM#	MY RESPONSE
1		17		4	
2		18		6	
3		20		8	
5		21		11	
7		23		13	
9		24		16	
10		26		19	
12		27		22	
14		28		25	
15		30		29	
Sum =		Sum =		Sum =	
÷10 =	= A	÷ 10 =	= B	÷ 10 =	= C

Because C indicates levels of disagreement with negative concepts, subtract C from 4. This becomes D, a positive indicator.

Now add A, B, and D and divide the sum by 3. Plot this number on the number line to see where you fall on a continuum of professional attitudes.

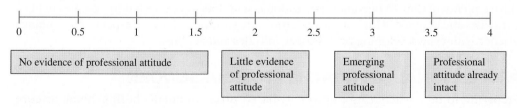

| 0 | 0.5 | 1 | 1.5 | 2 | 2.5 | 3 | 3.5 | 4 |

| No evidence of professional attitude | Little evidence of professional attitude | Emerging professional attitude | Professional attitude already intact |

Does your place on the number line accurately reflect where you think you are with regard to teacher professionalism? If so, why? If not, why not?

Teaching in Focus

As the English language arts and social studies teacher for Cario Middle School's CARE (Cario Academic Recovery and Enrichment) program, Deirdre Huger-McGrew has some unique challenges. Her students have experienced little academic success so far in school. Deirdre's responsibility is to provide learning opportunities for her students, along with the assistance necessary for them to progress to their appropriate grade levels in both knowledge and skills. Deirdre believes that computer skills are essential for her students and uses computer technology as an integral part of instruction. Deirdre is fulfilling her professional responsibilities by exploring, and then choosing and using, approaches that match the learning needs of her CARE students.

The Scholastic READ 180 program Deirdre chose for her students is designed to teach older students to read with fluency and comprehension. Reading intervention is accomplished through individualized instruction based on both ability level and specific need. READ 180 follows a comprehensive cycle of instruction that includes

1. a brief anchor video that provides background information to help the student understand what will be read

2. text about the video written at the student's predetermined reading level

3. prompts that allow the student to access help in decoding words, phrases, or whole passages

4. comprehension questions

5. a summary of how many words and phrases are correctly read and how many questions are correctly answered

6. opportunities to reread the passage with varying levels of support to build speed and accuracy (Hasselbring & Bausch, 2006)

The students in Deirdre's class have access to a library of books specifically related to the topics presented in the computerized videos and reading passages, as well as audiotapes of most of the books, allowing them to follow along as they listen. Focus student David McBeath's mom has encouraged him for years to listen to tapes and follow along in books to help increase his reading proficiency. So the instructional strategies used in Deirdre's classroom are reinforced at home.

Watch Deirdre Huger-McGrew's interview, room tour, and lesson as well as David McBeath's interview that includes his mom, in the Teaching in Focus section for Chapter 12 in MyEducationLab for this course.

Professionalism entails meeting responsibilities head on, as well as taking full advantage of opportunities involving teaching and learning. Responsibility and opportunity have a symbiotic relationship. You may recall from biology that when organisms are symbiotic, they have a close relationship that is advantageous to both. Responsibilities and opportunities are so close that they flow into one another. When responsibilities are fulfilled, opportunities are created; when opportunities are recognized and acted upon, their benefits incur responsibilities.

The close and mutually advantageous relationship between responsibility and opportunity is illustrated in Figure 12.1. Like the sand flowing from one chamber into the other in an hourglass, when responsibility is on top and is being fulfilled, it flows into opportunity. Similarly, when we make the most of opportunities, we are turning the hourglass over and watching each grain of our efforts create new responsibilities. This concept applies to each section of this chapter. Think of it often as you read.

How Can I Practice Professionalism During Teacher Preparation?

Many aspects of professionalism are discussed in Chapter 1 and referred to throughout the text.

This may be the first course in your teacher preparation sequence. You might be thinking, "I have plenty of time to become a professional, with lots of classes left to take and field experiences ahead of me." However, it's not too early to approach every aspect of becoming a teacher with ever-developing professional attitudes and actions.

PROFESSIONAL APPROACHES TO COURSEWORK

Preparing to be a teacher in a university-based program entails both general, or core, courses and courses that specifically address your future career as a classroom teacher.

Figure 12.1 The relationship between responsibility and opportunity

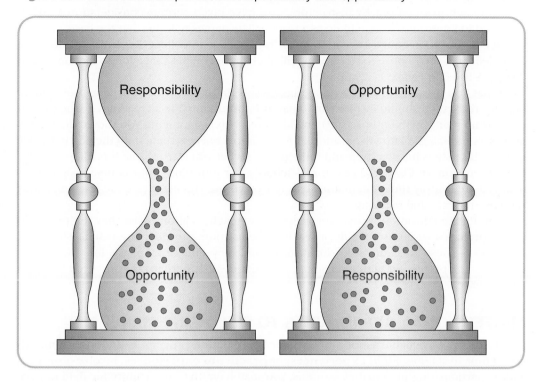

GENERAL EDUCATION COURSES. Most of your classes so far have likely been core courses required for most of the students who attend your college. They should not be viewed as fillers or as experiences that must be endured until you can enroll in classes specifically designed for teacher preparation. Because teachers need to be informed, interested, and interesting, core courses enhance teacher preparation by providing a wide spectrum of information and skills that are foundational for teachers and contribute to your status as a well-rounded adult. What you learn will help you put much of what you teach into context.

Some core courses provide opportunities for you to develop dispositions that determine attitudes and values you carry with you for life. Others lay the groundwork for a content area major required of most high school teachers, many middle-level teachers, and a growing number of elementary and early childhood teachers, depending on state licensure requirements and individual university programs. Table 12.1 may help you see more clearly the value of non-teacher-education coursework to your future as a teacher.

Points of Reflection 12.1

Which core courses do you enjoy or find exceptionally interesting? Which do you credit more for your affinity for these classes: the subject matter or the instructors' strategies? Why?

TABLE 12.1 Importance of non-teacher-education coursework	
Course	**Promotes an understanding of . . .**
Philosophy	pursuit of truth; nature of conflict; structure of knowledge
Psychology	nature of learning; knowledge of self; research methods; study of behavior
Sociology	socialization; socioeconomic status; social rules/processes; human social interaction
History	perspective from past; lessons of conflict; methods of problem solving
English	communication; literacy; persuasive writing
Math	logic; problem solving
Science	scientific method; experimentation; cause/effect

TEACHER EDUCATION COURSES. Your plan of study within a department of education has been mapped out by instructors who have given serious consideration to what you need to know and be able to do as a teacher. The names will vary, but the basic content of teacher education courses is fairly similar from college to college. Regardless of the level or subject area you choose to teach, you will likely have courses that address the topics and concepts listed in Figure 12.2 and more.

What you learn in your education classes lays the groundwork for your professional life. This realization should inspire you to pay attention, complete all readings, participate in class group work (with enthusiasm!), and keep up with assignments. You should do what is necessary to *own* the knowledge and skills, not simply *borrow* them until the end of the semester. This means internalizing and reflecting on what you learn through reading, lecture, class discussion, and experiences in real schools. Put more into your course assignments than required. Apply the content and skills to everything you know and are learning about schools, students, and teaching.

The Public Education Network surveyed new teachers about what they felt prepared and unprepared to do as a result of teacher preparation. Consider the results, shown in Figure 12.3. These areas of professionalism should be points of emphasis for you to help you enter the profession with a sense of preparedness that perhaps the surveyed teachers did not have.

PROFESSIONAL APPROACHES TO FIELD EXPERIENCES

One of the most valuable aspects of a teacher preparation program is the opportunity to spend time in schools. **Field experiences,** or **practicum experiences,** involve observing and/or participating in actual classrooms. You may have the opportunity for field experiences in early childhood, elementary, middle, and high school classrooms before you are

Figure 12.2 Topics/concepts addressed in teacher education coursework

Human growth and development	Educational technology
Exceptional learners	Curriculum development
Educational psychology	Instructional strategies
Education and society	Classroom management
Education and diversity	Schools, families, and community
Learning theory	Arts integration
Group dynamics	Techniques for teaching reading
History of education	Content/level-specific methods
Legal, governance, and financial aspects of education	courses

Figure 12.3 Survey results of perceived new teacher preparedness

New teachers feel most prepared to . . .

- create collaborative classroom environments
- teach all students
- develop curriculum that builds on student interests and needs
- understand how student development influences learning
- relate classroom experience to the real world

New teachers feel least prepared to . . .

- address learning needs of English-language learners
- work with families
- develop interdisciplinary curriculum
- address special learning needs
- assume leadership

Source: Public Education Network (2003). *The voice of the new teacher.* Washington, DC: Author.

required to declare your chosen level of certification. You may also have a chance to observe in related arts and special education classes. Ideally you will have the opportunity to visit rural, suburban, and urban schools. All of these experiences will help you decide who, what, and where you may want to teach.

Here are some general guidelines for professionally approaching field experiences. Following these guidelines with enthusiasm will make field experiences meaningful in schools with real teachers and real students.

1. Know your instructor's expectations.
2. Dress and behave with respect.
3. Remember you are a guest in the school.
4. Keep a detailed log of your experiences even if it is not required.
5. Spend time after each field experience reflecting on your time in schools. Write questions about what you observed.

EARLY FIELD EXPERIENCES. Early field experiences will likely be devoted to **structured observations.** This means you will be looking for specific things and responding to prompts that purposefully call attention to certain aspects of the classroom. If you are observing the learning environment, you may complete a form similar to Figure 12.4. You may be asked to focus on the students as a group, or perhaps on an individual student, using a form similar to Figure 12.5.

Field experiences that are associated with, or embedded in, **methods courses** will likely incorporate your first teaching experiences. Methods courses are those that emphasize particular strategies for specific subjects and will probably incorporate opportunities to actually apply what you are learning.

STUDENT TEACHING. Clinical practice, or student teaching, is the capstone internship experience of your teacher preparation program. The one- or two-semester experience will allow you to use what you have learned in your courses and practiced in your other field

Figure 12.4 Observing the learning environment and classroom management techniques

Name _____ Date _____ Time _____
Class observed _____ Teacher _____
School _____ Lesson topic _____

1. Describe the classroom. Include neatness, creative use of space/walls, arrangement of desks/tables, technology available, unusual features, student work displayed, etc.
2. Does the teacher have easy proximity to all the students?
3. What technique does the teacher use to get the attention of the students?
4. Is an established behavior plan in place? How can you tell?
5. Do any behavior problems become evident? If so, describe them.
6. How does the teacher handle behavior difficulties?
7. Do you sense that the classroom environment is conducive to learning? Why or why not?

Figure 12.5 Observing an individual student

Name _____ Date _____ Time _____
Student observed (first name) _____ Teacher _____
School _____ Grade _____ Lesson topic _____

1. What do you notice about this student (physical appearance, cultural background, language, social interaction, skills and abilities, motivation, attitude, self-concept, etc.)?
2. How is the student responding to the teacher's lesson?
3. Is the student interacting with other students? Describe.
4. What is the quality of the student's work?
5. Name something positive the student did during the lesson.
6. Name something negative the student did during the lesson.
7. What else did you observe about the student?

Your college supervisor during student teaching can be a valuable resource and confidant.

experiences. You will get to know a group of students well as you gradually take over full teaching duties. Your student teaching experience will probably require the hardest work you've ever done. George Posner (2005), a recognized expert on field experience, gives us six simple, practical goals for student teaching. He tells us that student teaching will allow you to:

1. find out what teaching is really like
2. see if you really like teaching
3. see if you really can do it
4. learn some skills and modify certain habits and characteristics
5. begin to develop your own approach or style
6. apply what you've learned in college to real students and to real classrooms (p. 16)

During student teaching, two people will fill very important roles. One is your cooperating teacher in whose classroom you will spend at least 10 weeks, and possibly a full school year. The other very important adult in your student teaching experience is your college supervisor. This instructor will visit you and your cooperating teacher numerous times to observe your lessons and give constructive feedback. In addition, your supervisor will probably have other clinical interns and will meet regularly with all of you as a group. These meetings provide opportunities for you to talk about your experiences in nonthreatening and empathetic circumstances.

Renee Ayers, our second grade focus teacher at Summit Primary School, has a growing concern about the student teachers she has met at her school. They're good teacher preparation students with lots of knowledge, skills, and enthusiasm for teaching. Renee's concern centers on what she perceives to be their lack of variety of field experiences. Read about her dilemma in this chapter's *Diversity Dialogue.*

DIVERSITY
DIALOGUE

Renee Ayers has had three student teachers so far. She has been asked by her principal, Laura Hill, to be the overseer of cooperating and student teachers at Summit. The professional expectation is that Renee will speak regularly with both the cooperating teachers and their teacher prep college students to help them plan for their time together and solve any potential problems. In exchange, Renee will be paid a small stipend.

After 9 years at Summit Primary, Renee is well aware that the teaching conditions there are superior to the conditions at many other schools in the Columbus, Ohio, area. The Summit student population poses more challenges now than when she first began teaching there, primarily because of the increase in language diversity. But in spite of increasing challenges, teaching at Summit is a pleasure, due in large measure to excellent colleagues and the leadership and support of Laura Hill. In fact, all the schools in the Licking Heights School District are good places to teach for many of the same reasons Renee enjoys at Summit.

Student teachers are placed in Licking Heights schools by area universities, one of which is a local 4-year college, with others in the Columbus vicinity. Renee developed a get-to-know-you form for the student teachers assigned to K–2 classrooms at her school. One question asks about the purposes of prior field experiences and where they were placed. Renee started noticing a pattern that she found disturbing. She created a table to record the student teachers' colleges and the locations of their field experiences. She discovered that almost all the field experiences of teacher candidates from the local college were exclusively in the Licking Heights School District, whereas the teacher candidates from the Columbus vicinity colleges had a balance of field experiences in rural, suburban, and urban schools. Licking Heights schools are rural and suburban only.

Generalizations about the differences among rural, suburban, and urban schools are discussed in Chapter 2.

As we know from *Meet the Focus Teachers and Students,* Renee's twin sister, Tara, teaches high school physics in an urban school. Her day-to-day professional life is different from Renee's in many ways. Obviously, grade level makes a difference. But so does the setting. Renee sees a need for the local college students to experience the diversity of urban settings as part of their teacher preparation.

Respond to these items by writing one well-developed paragraph for each.

1. Describe possible reasons for Renee's concern with regard to students, parental support, facilities, job openings for teacher candidates, and other aspects of diversity between urban and rural/suburban settings. While we know these are generalizations, it is still helpful to think about them.
2. Renee has decided to take her table of data and her concerns to the local college and talk with the department of education faculty. How could Renee begin the conversation in a professional way? What obstacles might the college face in diversifying field placements, even if they agree with Renee?

For a glimpse of Renee's teaching style, watch her lesson by going to the Teaching in Focus *section* for Chapter 12 in *MyEducationLab for this course.*

As with other field experiences, there are commonsense things you can do to make the most of student teaching. Here are some professional attitudes and actions that will be valuable to you.

1. *Keep a journal.* You will probably be asked to do this by your supervising instructor. Keeping a journal will help you reflect and learn more from your experiences.

2. *Keep up.* You will be very busy, with more responsibility and pressure than you've ever experienced. There will be lesson plans to write, materials to gather, paperwork to complete—all this while you are learning your craft, your profession. Don't let any aspect slide, and don't get behind.

3. *Be positive.* We choose our attitudes. Being positive is a choice. It doesn't mean glossing over difficulties but rather approaching each day with possibilities in focus.

4. *Be realistic.* Being realistic is not in conflict with being positive. It is acceptance that some of your lessons will not go as planned, nor are you going to solve all the problems of the students in your classroom. You are learning to be a teacher.

5. *Confide in someone you trust.* You will find that no one understands what you are experiencing as completely as another clinical intern. You should also confide in your supervisor.

6. *Be respectful.* Dress and speak respectfully; be respectful of the adults and students in your school. Earn their respect.

PROBLEMS IN REAL CLASSROOMS

It's very likely that you will see and hear things in schools that are contrary to what you are learning in teacher preparation. In real classrooms, the variables are many and teachers, as human beings, do not always approach responsibilities and opportunities in the best possible ways, or even in ways that seem acceptable. One of the purposes of field experiences is to let you see reality, reflect on what you see, and formulate possible solutions to the dilemmas you observe.

You will no doubt see what you consider poor instruction. You will probably hear a teacher or two scream at children or humiliate a child in front of the class. It is difficult to watch this type of behavior and say nothing. But you must remain calm. Remember: You are the guest. It is not your place to correct a teacher or act indignant in the face of teacher behavior you view as inappropriate. Also realize that you do not know the whole picture. You are seeing a snapshot. The time to express your dismay, or even outrage, is in your college class or student teaching seminar with an instructor and classmates. We learn a great deal from observing incorrect methods and behavior. Learning what *not* to do as a result of seeing its actual, or potential, damage is powerful.

Points of Reflection 12.2

Are you excited about field experiences? What aspects do you think you will enjoy most? What aspects do you think will cause some level of anxiety for you? Why?

TEACHER PREPARATION PORTFOLIO

A **portfolio for teacher preparation** is a cohesive package of representative products. In teacher preparation, a portfolio may either document growth or display best work, depending on its purpose. A teacher preparation portfolio may be composed of items such as lesson plans, student artifacts, sample assessments, journal entries, sample letters to parents, and your resume. A portfolio that documents growth will help you see areas of progress and detect areas of either weakness or lack of experience. A portfolio that displays your best work can be used to document accomplishments and may be an excellent tool when you begin looking for a teaching position.

If a portfolio is required, you will want to explicitly follow the guidelines you are given. If a portfolio is not required, it is advisable to create one on your own to exhibit what you know and can do. Although keeping a large notebook with hard copies is still acceptable if you develop a portfolio on your own, chances are that if your college requires a portfolio it will be in electronic form.

How Does Professionalism Look in the Various Relationships Involved in Teaching?

As a service, or "helping," profession, teaching involves relationships to a larger extent than almost any other profession. From students, to families, to the community, relationships are key to success. Within the profession, other adults in our schools and in the district present opportunities for mutually advantageous relationships. When we fulfill our responsibilities and take advantage of our opportunities involving relationships, we are doing so for the children and adolescents we teach. Building and maintaining strong relationships helps us ask and answer the recurring questions, "And how are the children? Are they all well?" in resoundingly positive ways.

PROFESSIONAL RELATIONSHIPS WITH STUDENTS

For teachers, students are absolutely at the top of the list of professional responsibilities and the primary focus of opportunities.

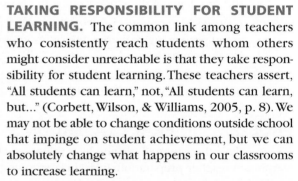

Focus teacher Tim Mendenhall maintains high expectations for his students while creating an inviting environment.

TAKING RESPONSIBILITY FOR STUDENT LEARNING. The common link among teachers who consistently reach students whom others might consider unreachable is that they take responsibility for student learning. These teachers assert, "All students can learn," not, "All students can learn, but..." (Corbett, Wilson, & Williams, 2005, p. 8). We may not be able to change conditions outside school that impinge on student achievement, but we can absolutely change what happens in our classrooms to increase learning.

Teachers who take responsibility for student learning take no excuses—from students, parents, or themselves. They find ways to engage students in learning. They use instructional strategies appropriate for both the content and the learners, and they model respect and enthusiasm. To them, "effective teaching means giving students no other choice but success" (Corbett et al., 2005, p. 12).

HIGH EXPECTATIONS. When we take responsibility for teaching all students unconditionally, regardless of the circumstances, we necessarily have high expectations for them (Gehrke, 2005). In his article "They Can Because They Think They Can," Richard Vacca (2006), noted expert in the field of reading instruction, states that providing learning experiences that allow students to be successful will increase their sense of **self-efficacy.** Vacca tells us, "Self-efficacy is an 'I can' belief in oneself that leads to a sense of competence" (p. 56). High expectations can foster this sense of competency. Unlike sometimes empty techniques that focus on building self-efficacy with words but are devoid of actual accomplishments, Vacca's concept of self-efficacy is solidly grounded in the accomplishment of a continuum of increasingly difficult challenges. As students master a concept or skill, they are encouraged to attempt even more difficult tasks. In this way, our high expectations for students lead to their own high expectations for themselves.

Focus teacher Craig Cleveland encourages students and helps build their sense of self-efficacy. Watch Craig's interview with focus student Guillermo Toscano, including a discussion with Guillermo's mom, in the Teaching in Focus *section for Chapter 12 in MyEducationLab for this course.*

PROFESSIONAL RELATIONSHIPS WITH FAMILIES

Involving families in the life of the school benefits the educational process in many ways. Parents are a child's first teachers. During the critically important years between birth and age 5, parents (and their choice of child-care providers) have great impact on children. In addition, for the rest of childhood and adolescence, parental modeling and attitudes influence students' success in school. "The way schools care about children is reflected in the way schools care about the children's families" (Epstein et al., 2002, p. 7). Throughout this section the words *parents* and *families* are used interchangeably to acknowledge the multiple ways people come together in a home.

Marzano (2003) tells us that parental involvement increases academic achievement and attendance rates and leads to more positive attitudes and behavior of students in the classroom. That's a formula for success! Although all students benefit from parental involvement, low-income and culturally diverse students are particularly more likely to succeed when family members communicate with, and are active in, the life of the school (Epstein et al., 2002).

Points of Reflection 12.3

Do you believe that what a teacher does in the classroom can overcome obstacles to learning that students face outside the classroom, such as poverty, lack of family involvement, and a background deficient in content and skills? Why or why not?

Family diversity is discussed in Chapter 3.

INVOLVING FAMILIES. Family involvement can take many forms, from consistently encouraging students to complete homework, to attending parent-teacher conferences, to volunteering regularly in the school or classroom, or even to serving on a district school board. James Comer (2005), a professor at Yale University School of Medicine's Child Study Center since 1968, endorses the development of "a yearlong, school-wide schedule of activities designed to support instruction and to create positive relationships in the school" (p. 40). This schedule may include

- parent volunteer opportunities that include materials preparation and working with students who may need extra help
- parent-student-teacher events, such as family math night and career exploration workshops
- student performances, such as chorus and band concerts, sports events, and club activities

Through participation, parents show support for both students and teachers. In turn, they gain a sense of connection with the education of their children.

Parental involvement can positively affect not only their own children but also whole classes and schools.

FAMILY COMMUNICATION. Teachers are responsible for communicating with families. Events such as Back-to-School Night, Open House, and parent conferences provide opportunities for teachers to talk about their curriculum, classrooms, and students. New teachers should ask experienced teachers about the format and general procedures for these events.

In addition to school-wide and regularly scheduled forms of communication, there are many other ways teachers can invite families to participate in their students' education, including:

1. *Welcome letter.* Sending a letter to families at the beginning of the school year is a good way for you to introduce yourself, inform parents about policies and procedures that are specific to your class, tell parents about volunteer opportunities, and let parents know how and when to reach you.

2. *Classroom newsletter.* Weekly or monthly newsletters sent home with students can keep parents informed and give them ideas for how to encourage students to complete school assignments and homework. Make sure the written communication you send home is error free.

3. *Homework hotline.* Many schools have a telephone system that allows parents to hear messages and homework assignments. The success of such a system depends on the regularity with which teachers update information.

4. *Phone calls.* Not all phone calls home signal trouble at school. Using the telephone to communicate good news is powerful. Imagine a parent hearing, "Good afternoon, Mrs. Lawson. This is Annie Morgan, Brandon's math teacher. I just wanted to tell you that Brandon took the lead today in his group's problem-solving activity. I was so proud of how he worked with the other students to come up with a unique solution!" Now imagine the smile that spreads across Mrs. Lawson's face, especially if Brandon is often the object of not-so-positive school communication. The teacher has taken an important step toward gaining Mrs. Lawson as a partner in Brandon's education and support should she need assistance in the future to help correct an undesirable trait Brandon might demonstrate. She has also encouraged Brandon to continue his positive behavior.

   Some phone calls home may be for reasons that include a negative change in a student's achievement or attitude, unacceptable behavior, and incomplete or missing work. These calls need to be handled professionally. If possible, it's best to have negative discussions in person so there can be face-to-face dialogue, but the initial call may be an invitation for such a meeting.

   Always prepare for phone calls, positive or negative, beforehand. Tips on how to do this are in Figure 12.6.

5. *Electronic communication.* Parent and teacher communication via email has become the norm. It can be done day or night, without disturbing the receiving party. When using e-mail, don't be sloppy. Use a salutation, as well as uppercase and lowercase letters. Do not use faddish abbreviations. The guidelines for both written and telephone communication apply to email communication as well.

PARENT-STUDENT-TEACHER CONFERENCES. For many beginning teachers, as well as a fair share of experienced ones, conference time is anticipated with dread. Rather than

Figure 12.6 Tips for calling parents

Here are some tips for making the most of phone calls to parents:

- Introduce yourself and make sure the parent understands who you are.
- Ask if the parent has a few minutes to talk.
- Be cordial.
- Try to begin with a positive statement.
- Be clear about the purpose of the call: simply to inform, schedule a conference, request return of forms or signed papers, or ask for some action needed at home.
- Listen actively.
- Thank the parent for his or her interest and willingness to do whatever you have asked.
- Be prepared to leave a concise message that may be heard by the student and other family members.

Figure 12.7 Guidelines for parent-student-teacher conferences

1. Consider parents allies, not enemies.
2. Ask that students attend when appropriate.
3. Arrange comfortable, nonthreatening seating, preferably around a table to increase the flow of communication.
4. Begin with positive statements about the students.
5. Present information as objectively as possible, including data when helpful.
6. Listen attentively, make eye contact, and encourage genuine interaction.
7. Avoid educational jargon.
8. Make a plan for success involving commitment and action from student, parents, and teacher.
9. Keep a written record of topics, decisions, plans, and so on, and send a copy to parents.
10. Follow through and follow up.

viewing conferences as responsibilities to be endured, approach them as opportunities to cultivate a partnership with parents for the sake of students. Figure 12.7 lists guidelines for conducting conferences that are more pleasant for everyone, as well as productive, and with the potential for longer-lasting impact.

One of the most helpful ways for new teachers to become comfortable with parent-student-teacher conferences is to sit in when experienced teachers are talking with parents and students. Ask teachers you admire if it would be possible for you to be a silent observer. You will pick up phrases, mannerisms, and strategies that will help guide your own conferences.

BARRIERS TO FAMILY INVOLVEMENT

Some barriers to parental involvement result from the attitudes and actions of parents, and some from the attitudes and actions of teachers. James Comer (2005), speaking of what he and his team of researchers experienced, tells us, "From the beginning of our work in schools, we were struck by this mixture of parents' hesitancy to get involved and educators' subtle and even unintentional resistance to parental involvement" (p. 39).

Parental Barriers. There are many legitimate barriers, such as work schedules, to parental involvement, regardless of socioeconomic status, culture, language, or educational background.

Socioeconomic Barriers. Money matters. Having it, or not having it, shapes many aspects of our lives. Some of the attitudes and actions of students and their families can be traced to their socioeconomic status, particularly when it comes to parental involvement.

> The relationship of socioeconomic status and school success is discussed in Chapters 3 and 10.

Families in low-income settings may be more mobile than other families. If a family is renting and one of its income earners loses a job, the family may leave the house or apartment before the next rent is due. Newsletters, forms, and other communication sent through the mail may not reach these families. Families may have a phone one week but not the next, or they may not have a phone at all. Many low-income homes do not have access to the Internet, so e-mail communication is not an option.

In addition, transportation may present a challenge for low-income families. They may have one car to accommodate five, six, or more family members, or they may have no vehicle at all. Some families depend entirely on public transportation, making getting to and from their students' schools very difficult. Finding or paying for child care can be difficult as well, and younger siblings may need to accompany parents to school functions.

Work can be a barrier to parental involvement at any socioeconomic level. Often in low-SES families, both parents may work two or three jobs, and their time is extremely limited. The unfortunate dilemma is that if these parents do show up to volunteer, it probably means they lost their jobs (Bradley, 2006). At the other end of the socioeconomic spectrum, parents who are highly paid professionals may also have severe limitations on their time. In both cases, showing up at school between 8:00 A.M. and 4:00 P.M. may be virtually impossible.

Cultural and Language Barriers.
Children do not choose the culture in which they are born. Their families may value education, or they may consider formal education unnecessary beyond the stage of being able to read and write at survival levels.

Watch interviews with the parents of Hector, Hugo, and Khammany that are part of the student interviews in the Teaching in Focus section for Chapter 12 in MyEducationLab for this course.

The language of a student's family may be a major barrier to parental involvement. The families of three of our focus students speak little English in their homes. Hector, our fourth grade student at Rees Elementary, is the only one in his family who speaks fluent English. He is the link between his family and the school. Hugo, a focus student at Roosevelt High School, speaks very little English himself, and his parents speak even less. Khammany, also at Roosevelt High School, is fluent in English, but her mother speaks no English at all. Engaging these parents in the life of the school is difficult.

Brenda Beyal talks about what parents can add to the lives of teachers. She tells us about a particular "deposit" a parent made to her career in *Teaching in Focus.*

Educational Background Barriers.
If parents were not successful in school, they are unlikely to be enthusiastic about stepping through the doors of their children's schools. If they quit school in sixth grade, or eighth grade, or if they never graduated from high school, they may be intimidated and hesitant to talk with teachers, believing that they are incapable of helping students with anything academic.

Table 12.2 consists of strategies for teachers and schools as they work toward increasing parental involvement.

Teacher Barriers.
Teacher-generated barriers to parental involvement are less legitimate than parent-generated barriers. A teacher's failure to invite parental involvement may stem from timidity, lack of conviction that parental involvement matters, and lack of effort.

Timidity.
Some teachers become nervous when they anticipate speaking to, or with, parents. You may hear them say, "I can be up in front of my sophomores all day long, but bring in their parents, and I freeze." A skilled communicator with students can become a skilled communicator with adults. Experience makes it easier.

Some teachers are uncomfortable having other adults watching and listening to them. They may worry about facing questions and possible criticism. They may find the presence of parents in their classrooms inhibiting and intimidating. This form of timidity can be overcome by planning excellent learning experiences for the classroom and being at your best

Teaching in Focus

Brenda Beyal, Grades 3–5 Multiage Classroom, Rees Elementary School, Utah. *In her own words. . . .*

Tucked away in a drawer I have a note that was given to me by a parent over 10 years ago. I take it out on occasion when I am having a particularly hard time with a school situation, or when I'm feeling ineffective. I read the salutation, "Dear Respected Madam." This is one of the most gracious openings to

a note that I have ever received. The note is from parents who had just emigrated from India. They had asked for help with a small matter, and I was able to help solve a dilemma for them.

The words still send a surge of renewal and recommitment within me for my chosen profession—teaching. Families and parents can make emotional deposits into our teaching lives, and then some can make deep withdrawals. As a teacher, I hold on to the unintentional deposits that parents make, and, with their help, I let the withdrawals slip away from my teaching so they will not keep me from making powerful teaching and learning connections.

TABLE 12.2 Strategies to overcome barriers to parental involvement

Barrier	Strategy
Frequent address changes	Organize student families into small groups, being careful to include a family that is rooted in the community. Devise ways to help these small groups stay in touch, with the more settled family taking the lead in communicating with the teacher when families move.
Disconnected phones	Using the group idea just described, establish a phone tree as a source of class information. In this way teachers learn about phone problems, perhaps before there is a need to call the family on a more urgent matter.
Lack of transportation	Make school events compatible with public transportation schedules. Have a teacher ride along on a route where many of the students live to serve as a welcoming guide to and from the event.
Time barriers	Schedule parent-student-teacher conferences at times that accommodate more parents. Split sessions could be 3:00–5:00 and 7:00–9:00 P.M. Provide ways for working parents to volunteer time, perhaps with weekend and evening projects that also involve students.
Child-care dilemmas	Provide child care onsite during school events and planned conference times. High school classes and organizations can be responsible for taking care of children while parents involve themselves in the life of the school.
Cultural differences	Acknowledge different perspectives and incorporate activities, artwork, and celebrations that draw families into the life of the school.
Language barriers	Find people who will serve as interpreters at events and conferences. Advertise the presence of interpreters to let parents know they will be able to communicate with teachers. Translate newsletters and forms into the languages spoken and read at home.
Limited education	Warm, friendly teachers who use jargon-free language in their communications help encourage parental involvement. Providing after-school homework help can ease parental guilt over not knowing how to help their children with assignments.

every day with the attitude that parents are your partners. The more hands and minds the better when it comes to increasing student learning.

Parents Matter. Some teachers appear to be unconvinced that parental involvement matters. Traci Peters is not one of them. She believes strongly in the value of parental involvement, as expressed in *Teaching in Focus.*

Lack of Effort. The most frustrating teacher barrier to parental involvement in schools and classrooms is lack of effort. There is no legitimate reason not to make that call, write that note, or invite parents into the classroom. If you are convinced that parental involvement matters and that parents are your allies in the education of students, you will draw parents into, rather than excluding or even alienating them from, the educational process.

Whatever the barriers to parental involvement, teachers need to continually strive to break them down by cultivating an invitational attitude. Parents are part of the larger community. With them as active participants in the life of the school, we are reaching out into the community.

PROFESSIONAL RELATIONSHIPS WITH THE COMMUNITY

Education is a public enterprise. Pick up a newspaper and you will find something in it that features, or refers to, schools and teachers. The community reads and hears about school, forming impressions along the way. Teachers, and those who work in and with schools, are

Points of Reflection 12.4

How might you overcome any reluctance you have to making parents your partners? How do you envision drawing parents into the process of educating their children? How would you overcome barriers to parental involvement?

Teaching in Focus

Traci Peters, Grade 7 Math, Cario Middle School, South Carolina. *In her own words. . . .*

When parents send you their children, they are sending you the best ones they have. They're not keeping their brighter, better behaved children at home. They are sending you their "babies," even in middle school. In an instant, teachers become the ones who spend more time each day with these children than the parents. Most parents want to be informed and involved, and they want what is best for their child. Parents and teachers are on the same side—the student's side. As teachers we need to reach out. There are many benefits to parental involvement for students, teachers, and the parents themselves.

There are many ways to involve parents, from simple occasional e-mail communication and a classroom newsletter, to more complex strategies such as home visits and family math nights. What matters is that we establish positive connections between the classroom and the homes of students. If you think of it as a give-and-take relationship, you may find very practical benefits to parental involvement. They can simplify some of your tasks by doing things such as copying and preparing materials, shopping for "fun with food" day, and displaying student work in the classroom or in the halls. They will enjoy their involvement and support your efforts in the classroom!

Points of Reflection 12.5

How do you envision being a community ambassador for schools? Do you think it's important to know what services are available for your students and their families? Should this be part of the professional responsibilities of teaching? Why or why not?

acutely aware of how public their endeavors are. For most people in a community, what they know from the media and their personal acquaintances about teachers, students, and classrooms is the sum total of their knowledge about schools. For this reason, teachers have the responsibility to be public relations agents for schools. We must put our best professional selves forward to represent education—in community groups, in places of worship, in social gatherings, in the grocery store—everywhere we go.

The community can provide support, resources, and services that are valuable lifelines for students and their families. Individuals can volunteer their time, give money and materials, and share their expertise as student mentors and guest speakers. Corporations can fund programs and events, offer employees release time to volunteer in schools, and provide political support for needed policy changes. Teachers should know what is available and, along with administrators and counselors, make sure families are aware of how to access community services such as health clinics, family counseling, and tutoring. When school, families, and the community work together, students receive optimum benefits, as illustrated in Figure 12.8.

PROFESSIONAL RELATIONSHIPS WITH COLLEAGUES

"One incontrovertible finding emerges from my career spent working in and around schools: The nature of relationships among the adults within a school has a greater influence on the character and quality of that school and on student accomplishment than anything else" (Barth, 2006, p. 9). This bold statement was made by Roland Barth, highly respected former teacher and principal and founding director of the Principals' Center at Harvard University. He continues by saying, "In short, the relationships among the educators in a school define all relationships within the school's culture" (p. 9). Is it possible that as a teacher, your relationship with another teacher down the hall affects these other relationships? Yes, according to Barth, who tells us we must find a way to confront this "elephant in the room": the relationships that loom so large within the school but are seldom addressed.

BASIC RELATIONSHIPS AMONG TEACHERS.
The four basic relationships among teachers as defined by Barth (2006) are parallel play, adversarial relationships, congenial relationships, and collegial relationships.

Figure 12.8 Optimum benefits for students

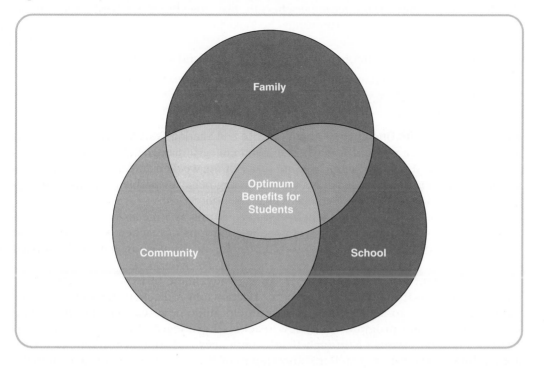

Parallel Play. When children sit on the floor just inches from one another, so absorbed in their own toys that they never acknowledge each other's presence or offer to share or play together in any way, we say they are engaged in parallel play. This behavior is considered normal development for 1- and 2-year-olds. Sadly, a sort of *teacher* parallel play is the norm in many schools. Too often teachers close their doors, hoard their lessons and materials, and infrequently share their tools of the trade—their knowledge of curricula and repertoire of instructional strategies. This isolating approach robs teachers of potential individual and collective growth.

Adversarial Relationships. Barth tells us that one reason so many teachers engage in a sort of parallel play is that they are attempting to avoid adversarial relationships, or those relationships characterized by blatant criticism, talking behind the backs of others, and unwarranted and destructive competition. This amounts to unprofessional behavior.

Congenial Relationships. You will no doubt develop congenial relationships with many of your colleagues. You will enjoy one another's company. People of different ages, personality types, interests, cultures, and races are teachers. You will find some with whom you have much in common and others very different from yourself. Developing congenial relationships makes school more fun. Students can sense when their teachers enjoy the people around them. That's being a role model in the most practical ways.

Teachers who share a congenial relationship are more likely to collaborate in collegial ways to engage learners.

Collegial Relationships. Relationships with other teachers that promote growth through sharing of professional expertise are **collegial.** Barth (2006) quotes famous baseball manager Casey Stengel: "Getting good players is easy. Getting 'em to play together is the

Points of Reflection 12.6

Do you recall teachers in your K–12 experience who genuinely appeared to enjoy one another's company? How could you tell?

hard part" (p. 11). There are lots of "good players," or competent teachers, in schools. Developing collegiality means getting teachers to "play" together. When Barth visits schools and looks for signs of collegial relationships, he looks for three components:

- Educators talking with one another about practice and sharing craft knowledge
- Educators observing one another while they are engaged in practice
- Educators rooting for one another's success

Educators Talking with One Another About Practice and Sharing Craft Knowledge. There is a difference between congenial conversation and collegial dialogue about what we do as teachers. When we talk about a movie or our plans for the weekend, we are engaging in congenial conversation; when we talk about a challenging behavior problem and listen to suggestions from colleagues, we are demonstrating collegiality.

James Beane (2005) suggests **teacher study groups** as a means of building professional, collegial communities within schools. Small groups of teachers select books and journal articles to read, talk about what they have read, and discuss how it might be applied to their teaching.

One excellent way for new teachers to take advantage of experienced teachers' craft knowledge is through a mentor-mentee relationship. A teacher **mentor** uses experience and wisdom to answer questions and help guide new teachers. Fresh out of a teacher preparation program, most new teachers have learned lots of instructional strategies in their classes or through field experiences and student teaching that they are anxious to try. A new teacher's knowledge of theory and research may actually exceed that of more experienced colleagues. In this regard, mentors have the opportunity to learn from their mentees. However, what experienced teachers have that new teachers don't have is what Berliner (2001) calls **case knowledge.** When experienced teachers face a new student, a new learning problem, or new materials, they have a memory bank of other similar situations on which to draw, or case knowledge. New teachers can take advantage of this case knowledge by asking questions, listening, and observing. Renee Ayers shares her case knowledge in specific ways. Read what she has to say in *Teaching in Focus.*

Teaching in Focus

Renee Ayers, Grade 2, Summit Primary School, Ohio. *In her own words. . . .*

Many wonderful people supported and helped me during my first years of teaching: the clever curriculum director who told me about the "question chair" to stop interruptions during reading groups; the kind principal who cheered me on even when I was in tears in his office; the caring special education teacher who would come to my classroom during her planning period to tutor a student with special needs; the 30-year-veteran teacher next door who taught me all of his "sing to learn" songs; and the school counselor who assisted me in doing hands-on science experiments with 27 second graders. I look back with such fondness as I consider the people who nurtured me.

As I grew in my career I decided I had a responsibility to pass this support on to other new teachers. In my sixth year of teaching I became a Praxis mentor with every intention of going into my protégés' classes and dishing out all my experience and advice. What I found from this experience was that by observing and supporting first-year teachers, I had created an opportunity for myself to learn. Every protégé has become a resource and friend to me. Their enthusiasm is contagious, their teaching practices are fresh, and their ability to persevere through the extreme pressure and demands of a first classroom never ceases to amaze me.

Educators Observing One Another While They Are Engaged in Practice. One of the most helpful things teachers can do is observe one another in the classroom and then describe what they see in nonevaluative, nonthreatening ways. As an observer, another teacher may be able to see dynamics between teacher and students, as well as between students and students, that the teacher instructing may miss. Observers can point out what they see and make suggestions for improvement. As teachers talk with one another and observe in colleagues' classrooms, they become more invested in one another's success.

Educators Rooting for One Another's Success. This characteristic of collegiality involves sincere support and encouragement of teachers for one another. When teachers keep students first and want them all to succeed, then they will be rooting for each other's professional success.

One teacher who has capitalized on his concern for teachers and their ability to meet the needs of their students creatively is Charles Best, the young man featured in this chapter's *In the News* feature. His program is benefiting teachers across the country.

PROFESSIONAL RELATIONSHIPS WITH OTHER ADULTS IN THE SCHOOL

It's a good idea to get to know each adult who contributes to the daily work in schools, including administrators, administrative assistants, cafeteria and custodial workers, counselors, social workers, nurses, media specialists, and teacher assistants. They all have the interests of students as priorities and can be our partners in teaching and learning.

Paraprofessionals are also known as teacher aides or teacher assistants. The people who hold these positions are typically not certified teachers. Paraprofessionals are most commonly employed in early childhood and elementary settings. They may be in one classroom full time or may rotate among teachers. For instance, a paraprofessional may be assigned to second grade in a school with five second grade teachers. These teachers may decide that the best use of another adult is to have the paraprofessional join the classes during the times when the children are in reading circles. Or the teachers may want extra help in their classrooms when students are working on projects that require the use of multiple materials.

> Teacher professional relationships with principals and assistant principals are discussed in Chapter 11.

In the News abcNEWS

Charles Best: Providing a Quality Education for All Students

Charles Best believes that teaching is one of the highest callings and, as he puts it, "just plain fun." This remarkable young man has made it his mission in life to make a difference in the lives of kids through teaching—and through a Web-based nonprofit organization he created called Donors Choose. This marvelous idea, to allow donors to choose personally to whom they give their money and resources and to know that what they give goes directly into the classroom, provides a satisfying experience for all involved.

To view this video, go to the In the News section of Chapter 12 on MyEducationLab for this text and watch the clip *Charles Best: Providing a Quality Education for All Students.* After watching the video, respond to these questions.

1. Charles describes both the student population and the staff at his school. Does the setting appeal to you? If so, why? If not, why not?

2. Charles expresses his initial concern that teachers wouldn't participate and ask for classroom resources. Why do you think he was concerned? Would you be willing to ask for donations on the Donors Choose Web site?

3. Why do you think Charles says he has to take complex ideas and reduce them to their essence in his classroom? What is he afraid will happen when he does this?

Some schools are fortunate to have paraprofessionals who have worked for 20 or 30 years in schools. They may know the community well and be valuable assets. If you are fortunate enough to have a teacher assistant in your classroom, treat him or her with respect. You have professional knowledge that may exceed that of a paraprofessional in some ways, but chances are your assistant has a lot of experience with students and families. Learn from them even as you direct their participation with the students in your classroom.

How Can I Develop as a Professional When I Am a Teacher?

Professional growth is an absolute necessity for teacher effectiveness. There is a documented relationship between professional self-growth leading to improved teaching quality and student achievement (Darling-Hammond & Youngs, 2002). In addition to professional opportunities to grow with help from colleagues and participation in professional organizations, a wealth of literature addresses the many aspects of teaching and learning. Reading articles and books pertinent to content and students, and then using ideas and advice, is another way for teachers to continue to grow professionally. Collegial conversations allow for sharing both questions and solutions.

ORGANIZED PROFESSIONAL DEVELOPMENT

Professional development is a phrase used to describe efforts to help teachers improve their knowledge and skills. Some districts refer to professional development as in-service training, staff development workshops, or teacher retreats. Many opportunities for professional growth will be presented to you. Some are required and others are optional.

You will likely hear more than a few teachers complain that a professional development workshop or staff retreat is sure to be a waste of time. They may have become jaded by ineffective sessions, or they may not be open to exploring new ideas. But remember, there is always something to be learned when teachers get together, regardless of the perceived quality or relevance of what is formally presented.

INFORMAL PROFESSIONAL DEVELOPMENT USING 21ST-CENTURY ACCESSIBILITY

Teachers don't have to actually go somewhere or be in a particular place to learn more about their craft. Twenty-first century technology allows teachers to access knowledge in a variety of ways, presenting options for ongoing and specifically tailored professional development.

Some schools and districts are using the Moodle format for e-learning. Moodle stands for Modular Object-Oriented Dynamic Learning Environment and is a course management system that allows teachers to share information and plans. Other e-learning vehicles include the wiki, blog, and Ning. Although face-to-face professional development will always have a place in teachers' careers, online learning has the capacity to reach more teachers in convenient, immediate ways (Huber, 2010).

ADVANCED DEGREES

Teachers can continue their professional education by seeking advanced degrees. Combinations of on-site and distance learning often allow coursework to fit more easily into a teacher's schedule. Master of education degrees are offered at numerous universities. Secondary teachers often seek advanced degrees in the subject area they teach; elementary teachers may seek advanced degrees in a more generic area such as curriculum and instruction. Not only does more in-depth study of content, curriculum, and instruction enrich teaching, but it also opens leadership doors.

NATIONAL BOARD FOR PROFESSIONAL TEACHING STANDARDS CERTIFICATION

One of the most recognized, state-endorsed opportunities for professional growth is certification through the **National Board for Professional Teaching Standards (NBPTS)**. The organization was created in 1987 to emphasize what teachers should know and do to positively affect student learning. The philosophical foundation of NBPTS (2010) is composed of five core beliefs:

- Teachers are committed to students and learning.
- Teachers know the subjects they teach and how to teach those subjects to students.
- Teachers are responsible for managing and monitoring student learning.
- Teachers think systematically about their practice and learn from experience.
- Teachers are members of learning communities.

In addition to the five core beliefs, NBPTS has specific standards that must be met in each of the categories of certification. There are 25 certification areas that align with content and the levels of school, including early childhood, middle childhood (elementary), early adolescence (middle school), and adolescence and young adulthood (high school).

As of 2010, over 55,000 teachers were certified through NBPTS. Formal certification requires teachers to

- undertake a year-long intense process involving self-reflection and assessment
- create a teaching portfolio
- complete an involved writing component
- perform successfully on a comprehensive exam (NBPTS, 2010)

In addition to certification and recognition, all states offer some sort of reward or incentive. Here are two examples. In South Carolina, NBPTS-certified teachers receive an additional $7,500 per year for 10 years, do not have to go through normal state certification procedures, and are reimbursed for the expenses involved in achieving certification. In Wisconsin, although not as extensive as South Carolina, the financial benefits are still good. Half of the cost of NBPTS certification is reimbursed, and certified teachers receive a $2,500 stipend each of the 9 remaining years of certification (NBPTS, 2010a).

TEACHER EVALUATION AS OPPORTUNITY FOR PROFESSIONAL GROWTH

It is perfectly normal to be apprehensive about being evaluated, especially in your first few years in the classroom. Evaluations should be viewed as opportunities for professional growth. There is always more to know and new skills to develop, even for experienced teachers.

Methods school districts use to evaluate teachers vary. Most involve elements such as observation of teachers with students, opinions of administrators concerning planning for instruction, evidence of collaboration with colleagues, attendance at professional development sessions, and classroom management skills. New teachers are usually assigned a mentor teacher who will informally observe and do a formative assessment, an ongoing look at how new teachers function, with no formal affirmation or unfavorable consequences. Formative assessments are used to promote growth.

Teachers usually receive an annual summative evaluation, one that will be accompanied by a written report of performance (as measured using whatever criteria the state and district choose) and used as the basis for continuing employment decisions. This summative evaluation will be conducted by a building-level administrator who may use a detailed form on which a kind of "score" is kept of both if and to what extent a teacher does certain things associated with effective instruction. Some evaluations are much less prescriptive, with the evaluator taking detailed notes about what's observed and then writing a description from the notes. Both methods will be the bases for follow-up conferences.

PROBLEMS WITH TEACHER EVALUATION. There is growing sentiment that teacher evaluation is not working. U.S. Secretary of Education Arne Duncan wrote in 2010,

> No area of the teaching profession is more plainly broken today than that of teacher evaluation.… In district after district, more than 95 percent of teachers are rated as good or superior, even in schools that are chronically underperforming year after year. Worse yet, evaluations typically fail to take any account of a teacher's impact on student learning.… As a result, great teachers don't get recognized, don't get rewarded, and don't help their peers grow. (Duncan, 2010)

The National Council on Teacher Quality (2009) reveals some disturbing evidence about teacher evaluations in general, including:

- Only four states require evidence of student learning as a major factor in teacher evaluations.
- Twenty-one states do not even require that evaluations include classroom observations.
- Only 24 states require that new teachers be evaluated more than once a year, with 9 states not requiring evaluation of new teachers at all.
- Only 15 states require annual evaluations of veteran teachers, with some states permitting teachers to go 5 years or even longer between evaluations.
- Forty-seven states allow teachers to receive tenure automatically (ongoing status with job security) after simply being employed for a period of time and without review.

Points of Reflection 12.7

With so many responsibilities and opportunities for professional growth, you will likely recognize the value of balance between your personal life and your professional activities. Have you considered how you might balance the personal and professional aspects of your life? What are your worries about this aspect of becoming a teacher?

INCENTIVE FOR IMPROVEMENT. The National Council on Teacher Quality findings and Secretary Duncan's assessment of teacher evaluation paint a bleak picture of what most school systems are doing to evaluate teachers. An unprecedented incentive for improvement in teacher evaluation is part of President Obama's plan to reauthorize the Elementary and Secondary Education Act (known as No Child Left Behind 2001–2010). In 2010 the federal government offered states $4.3 billion in grants for planning, among other things, ways to evaluate teaching that include levels of student learning and improvement. *Race to the Top* is designed to promote the development of teacher evaluation that is meaningful and may lead to ways of paying teachers based on more than longevity and levels of education. Perhaps pay-for-performance, or merit pay, that satisfies teachers' need for fairness will be in your future as part of the recognition of teacher effectiveness.

What Do I Have to Offer the Teaching Profession?

The teaching profession is bolstered every time an engaging lesson is taught or learning is facilitated in whatever way is appropriate for students. In this respect, effective teachers routinely contribute to the profession. In addition, there are specific activities that reach beyond the classroom to have positive impact on the teaching profession.

TEACHER INVOLVEMENT IN PROFESSIONAL ORGANIZATIONS

The effectiveness of any organization depends in large measure on its membership. Teachers are responsible for the effectiveness of professional teacher organizations, whether large and politically aggressive, like the National Education Association (NEA) and the American Federation of Teachers (AFT), or small, like a district social studies council with the purpose of providing resources and information for area social studies teachers. In most cases, membership in professional organizations is voluntary, although there are instances when teachers may feel pressured into joining specific groups.

Subject area organizations, such as the National Council of Teachers of English (NCTE) and the National Council of Teachers of Mathematics (NCTM), provide valuable information and resources. Being a member helps teachers do what they do more effectively; every teacher who belongs makes subject area organizations stronger. Most states have their own subject area organizations that are affiliates of the national subject area groups. State membership fees are generally less and conferences are more accessible because they are within the individual states. Membership in state organizations is a good place to begin.

It is important for teachers to take advantage of the opportunities professional organizations provide. In turn, teachers should feel a responsibility to join professional organizations to help build the teaching profession.

> Professional organizations are discussed in Chapters 1 and 4, with a list and contact information in Chapter 1.

SYSTEMIC INVOLVEMENT

Extending teacher influence at the local and district levels is what systemic involvement is all about. It is possible and desirable, although it consumes both time and energy, for teachers to have an impact on both adults and students well beyond the classroom door. You can grow into many of these responsibilities and opportunities with time and experience.

TEACHER INVOLVEMENT IN THE SCHOOL. Being an active participant in the collegiality of a school is a positive way to be involved. For new teachers this may mean benefiting from a strong mentor relationship with experienced teachers and maintaining a helpful, open spirit. When you become more confident in your new role, you will have opportunities to be part of committees and task forces with specific decision-making and action responsibilities, including

- planning special events
- choosing grade level or subject-area curricular materials
- selecting new books for the media center
- developing schedules
- working with business partners
- planning for future growth
- collaborating with other teacher groups (e.g., regular education with special education, core subjects with related arts)

> Teacher leaders are discussed in Chapter 11.

TEACHER INVOLVEMENT IN THE DISTRICT. Every district functions within state guidelines and with the use of state funds. Being informed about how your district functions begins with paying attention to who is in leadership roles and how the chain of influence works. After teaching for a few years you may have opportunities to participate in district-level committees that may make decisions and take action such as

- textbook selection (within state guidelines if applicable)
- curricular planning to incorporate state standards
- recommendations for creating activities to involve parents

Derek Boucher, one of our focus teachers at Roosevelt High School in California, chooses to contribute to the teaching profession by expressing his opinions in public ways. Read about his contributions in *Teaching in Focus.*

CONTRIBUTIONS TO THE PROFESSIONAL KNOWLEDGE BASE

Teachers have a responsibility to contribute to the professional knowledge base. When a teacher tries an instructional strategy that works well with a particular topic, or with a specific group of students, sharing the experience will help other teachers. This sharing can happen in

Teaching in Focus

Derek Boucher, High School History and Reading, Roosevelt High School, California. *In his own words. . . .*

In 2002 I read *Resisting Reading Mandates* by Dr. Elaine Garan. Her book exposed many of the biases and conflicts of interest that exist among those who make national policy decisions regarding K–12 reading instruction.

I was so inspired by her revealing work that I wrote an opinion editorial that was published in our local newspaper. What happened next shocked me. Attorneys from a large educational publishing company that was implicated in Dr. Garan's book contacted me. This company stood to benefit financially from the new reading policy. They wanted to stop me from expressing my opinion and the newspaper from publishing opinions that disagreed with their position. At that moment, I realized the power and responsibility teachers have to express their opinions about what works in the classroom.

Since that time, I have submitted opinion pieces to educational journals, as well as over a dozen letters to the editor of our local newspaper. Many outside the classroom feel they know what is best for our children and classrooms. It is our responsibility as professionals on the front line, who work with children on a daily basis, to share our experience and perspective.

a team or grade-level meeting, through a Moodle or other online vehicle, at a meeting of a professional organization, or in an article written for an education journal. Teachers who try a new strategy, develop a way to gather evidence concerning the effects of it, interpret the evidence, and make inferences from it, are conducting a kind of research referred to as **action research.** Reporting findings and continuing inquiry adds to the professional knowledge base.

What Is My Role as a Professional in Education Reform?

To reform is to change, to make different, or to improve. The word *reform* in education usually involves funding allocations, school choice, new instructional programs, and, basically, the promotion of one ideology or another. To be sure, reform initiatives can change the way some aspects of school operate, either permanently or for a period of time until the particular ideology falls out of favor. So how does a professional teacher respond to calls for reform?

Public schools continue to be works in progress. Reform of one sort or another will always be with us. Professional teachers know this. They also care deeply about students and the teaching profession and support ideas and efforts intended to increase learning. They do so with common sense. If a particular reform doesn't appear to make sense for the students they know well, they speak up concerning their objections, they work cooperatively with others even as they try to influence the course of events, and they continually keep the question "And how are the children?" at the forefront of all discussions.

Being an informed professional is a position from which to impact reform. There have been many reform efforts in the last few decades; there will be many more in the future, some that will advance student learning and others that will not. Here are summaries of three current reform efforts.

PERFORMANCE-BASED PAY

Performance-based pay is a hot topic in education involving paying teachers more when they produce whatever results are designated as desirable. In the first decade of this century one estimate puts the number of news stories on the topic of performance-based pay at almost 50,000 (Springer & Gardner, 2010). That's a lot of opinions from a lot of people, but, by most accounts, we aren't much closer to figuring out how to judge teacher performance accurately and fairly, and how to reward it, than we were in 2000. Is it what we observe teachers doing that counts? Are extra duties worth extra pay? Should teachers in hard-to-staff schools be paid more? Do high school science and math teachers deserve more money than fifth grade teachers? Or is the bottom line how teachers affect student learning? President Obama and the *Race to the Top* funding competition make planning for performance pay a major part of the decision for awarding money to states to promote teaching and learning (U.S. Department of Education, 2009).

Performance-based pay for teachers is not a new concept. Every 20 years or so the idea surfaces, some districts and states try it, flaws in the system emerge, and the idea is abandoned again. But performance-based pay makes sense, doesn't it? Simply put, the teachers who do the best jobs should be paid the most. From a business-model perspective, where production may be relatively easy to measure, performance-based pay may be incentive enough to see sustained positive results. In education, if results are longer hours or more graduate degrees, measurement would be easy. However, if sustained positive results are increased student learning, the questions remain: "How do we quantify student learning?" and "Which parts of student learning, by whatever measure we use to judge it, are directly attributable to a teacher who has the students in class for 9 months?" For instance,

- If a teacher's fourth grade students show marked improvement in math, who's to say that the foundation for the increased learning wasn't built in third grade and simply all came together in fourth grade?

- If tenth graders demonstrate improved writing skills, is it due at least in part to the ninth grade teacher's concentration on mechanics that the tenth grade teacher used in the process of teaching about idea development? Should the tenth grade teacher be rewarded but not the ninth grade teacher?

Can you see how complex the issue of performance-based pay becomes? Table 12.3 lists some of the beliefs of advocates and critics.

Performance pay will continue to be debated and attempted as part of ongoing efforts of educational reform. Some states are developing aggressive plans for performance pay, including Colorado, where Senate Bill 191 ties 50% of an evaluation for principals and teachers to student academic growth and changes the way teachers get and keep tenure. Bills such as this remain controversial.

Other states, such as New York, are debating how to approach teacher evaluation, and ultimately teacher pay, to reflect student learning. The issue is addressed in the opinion piece in Figure 12.9 written by the president of the New York State United Teachers

TABLE 12.3 Advocates and critics of performance pay based on student learning	
Advocates believe that performance-based pay	Critics believe that performance-based pay
can be a catalyst for change	amounts to tweaking, rather than fixing, the problem of uneven or lagging achievement
increases student learning	penalizes teachers who do not directly teach the tested subjects
motivates teachers who aren't trying hard enough	encourages teaching to the test, thereby narrowing the curriculum
makes teaching more competitive and increases effectiveness	fails to instill systemic responsibility for increasing student learning
is a fair way to differentiate among varying levels of teacher effectiveness	perpetuates measuring success by test scores alone

Figure 12.9 Opinion on teacher evaluation

Grade teachers, the right way

Richard C. Iannuzzi (an elementary school teacher for 34 years; president of the 600,000-member NYSUT)

October 22, 2009

Great teaching matters. In fact, research demonstrates that teacher quality may be one of the most, if not the most, important factors linked to student success. Teacher quality is something most parents, students and educators already understand. But, how do you measure it?

Beginning in the next few weeks, the Obama administration will seek to answer that question. It might even have a transformative impact on the nation's education system as it begins to award Race to the Top grants, eventually totaling $4.35 billion. This huge pot of money will be awarded based on how willing states are to embrace a short list of reforms, including using data to measure teacher effectiveness.

In New York, the discussion on Race to the Top has revolved around a bogus claim that has been fanned by critics trying to drive a wedge between unions and the Obama administration. The claim is that New York law prohibits the use of student test scores in measuring teacher effectiveness. It is simply not true. Nothing in state law prohibits school administrators from examining student test data to help determine teacher effectiveness.

To be absolutely clear, the 600,000-member New York State United Teachers [NYSUT] supports the appropriate use of student test scores as one of the multiple measures that should be part of comprehensive evaluations. The appropriate use of data can help us understand how teachers can make the biggest positive difference in the lives of children. As professionals, teachers and their unions must be willing to develop and accept sound, research-based changes even when those changes might make us uncomfortable.

At the same time, education unions owe it to their members, as well as to students, to distinguish meaningful reform from misinformed schemes and top-down, quick fixes that do more harm than good. Too often, well-intentioned ideas lack the necessary foundation in proven research and fail to appreciate the realities that exist in our classrooms.

That's why we have raised concerns about Race to the Top's over reliance on test scores, undervaluing of professional development, rapid expansion of charter schools and abbreviated timeline for developing common national standards.

We will always be resolute in rejecting proposals that are likely to be ineffective or could reverse the steady progress we've made toward closing the achievement gap.

The Board of Regents and the state Education Department have been working for more than a year on a comprehensive plan for improving teacher effectiveness that, among other factors, includes using data on student performance. It is anticipated that this model will be available for the next school year.

We hope New York will be ready with a comprehensive and fair system that recognizes the complexity of teaching. As part of our willingness to accept accountability and take charge of our profession, NYSUT has been an active participant in developing a model we hope will be fair and balanced and that will help to define excellence in our profession.

Education unions have always been at the leading edge of reform. Now we have as a partner an administration that understands that professional unions are a catalyst, not an impediment, to bringing well-thought out innovations to the nation's classrooms.

Every child deserves a great teacher, but how great teachers are measured matters greatly. For Race to the Top to get it right, New York and other states must develop systems that are supportive of excellent teaching, are transparent and accountable and require shared responsibility among all stakeholders.

The best way to achieve this will be to put political gamesmanship aside and to start putting children first.

It's not a bad place to start.

(NYSUT) that appeared in the Albany, New York, newspaper, *The Times Union.* Following the opinion piece is this chapter's **Letter to the Editor,** written by the director of research for the Foundation for Education Reform & Accountability (FERA), an independent, non-profit education reform organization with the mission of improving education in New York by promoting accountability, stimulating innovation, and supporting school-choice efforts (FERA, 2010).

Letter to the Editor

This letter appeared in the Albany, New York, newspaper, *The Times Union*. It was written by the director of research for the Foundation for Education Reform & Accountability in response to the opinion piece you just read.

Nov. 8, 2009 Prove Teachers Deserve Tenure

New York State United Teachers President Richard Iannuzzi misleads readers when he claims the union isn't standing in the way of using student achievement results to help evaluate teachers.

Despite claims that students' test scores are "one of the multiple measures" that can be used in teacher evaluations, the union was the primary force in getting a state law passed last year to ban the use of those scores as a factor in making tenure determinations for teachers.

One only has to go to the union's Web site to read of NYSUT touting its "leading role in securing language that bars the use of student test scores as a yardstick for tenure" and a statement by Iannuzzi that "student assessments are designed to assess students, not teachers."

Thanks to NYSUT, school districts are required to grant or deny tenure to teachers without even being able to consider how their students perform academically. This is a terrible disservice to students, to their families and to local taxpayers who ask for a little accountability.

Is it asking too much to require teachers to demonstrate that their students are learning before they are granted lifetime tenure in their job?

B. Jason Brooks,
Foundation for Education Reform & Accountability

Source: Times Union, Albany, New York.

Now it's your turn. Write a letter to the editor from the perspective of a future teacher expressing your views about what should be included in teacher evaluation. You may comment on any, or all, of the writer's expressed opinions. The following information and questions may help you frame your thinking but should not limit nor determine what you write.

1. These two writers seem to disagree on what should be fact, not opinion. How might you express this in a professional way that is not offensive to either one but that makes the point that there are ways to determine facts?
2. Mr. Brooks says that New York state law bans the use of test scores as part of tenure decisions. This is not the case. The law says that student progress must be used but only as a *partial* determinant of teacher evaluation and tenure decisions. Should your letter point out facts such as this?
3. Consider what Mr. Brooks says Mr. Iannuzzi stated: "student assessments are designed to assess students, not teachers." Do you agree with the statement? If so, why? If not, why not?
4. Mr. Brooks states that "school districts are required to grant or deny tenure to teachers without even being able to consider how their students perform academically," but this is only the case for the system of evaluating teachers until the school year 2011–2012. In the fall of 2011, 40% of teacher evaluation will be based on student growth. Should this information be included in your letter?
5. How would you answer Mr. Brooks's last question?

Write your letter in understandable terminology, remembering that readers of newspaper Letters to the Editor are citizens who may have limited knowledge of school practices and policies. Remember to refer to the letter assessment rubric in Chapter 1.

TEACHER PROFESSIONALISM AND PERFORMANCE-BASED PAY. Because pay based on performance has been attempted a number of times over the past four or five decades, almost always unsuccessfully, there may be considerable pessimism among veteran teachers who have seen plans come and go. Still, professionals remain optimistic that ways will be found to judge their competency, at least in part, on the degree of learning experienced by their students. They know, however, that the current method of measuring student learning solely by standardized test scores does not present the whole picture of their teaching effectiveness. Even so, professionals encourage exploration in education that may positively impact teaching and learning.

COMMON CORE STATE STANDARDS

The development of the Common Core State Standards was coordinated by the National Governors Association Center for Best Practices (NGA Center) and the Council of Chief

Curricular standards are discussed in Chapters 4 and 5, and levels of governance are discussed in Chapter 11.

State School Officers (CCSSO). These common standards were written through collaboration of content experts and state representatives including teachers, school administrators, and parents. The English-language arts and mathematics standards for grades K to 12 are intended for use throughout the United States, but states may volunteer to use them or not. In most cases, this state-specific decision is jointly made by a state board of education and a state department of education.

The NGA and CCSSO (2010) tell us that the Common Core State Standards

- are aligned with college and work expectations
- are clear, understandable, and consistent
- include rigorous content and application of knowledge through high-order skills
- build upon strengths and lessons of current state standards
- are informed by other top performing countries, so that all students are prepared to succeed in our global economy and society
- are evidence and research based

While some have wanted national standards for decades, the catalyst for their development now is largely the result of what have been shown to be uneven and inconsistent state standards that were adopted to comply with the No Child Left Behind Act of 2001. NCLB mandated that states develop curricular standards, test students based on those standards, and report percentages of students who score in the proficient range. Each state did just that, but results from the National Assessment of Educational Progress have made it quite clear that standards are not uniform from state to state. When some states reported high percentages of proficient students and NAEP reported low percentages for the same states, the idea of common standards picked up momentum (Common Core State Standards Initiative, 2010). The purpose of national common standards is to eliminate inconsistencies in expectations, so teachers and parents know what students are to learn and be able to do from grade to grade, regardless of their zip code.

The purpose and implementation of the National Assessment of Educational Progress are discussed in Chapter 5.

As with all reform efforts, there are people who are in favor of Common Core State Standards and others who object to them. Figure 12.10 presents a variety of views of both advocates and critics.

TEACHER PROFESSIONALISM AND COMMON CORE STATE STANDARDS. The common standards do not propose to tell teachers how to teach and are not a curriculum. States and districts can use the knowledge and skills of the standards as goals on which to

Figure 12.10 Advocates and critics of common core standards

Advocates believe that common core standards	Critics believe that common core standards
provide clear and consistent goals for learning, regardless of where in the United States students may live	take away states' rights to determine what is taught and learned
prepare U.S. children for success in college and work	are premature and that state standards have not had sufficient time to succeed
unite teachers and students across the United States as a cooperative effort	do not allow for local educational values and use of local resources
provide common ground around which strategies and programs may be shared	detract from individualism of states and teachers
build on strengths and lessons of current state standards	are unwieldy and will not be enforceable
level the academic playing field for all students	will bring all states' standards down to the lowest common denominator

build their grade-by-grade and subject-by-subject curricula. Instructional strategies can be developed by individual teachers or groups of teachers to best promote teaching and learning based on the standards.

Professionalism with regard to standards involves making standards come alive for our students. We do this by knowing their interests and needs, developing lessons and experiences that are standards based and appropriate for our students, and then engaging learners in knowledge and skills that build on prior learning.

REAUTHORIZATION OF THE ELEMENTARY AND SECONDARY EDUCATION ACT

Perhaps the most significant overarching reform elements that will affect your first years of teaching are part of *A Blueprint for Reform*, the reauthorization of the Elementary and Secondary Education Act (2010). Recall that the last reauthorization was the No Child Left Behind Act of 2001.

These are the key priorities of the reauthorization of the Elementary and Secondary Education Act:

- Promote college- and career-ready students
- Provide great teachers and leaders in every school
- Ensure equity and opportunities for all students
- Raise the bar and reward excellence
- Promote innovation and continuous improvement (U.S. Department of Education, 2010)

To accomplish these priorities, a variety of reform efforts will be put in place. One proposal in the ESEA reauthorization intended to turn around low-performing schools involves intervention models designed to bring about significant changes in the operation, governance, staffing, and instructional programs of schools deemed unsuccessful in educating students. Figure 12.11 briefly explains four intervention models that may be applied to schools as part of the ESEA reauthorization.

TEACHER PROFESSIONALISM AND *A BLUEPRINT FOR REFORM*. If you are teaching in a school that is placed on an intervention plan, you will no doubt experience upheaval in your professional life. This likelihood is slim, but possible, if the guidelines attached to the reauthorization of ESEA, *A Blueprint for Reform*, are enforced.

The five priorities of the reauthorization are sound principles of effective education. Teacher professionalism pushes us to be great teachers and leaders, to promote innovation and continuous improvement, and to help our students become ready for college and careers. *A Blueprint for Reform* calls for us to create equitable opportunities for all students.

Figure 12.11 Intervention models

- *Transformation model:* Replace the principal, strengthen staffing, implement a research-based instructional program, provide extended learning time, and implement new governance and flexibility.
- *Turnaround model:* Replace the principal and rehire no more than 50 percent of the school staff, implement a research-based instructional program, provide extended learning time, and implement new governance structure.
- *Restart model:* Convert or close and reopen the school under the management of an effective charter operator, charter management organization, or education management organization.
- *School closure model:* Close the school and enroll students who attended it in other, higher-performing schools in the district.

Source: U.S. Department of Education (2010).

REFORM IN PERSPECTIVE

"Educators are drowning under the weight of initiative fatigue—attempting to use the same amount of time, money, and emotional energy to accomplish more and more objectives" (Reeves, 2006, p. 89). Veteran teachers will tell you about initiatives and reform efforts that lasted maybe a year, maybe two, with lots of buildup and preparation, some with a flurry of activity but few with lasting positive effects. This doesn't mean we shouldn't keep trying, but it does mean we need to be steady, professional educators who care deeply about all children and their learning, even as initiatives and reform efforts come and go.

In his book, *So Much Reform, So Little Change*, Charles Payne (2008) laments the fact that so many reform efforts end in disappointment. Educators and others come up with ideas and programs that look good on paper, that may make sense from a business perspective, but that fail to view schools and school systems from the human perspective. Payne tells us that relationships and trust-building are foundational, rather than side issues. They matter to the success of any reform.

Payne urges as part of his *School Reformers' Pledge of Good Conduct* that when approaching any effort to improve schools we should not disrespect teachers or do anything behind the principal's back, nor should we expect change overnight. In other words, to contribute to the success of efforts aimed at school improvement, we need to be professionals.

Often the most effective reform is accomplished day by day through the attitudes and actions of teachers who live and teach in ways that are guided by professionalism. Such is the case with Traci Peters, one of our focus teachers at Cario Middle School, South Carolina. In *Teaching in Focus* Traci writes directly to you, giving advice based on her years as an effective, happy teacher of young adolescents.

Teaching in Focus

Traci Peters, seventh grade math, Cario Middle School, South Carolina. *In her own words. . . .*

Dear Teacher Candidate,
   What an exciting career you have chosen. I can assure you that your years as a teacher will be filled with memories that last a lifetime! Many things change each year as a new group of students enter your life. Yet many things must stay the same. Here are just a few things on my "have to do each year" list:

- Love your students as if they were your own children, even the ones that know just what buttons to push. In order to love them, you have to get to know them. So talk to them about things other than the textbook!

- Laugh with your students. If you don't enjoy teaching, then why do it? Middle school kids are especially funny and definitely want all the attention they can get.

- Follow a routine every day. This doesn't mean that you have to do the same thing every day, but it does mean that kids like structure.

- Stay organized—it saves lots of time and frustration!

- Plan with your colleagues. It'll make for more exciting lessons and give you some much needed "adult time." Don't forget to ask for help when you need it!

- Respect your students and their parents, and, in turn, they will respect you. Most importantly, respect yourself. A happy teacher makes a happy class!

- Be consistent with your discipline, from day to day and from student to student. Be sure you don't overuse the word "no" when "yes" is sometimes more appropriate. Remember to reward good behavior, and be sure the consequence fits the not-so-good behavior.

   Good luck to you in your first year of teaching. Be confident that you will make a difference in your students' lives and that all of your hard work does pay off!

Sincerely,
Traci

CONCLUDING THOUGHTS

It's possible to spend an entire career in the position of teacher and never accept the inherent professional responsibilities that accompany the position. How unfortunate and sad for the individual who chooses to go through the motions but never invests the commitment and care necessary to be a true professional.

On the positive side, it is possible to spend an entire career accepting responsibilities to families, community, colleagues, the educational system, the profession, self-growth, and students. Fulfilling each responsibility brings opportunities to affect students' lives and to enjoy a career filled with challenge and satisfaction.

Congratulations on completing this text and the course that made it required reading! For those of you who are sure that teaching is in your future, or who are still seriously considering the profession, you have quite an adventure ahead of you. If this is your first course in teacher preparation, you now probably have a sense of what's ahead in your college program. With each step in teacher preparation your passion for education will likely grow.

If, however, you have decided that teaching is not for you, thank you for opening your mind to what education in the United States is like and to the needs of the more than 50 million students who attend PreK–12 schools. You are more informed than most of the American public. Expressing your opinions will be easier (and hopefully more valid) now that you have a greater understanding of the challenges and opportunities that lie within U.S. schools. Be an advocate for children and their futures—and thus for the future of us all. Please frequently ask, "And how are the children? Are they all well?"

Each page in this book is written by the hands, and from the heart, of a teacher. There is no finer way to spend a lifetime. To be a teacher is to live in a world of possibility—to know that what we do matters. Join us.

After reading the *Chapter in Review,* read about Deirdre's plan to recruit minority teachers for Cario and respond to items in this chapter's *Developing Professional Competence.*

Chapter in Review

How can I practice professionalism during teacher preparation?

- When professional responsibilities are fulfilled, opportunities are created; when opportunities are recognized and acted upon, their benefits incur responsibilities.

- General education courses provide a wide spectrum of information and skills that help teachers put learning in context for their students.

- Teacher candidates should internalize and use education coursework content.

- One of the most valuable aspects of a teacher preparation program is the opportunity to spend time in schools.

- Clinical practice, or student teaching, is the capstone internship experience of your teacher preparation program.

- Keeping an ongoing and reflective log of observations and participation in field experiences will enhance their value.

- Learning from negative experiences can be valuable.

- A teacher preparation portfolio is a good way to exhibit what you know and can do with regard to classroom teaching.

How does professionalism look in the various relationships involved in teaching?

- Teachers should develop and maintain a sense of responsibility for student learning.

- To teach unconditionally means to accept all students for who they are rather than for what they do.

- Teachers need to maintain high expectations for all students, which, in turn, helps students expect more of themselves.

- Parental involvement increases academic achievement and attendance rates and leads to more positive attitudes and behavior.

- There are many ways to communicate with parents about opportunities for involvement.

- Both parents and teachers create barriers to family involvement.

- Teachers have the responsibility to be positive, productive public relations agents for their schools and education.

- The community provides valuable support and services for children and their families.

- When schools, families, and the community work together, students benefit.

- To be collegial requires overt efforts to create and maintain mutually beneficial relationships.

- There are tremendous opportunities for professional and personal growth through collegial relationships within a school.

How can I develop as a professional when I am a teacher?

- Professional growth does not happen automatically.

- Reading, talking with colleagues, and other informal avenues to professional growth are available, as well as formal opportunities such as advanced degrees and National Board of Professional Teaching Standards certification.

- It is important for teachers to balance their professional and personal lives by developing interests and friendships that promote healthy lifestyles.

What do I have to offer the teaching profession?

- The teaching profession is bolstered every time an engaging lesson is taught or learning is facilitated in whatever way is appropriate for students.

- Teachers have a responsibility to extend their influence beyond the classroom.

- New teachers can become actively involved in their schools.

- With a few years of teaching experience, teachers can extend their involvement to district, state, and even national arenas.

- The teaching profession is strengthened through teacher involvement in local, statewide, and national teacher organizations.

- Teachers have many opportunities to add to the teaching knowledge base through research, writing, and participation.

What is my role as a professional in education reform?

- Professional teachers support ideas and efforts intended to increase learning.

- Being an informed professional is a position from which to impact reform.

- Professionals remain optimistic that ways will be found to judge their competency, at least in part, on the degree of learning experienced by their students.

- Professionals encourage exploration in education that may positively impact teaching and learning.

- Teacher professionalism pushes us to be great teachers and leaders, to promote innovation and continuous improvement, and to help our students become ready for college and careers.

- Professional teachers need to be steady, professional educators who care deeply about all children and their learning, even as initiatives and reform efforts come and go.

Developing Professional Competence

Visit the Developing Professional Competence section on Chapter 12 of the MyEducationLab for this text to answer the following questions and begin your preparation for licensure exams.

Cario Middle School is considered a suburban school. The population is about 75% white students and 20% black students, with the rest a mix of students of Asian and Hispanic ethnicities. Of the 67 teachers at Cario, only 2 are African American. This has always bothered Deirdre a little, but now that she teaches the CARE students, most of

whom are black, she has become even more aware of the lack of diversity of the teachers with whom she works.

Deirdre received a master's degree from the College of Charleston (C of C), located about 15 miles from Cario. The college has a large teacher preparation program, with teacher candidates recruited by local schools because of their proven ability. Deirdre has decided she wants to do some recruiting herself, primarily among the nonwhite teacher candidates. Now she has some decisions to make.

Think through this scenario and answer the following multiple-choice questions:

1. Before Deirdre begins planning recruitment she should
   a. talk with several instructors at the C of C to gauge whether they will be open to her efforts
   b. discuss her desires with Cario principal Carol Bartlett
   c. determine the percentage of nonwhite teacher candidates at C of C
   d. contact the NAACP to ask if there are established procedures

2. From whom will Deirdre need to seek support for her recruiting activities?
   a. the dean of the C of C School of Education, Carol Bartlett, the NAACP, the state department of education
   b. Carol Bartlett, the NAACP, the state department of education
   c. the dean of the C of C School of Education, Carol Bartlett
   d. the dean of the C of C School of Education, Carol Bartlett, the NAACP

3. Which reason for applying to teach at Cario will probably have the least impact on C of C teacher candidates?
   a. Cario's administration supports teacher professional development.
   b. This is an opportunity to further integrate the teaching faculty of a school.
   c. Cario is known for quality relationships among teachers.
   d. They will have a chance to work with a majority of white teachers.

Now it's time for you to respond to two short essay items involving the scenario. In your responses, be sure to address all the dilemmas and questions posed in each item. Your responses should each be between one half and one double-spaced page. Consider the following teacher standards as you respond.

INTASC Principle 9, Performances

The teacher draws upon professional colleagues within the school and other professional arenas as supports for reflection, problem solving, and new ideas, actively sharing experiences and seeking and giving feedback.

NMSA, Standard 7 Middle Level Professional Roles, Performance 4

Middle-level teacher candidates engage in and support ongoing professional practices for self and colleagues (e.g., attend professional development activities and conferences, participate in professional organizations).

INTASC Principle 10 Performances

The teacher establishes respectful and productive relationships with parents and guardians from diverse home and community situations, and seeks to develop cooperative partnerships in support of student learning and well-being.

4. Deirdre is not sure her desire for more nonwhite teachers at Cario will be met with enthusiasm from her colleagues. She knows they won't object, but they likely won't share her passion. How might she approach them? What information could she present that would make her case in a professional way? Why is it important for the teachers at Cario to know about Deirdre's recruitment? How does INTASC principle 9 apply?

5. Deirdre thinks that some teacher candidates may be swayed toward Cario if they meet some of the parents of students who are in the racial minority. How should Deirdre go about arranging a meeting? Who would need to be involved? How does INTASC principle 10 apply?

Where DO I Stand NOW?

In the beginning of this chapter you completed an inventory that gauged your professional attitude. Now that you have read the chapter, completed exercises related to the content, engaged in class discussions, and so on, respond to the following items in your course notebook.

Write a well-developed paragraph that depicts your attitude toward each of the major questions addressed in this chapter.

1. How can I practice professionalism during teacher preparation?

2. How does professionalism look in the various relationships involved in teaching?

3. How can I develop as a professional when I am a teacher?

4. What do I have to offer the teaching profession?

5. What is my role as a professional in education reform?

MyEducationLab

The MyEducationLab for this course can help you solidify your comprehension of Chapter 12 concepts.

- Explore the classrooms of the teachers and students you've met in this chapter in the Teaching in Focus section.

- Prepare for licensure exams as you deepen your understanding of chapter concepts in the Developing Professional Competence section.

- Gauge and further develop your understanding of chapter concepts by taking the quizzes and examining the enrichment materials on the Chapter 12 Study Plan.

- Visit Topic 11, "Professional Development," to watch ABC videos, explore Assignments and Activities, and practice essential teaching skills with the Building Teaching Skills and Dispositions unit.

Glossary

A

Academic freedom A form of expression that allows teachers to use their judgment in making decisions about what to discuss, what to assign as readings, what teaching strategies to use, etc.

Academic rigor The content of what we teach is meaningful, and our expectations of the learning of that content are demanding.

Academies Early secondary schools designed to teach content intended to prepare students to participate in business and trade.

Accountability Holding a person or program responsible for an outcome.

Achievement gap Disparity among students, with some excelling while others languish with respect to learning and academic success.

Action research Research conducted by teachers in their classrooms around a concept or question that captures their interest; results of research may be added to the teaching knowledge base.

Active engagement Involving students in meaningful experiences that promote learning; providing an environment for creativity and collaboration, all with increased learning as the goal.

Adequate Yearly Progress School report that consists of a number of elements determined by each individual state with guidance from No Child Left Behind requirements. AYP data are kept by race, socioeconomic status, and gender. Typical components of the AYP report include graduation rate, attendance, math scores, reading/language arts achievement data, and other indicators of student progress.

Advocate for students Support and defend students, always putting their needs first.

Aesthetics The determination of what is beautiful and artistic.

Alternative assessment Generally any assessment other than traditional paper-and-pencil and/or forced-choice assessment.

Alternative school School designed for students who are not successful in a traditional school setting.

American Federation of Teachers (AFT) America's second largest professional association for teachers.

Analytic rubric Specifies separate parts of an assessment task, product, or performance and the characteristics of various levels of success for each.

A Nation at Risk: The Imperative for Educational Reform Report commissioned by President Reagan in 1983 that referred to U.S. public education as a "rising tide of mediocrity." In response, various proposals for reform and improvement surfaced.

Assessment Gathering evidence of student learning.

Assimilation Process of bringing persons of all races and ethnicities into the mainstream by having them behave in ways that align with the dominant culture.

Assistive technology Devices and services that benefit students with disabilities by helping them communicate, increasing their mobility, and aiding in multiple ways that enhance their capacity to learn.

Associative play Children begin to share toys and communicate verbally.

At-large election Voters may vote for any candidate regardless of the area in the district the candidate represents.

At-risk students Those who are in serious danger of not completing school and/or who may be heading toward nonproductive or counterproductive lifestyles.

Attention deficit hyperactivity disorder (ADHD) A learning disability in which students demonstrate three defining characteristics—inattention, hyperactivity, and impulsivity—in persistent patterns that are more severe than in others of the same age.

Authentic assessment Students show what they know and can do in a real-life setting or situation.

Axiology Branch of philosophy that addresses values, both in ethics and aesthetics. Ethics is the determination of what's right and what's wrong. Aesthetics is the determination of what is beautiful and artistic.

B

Backward design An approach to planning for teaching and learning that starts with deciding on the desired learning results (curriculum), then identifies how to collect the evidence necessary to know if the results have been achieved (assessment), and then proceeds to choosing how to help students acquire the desired knowledge and skills (instruction).

Benchmarks Statements of what students should know and be able to do at specific developmental stages.

Bilingual education The delivery of instruction in two languages.

Bilingual Education Act of 1968 Provided funds to assist non-English-speaking students (mostly Hispanic) who were dropping out of high school at a rate of about 70%.

Black Codes Prior to the Civil War, predominantly in the South, Black Codes were enacted to prohibit the education of slaves.

Block grants Grants that provide funding with few restrictions for its use, allowing states and school districts the freedom to use the money in ways that meet their specific needs.

Block schedule A schedule allowing for longer class periods; a block schedule may be composed of a wide variety of schedule options.

Bloom's taxonomy A classification system of thinking and processing skills that range from simple to complex; used to classify various levels of learning objectives and experiences.

Blueprint for Reform Part of the 2010 proposal to reauthorize the Elementary and Secondary Education Act.

Bond referendum Allows school districts to borrow money stipulated for specific projects. The school board asks voters in the district to approve the borrowing of the money (the bond) that will be repaid over a period of time.

Breach of contract Contracts are binding on both parties. If a person signs one and then backs out or takes a different job, or if the district backs out, the person or the district may be sued for damages.

Brown v. Board of Education In 1954 Chief Justice Earl Warren declared that segregating children based solely on race was wrong and illegal. Some schools integrated peacefully; others did not.

Buckley Amendment Also known as the Family Educational Rights and Privacy Act (FERPA) of 1974. Allows parents and guardians access to their students' academic records and requires written parental permission for the records to be shared with anyone else. When students turn age 18, they have control over who sees their records.

Bullying Relationally aggressive behavior; a type of emotional or physical violence where individuals use relationships to harm others.

C

Case knowledge When experienced teachers face a new student, a new learning problem, or new materials, they have a memory bank of other similar situations on which to draw.

Case law Based on the doctrine of *stare decisis*, a Latin phrase meaning "let the decision stand;" once a decision is made in a court of law, that decision sets a precedent for future cases of a similar nature until challenged or overturned.

Categorical grants Money that is allocated or funds that are earmarked for specific purposes.

Charter school A public school that is freed in specific ways from typical regulations required of other public schools.

Child abuse Any act that results in death, serious harm, or exploitation of children.

Child neglect A form of abuse resulting from the failure to act in the best interest of children.

Civil Rights Act of 1964 Stipulates that if schools discriminate based on race, color, or national origin, they are not eligible for federal funding.

Classroom assessment Encompasses every deliberate method of gathering information about the quantity and quality of learning.

Classroom climate The everyday environment of teachers and students working together.

Classroom community A classroom where students and teacher tend to be like-minded and have common beliefs, understandings, and aims.

Classroom management The establishment and enforcement of rules and disciplinary actions; teacher strategies to ensure an orderly classroom environment.

Clinical internship Also known as student teaching or clinical practice; involves extended fieldwork in which teacher candidates teach lessons and, for a designated period of time, take over all classroom duties.

Coleman Report Report written in 1966 that concluded that family and community factors such as poverty and parental levels of education prevented some children from learning, that no matter what schools did, some children would not be successful in school.

Collective bargaining Act of negotiating with employers and/or states to gain additional benefits for members of the bargaining group; a right practiced in most states by teacher associations and unions. States often allow unions to negotiate with school boards concerning elements of teacher contracts and working conditions.

Collegial Relationships with other teachers that promote growth through sharing of professional expertise.

Common Core State Standards Initiative Efforts to develop and promote common national standards by the National Governors Association (NGA) and the Council of Chief State School Officers (CCSSO).

Common schools Community-supported elementary schools for all children established in response to many economic, social, and political factors.

Community The neighborhood, town, city, and/or county in which a person lives.

Comprehensive high school High schools that attempt to meet the educational needs of all adolescents on a single campus.

Compulsory education law Requires children to attend school until a specified age.

Consequences Implies more natural ramifications for wrongdoing than the word *punishment*, which can be arbitrary.

Constructive correcting Assigning consequences in ways that serve as student learning experiences.

Constructivism A way of approaching instruction that builds on progressivism as students are challenged to construct, or discover, knowledge about their environments. Process is valued in progressivism, often more than product. The theory is that students who learn through the processes of construction, discovery, and problem solving will be better able to adapt to a changing world.

Content Knowledge and skills that are taught.

Content standards Specific knowledge students should have and skills they should be able to do.

Contract An agreement between parties that includes the rights and responsibilities of each. When teachers begin jobs in schools they sign initial contracts.

Cooperating teacher A classroom teacher who serves as the host and mentor during clinical practice.

Cooperative learning Loosely defined, any instance of students working together in small groups.

Cooperative play Children actively coordinate ways to keep interaction going.

Copyright laws Federal laws that protect the rights of a creator or author to own intellectual property and to prevent others from copying or distributing it without permission. Intellectual property includes written material, original audio and visual work, and computer programs. Copyright laws also provide guidelines for authorized use of someone else's intellectual property.

Core Knowledge An organization that proposes there is a body of lasting knowledge that should determine the curriculum in PreK–8 schools.

Core subjects Generally considered language arts, math, science, and social studies.

Corporal punishment Physical punishment practiced in some school settings.

Council of Chief State School Officers An organization composed of school superintendents and other school leaders.

Council for Exceptional Children (CEC) National organization that represents the needs of students with exceptionalities and fosters appropriate education for them.

Criterion-referenced test Student scores indicate levels of mastery of a subject and do not depend on how other students perform.

Critical thinking Higher-order thinking involving observing, comparing and contrasting, interpreting, analyzing, seeing issues from a variety of perspectives, weighing variables, and then making decisions and solving problems.

Cultural identity Results from the interactions of many factors, including language, religion, gender, income level, age, values, beliefs, race, and ethnicity.

Culturally responsive teaching What teachers do to make multicultural education a reality.

Cultural pluralism Involves the recognition that our nation is populated by a rich variety of people of varying races and ethnicities, and thus cultures, all with potential to contribute positively to our common goal of a productive, free society.

Culture A composite of social values, cognitive codes, behavioral standards, worldviews, and beliefs that characterize a group of people.

Curriculum The educational term for what students experience in schools.

Cyberbullying Using technology to bully.

Cybercitizenship Responsibly using technology in ways that do not harm others.

D

Dame schools In colonial days, dames were respected women who, usually without formal schooling, had learned to read and write and who turned their homes into schools where parents paid to have their children educated.

Deductive reasoning A process that begins with a general statement from which more specific statements are assumed to be true.

Democratic classroom A classroom setting that promotes choice, community, authentic learning, and a relevant, creative curriculum; students participate in the establishment of behavioral expectations.

Departmentalization School organizational pattern in which teachers teach their own subjects and meet occasionally with other teachers who teach the same subject.

Depression Mental illness characterized by a deep sense of sadness and a loss of interest or pleasure in activities.

Developmental appropriateness Teaching and learning that matches students' physical, cognitive, social, emotional, and character development.

Diagnostic assessment Assesses student knowledge and skill levels before beginning a unit of study; commonly referred to as pretesting.

Dialects Deviations from standard language rules used by identifiable groups of people.

Differentiation of instruction Varying instruction based on the needs of students.

Direct instruction A general lesson model that includes a distinct opening, presentation of information, practice, and teacher feedback and review.

Dispositions Attitudes and beliefs that guide and determine behavior.

Distance learning Involves the acquisition of knowledge and skills through instruction delivered using technology.

District school board Governing body composed of elected citizens responsible for setting policies that affect the operation of schools.

District superintendent Functions as the school district's chief executive officer; hired by the board and serves at its pleasure.

Dropouts Students who do not complete high school.

Due process The steps a district must take to pursue the charges when a tenured teacher is threatened with dismissal; important principle that requires guidelines to be followed to ensure that individuals are protected from arbitrary or capricious treatment by those in authority.

E

Early childhood education The care and education of the youngest students in the United States, typically considered birth through age 8.

Ebonics Black English, one of the best known and most controversial dialects in the United States.

Educational technology Any technology that assists teachers in teaching and students in learning.

Education for All Handicapped Children Act (Public Law 94-142) Federal law passed in 1975 that guaranteed a free and appropriate education to all children with disabilities in the least restrictive environment; renamed Individual with Disabilities Education Act in 1990.

Education Maintenance Organization (EMO) An organization contracted to take over the management of a public school for profit.

Education summit Organized meeting to advocate for school improvement.

Effective schools Schools that meet the learning needs of the students who attend them.

Effective Schools Movement Originated in the 1970s to develop research pertaining to the assertion that all children can learn; purpose was to find schools deemed effective for all children and identify common characteristics.

Elementary Level of school that usually includes grades K through 5.

Elementary and Secondary Education Act Enacted during the presidency of Lyndon B. Johnson to provide extra funding, called Title I funding, for schools with high numbers of children from low-income homes.

Emotional intelligence quotient (EQ) A set of skills that accompany the expression, evaluation, and regulation of emotions. A high-level EQ indicates a person's ability to understand others' as well as his or her own feelings, respond appropriately to them, and, in general, get along.

Encore courses Also known as related arts or exploratory courses; all courses other than what are considered the core courses of math, English language arts, social studies, and science.

English as a second language (ESL) Students receive individualized assistance; unlike bilingual education, ESL services are delivered only in English; little or no emphasis is placed on preserving native language or culture; and ESL teachers do not need to speak another language.

English-language learners (ELL) Non-English speakers and students with limited English proficiency.

Entitlements Grants given to certain segments of the population that have specific needs; the federal government deems these individuals entitled to extra assistance.

Epistemology Branch of philosophy that addresses the dilemma of determining truth and ways of acquiring knowledge.

Era of standards A time when content standards determined curricular learning goals; generally considered 1990 through the present.

Essentialism A philosophy of education based on the belief there is a core curriculum that everyone in the United States should learn. This core can shift in response to societal changes but should always be basic, organized, and rigorous.

Ethics Standards of conduct based on moral judgments; the determination of what's right and what's wrong.

Ethnicity An individual's country of origin and ancestry.

Eurocentric Contributions and traditions centered on European values.

Evaluation Judgments about, and the assigning of values to, the *results* of assessments.

Excise tax Tax on luxury items such as boats and travel trailers.

Exemplars *S*amples of work that fit various criteria for scoring so students actually see what a product looks like that earns a particular number.

Existentialism Primary emphasis is on the individual. As a philosophy of education, existentialism contends that teachers teach the whole person, not just math, reading, science, or any other particular subject. Each student searches for personal meaning and personal understanding. If learning about a subject area increases a student's sense of self, then it's worthwhile.

Expectations A word with positive connotations that may be used in place of *rules,* a word with negative connotations.

Expenditure per pupil The average amount of money spent from federal, state, and local sources on an individual student.

Explicit curriculum What teachers are expected to teach, what students are expected to learn, and what society expects of schools; also referred to as the formal curriculum.

Exploratory courses Also known as related arts or encore courses, all courses other than math, English language arts, social studies, and science; may include art, music, physical education, industrial arts, languages, drama, computer education, and others.

Expulsion Semipermanent or permanent dismissal from school for a semester or for an indefinite period.

Extracurriculum Includes the organized experiences students have that are beyond the formal curriculum.

Extrinsic incentives Incentives that are imposed or originate outside the individual.

F

Fair use Specific limitations on the use of copyrighted materials.

Family Educational Rights and Privacy Act (FERPA) of 1974 Commonly called the Buckley Amendment, allows parents and guardians access to their students' academic records and requires written parental permission for the records to be shared with anyone else. When students turn age 18, they have control over who sees their records.

Feeder system Configuration of schools in a district; typically in one feeder system of schools, early childhood/elementary schools feed into middle schools that feed into a particular high school.

5-E lesson plan A way for teachers to guide students through a cycle of inquiry learning; most commonly used for science exploration.

Field experience Observing and/or participating in actual classrooms; also referred to as practicum experiences.

Formal curriculum Encompasses what is intentionally taught, what is stated as the goals of student learning.

Formative assessment A series of assessments in a variety of formats that help monitor student progress.

For-profit schools Schools operated by private companies for profit.

Full-service school A public school that provides a comprehensive program of education and includes student and community services such as after-school and family education programs.

Functional behavioral assessment (FBA) A management plan through a team of educators using a process that looks for events and actions that may lead to misbehavior and devises strategies to help students abide by classroom expectations.

G

Gender The sense of being male or female, as opposed to sex, which refers to anatomical differences.

Gender bias The favoring of one gender over the other in specific circumstances.

Gender equity The fair and balanced treatment of males and females.

Gender stereotyping Occurs when perceived gender differences are assumed for all people.

Gifted and talented Exceptional learners who demonstrate high levels of intelligence, creativity, and achievement.

Global awareness Involves understanding environmental, societal, cultural, political, and economical concepts and issues that impact our world.

Graduation rate Percentage of students who graduate from high school with a regular diploma in the standard number of years.

Grade Judgment of assessment quality (evaluation) with a number attached to it.

Grant Funds provided by a source to pay for equipment or services requested by teachers and others.

Great Books The writings of those considered to be the great thinkers throughout the history of Western civilization, such as Homer, Shakespeare, Melville, Einstein, and many others.

Grievance A formal complaint filed by an individual teacher or group of teachers against a district.

Guided practice Opportunities for students to work independently on applying knowledge in a non-threatening setting that includes teacher feedback.

H

Head Start The largest provider of government-funded preschool education, employing one of every five U.S. preschool teachers.

Hidden curriculum Curriculum that is not explicit or openly expressed; similar to the informal curriculum but with negative connotations.

Hierarchy of needs Maslow's (1908–1970) theory that all human beings experience the same needs.

Highly qualified Those who meet government guidelines for teacher quality in public schools.

High school completion rate As defined by the U.S. Department of Education, the "percentage of students, measured from the beginning of high school, who graduate from a high school with a regular diploma in the standard number of years"; also known as graduation rate.

High schools Schools that most often encompass grades 9 to 12.

High/Scope An approach to early childhood education built on consistency and few transitions during the day.

High-stakes tests Standardized tests that have far-reaching consequences.

Holistic rubric A grading instrument that uses one scale for an entire project.

Homeschooled Refers to students who receive most of their academic instruction in their homes.

Homework Independent practice outside the classroom.

I

Idealism A philosophy based on the belief that ideas are the only reliable form of reality. Idealists believe the physical world changes continually and that ideas are what should be taught.

Implicit curriculum Curriculum that is implied and subtle; the informal curriculum.

Incentives A word that may be used in place of the overused and value-laden word *rewards*.

Inclusion Students attend their home school with their age- and grade-appropriate peers, participate in extracurricular activities, and receive special education and support services to the maximum extent possible in the general education classroom.

Individualized educational program (IEP) A plan developed for a student by educators, the family, and others as appropriate, involving details of how to reach specific goals. A student's IEP must be revisited annually and student progress evaluated.

Individuals with Disabilities Education Act (IDEA) Also referred to as PL94-142 (and the revised version of the Education for All Handicapped Children Act of 1975), this act made special education services a right, not a privilege, because it required schools to place students in least-restrictive environments within public schools.

Individuals with Disabilities Education Improvement Act Reauthorization of IDEA in 2004 that compiled all U.S. laws that affect children with disabilities into one statute.

Inductive reasoning Given specific statements, a general conclusion may be logically assumed.

Informal curriculum What students learn that isn't written in a lesson plan or necessarily intentionally transmitted to students.

Information literacy Involves recognition of when information is needed, knowing how to access information, and judging information credibility.

In loco parentis Serving in place of parents.

Inquiry learning When students pursue answers to questions posed by others or developed on their own, they are involved in inquiry learning. Observation, questioning, hypothesizing, and predicting are all part of inquiry-based learning.

Instruction Encompasses the strategies used to convey the curriculum with the desired end result of student learning.

Instructional software Software designed specifically for student use to learn about concepts and/or practice skills related to a subject area.

Instructional time Time available for teaching and learning.

Instrumental aggression Aggression based on attempting to meet a specific goal, such as grabbing a particular toy or establishing dominance in an activity; most common among boys.

Integrated curriculum Involves making connections among subject areas through the use of a unifying topic or theme.

Intelligence The capacity for knowing and learning.

Intelligence quotient (IQ) The results of a test that affixes a number to intelligence.

Intelligent design Includes a belief that certain features of the universe and of living things are best explained by an intelligent being (God), not by the process of natural selection espoused by evolution.

Interdisciplinary Term often used to describe curricular links or connections among subjects.

Interdisciplinary team The preferred organizational structure for middle-level education, involving a team of two to five teachers working with a distinct group of students for an entire year.

Intermediate grades Typically grades 4 and 5 in an elementary setting.

Internet Computer network that allows people around the world to search for information, share resources, and communicate.

Interstate New Teacher Assessment and Support Consortium (INTASC) Organization that sets standards for what new teachers should know and be able to do.

Intrinsic incentives Incentives that come from within and result from students' natural drives.

J

Jigsaw Strategy involving students becoming experts on particular topics and then teaching those topics to the other students.

Junior high Schools developed in 1909 to be a bridge between elementary and high school; typically grades 7 to 9.

K

Kalamazoo Case Established that the legislature could tax for support of both common and secondary schools, propelling public high schools into school systems in every state.

Kindergarten German for "children's garden," the school year that precedes first grade.

L

Language Primary means of communication; transmits knowledge and passes on culture.

Language minority students Students whose native language is other than English, regardless of their current level of English proficiency.

Latin grammar school First established in 1635 in Boston for boys whose families could afford to send them on for more education beyond the dame school; considered the forerunner of modern high schools and specifically prepared boys to attend Harvard University, established in 1636.

Learning A complex and dynamic process involving thinking, perception, experience, and memory.

Learning disabled (LD) A general category of students with disorders involving problems understanding or using language that results in significant differences between learning potential and achievement.

Learning modalities Auditory (hearing), visual (seeing), tactile (touch), and kinesthetic (movement); all four are used in the process of learning, but individuals tend to favor one or two over the others.

Learning styles Ways in which individuals learn most effectively and efficiently.

Least restrictive environment (LRE) The setting within which students with disabilities can function at capacity; generally the setting with students who do not have disabilities that also meets the educational needs of the students with disabilities.

Lesson plan Devising experiences for students as part of the formal curriculum.

Liable To be responsible for; liability is what teaching is all about—accepting responsibility for students while they are under our supervision.

Limited English proficiency (LEP) Students with LEP may speak and understand some English, but not enough to be successful in classes taught in English without additional assistance.

Literacy Involves ability to analyze and apply knowledge and skills necessary to solve problems within a discipline.

Logic Reasoning that attempts to avoid vagueness and contradictions. To use logic simply means to think clearly to understand a situation, solve a problem, or draw a conclusion. There are two basic kinds of reasoning, or logic, commonly addressed in school. One is **deductive reasoning,** a process that begins with a general statement from which more specific statements are assumed to be true. Another kind of logic, **inductive reasoning,** works the other way: Given some specific statements, a general conclusion may be assumed.

Long-range plans Lesson plans that may encompass a nine-week timeframe, a semester, or a year.

Looping School practice that keeps a teacher with a particular group of students for more than 1 year.

M

Magnet school A public school with a specific emphasis or theme and curriculum and instructional programs tailored with unique opportunities that attract certain students.

Manipulatives Hands-on objects that enhance and illustrate concepts and skills.

Massachusetts Act of 1642 First compulsory education law in the New World; required all white children to attend school.

Mentor An experienced teacher who uses experience and wisdom to answer questions and help guide new teachers.

Meta-analysis A research technique involving the analysis of multiple studies.

Metaphysics Branch of philosophy that addresses the search for reality and purpose. The word *metaphysics* means "beyond the material or the physical." Those who study metaphysics look for answers that go beyond scientific experiments.

Methods courses Courses that emphasize particular strategies for specific subjects and will probably incorporate opportunities to actually apply what you are learning.

Micromanagement Managing to a level of detail that is inappropriate for a particular position. For instance, when school board members go beyond policy making into what is considered day-to-day operations, they may be seen as micromanaging.

Middle school Schools for young adolescents with a distinct philosophy that embraces both academic rigor and developmental appropriateness; may include any combination of grades 5 to 9.

Mini-lecture Shortened, focused version of the lecture.

Montessori An approach to early childhood education with mixed-age grouping and self-pacing.

Morrill Act In 1862 the government granted states 30,000 acres of land for every senator and representative in Congress in 1860. The income the state generated from this land was to be used to support at least one college.

Multiage classroom Classroom where children in two, three, or more grade levels learn together.

Multicultural curriculum Curriculum that purposefully includes contributions and viewpoints from the perspectives of different cultures, ethnicities, races, genders, and socioeconomic levels.

Multicultural education An instructional approach that celebrates diversity and promotes equal educational opportunities.

Multimedia Using more than one medium to communicate information.

Multiple intelligences theory (MI) A theory developed by Howard Gardner that intelligence is multidimensional, that individual brains work in ways that give each of us our own personal intelligences; includes nine intelligences.

N

National Assessment of Educational Progress (NAEP) Only standardized test systematically administered to a sampling of students across the United States. The NAEP is administered to fourth, eighth, and twelfth graders in math, reading, writing, science, history, economics, geography, civics, foreign language, and a variety of the arts; often called the nation's report card.

National Board of Professional Teaching Standards (NBPTS) Board that sets standards, establishes policies, and issues certificates designating teachers with skills to perform effectively.

National Council for the Accreditation of Teacher Education (NCATE) Agency that scrutinizes university teacher education programs. About two thirds of states require university teacher education programs to be accredited (authorized to prepare teachers) through NCATE.

National Defense Education Act of 1958 Called for strengthening of science, math, and foreign language programs; teachers were given training in the use of new methods and materials in hopes of bringing American student learning up to, and beyond, the levels of learning in other countries.

National Education Association (NEA) The largest professional education association in the United States, with a total of over 5 million members including teachers, administrators, professors, counselors, and other educators.

National Governors Association Organization of governors enabling them to share expertise and tackle dilemmas collectively.

National Middle School Association (NMSA) Organization that provides standards for the preparation of teachers for grades 5 to 9, and advocates for the needs and education of young adolescents.

Nature Refers to the genetically inherited influences on who we are.

Neighborhood school Students in a geographic area attend school close to their home.

New England Primer First published in 1690 for children in upper elementary and secondary levels. Published for over 150 years with few substantial changes over its lifetime, the *New England Primer* included a spelling guide based on the alphabet denoted in brief rhymes and pictures, the Lord's Prayer, the Apostles' Creed, the Ten Commandments, a list of the books of the Bible, the Puritan catechism, and numbers 1 to 100.

No Child Left Behind Act of 2001 (NCLB) Federal law (2001–2010) that holds schools accountable for student learning, regardless of student diversity. States are required to test all students in grades 3 to 8 annually to determine progress.

Normal schools Publicly funded secondary schools specifically designed to prepare teachers for the classroom.

Norm referenced Tests used to compare students; administered to a group of students selected because they represent a cross section of U.S. students (norm group).

Norms Expectations that are foundational, including physical norms for preserving the health and safety of students, moral norms pertaining to respect for others, and societal norms for politeness and individual responsibility.

Northwest Land Ordinance of 1787 Divided federally owned land in the wilderness into townships and required that schools be built.

Null curriculum What is not taught in school.

Nurture Refers to the influence of the environment, including everything that happens except for what can be accounted for genetically.

O

Obesity Extreme overweight as indicated by body mass index (BMI), a measure of how much a person weighs relative to height.

Objective Concise statement about what students are expected to learn and be able to do as a result of the lesson.

Old Deluder Satan Act Because education was considered the best way to fight the devil, the act (also known as the Massachusetts Act of 1647) established that every town of 50 or more households must provide a school.

Open enrollment A plan that allows students to choose from among virtually all the schools in a school district.

Overlapping A teacher's ability to multitask, to take care of several things at once.

P

Pacing guide A document that dictates the timing of content coverage; helps ensure that all grade-level standards are part of the curriculum.

Parallel play Children agreeably sharing the same space but are not communicating.

Paraprofessional A teacher aide or assistant teacher; typically not a certified teacher.

Parochial schools Schools affiliated with religious organizations.

Partnership for 21st Century Skills Leading advocacy organization focused on infusing 21st-century skills into education.

Pedagogy The combining of curriculum and instruction to foster learning.

Perennialism A philosophy of education based on a core curriculum with themes and questions that endure, that are everlasting; as life changes and times change, the real substance and truths of life remain the same.

Performance assessment May be a project, a demonstration, a creation, or anything that requires the application of knowledge and skills.

Performance-based pay Involves paying teachers more when they produce whatever results are designated as desirable.

Performance standards Designated levels of the knowledge or skills that are considered acceptable at a particular grade level.

Philosophy *Philo* means "love," and *sophos* means "wisdom." Philosophy, then, means "love of wisdom." This love of wisdom, or philosophy, becomes a means of answering fundamental questions.

Philosophy of education The *love of wisdom* regarding teaching that expresses itself in attitudes and actions every day in the classroom.

Portfolio Assessment tool for which either students or teachers assemble a cohesive package of representative evidence of student learning.

Portfolio for teacher preparation A cohesive package of representative products; may either document growth or display best work, depending on purpose.

Postmodernism Grew out of a sense that those in power control those who don't have power. This control, postmodernists believe, is manifested through major institutions like schools.

PowerPoint Presentation program used by teachers to deliver instruction and by students to demonstrate skills and display project products.

Practicum experiences Involve observing and/or participating in actual classrooms; also referred to as field experiences.

Pragmatism A philosophy that says that student-centered perspectives integrated with firsthand experiences are most effective.

Praise Complimenting others for real or perceived positive actions or attributes.

Praxis Series Battery of tests published by the Educational Testing Service (ETS) that may be used to determine the qualifications of individuals to be licensed or certified to teach in a variety of disciplines and grade levels.

Preschool A semistructured environment for 3- and 4-year-olds housed in a school setting; care is enhanced by exposure to basic educational concepts.

Pretesting Assessing student knowledge and skill levels before beginning a unit of study; also called diagnostic assessment.

Primary grades Typically grades K to 3.

Principal Oversees every aspect of school life and answers to the district for all that occurs at the school. The principal's role involves administrative tasks such as facility maintenance, attendance, discipline, parent/community relationships and communication, transportation, and all manner of paperwork. Principals are also instructional leaders with knowledge of, and experience with, the teaching and learning process.

Private schools The two elements that make schools public—public funding and public accountability—are both absent in private schools.

Privilege gap Gap between the haves and the have-nots.

Problem-based learning (PBL) Focusing student attention and effort on a real-life problem that has more than one solution path or product.

Problem solving Process involved in finding a solution to a problem.

Processing Sending a student out of the classroom with the purpose of reflection and planning for better choices.

Process standards Processes that support content learning by explaining how the content might be best learned and how to use the content once it is acquired.

Profession An occupation that meets certain criteria, including (1) extensive training to enter, (2) inclusion of a code of ethics, and (3) service as the primary product.

Professional development Efforts to help teachers improve their knowledge and skills.

Professionalism A way of being involving attitudes and actions that convey respect, uphold high standards, and demonstrate commitment to those served.

Progressive education In 1896 John Dewey established a method of involving students in their own learning through cooperative groups, which grew into a major movement with far-reaching implications; interests guide what is learned about traditional subjects.

Progressivism A student-centered philosophy of education that focuses on curriculum of interest to students. Progressivists view education as more than preparation for the future; it is life itself. The progressive philosophy of education endorses experiential learning full of opportunities for student discovery and opportunities to solve problems.

Property taxes Values of property are determined, and a small percentage of the assessed amount (usually less than 1%) is collected annually and used for local services.

Proximity The accessibility of teacher to students.

Public domain A work is in the public domain if it is more than 75 years old or is published by a federal agency; work in the public domain is not protected by copyright.

Public Law 94-142 (PL94-142) Common way of referring to the Individuals with Disabilities Education Act (IDEA), an act that made special education services a right, rather than a privilege.

Public schools Public schools are funded through some form of taxation and are accountable to the community through elected or governmental officials who have policy and oversight responsibilities.

R

Race Term used to classify people according to their physical characteristics that are nature given. Race classifies people at birth.

Race to the Top A federal initiative challenging states to make bold efforts to improve teaching and learning; over $4 billion in federal money awarded to states on a competitive basis.

Racism A form of prejudice that may be perpetuated by individuals or governments stemming from a belief that one race is superior to another.

Reading across the curriculum Infusing the curriculum with reading, regardless of content area.

Realism Based on the belief that some facts are absolutes no matter who recognizes them. Realists contend that the only way to know these absolutes is to study the material world.

Reduction in force Occurs in schools when there are fewer students, budget cuts, or the cancellation of a program. Reduction in force (rif) may also apply to tenured teachers. The general rule of "riffing" is that the last hired are the first to go if it becomes necessary.

Reflection Thinking about what is done, how it's done, and the consequences of actions or inactions, all with the goal of being a better teacher.

Reflective practitioner A teacher who thinks critically about teaching and the consequences of actions or inactions, all with the goal of being more effective with students.

Reform To change, to make different, or to improve.

Reggio Emilia An approach to early childhood education for ages 3 months to 6 years based on relationships among children, families, and teachers.

Related arts courses Also known as exploratory courses or encore courses; all courses other than math, English language arts, social studies, and science; may include art, music, physical education, industrial arts, languages, drama, computer education, and so on.

Relational aggression Subtle actions that may hurt emotionally rather than physically; may include name-calling, gossiping, or saying mean things just to be hurtful; most common among girls.

Reliability The degree to which an assessment yields a pattern of results that is repeatable and consistent over time.

Resilience The ability to bounce back and meet life's challenges.

Resource teacher A special education teacher who helps students develop strategies for school success.

Ripple effect An effect that occurs when one action directly affects another.

Role play Getting students up and moving as they dramatize a scenario to make a point or prompt students to think in divergent ways.

Romanticism A philosophy of education that contends the needs of the individual are more important than the needs of society; also known as naturalism.

Routine An expected action that occurs in a given circumstance to accomplish a task efficiently.

Rubric Assessment tool that makes explicit what is being assessed, lists characteristics of degrees of quality, and provides a rating scale to differentiate among these degrees.

Rural Indicates an area with fewer than 2,500 people and a minimum of retail stores and services.

S

Scaffolding The support given to children to help them move through progressive levels of learning.

School choice Method of letting parents decide which schools their students attend.

School connectedness Student bonding and engagement in the school experience.

School culture The prevailing atmosphere of a school that provides the context of learning experiences; as places where people work together and learn to-gether, schools function according to their cultures.

School district An organizational structure of local schools defined by geographic boundaries.

School-to-Work Federal government program initiated to bring real-world, work-related skills and under-standing to students through courses and experi-ences that introduce them to career possibilities.

School venues The variety of ways Americans "do school" in the more than 120,000 schools in the United States. The most prominent venues are public schools and private schools.

Self-contained classroom An organizational structure involving one teacher and a group of students for whom the teacher is accountable much of the school day.

Self-efficacy An "I can" belief in oneself that leads to a sense of competence; the concept of self-efficacy is solidly grounded in the accomplishment of a continuum of increasingly difficult challenges.

Settlement houses Established by early American reformers to confront the problem of urban poverty; community service centers that provided educational opportunities, skills training, and cultural events.

Sexual harassment Behavior with sexual implications that is neither wanted nor welcome; may include obvious looks with lewd intent, taunts with sexual innuendo, touching, kissing, groping, and any behavior that has sexual connotations.

Sexual orientation The sex to which a person is romantically or socially attracted is considered a person's sexual orientation.

Single gender All male or all female.

Single-member elections Only those who live in a specific area can vote for the representatives in their area.

Sin tax Tax on items some consider vices, such as alcohol and cigarettes.

Site-based management Public school management structure in which governance is in the hands of those closest to it, generally teachers, administrators, and parents.

Social cognition Process of relating to others and thinking about them and oneself.

Socialization Occurs through a variety of influences including home, family, church, print and electronic media, peers, and school.

Social reconstructionism A philosophy of education that looks to education to change society, rather than just teach about it. Social reconstructionism as an education philosophy calls on schools to educate students in ways that will help society move beyond all forms of discrimination to the benefit of everyone worldwide.

Socioeconomic status (SES) Status based on economic level and other sources of power.

Software Computer programs that are written to perform specific applications; application software and instructional software are two basic types used in schools.

Special education services Services provided by schools to help students with disabilities function and learn in ways optimal to each.

Special education students Students with disabilities that require services enabling them to function and learn in ways optimal to each individual.

Special interest group Group of people with a common mission who work to have an impact.

Stages of cognitive development Jean Piaget (1896–1980) recognized distinct differences in children's and adolescents' responses to questions that directly correlated to their chronological ages and categorized these differences into stages.

Stages of moral reasoning Noted developmental psychologist Lawrence Kohlberg contends that people pass through distinct stages as they develop morally.

Standard English A composite of the language spoken by educated middle-class people in the United States.

Standardized test Test given to multiple groups of students, designed for specific grade levels, and typically repeated annually. These tests are administered and scored under controlled conditions, and their exact content is unknown to everyone except the test makers before they are administered.

Standards Expectations for what individuals should know and be able to do.

Standards-based reform movement Efforts to improve teaching and learning through content standards; another way of expressing the era of standards.

Standards-based test Test written using the content of a specific set of standards.

State board of education Volunteers who are either elected or appointed by the governor; state legislatures give state boards oversight authority; boards act in regulatory and advisory capacities.

State department of education Operates under the guidance of the governor, legislature, and state board of education; also known as state office of education or perhaps department of public instruction.

State superintendent The one person given responsibility for managing the state department of education; also known as chief state education officer or commissioner of education.

Structured English immersion Approach includes significant amounts of the school day dedicated to the explicit teaching of the English language, with other content supporting instruction but not as the primary focus.

Structured observation Early field experiences involving looking for specific things and responding to prompts that purposefully call attention to certain aspects of the classroom.

Student self-monitoring Students assume control of their own behavior as they develop a sense of ownership for that behavior.

Students with exceptionalities Learners with abilities or disabilities that set them apart from other learners.

Student teaching Also known as clinical internship or clinical practice; involves extended fieldwork in which teacher candidates teach lessons and, for a designated period of time, take over all classroom duties.

Substance abuse A pattern of alcohol or drug use that can lead to detrimental and habitual consumption, impaired functioning at school and work, and legal difficulties.

Suburban Indicates neighborhoods and small- to medium-size towns that are located on the fringe of cities or are their own distinct locations.

Summative assessment A formal assessment involving judgments about the success of a process or product; most often occurs at the end of a unit of study.

Superintendent A school district's chief executive officer; hired by the district school board; advises the board and carries out board policies.

Suspension Time out of school that may range from 1 day to less than a semester, but is usually for 10 days or less.

T

Tableau Freeze-frame role-playing with students choosing a book passage, striking a pose that depicts the passage, and holding the pose while a narrator reads the passage.

Tax cap An upper limit to taxation.

Teacher leader A teacher with additional responsibilities such as chairperson of a grade level of teachers or perhaps a subject-area specialist who works with other teachers to help them improve their knowledge and/or skills; more generally, teachers who prove to be leaders in their schools, as well as in their districts and states, simply by being dynamic, well-informed classroom teachers.

Teacher study groups Building professional, collegial communities within schools. Small groups of teachers select books and journal articles to read, talk about what they have read, and discuss how it might be applied to their teaching.

Teacher think-aloud An instructional strategy in which teachers think out loud about how to approach a problem, make sense of new information, use self-restraint in volatile situations, consider options, discard what doesn't work, and begin to refine what makes sense.

Teach for America Most widely known of all alternative licensing programs; TFA recruits individuals who are college seniors or recent graduates who agree to teach in high-needs rural or urban schools for at least 2 years.

Tenure Continuing contract status; a teacher with tenure is entitled to a contract each year unless the district has reason to not renew it or the teacher decides to go elsewhere. In most states tenure doesn't guarantee a particular position in a particular school, but it does guarantee employment in the district.

Thinking skills Skills that aid in processing information.

Think-pair-share Teachers expose students to information, give a prompt, ask a question, or provide an experience and then challenge them to think about it in a particular way and perhaps record their thoughts on paper (T). Students then choose a partner (P) and share their thoughts with another student (S).

Time-on-task Productive learning time.

Title I funding Federal compensatory funds provided through the Elementary and Secondary Education Act given to public schools where more than 50% of the students qualify for free or reduced-price meals; used to supplement regular school funding in schools with high numbers of students from low-income settings.

Title IX of the Education Amendments Act of 1972 Prohibits government money from being used for anything that discriminates on the basis of gender.

Token economy A system of giving symbolic rewards for appropriate behavior and withholding or taking away rewards for inappropriate behavior.

Town schools Early American schools established for whole communities; while some schools still limited curriculum to reading, writing, and the classics, specialized schools in the form of academies became popular.

Traditional public schools Schools that have no admission criteria, other than perhaps residency in a particular attendance zone.

Transition When students change activities or locations, they are in transition; generally a time when most classroom disruptions happen.

Transparent Decisions are made with full disclosure of information and reasoning.

Trends in International Mathematics and Science Study (TIMSS) International tests that compare students worldwide; administered every 4 years since 1995.

Truancy Nonattendance during compulsory education, not including excused absences generally granted for health reasons.

Tyler Rationale Ralph Tyler developed four questions that should be asked throughout the stages of curriculum development.

U

Unconditional teaching Accepting students for who they are, not for what they do.

Unfunded mandate A legally enforceable law without monetary support provided.

Unit of study Organizes curriculum, instruction, and assessment around a major theme or distinct body of content; provides planned cohesion.

Unobtrusive intervention Consequences that do not disrupt instruction.

Urban Indicates cities with large downtowns and dense populations.

V

Validity The degree to which an assessment measures what it is supposed to measure.

Virtual schools Schools that deliver instruction only through distance learning.

Vocational Education Act of 1963 Quadrupled the amount of money allocated for vocational education.

Voucher Government-issued piece of paper that represents part of a state's financial contribution for the education of a student; parents choose a school and present the voucher, and the government allocates funding to the school accordingly.

W

Watchdog group Community members who join forces to keep an eye on school district accountability by examining policies and practices.

Wayside teaching Teaching that occurs inside and outside the classroom through attitudes, values, habits, interests, and classroom climate.

Whole child Attending to student developmental stages and needs, along with teaching them grade-level and subject-area content.

Withitness Refers to a teacher's awareness of what's going on in the whole classroom, enabling the teacher to step in when needed to keep the environment positive; originated with Jacob Kounin.

Writing across the curriculum Infusing the curriculum with writing, regardless of content area.

Y

Young adolescents Students between ages 10 and 15.

Z

Zero tolerance School-imposed nonnegotiable consequences for certain infractions. For instance, the consequence for fighting may be automatic suspension for 3 days.

Zone of proximal development The level at which a child can almost, but not completely, grasp a concept or perform a task successfully; theory proposed by Lev Vygotsky.

References

Chapter 1

American Federation of Teachers. (2008). Survey and analysis of teacher salary trends (2006–2007). Retrieved February 1, 2010, from http://archive.aft.org/salary/

Berliner, D. C. (2000). A personal response to those who bash teacher education. *Journal of Teacher Education, 51*(5), 358–371.

Bushaw, W. J., & McNee, J. A. (2009). The 41st annual Phi Delta Kappa/Gallup poll of the public's attitudes toward the public schools. *Phi Delta Kappan, 91*(1), 8–23.

Codell, E. R. (1999). *Educating Esme: Diary of a teacher's first year.* Chapel Hill, NC: Algonquin Books of Chapel Hill.

Corbett, D., & Wilson, B. (2002). What urban students say about good teaching. *Educational Leadership, 60*(1), 18–22.

Council of Chief State School Officers. (1992). *Model standards for beginning teacher licensing, assessment, and development: A resource for state dialogue.* Washington, DC: Author.

Darling-Hammond, L. (2003). Keeping good teachers: Why it matters, what leaders can do. *Educational Leadership, 60*(8), 7–13.

Delaware Department of Education. (2006). Vision 2015. Retrieved July 28, 2010, from http://www.vision2015delaware.org/resources/Vision2015report1-26.pdf

Dewey, J. (1933). *How we think: A restatement of the relation of reflective thinking to the educative process.* Boston: D.C. Heath.

Duncan, A. (2009/2010, Winter). Evaluating the teaching profession. *American Educator, 33*(4), 1–5. Retrieved January 31, 2010, from http://www.aft.org/pdfs/americaneducator/ae_winter09.pdf

Feistritzer, C. E. (2009). Alternative teacher certification: A state-by-state analysis 2009. Retrieved January 24, 2010, from www.teach-now.org/overview.cfm

Fessenden, F., & Barbanel, J. (2005). The rise of the six-figure teacher. *The New York Times.* Retrieved May 20, 2005, from http://www.nytimes.com/2005/05/15/nyregion/15iteach.html

Ginott, H. G. (1993). *Teacher and child.* New York: Collier Books/Macmillan.

Haycock, K. (2003). Toward a fair distribution of teacher talent. *Educational Leadership, 60*(4), 11–15.

Howsam, R. B., Corrigan, D. C., Denemark, G. W., & Nash, R. J. (1976). *Educating a profession.* Washington, DC: American Association of Colleges of Teacher Education.

Ingersoll, R. (1997). *The status of teaching as a profession: 1990–1991.* Washington, DC: U.S. Department of Education.

Johnson, S. M., & Kardos, S. M. (2005). Bridging the generation gap. *Educational Leadership, 62*(8), 8–14.

Metropolitan Life Insurance Company. (2008). METLife survey of the American teacher. Retrieved August 24, 2010, from www.metlife.com/assets/cao/contributions/foundation/american-teacher/MetLife_Teacher_Survey_2009.pdf

National Center for Education Statistics. (2009). Fast facts. Retrieved August 4, 2010, from http://nces.ed.gov/fastfacts/display.asp?id=28

National Council on Teacher Quality. (2009). Evaluation and tenure policies do not consider what should count the most about teacher performance: classroom effectiveness in 2009. State teacher policy yearbook. Retrieved January 31, 2010, from www.nctq.org

National Education Association. (2001). *Attracting and keeping quality teachers.* Washington, DC: Author. Retrieved May 15, 2005, from http://nea.org/teachershortage.index

National Education Association. (2003). *Status of the American public school teacher 2000–2001.* Washington, DC: Author. Retrieved May 15, 2005, from http://www.nea.org/edstats/images/status.pdf

Nieto, S. (2009). From surviving to thriving. *Educational Leadership, 66*(5), 8–13.

Partnership for 21st Century Skills. (2009). About us. Retrieved November 17, 2009, from http://www.21stcenturyskills.org/index.php?option=com_content&task=view&id=42&Itemid=69

Phelps, P. H. (2003). Teacher professionalism. *Kappa Delta Pi Record, 40*(1), 10–11.

Public Agenda. (2003). Attitudes about teaching. New York: Author.

Public Education Network. (2003). *The voice of the new teacher.* Washington, DC: Author.

Ripley, A. (2010, January/February). What makes a great teacher? *The Atlantic.* Retrieved January 29, 2010, from http://www.theatlantic.com/doc/201001/good-teaching

Rowan, B. (1994). Comparing teachers' work with work in other occupations: Notes on the professional status of teaching. *Educational Researcher, 23*(6), 4–17, 21.

Stronge, J. H. (2002). *Qualities of effective teachers.* Alexandria, VA: Association for Supervision and Curriculum Development.

Teach for America. (2010). *Growth plan.* Retrieved January 24, 2010, from http://www.teachforamerica.org/about/our_growth_plan.htm

Tell, C. (2001). Who's in our classrooms: Teachers speak for themselves. *Educational Leadership, 58*(8), 18–23.

Webb, L., Metha, A., & Jordan, K. F. (2007). *Foundations of American education* (5th ed.). Upper Saddle River, NJ: Merrill/Prentice Hall.

Chapter 2

Barnett, W. S. (2003). Preschool: The most important grade. *Educational Leadership, 60*(7), 54–57.

Barth, R. S. (2001). *Learning by heart.* San Francisco: Jossey-Bass.

Carter, G. R. (2003). *NCLB and the diverse needs of rural schools.* Retrieved September 26, 2004, from www.ascd.org/cms/index.cfm

EdisonLearning, Inc. (2010). About us. Retrieved March 15, 2010, from http://www.edisonlearning.com/about_us

Eisner, E. W. (2004). Preparing for today and tomorrow. *Educational Leadership, 64*(6), 6.

Goodlad, J. I. (1984). *A place called school.* New York: McGraw-Hill.

Haycock, K. (2003). Toward a fair distribution of teacher talent. *Educational Leadership, 60*(4), 11–15.

Kostelnik, M. J., Soderman, A. K., & Whiren, A. P. (2004). *Developmentally appropriate curriculum: Best practices in early childhood education* (3rd ed.). Upper Saddle River, NJ: Merrill/Prentice Hall.

Kozol, J. (1991). *Savage inequalities: Children in America's schools.* New York: Crown.

Lezotte, L. W. (1991). *Correlates of effective schools: The first and second generation.* Okemos, MI: Effective Schools Products.

Merrow, J. (2004). Meeting superman. *Phi Delta Kappan, 85*(6), 455–460.

Morrison, G. S. (2008). *Fundamentals of early childhood education* (5th ed.). Upper Saddle River, NJ: Merrill.

National Center for Education Statistics [NCES]. (2003). *National elementary and secondary school enrollment model.* Retrieved August 2, 2005, from http://www.nces.ed.gov/pubs2003

National Center for Education Statistics [NCES]. (2004). *National household education survey.* Retrieved March 16, 2007, from http://nces.ed.gov/quicktables/result.asp?SrchKeyword=national+household+education+survey&topic=All&Year=2004

National Center for Education Statistics [NCES]. (2010). *Digest of education statistics, 2009.* Washington, DC: U.S. Department of Education.

National Middle School Association. (2010). *This we believe: Keys to educating young adolescents.* Westerville, OH: Author.

Roberts, P. L., Kellough, R. D., & Moore, K. (2006). *A resource guide for elementary school teachers* (6th ed.). Upper Saddle River, NJ: Merrill/Prentice Hall.

Scherer, M. (2005). Our cities, ourselves. *Educational Leadership, 62*(6), 7.

Snyder, T. D., Dillow, S. A., & Hoffman, C. M. (2009). *Digest of education statistics, 2008* (NCES 2009-020). National Center for Education Statistics, Institute of Education Sciences. Washington, DC: U.S. Department of Education.

U.S. Department of Education. (2010). Elementary and Secondary Education Act (ESEA). Retrieved July 31, 2010, from www2.ed.gov/policy/elsec/leg/esea02/beginning.html

Chapter 3

American Psychological Association. (2000). *Diagnostic and statistical manual of mental disorders* (4th ed., rev.). Washington, DC: Author.

August, D., & Shanahan, T. (Eds.). (2006). *Developing literacy in second language learners: Report of the national literacy panel on language minority youth and children.* Mahwah, NJ: Erlbaum.

Bandura, A., Barbaranelli, C., Caprara, G. V., & Pastorelli, C. (2001). Self-efficacy beliefs as shapers of children's aspirations and career trajectories. *Child Development, 72,* 187–206.

Banks, J.A. (Ed.). (2004). *The handbook of research on multicultural education.* San Francisco: Jossey-Bass.

Campbell, A., Shirley, L., & Candy, J. (2004). A longitudinal study of gender-related cognition and behavior. *Developmental Science, 7,* 1-9.

Capps, R., Fix, M., Murray, J., Ost, J., Passel, J., & Herwantoro, S. (2005). *The new demography of America's schools: Immigration and the No Child Left Behind Act.* Washington, DC: Urban Institute.

Clark, K. (2009). The case for structured English immersion. *Educational Leadership, 66*(7), 42-46.

Delgado-Gaitan, C., & Trueba, H. (1991). *Crossing cultural borders: Education for immigrant families in America.* New York: Falmer.

Diversity Data. (2000). *Principal Magazine, 79*(5), 18.

Feldman, R. S. (2008). *Development across the life span* (5th ed.). Upper Saddle River, NJ: Prentice Hall.

Gallahue, D. L., & Ozmun, J. C. (2006). *Understanding motor development: Infants, children, adolescents, adults.* Boston: McGraw-Hill.

Garcia, E., & Cuellar, D. (2006). Who are these linguistically and culturally diverse students? *Teachers College Record, 108*(*11*), 2220-2246.

Gardner, H. (1999). *The disciplined mind: What all students should understand.* New York: Simon & Schuster.

Gathercoal, P., & Crowell, R. (2000). Judicious discipline. *Kappa Delta Pi Record, 36*(4), 173-177.

Gay, G. (2000). *Culturally responsive teaching.* New York: Teachers College Press.

Glazer, S. (2005). Gender and learning. *Congressional Quarterly Researcher, 15*(19), 445-468.

Gober, D. A., & Mewborn, D. S. (2001). Promoting equity in mathematics classrooms. *Middle School Journal, 32*(3), 31-35.

Goldstein, L. (2003, April 16). Special education growth spurs cap plan in pending IDEA. *Education Week, 22*(31), 1-17.

Goleman, D. (1995). *Emotional intelligence.* New York: Bantam Books.

Gollnick, D. M., & Chinn, P. C. (2009). *Multicultural education in a pluralistic society* (8th ed.). Upper Saddle River, NJ: Merrill/Prentice Hall.

Hernandez, D. J., Denton, N. A., & Macartney, S. E. (2008). Children in immigrant families: Looking to America's future. *Social Policy Report, 22*(3), 3-22.

Heward, W. L. (2006). *Exceptional children: An introduction to special education* (8th ed.). Upper Saddle River, NJ: Merrill/Prentice Hall.

Hodgkinson, H. (2001). Educational demographics: What teachers should know. *Educational Leadership, 58*(4), 6-11.

Jackson, R., & Harper, K. (2002). *Teacher planning and the universal design for learning.* Wakefield, MA: National Center on Accessing the General Curriculum.

Kohlberg, L. (1984). *The psychology of moral development: Essays on moral development* (Vol. 2). San Francisco: Harper & Row.

Levine, M. (2003). Celebrating diverse minds. *Educational Leadership, 61*(2), 12-18.

Maslow, A. H. (1999). *Toward a psychology of being* (3rd ed.). New York: Wiley.

McDevitt, T. M., & Ormrod, J. E. (2010). *Child development and education* (4th ed.). Upper Saddle River, NJ: Merrill/Prentice Hall/Pearson.

Mukhopadhyay, C., & Henze, R. C. (2003). How real is race? Using anthropology to make sense of human diversity. *Phi Delta Kappan, 84*(9), 669-678.

National Association for Single-Sex Public Education [NASSPE]. (2010). Single-sex schools/schools with single-sex classrooms/what's the difference? Retrieved January 3, 2010, from http://www.singlesexschools.org/home-introduction.htm

Neuman, S. B. (1999). Books make a difference: A study of access to literacy. *Reading Research Quarterly, 34*(3), 286-311.

Neuman, S. B. (2003). From rhetoric to reality: The case for high-quality compensatory prekindergarten programs. *Phi Delta Kappan, 84*(4), 286-291.

Nieto, S. M. (2003). Profoundly multicultural questions. *Educational Leadership, 60*(4), 6-10.

Partnership for 21st Century Skills. (2009). Global awareness. Retrieved August 1, 2010, from http://www.p21.org/index.php?option=com_content&task=view&id=256&Itemid=120

Payne, R. (2008). Nine powerful practices. *Educational Leadership, 65*(7), 48-52.

Pew Forum. (2010). *U.S. religious landscape survey.* Retrieved August 1, 2010, from http://religions.pewforum.org/reports/

Powell, S. D. (2011). *Introduction to middle school* (2nd ed.). Boston: Allyn & Bacon.

Rance-Roney, J. (2009). Best practices for adolescent ELLs. *Educational Leadership, 66*(7), 32-37.

Richardson, R. C., & Norman, K. I. (2000). Intrinsic goodness: Facilitating character development. *Kappa Delta Pi Record, 36*(4), 168-172.

Rosenberg, M. S., O'Shea, L. J., & O'Shea, D. J. (2006). *Student teacher to master teacher: A practical guide for educating students with special needs.* Upper Saddle River, NJ: Merrill/Prentice Hall.

Scherer, M. (2009). In the neighborhood. *Educational Leadership, 66*(7), 7.

Short, D. J., & Fitzsimmons, S. (2007). *Double the work: Challenges and solutions to acquiring language and academic literacy for adolescent English language learners—A report to the Carnegie Corporation of New York.* Washington, DC: Alliance for Excellent Education.

Silver, H. F., Strong, R. W., & Perini, M. J. (2000). *So each may learn: Integrating learning styles and multiple intelligences.* Alexandria, VA: Association for Supervision and Curriculum Development.

Sternberg R. J. (2007). Who are the bright children? The cultural context of being and acting intelligent. *Educational Researcher, 36*(3), 148-155.

Turnbull, R., Turnbull, A., & Wehmeyer, M. (2010). *Exceptional lives: Special education in today's schools* (6th ed.). Upper Saddle River, NJ: Merrill/Prentice Hall.

Underwood, M. (2003). *Social aggression among girls.* New York: Guilford.

U.S. Census Bureau with U.S. Department of Education. (2006). *Income, poverty, and health insurance coverage in the United States: 2005.* Retrieved April 6, 2006, from http://www.census.gov/prod/2006pubs/p60-231.pdf

U.S. Census Bureau. (2008). U.S. population projections. Retrieved August 1, 2010, from http://census.gov/population/www/projections/summarytables.html

U.S. Department of Education. (2009). *Building the legacy: IDEA 2004.* Retrieved August 1, 2010, from http://idea.ed.gov/explore/home

Vermeer, H. J., Boekaerts, M., & Seeger, G. (2000). Motivational and gender differences: Sixth-grade students' mathematical problem-solving behavior. *Journal of Educational Psychology, 92,* 308-315.

Chapter 4

Allington, R. L. (2002). What I've learned about effective reading instruction. *Phi Delta Kappan, 83*(10), 740-747.

American Council for the Teaching of Foreign Language. (2005). *Standards for foreign language learning.* Retrieved July 1, 2005, from http://www.actfl.org

Anderson, L. W., & Krathwohl, D. R. (Eds.). (2001). *A taxonomy for learning, teaching, and assessing.* New York: Longman.

Banks, J. A. (2003). *Teaching strategies for ethnic studies* (7th ed.). Boston: Allyn & Bacon.

Core Knowledge. (2009). About core knowledge. Retrieved November 20, 2009, from http://coreknowledge.org/CK/about/index.htm.

Cornett, C. E. (2003). *Creating meaning through literature and the arts: An integration resource for classroom teachers* (2nd ed.). Upper Saddle River, NJ: Merrill/Prentice Hall.

Dewey, J. (1900). *The school and society.* Chicago: University of Chicago Press.

Dewey, J. (1902). *The child and the curriculum.* Chicago: University of Chicago Press.

Dewey, J. (1938). *Experience and education.* New York: Macmillan/Collier.

Eisner, E. (2002). *The educational imagination: On the design and evaluation of school programs* (3rd ed.). New York: Macmillan College.

Goodlad, J. I. (1984). *A place called school.* New York: McGraw-Hill.

Gregoire, M. A., & Lupinetti, J. (2005). Supporting diversity through the arts. *Kappa Delta Pi Record, 41*(4), 159-163.

Gunter, M. A., Estes, T. H., & Mintz, S. L. (2007). *Instruction: A models approach* (5th ed.). Boston: Allyn & Bacon.

Holloway, J. H. (2000). Extracurricular activities: The path to academic success? *Educational Leadership, 57*(4), 87-88.

International Society for Technology in Education. (2005). *Mission statement.* Retrieved July 1, 2005, from http://www.iste.org

Jensen, E. (2005). *Teaching with the brain in mind* (2nd ed.). Alexandria, VA: Association for Supervision and Curriculum Development.

Johnson, D. W., & Johnson, R. T. (1999). *Learning together and alone: Cooperative, competitive, and individualistic learning.* Boston: Allyn & Bacon.

Jones, R. (2000, December). Textbook troubles. *American School Board Journal,* pp. 18-21.

Krashen, S. (2002). Whole language and the great plummet of 1987-1992. *Phi Delta Kappan, 83*(10), 748-753.

Little, C. (2001). What matters to students. *Educational Leadership, 59*(2), 61-64.

Lounsbury, J. H. (1991). *As I see it.* Columbus, OH: National Middle School Association.

McHugh, J. (2005). Synching up with the kids. *Edutopia, 1*(7), 32-35.

Moats, L. C. (2001). When older students can't read. *Educational Leadership, 58*(6), 36-40.

National Council for the Social Studies. (2005). *Curriculum standards for social studies: Executive summary.* Retrieved July 1, 2005, from http://www.socialstudies.org/standards/execsummary/

National Science Teachers Association. (2005). *National Science Education Standards.* Retrieved July 1, 2005, from http://books.nap.edu/html/nses/6a.html

Noddings, N. (1992). *The challenge to care in schools: An alternative approach to education.* New York: Teachers College Press.

Osterman, K. (2002). Schools as communities for students. In G. Furman (Ed.), *School as community: From promise to practice.* New York: State University of New York Press.

Powell, S. D. (2010). *Wayside teaching: Connecting with students to support learning.* Thousand Oaks, CA: Corwin Press.

Powell, S. D. (2011). *Introduction to middle school* (2nd ed.). Boston: Allyn & Bacon.

Renard, L. (2005). Teaching the DIG generation. *Educational Leadership, 62*(7), 44–47.

Renzulli, J. S., Gentry, M., & Reis, S. M. (2004). A time and place for authentic learning. *Educational Leadership, 62*(1), 73–77.

Roblyer, M. D. (2006). *Integrating educational technology into teaching.* Upper Saddle River, NJ: Merrill/Prentice Hall.

Stipek, D. (2006). Relationships matter. *Educational Leadership, 64*(1), 46–49.

Tomlinson, C. A. (1999). *The differentiated classroom. Responding to the needs of all learners.* Alexandria, VA: Association for Supervision and Curriculum Development.

Tomlinson, C. A., & McTighe, J. (2006). *Integrating differentiated instruction + understanding by design.* Alexandria, VA: Association for Supervision and Curriculum Development.

Tyler, R. (1949). *Basic principles of curriculum and instruction.* Chicago: University of Chicago Press.

Vacca, R. T. (2002). From efficient decoders to strategic readers. *Educational Leadership, 60*(3), 7–11.

Wiggins, G. P., & McTighe, J. (2005). *Understanding by design* (2nd ed.). Alexandria, VA: Association for Supervision and Curriculum Development.

Wolk, S. (2007). Why go to school? *Phi Delta Kappan, 88*(9), 648–658.

Chapter 5

Johnson, J., & Duffett, A. (2003). *Where we are now: 12 things you need to know about public opinion and public schools.* New York: Public Agenda. Retrieved April 11, 2007, from http://www.publicagenda.org/research/PDFs/where_we_are_now.pdf

Kohn, A. (2000, September 27). Standardized testing and its victims. *Education Week,* pp. 60, 46–47.

Marzano, R. J. (2000). *Transforming classroom grading.* Alexandria, VA: Association for Supervision and Curriculum Development.

National Center for Education Statistics [NCES]. (2006). *The nation's report card.* Retrieved April 10, 2007, from http://nces.ed.gov/nationsreportcard/

National Center for Education Statistics [NCES]. (2010). *TIMSS 2007 results.* Retrieved August 2, 2010, from http://nces.ed.gov/pubsearch/pubsinfo.asp?pubid=2009001

National Council of Teachers of Mathematics. (1995). *Assessment standards for school mathematics.* Reston, VA: Author.

O'Connor, K. (2002). *How to grade for learning.* Arlington Heights, IL: Skylight Professional Development, Pearson Education.

Ohanion, S. (2003). Capitalism, calculus, and con-science. *Phi Delta Kappan, 84*(10), 736–747.

Partnership for 21st Century Skills. (2009). About us. Retrieved November 17, 2009, from http://www.21stcenturyskills.org/index.php? option=com_content&task=view&id=42&Itemid=69

Powell, S. D. (2011). *Introduction to middle school* (2nd ed.). Boston: Allyn & Bacon.

Reeves, D. B. (2004). *Accountability for learning: How teachers and school leaders can take charge.* Alexandria, VA: Association for Supervision and Curriculum Development.

Renzulli, J. S., Gentry, M., & Reis, S. M. (2004). A time and place for authentic learning. *Educational Leadership, 62*(1), 73–77.

Stiggins, R. J. (2001). Building a productive assessment future. *National Association of Secondary School Principals, 85*(621), 2–4.

Chapter 6

Boynton, M., & Boynton, C. (2005). *The educator's guide to preventing and solving discipline problems.* Alexandria, VA: Association for Supervision and Curriculum Development.

Darling-Hammond, L. (1997). *The right to learn.* San Francisco: Jossey-Bass.

DeVries, R., & Zan, B. (2003). When children make rules. *Educational Leadership, 61*(1), 64–67.

Dewey, J. (1944). *Democracy and education.* New York: Free Press.

Dunklee, D. R., & Shoop, R. J. (2002). *The principal's quick reference guide to school law: Reducing liability, litigation, and other potential legal tangles.* Thousand Oaks, CA: Corwin Press.

Erwin, J. C. (2003). Giving students what they need. *Educational Leadership, 61*(1), 19–23.

Farrell, C. (2010). *Corporal punishment in the United States.* Retrieved August 7, 2010, from http://corpun.com/counuss.htm

Glasser, W. (1998). *Choice theory.* New York: Harper Collins.

Kohn, A. (2005). Unconditional teaching. *Educational Leadership, 63*(1), 20–24.

Kounin, J. S. (1970). *Discipline and group management in classrooms.* New York: Holt, Rinehart and Winston.

Lemlech, J. K. (2004). *Teaching in elementary and secondary classrooms.* Upper Saddle River, NJ: Merrill/Prentice Hall.

Loeper, J. L. (1973). *Going to School in 1776.* New York: Macmillan.

Lumpkin, A. (2007). Caring teachers: The key to student learning. *Kappa Delta Pi Record, 43*(4), 158–160.

Manning, L., & Bucher, K. T. (2003). *Classroom management: Models, applications, and cases* (2nd ed.). Boston: Allyn & Bacon.

Marzano, R. J. (2003a). *Classroom management that works: Research-based strategies for every teacher.* Alexandria, VA: Association for Supervision and Curriculum Development.

Marzano, R. J. (2003b). *What works in schools: Translating research into action.* Alexandria, VA: Association for Supervision and Curriculum Development.

McCloud, S. (2005). From chaos to consistency. *Educational Leadership, 62*(5), 46–49.

Noddings, N. (1992). *The challenge to care in schools: An alternative approach to education.* New York: Teachers College Press.

Stevenson, C. (2002). *Teaching ten to fourteen year olds* (3rd ed.). New York: Longman.

Prensky, M. (2010). Shaping tech for the Classroom: 21st-century schools need 21st-century technology. Retrieved April 9, 2010, from http://www.edutopia.org/adopt-and-adapt

Ray, B. (2010). Guest Blog: Making the Case for Social Media. Retrieved April 9, 2010, from http://www.edutopia.org/social-media-case-education-edchat-steve-johnson

Weinstein, C. S., Romano, M., & Mignano, A. (2011). *Elementary classroom management: Lessons from research and practice* (5th ed.). New York: McGraw-Hill.

Chapter 7

Adler, M. (1982). *The Paideia proposal: An educational manifesto.* New York: Simon & Schuster.

Banks, J. A., & Banks, C. A. M. (Eds.). (2009). *Multicultural education: Issues and perspectives* (7th ed.). New York: Wiley.

Bloom, B. S. (1956). *Taxonomy of educational objectives: Handbook I. Cognitive domain.* New York: Longman, Green.

Boyer, P., & Stuckey, S. (2005). *American nation in the modern era.* Austin, TX: Holt, Rinehart and Winston.

Button, W. H., & Provenzo, E. F., Jr. (1989). *History of education and culture in America.* Upper Saddle River, NJ: Prentice Hall.

Carnegie Corporation. (1989). *Turning points: Preparing American youth for the 21st century.* New York: Author.

Chartock, R. K. (2004). *Educational foundations: An anthology* (2nd ed.). Upper Saddle River, NJ: Merrill/Prentice Hall.

Cohen, S. S. (1974). *A history of colonial education, 1607–1776.* New York: Wiley.

Cubberly, E. (1934). *Public education in the United States.* Boston: Houghton Mifflin.

Dewey, J. (1956). *The child and the curriculum, and the school and society.* Chicago: University of Chicago Press.

Eisner, E. W. (2000). *Prospects: The quality review of comparative education.* Paris: UNESCO Publication, 30(3).

Franklin, B. (1931). Proposals relating to education of youth in Pennsylvania. In T. Woody (Ed.), *Educational views of Ben Franklin.* New York: McGraw-Hill.

Good, H. G. (1964). *A history of American education.* New York: Macmillan.

Gutek, G. L. (2005). *Historical and philosophical foundations of education* (4th ed.). Upper Saddle River, NJ: Merrill/Prentice Hall.

Holmes, M., & Weiss, B. J. (1995). *Lives of women public school teachers: Scenes from American educational history.* New York: Garland.

Johnson, J. A., Musial, D., Hall, G. E., Golnick, D. M., & Dupuis, V. L. (2005). *Introduction to the foundations of American education.* Boston: Allyn & Bacon.

Kaplan, L. S., & Owings, W. A. (2011). *American education: Building a common foundation.* Belmont, CA: Wadsworth, Cengage Learning.

Kneller, G. F. (1971). *Introduction to the philosophy of education.* New York: Wiley.

Loeper, J. L. (1973). *Going to school in 1776.* New York: Macmillan.

McNeil, J. D. (1995). *Curriculum: The teacher's initiative.* Upper Saddle River, NJ: Prentice Hall.

McNergney, R. F., & McNergney, J. M. (2009). *Education: The practice and profession of teaching.* Boston: Allyn & Bacon.

Montessori, M. (1967). *The discovery of the child.* Notre Dame, IN: Fides.

Ornstein, A. C., & Levine, D. U. (2006). *Foundations of education* (9th ed.). Boston: Houghton Mifflin.

Orfield, G. (2009). *Reviving the goal of an integrated society: A 21st century challenge.* Los Angeles: The Civil Rights Project/Proyecto Derechos Civiles at UCLA.

Pulliam, J., & Van Patten, J. (2007). *History of education in America* (9th ed.). Upper Saddle River, NJ: Merrill/Prentice Hall.

Rippa, S. A. (1997). *Education in a free society: An American history* (8th ed.). New York: Longman.

Stanford News Service. (1994). *Ralph Tyler, one of the century's foremost educators, dies at 91.* Retrieved March 1, 2006, from Stanford University News Service Web site: http://www.stanford.edu/dept/news/pr/94/940228Arc4425.html

Takaki, R. (1993). *A different mirror: A history of multicultural America.* New York: Little, Brown.

Tehie, J. B. (2007). *Historical foundations of education.* Upper Saddle River, NJ: Merrill/Prentice Hall.

Tyler, R. (1949). *Basic principles of curriculum and instruction.* Chicago: University of Chicago Press.

U.S. Census Bureau. (2008). *American Factfinder: BO3001. Hispanic or Latino origin by specific origin.* Retrieved May 22, 2010, from http://factfinder.census.gov/servlet/DTTable?_bm=y&-geo_id=01000US&-ds_name=ACS_2008_3YR_G00_&-mt_name=ACS_2008_3YR_G2000_B03001

U.S. Census Bureau. (2009). *Facts for features: Asian/Pacific American heritage month 2009.* Retrieved May 24, 2010, from http://www.census.gov/Press-Release/www/releases/archives/facts_for_features_special_editions/013385.html

Webb, L., Metha, A., & Jordan, K. F. (2010). *Foundations of American education* (6th ed.). Upper Saddle River, NJ: Pearson/Merrill.

Chapter 8

Adler, M. (1982). *The Paideia proposal: An educational manifesto.* New York: Simon & Schuster.

Brameld, T. (1956). *Toward a reconstructed philosophy of education.* New York: Holt, Rinehart and Winston.

Chartock, R. K. (2004). *Educational foundations: An anthology* (2nd ed.). Upper Saddle River, NJ: Merrill/Prentice Hall.

Counts, G. (1932). *Dare the school build a new social order?* New York: John Dey.

Eisner, E. (Ed.). (1985). *Learning and teaching the ways of knowing: The eighty-fourth yearbook of the National Society for the Study of Education.* Chicago: University of Chicago Press.

Friere, P. (1970). *Pedagogy of the oppressed.* New York: Herder and Herder.

Greene, M. (1978). *Landscape of learning.* New York: Teachers College Press.

Greene, M. (1995). What counts as philosophy of education? In W. Kohli (Ed.), *Critical conversations in philosophy of education.* New York: Routledge.

Gutek, G. L. (2005). *Historical and philosophical foundations of education* (4th ed.). Upper Saddle River, NJ: Merrill/Prentice Hall.

Hirsch, E. D. (1987). *Cultural literacy: What every American needs to know.* Boston: Houghton Mifflin.

Illich, I. (1971). *Deschooling society.* New York: Harper & Row.

Jacobsen, D. A. (2003). *Philosophy in classroom teaching: Bridging the gap* (2nd ed.). Upper Saddle River, NJ: Merrill/Prentice Hall.

Neill, A. S. (1960). *Summerhill: A radical approach to child rearing.* New York: Hart.

Nelson, J. L., Carlson, K., & Palonsky, S. B. (2000). *Critical issues in education: A dialectic approach* (4th ed.). New York: McGraw-Hill.

Ornstein, A. C. (2003). *Pushing the envelope: Critical issues in education.* Upper Saddle River, NJ: Merrill/Prentice Hall.

Ozmon, H., & Craver, S. (2008). *Philosophical foundations of education* (8th ed.). Upper Saddle River, NJ: Merrill/Prentice Hall.

Perrone, V. (1991). *A letter to teachers: Reflections on schooling and the art of teaching.* San Francisco: Jossey-Bass.

Pulliam, J., & Van Patten, J. (2007). *History of education in America* (9th ed.). Upper Saddle River, NJ: Merrill/Prentice Hall.

Ravitch, D. (2000). *Left back: A century of failed school reforms.* New York: Simon & Schuster.

Sizer, T. R. (1985). *Horace's compromise.* Boston: Houghton Mifflin.

Webb, L., Metha, A., & Jordan, K. F. (2010). *Foundations of American education* (6th ed.). Upper Saddle River, NJ: Merrill/Prentice Hall.

Chapter 9

Alcoholism Information and Resources. (2010). Learn-about-alcoholism. Retrieved June 5, 2010, from http://www.learn-about-alcoholism.com/index.html

Alliance for Excellent Education. (2009). High school dropouts in America. Retrieved June 7, 2010, from http://all4ed.org/files/GraduationRates_FactSheet.pdf

Alliance for Excellent Education. (2009a). Understanding high school graduation rates in the United States. Retrieved June 4, 2010, from http://www.all4ed.org/files/National_wc.pdf

American Academy of Child and Adolescent Psychiatry. (2009). *Facts for families: Teen suicide.* Retrieved June 3, 2010, from http://www.aacap.org/cs/root/facts_for_families/teen_suicide

American Association of Suicidology. (2009). *Youth suicide fact sheet.* Retrieved June 3, 2010, from http://www.suicidology.org/c/document_library/get_file?folderId=232&name=DLFE-161.pdf

American Psychiatric Association. (2005). *Let's talk facts about depression.* Retrieved April 6, 2006, from www.healthyminds.org/multimedia/depression.pdf

American Psychiatric Association. (2005a). *Let's talk facts about teen suicide.* Retrieved April 6, 2006, from www.healthyminds.org/multimedia/teensuicide/depression.pdf

America's Promise Alliance. (2009). GradNation. Washington, DC: Author. Retrieved June 6, 2010, from http://www.americaspromise.org/Our-Work/Dropout-Prevention/Grad-Nation-Campaign.aspx

Ariza, E. N. (2002). Cultural considerations: Immigrant parents involvement. *Kappa Delta Pi Record, 38*(3), 134–137.

Bridgeland, J. M., Dilulio, J. J., & Morison, K. B. (2006). *The silent epidemic: Perspectives of high school dropouts.* Retrieved April 8, 2006, from http://www.civicenterprises.net/pdfs/thesilentepidemic3-06.pdf

Centers for Disease Control and Prevention. (2009). National trends in risk behaviors. Atlanta, GA: Author. Retrieved June 4, 2010, from http://www.cdc.gov/healthyyouth/yrbs/trends.htm

Century Council. (2008). Drinking pattern 2008. Retrieved June 2, 2010, from http://www.centurycouncil.org/learn-the-facts/underage-drinking-stats

Child Welfare Information Gateway. (2006). *Recognizing child abuse and neglect: Signs and symptoms.* Retrieved April 22, 2007, from http://www.childwelfare.gov/pubs/factsheets/signs.cfm

Craig, G. J., & Dunn. W. L. (2007). *Understanding human development.* Upper Saddle River, NJ: Prentice Hall.

DeAngelis, T. (2004). Size-based discrimination may be hardest on children. *Monitor on Psychology, 35*(1), 62.

Dinkes, R., Kemp, J., & Baum, K. (2009). *Indicators of school crime and safety: 2009* (NCES 2010-012/NCJ 228478). Washington, DC: National Center for Education Statistics, Institute of Education Sciences, U.S. Department of Education, and Bureau of Justice Statistics, Office of Justice Programs, U.S. Department of Justice.

Dynarski, M., Clarke, L., Cobb, B., Finn, J., & Rumberger, R. (2008). Dropout prevention. Retrieved June 8, 2010, from http://ies.ed.gov/ncee/wwc/pdf/practiceguides/dp_pg_090308.pdf

Education Vital Signs. (2006a). *As educators face a childhood obesity "epidemic," other indicators of well-being improve.* Retrieved March 30, 2006, from http://www.asbj.com/evs/06/studenthealth.html

Education Vital Signs. (2006b). *Graduation statistics and systemic reform spark a conversation among state leaders.* Retrieved March 30, 2006, from http://www.asbj.com/evs/06/studenthealth.html

Education Vital Signs. (2009). Leading children down a healthy path. Retrieved June 22, 2010, from http://www.asbj.com/MainMenuCategory/Supplements/EVS/2009-EVS.aspx

First Amendment Center. (2006). *Public schools and sexual orientation: A First Amendment framework for finding common ground.* Retrieved April 2, 2006, from www.firstamendmentcenter.org/pdf/sexual.orientation.guidelines.pdf

Focus Adolescent Services. (2006). *Youth who drop out.* Retrieved April 20, 2006, from http://www.focusas.com/Dropouts.html

Gollnick, D. M., & Chinn, P. C. (2009). *Multicultural education in a pluralistic society* (8th ed.). Boston: Allyn & Bacon.

Hall, D. (2005). *Getting honest about grad rates: How states play the numbers and students lose.* The Education Trust. Retrieved January 2, 2007, from http://www2.edtrust.org/NR/rdonlyres/C5A6974D-6C04-4FB1-A9FC-05938CB0744D/0/Getting_Honest.pdf

Haskins, R., Paxson, C., & Donahue, E. (2006). *Fighting obesity in the public school.* Policy brief of The Future of Children. Retrieved April 6, 2006, from http://www.futureofchildren.princeton.edu/briefs/FOC%20policy%20brief%20spr%2006.pdf

Haynes, C. C. (2006, March). A moral battleground, a civil discourse. *USA Today.* Retrieved March 23, 2006, from http://www.usatoday.com/news/opinion/editorials/2006-03-19-faith-edit_x.htm

Healthcommunities.com. (2010). *Overview, consequences of teenage pregnancy.* Retrieved June 4, 2010, from http://www.womenshealthchannel.com/teenpregnancy/index.shtml

Infoplease. (2004). *Teen birthrates continue to decline.* Retrieved April 7, 2006, from http://www.infoplease.com/ipa/A0193727.html

Infoplease. (2009). *Teen birth rates in the U.S., 1980–2006.* Retrieved June 2, 2010, from http://www.infoplease.com/ipa/A0193727.html

Infoplease. (2010). *Homicide rate (per 100,000).* Retrieved June 6, 2010, from http://www.infoplease.com/ipa/A0873729.html

Institute for Children and Poverty. (2009). *Quick facts: National data on family homelessness.* Retrieved June 8, 2010, at http://www.icpny.org/index.asp?CID=7

Jerald, C. D. (2006). Dropping out is hard to do. Washington, DC: Center for Comprehensive School Reform and Improvement. Retrieved June 9, 2010, from http://www.centerforcsri.org

Johnston, L. D., O'Malley, P. M., Bachman, J. G., & Schulenberg, J. E. (2005). *Monitoring the future: National results on adolescent drug use.* Retrieved April 15, 2006, from http://monitoringthefuture.org/pubs/monographs/overview2005.pdf

Landsman, J. (2006). Bearers of hope. *Educational Leadership, 63*(5), 26–32.

Lewis-Charp, H. (2003). Breaking the silence: White students' perspectives on race in multiracial schools. *Phi Delta Kappan, 85*(4), 279-285.

MacDonald, G. J. (2004, October 19). Schools lay tender trap for truants. *Christian Science Monitor.* Retrieved April 6, 2006, from http://www.csmonitor.com/ 2004/1019/plls02-legn.html

McCarthy, D. M., & Brown, S.A. (2004). Changes in alcohol involvement, cognitions and drinking and driving behavior for youth after they obtain a driver's license. *Journal of Studies on Alcohol and Drugs, 65*(3). Retrieved June 6, 2010, from http://www.jsad.com/jsad/article/Changes_in_Alcohol_Involvement_Cognitions_and_Drinking_and_Driving_Behavio/1062.html

Mukhopadhyay, C., & Henze, R. C. (2003). How real is race? Using anthropology to make sense of human diversity. *Phi Delta Kappan, 84*(9), 669-678.

National Center on Addiction and Substance Abuse. (2007, October). *Tobacco: The smoking gun.* Retrieved June 9, 2010, from http://www.casacolumbia.org/templates/PressReleases.aspx?articleid=508&zoneid=65

National Center for Education Statistics. (2005). *Common core of data.* Washington, DC. Author. Retrieved July 22, 2006, from http://nces.ed.gov/pubs2005/2005314.pdf

National Center for Education Statistics. (2005a). *Indicators of school crime and safety.* Washington, DC: Author. Retrieved March 22, 2006, from http://nces.ed.gov/pubs2005/2005002.pdf

National Center for Higher Education Management Systems. (2006). Public high school graduation rates—2006. Retrieved June 4, 2010, from http://www.higheredinfo.org/dbrowser/index.php?measure=23

National Coalition for the Homeless. (2006). McKinney-Vento Act NCH Fact Sheet #18. Retrieved from www.ct.gov/ccpa/lib/ccpa/Overview_of_Mckinney-Vento_Act.doc

National Coalition for the Homeless. (2009). *Homeless families with children.* Retrieved June 7, 2010, from http://www.nationalhomeless.org/factsheets/families.pdf

Obama, M. (2010, March 22). Michelle on a mission. *Newsweek,* pp. 40-41.

Ophelia Project. (2005). *Bullies, broken hearts . . . and the harsh reality of relational aggression.* Retrieved April 9, 2006, from www.opheliaproject.org

Paulson, A. (March 1, 2010). Obama pledges $900 million more to stem 'dropout crisis.' *Christian Science Monitor.* Retrieved June 11, 2010, from http://www.csmonitor.com/USA/Education/2010/0301/Obama-pledges-900-million-more-to-stem-dropout-crisis

Paxson, C., Donahue, E., Orleans, C. T., & Grisso, J. A. (2006). Introducing the issue. *The Future of Children, 16*(1), 3-15.

Polite, L., & Saenger, E. B. (2003). A pernicious silence: Confronting race in the elementary classroom. *Phi Delta Kappan, 85*(4), 274-278.

Rank, M. R., & Hirschl, T. A. (2009). Estimating the risk of food stamp use and impoverishment during childhood. *Journal of the American Medical Association: Archives of Pediatrics & Adolescent Medicine, 163*(11), 994-999. Retrieved June 1, 2010, from http://archpedi.ama-assn.org/content/vol163/issue11/index.dtl

Rothstein, R. (2008). Whose problem is poverty? *Educational Leadership, 65*(7), 8-13.

Schlozman, S. C. (2002). Why "just say no" isn't enough. *Educational Leadership, 59*(7), 87-89.

Simmons, R. (2002). *Odd girl out: The hidden culture of aggression in girls.* Orlando, FL: Harcourt.

Singh, G. K., Kogan, M. D., & van Dyck, P. C. (2010). Changes in state-specific childhood obesity and overweight prevalence in the United States from 2003 to 2007 (abstract). *Journal of the American Medical Association: Archives of Pediatrics & Adolescent Medicine, 164*(7). Retrieved June 1, 2010, from http://archpedi.ama-assn.org/cgi/content/short/2010.84

Snyder, T. D., Dillow, S. A., & Hoffman, C. W. (2009). *Digest of education statistics 2008* (NCES 2009-020). Retrieved June 9, 2010, from http://nces.ed.gov/programs/digest/

Story, M., Kaphingst, K. M., & French, S. (2006). The role of schools in obesity prevention. *The Future of Children, 16*(1), 109-131.

Sullivan, A. (2006). *White House pushes more schools to drug-test students.* Retrieved April 1, 2006, from http://www.infoshop.org/inews/article.php?story= 20060320104929207&mode=print

Tenneyson Center for Children. (2006). *The numbers are alarming . . . and growing.* Retrieved April 18, 2006, from http://www.childabuse.org/abuse%20stats.html

Thompson, M., & Grace, C. O. (2001). *Best friends, worst enemies: Understanding the social lives of children.* New York: Ballantine.

Thornburgh, N. (2006, April 17). Dropout nation. *Time,* pp. 30-40.

U.S. Census Bureau. (2008). National population projections, released 2008. Retrieved June 1, 2010, from http://www.census.gov/population/www/projections/summarytables.html

U.S. Department of Health and Human Services [DHHS]. (2010). *Child maltreatment 2008.* Retrieved June 4, 2010, from http://www.acf.hhs.gov/ programs/cb/pubs/cm08/index.htm

U.S. Substance Abuse and Mental Health Services Administration. (2009). Trends in substance use, dependence or abuse, and treatment among adolescents: 2002 to 2007. Retrieved June 5, 2010, from http://www.oas.samhsa.gov/2k8/youthTrends/youthTrends.htm

White, J. L., & Cones, J. H. (1999). *Black men emerging: Facing the past and seizing a future in America.* New York: Freeman.

White-Hood, M. (2006). Targeting the school bully. *Middle Ground, 9*(4) 30-32.

Chapter 10

American Association of University Women. (2001). *Hostile hallways: Bullying, teasing, and sexual harassment in school.* New York: Harris Interactive.

Dunklee, D. R., & Shoop, R. J. (2002). *The principal's quick reference guide to school law: Reducing liability, litigation, and other potential legal tangles.* Thousand Oaks, CA: Corwin.

Fischer, L., Schimmel, D., & Stellman, L. (2007). *Teachers and the law* (7th ed.). Boston: Allyn & Bacon.

Howe, K. R. (1996). A conceptual basis for ethics in teacher education. *Journal of Teacher Education, 37,* 6.

LaMorte, M. W. (2008). *School law: Cases and concepts* (8th ed.). Boston: Allyn & Bacon.

McNergney, R. F., & McNergney, J. M. (2009). *Education: The practice and profession of teaching.* Boston: Allyn & Bacon.

National Education Association. (2005). *About NEA.* Retrieved May 27, 2005, from http://www.nea.org/aboutnea

Pauken, P. D. (2006). Student rights. In C. Russo (Ed.), *Key legal issues for schools: The ultimate resource for school business officials.* Lanham, MD: Rowman & Littlefield Education.

Riley, R. W. (1998). *Secretary's statement on religious expression.* Retrieved November 12, 2006, from www.ed.gov/inits/religionandschools

San Antonio, D. M. (2006). Broadening the world of early adolescents. *Educational Leadership, 63*(7), 8-13.

Underwood, J., & Webb, L. D. (2006). *School law for teachers: Concepts and applications.* Upper Saddle River, NJ: Merrill/Prentice Hall.

Chapter 11

Azzam, A. M. (2005). The funding gap. *Educational Leadership, 62*(5), 93.

Biddle, B., & Berliner, D. (2002). Unequal school funding in the United States. *Educational Leadership, 59*(8), 48-59.

Brimley, V., & Garfield, R. (2004). *Financing education* (9th ed.). Boston: Allyn & Bacon.

Council of Chief State School Officers. (2006). *Chief state school officers method of selection.* Retrieved June 20, 2005, from http://www.ccsso.org/chief_state_school_officers/method_of_selection/index.cfm

Hess, F. M. (2002). *School boards at the dawn of the 21st century: Conditions and challenges of district governance.* Arlington, VA: National School Boards Association. Retrieved June 10, 2007, from http://www.nsba.org/site/docs/1200/1143.pdf

Hess, F. M. (2010). Weighing the case for school boards. *Phi Delta Kappan, 91*(6), 15-19.

Lambert, L. (2003). *Leadership capacity for lasting school improvement.* Alexandria, VA: Association for Supervision and Curriculum Development.

Mizell, H. (2010). School boards should focus on learning for all. *Phi Delta Kappan, 91*(6), 20-23.

National Association of State Boards of Education. (2005). *State education governance at-a-glance.* Retrieved June 20, 2006, from http://www.nasbe.org/Educational_ Issues/Governance/Governance_chart.pdf

National Education Association [NEA]. (2009). *Rankings of the states 2008 and estimates of school statistics 2009.* Retrieved June 18, 2010, from http://www.nea.org/assets/docs/09rankings.pdf

National Governors Association [NGA]. (2010). NGA center for best practices. Retrieved June 20, 2010, from http://www.nga.org/portal/ site/nga/menuitem.8274ad9c70a7bd616adcbeeb501010a0/?vgnextoid=e9e8fbc137400010VgnVCM1000001a01010aRCRD

North American Association of State and Provincial Lotteries. (2010). *Member lotteries.* Retrieved June 18, 2010, from http://www.naspl.org

Nylander, A. (2007). National school board survey. Retrieved June 23, 2010, from http://www.oldham.kyschools.us/files/reports/National_Surveys/National%20School%20Board%20Survey%202007%20Final%20Results_pdf.pdf

Sergiovani, T. J. (2001). *The principalship: A reflective practice perspective* (4th ed.). Boston: Allyn & Bacon.

Snider, J. H. (June 2010). It's the public's data: Democratizing school board records. *Education Week.* Retrieved from http://www.edweek.org/login.html?source=http://www.edweek.org/ew/articles/2010/06/16/ 35snider.h29.html&destination=http://www.edweek.org/ew/articles/2010/06/16/35snider.h29.html&levelId=2100

White House. (2010). *Education.* Retrieved June 17, 2010, from http://www.whitehouse.gov/issues/education

U.S. Census Bureau. (2009). *Public education finances 2007.* Retrieved June 17, 2010, from http://www2.census.gov/govs/school/07f33pub.pdf

U.S. Department of Education. (2001[A1]). *Statistics of state school systems: Revenues and expenditures for public elementary and secondary education*. Washington, DC: U.S. Department of Education, National Center for Education Statistics. Retrieved August 2, 2006, from http://www.nces.ed.gov.

U.S. Department of Education. (2006). *The federal role in education*. Retrieved July 27, 2006, from www.ed.gov/about/overview/fed/role.html

U.S. Department of Education. (2009). Characteristics of public, private, and Bureau of Indian Education elementary and secondary school principals in the United States. Retrieved June 18, 2010, from http://nces.ed.gov/pubs2009/2009323/tables.asp

Chapter 12

Barth, R. S. (2006). Improving relationships within the schoolhouse. *Educational Leadership, 63*(6), 9–13.

Beane, J. A. (2005). *A reason to teach: Creating classrooms of dignity and hope*. Portsmouth, NH: Heinemann.

Berliner, D. C. (2001). Improving the quality of the teaching force: A conversation with David Berliner. *Educational Leadership, 58*(8), 6–10.

Bradley, F. (2006). Answering the perplexities of parent involvement. *Education Update, 48*(6), 4.

Comer, J. P. (2005). The rewards of parent participation. *Educational Leadership, 62*(6), 38–42.

Common Core State Standards Initiative. (2010). *National Governors Association and state education chiefs launch common state academic standards*. Retrieved July 7, 2010, from http://www.corestandards.org

Corbett, D., Wilson, B., & Williams, B. (2005). No choice but success. *Educational Leadership, 62*(6), 8–12.

Darling-Hammond, L., & Youngs, P. (2002). Defining "highly qualified teachers": What does "scientifically-based research" tell us? *Education Researcher, 31*(9), 13–25.

Duncan, A. (2010). *Elevating the teaching profession*. Retrieved July 16, 2010, from http://www.educationvotes.nea.org/2009/12/09/elevating-the-teaching-profession/

Epstein, J. L., Sanders, M. G., Simon, B. S., Salinas, K. C., Jansorn, N. R., & VanVoorhis, F. L. (2002). *School, family, and community partnerships: Your handbook for action*. Thousand Oaks, CA: Corwin.

Foundation for Education Reform & Accountability [FERA]. (2010). *Welcome to FERA*. Retrieved July 16, 2010, from http://www.nyfera.org/?page_id=165

Gehrke, R. S. (2005). Poor schools, poor students, successful teachers. *Kappa Delta Pi Record, 42*(1), 14–17.

Hasselbring, T. S., & Bausch, M. E. (2006). Assistive technologies for reading. *Educational Leadership, 63*(4), 72–75.

Huber, C. (2010). Professional learning 2.0. *Educational Leadership, 67*(8), 41–46.

Marzano, R. J. (2003). *What works in schools: Translating research into action*. Alexandria, VA: Association for Supervision and Curriculum Development.

National Board for Professional Teaching Standards [NBPTS]. (2010a[A1]). *The five core propositions*. Retrieved July 3, 2010, from http://www.nbpts.org/the_standards/the_five_ core_propositions

National Board for Professional Teaching Standards. [NBPTS]. (2010b). State and local information. Retrieved July 8, 2010, from http://www.nbpts.org/resources/state_local_information

National Council on Teacher Quality. (2009). *2009 state teacher policy yearbook: Primary findings*. Retrieved July 5, 2010, from http://www.nctq.org/stpy09/findings.jsp

National Governors Association [NGA] and Council of Chief State School Officers [CCSSO]. (2010). Common core standards initiative frequently asked questions. Retrieved July 7, 2010, from http://www.corestandards.org

Payne, C. (2008). *So much reform, so little change: The persistence of failure in urban schools*. Boston: Harvard Education Press.

Posner, G. J. (2005). *Field experience: A guide to reflective teaching*. Boston: Allyn & Bacon.

Public Education Network. (2003). *The voice of the new teacher*. Washington, DC: Author.

Reeves, D. B. (2006). Pull the weeds before you plant the flowers. *Educational Leadership, 64*(1), 89–90.

Springer, M. G., & Gardner, C. D. (2010). Teacher pay for performance. *Phi Delta Kappan, 91*(8), 8–15.

U.S. Department of Education. (2009). Race to the Top application for initial funding, CFDA Number 84.395A. Washington, DC: Author.

U.S. Department of Education. (2010). *A blueprint for reform: The reauthorization of the Elementary and Secondary Education Act*. Retrieved July 14, 2010, from http://www2.ed.gov/policy/elsec/leg/blueprint/blueprint.pdf

Vacca, R. T. (2006). They can because they think they can. *Educational Leadership, 63*(5), 56–59.

Name Index

Note: Page numbers followed by *f* indicate figures; page numbers followed by *t* indicate tables.

Subject Index

Note: Page numbers followed by *f* indicate figures; page numbers followed by *t* indicate tables.

homosexuality, 247
host, 10
human capital, 32

idealism, 227
immigrant children, in nineteenth-century
    schools, 195-196
immigration, 251-253
implicit curriculum, curriculum, 107
incentives, 159, 161-163
inclusion, 84-85
Individualized Education Plan (IEP), 84, 169
individual needs, 32
Individuals with Disabilities Education
    Act (IDEA), 83-84, 100, 169
Individuals with Disabilities Education
    Improvement Act, 84
inductive reasoning, 217-218
informal curriculum, 107-108
informal professional development, 348
initiative, 172
in loco parentis, 280
inquiry learning, 111-112
instruction, 93-96
    implementation of, 110-118
    school levels and, 118-120
    See also curriculum
instructional decision making, 129
instructional time, 155
instrumental aggression, 66
integrated curriculum, 103-104
intelligent design, 105
intelligence, 79, 80f
intelligence quotient (IQ), 79
interdisciplinary curriculum, 103
interdisciplinary team, 45
interventions, unobtrusive, 164-165
intrinsic incentives, 161, 163
intuition, 217

job performance, personal conduct
    and, 278-279
junior high schools, in twentieth
    century, 197-198

Kalamazoo case, 192
Kappa Delta Pi Record, 15
kindergarten, 42, 43f, 192
knowledge, 17, 202
knowledge base, contributions to,
    351-352

labor unions, 276
language, 72
language arts, 101
language minority students, 73
laws, 272-274
leadership, 173
learning
    facilitation of, 16
    philosophy of education and, 219-227
    See also lifelong learning
learning differences, 79-82
learning disabled (LD), 82
learning environment, 147-150
    classroom management plan, 168-175
    consequences, 159, 163-168
    creation of, 150-155

expectations, 159-161
    incentives, 159, 161-163
    review, 175
    routines, 155-159
learning modalities, 80
learning preferences, 81fI
learning styles, 80-81
least restrictive environment (LRE), 84
legal issues
    laws, 272-274
    legal responsibilities of teachers,
        280-283
    legal rights of students, 285-294
    legal rights of teachers, 274-280
    review, 294-295
    schools and religion, 283-285
legal responsibilities, of teachers, 280-283
legal rights
    students, 285-294
    teachers, 274-280
legal support, for students with
    disabilities, 83-84
legislation, curriculum and, 99-100
legislatures, 305-306
lessons, components of, 117-118
level-specific professional organizations, 14t
liability, 280-281
lifelong learning, commitment to, 16-17
limited English proficiency (LEP), 73
literacy, 109
local funding, 319-323
local laws and policies, 273
logic, 217-219, 219t, 229t
long-range plans, 117
looping, 44
love, 164f

magnet schools, 35
manipulatives, 112
mathematics, 101, 135-136
McKinney-Vento Act, 241
melting pot, 70
mentor, 10, 346
metaphysics, 216, 219t, 229t
Mexican American children, 194
micromanagement, 311
Middle Eastern America students,
    in twenty-first century
    schools, 204-205
middle-level instruction, 119-120
middle school
    developmental appropriateness, 171
    educational routines, 158
    structure and organization of, 45-46
    twentieth century, 197-198
mini-lectures, 110
minorities, in nineteenth-century
    schools, 193-196
misbehavior, consequences of, 164-166
misconduct, with students, 280
Montessori method, 42, 198
moral development, 64
Morrill Act, 196
multiage classrooms, 44
multicultural curriculum, 104, 105-106
multicultural education, 71-72
multiple intelligences theory,
    80, 81t

Nation at Risk, A, 143, 200-201
National Assessment of Educational
    Progress (NAEP), 97, 136
National Association for Single-Sex Public
    Education (NASSPE), 67
National Board for Professional Teaching
    Standards Certification (NBPTS), 349
National Commission on Excellence in
    Education, 143
National Council of Teachers of Mathematics
    (NCTM), 97
National Defense Education Act of 1958, 198
National Governors Association (NGA), 97
National Middle School Association, 45
national standards, 97
Native American children, 193-194
nature, 60-61
NCES, 60
needs hierarchy, 61
needs, 164f
needs, individual and collective, 32
need-specific professional organizations, 14t
neighborhood school, 325
neighborhood schools, 34-35
No Child Left Behind Act (NCLB), 97, 100,
    137, 202, 319, 357
nondiscrimination, right to, 293
nonparticipation, student right of, 292-293
norm-referenced tests, 137
Northwest Land Ordinance of 1787, 189
null curriculum, 109-110
nurture, 60-61

obesity, 247-249
objectives, 117, 119
observation, 347
open enrollment, 40
organized professional development, 348
overlapping, 154

pacing guides, 117
parallel play, 63, 345
paraprofessionals, 347
parents
    curriculum and, 100
    involvement in schools, 339-340
    school governance and, 315-316
    single-parent homes, 77
    teacher effectiveness and, 21
parent-student-teacher conferences, 340-341
Parent Teacher Association (PTA), 316
parochial schools, 38
Partnership for 21st Century Skills
    (P21), 100, 109, 171-173
peer observation, 347
perennialism, 221-222, 229t
performance assessment, 131
performance-based pay, 352-353, 355
performance standards, 97
personal conduct, 278-279
personal lives, of teachers, 277-280
personal philosophy of education, 227-230
Pew Forum, 77
philosophy, 214, 215-219
philosophy of education, 211-215
    branches of, 215-219
    personal, 227-230
    review, 231
    teaching and learning, 219-227

philosophy trees, 220
physical development, 62, 65t
physical education, 102
physical space, 150-152
planning, for instruction, 116-118
portfolio, 131
portfolio assessment, 131
postmodernism, 227
power, 164f
practicum experiences, 334
pragmatism, 222
praise, 162
prayer in school, 284-285
preoperational thought, 62
preschool, structure and organization of, 42
presidential influence, on public
    education, 303-304
pretesting, 128
primary grades, structure and
    organization of, 43
principals, 311-313
privacy, of student records, 293
private donations, 322-323
private school venues, 38-39
privilege gap, 78
problem solving, 110, 119
process standards, 97
productivity, 173
professional associations, 13, 14t
professional development, 348-350
professional ethics, 268-270
professionalism, 329-332
    education reform, 352-359
    professional development, 348-350
    review, 359-360
    teacher contributions, 350-352
    teacher preparation and, 332-338
    teaching relationships, 338-348
professional knowledge base, contributions
    to, 351-352
professional organizations, teacher
    involvement in, 350-351
program evaluation, 129-130
progressive education, 197
progressivism, 222-223, 229t
property taxes, 319, 321-322
protective rights, of students, 289-293
proximity, 152
public domain, 282
Public Law 94-142, 51, 83
public schools, purposes of, 30-33. See
    financing; government
public school venues, 34-37
public-to-public school choice, 40
punishment, 165-166

quality, commitment to, 16

race, 69-70, 193-195
Race to the Top, 97
racial diversity, educational history
    and, 202-205
racism, society and, 250-253
reading, integrated curriculum and, 114-116
reasoning, 217
reconciliation, 167
Reggio Emilia, 42
related arts, 45

related arts courses, 101
relational aggression, 66
relationships, 63
reliability, 137
religion
    compulsory education and, 284
    legal impacts on, 283-285
religious diversity, 77-78
religious holidays, 285
religious organizations, meeting on
    school grounds, 285
resilience, 167
resource teacher, 83
responsibility, 143-144, 173
restructuring, 201
ripple effect, 155
romanticism, 227
routines, 155-159
rubrics, 133
rural schools, 48

sadness, boys and, 67
scaffolding, 63
school adults, professional relationships
    with, 347-348
school choice, 39-41
school connectedness, 108
school culture, 33-34
school districts, 307-311
school grounds, religious organizations
    meeting on, 285
schooling, education versus, 30-31
school levels
    instruction and, 118-120
    routines in, 156-159
school management structure, 311-315
school prayer, 284-285
schools
    bullying, 254-256
    childhood obesity, 249
    community and, 240
    different levels of, 41-48
    dropping out, 260-261
    effective, 50-52
    eighteenth century, 188-189
    family and, 237
    immigration, 252-253
    legal impacts on, 283-285
    neighborhood, 325
    nineteenth century, 191-192
    principal settings of, 48-50
    purposes of, 30-33
    seventeenth century, 183-187
    sexuality-related concerns, 247
    socioeconomic status and, 242-243
    suicide, 250
    theft and violence, 256-257
    truancy, 258
    twenty-first century, 202
    See also financing; government
School-to-Work, 103
school venues, differences between, 34-41
science, 101, 135-136
search and seizure, 289
seating arrangements, 151-152
secondary schools, 192
Seed Public Charter School, 36
self-contained classrooms, 43

self-direction, 172
self-efficacy, 339
self-monitoring, 163
sensory motor intelligence, 62f
settlement houses, 195-196
sex education, 106
sexual harassment, 289-291
sexuality-related concerns, 246-247
sexual orientation, 67
single-gender schools, 38
single-member elections, 308
site-based management, 35, 312
skills, 17, 202
social aspects, of gender, 66
social cognition, 63
social development, 63-64, 65t
socialization, 31
social media, 154
social reconstructionism, 223-224, 229t
social skills, 173
social studies, 101-102
societal contexts, 233-236
    bullying, 253-256
    classroom management and, 169-170
    community, 236, 237, 239-240
    dropping out, 257, 258-261
    family, 236-237, 238-239f
    health issues, 243-250
    racism, 250-253
    review, 262
    socioeconomic status, 240-243
    theft, 253-254, 256-257
    truancy, 257-258
    violence, 253-254, 256-257
societal participation, 31-32
societal reconstruction, 31
societal transmission, 31
socioeconomic diversity, 78-79
socioeconomic status, society and, 240-243
special education services, 82
special interest groups, school
    governance and, 316-317
stages of cognitive development, 62
stages of moral reasoning, 64
stakeholders, 53
Standard English, 72
standards, 97-98
standards-based reform movement, 97
standards-based test, 135
state board of education, 306
state court influence, on public
    education, 306
state department of education, 306-307
state funding, 319
state government, public education
    and, 304-307
state laws, 273
state legislatures, 305-306
state standards, 97, 355-357
state standards-based standardized tests, 137
state superintendent of education, 306
stereotyping, gender, 66, 68
structured English immersion (SEI), 75
structured observations, 335
student achievement, evaluation of, 129
student advocacy, 15
student collaboration, 112-113
student development, 62-64, 65t

Photo Credits

Provided by the Todd family, p. I-2 (bottom left, right); provided by the Francis family, p. I-3 (top left, center); provided by the Wiley family, p. I-5 (bottom left 3 images); provided by the Mancia family, p. I-6 (top left 3 images); provided by the Ford family, p. I-6 (bottom left 3 images); provided by the McBeath family, p. I-8 (bottom left 3 images); provided by the Sutton family, p. I-9 (top left 3 images); provided by the Kutcher family, pp. I-9 (bottom 4 images), 86 (all); Jessica O'Rourke, pp. I-10 (bottom), 47, 352; provided by the Reyes family, p. I-11 (bottom 4 images); provided by the Toscano family, p. I-12 (top left 4 images); provided by the Martinez family, p. I-12 (bottom left); provided by the Douangsavanh family, p. I-13 (left 3 images); Shutterstock, pp. 1 (bottom), 27 (bottom), 93 (bottom), 125 (bottom), 147 (bottom), 179 (bottom), 211 (bottom), 233 (bottom), 240, 265 (bottom), 299 (bottom), 322 (middle), 329 (bottom); Cody White, p. 42 (bottom); Fotolia, p. 57 (bottom); Scott Cunningham/Merrill, p. 85; provided by the author, pp. 147 (top), 191, 211 (top), 215, 228, 252, 280, 299 (top); Barbara Hairfield, pp. 171, 345; Getty Images Inc.–Hulton Archive Photos, pp. 187, 195 (top); CORBIS–NY, pp. 188, 189 (bottom), 197, 198 (top); Corbis RF, pp. 189 (top), 195 (bottom); North Wind Picture Archives, p. 192 (top); © Bettmann/CORBIS All Rights Reserved, p. 192 (bottom); courtesy of the Library of Congress, pp. 193 (top), 199 (top); © CORBIS All Rights Reserved, p. 193 (middle); The Schlesinger Library, p. 193 (bottom); The Prudence Crandall Museum, p. 194 (top); courtesy of Millican Art and Photography, p. 194 (bottom); The New York Public Library/Art Resource, NY, p. 198 (bottom); Ansel Adams/University of Chicago Library, p. 199 (bottom); University of Chicago Library, p. 200; Rebecca Dunbar, p. 223; David Young-Wolff/PhotoEdit, p. 244; Will Hart/PhotoEdit, p. 249; David Graham/PH College, p. 255; Philip James Corwin/CORBIS–NY, p. 276; Valerie Berta/Journal-Courier/The Image Works, p. 284; Mark Richards/PhotoEdit, p. 310; Patrick Watson/PH College, p. 322 (top); Getty Images–Stockbyte, Royalty Free, p. 322 (bottom). All other photos by Sara Davis Powell.